Great Migration Newsletter

Volumes 1 through 10
(1990-2001)

2002
The Great Migration Study Project
The New England Historic Genealogical Society
Boston, Massachusetts

International Standard Book Number: 0-88082-140-X
Library of Congress Control Number: 2002104060

Cover Design: Carolyn Sheppard Oakley

Published by the
New England Historic Genealogical Society
101 Newbury Street
Boston, MA 02116-3007

Printed by Daamen Printing Co., Inc., West Rutland, Vermont.

TABLE OF CONTENTS

Please note that the Newsletter has been repaginated consecutively, with the new number at the bottom of each page.

INTRODUCTION

When the Great Migration Study Project was initiated in 1988, we immediately began to plan for a quarterly newsletter, which would serve a number of purposes. First and foremost, the *Great Migration Newsletter* would provide useful information on the immigrants of the Great Migration, on the towns that they settled, and on the records that they created. Second, the Newsletter would provide interested readers with updates on the progress of the Project itself, and would thus generate and maintain interest in the Project.

We feel that the original reasons for creating this publication have been more than justified, and we have decided to collect the forty issues of the first ten volumes of publication into a single volume, with subject and place indexes and a consolidated name index. Those who have not been subscribers, or who do not own a full set, can now have the entire run to date of the Newsletter in one convenient volume. For those who have been subscribers from the beginning, or who have otherwise received all forty issues, the present compilation will make the material even more useful, bringing together the entire set in one unit, and easing access through a single index.

From the beginning, the Newsletter has adhered to a regular format. Most issues have been eight pages, with the outer four pages constituting one section of the Newsletter and the inner four pages another section. The outer section includes one or two feature articles, a column with editor's comments, and a review of recent literature on the Great Migration. The inner section is called the FOCUS section, with detailed coverage of one of the towns settled during the Great Migration, or of a specific critical record, or group of records. The FOCUS and feature articles frequently concentrate on a particular class of records for one or another of the early New England towns or colonies.

In the first volume of *The Great Migration Begins* and in each of the volumes of the second *Great Migration* series, a section entitled SOURCES provides brief comments on each of the major categories of records consulted in the writing of these volumes. The many articles in the *Great Migration Newsletter* may be considered an extension of this introductory material in *The Great Migration Begins* and the more recent books, inasmuch as it treats the records of each town and colony in more detail than has been possible in the books. The Newsletter articles provide much of the basis for the rules of evidence used in compiling the Great Migration sketches, so this collected set of the Newsletter should be used as a companion to the published volumes, to help the reader interpret the conclusions reached in the sketches.

Robert Charles Anderson

Great Migration Newsletter

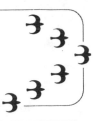

| Vol. 1 | January-March 1990 | No. 1 |

SEARCHING FOR PATTERNS OF MIGRATION

A pervasive theme of the Great Migration Study Project will be the search for patterns. Patterns of migration within New England will point to long-term patterns of association of certain families. These associations will provide clues to English origins, and to group migrations to New England.

We will be looking at all aspects of the migration process, and one area that will receive special attention is the frequency of return trips to England. A few people, usually merchants, made many crossings; Isaac Allerton of Plymouth comes immediately to mind. Others stayed only briefly in New England and returned to old England to stay, as for example Hugh Peter of Salem.

The "frequent flyers" and the sojourners are generally prominent persons, and well recorded. But what of those who made one or two return trips to England, but still remained wedded to their new home in New England? How many individuals and families fall within this group? What were their reasons for the visits to their home country?

Patterns are detected by collecting a large number of specific instances. We will present here a handful of examples as a first step in studying this particular aspect of the Great Migration.

1. EDWARD IRESON - In the passenger list of the *Abigail* in 1635 are Edward Ireson, aged 32, and Elizabeth Ireson, aged 27. Edward received a grant of land at Lynn in 1638, and lived there until his death in 1675. This all seems quite straightforward, except that in 1671 he deposed that "long since that is to say forty years ago" he had been a servant of "Mr. Johnson deceased living at Lynn." Thus it would appear that Edward Ireson had come to New England in 1630 with Isaac Johnson at the age of about 27, that he had within a few years returned to England, and then came again to Massachusetts in 1635. Some sources have claimed that the Elizabeth Ireson of the 1635 passenger list was Edward's wife, but she may well have been a sister, since Edward's known wife was named Alice.

2. EDWARD RAINSFORD - On the same ship with Edward Ireson was Edward Rainsford, aged 26, merchant. One of the earliest persons to join the church at Boston was Edward Rainsford, indicating that he had come with Winthrop in the summer of 1630, and recent research indicates that he had been born in 1609. Edward Rainsford had married twice in Boston between 1630 and 1634, so his return trip was not for the purpose of finding a wife.

3. STEPHEN TERRY - Among the first group of freemen admitted in 1631 was "Stephen Terre," afterwards seen at Dorchester, and then at Windsor. But then in the passenger list of the *Recovery*, dated 31 March 1633, along with several others who would settle in Dorchester and related towns, we find "Stephen Terrey." Although we have no direct evidence of the purpose for this trip, it may have been to find a wife, since his first child was born two years after this return trip.

4. JONATHAN GILLETT - Also on the *Recovery* was Jonathan Gillett, but, unlike Terry, he was making his first trip to New England. He must have returned to England almost immediately, since his marriage to Mary Dolbiar at Colyton, co. Devon, took place on 29 March 1634. All of this explains the later statement of his son that "My father Gille[tt] came into new-inglan the secon[d] time in June in the yeare 1634."

5. JOHN PEIRCE - From our analysis of the Watertown land records, we have concluded that John Peirce must have come to New England no later than 1634, and

[continued on page two]

EDITOR'S EFFUSIONS

The purpose of the *Great Migration Newsletter* is to inform you of the progress of the Project itself, to discuss the sources that will be studied in carrying out the research, and also to bring you information on recent genealogical discoveries pertaining to these earliest immigrants to New England.

A substantial part of the newsletter will be devoted to various regular features, such as this Editor's Column. Half of each issue, pages three through six, will focus on one major topic. Most frequently this will be a close inspection of one of the towns settled during the Great Migration. For this inaugural issue, Watertown is the focus. We examine the vital records which survive for the earliest years, and then discuss the process of granting land in this one town. Moving beyond this discussion of the records, we develop ideas which help interpret the lives of these early residents of Watertown.

Another regular part of the newsletter will be the review of Recent Literature, which will provide brief summaries of recent articles and books relating to the Great Migration, both genealogical and historical. On the genealogical side, we will be reporting on articles in the leading genealogical journals, and also on books which contain material on the immigrants of our period. In the historical literature, our greatest interest will be in those publications which attempt to use the genealogical literature to arrive at broad conclusions about early New England society, or else on items which will help us to better understand the lives of the participants in the Great Migration.

Material is already being gathered for the second issue of the *Great Migration Newsletter*. The Focus will be on the town of Cambridge, Watertown's closest neighbor. We will see many similarities, and also some important differences. In addition, we will report on some of the results of a recent research trip to England, which uncovered genealogical and biographical records of several New Englanders from the counties of Norfolk, Suffolk and Essex.

Robert Charles Anderson, FASG   Editor
Margaret F. Costello   Production Assistant

The *Great Migration Newsletter* is published quarterly by the Great Migration Study Project, a project of the New England Historic Genealogical Society, 101 Newbury Street, Boston MA 02116

The subscription rate is $8 for one year and $15 for two years.

[continued from page one]

probably in 1633. But he was absent for some of the land grants in 1636 and early 1637, and then he appears on a passenger list in 1637 with his wife and some of his younger children, two or three of his older children having made the trip to New England some years before.

6. RICHARD DUMMER - Richard Dummer first came to New England in 1632 as a member of the Company of Husbandmen, associated with Rev. Stephen Bachiler. After a few years residence in various Massachusetts towns, Dummer returned to his place of origin in Hampshire, and then came to New England a second time on the *Bevis* in 1638. The purpose of this return trip is not known, but he made at least one additional visit to his ancestral home about 1650, for he is seen at that time proving a will in the Prerogative Court of Canterbury.

Some returned to get married, some to collect the rest of their families, and (although we don't have a clear-cut example here) some to take care of unfinished business. Many more examples of these return trips will be documented as the Project proceeds, and as a result we will be able to construct a group of categories for this particular aspect of the migration process. This typology of return trips will then find its place within the larger pattern of migration in England prior to the transatlantic crossing, and migration in New England afterwards.

USING CAMBRIDGE CHURCH RECORDS

The records of the Cambridge, Massachusetts, church prior to 1658 have been lost, but the register compiled by Jonathan Mitchell (dubbed by Savage "Matchless Mitchell") is filled with clues to earlier events. The compiler of the published version of the Cambridge vital records made use of Mitchell's records, but did not always interpret them correctly.

Under Crackbone births we find "Benjamin, s. of Gilbert and Elizabeth, _____, 165_. C.R.1." The Cambridge church record reads "Gilbert Crackbone memb[er] in f[ull] C[ommunion] And Elizabeth His wife Joyned May. 22, 1659. His Son Benjamin was about 5 or 6 years old when His father Joyned here." The Cambridge VR compiler apparently interpreted this to mean that Gilbert had joined the Cambridge church in 1659, and that Benjamin was, therefore, born early in the 1650s. However, it was only Gilbert's wife Elizabeth who joined in 1659. Gilbert himself must have joined by 1636, for he was made a freeman on 25 May 1636. Thus the son Benjamin would have been born around 1630, in England. Should you encounter an item in the published Cambridge vital records which is based on these earliest surviving records of the First Church, take the time to consult the church records themselves, and verify that they have been properly interpreted.

Focus   on   WATERTOWN

EARLY VITAL RECORDS
OF WATERTOWN

During the nineteenth century two different versions of the earliest Watertown vital records were published. In 1852 and 1853 the *Register* carried a series on the "Early Records of Boston " which included Watertown for the years 1630 to 1644 (NEHGR 6:380, 7:159-62, 281-84). Then in 1894 the Historical Society of Watertown published its first volume of records, incorporating the early vital records, along with the land inventories and the early town meeting records.

By examining the entries for this period, we find that this was not a set of records that was maintained continuously, throughout the period in question, but was in the nature of a survey carried out toward the end of the period, probably during the winter of 1643-4. The principal reason for believing this is that vital entries which one might expect to find here, especially of those families who had left Watertown some years before 1644, are not found. For example, many of the families who settled in Watertown from 1630 to 1634 removed to Wethersfield in 1635 and 1636. Certainly some of these families must have experienced births, marriages and deaths during their sojourn in Watertown, but no trace of such families can be found.

Similarly, several of the earliest families of Dedham had spent a few years in Watertown, yet no records for these are found in the Watertown VRs at this date. The first birth entry for Dedham is for a son of John Dwight, born in 1635. Dedham did not yet exist as a town at that date, and John Dwight was a resident of Watertown in 1635, so this son would have been born in Watertown, yet no entry exists in the Watertown records.

Turning this around, we conclude that if a vital record appears in this set of Watertown records from 1630 to 1644, then the family in question was actually resident in Watertown at the time the town clerk, Simon Eire, collected this data. This helps us, for example, with widows who had remarried, and may have remained in town. John Tomson and his wife Margery had children born or buried in Watertown in 1635, 1636 and 1642, and John Tomson himself was buried in 1638. The land which had been granted to John Tomson later appears in the hands of William Clarke, who also in the years following John Tomson's death has wife Margery. The likely conclusion is that the widow Margery Tomson had married William Clarke, and the vital records appear in the 1644

summary because the Tomson family was still in Watertown, but now as part of the Clarke household. Had Margery Tomson moved out of Watertown before 1644, the Tomson events would not have been recorded in Watertown.

The records as published in the *Register* (for Watertown and a number of other towns beside Boston) ran under the title "Early Records of Boston." This is a misnomer, for the source of all these entries is a single book which included most of the towns of the newly organized Suffolk and Middlesex counties (Middlesex not having a separate existence until 1649). Not all these towns compiled their records in the same manner as Watertown. Some were arranged alphabetically and some chronologically. Thus, one must analyze and evaluate the records of each of these towns independently for this early period before drawing conclusions based on the appearance or non-appearance of a given family in the records. (In the years after 1644 the towns submitted their records annually, and different criteria apply.)

The records published by the town are clearly from a different source, as at least one entry does not appear in this version which is in the county copy (Isaac Stearns, born 1632). The editors of the town volume note this discrepancy, and refer to a version of the records at the Middlesex County Court House. Whether this is yet a third contemporary set of records, or a copy of one of the other two, awaits further research.

The town and county versions differ more significantly in the way they treat children who died young in years before 1644. In the town copy we find entries such as the following: [1636] "John Tomson the son of John & Mergrett Tomson Buried the 10d - 2m - aged three months." The county version provides us with a different entry: "John ye son of John & Margery Tomson borne 10 (11) 1635 buried 10 (2) 1636."

In the example above taken from the county copy, the interval from birth to death is precisely three months, from the tenth to the tenth. The way to resolve our problem would be to look at all cases in which the town copy gives the age at death in months or years, and see if the county versions always gives precise month or year intervals. If this is the case, then the compiler of the county version probably inserted his own calculations, since we would expect that more often than not the age at death would not be exactly a given number of months or years; and our conclusion would be that the county copy was derived from the town copy.

EARLY LAND GRANTING IN WATERTOWN

When Sir Richard Saltonstall and his associates arrived on the site of Watertown in the summer of 1630, they had a clean slate upon which to write when it came to parcelling out the land available to them. Any rights which the Native Americans might have had were ignored, and, except for a field of corn planted by the *Mary and John* passengers, no other European had made use of the land.

The actual actions of this earliest group of settlers will probably always be a matter of speculation, but apparently each of the thirty or so families of the Winthrop Fleet who settled in Watertown was given a modest piece of land, perhaps eight or ten acres, mostly along the river and in the vicinity of Mount Auburn. This arrangement sufficed for the next three summers, inasmuch as relatively few new immigrants appeared in Massachusetts Bay in 1631, 1632 and 1633. Presumably the town also allocated sizable tracts of land in common for pasture and meadow land.

The pace of migration picked up dramatically in 1634, and the population of Watertown was swelled by at least twenty families who arrived from Ipswich in England on the *Francis* and the *Elizabeth*. This nearly doubled the population of Watertown in the space of a few days in the summer of that year, and forced a reappraisal of the scheme of land usage. Although there is no explicit statement in the town records, study of the landholding patterns a few years later indicates that a more systematic distribution of land was made sometime in 1634, with blocks of houselots given out to the new arrivals, just to the west of the holdings of the older settlers (but still well within the modern bounds of Watertown).

Thomas Boyſon.

1. An Homeſtall of Sixteen Acres more or les bounded the Eaſt with Hill ſtreet the Weſt with Elliz Barron & James Cutler the North with Pequuſſet Common the South with Robert Sanders & Richard Linton.
2. Forty Acres of vpland being a great Dividend in the 1 Diviſion & the 18 Lott.
3. Three Acres of vpland oounded the North & Weſt with William Paine & the South with Thomas Haſtings.
4. Two Acres of Meddow in Rock Meddow bounded the North with Cambridge line the South with John Biſcoe & the Eaſt with the brooke.
5. Ten Acres of Plowland in the further Plaine & the 60 Lott.
6. Ten Acres of Meddow in the remote Meddowes & the 78 Lott.
7. Six Acres of vpland lying beyond the further Plaine & the 55 Lott.
8. A Farme of Seventy three Acres vpland in the 9 Diviſion.

Composite Inventory

More immigrants arrived in 1635, and the town began to feel land pressure. Sometime in 1635 each holder of a houselot was given one or two small parcels of meadow or of plowland, usually only an acre or two. These grants do not form coherent groupings, and no record was made of the distribution.

Late in the year, with the increased demand for land resulting from the arrival of more settlers, and the simultaneous departure of many families for the new settlement on the Connecticut River, the town meeting voted a new and important restriction on the granting of land [November (or December?) 30, 1635]:

Agreed, by the Consent of the Freemen (in consideration there be too many inhabitants in the Towne & the Towne thereby in danger to be ruinated) that no Foreainer comming into the Towne, or any Family arising among our selves shall have any benefitt either of Commonage, or Land undivided but what they shall purchase, except that they buy a mans right wholly in the Towne.

This decision by the town was of fundamental importance in establishing the proprietarial system in Watertown. First, a closed corporation was created, with a limited number of "rights" to receive new grants of land; as we shall see, this number was initially at least 120, and possibly a little higher. Second, it made these rights transferrable, stating that such a right was something that could be bought and sold. Third, as sons of landholders married and formed new households, they were not automatically eligible for grants of land; they could inherit the right of their father, or purchase that of another man, but no new right was created for "any Family arising among our selves."

The next grant made, and the first to be fully recorded, was of the Great Dividends, on 25 July 1636. These parcels, being generally of twenty acres or larger, were laid out in what would become northern Waltham, along the Cambridge line, and were granted "to all the Townsmen then inhabiting being 120 in number." Slightly more than half a year had passed since the order limiting the number of rights to new grants of land, so it is possible that some existing rights were bought in by some person who already held a right. These rights would then be consolidated into one, for in no case do we see a person who had purchased two, three or even four rights later receiving a like number of grants in any one new division.

The Great Dividend was followed by grants of the Beaverbrook Plowlands on 28 February 1636/7 and the Remote Meadows on 26 June 1637 (see below for further discussion of these grants). Then on 9 April 1639 a limited number of inhabitants were given grants, mostly of six acres, at the Town Plot; this was an attempt to settle a new town center away from the early nucleus of habitation. Since not all holders of rights were included in this grant, there was presumably some discontent, and a further grant was made to those not included in the Town Plot. These were called "the lands In Lieu of Township," also known as "the land beyond the further plain."

There was then a hiatus of some years in the granting of land, but in the meantime a few of the leading citizens of the town were granted "farms," which were sizable tracts, many of a hundred acres or more, in the far western part of what was then Watertown. Not surprisingly, this also led to dissatisfaction (a common condition in the early years of Watertown), and on 10 May 1642 all those not included in these earlier limited farm grants were also given similar tracts, which were eventually laid out in the area that would become the town of Weston.

Thus, by the winter of 1643-4, when Simon Eire was compiling the various inventories of Watertown landholding, the "standard" grouping of lands that one man should hold, assuming that he had been in Watertown for the entire series of grants, and had not sold or purchased any land, would be as follows:

* Houselot - about eight acres

* Small Lots - one or two small parcels of meadow or plowland, an acre or two apiece

---

Thurſton Rainer.

1. An Homeſtall of Sixteen Acres by eſtimation bounded the Eaſt & North wᵗʰ the highway the Weſt wᵗʰ Elliz Barron & James Cutler & the South wᵗʰ Robert Sanderſon & Richard Linton granted to him.

Gregory Stone.

1. Three Acres of vpland by eſtimation bounded the North & Weſt wᵗʰ William Paine & the South wᵗʰ Thomas Haſtings granted to him.
2. Forty Acres of vpland by eſtimation being a great Dividend in the firſt Diviſion & the Eighteen lott granted to him.
3. Two Acres of Meddow by eſtimation in Rockmeddow bounded the North wᵗʰ Cambridge line the South wᵗʰ John Biſcoe [145] & the Eaſt wᵗʰ the brooke granted to him.
4. Ten Acres of Plowland by eſtimation in the farther Plaine bounded the Eaſt wᵗʰ Thomas Brookes the Weſt wᵗʰ John Stowers the North wᵗʰ Commonland & the South wᵗʰ the highway granted to him.
5. Ten Acres of remote Meddow by eſtimation & the Seventy eight lott granted to him.

Thomas Boyſon.

1. Six Acres of vpland by eſtimation beyond the further Plaine & the Fifty third lott granted to him.

Inventory of Grants

---

* Great Dividend - most parcels about 35 acres, some smaller and some larger

* Beaverbrook Plowlands - based on family size, and value of cattle

* Remote Meadows - based on family size, and value of cattle

* Town Plot or Lieu of Township - usually six acres

* Farm - mostly 60 acres or more

Given this picture of how land in Watertown was apportioned among the proprietors, what can we learn from the actual holdings, as listed in the inventories prepared by Simon Eire? As an example, we will look at the case of Thomas Boyson (or Boylston). In the composite inventory of lands, which shows both those lands which a man had received from the town and retained, and those lands which he had inherited or purchased, Thomas Boyson appears as the possessor of eight parcels, and conforms to the ideal list given above (see inset on page four). Thomas Boyson had arrived in Massachusetts as a single man in 1635. The first volume of Suffolk Deeds (folio 67) contains a 1639 deed from Gregory Stone to a representative of Thomas Boyson, in which five parcels of land are transferred. Boyson then received a grant of land from the town in 1642, when he was given a 73 acre farm.

When we turn to the inventory of grants, showing only those parcels which a person had received directly from the town, we see Thomas Boyson credited only with the land "beyond the further plaine" [Lieu of Township]. But immediately above the Boyson entry is the entry for the grants to Gregory Stone, showing some but not all of the pieces of land sold by Stone to Boyson. One item only is not accounted for, and that corresponds to the entry in the inventory of grants which comes just above that of Gregory Stone, the entry of Thurston Rayner (see inset on this page).

Now we can begin to reconstruct what happened in this one instance, to this particular proprietary right. Thurston Rayner arrived in Massachusetts in July of 1634 as one of the passengers on the *Elizabeth*. He must have proceeded very quickly to Watertown, for he was granted the sixteen acre "homestall," which was part of the land division which we think was carried out in that year. But he was not granted any other parcels, and Gregory Stone is the grantee of record for the smaller parcels of meadow and plowland which were given out sometime in 1635.

We know that Thurston Rayner was one of the inhabitants who moved on to Wethersfield, and we also know that Gregory Stone came to New England in 1635. Based on the evidence of the inventory of grants, then, we can say that Thurston Rayner was one of the first contingent who went from Watertown to Wethersfield in 1635, and that he did not wait for the second group who made the move in 1636.

Rayner sold his land to the recent arrival Gregory Stone, who then was the recipient of all town grants through the Remote Meadows in 1637. Gregory Stone in 1639 sold this land to an agent of Thomas Boyson, and moved to Cambridge. The grant of Lieu of Township land to Thomas Boyson could only have come after he had acquired Stone's right to further divisions, so this implies that the Lieu of Township grants were actually laid out sometime after September 1639, even though the original order regarding the granting of these lands was made in July of 1638.

We are able to trace this one proprietary share through two changes of ownership in a space of ten years, and to pin down to a narrow range the time in which migrations within New England were made. We are aided here by the recording of the alienation by Gregory Stone, and this example was chosen because it is a model example, without any loose ends; other cases will not necessarily be so neat and clearcut.

We may derive a different sort of information from the recorded grants of the Beaverbrook Plowlands (28 February 1636/7) and the Remote Meadows (26 June 1637). These two tracts were granted in accord with the same formula: "Allowing one acre for a person, & likewise for cattle valued at 20lb the head." Most of the grants were in the range of one to ten acres, with a few larger. Do these grants accurately reflect family size in any way?

At the higher end, these allocations are certainly more for size of estate than of family. Such prominent citizens as Edward Howe and William Paine were granted twenty-four acres apiece. They certainly did not have twenty-two children; and we know from other records that these were both affluent men.

At the opposite end, there were about ten grants of one acre in each of these two tracts. Men such as Richard Sawtell and Henry Cuttriss had not yet acquired families in 1636 and 1637, so for these individuals the grants are accurate. Just this bit of information helps us with identifying the William Palmer who was resident in Watertown at this time. In these two divisions he is receiving one acre at a time, yet he has been consistently equated with the William Palmer from Ormesby, co. Norfolk, who appears in Hampton, New Hampshire, with wife and children. The fact that the William Palmer being granted land in Watertown in these years was a single man precludes this identification, and makes it much more

likely that the Watertown man was the one who appears soon after in Yarmouth, having married Judith Feake, niece of Robert Feake of Watertown.

In the middle ground, the situation is not so clear, and more extensive research will be necessary. As a tentative rule of thumb, one can be reasonably confident that those who received up to four acres were receiving land for the immediate family only. If the grant was for more than six acres, then probably some wealth (as measured by cattle) was being taken into account.

An interesting example in this middle range is Christopher Grant, who received three acres in the Beaverbrook Plowlands, and four acres in the Remote Meadows. Christopher Grant and Mary his wife had their first child, Abigail, born 6 February 1634/5, and second child, Joshua, born 11 June 1637, just before the granting of the Remote Meadows. Thus, the increase in the size of the family from three to four is directly accounted for in the Remote Meadows grant.

If an immigrant of interest to you passed through Watertown in this period prior to 1644, analysis such as that carried out above may reveal some interesting details of migration, land trading and family size.

SOURCES FOR WATERTOWN

The earliest surviving records of the town of Watertown have been published in *Watertown Records Comprising the First and Second Books of Town Proceedings with the Land Grants and Possessions also the Proprietors' Book and the First Book and Supplement of Births Deaths and Marriages* (1894). This volume includes three sections, containing town meeting, land and vital records. The vital records have been discussed on page three of this newsletter. The section on land records comprises the lists of five specific land grants between 1636 and 1642, the two inventories of 1643-4, and proprietors' records for the years 1714 to 1742. (See the April 1990 *New England Historical and Genealogical Register* for an analysis of the two inventories.) The town meeting records in this volume cover the years from 1634 to 1680, with an important gap from 1644 to 1646.

Records for the Watertown church do not survive prior to 1686, when Rev. John Bailey began his ministry. His predecessors (George Phillips [1630-1644] and John Sherman [1647-1685]) presumably kept such records, the fate of which is unknown. Although these records probably no longer exist, they may have remained with the estate of John Sherman upon his death, and possibly passed to his descendants.

RECENT LITERATURE

Janet Ireland Delorey, "The English Origins and Descendants to the Fourth Generation of Edward Wood of Charlestown, Massachusetts," *The Genealogist* 9 [1988]:90-159. Edward Wood appeared in Charlestown, Massachusetts, in 1639, with wife Ruth and children including Elizabeth and Obadiah; a family with these names, and of the appropriate ages, was found in Nuneaton, Warwickshire. Delorey presents this evidence, identifies the children of Edward Wood, and continues the Wood lines to the fourth generation.

Charles Fitch-Northen, "The Trowbridge Ancestry," *The Genealogist* 9 [1988]:3-39. Thomas Trowbridge is first of record in Dorchester, Massachusetts, in 1635, and his ancestry has long been known. Fitch-Northen here sets forth several further lines of ancestry, some reaching back to the Conquest; in the process he elucidates a number of points in medieval English genealogy. Of especial importance, this article includes newly discovered records on the immigrant's career in England, and also on his immediate Trowbridge ancestors (pp. 13-15).

[Neil D. Thompson], "Abell-Cotton-Mainwaring: Further Supporting Evidence," *The Genealogist* 9 [1988]:89. Provides additional evidence for identifying the mother of the immigrant Robert Abell as "the daughter of Richard Cotton by his first wife Mary Mainwaring."

Farley Grubb, "German Immigration to Pennsylvania, 1709 to 1820," *The Journal of Interdisciplinary History* XX [1990]:417-36. This item may seem out of place here, but it is commonly held that the German immigrants of the eighteenth century were closer in demographic composition to early New Englanders than was any other group. Articles such as this are useful for comparative purposes, to put the Great Migration in some perspective. Grubb, relying mostly on passenger lists, arrives at some conclusions about the changing nature of German immigration in the eighteenth century.

Thomas W. Cooper II, "The Cooper-Pierson-Griggs Connection," *The American Genealogist* 64 [1989]:193-202. Demonstrates that Henry Pierson of Southampton, Long Island, was stepson of John Cooper, rather than son-in-law, and then discusses additional evidence on these two families and the related Griggs family.

Frederick J. Nicholson, "A Clue to the English Origin of Thomas[1] Lincoln (the cooper) and William[1] Lane of Hingham, Mass.," *The American Genealogist* 64 [1989]:214-15. One would expect that all early settlers of Hingham, Massachusetts, came from Hingham, co. Norfolk, and vicinity. Parish register entries printed here strongly support the conclusion that Thomas Lincoln

(cooper) and his father-in-law William Lane emigrated from Beaminster, co. Dorset.

Gale Ion Harris, "Wyllys-Harris-Chambers-Hamlin-Smith," *The American Genealogist* 64 [1989]:226-32. Harris tackles and demolishes a number of erroneous statements about the various families of the title. Of most interest to this Project are the conclusions about George Wyllys of Connecticut.

Joan R. Kent, *The English Village Constable, 1580-1642: A Social and Administrative Study* [Oxford 1986]. Kent rehabilitates the image of the English village constable of early modern times, showing that he was of substantial economic status, and took his job seriously. The office of constable was one that also became important in New England towns, and Kent's study will help us understand the nature of the constable's work, and how the New England office differed from that in the parent country. On a more general level, the English constables were generally drawn from the town's yeomen and the more prosperous husbandmen. Since these are the same socioeconomic strata from which a large portion of early New Englanders came, Kent's descriptions of the positions of constables in their English settings should be of interest to us, even if we are not especially intrigued by the duties of the constable.

Sidney L. Paine, "The English Ancestry of Stephen Paine of Rehoboth, Plymouth Colony," *New England Historical and Genealogical Register* 143 [1989]:291-302. Stephen Paine and his family appear in New England in 1638, settling first at Hingham. Daniel Cushing's Record identifies Stephen Paine as being from Great Ellingham, co. Norfolk, but beyond this little was known about his ancestry. This article provides Paine with four generations of ancestry in the male line, and, like most research into English ancestry in the sixteenth and seventeenth centuries, makes heavy use of wills and parish registers. But the author also commissioned extensive investigation of the manorial records of Great Ellingham.

Douglas Richardson, "The Riddlesdale alias Loker Family of Bures St. Mary, Suffolk, and Sudbury, Massachusetts," *New England Historical and Genealogical Register* 143 [1989]:325-31. Henry Loker died in February of 1630/1 in the parish of Bures St. Mary, leaving behind a widow and four children who settled in Sudbury, Massachusetts, in 1639. Richardson has added significantly to the known ancestry of this Loker family (which also frequently added the alias Riddlesdale). An appendix presents additional data on Richard Newton, who married one of Henry Loker's daughters in 1636 and joined in the migration to Sudbury.

1646 MIGRATION FROM WATERTOWN

An important goal of the Great Migration Study Project is to identify groups of families or individuals who migrate together. Our main focus in this effort will be on the move from England to New England, but later group migrations within New England are also significant. Specifically, if we see several families moving together, we can reasonably hypothesize that they may have been associated at some time in the past.

The early migration from Watertown to Wethersfield on the Connecticut River in 1635 and 1636 is well known, and the later migration of some of these same families from Wethersfield to the new town of Stamford, around 1640 and 1641, is also documented. Some years later several families moved directly from Watertown to Stamford, as evidenced principally by their sale of Watertown lands in late 1645 and early 1646:

NICHOLAS THEALE - Sold to William Shattuck on 23 September 1645 [Suffolk Deeds 1:62]

WILLIAM POTTER - Sold to Nicholas Cady and John Knapp on 8 December 1645 [SD 1:66]

NICHOLAS KNAPP - Sold to Brian Pendleton on 7 May 1646 [SD 1:71]

ROBERT LOCKWOOD - Sold to Brian Pendleton on 7 May 1646 [SD 1:71]

JOHN ELLET - Sold to Thomas Wincoll on 29 June 1646 [SD 1:74]

JOHN WATERBURY - Sold to Robert Pearce on 15 October 1646 [SD 1:78]

RICHARD AMBLER - Last seen in Watertown in spring 1644, as evidenced by inclusion in earliest Watertown vital records; first seen in Stamford fall 1647, as stated in 1654 deposition [*New York Genealogical and Biographical Record* 64 (1933):17]

GREGORY TAYLOR - Last seen in Watertown in spring 1644, by same reason as Richard Ambler; arrival time in Stamford not known; died there 1657 [Huntington, *History of Stamford* (1868) p. 63]

We should not be surprised that, once Stamford was founded by migrants from Wethersfield who had even earlier lived in Watertown, a few Watertown families would also move to Stamford. One would not predict, however, that they would wait for several years after Stamford was founded, and that then eight families would all move within the space of a year, or two at most.

The conclusion that some of these families might share a common origin in England, although certainly not proven, does become a sound working hypothesis, and will direct research in English sources. As the Project proceeds, it should uncover many more clusters of families such as this, which are seen to move together in a concerted way.

Great Migration Newsletter

Vol. 1   April - June 1990   No. 2

WHEN DID THE GREAT MIGRATION END?

The Great Migration Study Project plans to survey all those persons and families who had arrived in New England between 1620 and 1643. The beginning date is obvious enough, being the year of arrival of the *Mayflower* at Plymouth. But the choice of 1643 as the terminus of the Project is less evident. Why not 1640, or 1645, or some other date?

After the landing of the *Mayflower*, immigration during the 1620s was fitful, and amounted to only a few hundred arrivals. In 1630 Winthrop brought about seven hundred passengers to Massachusetts Bay, but again the rate of migration slowed in the years immediately following. Only in 1634 did the movement of English men and women reach the level of two to three thousand in one year, and this rate continued for the rest of the decade.

In 1640 Winthrop noted in his journal that not as many new settlers had arrived in that year as in those preceding, and as a result New England was hit by its first depression. But Winthrop repeated virtually the same complaint in his journal under 1641, and the shipping registers in London show that several ships had been licensed to carry passengers to New England in 1640. For the moment, the interpretation seems to be that, because of the developing Civil War in England, migration dropped off by about half in 1640, and then in 1641 fell even further, perhaps to only a shipload or two. (See Marion H. Gottfried, "The First Depression in Massachusetts," *New England Quarterly* 9 [1936]:655-78.)

Thus we might choose 1640 or 1641 as our cutoff date for the Project, but there are other considerations. Since there are no passenger lists for these years, we have no immediate way of telling who came in 1640 or 1641. Thus, one reason for choosing a later date is to provide some time for the 1640 arrivals to show up in the records.

Another reason for delaying the cutoff date is that a number of convenient delimiting events occurred in 1643. Massachusetts Bay set up its county courts, and began a new series of records. The four Rhode Island towns decided to combine into one government. Massachusetts Bay, Plymouth Colony, Connecticut and New Haven decided to form the Confederation of New England. Plymouth compiled its list of men able to bear arms.

The final factor determining the cutoff date is the procedure for obtaining church membership and then freemanship. By the mid-1630s, the New England church had progressed to the point that each new member was required to make a confession of saving grace (see page fourteen). The process of admission as a church member was, then, time-consuming, and in Massachusetts Bay only after this process could a man ask to be made a freeman. Admission to freemanship could take place at any meeting of the colony court, but the largest number were admitted each May at the time of the court of elections of the General Court.

Most of the passenger traffic from England to New England took place in the spring, with ships arriving in Boston or some other port in June or July. Some ships arrived in the late autumn, but virtually no traffic occurred during the winter, with the exception of some fishing voyages. With very few exceptions, therefore, anyone appearing in the list of freemen made at the May court must have arrived in the previous year at the latest, since otherwise there would not be time for the transatlantic crossing, followed by admission to church membership.

The Great Migration Study Project, then, will examine all persons who appear in records of New England on or prior to 10 May 1643, the date of sitting of the court of elections in that year. The current phase of the Project, which will be completed by 1992, and which will comprise about ten percent of the whole, will study all those of record by the time of the court of elections of 1634.

EDITOR'S EFFUSIONS

This second issue of the *Great Migration Newsletter* contains a number of firsts. Most embarrassingly, we print below our first correction; these are unavoidable in the publishing process. Another first is the article on "Tracing Ministers' Careers," which reports some of the findings during a recent research tour in England. Similar accounts of other discoveries made on this tour will appear in future issues of the *Newsletter*; and longer and more detailed accounts of what has been learned about the Reverends Allin, Stoughton and Youngs will be published in the leading genealogical periodicals. Finally, the lead article is the first in a series which will explain what the Great Migration Study Project is intended to accomplish, and how. Other articles will describe various aspects of the research process, and what the final product will look like.

The next issue of the *Newsletter* will focus on the town of Lynn. This set of articles will be much different from the previous two, on Watertown and Cambridge. The latter two towns were both settled by East Anglians, and have substantial surviving town records from the time of the Great Migration itself. The early settlers of Lynn were a less cohesive group, and, with the exception of a few vital records, no records generated by the town survive prior to the last decade of the seventeenth century. The challenge will be to learn as much as possible about the early years of Lynn from colony, court and private documents.

CORRECTION

In the article on the first page of the last issue of the *Newsletter*, no account was taken of John Plummer's recent work which showed that the *Recovery* came to New England in 1634 and not 1633 (*National Genealogical Society Quarterly* 77 [1989]:249-55). Stephen Terry and Jonathan Gillett both sailed on this vessel, and although this adjustment of date does not affect the basic point that they were making a second trip, it does make sense of the marriage record for each.

Robert Charles Anderson, FASG   Editor
Margaret F. Costello   Production Assistant

The *Great Migration Newsletter* (ISSN 1049-8087) is published quarterly by the Great Migration Study Project, a project of the New England Historic Genealogical Society, 101 Newbury Street, Boston MA 02116

The subscription rate is $8 for one year and $15 for two years. The subscription year is the same as the calendar year.

TRACING MINISTERS' CAREERS

Most of the ministers who came to New England as part of the Great Migration had held livings in England before migration, some for a decade or more. Most were university graduates. Since many of these ministers were rallying points for groups of migrants of varying size, any knowledge we may have of their whereabouts prior to migration will help in identifying the origins of other families.

Research conducted late last year in the records of the Diocese of Norwich (Norfolk and Suffolk) and the Diocese of London (which includes Essex), and also in the Public Record Office, led to the discovery of the residences of three ministers connected with New England.

John Allin crossed the Atlantic in 1637 and settled in Dedham, where he was ordained as pastor of the newly-organized church in 1639. He had married in 1622 in Wrentham, co. Suffolk, and so it was assumed that he had graduated from university not long before that. Four men of that name had received both BA and MA degrees at Cambridge from 1618 through 1621, and John Allin of Dedham has long been identified as the one who had attended Gonville and Caius College.

Various sources claim that Allin had been beneficed in Ipswich, in South Elmham, and in Denton. The best clue was in notes at the end of Winthrop's journal, which showed that John Allin in 1635 was in "Surslingham" in Norfolk. There is a Surlingham, just east of Norwich, but no record of Allin was found there. Spreading the net wider, other possibilities were various parishes named Burlingham and Saxlingham. A search of records of these parishes soon revealed that John Allin had been rector of Saxlingham iuxta Mare, in north-central Norfolk, from 1624 through 1637.

But could we now find out which of the Cambridge men was our John Allin? Periodically the Bishop of Norwich (and all other bishops in England) would hold a visitation, in which their agents spread out over the diocese to perform various tasks of information-gathering and discipline. Among the records generated was a consignation book, which compiled the credentials of the ministers in each parish. These consignation books varied in nature from diocese to diocese, and in Norfolk they gave information only on the rector or vicar (or occasionally a curate, if he was serving alone). The data collected included the date and place of ordination, and the highest university degree obtained.

In the case of John Allin the consignation book stated that he was a Master of Arts, and that he had been or-

[continued on page sixteen]

Focus on CAMBRIDGE

THE BRAINTREE COMPANY

Unlike most of the towns of the Great Migration, Cambridge began as a planned community. In the fall of 1630 the leaders who had come over on the Winthrop Fleet held many discussions, and on 28 December they resolved "to build houses at a place a mile east from Waterton, near Charles River, the next spring and to winter there the next year, that so by our examples and by removing the ordinance and munition thither ... a fortified town might there grow up ..." (Thomas Dudley's letter to the Countess of Lincoln, March 1630/1).

Dudley may have thought that his colleagues among the Assistants had all agreed on this course of action, but Winthrop certainly didn't, or soon changed his mind. As a result only a few families, including two of the magistrates (Dudley and Simon Bradstreet), had settled in Newtown (as it was first called) by 1631. (The eight families who made this move are listed on the second page of the published Cambridge town records.)

Governor Winthrop entered in his diary in mid-August of 1632 an order of the General Court which changed the nature of Dudley's settlement: "The Braintree company, (which had begun to sit down at Mount Wollaston,) by order of court, removed to Newtown. These were Mr. Hooker's company."

Thomas Hooker, a graduate of Emmanuel College at Cambridge University, was one of the most prominent Puritan ministers in England, with a large following in Essex in the vicinity of Braintree. Although Hooker himself did not come to New England until 1633, some of his followers had sailed in July 1632 on the *Lyon*, and this is the group referred to by Winthrop as the Braintree company. Winthrop must have placed this entry incorrectly, since the *Lyon* did not arrive at Boston until mid-September, and the court order (which does not appear in the surviving court records) was probably made in October.

In the list of colony freemen for 6 November 1632 were nine men, most of whom had sailed on the *Lyon*, settled first in Cambridge, and later followed Hooker to Connecticut - William Goodwin, John Benjamin, John Talcott, James Olmstead, John Clark, William Lewis, Nathaniel Richards, William Wadsworth and Richard Webb. Since freemen first had to be church members, and since there was in November of 1632 no church at Cambridge, these members of the Braintree company must have been admitted to some other church, most likely Watertown.

In his journal for 4 September 1633 Winthrop notes the arrival of the *Griffin*, carrying two hundred passengers, including three ministers - John Cotton, Thomas Hooker and Samuel Stone. Cotton, of course, became teacher at Boston church, whereas "Mr. Hooker and Mr. Stone went presently to Newtown, where they were to be entertained." The *Griffin* also carried "Mr. Haynes (a gentleman of great estate) ... and many other men of good estates." John Haynes followed Hooker to Newtown, and undoubtedly many more of Hooker's Braintree followers sailed on this ship as well.

Little time was wasted in forming a church at Cambridge, for on 11 October Winthrop recorded "A fast at Newtown, where Mr. Hooker was chosen pastor, and Mr. Stone teacher, in such a manner as before at Boston." Although records of the Cambridge church for this period do not survive (see page fourteen), we can see from the list of freemen for 14 May 1634 who must have joined Hooker's congregation at its formation or soon after. At the head of this list is John Haynes, Esq., placed here because of his great wealth. Further down in the list are Mr. Thomas Hooker and Mr. Samuel Stone, followed immediately by twelve other men, most of whom were residents of Newtown at this time - men such as John Steele, Edmund Stebbins, Edward Muste and John Pratt.

The sojourn of Thomas Hooker and his Braintree company in Massachusetts Bay was a brief one, for in late May "Those of Newtown complained of straitness for want of land," and were granted permission to seek out land along the Merrimack River. They did not find anything here to their liking, and soon joined with like-minded men from Watertown, Dorchester and Roxbury in exploring new sites along the Connecticut River. In 1635 an advance party of Newtown men moved to the place that would become Hartford, and in 1636 Hooker and the rest of his followers also made the move.

Was this migration from Massachusetts Bay to Connecticut made strictly for reasons of land shortage? Probably not, for Hooker did not have as rigid a view of the connection between church and state as did Winthrop and some of the ministers associated with him. Our best evidence for this is the fact that in the colony of Connecticut church membership was not a prerequisite for admission to freeman status.

Whatever the motivations for the move, the history of the Braintree company in Massachusetts Bay spanned less than four years, from the arrival of the *Lyon* in September of 1632 to the departure of Hooker and the rest of his party in the spring and summer of 1636.

EARLY LAND GRANTING

Two contemporary sources exist which allow us to reconstruct much of the early land-granting process in Cambridge, and at the same time track the movement of early settlers in and out of the town. These are the records of the town meetings, and of the town proprietors.

Cambridge's first town clerk was Mr. William Spencer, who apparently arrived in New England and settled in Cambridge in 1631. The Cambridge town records are in his hand through October of 1636, shortly before his departure for Hartford (*The Records of the Town of Cambridge [formerly Newtowne] Massachusetts, 1630-1703* [Cambridge 1901]).

Although the published version of the Cambridge town records does not make it clear, the first few pages of this earliest volume are cluttered with a number of entries made by other scribes years later. In the midst of these extraneous entries is a list of names, written by Spencer, giving the earliest settlers of Cambridge, presumably those in residence prior to the arrival of the vanguard of the Braintree company.

The continuous series of records entered by Spencer begins with an undated agreement relating to the fencing in of some of the town's land, followed by an entry of 24 December 1632 in which the town's inhabitants agree on the scheduling of town meetings. This agreement was subscribed to by "Tho Dudley, John Haynes and others." Here we have the first clue that this entry at least was entered some time after its actual date, for two reasons: John Haynes did not arrive in New England until September of the following year; and, since the names of only two of the subscribers are included, this agreement must have been copied from an earlier version.

Examination of a microfilm copy of the original of these first few pages shows that all of William Spencer's entries through 7 April 1634 were written in a very regular fashion and in the same ink. This raises the possibility that the entire record down to this point was written at one sitting, or at least within a very brief period of time, more than a year after some of the meetings. We must be alert, therefore, for anachronisms and other problems with the entries before the spring of 1634.

The next item of interest after the 24 December 1632 entry is a list of names, under date of 7 January 1632/3, of those who were responsible for maintaining the fencing around the common, and the length of fencing each had to maintain and repair. Again, this list includes names of men who certainly were not in Cambridge at this date, leading off with John Haynes, Esq.; others on this list who apparently came with Haynes in late 1633 are Matthew Allen, Richard Lord and Andrew Warner (see town record for 4 November 1633).

This roster of January 1632/3 is the basis for many later claims for the presence of all these men in Cambridge in 1632. Among regularly consulted authors, Savage and Pope give 1632 as the earliest date for the arrival of most of these immigrants. But clearly this list too is anachronistic and, lacking corroborating evidence independent of the town records, we must not use this as evidence for the earliest date of arrival for anyone. Noting that the names are listed in order of length of fence to be tended, we may suggest that William Spencer compiled and arranged this list in late 1633 or early 1634, prior to or at the same time he was drafting this portion of the town records.

The next dated entry is a grant of cowyards (all for one acre or less) to twenty-eight individuals on 5 August 1633. This list appears more promising than the last, since it is not arranged in any regular manner, and no name on it can be immediately impeached. In order to assess the reliability of these names, we may divide them into four groups. First, there are those who may be placed in Cambridge (or elsewhere in Massachusetts Bay) prior to the arrival of the Braintree company [Denison, Dudley, Masters, Patrick, Sackett, William Spencer, and presumably Thomas Spencer, William's brother]. Next in order would be the members of the 1632 contingent of the Braintree company [Benjamin, Clark, Goodwin, Lewis, Olmstead, Richards, Wadsworth and White]. These two groups, containing just more than half the names on the list, were certainly in Cambridge by 5 August 1633, and so any doubt about the validity of this list depends upon our knowledge of the remaining thirteen.

The two remaining groups pose some problems. In the third group are seven names which first appear in other records on the 10 May 1634 list of freemen [Goodman, Hart, Muste, Pratt, Stebbins and John and George Steele]. Their presence in this list of freemen constitutes evidence that they had arrived during the 1633 sailing season, but not that they were in New England as early as 5 August of that year. Furthermore, Edward Muste appears in the May 1634 list of freemen, whereas his widow Hester is in the August 1633 list, clearly indicating again that this portion of the records was written later than its apparent date.

The fourth group consists of six men whose presence in New England prior to 1634 is not independently corroborated [Adams, Bosworth, Hosmer, Kelsey, Pantry and Westwood]. With Westwood especially there is difficulty, since he and his wife are on the April 1634 passenger list of the *Francis*. If the August 1633 cowyard grants are to be accepted as reliable, then we must postulate that Westwood had made an earlier trip (like others discussed in the first issue of this *Newsletter*), and that the 1634 sailing was his second voyage, certainly a possibility.

Some of these considerations make it difficult, but not impossible, to accept the conclusion that all these people were in New England by the summer of 1633. But there is at least one argument that does point towards the reliability of the list: On 4 November 1633 seven additional grants of cowyards were made to men who had arrived after August of that year; if the August list is not reliable, why would Spencer split up the cowyard grants in this way, and why would he not combine them into one list as he had already done for the fencing of the commons?

Pending further evidence, we will provisionally accept the thirteen names of the third and fourth groups above as immigrants before August 1633, probably on one of the ships that had arrived in the spring of that year. The English origins of many of these men remain unknown, and if future research should show that one or more of them was still in England in August 1633, we would have to revise this conclusion.

We turn now to a more general discussion of the granting of land in Cambridge. Looked at in one way, this process is not so clear in Cambridge as in Watertown, since we have fewer lists of the earliest grants of land. But in another way we learn much more here than we did in Watertown, since the surviving inventories are spread over a number of years; this gives us a glimpse of landholding both before and after the departure of the Braintree company, for example. The following discussion consists of preliminary observations based on a broad study of the early proprietors' records and close analysis of a few individual entries. Complete analysis of all entries here, and of relevant material in the town records, will reveal much more (*The Register Book of the Lands and Houses in the "New Towne"* ... [Cambridge 1896]).

Pursuant to court orders of April 1634 and March 1634/5, the first inventory was compiled between May and October 1635, listing the holdings of eighty-six individuals. Shortly after this inventory was taken, the majority of the inhabitants pulled up stakes and left for the Connecticut River Valley, having sold their lands to more recent arrivals in New England. Many of these transfers were recorded in this set of records, since no registry of deeds had yet been established.

After the recording of these transfers, the proprietors' records continue with a second compilation, apparently taken in 1638, which appears to contain only purchases or new grants made since 1635. Thus, this compilation is not properly an inventory; but since the turnover of population in 1635 and 1636 was almost total, it approaches being a full inventory, as virtually every piece of land changed hands during these few years. Of the eighty-six persons included in the 1635 inventory, only two (Abraham Morrill and John Masters) obtained additional land between 1635 and 1638.

There follows a similar but shorter compilation for the year 1639, presumably comprising transaction which had taken place in the previous year, as well as new grants made by the town. After a few more miscellaneous items, there is then copied into the proprietors' records "A Transcript of the houses and lands of the inhabitants of this town of Cambridge given in at a General Court holden at Boston the sixth day of the seventh month Anno Domini 1642." This again is a true inventory, and was probably prepared in obedience with the same court order which gave rise to the Watertown inventories of late 1643 and early 1644.

The history of a single houselot in the center of town illustrates the interrelationships among these various compilations, and also demonstrates the volatility of the land market in this first decade of settlement. Not all the details can be given here, but the interested reader can study the various entries, compare the boundaries, and see how a reconstruction is done. In the 1635 inventory, William Lewis owned "one house with backside about half a rood [one-eighth of an acre]" [p. 14]. In William Cutter's entry for the compilation of 1638 we learn that he "bought of Thomas Besbeech one house in the town with backside about half a rood ... which he bought of William Lewis" [p. 54]. But William Cutter must have surrendered this land to the town, for, still within the 1638 compilation, Sebastian Brigham "bought of the townsmen" this same lot [p. 59]. Finally, in the 1639 compilation, John Bridge is said to have bought this parcel from Sebastian Brigham [p. 65]. At this point things settle down somewhat, for John Bridge still has this property at the time of the 1642 inventory [p. 86]. In the space of four years (1635-1639), five different men owned this one plot. John Bridge remained in Cambridge until his death, but what of the other four? William Lewis joined the migration to Hartford in 1636, and Thomas Besbeech left the following year for Scituate. William Cutter remained in Cambridge, so must have given the land back to the town, and Sebastian Brigham went to Rowley.

One significant difference between Cambridge and Watertown in 1642 was that the latter had granted away virtually all its land by that date, whereas Cambridge had held much in reserve, and was still making substantial grants in the 1660s and 1680s. Some of this is accounted for by the fact that Cambridge had received from the General Court additional grants south of the Charles (in what would become Newton). Even so, Cambridge late in the century was still able to make grants in the western portion of its original territory, at about the same distance from the original town center as the Watertown Farms were from Watertown. Much is made by some historians of the differences in land granting in New England based on differences in regional origins in England; but both Cambridge and Watertown were settled by East Anglians,

CAMBRIDGE CHURCH RECORDS

Although no church records of the standard variety (vital events, membership, discipline) survive for the Cambridge church during the tenure of its first two ministers, we are lucky to have two other sets of records which allow us to reconstruct much of what happened in this church during its first decade.

The first of these were the confessions of faith gathered by Reverend Thomas Shepard. A confession of faith was a unique feature of the congregational system as developed in New England, and was necessary for admission to church membership. Since this confession was not a simple exercise, and since admission to freemanship in the Massachusetts Bay Colony was dependent upon church membership, the confession was an important hurdle for any Massachusetts Bay settler to get over. (See Edmund S. Morgan, *Visible Saints* [Cornell UP 1965] for the best discussion of the origin and development of the confession of faith.)

The largest surviving set of these confessions is that compiled and preserved by Thomas Shepard between 1637 and 1644, the manuscript of which is held by the New England Historic Genealogical Society. These confessions, fifty-one in all, have been edited and published by George Selement and Bruce C. Woolley (*Thomas Shepard's Confessions*, Publications of the Colonial Society of Massachusetts, Volume LVIII, Boston, 1981). (A smaller group of confessions from this church, covering the later years of the 1640s, has been discovered recently at the American Antiquarian Society, and is planned for publication in the *William and Mary Quarterly*.)

For the most part the confessions consist of a recounting of the steps by which the aspiring church member became satisfied that he or she had arrived at saving grace. Occasionally there would be embedded in this narrative a nugget or two of biographical or genealogical information. For instance, Christopher Cane indicated in his account that he had had the opportunity to hear the sermons of Reverend John Wilson while both were still in England. Wilson was minister of Sudbury in Suffolk from 1618 until his departure for New England in 1630, so we have a clue here for the general area within which Cane's English origin should be sought.

As a second example, Goodwife Crackbone (wife of Gilbert) told a sad story of living in London, and having a child die young, apparently not long before the family removed to New England. These clues may seem vague and inconsequential, but, in conjunction with other information, they may help to narrow the area of search required to solve a problem, or they may lead to additional information which will help corroborate a conclusion arrived at by other means.

The second set of records of the Cambridge church which provides information about the period of the Great Migration is the compilation made by Reverend Jonathan Mitchell, successor to Thomas Shepard after the latter's death in 1649. Mitchell began his record in January of 1658/9, when he carried out a sort of census of the members of his church, family by family (*Records of the Church of Christ at Cambridge in New England: 1632-1830 ...*, copied and edited by Stephen Paschall Sharples [Boston 1906]).

Mitchell's technique was to list first the name of the head of family and his wife, and give their membership status. This was followed by the names of the children and other members of the household, divided into three groups: first were any children born before the family arrived in Cambridge; second were those children born and baptized in Cambridge prior to 1659, without dates; and third were added those children baptized from 1659 on, with full dates. Information was also included about former marriages of spouses, and about marriages and residences of some of the children.

The genealogical value of this record is obvious, and many of the clues have already been used to establish various genealogical connections; but many clues remain to be exploited. One example of this sort, involving the family of Gilbert Crackbone, was demonstrated in the first issue of this Newsletter (page two). As another instance of the way in which Mitchell's records may be used, see the article on the English origin of Edward Shepard, discussed on page fifteen of this *Newsletter*.

Some of the best clues which remain neglected are those in which one or more of the children were born in England, for this can provide corroboration of an identification, and can also help to pin down more accurately the date of arrival of a family, and also the date when some of these immigrants first joined the church. One such example is that of Richard Champney and his family. The first child of Richard and his wife Jane is entered as follows: "Esther Champney now Convers living at Wooburne baptized in England aged about 6 years when her father joined here." Richard Champney came to New England late in 1635 with Thomas Shepard, and was made freeman on 25 May 1636; he most likely joined the second Cambridge church when it was organized in February 1635/6. Thus, we would be looking for a Richard Champney in England with a daughter Hester born about 1629.

The confessions and Mitchell's register are not adequate substitutes for a full set of baptisms, burials, admissions and other church matters. Taken together, however, and interwoven with other records of the town, county and colony, it is possible to recapture much of the early history of the Cambridge church under Hooker and Shepard.

RECENT LITERATURE

Lawrence I. Shepard, "In Search of English Origins: Edward Shepard of Cambridge," *Heritage Quest* #22:60-67, #23:48-54, 61, #24:38-40, #25:44-46, #26:35-38. The author has conclusively demonstrated that Edward Shepard, in Cambridge by 1639, married in Erwarton, co. Suffolk, in 1620 Violet Charnel (or Charnock). They had a daughter baptized in Mistley, co. Essex, in 1621, and four more children in nearby Lawford, co. Essex, from 1623 to 1631. Evidence is also presented which identifies the parents of Violet, and the probable ancestry of Edward. The author also clarifies the relationship of Edward Shepard to Gregory Wolterton, and, as a bonus, includes records which add to our knowledge of the English career of Nathaniel Merrill of Newbury. (Frequent references to "Appendix X" indicate that this article is an unedited excerpt from a larger work.)

Roger Howell, Jr., "A Note on the Publication Dates of Christopher Levett's *A Voyage into New England*," *Maine Historical Society Quarterly* 28 (1989):223-25. Traditionally, scholars have held that the first and only edition of Levett's narrative appeared in London in 1628. Howell presents proof of an earlier edition in 1624, and shows how this date is more in consonance with the internal evidence of the narrative itself.

Brice M. Clagett, "The Origin of Robert[1] Keyes of Watertown: A Correction," *The American Genealogist* 65 (1990):12. Demonstrates that the Robert Keyes in Watertown by 1633 was not the Robert Keyes baptized at Woburn, Bedfordshire, on 22 September 1617.

Edwin D. Witter, Jr. "Probable Fathers of Hannah and Joan Newton, Wives of Joseph[2] Phelps and Benedict[1] Alvord of Windsor, Conn.," *The American Genealogist* 65 (1990):13-16. Older sources identify the two women named in this article's title as daughters of Rev. Roger Newton of Farmington and Milford. Witter shows that this cannot be correct; he then produces a much more likely identification: that Joan Newton was sister of Anthony[1] Newton of Dorchester and Braintree, and Hannah Newton was Anthony's daughter.

Robert Charles Anderson, "The Daughters of Simon[1] Eire of Watertown and Boston, Mass.," with "Appendix: Nicholas[1] Guy of Watertown," *The American Genealogist* 65 (1990):17-23. Identifies Mary, the wife of Joseph[1] Tainter of Watertown as daughter of Simon[1] Eire. Tainter, in turn, was son of Jane, the wife of Nicholas[1] Guy, by an earlier husband. Jane (____) (Tainter) Guy also had a daughter Mary by her first husband who married Ephraim[1] Curtis. The suggestion is also made that Simon Eire's daughter Rebecca married Christopher Clark of Boston.

Frederick J. Nicholson, "The English Origin of Macuth[1] (or Matthew) Pratt and Edward[1] Bates of Weymouth, Massachusetts," *The American Genealogist* 65 (1990):33-43. Shows that Macuth Pratt and Edward Bates of Weymouth were from the parish of Aston Clinton, Buckinghamshire, and also that Pratt's wife was first cousin of Bates, both being grandchildren of William and Alice (Oslington) Bates. Furthermore, Nicholson argues that Pratt's given name was Macuth or some variant thereof, and not Matthew.

David Hackett Fischer, *Albion's Seed: Four British Folkways in America* (Oxford 1989). Hackett states his central thesis succinctly: "[T]he legacy of four British folkways in early America remains the most powerful determinant of a voluntary society in the United States today." These "folkways" are East Anglian Puritans to Massachusetts Bay (1629-40), a Royalist elite and their indentured servants from the south of England to Virginia (1640-75), Quakers from the North Midlands and Wales to Pennsylvania and New Jersey (1675-1725), and Scotch-Irish to the American backcountry (1717-1775).

For each of these four cultures, Fischer examines about twenty-five different "folkways." For New England these include such categories as speech, architecture, marriage, food, and child-rearing. To each of these folkways he devotes about three or four pages, surveying the secondary literature on the subject, and relating all this to his central thesis. Fischer contends that New England culture was the culture of East Anglia transplanted. For virtually every one of the folkways discussed, he claims that this feature was unique to East Anglia, and not found elsewhere in England.

There are two problems with Fischer's presentation. First, he overemphasizes the extent of the East Anglian element in the Great Migration. True, East Anglia sent more migrants to New England than did any other part of England, but there were also substantial migrations from the West Country and other regions. Surely these regions also affected the development of New England folkways, and made New England something different from East Anglia. Second, Fischer does not always give sufficient evidence for a unique East Anglian origin for many of the folkways. Closer analysis would probably show that some of these traits were more widespread, or represented Puritan rather than East Anglian traits.

This volume does synthesize an immense amount of secondary literature, and will lead the reader to a wide variety of interesting material. For all its shortcomings, *Albion's Seed* is essential reading for anyone interested in the Great Migration.

dained at Peterborough on 6 August 1620. This then necessitated a trip to the Northamptonshire Record Office at Delapre Abbey, where an inspection of the ordination registers of the Bishop of Peterborough showed that the John Allin ordained on that date had attended Christ's College at Cambridge, and not Caius. This identified the Dedham minister as the John Allin who had received his BA at Cambridge on 12 August 1616, whose parentage is not known, and not the Gonville and Caius graduate whose father was Reginald Allin of Colby.

Our second example is John Youngs, who sailed from Yarmouth in Norfolk in 1637, settled briefly in Salem, and then moved to Southold, Long Island, as one of the founders and the first minister. It has been known for many years that he was born in Southwold, co. Suffolk, where his father, Christopher Youngs, had long been the rector. But John's location in the early 1630s has remained unknown.

In this case, the record which came to the rescue was the Bishop's Register, which contains a chronological listing of the appointments to livings within the Diocese of Norwich. By reading this register for the early decades of the seventeenth century, it was simple enough to discover that John Youngs had been appointed rector of the parish of Covehithe (alias North Cove), also in Suffolk, and just a few miles from his place of birth. Examination of the parish registers for Covehithe verified this, and provided additional information on the Youngs family prior to migration to New England.

Last, we will look at a minister who was not an immigrant, but was father of several who did come to New England. Reverend Thomas Stoughton, father of Thomas and Israel Stoughton of Dorchester, served first, from 1586 to 1594, in the parish of Naughton in Suffolk, and then from 1600 to 1606, at Great Coggeshall in Essex. But where was he in the intervening six years, a period during which two or three of his children were probably born?

Several sources were tried, but the one that solved the problem was again the consignation books from the visitations made by the Bishop of London. But these were of a different form from those in the diocese immediately to the north. For the Archdeaconry of Essex and the Archdeaconry of Colchester, parts of the Diocese of London, these books, compiled every six months, listed all church officers, including churchwardens and sidesmen. Without this provision, Thomas Stoughton would not have been found; during these years he did not hold a beneficed living, but was instead the lecturer at Burstead Magna, the parish which contained the town of Billericay. The registers for this parish are not complete and are in other ways unsatisfactory, but they do provide clues which add to our knowledge of the family of the Reverend Thomas Stoughton.

Great Migration Newsletter

| Vol. 1 | July-September 1990 | No. 3 |

THE VALUE OF FREEMEN'S LISTS

In the English political system, a freeman held the freedom of a borough, city or company, and as such had a number of privileges and responsibilities. The Massachusetts Bay Company was a joint-stock company that was in the process of converting itself into an independent government, and the most valuable privilege of freemanship was the right to vote for company officers, such as governor or assistant. In the records of the General Court of Massachusetts Bay are lists of those admitted as freemen of the colony. Knowing that an individual in whom we are interested attained this status is a useful addition to our collection of biographical information, but what else can we learn from these lists?

The first thing to note is that the prerequisites for admission to freemanship were not always the same. A few of the more prominent of the settlers were freemen by virtue of having made a financial contribution to the Massachusetts Bay Company, including such luminaries as John Winthrop, Simon Bradstreet and Thomas Dudley. Then, in the fall of 1630, one hundred and eight men requested that they be granted freeman status, and on 18 May 1631 one hundred and eighteen were admitted, seventy of whom had been on the earlier list.

The thirty-eight men who requested freemanship in October 1630, but were not on the May 1631 list, deserve a closer look, and may be divided into five groups. Two of these men had died in the short interval between the two lists (Richard Garrett and Ralph Glover). Two more had returned to England in the spring of 1630, never to return to New England (Thomas Southcott and George Ludlow). There are five names which do not appear again in early New England records, and one assumes that they also fall in one of these first two groups, having died or returned to England.

Of the remaining twenty-eight applicants for freemanship who did not receive the honor in May 1631, eighteen did eventually become freemen, but ten never did (assuming that the surviving records are complete). Examples of those who eventually did become freemen are Richard Sylvester and Henry Wolcott, both of whom are on the list of 1 April 1634. These men are well-recorded in New

England in these early years, and were active in commerce. Of those who never became freemen, we might look at Samuel Freeman, who was known to have travelled to England in the spring of 1630 and returned many years later, or Richard Church, who may have moved at this time to Plymouth. The explanation for these twenty-eight men not immediately taking up their freemanship may in some cases lie in their absence in May of 1631 due to a trip to England, but this would probably not apply to all cases. (For further discussion of this group of men, see Robert Charles Anderson, "Some Doubts About the Parentage of John[1] Drake of Windsor, Connecticut," *The American Genealogist* 63 [1988]:193-206.)

These freemen of May 1631 had only to ask for the privilege. From that point on, and for the next thirty years, there was the added requirement that one must be a church member before one could apply to become a freeman. This condition allows us to extract additional information from the lists. For instance, on 6 November 1632 eighteen men were made free, the last nine of whom were from Hooker's Braintree Company, and known to have resided in Cambridge. But there was no church in Cambridge at this date, so one must assume that they were admitted as members of one of the neighboring churches. The most likely candidates would be Boston, Charlestown and Watertown. (There is little chance that these men would have been admitted to Dorchester church, since that town was inhabited exclusively by settlers from the West Country, and the Braintree Company were all East Anglians.) The records of the first two of these churches survive, and these nine men

(*continued on page 24*)

EDITOR'S EFFUSIONS

I very much appreciate all those who have written to the Project, some simply with words of encouragement, some with suggestions for new and different ways to do things, and some with offers of information and assistance. One of the more gratifying responses to the Newsletter was encountered several times recently during conversations at the NGS Conference in the States at Arlington, Virginia. A subscriber would say "I have enjoyed reading the Newsletter very much, and my spouse, who is not a genealogist, also enjoys it." Please keep writing with your comments and suggestions; I may not be able to answer every letter, but your thoughts and reactions are helpful.

On page 22 of this issue you will find an article on "Delayed Records," records from a period years or even decades after the Great Migration, which nevertheless provide direct information on the people and events of that period. One cannot search for records of this sort on a systematic basis, since they are buried in the most unlikely places. I would be pleased to learn of any "delayed records" which might be known to our readers, records such as a deposition made in old age by a man who had come over in the 1630s as a servant, but did not appear in the records of those years.

The next issue, completing the first volume, will focus on Dorchester. In addition to the usual material in the Newsletter, this phase of the Project's work will also generate an article attempting to establish objective and consistent criteria for determining whether a person or family should be listed as a passenger on the *Mary & John* in 1630; this article will be published elsewhere.

CORRECTION

On pages twelve and thirteen of the April-June 1990 issue of the Newsletter appears an article on Early Land Granting in Cambridge. This article ends in the middle of a sentence, and so the following should be added to complete the sentence: "... so some other explanation must be sought for the relative restraint of the Cantabrigians."

Robert Charles Anderson, FASG   Editor
Margaret F. Costello   Production Assistant

The *Great Migration Newsletter* (ISSN 1049-8087) is published quarterly by the Great Migration Study Project, a project of the New England Historic Genealogical Society, 101 Newbury Street, Boston MA 02116

The subscription rate is $8 for one year and $15 for two years. The subscription year is the same as the calendar year.

COMMENTS ON *DORSET PILGRIMS*

Several readers of this Newsletter have written in praise of a recently published volume, *Dorset Pilgrims: The Story of West Country Pilgrims Who Went to New England in the 17th Century*, by Frank Thistlethwaite (London 1989). The author has set out to write a narrative account of migration from the West Country to New England, and particularly of the movement led by the Reverend John White of Dorchester, co. Dorset.

Thistlethwaite sets the general background for migration to New England, and more particularly the conditions that prevailed in Dorset, Devon and Somerset. He then describes the gathering of the families who would travel on the *Mary & John,* their passage to New England in 1630, and the settlement of Dorchester. This is followed by a discussion of the move to Windsor, the early development of that town, and the lives of the first and second generations, concluding with the effect of King Philip's War on this settlement.

For the earliest years Thistlethwaite does for Dorchester what David Cressy has done on a larger scale, describing the manner in which the passengers on a given ship came together, how they crossed the ocean, and how their connections with the old country were maintained (Cressy, *Coming Over: Migration and Communication Between England and New England in the Seventeenth Century* [Cambridge, England, 1987]).

One point made by Thistlethwaite deserves further comment. He takes note of John White's claim that of "about 140 persons ... there were not six known either by face or fame to any of the rest." But Thistlethwaite has just expended a number of pages showing how far more than six of these passengers had known one another long before the gathering of the company of the *Mary & John*.

This passage is reminiscent of a similar statement made by the Reverend John Allin of Dedham, Massachusetts, regarding the earliest steps in founding the church there: "The township of Dedham consisting of about 30 families residing there 1637, being come together by divine providence from several parts of England, few of them known to one another before ..." Again, we know that most of the Dedham church founders had come from a limited region in East Anglia, and were as well known to one another as were John White's families from the West Country.

What were these ministers trying to tell us? In Allin's case, there was no question of trying to deceive the English authorities, since he composed this account decades after the event. Was this some sort of formula that was a common part of accounts of the forming of new settlements? Or do these claims have some deeper meaning, as yet uncovered?

Focus   on   LYNN

THE PROGRESS OF SETTLEMENT

The towns we have examined so far - Watertown and Cambridge - received a large number of settlers at one time and moved quickly into the category of full-fledged settlement, with a church, town officers, and the like. Lynn (which in its earliest years was known as Saugus) followed a more leisurely course.

From depositions taken many years later, we have solid evidence that there were residents in Saugus (or at least on Nahant Neck) as early as 1629. In the course of a dispute over earlier land grants, William Dixy deposed in 1657 that twenty-eight years earlier his master, Isaac Johnson, had written to John Endicott, seeking a place to keep their cattle. They were told that they could go wherever they pleased, and so chose Nahant, in what is now Lynn. Time intervals given in depositions should always be viewed with a jaundiced eye, but in this case we are told that Johnson wrote to Endicott, and this could only have taken place in 1629, so the date is confirmed. (See page 22 below for more details on this deposition.)

Isaac Johnson was one of the wealthiest men to sail with the Winthrop Fleet, having married a daughter of the Earl of Lincoln. Had he lived, Isaac Johnson might soon have turned Saugus into one of the leading settlements in Massachusetts Bay. But Johnson died in the first winter, and deprived Saugus of the leadership and nucleus of stability which any early town needed.

For the next few years, then, Saugus remained a very small community. This can be demonstrated in three ways, by comparing Saugus with the other Massachusetts Bay towns in three aspects: taxes, freemen and social composition.

TAXES - From time to time, the Massachusetts Bay General Court levied a rate on the various plantations, at first to cover some particular expense. Saugus appears for the first time in such a list on 5 July 1631, when the community was assessed for twenty shillings; this was far behind the five pounds demanded from Watertown and Boston, or the three pounds from Roxbury, and was only just ahead of the ten shillings asked of Nantasket or the fifteen shillings of Winnissimet. On 3 February 1631/2 Saugus was coupled with "Marble Harbour," so we cannot be sure of how much was asked of Saugus alone. By 1 October 1633 Saugus had moved ahead of Salem in the rate list, at thirty-six pounds, but still behind the eighty pounds for Dorchester and the forty-eight pounds for Roxbury, Charlestown and others. By this measure, then Saugus spent these early years of the

1630s growing slowly, from the level of such tiny and informal locations as Winnissimet, to the lower edge of the larger and more highly organized towns which were settled by the passengers of the Winthrop Fleet in 1630.

FREEMEN - Although the lists of men admitted as freemen of the colony do not indicate the town where each man resided, we can use other sources to draw up lists of freemen for each town. The first list of freemen, for 18 May 1631, contained 118 names, of which only three were certainly from Saugus: Mr. Edw: Tomlins, Mr. John Dillingham, and Tho: Dexter. By comparison, Dorchester and Boston each had more than a dozen. From that date until 14 May 1634 (when the rate of immigration and the rate of admitting freemen increased greatly), only three additional Saugus names can be identified: Mr. Nath: Turner, John Kirman and Timothy Tomlyns. Either Saugus men had some reason for avoiding freemanship, or the population of Saugus was much smaller in these years than the other Bay towns. One is hard-pressed to explain why Saugus would be a hotbed of political indifference, so the second explanation must be the correct one.

SOCIAL COMPOSITION - A central feature of the Great Migration is that it consisted largely of middle-class families, solid yeomen and husbandmen, with a wife, two or three children, and a servant or two. But the list of men and families which one could draw up for these first few years at Saugus would look quite different. Three of the six freemen listed above carried the honorific "Mr.," which designated the next social stratum above "Goodman," this latter category constituting the majority of most other towns. Other persons who can be placed in Saugus in these early years were single young men, servants to the more exalted men named above.

Taken together these features of life in Saugus from 1629 to about 1633 describe a settlement unlike that in Watertown or Cambridge. Saugus consisted of a few wealthy men, mostly agricultural entrepreneurs, each with a few male servants. These few men had suffered when Isaac Johnson died so soon after his arrival, and they also suffered because John Humphrey, who had also married a daughter of the Earl of Lincoln, did not come to New England as soon as expected.

John Humphrey had been associated with New England colonizing activities at least from the late 1620s, was expected to sail with the Winthrop Fleet in 1630, and was elected an Assistant for several years in anticipation of his arrival. When he finally did come, he immediately filled a position in Saugus like that held by Nowell in Charlestown, and Endicott in Salem, thus elevating the status of the settlement by his very presence.

THE CHURCH AT SAUGUS

A necessary element of every settled plantation in Massachusetts Bay was an orthodox church. The development of this institution in the early years of Saugus is another indicator of the way in which this town matured slowly by comparison with its neighbors.

One of the handful of passenger ships to arrive in the Bay during 1631 was the *Plough*, carrying the vanguard of a small group known as the Company of Husbandmen. This group had obtained a patent from the Council for New England for a tract of land in what is now Maine, but they were not well enough organized and not practical enough to take advantage of this asset. The *Plough* ended its journey ignominiously on the mudbanks of the Charles River, and the few people on board and their goods were soon dispersed over several Bay towns, with some of the passengers soon leaving for Virginia.

The following year more of the Company arrived, including their spiritual leader, the Reverend Stephen Bachiler, one of the more intriguing characters of these early years. Although close to seventy years old in 1632, Bachiler wasted no time getting on the wrong side of Winthrop and some of the other leaders of the colony. On 3 October 1632 the General Court issued the following order: "Mr. Bachelor is required to forbear exercising his gifts as a pastor or teacher publicly, in our patent, unless it be to those he brought with him, for contempt of authority, & till some scandals be removed." We do not know what happened in the ensuing months, but on 4 March 1632/3 we learn that "The Court hath reversed the last act against Mr. Batcheler, which restrained him from further gathering a church within this patent."

When exactly did Bachiler organize his church in Saugus? One of the signs of this event for other communities is the appearance in the list of admissions of freemen of a large group from the town in question, usually including the minister and other church officers. On 4 March 1632/3 two Saugus men were admited to freemanship (John Kirman and Timothy Tomlins, the first of whom is known to have been one of the Company of Husbandmen). No one else who can be identified as a Lynn resident was made free until 14 May 1634 when four men were admitted, at a time when well over a hundred were admitted from the whole colony. Among these four was Christopher Hussey, Bachiler's son-in-law, but this small grouping is still not the sign of an organized church.

Then in 1635 a rapid series of events brought the situation to a conclusion. On 15 March 1634/5 Winthrop includes a relatively long entry in his journal, detailing a dispute in Saugus church which clearly shows that there were two warring factions, one of which felt that Bachiler had not organized the church in a proper man-

ner. A conference of church elders found that "they were a true church, though not constituted, at first, in due order, yet after consent and practice of a church estate had supplied that defect." Then, in the 6 May 1635 list of freemen is a grouping of nine names, six of which were surely Saugus residents, and the last of which was "Mr. Steven Batchellor." Within months, however, dissension had broken out again, for on the 25th of February (or possibly January) 1635/6 Winthrop reports that "The distractions about the churches of Salem and Sagus, and the removal of other churches, and the great scarcity of corn, etc., occasioned a general fast to [be] proclaimed." Later in the same year a new church is organized with Reverend Samuel Whiting as minister, and Bachiler departs for a brief stay in Yarmouth.

This reorganization of the church at Saugus was not an isolated event. In the neighboring Salem church, Roger Williams was ejected late in 1635, and a new church was gathered the following year under Hugh Peter. With the migration of many settlers to the Connecticut River valley, new churches were organized in Dorchester and Cambridge in 1636. And during this same period a larger question revolving around admissions procedures in all the Bay churches was being worked out; each prospective member now had to present a confession of faith, detailing the pathway by which he or she had learned of having saving grace (see Edmund Sears Morgan, *Visible Saints: The History of a Puritan Idea* [New York 1963]).

More than half the churches in the Bay were affected by this series of events, with at least a rewritten covenant if not total reorganization. (On the same day that he noted the "distractions" relating to Salem and Saugus, Winthrop also noted that "The Church of Boston renewed their covenant this day, and made a large explanation of that which they had first entered into, and acknowledged such failings as had fallen out, etc.") But clearly Bachelor's church, which maintained a tenuous and not totally legitimate existence from 1632 to 1636, was in 1636 replaced with a church which met all the standards of orthodoxy demanded by the colony's religious and civil leaders.

Thus, by the middle of 1636 Saugus had at last gathered all the trappings of a mature town. It had a sizable population of families of the yeomanry, it had a resident magistrate (John Humphrey), and it had a settled church. A sure sign that Saugus had come of age occurred in a brief note in the records of the General Court on 20 November 1637: "Saugust is called Linn." The other settlements at the Bay had almost immediately exchanged their original Indian names for an English favorite; Mattapan became Dorchester, Shawmut became Boston, and Naumkeag became Salem. But Saugus had to wait seven years to become Lynn, a long journey from unsettled plantation to fully-fledged town.

LAND GRANTING

The absence of all early records for the town of Lynn obviously means that we do not have lists of grants of land, or a compiled book of possessions, as we do for most of the other towns of Massachusetts Bay. This means that a single document which is preserved in an Essex court case of 1661 takes on special importance.

In 1661 William Longley, earlier known as Richard Langley, sued the town of Lynn for land which he felt had been granted to him, but withheld. The main point in contention was whether this man now calling himself William Longley was the same as the Richard Langley who had indeed received a grant of town land in 1638. In the process of the suit, one of the documents introduced as evidence was an extract from the town records of the complete town grant of 1638, to all persons.

The list of parcels granted provides much useful information. This grant was described in one of the depositions as "the thirty and forty acre lots in Lynn Village," which tells us that these lots were in that area which became Reading. A few of these lots, however, were much larger, the largest being 800 acres for Lord Brooke (who never came to New England), with other large parcels going to various members of the town's elite. This grant also came at an interesting time in the town's development, a year after the departure of several families for Sandwich on Cape Cod, and two years before the migration of others to Southampton on Long Island. We see a picture of a town in process of change, and can study the intermingling of families who would stay in Lynn for decades with those who were only passing through.

If this is the only complete record of a grant of Lynn town land, how are we to reconstruct the larger picture? Certainly before this time there would have been grants of a houselot, with a parcel or two of marsh or meadow, and maybe a piece of plowland; this was the minimum that every English husbandman or yeoman would need to engage in his agricultural pursuits and supply the needs of his family. Much of this information can be found in the records of later transfers of this land, in the deeds and probates. No attempt is made here to search the Essex County deeds, but a survey of early Essex probate papers, along with one entry from a volume of notarial records, does supply the beginning of a pattern.

In August 1639, Francis Godsome sold to John Fuller a house and five acre home lot, three acres of meadow and thirty acres of wood and upland. [*Lechford's Note-Book* 152-3]

Inventory of Abraham Belknap, Sept. 1643: House, 5 a.; planting land, 2 a.; salt marsh, 2 a.; salt marsh at Fox Hill, 6 a.; and "at the village," 30 a. [*Essex Probate* 1:26-27]

Inventory of Hugh Churchman, 4 Aug. 1644: "House, lot and marsh appraised at 6li." [EP 1:33-34]

Inventory of Jane Gaines, widow, 14 Jan. 1644/5: House and lot of upland, 6 a., with a "small parcel of salt marsh lying before the door"; "salt marsh lying at Rumley marsh," 2 a. [EP 1:44-45]

Inventory of William Gouge, 28 Oct. 1645: House and lot (no acreage given); meadow, 2a.; and lot, 10a. [EP 1:50]

Inventory of Francis Lightfoot, 21 Dec. 1646: House and 2 a. of ground it stands on; and meadow, 3 a. [EP 1:56]

Inventory of Edward Ingalls, 1648: "House and lands 50li." [EP 1:100]

Inventory of Hugh Burt Jr., 8 Oct. 1650: "House and land belonging 22li." [EP 1:123]

Inventory of William Knight, 22 March 1654/5: Dwelling house, barn and 15 a. plowland; meadow in Rumley marsh, 6 a.; and meadow in the town marsh, 5 a. [EP 1:213]

From this we can begin to extract a picture of early land granting in Lynn. For each case where we have a list of each parcel of land, there is first a houselot, ranging from two to fifteen acres, but usually around five. There is then a piece or two of marsh or meadow, generally two or three acres. Finally, a few of the estates include a larger lot, of which we see here two of thirty acres and one of ten. This latter is the grant of 1638 which has been discussed above; although some of these people may have sold their share of this grant, the more likely explanation is that the land was not yet considered to have any value, and was ignored, much as was the case with the Watertown farm lands in the early years.

This tentative outline raises some interesting questions. Clearly, as compared with Watertown and Cambridge, the Lynn inhabitants have received very little land. By the time of most of the inventories summarized above, virtually all the land in Watertown had been granted out, with most proprietors holding eight or more parcels, amounting to well over a hundred acres.

What was the reason for this parsimonious policy? Was land held in reserve according to notions of land use which the immigrants had brought with them from England? Or was less land granted simply because Lynn had proportionately less land that was agriculturally useful? To answer this question more research will be necessary, both in identifying the English origins of Lynn settlers and the agricultural practices in the relevant parts of England, and in further characterizing the land granting policy in Lynn by studying the Essex deeds.

DELAYED RECORDS

We are always happiest if the fullest range of records for a given town have survived - church, vital, land and town meeting records. But this is not always the case, and certainly not with Lynn, for which no town records earlier than 1691 are extant. In such cases we have a number of alternative sources. We look, for instance, in the records of adjacent towns, or in higher jurisdictions. There will, for instance, be marriages of Lynn residents which take place in other towns, and much of what we have learned about Lynn on the preceding three pages comes from Massachusetts Bay Court or Essex County Court records.

There are, however, two other sources of records which can help us to reconstruct the earliest history of Lynn, or of any other town whose early records are lost. We search these not at some geographic distance from Lynn, and not in a higher jurisdiction, but at a later date. Much can be unearthed by looking for copies of documents made many years and even decades after the documents were originally generated, or by looking for depositions made by early settlers many years after the actual occurrence of the events described.

We have already seen a very important example of a copied document in the record of the 1638 land grant for Lynn, preserved in the records of the Essex County Quarter Court as part of a legal dispute which took place in 1661.

On a smaller scale we find other extracts from Lynn town records which find their way into the court records. For example, at a Quarterly Court at Salem on 28 June 1670, copies from two different sessions of the Lynn town meeting were introduced in evidence. Dated "12:11:1663" and "15:12:1669" these two entries relate to a particular land grant to an individual from the common, and encroachment on town land. Although these items date from a period long after the Great Migration, they do demonstrate the way in which these earlier records become embedded in later court proceedings.

Depositions are a second source of "delayed record entry." Since these depend on the vagaries of human memory rather than the scribal ability of a town or county clerk, they can be more difficult to interpret and evaluate. A useful example bears directly on the date of earliest settlement of Lynn. In a legal squabble which first came before the Essex court in 1657, William Dixy gives his version of his participation in the settlement of Lynn:

> The deposition of Ensign William Dixy aged 50 years or thereabout, sworn sayeth that about twentyeight years ago, Mr. Isaac Johnson being my master writ to the Honoured Governor as now is Mr. Endecott for a place to sit down in, upon which

Mr. Endecott gave me & the rest leave to go where we would upon which I went to Saugust now Linne ..." Dated 1 July 1657

Twenty-eight years prior to 1657 places this episode in 1629. In general time spans found in depositions should be taken with a grain of salt, and certainly the age which William Dixy provides for himself would seem to be only an approximation. But with regard to the date of the event itself, we have corroborating evidence. John Endicott was indeed governor in 1657, a post to which he was first elected in 1644. But prior to that date, the only time during which he was in a position to be approached by Isaac Johnson in such a matter was from Endicott's own arrival in mid-1628 until Winthrop's arrival in mid-1630, so that the time stated in the deposition jibes exactly.

A second deposition helps in dating the arrival of a man who would later become a prominent citizen of Lynn, Daniel Salmon. As part of the same dispute to which Dixy was deposing, Salmon gave the following information:

> The deposition of Daniell Salmon aged about 45 years sayeth, that he being Master Humphryes servant & about 23 years ago, there being wolves in Nahant, commanded that the whole train band to go drive them out, because it did belong to the whole town, & Farmer Dexter's men being then at training went with the rest ..." Dated 1 July 1657

This tells us in the first place, if we can believe the span of twenty-three years, that Salmon was in Lynn as early as 1634; his earliest appearance in contemporary records is in a lawsuit of 1639, so this deposition places him in Lynn five years earlier. We also may infer that Salmon was not just an ordinary manservant, but was more likely Humphrey's agent, or perhaps steward, for otherwise he would have been in no position to give orders to the train band.

A third deposition, by John Sibley, raises some interesting questions:

> The testimony of John Sibley saith that about 28 yeares agoe dwelling with Sr Richard Saltingston, that my masters cattell with Mr. Johnson, was kept in Nahant without molestation by the Indians ..." Dated 1 July 1657

Again, twenty-eight years would put us in 1629, but Richard Saltonstall did not arrive until 1630. Was Sibley off by a year or two, or in saying that he dwelled with his master, did he really mean that he was in the service of Saltonstall?

Much of the earliest history of New England can be reconstructed by taking advantage of these two important classes of "delayed records." These documents are frequently more difficult to interpret than surviving contemporaneous records, but the rewards can be very great.

RECENT LITERATURE

John B. Carney, "In Search of Fayerweather: The Fayerweather Family of Boston," *New England Historical and Genealogical Register* 144 (1990):3-21. Thomas Fayerweather first appears in New England when he was admitted to the Boston church in the winter of 1630/1, indicating that he had arrived with the Winthrop Fleet, apparently as a single man. He resided in Boston, soon married and died late in 1638. The present article is the first installment in a six-generation genealogy of Thomas and his descendants.

Ruth Wilder Sherman, "The Mary Atwood Sampler: More About Mary (Wood) (Holmes) Bradford of Duxbury and Plymouth, Massachusetts," *New England Historical and Genealogical Register* 144 (1990):22-28. In discussing an early sampler, covers the families of Richard Masterson, in Plymouth by 1633, and of John Wood alias Atwood, first noted at Plymouth in 1636, who married Masterson's daughter.

David S. Lovejoy, "Plain Englishmen at Plymouth," *The New England Quarterly* 63 (1990):232-48. Robert Cushman, during his brief stay in Plymouth in 1621, delivered a sermon exhorting the settlers to persevere in their endeavors. This sermon was later published, and Lovejoy here examines this document in detail, comparing it to Winthrop's Model of Christian Charity of nine years later. Although Winthrop's sermon was more subtly composed, both placed great stress on the need for cooperation among the settlers, and the dangers of individualism and selfishness. Lovejoy points out that as a group, the Plymouth planters were more homogeneous than the Massachusetts Bay settlers, and from a slightly lower social stratum.

Robert Charles Anderson, "The English Origin of John Hunting (1602-1689) of Dedham, Massachusetts," *National Genealogical Society Quarterly* 78 (1990):85-97. Demonstrates that John Hunting, who arrived in Dedham in 1638, was born in Thrandeston, co. Suffolk, in 1602, moved with his family to Hoxne in the same county, and lived briefly in the adjacent parish of Oakley before sailing for New England. Also provides three generations of his ancestry, and shows that Susanna Hunting who married Edward Richards and Anna Hunting who married Henry Phillips, both at Dedham, were sisters of John.

Glenn W. LaFantasie, "Roger Williams and John Winthrop: The Rise and Fall of an Extraordinary Friendship," *Rhode Island History* 47 (1989):85-95. LaFantasie, editor of the correspondence of Roger Williams, traces in detail the ups and downs of the relationship between Winthrop and Williams. The two men generated great friction when they were in the same spot; but in their correspondence they exhibited much friendship. In the last four years of his life, however, Winthrop broke off all communication with Williams, which the latter was never able to understand.

Thomas W. Cooper II, "The Olney, Bucks., Emigrant Cluster: The Buckinghamshire Origin of the New England Families of Worcester, New(h)all, Kirtland, Farrington, Fuller, Gaines, Partridge, and Purrier," *The American Genealogist* 65 (1990):65-69. Expanding on his earlier work on the Cooper, Griggs and Pierson families, Cooper presents data on several emigrants to Lynn and Salisbury, Massachusetts, from the parishes of Olney, Sherington, and Clifton Reynes, all in northern Buckinghamshire: Rev. William Worcester of Salisbury, Philip and Nathaniel Kirtland of Lynn, Edmund Farrington of Lynn, John Fuller of Lynn, Henry Gaines of Lynn, William Partridge of Lynn and Salisbury, and William Purrier of Ipswich and Salisbury.

Robert Charles Anderson, "Drake Redux," *The American Genealogist* 65 (1990):87-88. Corrects an error in an earlier article on the ancestry of John Drake of Windsor, and provides additional evidence that this John Drake is not son of William Drake of Ashe, co. Devon.

Frederick J. Nicholson, "The English Origin of Macuth[1] (or Matthew) Pratt and Edward[1] Bates of Weymouth, Mass.," *The American Genealogist* 65 (1990):89-96. Completes an article begun in the previous issue of TAG, giving the English origins of these two emigrants to Weymouth, and showing how they were related to one another.

The Editors, "Thomas[1] Lincoln (the cooper) of Hingham and William[1] Lane of Dorchester (not Hingham)," *The American Genealogist* 65 (1990):106. Corrects and adds to an earlier article on this same subject.

Robert L. French, "John Tilley, 1599-1636," *The Mayflower Quarterly* 56 (1990):118-21. Men by the name of John Tilley appear in Salem, Dorchester and Windsor in the 1620s and 1630s. French claims that these various records all apply to one man, and that he is the son of John Tilley of the *Mayflower*. This latter claim is certainly wrong, since John Tilley of the *Mayflower* was from Bedfordshire, his son is not accounted for in any Plymouth records which should include him (such as the 1627 division of cattle), and the other John Tilley(s) had strong West Country associations. The prior claim, that there was one John Tilley in Salem, Dorchester and Windsor, is possible, but unlikely, and certainly unproved.

(*continued from page 17*)
were not admitted to Boston or Charlestown churches. The most probable conclusion, then, is that this advance group of the Braintree Company were admitted to the Watertown church, thus giving them the grounds to apply for freemanship.

Although the lists for each date are not organized in a totally systematic way, there are patterns. Frequently, persons of the same town were listed in sequence, although this is not always the case. For example, on 4 March 1632/3, eighteen freemen were admitted. The first five were Roxbury men, followed by five from Dorchester, two from Cambridge and two from Lynn. The last four are scattered, including another Dorchester man.

This arrangement can help us in a number of ways. On 1 April 1634 the list of freemen ends with six names, five of which are from Dorchester. The fifth of these six names, though, is Richard Sylvester, known to be residing at the embryo settlement of Wessaguscus (later Weymouth) at this time. From this we can conclude that Richard Sylvester had been admitted by this time as a member of the Dorchester congregation, and this is one of the many clues that indicates a strong connection between Dorchester and Weymouth at this time.

Study of groupings by town can also help in sorting out two or more men of the same name. In his *Planters of the Commonwealth*, Banks lists two Robert Days. He has the first sailing from Ipswich in England in April of 1634, and says this is the Robert Day later of Ipswich in Massachusetts. The second Robert Day came on the *Hopewell*, which arrived in Boston in June of 1635; this man, says Banks, settled in Cambridge.

In the freemen's records however, we find on 6 May 1635 (a month before the arrival of the *Hopewell*) a Robert Day sixth in a grouping of eight from Cambridge (beginning with Thomas Hosmer and ending with Joseph Maggot [i.e., Mygate]). Then on 2 June 1641 is another Robert Day in a series of Ipswich men. The conclusion is that Banks has mixed his identifications of these men.

More briefly, and of less consequence, the two John Bernards, of Cambridge and Watertown, may be assigned their correct dates of admission as freemen. The first John Bernard appears in the lists on 3 September 1634, in a long list of Watertown men, beginning with Brian Pendleton and ending with Nathaniel Foote. Then, on 4 March 1634/5, the second John Bernard is found in an even longer list of Cambridge men, running from Mr. William Andrews to John Wolcott.

These examples do not exhaust the possibilities for analyzing the lists of freemen, one of the more valuable records we have for the earliest years of Massachusetts Bay Colony.

Great Migration Newsletter

Vol. 1   October-December 1990   No. 4

MIGRATION IN 1631 AND 1632

Most accounts of the Great Migration assume, without always making an explicit statement, that the rate of migration was more or less constant during the 1630s. Closer examination of the records shows, however, that after the arrival of the Winthrop Fleet in 1630, very few new immigrants arrived over the next three years; not until the spring of 1634 did large numbers of ships and passengers arrive in Massachusetts Bay. (See Robert Charles Anderson, "A Note on the Changing Pace of the Great Migration," *New England Quarterly* 59 [1986]:406-07.)

What is the basis for this claim? Some have argued that we merely lack the records, and that we cannot say for sure how many did arrive in these years. In order to see more clearly what was happening in this period, we will look closely at the single year of 1631. The sources available to us for this year are quite limited: General Court records (including freemen's lists); Winthrop's Journal; the Winthrop Papers; and church records for a few of the towns. By blending our knowledge from these sources, a clearer picture will emerge.

For 1631, unfortunately, we have no passenger lists, no entries in the English port books for vessels sailing to New England with passengers. Our best substitute, as so often is the case in this early period, is Winthrop's Journal. Winthrop reports the arrival of three ships with immigrants in our year of interest. One of the points we will be testing is whether Winthrop was selective or comprehensive in his listing for these early years. (In 1634 and after, as the pace of immigration increased manyfold, Winthrop satisfied himself in some years simply with noting the number of passenger ships arriving; in other years he made no comment on this matter at all.)

On 5 February 1630/1 Winthrop notes that
"The ship Lyon, Mr. William Peirce, master, arrived at Nantasket. She brought Mr. Williams (a godly minister) with his wife, Mr. Throgmorton, [blank] Perkins, [blank] Ong and others, their wives and children, about twenty passengers ..."
On 6 July 1631
"A small ship of sixty tons arrived at Natascott ... She brought ten passengers from London ... These were the com-

pany called the Husbandmen ... Most of them proved familists and vanished away."
Finally, on 2 November Winthrop reports the arrival, for the second time in the year, of the *Lyon*.
"There came in her the governour's wife, his eldest son, and his wife, and others of his children, and Mr. Eliot, a minister, and other families, being in all about sixty persons ..."
(Winthrop also records the arrival of two other ships, which appear to have brought provisions and cattle, but no passengers - the *Friendship* and the *White Angel*.)

We have, then, three passenger vessels carrying a total of about ninety persons. Can this really be all the immigrants for the year of 1631? To begin to test this, let us look first at the freemen's lists for this year. The first list of freemen is that of 18 May 1631, which comprises mostly those who had arrived in 1630 or earlier, and had requested freemanship in the previous October. In this list we do find at least two of the adult male passengers on the first 1631 passage of the *Lyon*: John Perkins and George [i.e., John] Throckmorton. (Of the other adult males named on this vessel, Simon Onge died almost immediately after arrival, and Reverend Roger Williams never became a Massachusetts Bay freeman.)

Prior to the next sailing season, freemen were sworn on only two other dates - ten on 6 March 1631/2, and four on 3 April 1632. On the assumption that nearly all passenger ships left England in April and arrived in New England in June or later, the freemen of these dates must have arrived in 1631 or earlier. Of these fourteen, two are named as passengers on the *Lyon* on its second sailing: John Eliot and John Winthrop Jr. Presumably Jacob Eliot, John's brother, came on this vessel; and since

(continued on page 26)

EDITOR'S EFFUSIONS

This issue of the *Great Migration Newsletter* brings us to the end of our first year and our first volume. We have looked closely at four of the earliest towns of Massachusetts Bay (Watertown, Cambridge, Lynn and Dorchester). For each town we have examined the founding and early history of the church, the initial process of land-granting, and unusual features of the migration patterns relating to that settlement.

Aside from the focus on towns, we have covered a number of other topics of more general interest. Sometimes this has been the investigation of a specific source, such as the freemen's lists; at other times we have featured a discussion of broader aspects of the Great Migration.

As each of the towns is studied, information is gathered on the families who resided there. This information will be used to write the genealogical sketches which will be the final product of this phase of the Great Migration Study Project. For the period down to 1634, there will be about seven hundred sketches, of which one hundred have already been prepared. The principal activity of the Project in 1991 will be the drafting of the remaining six hundred sketches.

The first issue of the second volume of the *Newsletter* will focus on Charlestown. This will provide some contrast with our earlier discussions of towns, since Charlestown was a port town. Because of the high level of maritime commercial activity, we should expect to uncover migration patterns different from those we have seen in the other towns with a greater agricultural focus. A later issue will cover Roxbury, with the remaining two towns to be determined later.

For those of you who initially subscribed for one year only, the time has come to renew. We hope that you have been satisfied and informed by the four issues to date, and encourage you to continue with us for another year, or better yet for two.

Robert Charles Anderson, FASG   Editor
Margaret F. Costello   Production Assistant

The *Great Migration Newsletter* (ISSN 1049-8087) is published quarterly by the Great Migration Study Project, a project of the New England Historic Genealogical Society, 101 Newbury Street, Boston MA 02116

The subscription rate is $8 for one year and $15 for two years. The subscription year is the same as the calendar year.

(*continued from page 25*)

James Penniman's marriage took place in England in the summer of 1631, in the Nazing area, he also came on the *Lyon* at this time. Some of the fourteen men on these two lists had requested freemanship in October 1630, and thus had arrived prior to 1631: William Frothingham, John Mills, William Aspinwall and William Hulbert. On this analysis alone, then, we are left with only six other names from this source that might have arrived in 1631: Abraham Browne, Isaac Perry, Gregory Baxter, Samuel Moore, John Black and John Sanford.

Reverend John Eliot, after he removed to Roxbury and helped organize the church there, began a register of church members, which was arranged roughly in chronological order of arrival, and in many cases gave the month and year of arrival. In those records we are told specifically that Richard Lyman (with wife and four children) and Samuel Wakeman (with wife and one child) arrived in November 1630. This places them also on the *Lyon*, apparently as part of Eliot's party from the Nazing area in co. Essex. Most of the others in this part of the Roxbury church record are known to have come in 1630 and 1632, but a few remain unplaced as to date of arrival. For example, Gregory Baxter, one of the freemen noted above, was admitted to the church about this time.

The Boston church records for this period are arranged in chronological order, although no specific dates are found before 1633. However, by studying the list carefully, some conclusions may be reached. John Perkins and his wife Judith, passengers on the February voyage of the *Lyon*, are in positions 107 and 108 on this list. Just after this are John Eliot and Margaret Winthrop (passengers on the *Lyon* in November) in positions 110 and 111. Further down the list, in positions 132 and 133, are Thomas Oliver and his wife Ann, passengers on the *Lyon* in a later voyage of June 1632. The persons in between, from places 112 through 131, are possible 1631 arrivals. In this range we do find Jacob Eliot, John Sanfort, James and Lydia Penniman, Isaac Perry and John Winthrop Junior, all known or likely passengers on the *Lyon* in November 1631.

In the Charlestown records are lists (of dubious validity) of those admitted inhabitants of the town, year by year. For 1631 there are sixteen names, and many of these are known to have been in Charlestown in 1630 or earlier (e.g., Ralph Mousall, William Frothingham, Thomas Beecher, Robert Moulton, Abraham Pratt, and Mrs. Anna Higginson). Some of the remainder may have arrived in 1631, but probably not all.

For the other towns of Massachusetts Bay we do not have similar contemporary lists which are as useful as these, but there is no evidence that any of the other towns

(*continued on page 32*)

Focus   *on*   DORCHESTER

WEST COUNTRY MIGRATION

The settlement of Dorchester is associated in most people's minds with the arrival of the *Mary & John* in June of 1630. But this vessel and its passengers were only one group of several which came from the West Country (defined here as the counties of Devon, Dorset and Somerset), and formed the second largest grouping of immigrants to New England during the Great Migration, behind only the East Anglians.

The beginning point for this strand of migration was the colonizing activity of the Reverend John White of Dorchester, co. Dorset. (An account of his life and particularly of his participation in the settlement of New England is presented by Francis Rose-Troup in *John White: The Patriarch of Dorchester ... and the Founder of Massachusetts, 1575-1648* [New York 1930].) John White early grasped the idea of sending out colonists with the fishing ships, and wanted also to ensure that these colonists had access to a minister.

The group of speculators organized by White, the Dorchester Company, sent out several ships in the early 1620s, but very few of the colonists from this period remained in New England. These were led by Roger Conant, and were the group known as the Old Planters. When the Dorchester Company failed, White and some of his associates threw in their lot with some like-minded men of London and of East Anglia and formed the New England Company, which soon became the Massachusetts Bay Company.

Under the aegis of these corporations migration continued, and in 1629 the few passenger ships sailing for New England included the *Lyon's Whelp*, which left from Weymouth in Dorset and carried such passengers as the Sprague brothers of Fordington, co. Dorset, who participated in the settlement of Charlestown. The Old Planters and the passengers on the *Lyon's Whelp* were the West Country precursors of the *Mary & John*.

After the *Mary & John*, the next group of passengers from the West Country apparently came in 1632, on a ship whose name is uncertain. In the freemen's lists for 1632 are about half a dozen men who settled in Dorchester and are known to have had West Country connections. Giles Gibbs came from St. Sidwell, Exeter, co. Devon, and since he had a child baptized there in 1631, and he was made a freeman in late 1632, his date of arrival was most likely the summer of 1632. With him were probably such men as Eltweed Pomeroy, Nicholas

Denslow, George Hull, John Branker, and perhaps one or two others.

Another vessel was announced by Winthrop in his journal entry for 24 July 1633: "A ship arrived from Weymouth, with about eighty passengers, and twelve kine, who sat down at Dorchester." On this same ship came a letter from Henry Paynter of Exeter in Devon, dated 14 March 1632/3 and addressed to John Winthrop Jr., in which the latter was asked to "take notice of Mr. Cogan and Mr. Hill and Mr. Pinny ..." These would be William Hill, Humphrey Pinney and John Coggan, all of whom first settled in Dorchester, however briefly.

In 1634 the *Recovery* sailed from Weymouth, carrying many passengers for New England, including such Dorchester settlers as Thomas Newberry, Robert Dibble and Thomas Swift. On this vessel also was William Bowne (Bound) who first appears at Salem. (The record of this ship as originally published was misdated in 1633, but this has since been corrected; John Plummer, "Identifying George P___?___ of the *Recovery*, 1633 [1634]" [*NGSQ* 77 (1989):249].)

According to the port books, three ships left Weymouth in 1635, the *Marigold*, the *Hopewell*, and the *Unity*. More relatives of earlier arrivals on the *Mary & John* appear in the lists for these vessels, such as Edward Clap. Others came from the same regions in the West Country, such as John Strong and John Rockwell. In addition a fourth, unnamed vessel sailed from Weymouth, carrying the Reverend Joseph Hull and about twenty other families. Most of these families moved upon arrival in New England to the small settlement of Wessaguscus, which was renamed Weymouth. Finally, in 1637 we have lists from two more ships from Weymouth, carrying such immigrants as Elizabeth Poole, the founder of Taunton, Richard Babson, who settled at Salem, and more for Dorchester.

Thus, over a span of more than a decade, at least fourteen ships sailed from Weymouth and other West Country ports to New England. The *Mary & John* was the most famous of these, but all brought a genealogically intertwined group of immigrants who added a West Country flavor to several towns in New England, including Salem, Charlestown, Dorchester and Weymouth in Massachusetts Bay, Taunton in Plymouth Colony, and Windsor in Connecticut. Immediately after the arrival of the *Mary & John* most of these immigrants came to Dorchester; but with the departure of so many West Country folk to Windsor in 1635, the newer arrivals moved out to other settlements, such as Weymouth and Taunton.

EARLY DORCHESTER ALLOTMENTS

As with all the other early towns in the Massachusetts Bay Colony, the records of the earliest allotments of Dorchester lands, and in particular the granting of the house lots, no longer exist. With Dorchester we are better off than with Lynn, for instance, in which we have very little information about the land-granting of the first generation; but we are not so fortunate as we are with Watertown and Cambridge, with several lists of grants, and with periodic inventories of land-holding.

As with Lynn we can begin to reconstruct the land-granting process by studying early deeds which record the transfers between early emigrants from Dorchester to new arrivals. For Dorchester these are embedded in the ordinary run of town records, as they are in many of the towns before the establishment of the county registries, and even long after.

The first that we encounter are made on 12 August 1635 when Thomas Holcomb and Thomas Dewey, both about to depart for Windsor, convey their land to Richard Jones, a more recent settler in Dorchester. Each sells four parcels. Holcomb disposes of a four-acre house lot, an eight-acre great lot, and two pieces of meadow, six acres this side of Neponset and three acres on the other side. Dewey's holdings are similar: a four-acre house lot, eight-acre great lot, and two meadow lots, four acres this side of Neponset and two acres the other. The total acreage for Holcomb is twenty-one, and for Dewey eighteen.

The basic arrangement here falls in line with what we have seen in other towns: a house lot, some meadow, and some upland for plowing (in this case called great lot, although the parcels here are not so large as at Watertown). The first four pages of the Dorchester town records have been lost, and what now survives begins in January 1632/3. One of the first orders, on the 21st of January, provides for "marsh ground by the river Naponsett, according to the quantity of their home lots." This would appear to refer to the meadow sold by Holcomb and Dewey, although the proportion between home and meadow lots is not observed. What we do see is the usual employment of the house lot as the point of reference.

The grants of house lots to the *Mary & John* arrivals were apparently made prior to the date of the surviving records, but on 6 August 1633 several persons, including such 1633 immigrants as John Coggan, William Hill, Humphrey Pinney and Thomas Richards, but also including a few earlier settlers, such as Nicholas Upsall, received grants that appear to be house lots. (The appearance of Upsall in this list is puzzling, for he should have received his house lot some time before; perhaps this grant simply reflects an exchange of lands.) The

range in size of house lots is comparable to that in other towns, being usually four, six or eight acres.

Meadow and marsh lots were laid out wherever such land was available, but the bulk of the early grants were laid out on either side of the Neponset River (as noted above). The rule seems to have been that the amount of meadow accruing to each house lot would be laid out with two-thirds on this side (the west side) of the Neponset and one-third on the far side of the Neponset.

The map which appears facing page 322 in the published Dorchester town records gives a rough representation of these meadow lots beyond the Neponset. The suggestion has been made (p. 321) that this map was made "probably not later than 1637." But the lots shown include those of Thomas Holcomb and Thomas Dewey, who sold out in August of 1635. We do find in the list persons who first appear in Dorchester in 1634 (i.e., Thomas Newberry), but none who are known to have arrived in 1635. The likely date for the map, then, is late 1634 or early 1635.

Although the total acreage held by the ordinary settler, as exemplified by Holcomb and Dewey, was not great, Dorchester did establish extensive common fields, described here more explicitly than elsewhere. In 1745 the antiquarian and Dorchester town clerk James Blake took some brief notes from the town records, including pages three and four, now lost (*NEHGR* 32 [1878]:58). One of these notes, on page three, probably dating from sometime in 1632, says simply: "Fields to be kept in severalty." On 8 October 1633 orders were given for men to view the fences in four fields, given the names of the cardinal points of the compass; and orders for such fenceviewers were given for many years thereafter.

At about the same time that Roger Ludlow was organizing the move to Windsor, and many of the early West Country settlers were selling their various lots to the newer settlers who came with the Reverend Richard Mather, the town decided to make the number of proprietors a closed group. The word proprietors is not used, but on 18 January 1635/6 "It is ordered that all the home lots within Dorchester Plantation which have been granted before this present day shall have right to the Commons and no other lots that are granted hereafter to be commoners." (Compare Watertown town records for 3 January 1635.)

With the total number of proprietors limited to a fixed number, and with the turnover of lands consequent upon the removal to Windsor behind them, the town meeting of Dorchester began to give out more lands. There are some small grants made to individuals here and there in the records, and then on 18 March 1637/8 is recorded a single set of grants to all the proprietors, with each proprietor getting two parcels, one in the Neck and one in the Cow Pasture. The sizes of the lots were more variable than any of the previously recorded distributions, with Israel Stoughton receiving two lots of more than twenty-six acres each, although most grants were in the two to four acre range.

These new grants, however, must not have been laid out immediately. Thomas Hatch had received lots along with everyone else on 18 March 1637/8; but when he sold his lands, apparently on 31 October 1639, these grants on the Neck and in the Cow Pasture are not mentioned in detail. He conveys a great lot, parcels of meadow on either side of the Neponset, "and all his Commons except that in the neck." The land held in common clearly includes the grants in the Neck, and presumably also comprises the Cow Pasture grants.

Land granting in Dorchester, then, is just another variation on a theme we have already seen. The house lot is granted first, and is the basis for later grants of meadow (or marsh) and upland (or plowland). Parcels are smaller in Dorchester than elsewhere, but the use of common fields is more evident here.

DORCHESTER CHURCH

As in so many other ways, the formation of the first church at Dorchester was different from that of the churches in the other Bay towns. Whereas Boston or Watertown, for instance, organized their churches in August of 1630, a month or two after arriving in Massachusetts Bay, the soon-to-be settlers of Dorchester had organized their church at Plymouth in England in March, just before boarding the *Mary & John* for the voyage across the Atlantic.

Undoubtedly through the services of the Reverend John White, two ministers had been obtained to join the *Mary & John* group: John Warham, who had been minister at Crewkerne in Somersetshire and at Exeter in Devonshire; and John Maverick, rector at Beaworthy in Devonshire. When Dorchester was settled later in 1630, then, no additional effort was necessary to establish the church.

The earliest records of the town of Dorchester show that the town was something of a theocracy. All town orders from January 1632/3 (the first surviving) through June 1634 are signed by Maverick, Warham, and two other men - William Gaylord and William Rockwell. From other sources, we know that these men were the first deacons of the Dorchester church. After June 1634, town affairs were run by a larger group of men selected from the town at large, the group later to be known as selectmen. There is no indication in the town records of any discussion or controversy which led to this change in government.

When the move to Windsor was underway in 1635, John Warham chose to make the trip, but John Maverick resisted. Maverick died late in the year, and by 1636 Dorchester was without a settled minister. No records of the Dorchester church for this period survive.

During these earliest years the church at Dorchester briefly served two other neighboring communities. As with other churches, some information can be gained by analysis of the freemen's lists; for instance, a few settlers at Weymouth must have been admitted to Dorchester church, such as Richard Sylvester, for his name appears in a list among the names of other Dorchester men. Presumably, settlers at Wessaguscus, as it was then known, resorted to Dorchester church until the arrival of the Reverend Joseph Hull and the establishment of a church at Weymouth in 1639.

For a shorter period, Dorchester also served the small group of families who settled early at Roxbury. We learn this mostly from clues in John Eliot's records of the church at Roxbury. In his entry for George Alcock, a passenger in the Winthrop Fleet, Eliot states that
"... when the people of Rocksbrough joined to the church at Dorchester (until such time as God should give them opportunity to be a church among themselves) he was by the church chosen to be Deacon esp[ecially] to regard the bretheren at Rocksbrough ..."
This special arrangement would explain some other connections between Dorchester and Roxbury which appear in these records, such as the baptism of a child of Thomas Lamb at Dorchester in October of 1630, and the marriage somewhat later of William Pynchon of Roxbury to Mrs. Frances Samford, "a grave matron of the church at Dorchester."

The question has been raised many times as to whether the church organized at Plymouth in England in March 1630 moved to Windsor in 1635, or remained in Dorchester. In other words, was the church presided over by Richard Mather from 1636 onwards a newly organized church, or was Mather simply reorganizing the pre-existing church? This matter is discussed by Samuel Barrows and William Trask in the introduction to *Records of the First Church at Dorchester in New England:1636-1734* (Boston 1891). They seem to want to have it both ways, stating finally that "The churches at Dorchester and Windsor are thus both heirs of the same parentage" (p. xxiii).

The statement by Winthrop that this was a new church, and the readmission of many persons who must have been admitted to the Dorchester church under Warham and Maverick, both speak strongly in favor of those who contend that the church organized at Dorchester by Richard Mather was a totally new congregation, and that the existing church had moved to Windsor, leaving some of its members behind.

DORCHESTER TO BOSTON

Previous articles in the *Newsletter* have pointed out various features of migration from one town to another within New England, after the immigrants had arrived in the New World. In the very first issue, we presented data on the movement of eight families from Watertown to Stamford, Connecticut, in a period of just one or two years. More generally, reference has been made to the movement from Massachusetts Bay to the Connecticut River valley in 1635 and 1636. This migration, the largest concerted movement of the first generation of English settlers, was really composed of four lesser migrations: from Cambridge to Hartford; Watertown to Wethersfield; Dorchester to Windsor; and Roxbury to Springfield.

One of the peculiarities noticeable in this whole discussion of town-to-town migrations is that two early Massachusetts Bay towns do not appear - Boston and Charlestown. The obvious thought is that these were port towns rather than agricultural towns, and this is probably the correct answer; but we shall have to wait upon detailed studies of each of these towns to see just how Boston differs from Watertown, say, in the matter of migrations in and out.

The investigation of the earliest families of Dorchester does provide insight, however. Among all those families or individuals resident in Dorchester before May 1634, eighteen left Dorchester for some town in New England other than Windsor (thirty-four families from this time period had gone from Dorchester to Windsor). Of these eighteen families, seven moved to Boston, by far the most popular destination after Windsor. By looking at each of these seven families, we will get a first glimpse of the ways in which Boston added to its population.

JOHN COGGAN crossed the Atlantic in 1633 and settled first in Dorchester, but within a few months he had moved to Boston. Along with some other of the 1633 arrivals, he was granted a lot in Dorchester on 5 August of that year; but by the spring of the following year, Winthrop noted in his journal that "John Cogan, merchant, [set up] the first shop" in Boston. Coggan was a prominent citizen and businessman of Boston for the remainder of his life, and he died in Boston on 27 April 1658.

JOHN PHILLIPS was a passenger on the *Mary & John*, and requested freemanship in 1630. He resided in Dorchester from his arrival until the mid-1640s, at which time he made the move to Boston, where he was referred to in deeds as biscuit-baker. He did not confine his activities to the baking of biscuits in Boston, however, but also speculated in land as far away as Falmouth in Maine. He died in Boston 16 December 1682, having been since 1670 deacon of the Second Church.

NICHOLAS UPSALL was also a passenger on the *Mary & John* and remained in Dorchester until 1644, in which year he moved to Boston and soon became an innkeeper. Upsall also became notorious as a defender of the Quakers, and spent several years in jail as a result. He died in Boston in August 1666, and was buried at Copp's Hill.

CHRISTOPHER GIBSON also lived in Dorchester as early as 1630, but it is not certain that he was on the *Mary & John*, since his origins were in Berkshire and not the West Country. Gibson left Dorchester about 1646, and took up residence in Boston until his death in 1674, at which time he left a will naming many relatives in Boston and Dorchester. His occupation while in Boston was that of chandler.

NATHANIEL DUNCAN arrived in 1633, probably on the same ship with John Coggan, and settled in Dorchester. Unlike Coggan, he remained in Dorchester for a number of years, but moved to Boston about 1646, where he was a merchant and died in 1668. He was frequently associated with John Coggan, and in fact the two men had married sisters in England.

JOHN PIERCE was another passenger on the *Mary & John*, who settled first in Dorchester. He was twice chosen selectman, but moved to Boston about 1642. While in Boston he was referred to as a cooper; he died on 17 September 1661.

RICHARD COLLICOTT came to New England in 1633, settled in Dorchester, was at various times selectman and Dorchester's representative to the General Court, and moved to Boston by 1656. In Boston he was a tailor, and, like John Phillips, was active in affairs in Falmouth and Saco. He died in Boston on 7 July 1686.

Comparing this migration from Dorchester to Boston with the movement from Watertown to Stamford noted above, some interesting differences appear. First, whereas the move to Stamford took place in the space of just one or two years, the drift from Dorchester to Boston (for these seven families) is spread over a period of nearly a quarter of a century. Second, each of the seven men who made the move to Boston was engaged in an urban, non-agricultural occupation: two merchants, a baker, a cooper, a chandler, a tailor and an innkeeper.

Not surprisingly, then, we find that Boston is a steady magnet which draws men away from an agricultural setting, perhaps men with a bent for urban pursuits who could not be satisfied in a town like Dorchester. Presumably as we study other towns we will see similar patterns of movement into Boston. What will be more interesting will be to see what drew people away from Boston, and what sort of towns they went to.

RECENT LITERATURE

Myrtle Stevens Hyde, "The English Ancestry of Elizabeth Aldous, Wife of Henry Brock of Dedham, Massachusetts," *New England Historical and Genealogical Register* 144 (1990):124-37. Organizes records for three generations of an Aldous family of co. Suffolk in England, leading to Elizabeth Aldous, baptized at Stradbroke 6 January 1593/4, who became the wife of Henry Brock, the immigrant to Dedham, Massachusetts.

Melinde Lutz Sanborn and Dean Crawford Smith, "Mary Leathers, Ann Hoyle, Martha Dutch Jewell, Christian Abbott, and Margaret Crowell: Daughters of Robert[1] and Mary Knight of Manchester and Marblehead, Massachusetts," *New England Historical and Genealogical Register* 144 (1990):138-42. The 1691 will of Robert Knight, "misplaced" in the Essex County court records rather than in the probate records, names three sons and five daughters, thus proving the identities of the wives of several Essex County men.

Ken Smallbone, "The English Ancestry of Hezekiah Hoar of Taunton, Massachusetts: Part II: Proof of Medieval Ancestry Through Evidence of a Seal," *New England Historical and Genealogical Register* 144 (1990):143-46. Following up on the earlier work of Lyon J. Hoard (*NEHGR* 141 [1987]:22-33), the author uses the evidence of a personal seal to propose an extension of the paternal ancestry of Hezekiah Hoar.

Robert Charles Anderson, "Early Watertown Land Inventories," *New England Historical and Genealogical Register* 144 (1990):147-50. Discusses the relationships among the three Watertown land inventories of the 1640s, and suggests a narrower range of dates for their creation.

Betty Groff Schroeder, "The True Lineage of King Philip (Sachem Metacom)," *New England Historical and Genealogical Register* 144 (1990):211-14. Using published versions of seventeenth-century treaties between the English and the Massachusetts Indians, Schroeder demonstrates that King Philip was grandson of Massasoit, rather than son.

Joy Wade Moulton, "Some Doubts About the English Background of the Moulton Family," *New England Historical and Genealogical Register* 144 (1990):245-63. Improves on an earlier article in the *Register* on this family (141 [1987]:313-28). By correcting the date on a rent roll, the author demonstrates first that there was no separate Scratby line. She then proposes a different arrangement of the Ormsby Moultons, including a placement in this family of James Moulton, who arrived in Salem in 1637.

James C. Riley, "The Sickness Experience of the Josselins' Children," *Journal of Family History* 14 (1989):347-63. Although the Reverend Ralph Josselin never left England, he did succeed Thomas Shepard as chaplain to the Harlakenden family in Earls Colne, co. Essex, and so he was part of the social matrix which contributed so much to the East Anglian migration to New England. His diary has been used for many historical purposes, and here it is employed to provide information on the incidence and duration of childhood illness in seventeenth-century England. Although most of the conclusions are very general and not very helpful genealogically, a table which compares birth intervals and ages at weaning yields some interesting guidelines for reconstructing families.

Myrtle Stevens Hyde, "The English Origin of William[1] Phelps of Dorchester, Mass., and Windsor, Conn., with Notes on His Marriages," *The American Genealogist* 65 (1990):161-66. Hyde shows conclusively that William Phelps resided in Crewkerne, co. Somerset, from 1618 until 1629, just before his departure for New England. His only known wives were Mary _____ and Ann Dover, who were not sisters. The previously proposed connection with Porlock in the same county is proven incorrect, and some comments are made on George Phelps of Windsor, who has been claimed without proof as brother of William.

Dean Crawford Smith, *The Ancestry of Samuel Blanchard Ordway*, ed. by Melinde Lutz Sanborn (Boston:New England Historic Genealogical Society 1990). Provides new information on nearly two dozen families of Essex County, Massachusetts, and further north. A large portion of the volume is devoted to Ordways in England, especially in Worcestershire, with extensive extracts from parish registers, will registers and other sources. The ancestry of James Ordway of Newbury, and of Abner Ordway of Boston and elsewhere, is presented in standard form. Other Great Migration families included are Aquila Chase of Newbury, Philip Watson-Challis of Salisbury and Amesbury, Thomas Hardy of Ipswich, Bartholomew Heath of Haverhill, George Corliss of Haverhill, William Bennett of Manchester, Robert Cross of Newbury, and Robert Knight of Salem, Marblehead and Manchester. English origins are provided for Jane (_____) Bennett, wife of William Bennett, and, among later arrivals, for Roger Hill of Beverly, his uncles Zebulon and John, and his aunt Eleanor (Hill) Babson, and for John George, Ann Swaddock and John Swaddock of Haverhill. All families are treated in great detail, with genealogical and biographical details gathered from a wide range of sources, including some very entertaining material from county court records.

(continued from page 26)

received any significant addition of settlers in 1631. In Saugus (Lynn) and Cambridge in particular, as we have seen in earlier issues of this *Newsletter,* there were very few residents at all until a few years later. Cambridge, the only town founded in 1631, was begun not as a result of population pressure caused by new immigrants, but because of a political dispute between Dudley and Winthrop.

Thus, although it is not possible to match the names precisely from the freemen's lists to the church admission records, for example, there is considerable correlation among the various sets of records available. We do not have large numbers of new names coming into the churches who do not show up as freemen, and vice versa.

The conclusion is that Winthrop was complete and accurate in his reporting for 1631, and that only three passenger ships arrived, with fewer than a hundred new immigrants for Massachusetts Bay. Since mortality in the first winter after the Winthrop Fleet was relatively heavy, and since a number of the 1630 arrivals returned with the *Lyon* on its various voyages in 1630 and 1631, the number of new settlers was not enough to replace the losses. Even taking into account births in 1630 and 1631, the population of Massachusetts Bay, and of all of New England, was probably lower in the spring of 1632 than it had been in the summer of 1630.

For 1632 Winthrop records the arrival of five ships with passengers: the *Whale* on 26 May from Southampton with 30 passengers; the *William and Francis* on 5 June from London with sixty on board; the *Charles* from Barnstable on the same day with twenty persons: the *James* from London on 12 June with twelve passengers; and the *Lyon* (again) on 16 September with 123 immigrants.

There is not room here to carry through for 1632 the same exercise which was just performed above for 1631. Suffice it to say that the results are the same, and that the number of new persons and new families appearing in the town, church and colony records in 1632 and early 1633 is consistent with the arrival of about 225 new settlers on the five ships listed above.

In the winter of 1631 the mortality was not as high as it had been the previous year, nor does it appear that many people returned to England around this time. Thus, these new immigrants of 1632 really did increase the total population of New England, but only by a small amount. The Winthrop Fleet brought about seven hundred passengers in 1630, to join about three hundred still remaining from arrivals of previous years. The additions of 1631 and 1632 were probably about enough to replace the deaths and departures of the same time period, so that the total population going into the winter of 1632 was still probably not far from one thousand.

Great Migration Newsletter

| Vol. 2 | January-March 1991 | No. 1 |

INTERPRETING PASSENGER LISTS

Any genealogist, when approaching the study of an immigrant ancestor, will want to know the name of the ship that brought that ancestor to the New World. Since all the subjects of the Great Migration Study Project are, by definition, immigrants, this variety of record will be of central importance for us.

Over the last two centuries American and British genealogists have diligently searched the Public Record Office in London, and many other repositories, and have published many lists from the 1630s. Our discussion here will be based on three of the most important and most readily available volumes: John Camden Hotten, *The Original Lists of Persons of Quality ...* (New York 1880; rpt. Baltimore 1962, 1968); Charles Edward Banks, *The Planters of the Commonwealth* (Boston 1930; rpt. Baltimore 1961 and later); and Peter Wilson Coldham, *The Complete Book of Emigrants: 1607-1660* (Baltimore 1987).

One matter to be noted immediately is that the lists that we find for the early seventeenth century are nothing like the passenger lists that we are accustomed to from two centuries later. In the nineteenth century, we frequently have lists made up by the shipping company or the ship's captain, and also lists made upon embarkation in England or Europe and debarkation in America. Because of this we often have a good check on who actually sailed on a given vessel, and who actually arrived at the American port.

For the seventeenth century the records are different. We have absolutely no official lists generated in the New World upon the arrival of a ship. What does survive was created at dockside in England, in two closely related sets of documents - the Port Books and the Licenses to Pass Overseas. Examples of the lists from Port Books are found in the material recently uncovered by Coldham for some of the West Country ports; this material has been incorporated in *The Complete Book of Emigrants*, as for example the Weymouth list on page 183. The most extensive record of passengers we have for any year is for London in 1635, and this consists entirely of the Licenses to Pass Overseas granted for that year.

One immediate consequence of records of this nature is that those appearing on such lists did not necessarily emigrate. Many times a ship would sit at the docks in London for four or six weeks, and throughout that period people would appear in groups of varying sizes, bearing their licenses and signing up for this or that ship. Given the time that could elapse between the arrival of a potential passenger, and the actual date of sailing, there was ample opportunity for people to change their minds.

This feature of the lists has some consequences in our attempts to make identifications. A number of families, especially those from the 1635 lists, will not appear at all in New England records. For example, William Bentley, and John and Alice Bentley, apparently his children, are on the list for the *Truelove*, but they are not seen in any New England record, and in fact Savage observes, "but where he pitched his tent is unknown to me." Conceivably all three died on shipboard during the passage; but since shipboard mortality was generally low on the voyages to New England, and since there are many other similar examples, the more likely explanation is that the family had a last minute change of heart. If we could learn where this family, or some of the others who also leave no other trace, came from in England, it would be interesting to search that place of origin to see if they simply returned home and picked up life where they had left off a few weeks or months earlier.

Another aspect of this arrangement was that some people apparently chose to switch from one vessel to another while waiting for their sailing date. On an uncertain date, near the middle of April 1635, a William

(continued on page 8)

EDITOR'S EFFUSIONS

As the *Great Migration Newsletter* enters its second year, the Project itself is well past the halfway point in its first phase. That first phase will cover all settlers who arrived in New England by the spring of 1634, a population of more than eight hundred families and unattached individuals. Most efforts of the Project, aside from the production of the *Newsletter,* are now devoted to the preparation of the genealogical and biographical sketches which will be the core of the publication, probably in two volumes, which should appear in 1992.

In its first year the *Newsletter* examined closely four towns: Watertown, Cambridge, Lynn and Dorchester. This issue looks closely at Charlestown, and the likely towns to be covered in the remaining issues for this year will be Roxbury, Salem and the Piscataqua settlements. Also, a later issue this year will include an index to Volume One, and two or three samples of what the sketches will finally look like.

On the other half of this page appears a discussion of some publications which present to the public the results of extensive historical archaeological work undertaken in the last decade or two, in this case on various early settlements in Maine. This sort of work has become quite widespread in recent years, but there has been, unfortunately, little cross-communication between the two disciplines of genealogy and archaeology.

In the bibliographies in the publications of the Maine Archaeological Society are many references to publications on other sites occupied during the Great Migration. As most of these publications are hard to come by, a more extensive search will be carried out, and a bibliography of such articles and monographs will be published in a future issue of the *Newsletter*.

Response to the Project, including renewals for the *Newsletter* by those who originally subscribed for one year, have been most heartening, and I want to thank everyone who has in any way expressed interest.

Robert Charles Anderson, FASG   Editor
Margaret F. Costello   Production Assistant

The *Great Migration Newsletter* (ISSN 1049-8087) is published quarterly by the Great Migration Study Project, a project of the New England Historic Genealogical Society, 101 Newbury Street, Boston MA 02116

The subscription rate is $8 for one year and $15 for two years. The subscription year is the same as the calendar year.

THE ARCHAEOLOGY OF PLYMOUTH ON THE KENNEBEC

The seventh volume of Occasional Publications in Maine Archaeology, published by The Maine Archaeological Society in cooperation with two other organizations, is *Cushnoc: The History and Archaeology of Plymouth Colony Traders on the Kennebec*, by Leon E. Cranmer (Augusta ME 1990). The principal purpose of this monograph is to set out the results of archaeological excavations carried out in recent years at Cushnoc, now in the city of Augusta, the site of an early fur trading post on the Kennebec established and run by the settlers of Plymouth Colony. The archaeological evidence is compared with the slender historical documentation to produce a rounded portrait of this post and the activities circulating around it.

These excavations revealed a building on the east bank of the Kennebec, very close to a site later occupied in 1754 by Fort Western. The dimensions of the trading post were about twenty by forty-four feet, divided into three bays, in what is known as a "cross-passage" house plan. The central bay was an entrance hall, with doors on both sides of the building. The bays on either end were a storage room, and a living room, which probably was heated and had a raised floor. Like other buildings of the time, this one was probably prefabricated in Plymouth, shipped north in parts, and quickly erected at its new location, where it rested on posts sunk into the ground.

Various smaller artifacts help in portraying something of daily life at this outpost, and also in attempting to date more accurately the period of occupation of the site. Some of the objects found were nails, bits of pottery, fragments of glass bottles, clay pipes, lead shot and various oddments of trading goods.

Among the more useful artifacts for the purposes of dating are clay pipes, many features of which changed rapidly from decade to decade. The most recent estimate prior to the present work was that the building dates from about 1650, but Cranmer argues for an earlier date, perhaps even 1628, not long after trading activity began on the Kennebec.

Other volumes of interest in this same series are Emerson W. Baker, *The Clarke & Lake Company: The Historical Archaeology of a Seventeenth-Century Maine Settlement* (Number 4), and Alaric Faulkner and Gretchen Faulkner, *The French at Pentagoet 1635-1674: An Archaeological Portrait of the Acadian Frontier* (Number 5). The first of these discusses another trading post, further up the Kennebec and somewhat later in the century; the second describes a French undertaking which supplanted a short-lived outpost which the entrepreneurs of Plymouth established on the Penobscot in the late 1620s.

Focus   on   CHARLESTOWN

TOWN RECORDS

The earliest records of the town of Charlestown present a number of interesting problems in literary detection. Because the volume that has come down to us was compiled in 1664 from a variety of sources, we must inquire as to the validity of these various sources, and we must also pay close attention to the chronology.

On 18 April 1664 the Charlestown selectmen noted that John Greene, acting on earlier instuctions, had completed a transcript of the earliest records of the town as far as folio eight,

> most whereof is gathered by information of known honest men that lived & were actors in these times, and all except some court orders and some few town orders in the seven first pages not being of that concernment as the grants of land which happened after, we do approve of the same.

The selectmen then went on to instruct Greene to proceed with his transcript, concentrating on land grants, which he was to copy verbatim, although he could include such other factual matter as he thought relevant. Under these constraints, Greene completed a transcript which ran down to November of 1661.

This "reconstituted" record volume has been used by many historians since that day. Alexander Young, in compiling his *Chronicles of the First Planters*, copied the first few pages of this volume; and in a note at the end of this section he tells us that Thomas Prince used these records as one of his sources in compiling his *Annals of New England*.

Young noted that Greene had muddled his chronology, getting the earliest events all a year early, to the extent of claiming that Winthrop arrived in 1629. But Young adds to the confusion by not telling us just what he has copied. For the most part Young published an accurate transcription, without omissions, of the first few pages of the Greene compilation. Down to the break on page 385, in fact, Young is complete and accurate. But at this point he skips a large portion of the records, and his last three paragraphs are plucked out of later pages.

Closer examination of the records, including study of the pages not copied by Young, allows us to clear up some of the confusion. In the portion printed by Young, Greene is consistently one year too early. The settlement of Charlestown, of course, occurred in 1629, under the direction of the Sprague brothers, and the Winthrop Fleet arrived in 1630. The lists of inhabitants (to be discussed in more detail later) for 1628 and 1629 should thus also be advanced one year.

This chronological shift remains consistent until the account of the arrival of the *Lyon* in February 1630/1, an event which is accurately recorded in Winthrop's *Journal*. And this is also the point at which Young broke off his continuous and complete publication of Greene's transcript. The first item of Greene's which Young did not copy was a list of newly admitted inhabitants which in the manuscript is attributed to 1630. This is followed by two entries about persons allowed to build outside the Neck, and an order about building the fort; these items are all said to fall in 1630.

Then, under 1631 comes an agreement on fencing two of the fields, followed by a list of inhabitants said to be of 1631, and then another order on building the fort. We then move to 1632, where there is first a town agreement about hiring Henry Harwood as town herdsman, and then the admission of several persons as inhabitants, with specific months of admission given.

Here at last we seem to be back on solid ground, although these admissions are followed by the remaining discursive passages which conclude the material published by Young. What we may conclude is that all the material ascribed by Greene to 1630 and 1631 applies to 1631, and that only in late 1632 is the chronology back on track. Thus the two lists of inhabitants for 1630 and 1631 should be dated as 1631; and in fact many of the names on these two lists are known to have been in New England in 1630.

Greene's problems weren't just with dates, but with names as well. For example, Greene repeatedly refers to John Wignall, but the General Court records, including his admission to freemanship, call him Alexander Wignall; more will be heard about this gentleman two pages hence. In the list of inhabitants for 1629 (properly 1630) is Mr. John Glover. This is included in the material published by Young, and has led many to claim that this is the first appearance of John Glover of Dorchester, who is otherwise unseen until much later in the decade. But there are records, again from the General Court, which relate to a Mr. Ralph Glover. His residence is not given in the court records, but he is consistently associated with others from Charlestown, Medford, and vicinity. He died in 1633, and the General Court administered his estate. Clearly, Ralph Glover and not John was the Charlestown settler. Finally, George Hutchinson appears in both the "1630" and "1631" lists. Might one of these in fact be meant for Thomas Hutchinson, who appears in the

October 1630 list of those wishing to be made free immediately after George Hutchinson, but is seen in no other record in New England?

Aside from correcting the factual errors made by Greene, we may learn much from a dissection of the sources upon which he relied. The selectmen, when they revised Greene's instructions in 1664, noted that he had copied court and town orders. The court orders are usually identified as such in Greene's transcript, and can be matched with entries in the court records themselves. The town records are not always so easy to identify, but are usually, at least in 1633 and later, dated precisely, and begin with some phrase such as "Agreed and concluded by the inhabitants of the town..." These may not be precise quotes from the previously existing records, but we can safely assume that Greene had an actual written, contemporaneous record before him as he prepared his transcript.

Two more types of entries are worth further attention, as their sources are not so clear. First are the narrative and in some cases highly romantic passages which constitute so much of the portion of the record published by Young. In these sections Greene was truly a historian, and was working in the same mode as did William Hubbard a decade later. These were the very sections which displeased the selectmen, and we may regret the result that we do not have similar narrative accounts for a later date. Presumably some of this material was acquired from the "known honest men" whom Greene consulted.

Lastly, what of the lists of inhabitants? These are unique to the Charlestown records, and, in view of the manner in which the Greene transcript was produced, we would be right to exercise some skepticism. Are these lists copied from older records, or are they synthetic lists based on the decades-old memories of the "known honest men that lived and were actors in these times?" It may never be possible to answer this question satisfactorily, but at this point, comparisons of the names with other records, such as passenger lists and court and church records, have produced no inconsistencies or contradictions. For the moment, they may be taken as highly reliable, subject to the adjustment of dates set forth above.

John Greene may be likened to a monastic scribe, directed by his abbot to produce the chronicles of a monastery. Like the monk with his charters, his saints' calendars, his older chronicles and his oral tradition, Greene pieced together the early history of Charlestown as best he could with the materials at hand, the official town and court records, the living memories of survivors of the immigrant generation, and probably other records of which we now have no other trace. Greene deserves respect as one of the earliest true historians of New England, and his transcript will reward even deeper inquiries into its composition and content.

CHARLESTOWN CHURCH

In one sense, the first church to be established in Charlestown was that organized in August of 1630 by John Winthrop and the other luminaries of the Winthrop Fleet. But that church was soon carried off to Boston with its leading members, and for the next two years residents of Charlestown attended and became members of the church in Boston.

Charlestown was able to break away from Boston and establish its own congregation, "in regard of the difficulty of passage in winter, and having opportunity of a pastor," according to Winthrop. This occurred on 14 October 1632, when sixteen couples, and three single men, were dismissed from Boston church to found the new church across Charles River. (A few of these persons do not appear as having been admitted to Boston church. It remains unclear whether this represents a defect in the surviving Boston records, or the admission of a few people as founding members at Charlestown, without first having been members at Boston.)

The first minister was Thomas James, a graduate of Emmanuel College, Cambridge, who had come over in the summer of 1632. His tenure was brief and stormy, and by March of 1635/6, as we hear from Winthrop,

> most of the brethren had taken offence at diverse speeches of his (he being a very melancholic man and full of causeless jealousies, etc.)...they advised that, if they should not comfortably close, ... [he] should desire dismission ...but if he persisted, etc., the church should cast him out.

This was apparently done soon after. Whether this was strictly a matter of personality, or a deeper reflection of the controversy sweeping all the Bay churches in that year, does not appear in the church records.

The earliest records of the Charlestown church survive in published form (James Frothingham Hunnewell, *Records of the First Church in Charlestown, Massachusetts, 1632-1789* [Boston 1880]). Unfortunately the original first volume, long on deposit at the Congregational Library in Boston, was in recent years returned to the Charlestown congregation, and has since been lost.

The current unavailability of the originals is distressing for many reasons, not the least of which is the uncertainty expressed in the last century by Savage as to the contemporaneity of those records. In his discussion of Richard Kettle and his wife Esther, who according to the records joined Charlestown church in July of 1633, Savage notes that this wife was Esther Ward, who was admitted to Boston church under that name as a servant of Atherton Haugh six months later (3:15)! This and other nagging questions about early Charlestown families might be answered if we still had access to the original.

UNSETTLED PLANTATIONS

The list of those admitted as inhabitants of Charlestown in 1630 contains twenty-seven names. At the end of the list, four of those names are set off with a bracket, and the notation that they had "built in the main on the northeast side of the northwest creek of this town." These four men were Mr. Edward Gibbons, Captain [Walter] Norton, Alexander Wignall and Mr. William Jennings [i.e., Jennison]. Further examination of this little grouping of habitations will add to our knowledge of early Charlestown, and will also have something to say about the development of early New England settlements in general.

By studying the Charlestown town records and the 1638 Book of Possessions, we may deduce that all four of these houselots had passed to other hands within a very few years. In the town records for 1630, but probably referring to 1631, Walter Pope was admitted an inhabitant, with the notation that he had bought Wignall's house and land; Pope was succeeded by Richard Miller, who had apparently married Pope's daughter. In a list of those admitted inhabitants in 1634 we learn that Mrs. Crowe (or Crowell) "bought Mr. Wm. Jennings his house at her arrival." On 16 June 1638 Mr. John Crow sold this land to Matthew Avery. On 30 July 1638 the town records note that "Mr. Edward Paine was admitted a townsman having bought Mr. Gibbon's house and land." By elimination, this would indicate that Walter Norton's lot was acquired by Mr. John Hodges; although there is no record of this transaction, Hodges does appear in the town records shortly after Norton's death.

Comparing the descriptions of these four lots, we see that they were aligned in a row, along the banks of Gibbon's River, clearly named in honor of Captain Edward, who could only have resided there a few years. This body of water was later named Miller's River, and virtually disappeared when so much of the lower Charles River was filled in during the nineteenth century; a small part of this river survives as a channel near Lechmere Point. These lots were in an area that is now part of the town of Somerville, probably near the point where the McGrath Highway crosses the commuter rail line to Lowell and Haverhill.

William Wood, in his travelogue account of New England published in 1634, gets muddled up when he comes to this settlement. Having described the south shore plantations and then Boston and Charlestown, he swings into the lower Charles River basin, and proceeds as follows:

Towards the southwest in the middle of this bay is a great oyster bank. Towards the northwest of this bay is a great creek upon whose shore is situated the village of Medford, a very fertile and pleasant place and fit for more inhabitants than are yet in it.

The "great oyster bank" is the Back Bay, and the "village of Medford" is in fact our little grouping of independent settlers. Medford would not be seen by Wood from his vantage point in the middle of the Charles River, and he does correctly come to the town a page later when he describes the settlement of Mystic, along with the farms of Matthew Craddock and John Winthrop (William Wood, *New England's Prospect*, Alden T. Vaughan, ed. [University of Massachusetts Press: Amherst 1977] pp. 60-61).

The population of this little enclave "on the main" turned over rapidly. In the records of the Massachusetts Bay General Court for 6 September 1631 we find the following order:

Mr. Alex: Wignall is fined 40s., bound to his good behavior, & enjoined to remove his dwelling to some settled plantation before the last of May next, for drunkenness and much misdemeanor by him committed at the plantation where now he dwelleth.

As we have seen, Wignall was about this time succeeded at this location by Walter Pope.

The other three original inhabitants of this little "plantation" soon scattered in various directions. Gibbons, in the long run the most reputable of the lot, soon moved to Boston, and Jennings/Jennison to Watertown. Walter Norton was a patentee of Agomenticus (which would become York, Maine), and was killed in 1633 by Indians in Connecticut.

The common thread with these men is that they were not of the mainstream of Puritan yeomen, tradesmen and artisans who made up the bulk of the population of New England at this time. Admittedly, early Charlestown had a relatively high percentage of mariners, but this little grouping on the mainland apparently wanted to stand off from the larger community on Charlestown Neck. Gibbons, Norton and Jennison were military men and seafaring traders, and the transgressions of Wignall are noted above.

The four men who succeeded Gibbons and company were not as objectionable to the Puritan authorities, but they, too, were outside the mainstream. John Hodges was frequently before the magistrates for drunkenness and blasphemy. Avery and Paine were recently arrived mariners who were clearly more interested in business than in planting the holy commonwealth in the New World. Of Richard Miller relatively little is known.

Returning to the court order against Alexander Wignall, we note that he was enjoined to remove to a "settled plantation," implying that the area occupied by himself and the other three men was somehow "unsettled." What did this mean? We get a further clue from a letter of December 1634 from James Cudworth of Scituate to his stepfather in London, Dr. John Stoughton (brother of Thomas and Israel Stoughton of Dorchester). In the middle of his letter, Cudworth lists the ten plantations which have churches, naming for each the pastor and teacher. He then goes on to take note of "those plantations that are not yet settled and are newly begun," enumerating Duxbury, Scituate, and Bear Cove (Hingham) (Everett Emerson, ed., *Letters from New England: The Massachusetts Bay Colony, 1629-1638* [University of Massachusetts Press: Amherst 1976] p. 141).

The word "settled," then, does not simply refer to a location where people have established a residence; this condition is described by the word "plantation." "Settled" denotes a plantation which has attained a certain degree of organization and advancement. Looking back to the third issue of this *Newsletter,* in its discussion of the early years of Saugus, or Lynn, we see that that plantation might well have been described as unsettled in its early years. There was no properly organized church, no resident magistrate, and a population limited to a few wealthy men with their male servants.

The small plantation along Gibbon's River was clearly "unsettled" by these criteria, even though these houselots fell within the bounds of Charlestown. These families were, as noted above, not within the Puritan mainstream. The court order for Alexander Wignall to move to a settled plantation gave evidence of the desire of the civil and church leaders to bring all inhabitants under their control; independent souls who tried to evade the system were not encouraged.

CHARLESTOWN LAND

As with several of the other Massachusetts Bay towns of the first decade, the town of Charlestown, presumably in response to an order of the General Court, compiled an inventory of landholding. In the case of Charlestown, this compilation was made in 1638, and was called the Book of Possessions (*A Report of the Record Commissioners Containing Charlestown Land Records, 1638-1802, Third Report of the Record Commissioners* [Boston 1883]).

For the average landholder, this inventory in 1638 included seven or eight parcels of land, although many Charlestown proprietors had more than eight, whether through grant or purchase. As a probe of the landgranting process in Charlestown, we will study the inventory of William Dady. Dady had arrived in 1630, probably as part of the Winthrop Fleet; he was neither very high nor very low on the social and economic scale. In the Book of Possessions he holds eight pieces of land.

In order to illuminate the earliest landgranting, we will analyze Dady's holdings in reverse chronological order. Just before the compilation of the 1638 inventory, the town made a large grant of land, in two parcels per proprietor, on the north side of Mystic River, called at this time Mystic Side, later to become Malden and parts of other towns. Dady's allotment appears on page 36 of the earliest volume, under date of 23 April 1638. He receives Lot #51, with a line reading "5-30-5"; this is to be interpreted to mean that he received five acres on Mystic Side, thirty acres "above the Ponds," and had received five acres in a previous related grant. The first two of these three parcels correspond to numbers seven and eight in the inventory.

Parcel six is noted as the third item in the above grant, but was in fact granted more than a year earlier, on 6 March 1636/7 (p. 27). This was billed as the "First Division of lands on Mistickeside."

The fifth entry in the inventory is a half acre of meadow in Mystic Field. This meadow land was granted in 1635, and William "Dade" receives Lot #49, between the lots of Thomas Squire and George Felch, which corresponds with the description in the inventory (p. 19). The fourth item is "common for two milch cows." The granting of these proportional, proprietary rights in pasturage was recorded in 1637, but without an exact day and month given. William Dady received two "shares."

This 1635 grant of meadow is the earliest direct grant to William Dady which is found in the town records, leaving three parcels unaccounted for - a houselot and two two-acre parcels of arable land in the East Field. All of these parcels were on Charlestown Neck itself. We may assume that these were the earliest grants to William Dady, and were granted at a time before it was felt necessary to record such grants; in this way Charlestown landgranting is similar to that in all other towns studied to date.

There were a few other recorded grants prior to the 1635 meadow grant in which Dady participated, but these were made to a limited number of the proprietors, and correspond to what are labelled as land in the Line Field in the inventories. Why these grants were limited is not clear.

Scanning several other inventories similar to Dady's shows a similar pattern. In the first five years of Charlestown, most of the proprietors received a houselot, usually on the Neck, and a piece or two of arable land, sometimes on the Neck and sometimes not. No meadow was granted until the town was five years old, which implies that prior to that time meadow was used in common. This arrangement was formalized in the grant of the "milch cow commons," which correspond to later references to the stinted commons. In this way Charlestown was different from its neighbors Cambridge and Watertown, where a piece or two of meadow was granted early along with the houselot and the arable land.

RECENT LITERATURE

Frederick J. Nicholson, "Alice Grant(h)am, Probable Wife of John[1] Emery of Newbury, Massachusetts," *The American Genealogist* 65 (1990):211-13. Presents an English will and parish register entries which strongly support the contention of Walter Goodwin Davis that the wife of John[1] Emery was Alice Grantham; her father was very likely Walter Grantham of West Dean, Wiltshire.

George Ely Russell, "Mark Manlove Addenda," *The American Genealogist* 65 (1990):228-29. Adds to an earlier article by the same author on Mark Manlove, by providing new information on his later life in New Netherland and Delaware.

Harold F. Porter, Jr., "The Strutt-Biggs Relationships," *The American Genealogist* 65 (1990):240-47. Porter expands and embellishes the network of English ancestors and kinsmen of Thomasine Frost, wife of Edmund[1] Rice of Sudbury, Massachusetts.

Richard Archer, "The New England Mosaic: A Demographic Analysis for the Seventeenth Century," *The William and Mary Quarterly, Third Series* 47 (1990):477-502. Archer has compiled a database on more than twenty-thousand residents of New England prior to 1650, and uses this to reach a variety of demographic conclusions. His principal source is Savage "supplemented, modified, and corrected by genealogies and passenger lists (particularly those of Charles Edward Banks and John Camden Hotten)" and some other primary materials. Since the exact listing of the sources used is not known, and the methods of evaluation are not stated, the conclusions reached here are of limited value.

Lindsay L. Brook, ed., *Studies in Genealogy and Family History in Tribute to Charles Evans on the Occasion of His Eightieth Birthday* (Association for the Promotion of Scholarship in Genealogy, Ltd.: Salt Lake City 1990). In keeping with the broad range of interests of the man being honored by this volume, the twenty-three essays here published cover a wide range of times and places, with heavy emphasis on medieval European and English subjects. For students of the Great Migration, however, there are two articles of particular interest. First is "The Pyssing Ancestry of the Hulls of New England" by John Insley Coddington (pp. 44-51). Joan Pyssing was wife of Thomas Hull of Crewkerne, co. Somerset, and mother of the New England immigrants Joseph Hull of Barnstable and George Hull of New Haven. Coddington provides English records which identify her father, grandfather and many other relatives. Second, George E. McCracken writes at length on "The Vassalls of London and Jamaica" (pp. 217-49). The Vassall family produced a number of illustrious colonists up and down the Atlantic

seaboard. Among them was William Vassall who first came to New England in 1630 as an Assistant of the Massachusetts Bay Colony; he soon returned to England, came again to New England in 1635, and finally removed to Barbados where he died in 1655.

Johan Winsser, "Mary (Dyre) Ward: Mary (Barrett) Dyre's Missing Daughter Traced," *New England Historical and Genealogical Register* 145 (1991):22-28. Winsser shows that Mary Dyer, daughter of William Dyer and his wife Mary, the Quaker martyr, married one Henry Ward and resided in Maryland and Delaware in the 1670s. She was probably born about 1650 in Newport, Rhode Island, and died about 1679, having had two children by Ward.

Laurence M. Hauptman and James D. Wherry, ed., *The Pequots in Southern New England: The Fall and Rise of an American Indian Nation* (University of Oklahoma Press:Norman OK 1990). This publication is Volume 198 in The Civilization of the American Indian Series, and comprises the texts of a number of presentations made at a conference held in 1987 by the Mashantucket Pequot Tribe of Connecticut, in commemoration of the 350th anniversary of the Pequot War. The papers presented do not limit themselves to yet another discussion of the Pequot War itself (although this is included). There is much discussion of the later history of the tribe, which was one of the first in New England to gain recognition of tribal status in the modern era. There is also great emphasis on the importance of the Pequots in the earliest years of the New England economy, most importantly in the growth of the trading in wampum.

Eugene Chalmers Fowle, *Descendants of George Fowle (1610/11?-1682) of Charlestown, Massachusetts* (New England Historic Genealogical Society:Boston 1990). Presents the descendants of the immigrant George Fowle in standard format, with strong emphasis on the first six generations. Fowle is plausibly derived from Wittersham, co. Kent, although this suggested origin is far from proven.

Edward H. L. Smith III, "The Identity of Sarah, Wife of Richard[1] Smith of Smithtown, Long Island," *New York Genealogical and Biographical Record* 121 (1990):19-22. The author argues that Sarah, the wife of Richard[1] Smith of Smithtown, was a daughter of William Hammond of Watertown, Massachusetts. The principal evidence in favor of this identification is the will of William Hammond, which names daughter Sarah Smith, and her son Adam Smith. There is other circumstantial evidence, including other connections between the Hammonds of Watertown and the Smiths of Long Island.

(continued from page 1)

Hubbard, aged 35, with a Thomas Hubbard, 10, joined the *Elizabeth and Ann*, while on the 17th of the same month a William Hubbard, aged 35, and John, 10, signed on to the *Elizabeth*. While these might be two different Williams, Banks and Savage agree that they are more likely two entries for one man. (Comparison of Banks and Hotten on these entries is most informative.)

An exceedingly important feature of the 1635 lists, as noted above, is that they represent a daily log of families and individuals arriving at the London docks, with an appropriate certificate of conformity from a minister. Sometimes a group of families arriving on a given day for a given ship will record their parish of origin, but not always. On those occasions when no origin is given, we should view the groupings at dockside as a possible clue to origins. An example where the last parish of residence is supplied is the grouping of families which signed up on 1 April 1635 for the *Hopewell*, including John Cooper, Edmund Farrington, William Purrier, George Griggs, and the Kirtland brothers. These families were all from a limited area in northern Buckinghamshire, and continued connections in New England, especially at Lynn and Southampton.

On 15 April a similar cluster of families shows a desire to board the *Increase*. No parish of origin is given, but from other sources we know that several were from Essex and neighboring parts of Suffolk. Furthermore, several of these families settled initially in Watertown. On this basis we would be wise to begin searching for the remaining families of this cluster in the same region of England.

The importance of the arrangement of the original records leads to a discussion of the utility of the various published versions of these lists. The oldest of the three, Hotten, remains the most valuable in this regard, since he retained the original sequence of the lists, and in general remained most faithful to the original. Banks, on the other hand, took vast liberties with the records, rearranging them to suit his judgments, and adding extensive editorial notations in a manner not easy to distinguish from the records themselves. Coldham, for the 1635 lists, is less useful than Hotten, since he gathered all entries for a given ship, and omitted the day-by-day grouping of arrivals. However, Coldham surveyed many sources not used by Hotten, such as Admiralty cases and the various series of State Papers. For this reason, Coldham's collection is more broadly valuable for the whole period.

Until someone undertakes the preparation of a complete edition of passenger lists according to modern editorial standards, the best results will be obtained by a careful correlation of Hotten and Coldham, with a cautious dash of Banks.

Great Migration Newsletter

Vol. 2   April-June 1991   No. 2

JOHN CARMAN AND JOHN KIRMAN

How many John Carmans were there in New England before 1634? How many John Moores? How many John Smiths? This question arises again and again in the Great Migration Study Project, and, indeed, in genealogical problems of any time and place. By studying the case of John Carman and John Kirman, we will see how such problems are resolved; at the same time, we will be able to apply some of the lessons learned in previous issues of the *Newsletter* about various categories of records.

Our starting point is the relevant entry in the Roxbury church records, maintained by Reverend John Eliot. These records were obviously written at a late date, but appear to be quite faithful in entering church members in their proper order of admission. Of interest to us is an early entry: "John Carman. He came to N.E. in the year 1631. He brought no children." The entry goes on to list the births of three children in 1633, 1635 and 1639 (presumably 1639/40). Although the record does not so state explicitly, the implication is that Carman resided in Roxbury continuously from 1631 to 1640, at a minimum. Somewhat later than John, but not more than a year or so, Florence Carman, wife of John, is admitted to Roxbury church.

This Roxbury church record serves as an anchor, to which other data may be added. Additional records for John Carman, or Kirman, or other variants, appear in Lynn, Cambridge, Sandwich and Hempstead. Our task is to sort through these and see if they all relate to the Roxbury man, or whether a second John Carman/Kirman must be postulated. (Half a century ago, Edith Carman Hay and Sidney Wilson tackled these records, and came to the conclusion that there was only one John Carman [*New York Genealogical and Biographical Record* 60 (1939):332-36]; this article should be compared with the conclusions reached here.)

Our first point of departure is the lists of deputies to the General Court, where we find a John Kirman on 4 March 1634/5, and again on 7 December 1636. Was this the Roxbury man, representing that town? At this date, nine towns could send deputies (Boston, Charlestown, Dorchester, Roxbury, Watertown, Cambridge, Lynn,

Salem and Ipswich), and each town was permitted three representatives. There should, therefore, have been twenty-seven deputies at this court, but only twenty-five appear in the list, since the first order of business of the court was to examine the credentials of the delegates from Ipswich and reject two of them (Mr. Easton and Henry Short) as being "unduly chosen," leaving only Mr. John Spencer as legally elected.

The remaining twenty-four men must be allocated to the eight older towns. There is no difficulty finding three deputies from Roxbury (Lt. Richard Morris, William Dennison and John Johnson), so Kirman cannot be from that town, as some have thought. When we have sorted through the remaining twenty-one, the slots for Boston, Cambridge, Salem, Dorchester, Watertown and Charlestown are filled with well-known names, leaving only Capt. Nathaniel Turner, Mr. Timothy Tomlins and John Kirman. The first two are readily associated with Lynn, and we conclude that Kirman is the third representative from that town.

On 7 December 1636 Goo[dman] John Kirman was again a deputy to the General Court. By this time the number of deputies that any town could send had been changed, and was now determined as a proportion of the number of freemen in the town. Thus, there might be one, two or three representatives per town. Charlestown, Watertown and Boston, as the largest and wealthiest of the Bay communities, sent three delegates each to this court. Most other towns sent two, but between the two men from Dorchester and the two from Salem are two names: Kirman, and William Reade. The latter was an

(continued on page 10)

EDITOR'S EFFUSIONS

The cover article for this issue takes a different approach than have its predecessors. The previous five feature articles have addressed a particular type of record, or have explored some aspect of the migration process. This quarter some of the principles developed in earlier issues of the *Newsletter* are applied to the particular case of two men of the same name who have in the past been frequently confused and conflated into one individual.

This different emphasis (although it does not necessarily mean that future lead articles will take the same approach) reflects the fact that the main emphasis of the Project now and in the coming months is the compilation of the hundreds of sketches of families and individuals to be covered in this first phase of the Project. First drafts of more than a quarter of these sketches are now complete.

Partially as a result of this natural shift of emphasis at this stage, the July-September issue of the *Newsletter* will include a four-page bonus section, half of which will be the presentation of two or three preliminary samples of what these sketches will look like. The remainder of the extra section, intended as a pull-out to be filed with Volume One, will be an every-name index to the first four issues of the *Newsletter*.

In addition, a tentative schedule has been determined for the Focus sections of the next four issues. The last two issues of Volume Two will treat Salem and the Piscataqua settlements, and the first two issues of Volume Three will cover Boston and Plymouth.

CORRECTION

John Plummer of Waterbury, Connecticut, kindly points out that in Volume One, Number Four, on page 26, column two, first complete paragraph, line eight, "November 1630" should read "November 1631."

Robert Charles Anderson, FASG   Editor
Margaret F. Costello   Production Assistant

The *Great Migration Newsletter* (ISSN 1049-8087) is published quarterly by the Great Migration Study Project, a project of the New England Historic Genealogical Society, 101 Newbury Street, Boston MA 02116

The subscription rate is $8 for one year and $15 for two years. The subscription year is the same as the calendar year.

(*continued from page 9*)

associate of Joseph Hull in the early settlement of Weymouth, and was the sole representative of that town at this particular court. Kirman, then, was the only one on the list who could have been sent by Lynn.

Only a few of the most prominent men were deputies, but even so, much useful information is obtained by analysis of these lists. For example, Mr. John Spencer represented Ipswich on 6 May 1635 and Newbury on 2 September 1635, and Mr. Daniel Dennison sat for Cambridge on 2 September 1635 and Ipswich on 3 March 1635/6, so for these two men we have relatively narrow time frames for their migrations within New England. At the court for 6 May 1635 appears a deputy by the name of William Parker, a name that appears nowhere else this early in New England; by the same process of allocation and elimination described above, it appears that he must have served from Roxbury, which leads to the conclusion that the name should actually be William Parkes, a prominent Roxbury resident.

On 3 September 1634 the General Court appointed John Kirman to a committee "to set out the bounds of all towns not yet set out, or in difference betwixt any town." Appointments to such committees were frequently made so that each town would have one member, and such an arrangement would seem to be especially appropriate for a committee with responsibility for boundaries. (For a similar example see on the same date the committee of "overseers of the powder and shot, & all other ammunition, in the several plantations where they live.") The members of the committee on boundaries are Mr. [John] Oldham (Watertown), Mr. Daniel Dennison (Cambridge), Ralph Sprague (Charlestown), Edmond Quincy (Boston), Mr. [Richard] Dummer (Roxbury), Ensign [Israel] Stoughton (Dorchester), John Kirman, and Mr. John Spencer (Ipswich), and again John Kirman must be the member for Lynn.

On 4 March 1632/3 John Kirman was thirteenth in a list of eighteen men made free on that date. The first five were from Roxbury, followed by five from Dorchester, two from Cambridge (John White and William Spencer), and then John Kirman and Timothy Tomlins. At this date neither Cambridge nor Lynn had an organized church, so residents of these towns must have joined other churches prior to admission as freemen. For Cambridge the most likely choice would be Watertown, and for Lynn, Salem. John Kirman is followed immediately by Timothy Tomlins, a Lynn resident and his colleague as deputy on 4 March 1634/5, so it is likely that this John Kirman was a resident of Lynn and member of Salem church, and this also meshes with the requirement that all deputies be freemen. (There is a possibility that at this point he should be associated with the Cambridge men, since John Kirman, almost certainly the Lynn man, appears on the

(*continued on page 16*)

Focus   *on*   **ROXBURY**

THE EARLY YEARS OF ROXBURY

Roxbury, like Dorchester, Boston and Watertown, was founded in 1630 as an immediate consequence of the arrival of the Winthrop Fleet; but there are differences between the earliest years of Roxbury and those of the other 1630 towns. Dorchester was settled by the passengers of the *Mary & John* directly upon their arrival, in mid-1630. Boston and Watertown were settled soon after, as the members of the Winthrop Fleet dispersed from their first location at Charlestown in July of that year. As Thomas Dudley put it in a letter written in the spring of 1631,

... we were forced to change counsel, and for our present shelter to plant dispersedly ... This dispersion troubled some of us; but help it we could not, wanting ability to remove to any place fit to build a town upon, and the time too short to deliberate any longer, lest the winter should surprise us before we had builded our houses.

According to Dudley this dispersion created the settlements of Boston, Medford, Watertown, Roxbury, Saugus and Dorchester. The implication in this letter is that these places were all occupied more or less simultaneously; but there are bits of evidence that indicate that the process was in fact spread out over two or three months.

We have noted already that the immigrants to Dorchester went there immediately, and did not pass through Charlestown; they should not be included in Dudley's list

The first Court of Assistants to be held in Massachusetts sat at Charlestown on 23 August 1630, before Winthrop and others moved across to Shawmut, which would become Boston. The first order of business at this court was to provide maintenance for the two ministers, John Wilson and George Phillips. We learn that "Sir Richard Saltonstall undertook to see it done at his plantation for Mr. Phillips, and Mr. Governor, at the other plantation, for Mr. Wilson." Since Salem and Dorchester already had their own churches, Salem's organized in 1629 and Dorchester's brought along on the *Mary & John,* the implication of "the other plantation" is that on 23 August 1630 only Charlestown and Watertown were in existence, and therefore in need of church government.

When the next Court of Assistants was held, on 7 September, just two weeks later, the settlement of Boston had begun, as we learn from the statement of the court that "It is ordered that Trimountain shalbe called Boston; Mattapan, Dorchester; & the town upon Charles River, Waterton." One would think that, had Roxbury been founded by this date, it would have been included in this

list, which amounts to a recognition of the existence of these towns.

Roxbury first appears at the next Court of Assistants, held on 28 September 1630, when it is included in a list of plantations being taxed, with an assessment of five pounds. This is lower than Boston, Watertown, Charlestown and Dorchester, but higher than Medford, Salem, and the small settlements which would later become Weymouth and Hull. On this basis, the settlement of Roxbury can be dated between 7 and 28 September 1630. Much of the wealth for which Roxbury was assessed would have been the estate of William Pynchon, so the actual population of Roxbury must have been considerably smaller than that of the four towns which had a much higher assessment.

After the arrival of John Eliot in 1632, the population of the town was swelled by the addition of many families who had been his followers in England, known familiarly as the "Nazeing Christians"; these will be discussed further in the next section on the Roxbury church.

Roxbury shared with Cambridge, Dorchester and Watertown the experience of losing a number of its earliest settlers to the westward migration in 1635 and 1636. In the case of Roxbury, this resulted from the decision of William Pynchon, the wealthiest citizen of Roxbury during his years in that town, to move to the Connecticut River Valley, to establish the town of Springfield. Pynchon was motivated by a desire to monopolize the beaver trade on the Connecticut.

But whereas Cambridge lost virtually all of its pre-1635 population to the westward trek, and Dorchester and Watertown very high proportions, only a few of the early Roxbury inhabitants went west. Among the earliest settlers of Springfield, only Thomas Woodford, Thomas Ufford and Jehu Burr joined with Pynchon. Even with Roxbury's small population this would not have been disruptive, and would not have led to a large turnover in landholding, or pressures to move the church to Springfield, as happened with Cambridge and Dorchester.

The departure of Pynchon created something of a social and power vacuum in Roxbury, but after a short interval Thomas Dudley, probably the most powerful man in the Bay after Winthrop, settled in Roxbury. Under the leadership of Dudley, Weld and Eliot, Roxbury continued through the years of the immigrant generation as a small but significant community, with many connections to the other towns with large complements of East Anglians.

ELIOT'S ROXBURY CHURCH

The church at Roxbury was not founded until 1632, but, because of the unique set of records maintained by the Reverend John Eliot, we know things about this church that we do not know about any other of this period. (These records, along with the earliest Roxbury land records, have been published in the Sixth Report of the Boston Record Commissioners, *A Report of the Record Commissioners Containing the Roxbury Land and Church Records* [Boston 1884].)

Two years passed after the settlement of Roxbury before it had its own church, and in the interim those inhabitants of Roxbury who wished to join a church went to Dorchester. This arrangement is stated explicitly in Eliot's account of the admission of George Alcock to the Roxbury church, where we learn that

when the people of Rocksbrough joined to the church at Dorchester (until such time as God should give them opportunity to be a church among themselves) he was by the church chosen to be a Deacon, especially to regard the brethren at Rocksbrough.

Thus, not only did the church leaders at Dorchester admit members from Roxbury, but they were willing to give the Roxbury members a considerable voice in the running of the church.

Other entries in Eliot's records amplify our knowledge of this arrangement. Thomas Lamb's third son, born in Roxbury in October 1630, was baptized in the Dorchester church. This would indicate that Lamb had joined the Dorchester church not long after his arrival in New England. In a different sort of proceeding, William Pynchon, whose first wife died after only a few months in New England, "after some years married Mrs. Francis Samford, a grave matron of the church at Dorchester." This had further ramifications, in that Henry Smith, a son of Francis Samford by an earlier husband, married one of Pynchon's daughters, and thus became one of the leading citizens of his father-in-law's new settlement at Springfield.

John Eliot arrived in New England on 2 November 1631 on the *Lion,* travelling in company with several members of John Winthrop's family. Eliot soon joined the Boston church and was made a freeman on 6 March 1631/2. At the end of his entries for October 1632, Winthrop notes that the Boston church was planning to invite Eliot to take the position of teacher (a position that involved mostly preaching sermons, and which was to be filled the following year by John Cotton), and that

though Boston labored all they could, both with the congregation of Roxbury and with Mr. Eliot himself, alleging their want of him, and the covenant between them, etc., yet he could

not be diverted from accepting the call of Roxbury, November 5. So he was dismissed.

Eliot had not held a living in England, but had taught under Thomas Hooker at Little Baddow in Essex, not far from his youthful residence of Nazeing, on the Hertfordshire border. Eliot must have had a very forceful and attractive personality even in his twenties, for he was followed by several other families who would collectively become known as the "Nazeing Christians." On the *Lion* with him were his brother Jacob, and brother-in-law James Penniman, both of whom chose to remain in Boston when Eliot removed to Roxbury.

The following summer the *Lion* made another voyage, and most of the passengers on that trip were from the western part of Essex. We can see here clearly the results of the work of both Hooker and Eliot, since this ship in 1632 carried both the advance party of Hooker's Braintree Company (as we have seen in a previous *Newsletter* in our discussion of Cambridge) and many followers of Eliot. For 1632 these were William Curtis, William Heath, Isaac Morrill, John Perry, Daniel Brewer, Thomas Offitt (Ufford) and John Watson. English origins for all of these are not known, so they may not all have been from the Nazeing area; but this would be a likely place to start a search.

The next large group from the Nazeing area came in 1635, many on the *Hopewell*. Among these were the families of John Ruggles, Giles Payson and Isaac Heath, brother of William who had come in 1632. (Another probable arrival in 1635 was John Graves. The church records state that he came in 1633, but this entry is in a sequence of others who came in 1635, and John Graves was made a freeman on 18 April 1637 along with five other Roxbury men, some of whom had come in 1635.)

The grouping of all these families as the "Nazeing Christians" was not just an artifical construct applied to them by the filiopietistic writers of the nineteenth century. Evidence that they conceived of themselves as a special group is seen in one of the burial entries in Eliot's church records, under November 1644:

Day 4. John Grave, a godly brother of the church, he took a deep cold, which swelled his head with rheum & overcame his heart.

Day 15. Thomas Ruggles a godly brother, he died of a consumption.

These two brake the knot first of the Nazing Christians. I mean they first died of all those Christians that came from that town in England.

A point needs to be made here about group migrations. In an instance like this, from Nazeing, or similarly with Hingham in Norfolk, there is the appearance that large numbers of families are coming from a single parish, and seemingly depleting seriously the population in that place. In the case of Nazeing, and probably for most other examples of this phenomenon, this appearance is misleading.

What is actually happening is that a small nucleus of persons, usually attracted to a particular Puritan minster, is augmented by like-minded persons from neighboring parishes. In the case of Nazeing, we find that William and Isaac Heath, for example, were earlier from the nearby Hertfordshire parishes of Ware and Great Amwell, and that William Heath moved to Nazeing only in the mid-1620s. He, and perhaps some of the others designated "Nazeing Christians," was not a long-term resident of Nazeing at the time he migrated. The overall picture, then, is of a sizable group of immigrants being built up around a focal point by a slow process of accretion, with one or two families coming in from one neighboring parish, and then another one or two from another parish.

Eliot's records themselves deserve some comment. Although they are filled with useful (and unusual) information, they must be used with care. Worthley, in his survey of Congregational church records, states that the published version

omits the records for 1751-1775 as "containing nothing of interest to the public," bowdlerizes many of the disciplinary notices and drops other entries, all without indicating that the original text has been tampered with (*An Inventory of the Records of the Particular [Congregational] Churches of Massachusetts Gathered 1620-1805* [Cambridge 1970] p. 99).

Although the most interesting part of Eliot's church records is the list of admissions, with accompanying notes and commentary on those admitted, which includes people arriving throughout the 1630s, it would appear that the records were not begun until 1641. The records also include baptisms, burials, and church disciplinary matters, and all three of these categories begin in that year.

The explanation would seem to lie in the succession of ministers at Roxbury. When the church was founded, Thomas Weld was pastor, and senior to John Eliot as teacher. When Weld left in 1641, Eliot was the only ordained minister at Roxbury until the arrival of Samuel Danforth in 1650. Whether Thomas Weld kept records which have been lost, or never kept records at all, we do not know; but apparently Eliot, when left to his own devices, decided to begin a register of church matters.

For most affairs, he was content with beginning with current events, but with the admissions he may have felt a desire to report the growth of his church by taking notice of each person admitted, even though he had to go back nine years. We cannot now say for certain just how he composed these records, perhaps a combination of notes, memory and interviewing of living members. However, we may be thankful for Eliot's efforts, while at the same time interpreting these early entries with caution.

ROXBURY LAND

As with most other early Massachusetts Bay towns, Roxbury produced a Book of Possessions. But, because of the destruction of all early town records, Roxbury's earliest land inventory was created nearly a decade after those of other towns. Toward the end of the inventory is the following statement:

We whose names are underwritten being chosen by the town upon the twenty-ninth of January fiftyfour to examine the transcript which Edward Dennison was to write out according to the copies delivered to him, having examined the said transcript upon the fourteenth of February fiftyfour, and we find that he hath performed exactly according to the copies committed to his charge what he was betrusted with to write for the town, as far as we are able to discern.

This was signed by John Johnson, William Parkes, Griffin Crafts and Edward Riggs. What these men examined had clearly been produced by January of 1654, but how much earlier had it actually been prepared? This is one of the questions we will attempt to answer as we study the Roxbury land records.

The Book of Possessions is set up with one or two persons per page, frequently leaving much blank space on the pages of the original. With the destruction of all the earliest town records (pre-1646) we do not have records of any of the actual distribution of lands to the proprietors; but by analyzing the records of landholding we can reconstruct some of the process of land granting in Roxbury, although not in as much detail as we would like.

We can identify the proprietors as those who hold several parcels of land, usually about seven as a minimum, entered in a certain order. First, as one might expect, are the houselots. These are generally about three to five acres in size, although some of the grandees have much larger houselots. As we will see throughout this analysis, our conclusions must be hedged by the statement that with the passage of ten or more years since the lands were originally granted, there has been sufficient time for much purchase and consolidation of land, so that the specific entries in the inventory will frequently not reflect the original grant.

After the houselot, we generally find a series of small parcels, some of meadow and some of plowland. Then will come a larger piece of land, in the tens of acres usually, which are in the "last division," always designated as in the Second Allotment, or in the First and Third Allotment; this "last division" apparently was not sufficient to satisfy all the proprietors, for some inventories will contain instead a parcel of similar size in the Nooks toward Boston or the Nooks toward Dorchester. Lastly, the inventories, in the portion that apparently relates to the original grants to proprietors, will contain a much larger piece in the "thousand acres next to Dedham," or more rarely, and usually for the wealthier citizens, in the "four thousand acres." These last two parcels in the ordinary inventory, the "last division" (or Nooks) and "thousand acres" (or "four thousand"), are roughly equivalent to the Great Dividend and Farms in Watertown.

Two good examples of straightforward grants to proprietors are seen in the inventories of John Perry and Francis Smith, both of whom were in Roxbury early in the 1630s, and were therefore the original grantees of each of these lots. Perry has a houselot of two acres, three additional small parcels of six, four, and five acres (the last being described as "salt marsh and upland"), eighteen acres and a fraction in "the division of the Nooks next Boston," and twenty-one acres in "the thousand acres near Dedham." Francis Smith held a houselot of three-and-a-half acres, an acre-and-a-half of pasture, a ten acre woodlot, twenty-one acres and a fraction in "the first and third allotments in the last division," and twenty acres in "the thousand acres near Dedham."

Most of the individual inventories are not, however, so simple and straightforward. In many cases, after the usual listing of direct grants, as seen above for John Perry and Francis Smith, there will be one or more additional entries, some stating that the land had been purchased from some earlier owner, some giving no clue as to how the land was acquired. These entries, found after the grant in the thousand acres or in the four thousand acres, are meant to be a summary of the land transactions which have taken place since the original grants were handed out by the town to the proprietors.

Edward Bugby serves as a good example of such an augmented landholding. The first few entries are of the usual nature, showing a houselot, two smaller parcels, and grants in the last division and in the thousand acres. Following this series, however, are descriptions of seven additional parcels, in no particular order. In some cases the entry identifies the person from whom Bugby obtained the land, and in one instance some highly useful genealogical information is included, for we are told that the land was acquired by "exchange with my son Richard Chamberlain."

Examination of the original of this Book of Possessions (available on microfilm) shows that most of the entries were written at one sitting, in the same hand and with a constant intensity of ink. But a few entries, just one or two at the end of some of the individual inventories, are in a lighter ink, although in the same hand. These were presumably entered after the original compilation of the Book of Possessions by Edward Dennison, and examination of some of these late additions will help us with the problem, stated at the beginning of this article, of dating more exactly the labors performed by Dennison.

Some examples of these late entries are the last piece of land in the inventories for Giles Payson (bought of Richard Sutton), John Stebbins (bought of William Lyon), Isaac Johnson ("lately Hugh Prichard's"), and Griffin Crafts (bought of Peleg Heath). A search of deeds in Suffolk County reveals one of these transactions, the sale by Hugh Prichard to several men, including Isaac Johnson, of a parcel of marsh, which sale took place before 25 June 1651 (Suffolk Deeds 1:144).

Another probe of the dating of this document is to look at the entries for those who had died before the inventory was compiled. Nine of the individual inventories begin with a phrase such as "The heirs of Thomas Ruggles." Eliot's church record includes detailed records of burials, and for these nine men, the last to die was John Levens, who was buried on 15 November 1647.

No adult males died in 1648 or 1649, and the only two to die in 1650 and 1651 were John Woody and John Roberts, neither of whom held land. The next proprietor to appear in Eliot's death records was William Heath, who was buried on 29 April 1652. There is no inventory for him in the Book of Possessions, but there are separate entries for his two sons Isaac and Peleg, who were by the terms of William's will to receive the land.

The next death of a proprietor is that of Thomas Dudley, at that time the leading citizen of Roxbury and the leading entry in the inventory; he was buried on 31 July 1653. This entry is written as if Dudley were alive, as is that of Robert Potter, who was buried on 17 January 1653/4. The picture is clouded somewhat by the fact that the land of William Dennison, who was buried just eight days after Potter, is in the inventory in the hands of his son Edward; but as William did not leave a will, he may have transferred the land during his lifetime.

The final picture, then, is not as clear as we might like, but it would seem that Edward Dennison carried out his mission in late 1652 or early 1653, after the death of Heath and before that of Dudley. The late entry of a land transaction which took place in 1651 could be the result of late registration of the document with the register of deeds, although one would think that Dennison would have known about this transfer, since so many Roxbury men were involved.

Like Watertown, and unlike Cambridge, Roxbury seems to have distributed all lands available within the first ten to fifteen years of the town's existence, with nothing left for later use. New lands for the rising generations would not become available until late in the century, when Roxbury was granted by the General Court the lands in the west which would at first be known as New Roxbury, but eventually as Woodstock, which would in time be ceded to Connecticut.

RECENT LITERATURE

Helen S. Ullmann, "Elizabeth New(h)all, Wife of Edmund[1] Farrington of Lynn, Massachusetts," *The American Genealogist* 66 (1991):9. Building on the recent work of Thomas Cooper, Ullmann cites an Essex County probate document which completes the proof that the wife of Edmund Farrington was the sister of Anthony and Thomas Newhall.

Dorothy Chapman Saunders, "The Origin of Robert[1] Chapman of Saybrook, Connecticut: A Theory Nipped in the Bud," *The American Genealogist* 66 (1991):30-32. In an effort to avoid duplication of effort by genealogists who might in the future follow the same dead end, Saunders presents here the results of extensive research which shows that Robert Chapman, the immigrant to Saybrook, was not the man of that name baptized at Kingston upon Hull, Yorkshire, on 1 January 1616/7.

Thomas W. Cooper, II, "The English Origin of Ellis Mew and Benjamin Ling of New Haven, Conn., and of Sarah (Mew) Cooper of Southampton, Long Island," *The American Genealogist* 66 (1991):45-48. Although Ellis Mew and his sister Sarah arrived in New England well after 1643, their connection with Benjamin Ling and other Great Migration families is sufficient reason for us to be interested in them. The two men were cousins through maternal lines of each, were both salters, and had immediate origins in London parishes.

Sargent Bush, Jr., "John Wheelwright's Forgotten *Apology*: The Last Word in the Antinomian Controversy," *The New England Quarterly* 64 (1991):22-45. *A Brief, and Plain Apology by John Wheelwright* was published in London in 1658, and "has gone unnoticed by Wheelwright scholars." Bush analyzes this pamphlet, and concludes that Wheelwright, twenty years after his banishment as one of the principal actors in the Antinomian controversy stimulated by Anne Hutchinson, was still holding to the positions which had led to his downfall at that time. Although he is not the first to do so, Bush also maintains that *Mercurius Americanus,* published in London and held by many to be written by Wheelwright as an earlier defense, was in fact written by his son, John Jr.

John Brooks Threlfall, *Fifty Great Migration Colonists & Their Origins* (Madison WI 1990). Threlfall provides extensive treatment of the immigrant generation, and English ancestry where known, of fifty early immigrants to New England, many of whom came before 1643. Documents are quoted extensively. While most of the material presented represents Threlfall's own work, there are also contributions by William Haslet Jones, Harold F. Porter, Jr., John Plummer and Douglas

Richardson. Of the newly discovered English origins first printed here, the most exciting is that of Anthony Colby, said by Threlfall to be from Horbling, Lincolnshire. Although such an origin seems likely, the evidence for the identification is not given here. If Colby's origin can be positively proved, it would be a great advance, since a longstanding but false royal descent, although exposed by Threlfall and others years ago, continues to crop up.

James Gilreath, ed., *The Judgment of Experts: Essays and Documents about the Investigation of the Forging of the* Oath of a Freeman (Worcester: American Antiquarian Society 1991). The Oath of a Freeman is the earliest item printed in British North America, having come off the Cambridge press in 1638 or 1639, but no copy of it exists today. When Mark Hofmann claimed in 1985 to have found a copy in New York, there was much excitement in the book world, but, as with earlier such discoveries, this turned out to be a false alarm, and, in this case, a fraud. There have been several accounts of the full range of Hofmann's misdeeds, but this is the first volume to focus on his forgery of the Oath. Although the most important evidence for the forgery is now Hofmann's own confession, the leading independent element in the unravelling of the crime was the discovery of the photographic negative for the printing plate used by Hofmann. For the most part, the modern scientific tests did not dispute the authenticity of the document.

Frank Elwood Potter, comp., *Descendants of Nicholas Potter of Lynn, Massachusetts* (Baltimore 1991). The compiler sets forth the descendants of Nicholas Potter in standard Register form, and prefaces the book with extensive extracts from the parish register of Newport Pagnell, Buckinghamshire, which show that the immigrant was baptized in that parish on 1 April 1604, and that he married in that same parish and had baptized there the three children who came with him to New England in 1634 or 1635.

The Essex Genealogist, quarterly publication of the Essex Society of Genealogists, Lynnfield Public Library, 18 Summer Street, Lynnfield MA 01940. For some time now *The Essex Genealogist* has been publishing a series of compiled genealogical accounts of the descendants of the earliest settlers of Lynn, most of whom fall within the period of the Great Migration. Those immigrants with installments in the February 1991 issue are Thomas Stocker, John Ramsdell, William Tilton, Peter Twiss and Henry Collins. Although these installments are all for the third generation or later, the opening installment in an earlier issue did treat extensively the lives of the immigrants.

(continued from page 10)
earliest list of Cambridge residents, presumably for 1632, along with William Spencer; in any case, this freeman is not the Roxbury man.)

We now have John Kirman associated with Lynn on four different dates, spanning a period from March 1632/3 to December 1636. During this same time frame John Carman in Roxbury had a son John born 8 July 1633 and daughter Abigail born in July 1635. The conclusion is inescapable: there were two men of the name John Carman/Kirman in New England at this early date. One of the "ten men of Saugus" authorized by the Plymouth Court on 3 April 1637 to settle Sandwich was John Carman, who appears in the Plymouth records several times in 1638 and 1640; again this conflicts with the birth of Caleb, son of John Carman, in Roxbury in March 1639/40. After 1640 John Carman disappears from the Plymouth records, and he may have returned to England. On the other hand, an associate of Robert Fordham in the founding of Hempstead on Long Island in 1643 is John Carman, and since this man has wife Florence and children John, Abigail and Caleb, it is easy to see that he is the Roxbury man.

There is much more to the story than this. Much of the confusion arises because both men arrived in New England in 1631, a year in which fewer than one hundred new immigrants arrived. John of Roxbury and Hempstead apparently came on the *Lion* in November with John Eliot, his pastor at Roxbury, while John of Cambridge, Lynn and Sandwich was a passenger on the *Plough*, and a member of the Company of Husbandmen, a fascinating group associated with the Reverend Stephen Bachiler.

Furthermore, Richard Dummer, who had travelled with Bachiler and who was also associated with the Company of Husbandmen, settled first at Roxbury. Thus, a prominent member of the Company was at each of the towns in which resided a John Carman or Kirman. Nevertheless, the analysis presented above shows that the *Plough* passenger must have gone to Lynn.

Because John Kirman of Lynn and Sandwich had no children, he could easily be combined with John Carman without any dire genealogical consequences. But a search for John Kirman of Sandwich after 1640 would be worthwhile, and should be feasible since he was a man of some prominence. Perhaps he returned to England to participate in the events of the Civil War.

In any case, the analysis displayed here in sorting out two men of the same name is being applied to all participants in this early phase of the Great Migration, in order to answer a wider range of questions relating to the details of residence, of time of migration, and of association with other immigrants.

Great Migration Newsletter

Vol. 2   July-September 1991   No. 3

EARLY VITAL RECORDS

In the first issue of the *Newsletter,* in the course of our discussion of Watertown, we commented on the earliest vital records of that town, and referred to the so-called "Early Records of Boston," which in fact have only a limited connection with Boston. Many of the comments made about the Watertown portion of these records is relevant to the records of other towns included in this document. But as there are also differences from town to town, a more detailed look at this earliest set of Massachusetts Bay vital records will be worthwhile.

The document in question is in fact a compilation of those vital records submitted to the county court by the towns of Suffolk County, beginning in 1644. Massachusetts Bay Colony established counties in 1643, two of them being Suffolk and Middlesex, but Middlesex did not take on an independent existence until 1649. Thus for years prior to 1649 this book of records includes submissions from the towns of Boston, Roxbury, Dorchester, Braintree, Weymouth and Dedham (which then made up Suffolk County), and Cambridge, Charlestown, Watertown, Concord, Woburn and Sudbury (then Middlesex). Hingham, which should have begun sending in its records in 1644, did not in fact do so until 1649. Even then, it did not include items retrospectively, as did the other towns. Also in 1649, Springfield sent in some vital records; it was for the moment part of Middlesex County, prior to the establishment of Hampshire County.

The probable reason for calling these the "Early Records of Boston" is that they are now, and have long been, in the custody of the Boston City Registrar. They are properly records of Suffolk County and should be returned to that jurisdiction. This volume was transcribed in the last century by David Pulsifer, and published in many installments in the *Register*, beginning with the first issue of the second volume.

The General Court had tried more than once to get the towns to be more diligent in recording vital records. The order which apparently prompted action after many years was made on 14 June 1642, referring back to a previous order of 1639 and noting that this order was "much

neglected in many towns," and directed the clerks of the writs (i.e. town clerks) to record births and deaths,

and for time past it is ordered, they shall do their utmost endeavor to find out in their severall towns who hath been born, & who hath died, since the first founding of their towns, & to record the same as aforesaid.

This same court order required the "magistrates and other persons appointed to marry" to keep the marriage records, which explains why the county court copies of the vital records for this early period are limited to births and deaths.

For several of the towns the record tells us that the register of births and deaths runs "until the first of the first month 1644." Given the problems with the calendar at this time, we want to know just what is meant by this limit on the first group of records, which supposedly includes everything back to the "first founding of their towns."

Examination of several of the towns shows that in this record the year began on the first of March, and not on the 25th, as in many other records. One specific example which helps in this determination comes from the entries from Dedham, in which Mary Aldridge, daughter of Henry and Mary, was born on the tenth of the first month (March) 1643, and died on the 24th of the second month (April) 1643. This sequence is possible only if the first of March is New Year's Day. Thus, the announced terminus for this first set of records, in the notation of double-dating, would be 1 March 1643/4.

(*continued on page 18*)

EDITOR'S EFFUSIONS

You will notice that this issue has a bonus section, four pages in the center which may be removed and placed with the issues for Volume One. This supplement contains an index to Volume One, and two sample sketches of the sort that will appear in a two-volume set next year. The two-volume set will contain more than eight hundred of these sketches. Some will be like the first of the two samples seen here, in that they will provide an outline of what is known about those families which stayed in New England for some time and generated a sizable number of records. Others will be like the second sample, in that they provide the evidence for persons or families which made a very brief appearance in New England, and left only two or three traces in the records.

The April 1991 issue of *William & Mary Quarterly* contains several items of interest to readers of this *Newsletter*. First, several colonial scholars, experts in different regions of colonial America, take David Hackett Fischer to task for some of his conclusions in *Albion's Seed* (noticed in this *Newsletter* in the April-June 1990 issue), and Fischer responds at length and with gusto. Second, this editor and William Thorndale wrote to the editor of *William & Mary Quarterly* with comments on the article by Richard Archer that was noticed in the January-March 1991 issue of the *Newsletter,* and Archer responds to those two letters.

The Focus section for this issue looks at the town of Salem, but not in the usual way. Since the analysis of the two land grants produced such unusual results, this feature of the town's early years is examined in great detail, rather than providing the usual even-handed survey of land and church records, along with a summary of the chronology of settlement, with comments about migration patterns. The Focus section in the next issue will also be different from the usual style, since the subject will be the settlements on the Piscataqua, for which the records are not at all like those for the towns already studied.

Robert Charles Anderson, FASG   Editor
Margaret F. Costello   Production Assistant

The *Great Migration Newsletter* (ISSN 1049-8087) is published quarterly by the Great Migration Study Project, a project of the New England Historic Genealogical Society
101 Newbury Street, Boston MA 02116

The subscription rate is $8 for one year and $15 for two years. The subscription year is the same as the calendar year.

(continued from page 17)

Despite this supposed cutoff date, not all the towns included all records down to that date. In Boston, for instance, there are (aside from a few entries for the Dutchfield family, which appear to be later additions) three entries for November, one for December, and none for January and February of 1643/4. Then, when the "second round" of Boston records is entered, we are told that they begin in the eighth month of 1643, October. Dorchester, on the other hand, seems to have felt that the earliest grouping of records should include the first month of 1644, and so there are three entries for March 1643/4, all before the 25th. Perhaps the Dorchester town clerk chose to report as if Lady Day were the first of the year, and then the county clerk "corrected" the dates.

In the discussion of the Watertown section of these records, we saw that the clerk of the writs did not report all births and deaths which had occurred in that town prior to 1 March 1643/4, but only those for families which still resided in Watertown at that later date. And for those families, only events which had taken place while the family actually resided in Watertown were recorded.

This same phenomenon extends to most of the other towns included in this volume, and certainly to all those established in the immediate aftermath of the arrival of the Winthrop Fleet (Boston, Charlestown, Cambridge, Watertown, Roxbury and Dorchester). An excellent demonstration of this principle may be seen in the family of George Ruggles. This man first appears in the records of the Boston church, where he is admitted in November of 1633. He then has children baptized at this church on 8 December 1633, 3 January 1635/6, and 31 December 1637. Not long after this last baptism he moved to Braintree. In the Braintree section of the vital records volume under discussion are listed children of George Ruggles born on 5 May 1640 and 15 February 1642/3. The children born to George Ruggles in Boston do not appear in the vital records of that town, since he had moved away well before 1644, and we are fortunate in this case to have them recorded in the church records. The Braintree records for this period, on the other hand, contain only those births which actually occurred in Braintree, after his removal from Boston, even though the earlier births would not be recorded anywhere in the civil records.

The records in this volume are beset by another problem as well. Since they were obtained from the town clerks by the county clerk, they have been copied over a number of times, which has allowed many errors to creep in. In the best of circumstances, the county clerk might have copied directly from the original record prepared by the town clerk. But more frequently it is likely that the town clerk made a copy of his records, which was then

(continued on page 24)

Focus   *on*   **SALEM**

EARLY SALEM CHURCH RECORDS AND THE 1636 SALEM LAND GRANT

Neither the earliest church records nor the earliest grants of town land in Salem are as complete as we might like. Nevertheless, careful analysis of the surviving portions of each reveals some interesting conclusions, and shows that these two types of records interact, at least in this community, in unexpected ways.

The church in Salem was organized in 1629, but suffered an uncertain existence for its first few years. The earliest ministers died or left soon, to be replaced by the redoubtable Roger Williams, whose approach to his ministry did not please the colony authorities, or many of the inhabitants of Salem. In 1636, after Williams had left for his permanent exile in Rhode Island, the church at Salem was reorganized under the leadership of the Reverend Hugh Peter. Like his predecessors in this office, Peter did not remain for very long, but he did establish a firm foundation, and the complete and continuous church records date from the beginning of his tenure.

All that survives from the years from 1629 to 1636 is a list of names of members of the church during this period, recording all men in one column and all women in another. There are 47 men in this record and 34 women, but, as we shall see, there are many omissions from this list, for a variety of reasons (Richard D. Pierce, ed., *The Records of the First Church in Salem, Massachusetts: 1629-1736* [Salem 1974] pp. 5-6).

As with so many of the other early towns, there is no consolidated record of the earliest grants of houselots, and some small parcels of meadow and arable land (although a few of these grants after 1634 do appear in the town records). The earliest surviving records of grants to the entire population are two lists, one for 1636 and one for 1637. Both have been published more than once, but not always in the same form. They may be found as appendices at the back of the first volume of Perley's *History of Salem*, and also in the first published volume of Salem town records (Sidney Perley, *The History of Salem, Massachusetts* [Salem 1924] 1:454-59; Wm. P. Upham, "Town Records of Salem, 1634-1659", *Essex Institute Historical Collections*, Second Series, Volume 1 [1868], pp. 18-27).

The starting point for our analysis of these sources will be the land grant of 1636. As published by Perley, this is a straightforward list of names, but with many footnotes, indicating that various names had originally appeared in the record, but had been crossed out; comparison of the names shows that all those crossed out appear somewhere else in the list. The version published in the Salem town records attempts to adhere more closely to the original, for it shows the deleted names in their proper location. The largest grants were of three hundred and two hundred acres, to a few of the community leaders. Most of the grants were in the range of thirty to eighty acres, with many as low as ten or twenty.

In the surviving manuscript volumes of the Salem town records, as examined on microfilm, this list exists in three forms: a rough, seventeenth-century version, which corresponds to the record as printed in the published town records; a nineteenth-century copy of this version; and a seventeenth-century list, which appears to be a fair copy of the first item above, without the deletions.

Our analysis will depend for the most part on the first of these manuscript copies, the rough, seventeenth-century record. There are many indications that this document is in fact three separate lists, all referring to the same distribution of land in 1636, and that this record began as a single list, which was then added to and extended, to reach its present form.

First, the list is spread over eight leaves of the manuscript volume, and is not continuous over this space. The record begins on leaf three, and covers both sides of that leaf, the front of leaf four, but only a small part of the back. The next section begins on leaf five, covering both sides of leaves five and six, but the front only of leaf seven. The back of leaf seven, and all of leaf eight, are blank. Finally, the third section of the list covers the front of leaf nine, a small portion of the back, and the front only of leaf ten.

Second, the middle portion of the list is in rough alphabetical order, whereas the beginning and the end of the list are in no discernible order whatever. This alphabetical section corresponds to the middle section described above, on leaves five through seven.

Third, there are marginal annotations for most of the entries on leaves three and four indicating that they have been transferred to leaves nine and ten, and corresponding cross-references on nine and ten, referring back to three and four. There are no such marginal notations on the middle section.

How do these three lists-within-a-list relate to one another? The first portion, that on leaves three and four, seems to have been prepared first. The reason for this statement is that some names (i.e. Roger Conant and John Endicott) appear in this section only. The names in this first portion which are lined through (and which are noted in the footnotes in the version of the list published by Perley) all reappear in the second or third part of the list. With a few exceptions, all the names in the third section of the list were brought over from the first part, and virtually all are cross-referenced with marginal annotations in both parts. Some of the names in the second part have also been brought over from the first section, but most of the names in this alphabetical sequence appear here only.

The third section of the list has the heading "Freemans Land," and all the entries which were transferred from the first section to this section are followed in the first section by the letter "f," which has been interpreted to mean freeman. The most obvious way to check this is to compare the names in this part of the record with the lists of freemen in the court records of Massachusetts Bay Colony. As one might expect, more than half the names in the third section of the 1636 land grant appear also in the colony lists of freemen, but there are many that cannot be found. Are the colony lists grossly incomplete, or is there some other explanation?

One helpful clue is found by direct examination of the list. In this section of "Freemans Land" appear two widows, Widow Felton and Widow Skarlet. Both of these women were apparently widowed before arrival in New England, for there is no evidence to show a husband for either of them on this side of the Atlantic. In that portion of the list of those admitted to Salem church before the reorganization in 1636, however, we find Ellen Felton and Anne Skarlett, and these are presumably the two widows of the land grant.

Among the men in this third part of the land grant are some who were not among the colony freemen, at least by 1636. Hugh Laskin, for instance, was not made free until 22 May 1639, but he does appear on the Salem church records as having been admitted before 1636, and he does receive a portion of the "Freemans Land."

In Salem, then, a person received "Freemans Land" if he or she was a member of the Salem church at the time, regardless of whether or not colony freeman status had been conferred (and of course such status could not have been give to women). This is a usage of the term "freeman" not seen elsewhere, and perhaps idiosyncratic to Salem.

A systematic comparison of this third part of the 1636 land grant, the Salem church membership list, and the colony lists of freemen turns up a few who received "Freemans Land," but do not appear as church members or as colony freemen. Among these are John Talbie, Mr. [Charles] Gott and William Dodge. But there is good

evidence that these men, and others like them, had been admitted to Salem church by 1636. The regular recording of baptisms begins on Christmas Day 1636, with each entry giving the name of the child or children baptized, and the name of one parent. This is usually the father, but occasionally the mother. This sort of arrangement is seen in other church records (Dedham, for instance), and the reason generally is that the child must be baptized on the account of a parent who is a member of the church, and when the father is not a member, the record will be in the name of the mother. With regard to the three cases above, a child is baptized in the name of each of these men: Difficulty, daughter of John Talby, 25 December 1636; Deborah, daughter of Charles Gott, 12 February 1636/7; and John, son of William Dodge, 25 December 1636.

For two of these men there is additional evidence for early church membership. Charles Gott was known to be intimately involved with the foundation of the Salem church in 1629. He wrote a letter to William Bradford shortly after the event, giving Bradford a detailed account of the election of Skelton and Higginson as pastor and teacher. Although Gott in this letter does not state directly that he became a member of the Salem church at its founding, he does say that he was one of those who voted for the church officers, and it would be surprising on this basis if he were not one of the founders (Perley, *History of Salem*, 1:154-56). John Talby, whose wife was executed for murdering their daughter Difficulty, was excommunicated from the Salem church prior to 1 May 1639, which clearly implies that he had earlier been admitted to the church (Perley 1:272).

The conclusion, then, is that the surviving list of Salem church members is incomplete, and is missing a number of men (and presumably women as well) who joined the church prior to 1636, who were still resident in Salem in that year, and who in most cases were in Salem for many years thereafter.

If the third part of the 1636 land grant represents the apportionments for the members of the Salem church, known in local parlance as "freemen," who were the people in the second part of the list? Again checking these names against the list of early Salem church members and the lists of freemen of the colony, we find that almost all the names in the alphabetical portion of the 1636 land grant are not in either place. But there are a few names here which do appear as freemen of the Massachusetts Bay Colony, and these must be accounted for.

The names to be explained (with dates of freemanship) are: Anthony Dixe (18 May 1631), Robert Cotty (6 May 1635), Elias Stileman (3 July 1632), and Philip Veren (2 September 1635). The latter two are an illusion, since in each case there was a father and adult son of the same name by 1636; the freemanship is for the father, the name in the second part of the list is for the son. The elder Philip Veren appears in the first section of the list, receiving 160 acres, and the son gets nothing; the elder Elias Stileman receives 100 acres in the third part of the grant, and the son thirty acres in his position in the middle portion of the grant.

The explanations for Anthony Dixe and Robert Cotty are different. Dixe was made a freeman on 18 May 1631, the last date upon which one could be made free without first being a member of a church. Thus, although he was a freeman by colony standards, he apparently did not meet the standards set by Salem for receipt of "Freemans Land." Robert Cotty was made free at a time when church membership was necessary, but he appears in a sequence in the list for 6 May 1635 with several others being admitted from the church at Lynn. Cotty (or Cotta) in fact appears in all three sections of the 1636 list. In the first section his name is crossed out, and it is followed by the letter "f" and a grant of thirty acres. In the second section the name is crossed out. And in the third section he appears with a grant of thirty acres, and a marginal notation indicating transfer from the first section. Perhaps he had recently been dismissed from Lynn church and admitted to Salem church, and so had only recently become eligible for "Freemans Land." Note that he too had children baptized in Salem on his own account, the earliest being on 28 January 1637/8, indicating that by that date he had been admitted to Salem church, if not earlier.

The second part of the 1636 list, then, includes those persons being considered for land grants who were not members of the Salem church. Some of these, but not many, had been included in the first portion of the list. When that section of the list was purged, the names of non-church members were lined through, but no marginal annotation of transfer was made, as had been done for the church members who were removed to the last section. The second section differs from the parts which went before and after in that it was alphabetically arranged, and in that there are relatively few erasures, as compared with the other parts.

Another feature of the middle section of this land grant list is that it included a number of the persons who received no grant at all. Presumably these were persons who were still quite young, and perhaps also still serving out a term of servitude. We have seen already that the younger Philip Veren appeared on the list, but received no land; he was just barely seventeen at the time of this grant. George Roaps appears in this part of the 1636 list, but in the town records on 17 April 1637 we are told that "George Roaps cannot yet be received [as an inhabitant, and therefore eligible for grants of land] because he hath a year to serve."

As noted earlier, the original town record volume also contains another contemporary copy of the 1636 land grant list, but as a single, continuous run of names, without the deletions or the differences between sections described above. This appears to have been created simply by listing the non-deleted entries from the rough list, skipping over those which did not receive any grant. This list is in a different hand than the rough list which we have been discussing, but it has the appearance of having been written down at about the same time.

This consolidated list itself deserves further study, but only one additional observation will be made here. In the rough list, and in the published version in the town records, the phrase "at Jeffrys Creek" appears twice. Upham interpreted this to apply both to the entry for Thomas More's widow and to a list of eight men beginning with Samuel Archer. The consolidated list does not attach this phrase to Thomas More's widow, which is consistent with the ambiguous appearance of the original. The contemporary consolidated list should be followed in preference to Upham on this point.

We are now in a position to summarize what we have learned about the land grant of 1636, and about the list of pre-1636 church members. The land grant list was begun as a single list, with Roger Conant and other prominent inhabitants of Salem at the beginning. This list included both church members and non-members, but not all of the latter. Apparently as this list was being compiled, it was decided that church members should be treated differently from non-members, and so all grants for the former, except a few which had already been given to the town's leaders, would be drawn off to a separate list, which is part three of the document as we now see it. The non-church members were then accommodated by the second part of the list, and to these were added others not already in the original compilation; not all of the non-church members received land in this grant. (In the list as published by Perley, the first section extends from Roger Conant to widow Turner, the second part from John Alderman to "Mr. Peeters," and the third part from Thomas More's widow to "Mr. Peters.")

All that survives of the church records prior to December of 1636 is the list of members, and this is defective in at least two different ways. First, many men and women who had been admitted to Salem church prior to that date, and were still residing in Salem at much later dates, are missing from this list. Second, all who had joined Salem church prior to 1636, but had died or moved away prior to that date, are not in the surviving list. An obvious example in this category would be Roger Williams. As a consequence of these various deficiencies, less than half, and possibly only a third, of those admitted to Salem Church in its first seven years were retained on the records at the time of reorganization. For this period, the list of members of Salem church cannot be used in the same way as the lists for Boston, Charlestown and Roxbury, the only other churches with records this early.

THE 1637 SALEM LAND GRANT

The 1637 grant of Salem land, also published by Perley as an appendix to his first volume (1:460-65), is not so problematic as the 1636 grant, but it is equally interesting, and in some ways more informative.

This was apparently a record of a town grant of marshland to all inhabitants, ordered in December 1637. In the column for amount of land, the number "2" is intended for half an acre, and the number "3" for three-quarters of an acre. The number to the left of the name gives the size of the household at that time.

Unlike the 1636 list, there does not appear to be any pattern to the arrangement in 1637. There is only a single list, with no interlineations, deletions, or cross-references. This is a completely independent list, which was not made with any reference to the record of a year earlier.

Some useful information does emerge, however, if we simply compare the two lists to see which names are common to both, and which appear in only one list or the other. On the one side, there are seventeen names which are seen in 1636 and not in 1637. From the other direction, sixty-six names are in the 1637 list only.

We will first examine a few of the sixteen who are present in 1636 but not in 1637. Two may simply be variants of the same name; John Bradley of 1636 may well be John Brittell of 1637; and there is a slight possibility that Thomas Tuck of 1636 is Thomas Tracy of 1637. Mr. Moses Maverick is in the 1636 list, but his absence in the following year is not surprising, since his commercial activities had him on the move throughout his life. John Leach Jr. was one of those who was on the 1636 list but did not receive a grant, probably because he was too young, and he was probably still too young a year later. The 1636 entry for Mrs. Higginson (widow of the Reverend Francis) allots her land only if she were to come to Salem to live, and clearly she did not. Arguments along these lines would probably explain the remaining eleven cases in this category.

The sixty-six who appear only in the 1637 grant are a more interesting group. Many of them sailed to New England in 1637 on one of the three vessels which left Yarmouth, co. Norfolk, in that year (John Camden Hotten, ed., *The Original Lists of Persons of Quality* ... [London 1874 and later reprintings], pp. 289-95). Among these were Mr. [John] Youngs, John Gedney, Francis Laws and William Williams. There are others in this category who are known to have come from the same areas in southeastern Norfolk and northeastern Suffolk as did the above persons, but who are not on the passenger lists for these ships. Examples would be Christopher Youngs, brother of Reverend John, and James Moulton, closely related to the other Moulton families which sailed

at this time. These persons, and their families, can be safely added to the passenger lists for the ships from Yarmouth, which in any case appear to be incomplete.

Also among the sixty-six are sons of earlier immigrants, now just coming of age. Toward the end of the 1637 list appear Thomas Gardner and George Gardner, each shown as a household of one, i.e. each a single man living alone. These are the sons of Mr. Thomas Gardner, who appears elsewhere in the list shown as a household of seven. John Hardy Junior, also with a household of one, receives a grant, as does his father.

We also find in this group of sixty-six evidence for migration within New England. At the end of the list is Goodman Holiman, with a family of two. This would be Ezekiel Holiman, who appears regularly on the Dedham records in 1636 and late 1637. From this record we learn that he sojourned briefly in Salem, before moving on to Providence to join Roger Williams. Also toward the end of the list are two consecutive names making their first appearance in New England: Ezekiel Knight, with a family of five, and Thomas Flatman, with a family of three. These two families stayed only briefly in Salem, and both appear next in Braintree. This is good evidence that the two were associated in England, and that a search for the origins of one would turn up the other as well.

The most important information in this record is the indication of household size, the number immediately preceding the name. How accurate is this number? We must first remember that it is not necessarily limited to the nuclear family, but may also include relatives more distant than wife and children, as well as servants.

The best check we have on the family size is again from the 1637 passenger lists, since these are arranged by family, with all persons given, and they were compiled just a few months before the grant in question. On the 1637 land grant, Mr. [John] Young has a family of eight, and on the passenger list we find him, his wife, and six children. William Williams is granted land based on a household of four, and the passenger list shows William with wife Alice and two children. Francis Lawes appears in the Salem record with a household of four, and on the passenger list he is accompanied by his wife, one child, and two servants. John Gedney has seven persons in his Salem household in late 1637, and the passenger list entry includes John, wife Sarah, three children, and two servants. Thus three of the families examined match exactly, and the fourth is easily explained if one of the servants died, or was transferred to another master.

We can conclude, then, that the 1637 Salem land grant is quite reliable with regard to household size, and this record may be used in much the same way as the grants of Beaverbrook Plowlands and Remote Meadows in Watertown.

RECENT LITERATURE

Vera Main Robinson, "A Clue to the Identity of Mrs. Ezekiel Main," *Rhode Island Roots* 17 (1991):16-19. Presents evidence that Mary, wife of Ezekiel Main (d. 1714) of Scituate, Massachusetts, and Stonington, Connecticut, was daughter of Thomas Hatch, immigrant in the 1630s to Scituate. This Mary had earlier been wife of Daniel Pryor of Scituate.

Wayne Howard Miller Wilcox, "The Ancestry of Katherine Hamby, Wife of Captain Edward Hutchinson of Boston," *New England Historical and Genealogical Register* 145 (1991):99-121. Captain Edward Hutchinson, son of William and Anne (Marbury) Hutchinson, immigrants to Boston in 1634, married in England (probably at Lawford, co. Essex) Katherine Hamby. Wilcox has compiled a detailed account of four generations of her ancestry in the paternal line, the Hambys being prominent in Suffolk and earlier in Lincolnshire. A second installment of this article will present the children and grandchildren of Edward and Katherine, and three lines of royal descent for Katherine.

Jane Fletcher Fiske, "A Clue to the English Background of the Cor(e)y Family of Rhode Island," *New England Historical and Genealogical Register* 145 (1991):122-24. John Roome, who appears in the records of Newport and Portsmouth, Rhode Island, as early as 1638, married the widow Anne Corey. The John Corey who is seen in Rhode Island court records of 1643 may or may not be Anne's son, but the William Cory who appears in Portsmouth in 1657 is certainly her grandson. The author points out records that indicate the Coreys probably came from Bristol in England.

Gerald James Parsons, "Were Joseph and Benjamin Parsons and David Wilton of Beaminster, Dorset, England, the New England Colonists?" *New England Historical and Genealogical Register* 143 (1989):101-19. The author provides records for a Parsons family in Beaminster, Dorsetshire, which leave little doubt that the immigrants to New England, Joseph and Benjamin Parsons of Springfield, Massachusetts, came from that parish. Aside from the usual evidence of parish register entries which are in chronological agreement, there are a number of connections with other West Country immigrants to Dorchester, which ties in with the marriage of William Pynchon, founder of Springfield, with a widow from Dorchester not long before 1636. There is also excellent evidence that David Wilton, another early settler of Dorchester and Springfield, was from Beaminster. There are in Beaminster as well many records of a Hoskins family, but none that can with assurance be connected with the Hoskins family of Dorchester.

Jane Thayer Friedman, "Richard Johnson of Lynn and His Descendants," *The Essex Genealogist* 11 (1991):82-89. The latest in the series of articles in this journal on the earliest settlers of Lynn, this first installment covers the immigrant Richard Johnson and his two sons Samuel and Daniel. He first appears in Lynn in 1638, and may be the man of the same name who is seen the year before in Salem. It is, however, highly unlikely that the Richard Johnson discussed here is identical with the man of that name who appears twice in 1630, associated with Watertown and Charlestown.

Andrew B. W. MacEwen, "A Blaisdell Note," *The American Genealogist* 66 (1991):74. The author points out a record which places the widow of Ralph[1] Blaisdell, immigrant to Salisbury, in Boston in 1658, and notes that this explains "the presence of her daughter there."

John Plummer, "The English Origin of John[1] Moore of Sudbury, Massachsetts," *The American Genealogist* 66 (1991):75-77. Plummer has found the marriage in 1633 in the parish of Little Gaddesden, Hertfordshire, of John Moore and Elizabeth Rice. He identifies these as the immigrants to Sudbury, Massachusetts, about 1640, and notes that this strongly supports an earlier argument that John Moore's wife was stepdaughter of Philemon Whale and not daughter. The author then adds a number of English baptismal records which belong to this family, and help to clarify the chronology.

David L. Greene, "Enigmas: Was Tabitha, Wife of William Howard of Ipswich, Mass., a Daughter of Robert[1] Kinsman?" *The American Genealogist* 66 (1991):111-18. William Howard or Hayward of Ipswich had by 1666 acquired a wife with the given name of Tabitha. Previous writers had claimed that she was daughter of Robert[1] Kinsman, early settler of Ipswich, but without providing adequate evidence. The author has examined the available evidence in great depth, and concludes that the proposed identification is correct, but not yet totally proven, and so he presents this as a problem for others to ponder, and to add to, if possible. The article concludes with a discussion of connections between Roxbury and Ipswich, focussing on the Dane family.

John Plummer, "East Anglian Immigration to New England in 1637: A Hypothesis," *National Genealogical Society Quarterly* 79 (1991):123-27. The author argues that in addition to the three ships known to have sailed from Yarmouth, co. Norfolk, for New England in 1637, there were an additional three to five ships which made the passage from East Anglia in that year. The evidence is suggestive, but not compelling, and more work needs to be done to support or disprove this hypothesis.

(continued from page 18)

carried to Boston to be copied again by the county clerk into the single volume for the whole county. And there may have been other steps of which we are unaware. The opportunities for scribal errors were abundant.

The earliest vital records of Dedham are among the most carefully maintained, and comparison with the county copy will tell us much about the intrusion of error into the latter. In the first place, the town copy of the vital records was maintained in chronological order, whereas the county version has been alphabetized for the whole period from 1635 to 1642, and this process of rearrangement is certainly another occasion for errors to creep in. (For some reason, Dedham submitted its records for 1643 separately; perhaps the Dedham town clerk had his copies for submission to the county ready before those of any other town.)

Other errors in the Dedham comparison are plentiful. Without citing specific examples, there are many dates, sometimes of month or year but mostly of day only, which are not in agreement in the two versions. Other errors are more serious, as with the omission in the county copy of the birth of Mary Barstow, daughter of William, on 28 December 1641, and of several death records, such as that of Thomas Fisher on 10 August 1638. Robert Woodward, who died on 30 December 1638, is recorded by the county as Robert Wood!

Two other errors are even more serious. The town records show one child born to Austen Kalem, a son Lot born 11 September 1641; the county copy gives his birth on the same day and month, but a year earlier, and then tells us of a daughter Sarah, born 4 January 1641/2, of which the town knows nothing. Without further research, it is not clear which version is correct here. Finally, the county version has great difficulty with the family of Thomas Ames or Eames. There are two entries under Eams, a death of a John in 1641, and a birth of a John in 1642. These correspond with similar entries in the Dedham town records, but there we also find another birth of a son John in 1641, prior to the death record. In the county record is a birth of a John James, son of Thomas, on the same date as the John Ames of the town record. The county record has created a new family in Dedham!

In general, then, the county copy, as represented by the misnamed "Early Records of Boston," is much inferior to the copy retained by the town. Savage makes this point frequently in his *Genealogical Dictionary of New England,* when comparing this county copy (which is all that exists for Boston of civil vital records at this date) with the record of church baptisms. If there is an existing alternative to the county copy for this period down to 1644, and a discrepancy appears, the first thing to do is to check the originals. If the discrepancy persists, the alternative source should be preferred to the county copy.

Great Migration Newsletter

Vol. 2   October-December 1991   No. 4

MILITARY MEN

Both Plymouth Colony and Massachusetts Bay Colony, in their preparations for the settlement of New England, took great care to provide for their defense. In both cases the leaders looked principally to men who had experience in the fighting in the Low Countries in the early decades of the seventeenth century. Perhaps the most famous of these fighting men was Myles Standish, recruited by the Pilgrim leaders of Leyden for the colony at Plymouth. Our spotlight in the current article will be on the military men hired and appointed by the Massachusetts Bay Colony, and the organization created for the defense of the colony.

One of the first actions of the Court of Assistants of Massachusetts Bay Colony, on 7 September 1630, was to arrange provisions for Daniel Patrick and John Underhill. Both of these men had served in the Low Countries, and had acquired Dutch wives in the process. As later events would show, neither was particularly sympathetic to the Puritan cause. They were obviously hired by Winthrop and his associates to perform a particular function for the colony, and not because of religious compatibility.

There were others who had seen service in the Low Countries in the 1620s, but, for one reason or another, most of them did not last long in New England. Captain Walter Norton had served long and faithfully in the Low Countries, in Ireland, and at the Battle of Rhe, where he had lost a son. He first appeared in 1630 in Charlestown, but he was clearly not in sympathy with the Puritans, for he soon joined with several others to obtain a charter for what would eventually become the town of York in Maine, later the focus of activities of the Gorges family. Norton had probably only lived in York for a year when he accompanied a few other men on a trading expedition to Long Island Sound and was killed by Indians.

A very different man was Jost Weillust, a German who on 1 March 1630/1 was by the General Court "chosen surveyor of the ordinance and cannoneer, for which he is to have allowed him £10 per annum." But on 3 July 1632 he was allowed "£5 towards his transportation into his own country, whither, according to his desire, he hath free leave to go," and he was never seen again.

On 28 September 1630, a rate was levied on nine Massachusetts Bay settlements for the support of Patrick and Underhill. Conspicuously absent from this list of towns was Salem, which had also been excluded earlier when support for the ministers of the Bay towns was organized. Salem had its own ministers, and presumably had already arranged for its own defenses; certainly this was true by 7 November 1632 when William Trask was referred to as captain in the court records.

Then on 26 July 1631 the court ordered that

every first Thursday in every month there shalbe a general training of Captain Underhill's company at Boston & Roxbury, and every first Friday in every month there shalbe a general training of the remainder of them who inhabit at Charlton, Mistick & the newe towne [Cambridge].

Presumably "the remainder" were to be drilled by Captain Patrick. Note that in addition to Salem, Dorchester and Watertown were absent from this list. The omission of Watertown is probably just an oversight, but Dorchester may also have had its own captain already, in Captain Southcott (see below).

At first sight this looks similar to the arrangement with the ministers, where John Wilson and his church served the settlements at Boston and Charlestown, George Phillips ministered to the population of Watertown, Cambridge and probably Medford, and Roxbury came under the care of Dorchester church. Salem, being an older town and already having its own church, was left out of this arrangement. With regard to military matters, it appears that again Salem and Dorchester were on their

(continued on page 26)

EDITOR'S EFFUSIONS

With the current issue we complete our second year of publication, and look forward to a third. The Focus section in this issue, on the settlements along the Piscataqua river, is different from previous Focus articles. The nature of the settlers on the Piscataqua, and the records they created, are of a different nature from those created to the south. As a consequence, our inquiries into the earliest years of these settlements bring forth quite different results. Rather than being able to analyze in great detail the land-granting policies of the Piscataqua settlements, or study the development of the church, we have to look to records of a more literary nature to ask much broader and more basic questions, such as how many settlements were there, and just where were they.

For the first issue of Volume Three we will return to more familiar themes, with the Focus on Boston. In this case, though, there will be the difference that Boston was much larger than the other early Bay towns. Furthermore Boston, as the largest and most important town in Massachusetts, and the home of most of its leaders, has generated much more writing about and analysis of its earliest records, and for this reason our treatment of Boston will be more of a reaction to the analysis of earlier writers, rather than the new inquiry which has been possible with some of the other, more neglected towns.

In the second issue of 1992, the Focus will be on Plymouth. Here again the approach will differ, since the town of Plymouth was identical with the colony of Plymouth for the first twelve years, but the records for these earliest years are quite sparse. Only at the time of the earliest movement out to new settlements in Plymouth Colony (Duxbury and Scituate) do the records become more voluminous.

Once we have presented our views on Boston and Plymouth the discussion of the towns settled before 1634 will be nearly complete, and in the April-July 1992 issue of the Newsletter plans for the future of the Focus section will be announced.

Robert Charles Anderson, FASG   Editor
Margaret F. Costello   Production Assistant

The *Great Migration Newsletter* (ISSN 1049-8087) is published quarterly by the Great Migration Study Project, a project of the New England Historic Genealogical Society
101 Newbury Street, Boston MA 02116

The subscription rate is $8 for one year and $15 for two years. The subscription year is the same as the calendar year.

(continued from page 25)

own, but the implication is that the remainder of the towns were to be under the military care of one of two men - either John Underhill or Daniel Patrick.

The records very soon make it clear, however, that this was not the case (or that the originally intended arrangement was very soon changed). On 12 April 1631 the General Court ordered that "every captain shall train his company on Saturday in every week."

Phrased in this way it certainly sounds as if there were more captains of the military than just Patrick and Underhill, and succeeding records show that to be the case. We have already seen that by 7 November 1632 William Trask was referred to as captain, and on 14 May 1634 "Richard Damford [Davenport] was chosen ensign to Capt. Traske." On 4 March 1633/4 "Mr. Nathaniel Turner is chosen captain of the military company of Saugus." The last of these items shows that even one of the smallest of the settlements had its own military company, even though there is no record that such an organization was established, or set off from the company headed by Patrick or Underhill. The Salem item, coupled with that town's omission from the tax assessment in support of Patrick and Underhill, supports the idea that they may have had their own unit since the beginning.

The record relating to Salem also indicates that a hierarchy was developing within each company, and that there were officers other than just the captain. In fact, in these early years we can identify the ranks of captain, lieutenant, ensign, sergeant and corporal. Many of the men who held these offices in the early years moved up rapidly in rank, as the military companies took solider form.

To show this system at work, let us look more closely at one town, Dorchester. As with the church, Dorchester seems to have been left out of the system established for defense, for we find that on the *Mary & John* was one Captain Southcott, also a veteran of the wars in the Low Countries. (This man was named either Richard or Thomas; both applied for freemanship on 19 October 1630, but only one, with the military title but without a forename, was admitted on 18 May 1631.) But already on 26 July 1631 the General Court ordered that

Mr. Frauncis Aleworth is chosen Lieutenant unto Captain Southcoate, & Captain Southcoate hath liberty granted him to go for England, promising to return again with all convenient speed.

Captain Southcott never did return to New England, and in the following year, on 3 October 1632, the Court agreed that "Lieutenant Aleworth hath liberty granted him to return to England by the ship Lyon." This left the

(continued on page 32)

Focus on THE PISCATAQUA

PISCATAQUA AND PORTSMOUTH

The name Piscataqua, or Piscataway, or any of its many variants, was in the middle of the seventeenth century one of the most flexible and indefinite geographic terms in use. It could refer to the entire inhabited length of the Piscataqua River, and to much of the mainland beyond, or it could refer to one or another of the several settlements along the river. Close attention to context is necessary in order to determine what it might mean in any given instance.

Aside from the uncertainty in the name Piscataqua, there is an accompanying cloud over the details of settlement in the 1620s and 1630s, because of the lack of reliable records. Unlike the Puritan towns and colony founded to the south a few years later, the Piscataqua settlements did not create town records until well into the 1640s. The records that do survive are more of a private nature, reflecting the business activities of the principal settlers. In addition, because of disputes over the claims of the heirs of John Mason, stretching well into the eighteenth century, many forged documents were created in support of various law suits (see discussion on page 30). Great care is needed in interpreting the records that we do have.

In 1622 the Council for New England, at that time controlled by a group of West Country merchants, granted to Sir Ferdinando Gorges, Captain John Mason, and several others a stretch of New England coastline, which included the Piscataqua River (now the boundary between New Hampshire and Maine), and extended to the "western sea."

Associated with Gorges and Mason was David Thompson, a merchant, mariner and gentleman of Plymouth, Devonshire, where in 1613 he married Amias Cole. In 1623 he set out for New England in the *Jonathan,* with his wife, children and a group of servants. He was given a patent for some of the land around the mouth of the Piscataqua, but he was also an agent of Gorges and Mason in this venture. Thompson established himself near the mouth of the Piscataqua, on the southern side of the river, at Little Harbor and Odiorne's Point. These sites eventually became part of Portsmouth, and were then set off as part of the town of Rye.

Thompson was still at Piscataqua in 1626, according to Bradford, but he soon moved to the island in Boston Harbor which bears his name, and very soon after that he died. His widow would later marry Samuel Maverick, another early settler of Massachusetts Bay, and an individualist of the highest order.

We get a fuzzy snapshot of the situation on the Piscataqua in 1628, as a result of activity occurring on the south shore of Massachusetts Bay. Thomas Morton, the decidedly non-Puritan inhabitant of Merrymount, who had to the great consternation of the Pilgrims erected a maypole at that location, had been taken into custody and was to be sent back to London in the custody of John Oldham, yet another of the great characters of New England in the 1620s. In order to finance that quasi-legal activity, Bradford organized a tax assessment on all the communities from Plymouth north to Piscataqua.

In this tax list, which may be found in Bradford's Letterbook, are eight entries: "Plimouth £2 10s; Naumkeak £1 10s; Pascataquack £2 10s; Jeffrey & Burslem £2; Natascut £1 10s; Mrs. Thomson 15s; Blackston 12s; Edward Hilton £1." Aside from Plymouth, each of these needs a little explanation. "Naumkeak" is the recently established settlement whose name would change to Salem; at the time of this assessment it is still under the control of Roger Conant, with John Endicott already on his way under instructions from the Massachusetts Bay Company. "Natascut" is Nantasket, later Hull, a small fishing community established some years earlier by Lyford and others who had left Plymouth after a dispute with Bradford and others; this plantation straggled along for nearly two decades before attaining full status as a town. "Jeffrey & Burslem" represents William Jeffrey and John Bursley, who with a few servants were running a fishing community, and probably trading with the Indians, at Wessaguscus, or Weymouth; they may be the remnants of the Robert Gorges expedition of 1623. And "Blackston" is the Reverend William Blackstone who enjoyed for some years a solitary existence on Shawmut peninsula, the future site of Boston, prior to the arrival of Winthrop; again, he probably had with him his wife, child, and a few servants.

As can be seen from the entities discussed above, some of these small settlements were known simply by the name of the principal resident. In this light, the remaining three entries are of immediate interest to us: Pascataquack £2 10s; Mrs. Thomson 15s; and Edward Hilton £1. This listing confirms that David Thompson had died, and his widow was living at a site other than Piscataqua - in fact, on Thompson's Island in Massachusetts Bay. David Thompson had left Piscataqua a year or two before, and had presumably left the employ of Gorges and Mason. The assessment for Piscataqua is the largest of the three, and in fact is the same as the assessment for Plymouth itself. This cannot mean that the population at Piscataqua was as great as that at Plymouth (which in 1627 had been at least 156, based on the cattle division listing of that year). The high rate of taxation for Piscataqua in 1628 must be based on the value of the goods at that location, mostly the property of Gorges and Mason. The entry for Edward Hilton is in fact for the whole settlement at Hilton's Point in present-day Dover (see more detail on page 29).

Gorges and Mason had sent David Thompson to take possession of their territory in 1623, and he had carried out this mission for a few years, but had then abandoned the Piscataqua. In 1630 the proprietors sent over Walter Neal, Ambrose Gibbons and others to look after their interests. This raises the interesting question of who was in charge at Little Harbor and Odiorne's Point in the closing years of the 1620s. The assessment in 1628 tells us that there was activity, and that there was some population at that settlement, but we do not know the name of the leader for the few years between Thompson and Neal. Nor do we know the names of any of the settlers for this period. We have the names of many people who were on the Piscataqua in the earliest years, and undoubtedly some few of these had been present in the years just before 1630, but which ones?

For the period beginning in 1630 we have the papers associated with the adminstration of Ambrose Gibbons, many of them in Gibbons' own hand. Also associated with Gibbons were Walter Neal, Edward Godfrey, Thomas Wannerton and, somewhat later, Henry Josselyn. They greatly expanded the trading and fishing activities carried on at various places along the Piscataqua in the interests of the proprietors.

Even so, the returns were not as great as had been hoped, and in 1633 Neal was recalled to England. In a letter of 5 December 1632 the Laconia Company (as the Gorges/Mason operation on the Piscataqua was called) instructed Gibbons as follows:

We pray you to take care of our house at Newichewanick, and to look well to our vines; also, you may take some of our swine and goats, which we pray you to preserve.

We have committed the choice care of our house at Pascattaway to Mr. Godfrie and written unto Mr. Warnerton to take care of our house at Strawberry Bancke, our desire is that Mr, Godfrie, Mr. Warnerton and you should join lovingly together in all things for our good ...

This is the first evidence we have of three separate locations built and controlled by the Laconia Company. In this instance "house" means not a single-family dwelling, but a larger building, which served as warehouse for the trading goods and the items acquired in trade, and also as sleeping quarters for many of the servants, especially the single men. Similar buildings were found at

other fishing settlements, with a well-known example at the Isles of Shoals.

Here also we have a clear instance where the name Piscataqua referred not to the whole length of the river, but to one specific site. Where were these three spots in 1632: Newichawannock, Strawberry Bank and Piscataqua?

Strawberry Bank is the easiest, for this was the house that was on the site of the present location of Strawbery Banke Museum, on the waterfront in downtown Portsmouth. But in 1633 this was probably the least of the three locations, and the most recently built. This is suggested by the inventory of trade goods which was created in 1633 by Gibbons and his associates, presumably to inform the proprietors of the state of their economic affairs at that time. There are extensive inventories for Piscataqua and for Newichawannock, but none for Strawberry Bank. This would not appear to be a result of the accidents of document survival, for the two inventories are contained on the same sheet of paper, and contemporaneous copies were made.

Piscataqua of the 1632 and 1633 Gibbons documents, then, is the oldest of the three locations, the original site of the Thompson settlement on Odiorne's Point. This was the site also known as Mason's house, and became the focus of the claims of the widow and heirs of John Mason over the years. The site of this house is in the present town of Rye.

Newichawannock, the third of the three sites of 1633, has been a subject of much contentious writing, some claiming that it was on the Maine side of the river, in the present town of South Berwick, and others arguing in favor of a location on the other side of the river, more or less opposite. The South Berwick site has far the better credentials for being the correct location, as is evidenced in an article by Everett S. Stackpole ("The First Permanent Settlement of Maine," *Sprague's Journal of Maine History* 14 [1926]:190-215, later issued as a separate pamphlet). The most important documentary evidence for this location is the division of the Mason lands, which enumerates the various properties on the New Hampshire side of the river, and then separately (albeit not unambiguously) names Newichawannock.

With the departure of Neal in 1633 and the death of John Mason in 1635, the control of the proprietors along the Piscataqua failed, and the various settlements began to go their separate ways. Piscataqua, defined narrowly as the house at Odiorne's Point, as noted above, became the focus of the Masonian claims for a period, and lost importance as a center of trading and fishing activities. Strawberry Bank grew and, with the arrival of a new generation of merchants, became the thriving seaport of Portsmouth, the metropolis of New Hampshire throughout the colonial period. Newichawannock developed into a center for milling and lumbering activities, and eventually fell within the original bounds of Kittery, then in that part set off as Berwick, and finally as South Berwick.

As will be seen below, a number of the early documents relating to the Piscataqua are forgeries. But among those that are genuine, for genealogical purposes, the most important of the documents written by Gibbons is the letter of 13 July 1633, addressed to the proprietors of the Laconia Company, in which he reports on the steps he has taken to carry out their instructions of the previous December (New Hampshire Provincial Papers 1: 81-82). We do not hear of the house at Strawberry Bank in this letter, but we do have a specific statement about each of the other houses, and the names of those left in residence:

Mr. Wanerton hath charge of the house at Pascatawa, and hath with him William Cooper, Rafe [Ralph] Gee, Roger Knight and his wife, William Dermit, and one boy.

For your house at Newichwanicke, I ... will do the best I can there and elsewhere for you, until I hear from you again... These 4 men with me is Charles Knel, Thomas Clarke, Steven Kidder and Thomas Crockit.

Some of these names, as printed, are simply misreadings. William Dermit, for instance, is William Donnil or Darnil (perhaps Daniels), not seen again, and Thomas Clarke is correctly Thomas Blacke, identical with the Thomas Blake seen in another document in the collection (#5, p. 71). Most of these people with Gibbons and Wannerton soon disappeared and did not leave descendants in New England, but Thomas Crockett did remain, removed to Kittery where he became the ferryman, and left behind several children and many descendants.

RECOMMENDED READING: The so-called Gibbons documents, including the forgeries, have been published more than once. The best place to read them, even though there are some errors in a few of the names, is Volume One of the *Documents and Records Relating to the Province of New-Hampshire ...* (Concord 1867), better known as the New Hampshire Provincial Papers, 63 through 102. A selection of these same papers, apparently taken from this published version and not from the originals, since the same errors in reading are repeated, is in *Capt. John Mason*, which is Volume 17 of the publications of the Prince Society (Boston 1887). Other documents which supplement the Gibbons papers, found in the Public Record Office, were published in Volume 17 of the *New Hampshire Provincial and State Papers* (Manchester 1889), beginning on page 475 (the earlier pages of this volume being taken up with Revolutionary War records); these documents had earlier been issued as a separate publication, now very rare, by John Scribner Jenness.

DOVER

The confusion over the name Piscataqua did not end with the departure of Neal and the death of Mason, and even though the name continued to be used for all settlements on the river, there were a number of uses which related to the settlement at Hilton's Point. At a court held at Saco in 1640, a list was appended of those from Piscataqua who did attend court and those who did not. Among the list of those not attending were mostly persons from Kittery, but also many from the New Hampshire side of the river, including some from Dover.

Winthrop frequently referred to Piscataqua in his Journal, and for the most part these references were intended for Dover. A few examples follow:

22 October 1631: The governor received a letter from Capt. Wiggin of Pascataquack ...

10 October 1633: He brought Capt. Wiggin and about thirty, with one Mr. Leveridge, a godly minister, to Pascataquack ...

8 November 1638: ... the governor wrote a letter to Mr. Burdet, Mr. Wiggin, and others of the plantation of Pascataquack ..."

Dover, among all the settlements on the Piscataqua, was always a place apart. Edward Hilton was not an agent of Gorges and Mason, nor were any of his successors (despite statements to the contrary in some histories). He did obtain a grant from the Council for New England, for the so-called Squamscot Patent, but he soon sold this to a group of Bristol merchants (unnamed), and they sold this within a very short time to Lords Say and Brook.

Lords Say and Brook had been, and would continue to be, deeply involved in Puritan attempts to colonize the New World, and as such would naturally be in conflict with Sir Ferdinando Gorges, his ideals, and the men around him. They had been interested in the Massachusetts Bay Company from its earliest stages, and soon after their acquisition of the Squamscot Patent they organized and financed a settlement at the mouth of the Connecticut River, which would become Saybrook.

As their agent at Dover they appointed Captain Thomas Wiggin, who had been in New England in 1630 and 1631, but had returned to England in 1632, partly for business reasons, but also to get married. While in England he testified before the Privy Council in favor of Winthrop and the rest of the settlers in Massachusetts Bay, and against all the gathered enemies of the Puritans, including Sir Ferdinando Gorges, Thomas Morton of Merrymount, Sir Christopher Gardiner, and others. As noted by Winthrop,

through ... the good testimony given on our behalf by one Capt. Wiggin, who dwelt at Pascataquack, and had been diverse times among us, their malicious practice took not effect.

FORGED DOCUMENTS

The various attempts by the Masonian heirs to make good their claim to all of New Hampshire provided the opportunity and the incentive for the creation of evidence which did not exist earlier. *The Genealogical Dictionary of Maine and New Hampshire*, in presenting the list of those sent over to the "Laconia and Mason Plantations" (8), notes that "six forged documents now kept with the Gibbins papers are disregarded," but does not tell us which six documents these are.

The Gibbins (or Gibbons) papers are those published in New Hampshire Provincial Papers, Volume One, pages 63 through 102; but which ones are forged? As a start, Document #17 (pp. 83-86) is certainly not authentic. In the first place, it uses many place-names which were not yet then in use. Strawberry Bank did not become Portsmouth until 1651, and Northam and Exeter were not used until several years after 1633. Also we find in this document that Walter Neale and Thomas Wiggin are made to appear as cooperating in the division of land into the four towns that would later make up the basis of seventeenth-century New Hampshire, when, as we have seen, Neale and Wiggin in actuality represented diametrically opposed parties, and would never have cooperated in such a fundamentally important activity at that date.

In addition this supposed land division of 1633 depends upon, and is related to, the infamous forged Wheelwright deed of 1629. Savage expends great energy in exposing this fraudulent document, concentrating especially on the whereabouts of the supposed witnesses to this deed, showing that most of them could not have been anywhere near New England at the time in question. (See Savage's 1853 edition of Winthrop's Journal, Appendix H, pp. 486-514.) The exposure of the 1629 deed as a fake leads to the same conclusion for the 1633 land division.

Once we know that Document #17 was forged, we are led to a few others that are directly connected. Document #24 (p. 95, George Vaughan to Ambrose Gibbons, 20 August 1634) has as an enclosure a copy of this same purported division of lands. In the cover letter Vaughan states that he had found the enclosed while going over his papers, and sends it along in case Gibbons might be interested. This comes across as altogether too convenient, and in addition there is evidence that Vaughan was already in England when he supposedly wrote this letter from Boston. And this then leads to a second letter from Vaughan to Gibbons, in the same hand (and apparently even in the same ink, although it was dated two years later) (pp. 97-98), which again tends to support the Masonian claim too neatly to be believable.

We have, then, identified four of the six forged documents. Most of the rest are authentic and reliable, and most definitely those composed by Ambrose Gibbons,

and in his hand, may be relied upon. Among these are some of the inventories of goods at the houses at Piscataway and Newichawannock, and also some reports to the proprietors in England.

COUNCIL FOR NEW ENGLAND

The Council for New England was incorporated on 3 November 1620, its full name on the original charter being "The Council established at Plymouth, in the County of Devon, for the planting, ruling, ordering, and governing of New England in America." The leading lights among the patentees were mostly merchants from the West Country in England, and among these the most important for the history of New Hampshire and Maine would be Sir Ferdinando Gorges.

The surviving records of the Council for New England were published in 1867 in the *Proceedings of the American Antiquarian Society*, pages 59 through 131. The records are, unfortunately, not complete, and cover parts of the years 1622, 1623, 1631, 1632, 1634 and 1635. In 1635 the Council ceased to exist and made no further grants.

The fact that the records for 1622 and 1623 have survived is most fortuitous for our study of the Piscataqua, since a number of relevant grants were made in that period. For instance, on 16 November 1622 we find the brief notation that "Mr. Thompson's patent was this day signed by the abovesaid Council" (p. 73). Although the meaning of this sentence is not totally clear, this would appear to be the grant given directly to David Thompson, just prior to sailing for New England and settling at the mouth of the Piscataqua. During these same years will also be found a number of entries relating to the patent of the settlers at Plymouth, whose agent before the Council was Mr. John Peirce of London.

An excellent discussion of the Council for New England, including a brave attempt to sort out the evidence available for all the grants supposed to have been made by the Council, may be found in a pamphlet by Samuel F. Haven, *History of Grants under the Great Council for New England* (Boston 1869). The actual texts of the grants made by the Council are not found in the Council's own records, but must be sought out in the various places where they were recorded, such as in Suffolk Deeds; and Haven gives citations to many of these.

For example, the grant to Edward Hilton for Hilton's Point, which he had occupied already for some years, was dated 12 March 1631, a date for which the Council records do not survive. Haven provides specific details on the patent, with citations to printed versions of the patent (p. 32).

RECENT LITERATURE

John Plummer, "English Notes on Isaac Cummings of Essex County, Massachusetts," *New England Historical and Genealogical Register* 145 (1991):239-40. Plummer has discovered, in the parish of Mistley, co. Essex, baptisms of four children of an Isaac Commen, which match completely with the known children of Isaac Cummings, present in Watertown by 1634, and then later of Ipswich. The correctness of the claimed identity is supported by the fact that Henry Kimball, also a resident of Watertown in 1634, was also from the parish of Mistley.

George Freeman Sanborn Jr., "Rev. Stephen Bachiler of Hampton: Some Additional Information," *The New Hampshire Genealogical Record* 8 (1991):14-17. Sanborn reviews the evidence relating to the later years of the Reverend Stephen Bachiler, that most remarkable of early New England settlers. He confirms the record of Bachiler's burial on 31 October 1656 in the parish of All Hallows Staining, London, and adds a record from the churchwardens' account for that parish, in which receipt is noted of payment for a "knell" for Stephen Bachiler. Sanborn notes that, contrary to tradition, it is unlikely that Bachiler married for a fifth time in his brief stay in England prior to his death.

Simon P. Newman, "Nathaniel Ward, 1580-1652: An Elizabethan Puritan in a Jacobean World, *Essex Institute Historical Collections* 127 (1991):313-26. Newman points out that, unlike most of his other colleagues in the early New England ministry, Nathaniel Ward had been nurtured and educated in Elizabethan rather than Jacobean England. The religious and political atmosphere of late-sixteenth century England is portrayed as being more moderate and accommodating than it was to become a generation later when men like John Cotton and Thomas Hooker were coming to maturity. As a result of this difference in upbringing, there was also a difference in outlook, which led to differences between Ward and other ministers in New England. For example, when it came time to draw up a code of laws for Massachusetts Bay, Ward produced a document that was largely based on English common law, and stressed the ancient liberties and privileges of Englishmen, whereas Cotton based his compilation almost wholly on the Old Testament, making a clean break with English tradition. Ward's more moderate outlook was also seen in his reaction to the English Civil War, and on this occasion he was pitted against Hugh Peter in a pamphlet battle between New Englanders who had repatriated themselves in the 1640s.

Dean Crawford Smith and Melinde Lutz Sanborn, "The Angells and Roger Williams: Thomas[1] Angell of Providence, R.I., Was Not a Son of James Angell of London," *The American Genealogist* 66 (1991):129-32. Through chronological argumentation and the analysis of wills, Smith and Sanborn demonstrate conclusively that Thomas Angell of Providence could not be son of James Angell of London, and furthermore show that the remaining possibilities for Thomas to be a descendant of the Peakirk Angells are limited. In addition, they debunk the traditional statement that Thomas Angell was the "lad of Richard Waterman" who accompanied Roger Williams to Providence in 1636.

Robert Charles Anderson, "English Records of Joshua[1] Fisher of Dedham, Massachusetts," *The American Genealogist* 66 (1991):133-34. Presents baptismal and burial records which show that Joshua Fisher, after the baptisms of his first two children in Syleham, co. Suffolk, resided from about 1622 to 1638 in the parish of Redenhall, co. Norfolk, just across the Waveney River. Also shows that at marriage the name of his second wife was not Anne Luson, but Anne Orfor (presumably a variant of Orford).

Mary Rhinelander McCarl, "Thomas Shepard's Record of Relations of Religious Experience, 1648-1649," *The William and Mary Quarterly,* 3rd ser., 48 (1991):432-66. McCarl transcribes and annotates a slim volume which contains sixteen religious relations, or confessions, of early members of the Cambridge church; these supplement an earlier and larger group for the same church (George Selement & Bruce C. Woolley, *Thomas Shepard's* Confessions, Publications of the Colonial Society of Massachusetts, Collections Volume 58 [Boston 1981]). A relation of religious experience was, by 1636, a necessary prerequisite to church membership in Massachusetts Bay Colony, but remarkably few of these narratives have survived. By 1648, the date of this new set of relations, most of those who were adult at the time of the Great Migration had already become church members, but this new group of sixteen does include some who had come a decade earlier as children, and were just now reaching adulthood, such as John Shepard, son of Edward, and Elizabeth Stone, daughter of Gregory.

Steven T. Katz, "The Pequot War Reconsidered," *The New England Quarterly* 64 (1991):206-24. One strand of the radical revisionist historical writing of the past two decades has been an attempt to portray the Pequot War as an example of premeditated genocide. Katz looks at the evidence again and argues that, as extensive and unnecessary as was some of the violence heaped upon the Pequots, the various accounts of the battles do not permit the conclusion that the New Englanders, not John Winthrop, not John Endicott, not John Mason, had set out to exterminate the Pequots.

(continued from page 26)
military company at Dorchester without any leadership, a situation which was soon rectified. On 2 July 1633 John Mason was referred to by the Court as Lieutenant Mason, when he was reimbursed for his activities in the chase after the pirate Dixy Bull. Sometime in the next four months Mason must have been elevated to the position of captain of this company, for on 5 November 1633 the court ordered that "Sergeant Stoughton is chosen Ensign to Captain Mason." This set of records is typical, in that what survives only reflects about half of the promotions, for we do not see when Mason was made captain or when Stoughton was made sergeant.

By 9 March 1636/7 Dorchester had its full complement of officers, with Israel Stoughton as captain (we do not know whether he had been lieutenant in the interim), Nathaniel Duncan as lieutenant and John Holman as ensign. This entry for Dorchester was part of the listing of officers for ten towns, all now with captains, the whole being the order of battle for the Pequot War.

John Underhill and Daniel Patrick are still seen in charge of this whole burgeoning military apparatus, appearing at the end of this list of officers, where they are stated to be "For the country's service." But this was the swan song for the old warriors from the Low Countries, for not long after the Pequot War Underhill became embroiled in the Antinomian Controversy, supporting Wheelwright, and following him in 1638 to Exeter. After brief residence in Exeter and Dover, Underhill moved to Stamford, Connecticut, where he lived out his life, and defended Massachusetts Bay no more. Daniel Patrick, likewise, took advantage of the changing situation after the Pequot War and departed for Greenwich and New Amsterdam in 1638, also not to return.

After the Pequot War the military defense of Massachusetts Bay attained a more mature level. Each town now had its own military company, with a full complement of officers, and even a company clerk to keep track of men and equipment. Most of the officers were "home-grown" and not veterans of foreign wars. The experienced men from the Low Countries had served their purpose; they had built up the military organization, and had seen the colony through its first real crisis in the Pequot War. With the founding of the Ancient & Honorable Artillery Company soon after the Pequot War, the leaders of Massachusetts Bay were making a statement that they felt secure militarily.

CORRECTION

In Volume Two, Number One, page 5, it is stated that the 1630 list of Charlestown inhabitants has twenty-seven names; the correct number is seventeen. (My thanks to Gwen Epperson of Ogden, Utah, for this correction.)

Great Migration Newsletter

Vol. 3   January-March 1992   No. 1

SHIP ARRIVALS IN 1633

Among the many things we would like to know about the Great Migration is the frequency of arrival of ships from England. Our first concern here is with the arrival of passengers, but we will also learn much about the ways in which the immigrants maintained communication with England, and about the sorts of goods which were imported to New England.

As usual, our best source for this information is the various papers of the Winthrop family. First among these is Winthrop's Journal (abbreviated here as WJ, with page citations to the 1853 Savage edition), in which the arrivals of most of the ships are announced. A valuable check on the journal is provided by the papers collected by the Winthrop family, many of which were endorsed as to ship or master that carried the letter, and the date of arrival in New England. (The letters received in 1633 are printed in Volume Three of the Winthrop Papers, abbreviated here as WP.) Not all ships impinged directly on the Winthrop family, and we learn of a few ships from other sources. Our aim here is to assemble a complete list of all ships which arrived in 1633, not taking into account smaller vessels involved in the coastwise trade.

The *William*, William Trevor master, arrived at Plymouth on or about 22 February 1632/3 "with some passengers and goods for Massachusetts Bay" [WJ 1:119]. A letter from Emmanuel Downing to John Winthrop Jr., dated 21 November 1632, was endorsed by Winthrop "Recd. Feb: 23: 1623 [sic, 1632/33] These letters per the ship Mr. Trevore master, Mr. Hatherly, merchant, arrived at new-Plymouth" [WP 3:93]. Other letters dated in late November and early December 1632 are endorsed with the same date of receipt, and probably all the letters dated between 19 October and 3 December came on this ship. Of the passengers, we can only be sure of Hatherly. However, as Winthrop tells us that the ship "came to set up a fishing at Scituate," and this is where Hatherly settled, it may be that a few others of the early Scituate inhabitants were on this ship as well.

The *Welcome*, John Winter master, arrived at Richmond Island on 2 March 1632/3 [*Collections of the Maine Historical Society*, Second Series 3:22-24].

On 18 April 1633 William Hilton reported to John Winthrop Jr. that there

arrived a fishing ship at Pascataque about the 15th of this month wherein is one Richard Foxwell who hath formerly lived in this country ... The master's name of the ship is John Corbin of Plimouth [WP 3:119].

The *William & Jane*, William Bundock master, arrived at Boston sometime in May 1633 with thirty passengers, having come "in six weeks from London," implying a departure date in late March or early April [WJ 1:121]. Following the letter dated 3 December 1632, which presumably came on the *William*, the next letter received by the Winthrops was dated 25 February 1632/3, followed by two more dated 6 and 14 March; these three letters probably came on the *William & Jane*.

The next ship to arrive was the *Mary & Jane*, Mr. Rose master, which came into Boston probably in late May 1633 with 196 passengers, having left London seven weeks earlier [WJ 1:121]. The only passengers on this vessel mentioned by Winthrop were William Coddington and his wife. Three letters dated 26 March 1633 are endorsed as having come on this ship [WP 3:114-18].

On 15 June 1633 the "*Elizabeth Bonadventure*, from Yarmouth, arrived with ninety-five passengers," having left Yarmouth six weeks earlier [WJ 1:124]. She probably carried passengers from southeast Norfolk and northeast Suffolk, as did other ships sailing from this port.

On 24 July "a ship arrived from Weymouth, with about eighty passengers ... they were twelve weeks com-

(continued on page 2)

EDITOR'S EFFUSIONS

The Recent Literature section in this issue is different from the eight that have gone before. Instead of discussing eight or ten journal articles that have appeared in the previous quarter, we look in greater detail at two books, *New England's Generation*, by Virginia DeJohn Anderson, and *The Long Argument,* by Stephen Foster. These are by far the most important book-length studies of the Great Migration to appear in 1991.

While a description of the detailed subject matter of each appears on pages seven and eight, we will take the opportunity here to note briefly how the two volumes interact with one another, and with the Great Migration Study Project. Foster emphasizes the important difference in attitudes between the immigrants before and after 1633, relating mostly to the fact that the later arrivals experienced directly the draconian policies of Laud, while earlier immigrants did not. All of the ship passenger lists used by Anderson in her study date from 1635 or later, so her entire sample consists of immigrants from the Laudian period.

One element not taken into account by either Foster or Anderson is the great difference in the numbers of immigrants arriving before and after 1633, with about two thousand coming in the years up to 1633, and about fifteen thousand in the years from 1634 through 1640. While the differences in attitudes between the arrivals before and after 1633 would help to explain the disputes that arose in the latter years of the 1630s, the vastly larger numbers of the later immigrants should also help in explaining the way in which these disputes were resolved. While the studies of Foster and Anderson are more subtle and sophisticated than those that have gone before, a full interpretation of the Great Migration requires that the differential in numbers, as well as the differential in attitudes, be taken into account.

In the next issue of the Newsletter, we will return to our usual Recent Literature section, and the Focus section will be on Plymouth.

Robert Charles Anderson, FASG   Editor
Margaret F. Costello   Production Assistant

The *Great Migration Newsletter* (ISSN 1049-8087) is published quarterly by the Great Migration Study Project, a project of the New England Historic Genealogical Society
101 Newbury Street, Boston MA 02116

The subscription rate is $8 for one year and $15 for two years. The subscription year is the same as the calendar year.

(continued from page 1)

ing" [WJ 1:125]. This was the *Recovery,* which sailed from Weymouth sometime after 31 March [*National Genealogical Society Quarterly* (hereafter NGSQ) 71 (1983):171, which includes a list of the heads of household who sailed on the ship]. A letter to John Winthrop Jr. dated at Exeter on 14 March 1632/3 was endorsed "Father Painter July 27 per Waimouth ship" [WP 3:110].

The next ship to arrive was one of the more important in early New England history, being the *Griffin* which came into Boston on 4 September "having been eight weeks from the Downs" [WJ 1:128-30]. This ship carried two hundred passengers, including John Cotton, Thomas Hooker, Samuel Stone, John Haynes and Atherton Hough. A grouping of eight letters dated between 5 June and 22 June 1633, all addressed to John Winthrop Jr., probably came on this ship [WP 3:124-31].

Also on 4 September arrived the *Bird*, Mr. Yates master; unfortunately Winthrop does not tell us how many passengers were on this ship [WJ 1:132].

Finally, on 10 October 1633 the *James,* Mr. Grant master, arrived at Salem, "having been but eight weeks between Gravesend and Salem" [WJ 1:137]. On this ship were Captain Thomas Wiggin, Mr. William Leverich and about thirty passengers for Piscataqua, about thirty for Virginia, and "about twenty for this place" (i.e., Massachusetts). The final group of letters to arrive for the Winthrops, dated at London between 5 and 13 August, probably came with this vessel [WP 3:133-37].

There were at least three ships which made preparations to sail to New England, but which may never have done so. William Hilton on 18 April 1633 tells of "two ships making ready at Barstaple [Barnstaple, Devonshire] who are to bring passengers and cattle for to plant in the Bay" [WP 3:119]. In the Weymouth port book is the record of the *Neptune* which on 3 April 1633 took on cattle for New England, but apparently not passengers [NGSQ 71:171].

For six of the ten ships known to have arrived in New England we are told the number of passengers, the total being 651. The two ships for Piscataqua and Richmond Island probably did not have many passengers, and the William had "some." If we arbitrarily assume that the Bird was an average passenger ship, it probably had about one hundred souls aboard. This would bring the total for the ten ships to about eight hundred, which would be in the same range as the Winthrop Fleet year of 1630. These two years, 1630 and 1633, were the years of heaviest migration up to that point, but they would immediately be surpassed by the two thousand or more who came in the spring of 1634, and in the spring of every year for the rest of the 1630s.

Focus on BOSTON

EARLY LAND RECORDS

Like the other early towns in Massachusetts Bay, the earliest settlers received grants of a houselot and a parcel or two of marsh or arable land. These grants (if there were in fact formal grants) took place before town records were kept, or at least prior to the date of the surviving records.

As one might expect, Boston was different from the other towns in many ways. Most immediately, Boston, unlike all other towns except Charlestown, was confined to the neck of land known as Shawmut, and did not have much land to give beyond the houselots and small lots. Charlestown was able to overcome this simply by expanding beyond its neck into the adjoining "mainland." But in the case of Boston the land adjoining the neck was part of Roxbury and Dorchester.

This problem was solved for Boston (with the assistance of the General Court) by grants of land at various places around the Bay, in the gaps not taken up by the other early towns. Thus, Boston was able to make grants to the south, at Mount Wollaston (later Braintree), to the west at Muddy River (later Brookline), and to the north at Pullen Point and Rumney Marsh (later Chelsea). Boston was also able to make use of many of the islands in the Bay.

Many of the towns we have examined in past issues have had a Book of Possessions or the equivalent, and this has always provided great assistance in resolving many problems about residency and even family size. Again, Boston is different in this respect. There is a Book of Possessions, but it is unlike those of other towns.

The most important difference is implicit in the formula used to introduce each individual holding. An example would be "The possession of Mr. Thomas Olliver within the Limits of Boston." Oliver was one of the leading citizens of Boston, ruling elder of the church, and the head of a large household. Even so, his holdings in this listing ran to only three parcels: a house and garden adjoining; an acre and a half in the New Field; and a garden plot. What does not appear here is land held by Oliver outside of Boston neck, in his case totalling well over a hundred acres.

Although grants at Mount Wollaston, Muddy River and Rumney Marsh do appear in a very few of the listings, the Book of Possessions for the great majority of Bostonians only tells us of the houselot and small lots on

Boston neck. This must be the meaning, at the date of compilation, of "within the limits of Boston."

What was the date of publication? Whereas for other towns it has sometimes been necessary to engage in extended argumentation to learn this date, in the present case the work has already been done for us. William H. Whitmore and William S. Appleton, noted antiquaries of the latter half of the nineteenth century, Record Commissioners for the City of Boston, and editors of the Boston Book of Possessions, had originally thought that the volume had been compiled in 1652, after William Aspinwall's term as town clerk.

When they published the second edition of the Book of Possessions, however, Whitmore and Appleton reconsidered their position, and in five concise pages demonstrated decisively that the record must have been made by Aspinwall himself, sometime during 1645. They note that the first 111 pages of the original were all in one hand, and had the appearance of having been written at one time. Beginning with page 112, the entries have a date associated with them, the earliest date being 20 January 1645/6, and with each succeeding page at a later date. Furthermore, in earlier entries a number of later transactions, some of which may be compared against entries in the Suffolk Deeds, have been noted, and the earliest among these is dated 19 January 1645/6.

Thus, the Boston Book of Possessions was compiled in 1645, probably in the latter part of the year, and for the most part is limited to the houselots and small lots on Boston neck. Since in many instances this is ten or more years after the original grants of these parcels, and most of them have changed hands one or more times, much work is needed to reconstruct the original owners of some of the parcels.

Fortunately, this work has already been done. Annie Haven Thwing spent many years early in this century sifting through the records, with the result that in 1925 she was able to claim "that every estate has been traced between 1630 and 1800, with the authority for each fact recorded." The results of this work are summarized in her book *The Crooked and Narrow Streets of Boston* (Boston 1925). The details and documentation are housed at the Massachusetts Historical Society in a collection comprising a card index arranged alphabetically by landowner, and a series of volumes setting forth the chain of title for each parcel of land on Boston neck.

So far we have been talking only about the land on Boston neck. What about the other grants made at locations at a greater distance on the mainland? On 14 December 1635, the town in a general meeting agreed to grant farms at Mount Wollaston and Muddy River to a number of the leaders of town and church: William Coddington, Edmund Quincy, John Cotton, William Colborne, Thomas Oliver and Thomas Leverett. The town then went on the order that "the poorer sort of the inhabitants such as are members or likely to be so, and have no cattle, shall have their proportion of allotments for planting ground ... laid out at Muddy River."

This order was not carried out until the eighth of January 1637/8, when the bounds of the Great Allotments were brought in and included in the town records. Fifty-four lots were laid out at Muddy River, ranging from eight to eighty acres, in addition to the grants of farms to the leaders. This list was followed by a long list of grants of Great Allotments at Rumney Marsh and Pullen Point; these grants were generally larger than those at Muddy River, and included extensive tracts given to John Winthrop and Henry Vane.

These two locations, Muddy River and Rumney Marsh, would remain a part of Boston for many years. Muddy River was set off as the town of Brookline in 1705, and Rumney Marsh, Pullen Point and Winnissimet were set off as Chelsea in 1739.

The fate of Mount Wollaston was different. As we have seen, two large grants were made to William Coddington and Edmund Quincy, but in the grants of January 1637/8 there was no long list of Great Allotments as there had been for the other two locations. But very soon after this, later in January, there began to appear in the town records individual grants at Mount Wollaston, such as the following: "To William Mawer a Great Lot at the Mount for nine heads," or "To Abell Porter ... a houseplot and a Great Lot at the Mount for two heads." Already by this time there was no further room on the neck for additional houselots, and new arrivals had to be accommodated elsewhere. A church was orgainized at Mount Wollaston on 16 September 1639, and then the area was set off as Braintree on 13 May 1640.

RECOMMENDED READING: One could create a very long list of additional books and articles which have been written about early landholding in Boston, but only two more will be mentioned here. Justin Winsor, *Memorial History of Boston* (4 vols., Boston 1881-83): This monumental, cooperative work has chapters on all aspects of Boston history, including landholding, some written by some of the leading antiquarians of the nineteenth century. Darrett B. Rutman, *Winthrop's Boston: A Portrait of a Puritan Town, 1630-1649* (Chapel Hill, NC, 1965): Rutman gives a modern interpretation of the first two decades of Boston's existence, and in chapter four provides an excellent, brief discussion of land granting.

EARLY CHURCH RECORDS

The First Church of Boston was actually organized in Charlestown, for Winthrop and others who came with him had settled there first. As noted below four of these leaders formed the church in late July of 1630, and then on 27 August the congregation chose their officers: John Wilson, teacher; Increase Nowell, elder; William Gager and William Aspinwall, deacons. (The early churches of Massachusetts tried to have two ministers, a pastor to perform most duties, to include the administration of the sacraments, and a teacher, whose principal duty was to deliver sermons. In 1632 Wilson was made pastor, and in 1633 John Cotton was chosen teacher.)

When Winthrop and most of the rest of the 1630 inhabitants of Charlestown moved to Shawmut in September, the church went with them. Those who stayed behind in Charlestown now became, and remained for the next two years, members of the Boston church.

The earliest records of the Boston church include baptisms, and a list of admissions. The latter is initially just a list of names without dates (although this list is clearly arranged in the order in which the men and women were admitted), but it soon becomes a multi-purpose record, including also records of dismission and disciplinary actions. These records, and later records of this church, have been edited by Richard D. Peirce and published as *The Records of the First Church in Boston 1630-1868*, Volumes 39, 40 and 41 in the Publications of the Colonial Society of Massachusetts (Boston 1961). (The admissions begin on page 13, the baptisms on page 277, and the index is at the end of the third volume.)

Like so many of the New England records of the 1630s, these records, at least in the earliest years, are not the originals. Savage thought that the surviving manuscript was created about 1636, and that all entries prior to that date should be treated with some suspicion. As we shall see, there are some errors and omissions in these records; but by comparison with Boston's civil vital records for the same period, and with the church records of other towns, the Boston church records are very reliable.

Much useful information, especally on dates of arrival, can be obtained from the list of admissions to Boston church. Prior to 8 September 1633, when John Cotton and his wife were admitted, the admission entries are undated, but there are a number of clues along the way. In this period, covering nearly three years, 162 persons were admitted to Boston church.

The first four members, who constituted the church between 26 July and 2 August 1630, were John Winthrop, Thomas Dudley, Isaac Johnson and John Wilson, and by August 2 five more had joined.

The twenty-third and twenty-fourth members to join were "John Waters and Frances his wife." In one of his letters home late in 1630, Winthrop reports that this couple had died before 9 September 1630 [Winthrop Papers 2:312]. From this we can conclude that the members from ten to twenty-two all joined between 2 August and 9 September.

Our next checkpoint is member #55, Richard Garrett, who died a terrible death after being caught in an open boat during a winter storm. He died on 28 December 1630, so all members before #55 would have joined by that date [Winthrop's Journal 1:47].

The first passenger ship to arrive in the Bay after the Winthrop Fleet was the *Lyon*, which arrived on 5 February 1630/1, carrying about twenty passengers, most of whose names are known. Among these was John Perkins, presumably accompanied by his wife. "John Perkins and Judith his wife" were admitted to Boston church as members #107 and #108. Although we cannot be certain, it is reasonable to assume that all admitted prior to John Perkins and his wife had come in the Winthrop Fleet (or earlier), since there were so few arrivals in 1631, and the names of most are known. We may by this method convert a few 1631 arrivals into 1630 arrivals, but chances for error are small.

Immediately after the Perkinses in the list of admission is Ryce Cole, whose date of arrival is not known, although on the evidence of this list alone we can say he was here by 1631. Next on the list are John Eliot and Margaret Winthrop (wife of the Governor), both of whom are known to have come on the *Lyon* on its second voyage in 1631, landing at Boston on 2 November. Other passengers from this same voyage were Jacob Eliot (#114), James and Lydia Penniman (#117 and #118), and John Winthrop Junior (#121).

The pace of immigration picked up slightly in 1632, and there are a few signposts for events occuring in that year. John Ruggles, member #129, was made a freeman on 3 July 1632, which by this date implied church membership, so his admission (and that of all preceding him) must have been before 3 July. Very shortly after John Ruggles were admitted "Thomas Oliver and Anne his wife" (#132 and #133), who arrived on the *William & Francis* on 5 June 1632, so they must have been admitted after that date. And then member #135 was John Willis, who was made a freeman on 6 November 1632, and so must have been admitted to church at an earlier date.

In fact, however, John Willis must have been admitted to Boston church at least a month earlier than November, for we have a better marker after William Peirce, who is member #151. After the entry for Peirce, the church records note the dismissal on 14 October 1632 of those persons who had decided to form a new church in Char-

lestown, including such persons as Increase Nowell, Ralph Sprague, William Frothingham and several others, most of them with wives. Thus everyone prior to and including William Peirce would have been a church member by 14 October.

Following the list of those dismissed to Charlestown church, and prior to 8 September 1633, are eleven more names, the only persons admitted in a period of eleven months. Some of these may have been in Boston for a year or two, such as John Oliver, who had probably come with his father Thomas Oliver in June of 1632. Others had come on the ships arriving early in 1633, among whom would have been Mary, the new wife of the returning William Coddington, who landed in Boston in late May 1633 on the *Mary & Jane*. Anne Newgate, wife of John Newgate, must have been admitted by 6 August 1633, for she had a daughter baptized on that date.

Beginning in September 1633 admissions to Boston church are dated (although initially to month only) and close analysis is no longer needed to determine when someone might have joined the church. But with the guideposts noted above, it is possible to assign to any of the first one-hundred-and-sixty-two members of the Boston church a date of admission which is accurate to within a few months at least.

We want to know, of course, how complete this list of admissions is. With Salem, for example, we have seen that the surviving list of early admissions omits those who had removed early from town, and also many of those who had remained. In the case of Boston, the list as we see it does include many who did not reside in Boston at the time the list was apparently recopied. This would include those who remained behind in Charlestown, and also persons who had died or departed for other towns.

In Salem there were of a number of examples of people having children baptized, without any indication that the presenting parent was a church member. In Boston we do see that Richard Gridley is called "our brother" when a daughter was baptized in 1632, and on other later occasions, even though he is not in the list of admissions. But this is the only such case noted, whereas many similar examples were found for Salem.

Finally, we can make some judgments about the completeness of church records by studying the lists of freemen. On those occasions when the lists are grouped by town, we can look to see whether all those being admitted from Boston are also in the church admission lists. Examination of all lists through 1636 shows that for every Boston grouping, all the names of freemen also appear in the church list.

In general, then, the list of admissions for Boston is remarkably complete, and is the best we have for this early period, exceeding in quality the lists for Charlestown, Roxbury and Salem.

We turn now to the less problematic matter of the baptismal records of the early Boston church. These records show clearly some of the effects of the copying of the original. First, whereas almost all the baptismal entries identify the presenting parent as "our brother" or "our sister," seven of the entries prior to 1633 do not. Five of these children were from families who had been dismissed to the Charlestown church in late 1632, and were no longer brothers and sisters in the Boston church. A sixth entry is for a daughter of John Perkins, and the seventh is for a daughter of "John Foxall." The latter is a mystery, for no one of that name appears elsewhere in New England records of this date, but it may be intended for Richard Foxwell, admitted to Boston church in 1630, but removed to Scituate by 1635. John Perkins had gone to Ipswich with the early party in 1632, although there is no record of his dismissal to that church.

Second, a few of the entries in this same period are misdated. One indication of this is seen in the two consecutive entries for children of Increase Nowell, baptized, according to the record, on 21 November 1630 and 3 June 1631, little more than six months apart. The explanation is found in the itinerary of Reverend John Wilson, the first and, until the arrival of John Cotton, the only minister of the Boston church. Having arrived in New England in 1630 as part of the Winthrop Fleet, he returned to England in the spring of 1631 on the *Lyon*. He then made a second voyage to New England, bringing with him his wife, in early 1632. Thus, for about a year there would have been no one to baptize children in the Boston church.

During the period when Wilson was in England, the records contain the baptisms of ten children, between 3 June 1631 and 23 September 1631. Our conclusion must be that all these baptisms were actually for 1632, beginning shortly after Wilson's return, and meshing with the records beginning on 11 November 1632. As further evidence that this is true, note especially the baptism of William, son of Governor John Winthrop, on 26 August 1631. The birth of this child is noted by Winthrop himself in his Journal, in August of 1632.

There are, then, a few small problems with the early baptismal records of the Boston church. But in this case our main point of comparison is with the town's civil vital records, which, as we shall soon see, are among the most unreliable of the records available to us for this early period. In many instances a birth record in the 1630s in Boston will appear to be some days or weeks after the baptism. Barring external evidence to the contrary, the baptismal record should be accepted as correct in such instances, and the birth record should be simply ignored, or possibly reinterpreted.

EARLY VITAL RECORDS

In a previous issue of the *Newsletter* we discussed the general problems of the early vital records of Massachusetts Bay *(Great Migration Newsletter* 2:17). The earliest civil vital records for Boston are included in a larger grouping of records which are in fact the county copies of vital records for this period.

As noted in the earlier article, all records for 1643 and before were collected at one time, and, as with the other Bay towns, represent vital events only for those families resident in Boston in late 1643. Someone like Thomas Matson, for instance, who was in Boston as early as 1630, and moved from Boston to Braintree about 1639, would not have the births of his sons Thomas and John recorded in these Boston records, even though they were born in that town, and their baptisms are recorded in the Boston church records.

Although the records for all of the towns included in these early county copies were collected some years after the event actually took place, the Boston records seem to be subject to more error than any of the other towns. For instance, there appear to be an unusually large number of entries in Boston in which only the month and year of birth are given, and not the day. This would seem to indicate that these records were based more on memory than on a private written record.

As an example, take the case of the family of Gamaliel Wait, who had four children born by 1643. The first of these, a son Moses, was born in June 1637 according to the civil record, and baptized on 3 September 1637; although this is certainly possible, a delay of three months before baptism is highly unlikely. The second child, Grace, was baptized ten days after the recorded birth, but the third child, another Moses, was recorded as born in September 1640, but baptized on 23 August of the same year! The fourth child, a son Samuel, is given only a year of birth, 1641, and was baptized 7 November 1641. Thus, of these four children, the date of birth of one is clearly wrong, another probably wrong, and a third incomplete. Only one birthdate is complete and in good accord with the baptismal date.

Savage frequently took note of these discrepancies in the Boston records, and made some sort of barbed comment. In the case of Gamaliel Wait, in reporting the records for the second son Moses, he gave the baptismal date, and then continued "though that of the town pretends he was not born before September yet it may be more trustworthy in mentioning his death September of next year." The Boston civil vital records should be treated with special care for these early years, and in most cases the church records should be preferred in case of conflict.

RECENT LITERATURE

Virginia DeJohn Anderson, *New England's Generation: The Great Migration and the Formation of Society and Culture in the Seventeenth Century* (Cambridge University Press: Cambridge 1991), pp. x + 232, index. Order from Cambridge University Press, 40 West 20th Street, New York NY 10011. $34.50.

Over the last two decades a number of investigators have examined the Great Migration and its immediate aftermath using a community-based approach, with studies of such towns as Dedham and Andover, for example. Anderson points out that the study of any one town may result in biased conclusions, since there is no assurance that any one town is representative of the whole. She has undertaken a study based on nearly seven hundred passengers arriving in New England on seven vessels, three in 1635, three in 1637 and one in 1638.

This volume is divided into five chapters, the first of which, Decision, looks at the passengers in their English setting prior to migration, and addresses the question of the motivation for making the move to New England. Anderson comes down strongly on the side of those who believe that religion, the desire to practice their Puritan beliefs without interference, was the strongest element driving the migrants, although she recognizes that other factors went into the decision as well. (Because the error is repeated so often by so many historians, it is necessary to point out that the Edward Johnson who sailed to New England in 1637, the author of the *Wonder Working Providence,* was not the same as the Edward Johnson in Charlestown in 1630. The latter man left Massachusetts about 1632 and had a long career as a trader in Maine.)

The second chapter, Passage, explores the details of the transatlantic crossing itself. The aspects of the act of migration explored are the details of closing out business affairs and landholding in England, and gathering those items which would be needed for the crossing itself, and for setting up in the New World - food, clothing, tools, household goods, and so on. The chapter then concludes with a discussion of the experience aboard ship during the crossing. (In this chapter Anderson treats from a different angle some of the same themes covered recently by David Cressy in *Coming Over* [see *Great Migration Newsletter* 1:18].)

Chapter Three, Transplantation, examines the activities of the immigrants immediately after arrival, and the ways in which they reacted to their new environment. Much of this chapter is taken up with an excellent discussion of the development of the proprietary system of distributing land, and how this led to much internal

migration within New England in the years shortly after arrival (termed by Anderson "The Great Reshuffling").

This then leads to the fourth chapter, Competency, which takes the immigrant generation through the remainder of their lives. The emphasis is on the acquisition of a "competency," a central theme in Anderson's work, defined at one point as "a sufficiency, although not an abundance, of this world's goods." Competency is related to a number of tenets of Puritanism, and it is shown that even for many skilled artisans, this state of being was most readily attained in an agricultural setting.

Finally, Legacy, the last chapter, describes briefly the consequences of the migration and the activities of the first generation for the second and even the third generation of New Englanders. The second generation were in most cases assured of inheriting the competency which had been the principal achievement of their fathers, but since they did not share in the migration experience directly, they tended to fall away from the religious and moral standards of the first generation. By the time the third generation came along, very few direct connections with the immigrants remained, and the time was ripe for the actors in the Great Migration to be mythologized, and for this myth to be assimilated to other more pressing concerns, many of which would not have been seen as compatible by the first generation.

This volume is the most comprehensive and even-handed treatment of the Great Migration available, in that it successfully combines the spiritual and secular concerns and activities of the migrants themselves. Anyone interested in the Great Migration should read this book.

Stephen Foster, *The Long Argument: English Puritanism and the Shaping of New England Culture, 1570-1700 (*University of North Carolina Press: Chapel Hill NC 1991), pp. xx + 395, index. Order from University of North Carolina Press, P.O. Box 2288, Chapel Hill NC 27515-2288. $39.95.

Foster covers much the same time period as does Anderson, and many of the same topics, but from a far different perspective. He traces the various strands of Puritan theology, and the related philosophy of church government, from Elizabethan days, through the the Great Migration, and on to the time of the third generation in New England, showing along the way how the development of Puritanism in England and New England diverged after the Great Migration.

(*continued on page 8*)

(continued from page 7)

In his first chapter, Foster describes the flourishing of Puritanism under Elizabeth, especially in the years from 1570 to 1590. The conditions of Puritanism at this time were far different than they would be under James or Charles in the early decades of the seventeenth century. For example, the term Presbyterian could be applied to all Puritans, for the Civil War distinction between Independents (Congregationalists) and Presbyterians simply did not yet exist. The Puritan and other elements in the English church had reached an accommodation which lasted for much of the last third of the sixteenth century.

Foster uses his second and third chapters to look at what happened to Puritanism under King James. The author first shows that there was considerable continuity between Elizabethan and Jacobean Puritanism, even if in the latter period this strain of religiosity could not be practiced so openly. Many Puritans maintained their principles by reading Puritan tracts, and by taking advantage of the sermonizing of ministers who had been deprived of their living within the established church, but still preached privately, perhaps being subsidized by one or another of the Puritan gentry. Foster then shows how under James, and then during the early years of Charles, the politics of Puritanism became more closely tied to the politics of taxation, as James and Charles attempted to conduct a vigorous foreign policy without the full support of Parliament.

With the fourth chapter Foster reaches the heart of his argument, and the subject matter that is of most interest to us with relation to the Great Migration. He argues that the migrants who came with Winthrop in 1630, and for a few years on either side, were leaving an England with which they did not agree, but which had not yet officially rejected Calvinism.

With the elevation of Laud to Archbishop of Canterbury in 1633, the attack on Calvinism and Puritanism reached a new level, Puritans saw little hope at home, and migration to New England increased tenfold. The result, as Foster notes, was that the "style of Puritanism" Winthrop and others "transferred to the first New England towns in the early 1630s was not exactly the same as the more militant, more explicitly sectarian faith imported later in the same decade by exiles in flight from the full force of Laudian repression" [p. 139]. The different experiences of migrants to New England at the beginning and end of the 1630s would lead to different attitudes about how the new churches in New England should be organized and how they should function.

Foster closes with discussions of the second generation in New England (the Halfway Covenant and the jeremiads of declension) and the third generation (realignment of the elements of Puritanism in ways which would be unrecognizable to the first generation, and the rise of the "glacial generation" in the ministry).

Great Migration Newsletter

Vol. 3   April-June 1992   No. 2

RECONSTRUCTING A PASSENGER LIST

On 24 July 1633 Governor John Winthrop reported that

A ship arrived from Weymouth, with about eighty passengers, and twelve kine, who sat down at Dorchester. They were twelve weeks coming, being forced into the Western Islands by a leak, where they stayed three weeks, and were very courteously used by the Portugals; but the extremity of the heat there, and the continual rain brought sickness upon them, so as (blank) died (WJ 1:129).

No passenger list survives for this vessel, although Colonel Banks attempted a partial reconstruction (Planters of the Commonwealth p. 104). What sources does one use in an attempt to produce a synthetic passenger list for this period? Since we know that the eighty passengers "sat down at Dorchester," we would of course examine the records of that town, which do survive for the time of the arrival of this ship. In addition, we would want to see who appeared as a freeman from Dorchester in the year or so after July 1633.

Sources such as these would be the starting point for any reconstruction of an early passenger list. In the present instance, however, we have two other pieces of evidence, leading us more directly to an identification of some of the passengers on the Weymouth ship of 1633. First, in his diary William Whiteway of Dorchester in Dorsetshire tells us under date of 26 February 1632/3 that

This day Christofer Gould married with Rachell Beake, and shortly after, when Aquila Purchas, Bernard Gapen and others went for New England, he was by Mr. White chosen clerk of Trinity Parish, and by the town made schoolmaster of Trinity School (Whiteway Diary p. 129).

Counting backwards twelve weeks from 24 July takes us to late April of 1633, about two months after the marriage of Gould and Beake. Assuming that two months qualifies as "shortly after" for William Whiteway, this places Aquila Purchase and Bernard Capen as passengers on the Weymouth ship, since no other ship is known to have come from the West Country in the summer of 1633.

Capen and Purchase were brothers-in-law, for Capen had married Joan Purchase, sister of Aquila. Aquila Pur-

chase was very likely one of those who had died during the voyage, perhaps during the layover at the Western Islands, for on 5 August 1633, barely two weeks after the ship's arrival, "Widdow Purchase" was granted four acres by the town of Dorchester. Oliver, son of Aquila Purchase, also appears in Dorchester records at this time, and there are known to be two daughters - Sarah and Abigail. This gives us four of the passengers on the Weymouth ship (assuming that the number of eighty accounts only for those who survived the voyage and actually settled at Dorchester): Widow Purchase and her three children.

Obviously, Bernard Capen was another passenger on this ship. Who else might have come with him? His wife Joan outlived him by fifteen years, and presumably accompanied him in 1633. His only surviving son was made a freeman on 14 May 1634, which would indicate arrival no later than 1633. Bernard Capen had four daughters known to have lived to adulthood. One of these, Honor, married William Hannum of Dorchester and Windsor about 1635, so she very likely accompanied her parents in 1633.

The other three daughters had married in England: Susanna to William Rockwell in 1624; Dorothy to Nicholas Upsall in 1630, just a few weeks before the sailing of the Mary & John; and Elizabeth to Thomas Swift in 1630. Rockwell and Upsall were in New England by 1630, and Swift is on the passenger list of the Recovery in 1634, so we might think that none of these daughters came in 1633. But for one at least we have contradictory evidence. The earliest child recorded to Nicholas and

(continued on page 10)

EDITOR'S EFFUSIONS

Three years ago John Plummer published an excellent analysis of the passenger list of the *Recovery*, said to have sailed from Weymouth to New England in 1633. Plummer demonstrated conclusively that this sailing must have taken place in 1634. Twice in the pages of this Newsletter the original error has been repeated, most recently in the article in the last issue on the ships of 1633.

When Plummer showed that the *Recovery* had actually sailed in 1634, this left the unnamed Weymouth ship of 1633 without a passenger list. As a penance for making the same mistake twice, we present here as the lead article an attempt to reconstruct partially the passenger list for this ship. This same sort of analysis can be performed for other ships, although it becomes more difficult beginning in 1634 when the pace of migration increases. Aside from its intrinsic interest for descendants of passengers on this ship, the article is intended to show what conclusions can be drawn from a few clues, as long as one is guided by consistent principles, and not by guesswork.

Another error in a recent issue which was noted by several readers was the claimed death of John Underhill in Stamford, when in fact he lived for many years at Oyster Bay on Long Island and died there.

With the Focus section on Plymouth in this issue, we come to an end of our treatment of those towns founded during the first phase of the Great Migration, down to 1633. In the next issue we will examine Ipswich, a transitional town in a sense, since it was founded in 1633, but did not really become heavily populated until the next year. Then, beginning with the fourth issue of this volume, we will begin to look at towns from all over New England, founded in the years from 1634 to 1643. This will allow us to move beyond the immediate vicinity of Massachusetts Bay, and include towns from Connecticut and Rhode Island.

Robert Charles Anderson, FASG   Editor
Margaret F. Costello   Production Assistant

The *Great Migration Newsletter* (ISSN 1049-8087) is published quarterly by the Great Migration Study Project, a project of the New England Historic Genealogical Society
101 Newbury Street, Boston MA 02116

The subscription rate is $8 for one year and $15 for two years. The subscription year is the same as the calendar year.

(*continued from page 9*)

Dorothy (Capen) Upsall in Dorchester, and the earliest known child of this couple, was born in 1635. This at least suggests that when Nicholas came in 1630 he left his new bride behind. There are no records for Nicholas Upsall in New England in 1632, and it is possible that he returned to England in that year, rejoined his bride, and travelled with her and the rest of the Capen family in 1633. Thus, for the Capen family we have at least four members (Bernard, Joan, John and Honor), and possibly the Upsalls as well.

Turning now to the second piece of evidence created in England, we learn of three more families who must have been on the Weymouth ship. In a letter to John Winthrop Jr., dated 14 March 1632/3, Henry Paynter of Exeter, Devonshire, made the following request:

I desire you to take notice of Mr. Cogan and Mr. Hill and Mr. Pinney our pious and loving neighbors and good friends that now come unto you ... (Winthrop Papers 3:109).

Winthrop added an endorsement to this letter: "Father Painter July 27 Waimouth ship." The letter itself, then, came on the unnamed ship from Weymouth. These three men can be identified as John Coggan, William Hill and Humphrey Pinney.

John Coggan was a merchant who in 1630 resided in the parish of St. Petrock in Exeter, and after his arrival in New England, and a brief residence in Dorchester, he opened the first shop in Boston. He had three children born before his departure from England, John, Mary and Elizabeth, and presumably these were all passengers on this ship along with their father. The question of John Coggan's many wives is extremely involved, but if Anne, by whom he had two children in Boston, was also the mother of these three children, she would have been on the ship as well (NEHGR 111:10-16).

Two men with the surname Hill were resident in Dorchester in the early days - John and William. Since William is frequently given the honorific "Mr." in New England records and John is not, we should conclude that William was the passenger on this ship. He had married at St. Mary Arches, Exeter, in 1619 Sarah Jourdain, daughter of Ignatius Jourdain. They had six children, most, and perhaps all, born in England. The Sarah Hill who is in the passenger list for the *Recovery* of Weymouth a year later is probably this wife, and we cannot tell from this distance whether the children came in 1633 or 1634.

Claims have been made in the past that Humphrey Pinney came on the *Mary & John* in 1630, but the earliest record of him in New England is the 5 August 1633 grant of land to him in Dorchester, along with several others

(*continued on page 16*)

<table>
<tr><td colspan="2">Focus   on   PLYMOUTH</td></tr>
</table>

Focus on PLYMOUTH

Approaching the early records of Plymouth is a different matter from anything we have faced for the other towns of the earliest years of the Great Migration. For the first decade and more, the town of Plymouth and the colony of Plymouth were coterminous, and perhaps for that reason the leaders and inhabitants felt no need to keep records. There was no formally organized church and no settled minister, there was no large-scale granting of land with attendant proprietors' records, and there were no vital records, except for those few events recorded by Bradford in his various writings.

On the other hand, more has been written about these early years of Plymouth than about any other colonial group of equal size. This was true virtually from the beginning of settlement, and certainly has been the case for the past two centuries, during which many of the earliest Plymouth settlers have taken on mythical and legendary status.

Our procedure here will be to look at the first fifteen years or so of Plymouth's existence from a variety of angles, to make it easier to understand just what the records are telling us. We will look at the ships that brought those associated with Leyden, and this will provide some insight on the population of Plymouth in its first decade. We will look carefully at two important records generated in the 1620s: the 1623 Land Division and the 1627 Cattle Division, and then at the first few years of the records of the Plymouth Court, with emphasis on the lists of freemen. Third, we will describe briefly the splitting off of the first daughter towns in Plymouth Colony - Scituate and Duxbury. Lastly, we will engage in a bibliographic discussion, and point out a few of the most valuable of the items in print on Plymouth Colony.

PASSENGERS TO PLYMOUTH

After more than a decade in Leyden, Holland, the Pilgrims had decided that they had to find a new home, and obviously this could not be England. The story of the sailing of the *Mayflower* and its arrival, whether by accident or design, off Cape Cod in November of 1620 is well-known. This first movement of the Pilgrims from Leyden to Plymouth did not, of course, bring to New England all those who wanted to come. A second ship, the *Speedwell*, set sail with the *Mayflower*, but had to return to England, and some passengers on this ship had to be left behind.

The exact passenger list for the *Mayflower* was for many years not known, but with the reemergence of Bradford's *History of Plymouth Plantation* in the mid-nineteenth century, a reliable, contemporary list became available, showing that there were one hundred and two passengers. Even after this list became available, however, many inaccurate inventories of the passengers of 1620 were printed, and one has to be careful in consulting such lists. The most readily available at this time are in the Ford or the Morison editions of Bradford's *History*, and in Stratton's *Plymouth Colony* (see section on Bibliography on page 14 below).

The Pilgrim leaders were able to arrange for a second group of passengers to come to New England in 1621; the *Fortune* brought thirty-five new settlers, mostly from London. Then in 1623 two more ships arrived, the *Anne* and the *Little James,* this time with about sixty passengers, again a medley of Londoners and Leydeners. While we know about the sailing of these vessels from Bradford, our knowledge of the names of the passengers comes from a very different source. In 1623 the Pilgrims had finally been forced by reality to give up their ideal of communal landholding, and grant an acre of land to each member of a household. This 1623 Land Division provided the names of those who came on these three ships in 1621 and 1623.

For the next six years there were no more ships and no additional members of the Leyden congregation made the crossing of the Atlantic. In May of 1629 the London partners of the Pilgrims arranged for a second *Mayflower* to make the voyage, with arrival in Plymouth in August, and then in March of 1630/1 a last grouping of the Leyden Pilgrims joined the passenger contingent on the *Lyon,* which arrived in Massachusetts Bay in late May of 1630. The total number of passengers bound for Plymouth on these two ships was slightly more than a hundred.

Thus, over a period of ten years the organized migration from Leyden to Plymouth was carried out on six ships (*Mayflower* 1620, *Fortune* 1621, *Anne* 1623, *Little James* 1623, second *Mayflower* 1629, *Lyon* 1630), bringing a total of about three hundred passengers. These were not all members of the Leyden congregation, but a mix which included a number of hired hands from London. There may have been others connected with the Leyden church who came later, but they were totally submerged in the larger body of migration to Massachusetts Bay in the 1630s. Thus ended one phase of the Great Migration, no more than a few percent of the whole, but with an impact out of proportion to their numbers.

PLYMOUTH COURT RECORDS

In Massachusetts Bay, because John Winthrop had brought with him the charter of the Massachusetts Bay Company, court records were kept from the beginning, with the first session being held on 23 August 1630, just a few weeks after arrival from England. In Plymouth, by contrast, the continuous recording of court sessions did not begin until 1 January 1632/3, twelve years after the landing at Plymouth. Most of the records generated by Plymouth Colony were published in the last century as a twelve-volume set, transcribed and edited by Nathaniel B. Shurtleff and David Pulsifer, under the title *Records of the Colony of New Plymouth in New England* (hereafter PCCR, with volume and page citation).

Despite the late beginning, there are a few scattered records which were created before 1633. The first of these, and one of the most important, was the land division of 1623. By the fourth year of the colony's existence, the leaders realized that the ideal of holding all land communally would not work, and so they decided to allot to each member of each household one acre of planting ground. Luckily for us, the record of this first land allotment in Plymouth is not simply a list of names, but is arranged according to the ship upon which a given settler sailed. Thus, there are separate groupings for the *Mayflower* passengers, for those on the *Fortune* in 1621, and for those on the *Anne* and *Little James* in 1623 (the latter two sets of passengers being lumped together).

In 1974 Robert S. Wakefield FASG carried out a careful analysis of this land division (*Mayflower Quarterly* 40:7-13, 55-62). Wakefield points out that the land division may actually have taken place in January of 1624 (although this would still be 1623 by the old calendar). He then sets forth his reconstruction of the rules that were used for allocating the land. Finally, he attempts to identify who was in each household at the time of the land division.

The next important document created was the 1627 Division of Cattle (PCCR 12:9-13). The court decided that it would be more equitable and more efficient if the colony's small herd of livestock were parcelled out to designated individuals, who would then have a stake in the care of that particular animal. As a result the Plymouth population was divided into twelve "companies" of thirteen members each. These companies might include more than one family, and a few unattached individuals. This list, dated 22 May 1627, includes the names of all persons, and not just heads of household. As a result genealogists have long made effective use of this list in deducing approximate dates of marriage and birth for many members of the community.

Aside from the 1623 Land Division and the 1627 Cattle Division, the only records which survive prior to 1633

are a few deeds, printed on pages seven, eight and fifteen through eighteen of PCCR 12. This last volume of the published Plymouth Colony records contains the first volume of Plymouth Colony deeds. Volume Two of the deeds, and a portion of Volume Three, have been published in an ongoing series in the *Mayflower Descendant*. The rest of Volume Three, and Volumes Four and Five, remain unpublished, and are available at the County Commissioners' Office in Plymouth, or on microfilm. Aside from these volumes of land records, the only official records of Plymouth Colony which remain unpublished are the probate records; abstracts of some of these have appeared in various periodicals.

The surviving court records begin on 1 January 1632/3, and run continuously for the remainder of the existence of Plymouth Colony. These records are much like the records of the General Court of Massachusetts Bay, including general matters, and items of legislation, as well as more particular entries relating to land disputes, criminal activities, appointments to office and so on. Unlike the Massachusetts records, there are some marriage records scattered through these court records.

These Plymouth records differ from their Massachusetts Bay equivalents in an important manner. In the very earliest days in Massachusetts Bay civil disputes were heard by the General Court, and then in the Quarter Courts after those had been established in 1636. In Plymouth these matters frequently appear in a separate series of records, called Judicial Acts. These have been published as Volume Seven of PCCR.

Of particular interest in the earliest pages of the court records are two tax lists, one dated 25 March 1633 and the second dated 27 March 1634 (PCCR 1:9, 27). Each of these lists contains more than eighty names, and here we find recorded for the first time the names of many of those who came on the *Mayflower* in 1629 or the *Lyon* in 1630. Reconstructing the lists of passengers who came on these two ships will not be easy, but these tax lists constitute one of the basic resources to be used in this effort.

Preceding the record of the court session of 1 January 1632/3 are two pages of freemen of Plymouth Colony, the first of several such lists. Ninety-one names appear on this list, and after the sixty-eighth is the notation "The rest admitted afterwards." Since the list purports to be for 1633, and since some towards the very end have next to them a date in 1635, we might suppose that the first sixty-eight were all freemen by 1 January 1632/3. But this is not so.

In the record of the court for 1 January 1632/3 four men were admitted as freemen: Kenelm Winslow, Josiah Winslow, Samuel Eddy and Philip Delano. In the list of freemen these four names do not appear together; Kenelm Winslow is forty-sixth on the list followed by his brother Josiah, while the other two men come about a dozen positions later. The next group of men admitted as freemen are recorded at the court of 1 January 1633/4: Mr. William Collier, Thomas Willet, John Cooke and Thomas Cushman. These are the last four names in the list prior to "The rest admitted afterward." Another year later, on 1 January 1634/5, seven more men were admitted, and they appear further down on the list. But in between these last two groups are five more names (John Barnes, George Watson, Isaac Robinson, James Cole and Samuel Fowler [Fuller]), for whom there is no record of admission to freemanship.

Quite clearly men were being admitted as freemen at other times of the year than at the January court, but were not being recorded. Based on the arguments in the paragraphs above, we can conclude that the first sixty-eight on the list were freemen by 1 January 1633/4, and we can also conclude, with somewhat less certainty, that all those on the list prior to Kenelm Winslow were freemen before 1 January 1632/3. With even less certainty, we may suggest that those men on the list between the Winslows and Samuel Eddy were admitted sometime in 1633, but there may be some other undetected distortion of the list taking place here.

We find, then, that the Plymouth Colony lists of freemen require a different sort of analysis than is used on the Massachusetts Bay lists, and as a result the information we derive from them is of a different nature. For example, we are not able to date precisely when all freemen were created in Plymouth Colony, and thus we are not able to make the same sorts of statements about when they first appear in the records, as we can often do in Massachusetts Bay. Also, in Plymouth Colony we have more than one list, and only one has been analyzed here. The other lists are constructed differently, and most be approached differently.

DUXBURY AND SCITUATE

Because the population of Plymouth grew so slowly during the 1620s, there was no need to settle additional towns within the colony. But with the coming of the last remnants of the Leyden brethren, and with the encroachment of some portion of the larger number of settlers in Massachusetts Bay to the north, the movement away from Plymouth began.

Bradford noted this in his account for the year 1632 (Morison ed., pp. 252-54). A number of families who had begun to live across Plymouth Bay now found it difficult to come to church at Plymouth, and asked to be set off as a separate congregation. This became the town of Duxbury.

At about the same time that Duxbury was splitting off as a separate entity, Scituate, at the northern extremity of the colony, was settled as well. Some of the first settlers had earlier been residents of Plymouth, while others came with Timothy Hatherley upon his return to New England in 1632. (Some secondary sources claim that Scituate was founded by 1628, but this is based on a single erroneous item in the Plymouth land records. A deed ostensibly dated 10 April 1628 refers to an earlier transfer of land from Thomas Bird to Henry Merritt, which Merritt then sold to Nathaniel Tilden. As none of these men were otherwise recorded until well into the 1630s, the date of this deed must be in error, and should likely be 1638 [PCCR 12:103].)

The strongest evidence for the foundation of these two settlements comes from the court records, where we find on 1 January 1633/4 that Christopher Wadsworth was chosen constable for the "ward of [blank] bounded between Jones River & Greens Harbour," and Anthony Annable was chosen to the same office for the "ward of Scituate" (PCCR 1:21). Exactly a year later, on 1 January 1634/5, the court agreed that "the same constables of Duxbery and Scituat, Christopher Wadsworth and Antony Anible" would continue for another year.

Another document that tells us something about the early history of these towns is the December 1634 letter of James Cudworth of Scituate to his stepfather in London (*Register* 14:101). Toward the end of this letter Cudworth lists the ten settled towns in New England (i.e., those with ministers), of which nine were in Massachusetts Bay and the tenth was Plymouth itself. He then appends the names of three locations which were inhabited but did not yet have a minister: Scituate, Duxbury and Bear Cove (Hingham).

Unfortunately, in his 1632 account of the founding of Duxbury, Bradford also included a description of the similar movement to Green's Harbor, which later became Marshfield. This has led many later writers to claim 1632 as the date of settlement of Marshfield, but this event must actually have occurred some years later. There is no record of Green's Harbor as a settlement until at least 1638 (PCCR 1:117), and no constable until 1641 (PCCR 2:9). (The record above of Christopher Wadsworth as constable in 1632 of a district between Jones River and Green's Harbor should not be interpreted as evidence for the existence of Marshfield at this time; these were merely the bounds of what would become Duxbury.)

Like Ipswich further to the north, Scituate and Duxbury were transitional towns, formed as the slow pace of migration down to 1633 began to give way to the much greater immigration of the late 1630s. These towns have been briefly examined here to provide some perspective on the state of Plymouth Colony in 1633; in due course Scituate and Duxbury will get the full treatment they deserve in this Newsletter.

RECOMMENDED READING

The volume of literature relating to Plymouth Colony is immense, and there is not room to discuss even the most important items here. We will only touch on the most important contemporary writing, and on a few more recent publications which provide the best current interpretations, and also lead us back into all the literature of the past three centuries.

The fundamental text for understanding the early years of Plymouth Colony is Governor William Bradford's *History*, which, since its rediscovery in London in the middle of the nineteenth century, has appeared in many editions. The most recent and the most accessible edition is that prepared by Samuel Eliot Morison (Alfred A. Knopf: New York 1952). Another edition, older and more difficult to come by, is the two-volume version edited by Worthington Chauncey Ford (Massachusetts Historical Society: Boston 1912); the advantage of this edition is the extensive annotation and the inclusion of many related documents which are not easily found elsewhere.

What Bradford gives us is the best and most extensive account by a participant in the Leyden years and in the first three decades of Plymouth Colony itself. Unfortunately, Bradford did not have as well-developed a sense of chronology as did Winthrop, with the result that it is sometimes difficult to work out the sequence and exact dating of many of the events which Bradford narrates. (The dates of the founding of Duxbury and Marshfield, discussed above, provide an example of this problem.)

As noted in a previous section, an important feature included in both the Ford and Morison editions of Bradford is the passenger list of the *Mayflower*. This is not, however, a list compiled in 1620 at the time of sailing, but two lists prepared by Bradford thirty years later. The first part is the list of those who did sail on the Mayflower; the second is a reckoning after three decades of the births and deaths in each family. Although it does not always give details of names and dates, it provides much information available nowhere else which can help the genealogist reconstruct these families.

Of all the modern writings there are two which demand our attention, because they are the most comprehensive of the available histories, but each approaches the material from a different perspective, one historical and one genealogical.

In 1966 George D. Langdon Jr. published *Pilgrim Colony: A History of New Plymouth, 1620-1691* (Yale University Press, New Haven). Langdon was the first modern scholar to treat the full span of Plymouth Colony, in all its aspects, in a comprehensive and evenhanded manner. He covered not only the familiar subjects of the political and religious history of Plymouth, but also looked into social and legal history, as well as the relations of the Englishmen with the native population.

Langdon had prepared an extensive bibliography on Plymouth Colony, which for some reason was not published in the first edition of *Pilgrim Colony*. It was issued in July 1969 as part of the first number of *Occasional Papers in Old Colony Studies*, published by Plimoth Plantation. This bibliography was then included in the paperbound edition of *Pilgrim Colony*, making this cheaper edition in some ways more valuable than the hardbound version. This bibliography covers not only the printed literature on Plymouth Colony, but also surveys the surviving manuscript material, including the town and church records of each of the pre-1692 settlements in Plymouth Colony. All persons interested in Plymouth Colony should acquire a copy of this bibliography in some form.

The second modern publication which should come to our attention is Eugene A. Stratton's *Plymouth Colony: Its History & People, 1620-1691* (Salt Lake City 1986). Like Langdon, Stratton set out to provide a comprehensive history of Plymouth Colony, but this time from a genealogical point of view. In the first half of the book, Stratton takes up many of the same topics as were covered by Langdon, but with greater emphasis on our knowledge of family connections. The second half of the book consists of biographical sketches, with much genealogical information, extensively documented, for most of the immigrants to Plymouth down to 1634.

Stratton does a number of new and interesting things in *Plymouth Colony*. In the biographical sketches, he develops many new interpretations and solutions of old problems; while these are not always correct, they are stimulating. In addition, he provides several appendices, which bring together all the lists discussed in this Focus section, as well as the 1643 list of men able to bear arms.

Research and writing on Plymouth Colony continue at a rapid rate. In the last year or two the General Society of Mayflower Descendants, after a hiatus of more than a decade, has resumed publishing the silver volumes in its Five Generations Project. Volume Five treats the descendants of Edward Fuller, Volume Six covers John Billington and Edward Winslow, and further volumes are in preparation.

On the 10th and 11th of April, 1992, a conference on Plymouth Colony was held at Plimoth Plantation, jointly sponsored by the Colonial Society of Massachusetts, the Pilgrim Society and Plimoth Plantation. More than a dozen papers were delivered, on such diverse aspects of the Pilgrim experience as architecture, printing, furniture making, Indian relations and theology. These papers will be published in the near future by the Colonial Society of Massachusetts.

RECENT LITERATURE

Gale Ion Harris, "John Edwards of Wethersfield, Connecticut," *New England Historical and Genealogical Register* 145 (1991):317-41. Harris discusses in great detail the family and career of John Edwards, who first appeared in Wethersfield in 1638 (and may have been there as early as 1636), and then follows the lives of all seven of John's children. In the process, Harris provides additional evidence showing that Edwards' second wife, the widow of Abraham Finch, was the daughter of Robert Moulton of Charlestown and Salem.

Henry L. P. Beckwith, "Heraldic Intelligence: The English Ancestry of Hezekiah Hoar of Taunton, Massachusetts," *New England Historical and Genealogical Register* 145 (1991):373. A brief note expressing doubt about the significance of a dated seal in establishing a link in the English ancestry of Hezekiah Hoar.

Douglas Richardson, "The Widow Frances (Albright) Wells, Wife of Thomas Coleman of Wethersfield and Hadley," *New England Historical and Genealogical Register* 146 (1992):28-34. It has long been known that Frances, the wife of Thomas Coleman, who came to Wethersfield by 1639, was a widow Wells. Richardson shows that her first husband was Thomas Wells of Evesham, Worcestershire, who died there in 1637, and that she was Frances Albright, daughter of Richard Albright. The author also points to evidence which indicates that Thomas Coleman himself was of Evesham.

Frederick J. Nicholson, "The Norwich Ancestry of Margaret Chenery, Mother of John Moody and Frances (Moody) Kilbourne of Connecticut," *The American Genealogist* 66 (1991):197-204. In a previous article Nicholson had set forth the ancestry of Margaret Chenery who was mother of the two immigrants, John Moody and Frances (Moody) Kilbourne, wife of Thomas Kilbourne. He now presents evidence on the father, grandfather and greatgrandfather of Elizabeth Norwich, mother of Margaret Cheney. This family is found in a number of parishes in western Suffolk and eastern Cambridgeshire.

"Torrey Marriage Number," *The American Genealogist* 67 (1992), Number One. The editors of *The American Genealogist* have put together a theme issue, collecting several articles about New England couples in the seventeenth century, thereby adding to or correcting Torrey's Index of New England Marriages. As one might expect, most of these articles relate to participants in the Great Migration. Brief outlines of these articles follow:

Douglas Richardson, "Thomas[1] Marshfield's Wife Mercy; Did Their Daughter Mercy Marry John[1]

Dumbleton?", pp. 11-15. Richardson publishes a death record for the widow of Thomas Marshfield, showing that her given name was Mercy. With this and other onomastic and associational evidence, he then argues that Thomas and Mercy (_____) Marshfield had a daughter Mercy who married John[1] Dumbleton.

Robert C. Anderson, "English Marriages of New Englanders: Hobart, Fisher," pp. 28-29. It had been known that Peter Hobart of Hingham had married Elizabeth Ibrook, and Thomas Fisher of Cambridge and Dedham had married Elizabeth Allen, both in England. Anderson presents here the records of those marriages.

Penny G. Douglass, "Thankslord Perkins, Wife of Ralph[1] Shepard of Dedham, Massachusetts," p. 29. Douglass has found the marriage record, in Stepney, co. Middlesex, for Ralph Shepard of Dedham and his wife Thankslord, now seen to be Thankslord Perkins.

Robert S. Wakefield, "Additions and Corrections to Torrey's New England Marriages," pp. 30-31. Based largely on his work for the Mayflower Society's Five Generations Project, Wakefield gathers together brief notes on about two dozen couples, several of them immigrants to New England by 1643.

Gale Ion Harris, "Captain Richard Wright of Twelve-Mile Island and the Burnhams of Podunk," pp. 32-46. Harris brings together evidence from the records of several colonies to show that the Richard Wright who first appeared in Lynn (Saugus), and then moved to Rehoboth, was the same as the "Captain Wright" who appeared in the Connecticut River valley in the 1660s. He then provides a complete reconstruction of this man's family, indicating as many as six daughters, who married men at various places in Massachusetts and Connecticut.

Eleanor Cooley Rue, "Widow Joyce Wallen of Plymouth (1645) and Widow Joyce Lombard of Barnstable (1664): One and the Same?", pp. 47-53. Rue argues convincingly that Joyce, the wife and widow of Ralph Wallen of Plymouth, became about 1645 the second (or third) wife of Thomas Lombard of Dorchester and Barnstable. She then discusses the evidence for the marriage of Mary, daughter of Ralph and Joyce (_____) Wallen, first to John[2] Ewer, then to John[1] Jenkins.

Robert Charles Anderson, "Marriages of Promise: Killam, Houchin, Lusher," pp. 53-54. Anderson sets forth English marriage records which may be those of the immigrants Austin Killam of Salem, Dedham and Wenham, Jeremiah Houchin of Dorchester and Boston, and Eleazer Lusher of Dedham.

(continued from page 10)
who were certainly passengers on the 1633 ship from Weymouth. Pinney was unmarried at the time of his migration to New England, so we cannot place any other family members with him on this ship (Dawes-Gates 2:659-62).

Going beyond the immediate evidence of the Paynter letter, we note that Nathaniel Duncan, who had married Elizabeth Jourdain, a sister of the wife of William Hill, first appears in New England in 1633, being granted land in Dorchester on 5 August of that year; he was made a freeman on 6 May 1635. This couple had two sons born in England, Nathaniel and Peter, so this family accounted for four of the passengers.

As a final example, in the records of the Massachusetts Bay General Court we find the nuncupative will of Mr. John Russell, who died in Dorchester on 26 August 1633, having been granted land there on 5 August 1633. In early 1634, his former servant, Robert Fibben, was granted freedom "in consideration of some service performed at sea." Furthermore, Russell in his brief list of bequests, which did not include a wife or children, specifically names Bernard Capen as one of the "old Dorchester" persons who should get special consideration (Massachusetts Bay General Court Records 1:107, 121, 153). Thus, Mr. John Russell and his servant Robert Fibben should be placed on this ship as well.

Without coming close to exhausting the sources, then, we have with some confidence identified about a quarter of the eighty passengers who sailed from Weymouth in the spring of 1633. Further examination of Dorchester town records and the colony court and freeman records might well double this number. In particular, study of all those persons granted land in Dorchester on 5 August 1633 should provide the identities of more passengers. (Unfortunately, the Dorchester church records, which might show who had recently arrived, do not survive for these early years.) Other sources which would help with the reconstruction would be the Massachusetts Bay court records, the Winthrop Papers, and possibly later depositions which might claim immigration in 1633.

Earlier we noted that Banks had attempted a partial list for this ship. He did include both John Cogan and Aquila Purchase, but did not have the families totally correct in either case. And he must not have been aware of either the Whiteway diary or the Paynter letter, for he does not include those who clearly came with Cogan and Purchase.

Banks does include in his list such men as Philip Randall, Elias Parkman and John Rockett, all of whom were granted land on 5 August 1633, and do not appear earlier in New England records. But there are others granted land that day who are not included by Banks. Whether the other names suggested by Banks should be included awaits further research.

Great Migration Newsletter

Vol. 3   July-September 1992   No. 3

MINISTERIAL CONNECTIONS

As Roger Thompson demonstrates in his recent article on "Social Cohesion in Early New England," a large proportion of the East Anglian participants in the Great Migration came as part of extended networks, referred to by Thompson as "companies." Among the most important of the companies were the "clerical companies," organized around one or two ministers of Puritan inclinations (*New England Historical and Genealogical Register* 146 [1992]:235-53).

The clerical companies were especially evident in the latter phases of the Great Migration, the period from 1634 to 1640 when as many as three-quarters of all those who took part in the Great Migration arrived. Since, as we shall see, clerical companies were also quite common outside East Anglia, it is clear that a large proportion of the early arrivals in New England came as members of a clerical company. In fact, it may be that more than half of the twenty thousand or so immigrants were attached to such a group.

One very well-known clerical company was the group of persons who sailed from Dorsetshire in 1630 on the *Mary & John*; this group had been organized by Reverend John White of Dorchester in Dorsetshire, and was accompanied by two ministers, John Warham and John Maverick, who had been known earlier to many of the passengers.

There were other clerical companies from the West Country. In 1635 a ship sailed from Weymouth, also in Dorsetshire, carrying a little more than a hundred passengers, many of them from the parishes of Broadway and Batcombe in Somerset. At the head of the list of passengers was Reverend Joseph Hull, along with his large family. Hull was known to have been from this same area, having been born in Crewkerne, and having served as minister at Northleigh in Devonshire until his resignation in 1632. Recent research in ecclesiastical archives in England, however, has shown that in the years 1633 and 1634 Joseph Hull was curate at Broadway, and thus had within his care several of the families who accompanied him to New England in 1635. The minister at Batcombe at this time was Richard Bernard, who never left

England, but on the ship with Hull, among the Batcombe families, was Musachiell Bernard, son of the minister. Thus, the passenger list of this ship represents elements of two clerical companies, gathered from parishes in different parts of Somerset.

Clerical companies were also formed in parts of England outside of East Anglia and the West Country. In articles published in 1989 and 1990, Thomas W. Cooper II delineated a sizable group from the neighborhood of Olney, in the northern part of Buckinghamshire, who coalesced around Reverend William Worcester, vicar of that parish (*The American Genealogist* 64 [1989]:193-202, 65 [1990]:65-69).

William Worcester did not come to New England when so many of his parishioners did, but delayed his migration until 1639. Upon arrival, he soon became minister at Salisbury. But among those of his parishioners and neighbors who made the voyage in and about 1635, most of them settling first at Lynn, were: John Cooper with his wife and four children, Edmund Farrington with his wife and four children, William Purrier (or Parrier) with his wife and three children, the brothers Philip and Nathaniel Kirtland, the brothers Anthony and Thomas Newhall, and several others. Many of these families joined together in a later migration to Long Island.

Not only were these clerical companies found in all those parts of England which gave rise to substantial numbers of immigrants to New England at this time, but there was considerable communication between ministers in different parts of England, indicating that these clerical

(continued on page 18)

EDITOR'S EFFUSIONS

With this issue of the *Newsletter*, we begin to reach beyond those towns settled at the very beginning of the Great Migration. Ipswich had its earliest beginnings in the spring of 1633, but this was only a handful of settlers. Not until the following year did the town really begin to grow, with the large influx of new settlers to New England in the spring of 1634, and then again in 1635. Thus, Ipswich can be seen as a transitional town, having its origins in the migrations connected with the arrival of the Winthrop Fleet, but taking on its full flavor from the immigrants generated by the persecutions of Archbishop Laud, beginning in 1633.

In the next issue, we will for the first time treat a Connecticut town in the Focus section. We will look at Wethersfield, showing how it took shape from the removal of many families from Watertown in Massachusetts Bay. At the same time, we will see how this movement affected Watertown.

Beginning with Volume Four of the *Great Migration Newsletter,* the Focus section will range over all of New England, and over the entire time period down to 1643. Each year, at least one town each from Connecticut and Rhode Island will be featured, with occasional excursions to the north of Massachusetts.

The Recent Literature section in this issue takes up more space than usual, flowing over onto the back page. This is partly the consequence of attempting to treat a number of books and articles from outside the normal run of genealogical periodicals, and partly the result of a large number of genealogical articles in recent months on Great Migration immigrants.

For various reasons, mostly deriving from the change of residence of the editor, this issue of the *Newsletter* is somewhat later than usual. The fourth issue will be produced on a short schedule for delivery sometime between Thanksgiving and Christmas, and in that issue will be an announcement about the first book-form publication of the Great Migration Study Project.

Robert Charles Anderson, FASG   Editor
Margaret F. Costello   Production Assistant

The *Great Migration Newsletter* (ISSN 1049-8087) is published quarterly by the Great Migration Study Project, a project of the New England Historic Genealogical Society
101 Newbury Street, Boston MA 02116

The subscription rate is $8 for one year and $15 for two years. The subscription year is the same as the calendar year.

Copyright © 1992 by the New England
Historic Genealogical Society

(*continued from page 17*)

companies were not formed in total isolation from one another. One excellent example comes from the career of Reverend John White of Dorchester, Dorsetshire.

John White's elder brother was Josias White, also a minister. After Josias died late in 1622, his widow Anna married Francis Drake of Esher in Surrey, a member of the prominent Drake family of Ashe in Devonshire. In the household of Francis Drake only a few years before had been Thomas Hooker, who would come to New England in 1633, where he ministered first at Cambridge and then at Hartford. In his will of 13 March 1633/4, Francis Drake made bequests to his cousin John Drake (*not* the John Drake of Windsor, Connecticut), who was briefly in New England, and to Joanna Hooker, daughter of Reverend Thomas.

The Stoughton family provides another useful example. Thomas and Israel Stoughton were prominent settlers of Dorchester, Massachusetts, and Thomas very likely arrived in 1630 on the *Mary & John*. But the father of these two men was Reverend Thomas Stoughton, who had ministered to various churches in Suffolk and Essex. How did the East Anglian Stoughtons become involved with a West Country group of emigrants?

The elder brother of the immigrants Thomas and Israel Stoughton was John Stoughton, like his father a minister. About 1625 he married the widow of Reverend Ralph Cudworth, who had preceded Thomas Stoughton as minister at Great Coggeshall, Essex, but who was at the time of his death minister at Aller, Somersetshire. John Stoughton's brother Thomas moved to Aller by 1625, for in the register of that parish we find the baptism on 21 August 1625 of Thomas, son of Thomas and Elizabeth Stoughton, and then the burial on 29 December 1627 of Elizabeth, wife of Mr. Thomas Stoughton. Thus, Thomas Stoughton, despite being East Anglian in origin, was well placed to become acquainted with the organizers of the voyage of the *Mary & John* in 1630.

One may conclude from all of this that like-minded Puritan communities throughout England were connected through a grapevine of ministers and prominent laymen. They no doubt shared information about prospects in New England, and about the advantages of travelling in groups. This would include the ability to move aggressively upon arrival in New England in the matter of obtaining a grant of a township, and therefore keeping the group intact in the New World.

These various examples of clerical companies, and of wider connections between Puritan communities, are obviously of great importance to the study of the Great Migration. The discovery and delineation of clerical companies of immigrants will be one of the principal objectives of the Great Migration Study Project.

Focus   *on*   IPSWICH

SETTLEMENT OF IPSWICH

Ipswich is one of the few early New England towns for which we have a contemporary record of the first organized settlement. In the records of the Massachusetts Bay General Court is the following entry:

1 April 1633: It is ordered, that no person whatsoever shall go to plant or inhabit at Agawam without leave from the Court, except those that are already gone, viz: Mr. John Winthrop, Junr., Mr. Clerke, Robert Coles, Thomas Howlett, John Biggs, John Gage, Thomas Hardy, William Perkins, Mr. Thornedicke, William Srieant [Sergeant] [1:103].

Even at this early date the General Court was probably unable to enforce this command that no others settle at Ipswich. A few months later, though, they did allow Thomas Sellen to join the others at the new settlement. There may have been others who joined this vanguard during the first year, but we do know that in May of 1634 the *Mary & John* arrived with many passengers from Wiltshire and Hampshire, several of whom settled at Ipswich and, as we shall see shortly, founded the first church there.

In the spring of 1635 the population changed again, when many of the 1634 arrivals, led by the ministers Thomas Parker and James Noyes, moved a little further north to organize the town of Newbury. The places that they had made in Ipswich were soon filled by passengers arriving in 1635, mostly from East Anglia. On the *Planter,* for example, which arrived at Boston on 7 June 1635, were a number of persons who settled at Ipswich, including families headed by John Tuttle, George Giddings and Richard Haffield, and a number of single males such as Palmer Tingley and Francis Peabody. Many of these East Anglians had close connections with the settlers of Watertown, large numbers of whom were from the same part of England; in addition, some families which had been in Watertown for a few years made the move to Ipswich, including Richard Saltonstall Jr.

These changes of early 1635 set the tone for Ipswich for decades to come, and the town became an outpost of East Anglians in a county which was largely made up of emigrants from other parts of England (Salem being largely West Countrymen, Lynn residents from the smaller counties north of London, Newbury settlers from Hampshire and Wiltshire, Rowley immigrants from Yorkshire, and so on). Ipswich, despite the fact that it was in Essex County, had more the feel of a Middlesex County town.

FIRST CHURCH OF IPSWICH

There are no records for the Ipswich church for the first century of its existence, and there are no strictly contemporary accounts of the founding of the church. We must, therefore, rely on the few clues scattered through the Winthrop papers, the colony records and the writings of the early New England historians in order to piece together the history of the first years of the church at Ipswich.

Harold Worthley, in his inventory of Congregational church records, places the establishment of the Ipswich church in June of 1634, but he does not provide any documentation for this claim. (Worthley's book, with the cumbersome title of *An Inventory of the Records of the Particular [Congregational] Churches of Massachusetts Gathered 1620-1805* [Cambridge 1970], is an essential reference work for anyone working in this period, and should be consulted for information about the existence, location and published versions of church records, for lists of ministers and church officers, and for dates of founding, merger and extinction of churches.)

Worthley (or some earlier historian) may have settled on this date based on a letter which John Winthrop Senior wrote on 22 May 1634 to Sir Nathaniel Rich. In a postscript, Winthrop noted that "we have settled a plantation 20 miles to the northward, near Merrimack. Mr. Parker is to be minister there" (*Winthrop Papers* 3:168). In the spring of 1634 the plantation referred to could only be Ipswich.

Thomas Parker had sailed for New England on the *Mary & John* (not the same as the ship which had made the voyage in 1630), which had left England on 24 March 1633/4. Winthrop noted in the same postscript quoted from above that the ships recently arrived had mostly come in six weeks, so Parker could have been in New England for no more than two weeks, and perhaps somewhat less. To assume that a minister and associated group of laymen founded a church within a month or so of arrival may be pushing the chronology too far, as few other churches were founded so expeditiously.

We can say, however, that the church must have been founded by 3 September 1634, for on that day a large number of men were admitted to freemanship in Massachusetts Bay Colony, and in the list were two groupings of men who were at this time clearly of Ipswich. In about the middle of the list were Mr. John Spencer, Robert Mussey, Henry Short and Philip Fowler, and toward the end were three more, Mr. Thomas Parker, Mr. Nicholas Easton and Mr. James Noyes. (All of these men were passengers on the *Mary & John* except for Robert Mussey, although there were passengers named Abraham and John Mussey.) Thus the outside dates for the founding of the Ipswich church are no earlier than 22 May 1634, and no later than 3 September 1634.

The church grew very quickly after this. Presumably some of those who had made the move to Ipswich in early 1633 were admitted to the church, but as most of them were already freemen from an earlier date, they would not appear in the lists along with the new arrivals. Then, in the list of freemen for 4 March 1634/5 was a grouping of nine Ipswich men: Thomas Scott, Thomas Boreman, Roger Lanckton, John Webster, Hugh Sheratt, Joseph Metcalfe, William Bartholomew, Thomas Dorman and Richard Kent. Thus, by the spring of 1635 there were probably more than twenty male members of the Ipswich church, and presumably as many more females. (In most churches at this early date, husbands and wives were admitted together; in addition unattached men and women, mostly servants, were readily admitted also.)

Who were the first ministers of this church? Worthley begins his list with Thomas Parker and Nathaniel Ward, stating that both were ordained in 1634. We have seen from the 22 May 1634 Winthrop letter that Thomas Parker was already slated to be minister of the new congregation. But in the 3 September 1634 list of freemen we do not find Nathaniel Ward, although we do find James Noyes, who would soon accompany Parker to Newbury and join him in the ministry there.

Two early New England historians give us conflicting statements about the early ministry at Ipswich. Edward Johnson, writing in 1651 about events of 1634, states that in this year "Mr. Nathaniel Ward ... took up his station at the Town of Ipswich, where the faithful servants of Christ gathered the Ninth Church [in Massachusetts Bay]" (J. Franklin Jameson, ed., *Johnson's Wonder-Working Providence 1628-1651* [New York 1910] pp. 95-96). There is no mention of Reverend Thomas Parker at this point, but in the discussion of Newbury, still under 1634, he reports that Mr. James Noyes and Mr. Thomas Parker came over late in the year "and began to build the Tenth Church of Christ at a Town called Newberry" (p. 98).

Johnson, who was always more concerned with the providential interpretation of history than with chronological and factual accuracy, errs in placing the arrival of Noyes and Parker late in 1634, rather than in the spring, and in suggesting that they began the church at Newbury a year before the town was founded. Johnson did not arrive in New England until 1637, and he could not have had firsthand or contemporary knowledge of the events surrounding the founding of the Ipswich church.

William Hubbard wrote his *General History of New England* in 1682, the first comprehensive historical narrative covering this region. In his account of ecclesiastical affairs from 1631 to 1636 (Chapter XXVIII), he tells us that "The reverend and learned Mr. Parker was at first called to Ipswich, to join with Mr. Ward," but afterwards moved with many of his fellow Wiltshiremen to Newbury. William Hubbard arrived at Ipswich in 1635, became minister there in 1658, and has a high reputation for accuracy, so his account should be given greater credence than that of Johnson.

However, we have to set against Hubbard's version the data which we have from the records created in 1634. First, Winthrop on 22 May 1634 says that Parker will be minister at Ipswich, saying nothing of Ward. Second, in the 3 September 1634 list of freemen, the first after the founding of the church, we find Thomas Parker (and James Noyes), but not Nathaniel Ward. Third, in a letter of 12 December 1634 to his son John Jr., John Winthrop Sr. reports that "Mr. Ward continues at your house this winter" (*Winthrop Papers* 3:177). Finally, in a journal entry under 19 January 1634/5 describing a gathering of ministers, Winthrop tells us that "All the ministers, except Mr. Ward of Ipswich, met at Boston ..." (*Winthrop Journal* 183).

None of this is inconsistent with either Hubbard's or Worthley's claims, but another interpretation is possible. It may be that when the Ipswich church was founded in the summer of 1634 (probably in July or August), Thomas Parker and James Noyes were the organizers and first ministers, but they soon realized that they wanted to move on and found their own town. With this change in view, Nathaniel Ward, another 1634 arrival, was brought in to lead the church, which he was certainly doing by the time of the December and January records.

What we can be sure of is that Thomas Parker was pastor of the church at its founding in the summer of 1634, that Nathaniel Ward was minister there by the end of 1634, and that by early 1635 Parker had moved on to Newbury and the church was totally in the hands of Nathaniel Ward.

Nathaniel Ward had years of experience as a minister in England, and was one of the great scholars of early New England, but he did not have great success as pastor at Ipswich. Very few new church members were added in 1635 and the years immediately following (as evidenced by the lists of freemen), and by 1638 Ward was no longer in office.

In 1638 two new ministers were installed at Ipswich, Nathaniel Rogers as pastor and John Norton as teacher. With these two men in place the Ipswich pulpit was stable for fifteen years, and membership again began to grow.

EARLY IPSWICH RECORDS

As we have seen in earlier Focus sections, many of the early Massachusetts Bay towns had land inventories, or books of possession, mostly compiled in the years from about 1638 to 1643. For Ipswich there is no such record.

The early Ipswich records are an incomplete jumble of copies and partial copies. In 1859 George A. Schofield of Ipswich edited and published some of these records, under the title *The Ancient Records of the Town of Ipswich*, Volume 1, from 1634 to 1650 (referred to hereafter as *Ancient Records*; Volume 2 never appeared). Most of these had earlier been published in a local newspaper, and Schofield apologized for the crude form of these transcripts, including the fact that the published version was unpaginated. (For purposes of reference here, the page headed "Agawam Named Ipswich" will be considered as page one, with later pages numbered appropriately.)

The material published in this volume consists mostly of land grants, with a few other town matters, such as choice of selectmen (but only occasionally). As will be seen, Schofield selected his transcripts from more than one ancient volume, without noting his sources.

Among the microfilm reels of Ipswich town records are three which give as earliest date 1634: 1) Ipswich Grants - Town Meetings, 1634-1660; 2) Ipswich Town Records and Land Grants, 1634-1757; 3) Ipswich Commoners Record, 1634-1720. The last of these actually begins in 1702 and, although it does contain some brief references to earlier land transactions, we will ignore this item here. The remaining two volumes will be referred to here as Book One and Book Two.

The early pages of Book One correspond to the early pages of *Ancient Records*. These are mostly individual grants of land, with a few other items of town business thrown in. Each grouping of records is headed by the description "At a town meeting of" such-and-such a date, but it is clear that these are not the full records of the town meetings, for there are many things omitted which would normally be found in town meeting records of this date. The conclusion must be, then, that what survives for this early period are extracts from an original which is now lost.

Unfortunately, the published transcript is filled with errors. For instance, on page five there is an invented entry for John Gadge (Gage). The last complete entry on the page begins with a description of a grant of six acres to John Gadge, but halfway through Schofield allowed his eyes to wander back up the page, and finished with the last two lines from the Thomas Howlett entry above. He then began again with the John Gadge entry, and this time got it right. (In technical terms, this is referred to as "dit-

tography," the duplication in a transcript of something in the earlier text.)

On page eight, the transcriber commits the opposite error (known as "haplography," the omission in a transcript of a portion of the earlier text, usually the result of skipping directly from one occurrence of a word or phrase to a later occurrence of the same word or phrase). The entry for Robert Mussey is defective, in that it contains the first half of his grant with the second half of a grant to Henry Short. The lands entered on the top half of this page are laid out adjacent to one another, and a clue to the missing information is seen in the reference at the end of the incorrect Robert Mussey grant to adjoining land of John Satchwell, whereas the entry for Satchwell immediately following has this piece of land next to that of Henry Short.

There are simpler mistakes as well. On page eleven we find a grant to "Thomas Finnan," when the surname should be Firman. Furthermore, the transcript omits marginal notations entirely, so that for this same entry we do not learn that Thomas was "Mr. Firman," potentially a valuable piece of evidence.

After a few more pages in Book One, we begin to find records that look more like complete town meeting records, as they refer to "the seven men," or selectmen. Then we come upon several pages which are not records generated by the town of Ipswich, but are in fact the minutes of the Ipswich Quarterly Court for 1641; these have been included in the published version of the Essex Quarterly Court records, as apparently no other copy survives. Book One then reverts to complete records of town meetings from the early 1640s down to about 1659 or 1660.

Book Two picks up where Book One leaves off, with town meeting records from 1660 to 1704. But when the volume is turned around and read from the back, we find more copies of the Ipswich land grants from the 1630s and 1640s. They are in a seventeenth-century hand, of about the same time or somewhat later than the writing in Book One. Many of these copied entries are the same as those found in the early pages of Book One, and in *Ancient Records*.

What is disturbing is that in *Ancient Records*, items from Book Two are mixed in with items from Book One, without any notation to that effect. For example, on page eighteen, the grant to "Thomas Wells Anno 1635" is lifted from a page in Book Two, leaving other seemingly contemporaneous material behind, and placed in the middle of a sequence from Book One.

Looking back at Book One, we find that at some time in the past the book was disbound, and the individual leafs of paper were enclosed in silk, after which the silked pages were rebound. The loose pages are clearly not in their original order, and do not correspond to the sequence in which they were transcribed for *Ancient Records*. Furthermore, large chunks have been lost from the corners of some pages, even though the missing text appears in *Ancient Records*. Some of this, but not all, may have been supplied from the copies in Book Two.

Did Schofield copy these records before the rearrangement, or did he see yet another version of the town records which no longer exists (or at least is not on microfilm), or did he simply indulge in some creative editing?

By all measures, then, the published version of some of the early Ipswich records is highly defective. Given the importance of Ipswich to the early years of Essex County, and to New England in general, Ipswich deserves better, and awaits an editor who is willing to take on the very delicate and painstaking job of producing a modern, reliable transcript of these records.

EARLY IPSWICH LANDHOLDING

Since there is no inventory of lands or book of possessions for Ipswich, and no lists in which land is granted at one time to all proprietors, we must approach the question of landholding in early Ipswich indirectly. As with Lynn we can examine inventories in the Essex County probate records. In addition we do have the town records (described above), as muddled and confused as they are.

For the purposes of this article we will use the published Essex County probate records, *The Probate Records of Essex County, Massachusetts*, Volume One, 1635-1664 (Salem 1916), abbreviated here as EPR 1. The first Ipswich inventory we encounter is that of Sarah Dillingham, widow of Mr. John Dillingham, dated in 1636 [EPR 1:3-10]. Three parcels of land were included: six acres planting ground near the house, thirty acres of upland, and sixty acres of meadow. Next is the 1639 inventory of Humphrey Wise, listing the house and house lot of an acre, a six acre planting lot, and a farm of 120 acres [EPR 1:11].

After a gap of seven years, we begin to get a regular series of Ipswich probates, all of the following being from 1646. John Webster had a dwelling house and six acres tied to it, a farm of about thirty-two acres, and an island bought of widow Andrews [EPR 1:52-53]. The listing for Joseph Morse included a house and ground (area unspecified) bought of widow Perkins, one other old house and eight acres of ground and a barn, ten acres of upland and five acres of marsh [EPR 1:53-55]. Michael Carthrick owned a house with barn, yards and garden (area unspecified), twelve acres of land within fence and

another twenty-six acres of land [EPR 1:62-64]. Matthew Whipple, a wealthier man than the other Ipswich residents who died in 1646, held a dwelling house with four acres ground, a barn and other outhouses, a six acre lot, a four acre lot, six acres of marsh, another six acres of marsh with waste land adjoining totalling twenty acres, and a farm of 160 acres upland with thirty acres meadow attached [EPR 1:87-91].

Although there is great variety here, there are some patterns. Everyone had a houselot, probably an acre or less, for the house, a few outbuildings, and perhaps a kitchen garden. Most had a piece of planting ground attached to or near the house, usually six acres. In addition, a common holding would include a sizable parcel of meadow, and a piece of upland. Some of those inventoried had a farm, ranging in size up to 160 acres.

What do we learn from the land grants printed in *Ancient Records*? Does a comparison with these grants conform or conflict with this picture? Many of the grants of land are single parcels, and to obtain a complete picture we would have to bring together a number of grants from various parts of the surviving books. This could certainly be done, but given the confused nature of the records, we wouldn't be certain that we had all of a person's grants.

Fortunately, at various places there are entries which seem to list all the holdings for a given grantee. For example, on page eighteen of *Ancient Records* is a compilation of lands granted to Thomas Wells in 1635 (the same item referred to in the article above on early Ipswich records). From this we learn that Wells had a house lot with an acre-and-a-half of land, a six acre planting lot, twenty-four acres of upland, and eight acres of meadow. On page twenty-three there is a similar entry for William Warner, giving him a house lot with one acre of land, a six acre planting lot, a farm of ninety-seven acres, and fourteen acres of meadow. (These entries from *Ancient Records* have been verified against the manuscript entries in Book Two.)

The pictures derived from probate inventories and town records are reasonably similar then: a house lot with about an acre, a six acre planting lot, varying sized lots of meadow and upland, and for some a farm.

Bibliographic Note: Over the last few decades Ipswich landholding patterns have been studied by two practitioners of the new social history, on a broader basis than we are attempting here. Edward Perzel's 1967 doctoral dissertation at Rutgers was titled "The First Generation of Settlement in Colonial Ipswich, Massachusetts: 1633-1660," and from this he prepared an article, "Landholding in Ipswich," in *Essex Institute Historical Collections* 104 (1968):303-28. David Grayson Allen studied Ipswich landholding in *In English Ways* (Chapel Hill 1981), in Chapter Five and Appendix Four.

RECENT LITERATURE

William Whiteway, *William Whiteway of Dorchester, His Diary 1618 to 1635,* Dorset Record Society, Volume 12 (Dorchester, England 1991), pp. 195, index. William Whiteway was born into a wealthy family of Dorchester in Dorsetshire, and as such he was on a familiar basis with all the prominent persons of that town. Furthermore, his brother married a niece of Reverend John White, the great promoter of migration to New England. For more than a century brief excerpts from this journal have been appearing in print, giving hints about families who made the voyage to New England. Now we have the entire text, and, although there are not a large number of direct references to New England immigrants, the diary does tell us much about the environment in which so many of the West Country emigrants lived at the time they made the decision to leave England.

Arnold P.G. and Carolyn Bryant Peterson, "Edward Converse of Woburn, Massachusetts: Notes on His Birthplace and Ancestry," *New England Historical and Genealogical Register* 146 (1992):130-32. Combining new research with evidence already in print, the authors demonstrate that Edward Converse, a 1630 immigrant to Charlestown, was baptized in Navestock, co. Essex, that he was married in Great Burstead, co. Essex, and that he and his wife had three children baptized in South Weald, co. Essex. These three parishes are very close to one another, in southwestern Essex, an area which supplied many other participants in the Great Migration.

Robert Charles Anderson, "The Wives of Michael Barstow and Richard Carver of Watertown, Massachusetts, and The Identity of the Wives of William Randall of Scituate and William Perry of Marshfield," *NEHGR* 146 (1992):230-34. The author argues that Richard Carver and Michael Barstow had three wives each, and that the third wife of Carver became the third wife of Barstow. From this it follows that the wives of William Randall and William Perry were daughters of Carver, and stepdaughters of Barstow.

Roger Thompson, "Social Cohesion in Early New England," *NEHGR* 146 (1992):235-53. Using data drawn from many sources, Thompson examines one aspect of social cohesion in New England in its earliest decades: group migration from England to New England, in this case focussing on 2200 emigrants from East Anglia. Thompson discusses in detail three types of group migration, or "companies": gentleman's companies, clerical companies and extended family companies. He concludes that the result of this mode of migration was retention of ties with the mother country, and a lack of what others have seen as "modernizing" tendencies.

Douglas Richardson, "The Heath Connection: English Origins of Isaac and William Heath of Roxbury, Massachusetts, John Johnson, Edward Morris and Elizabeth (Morris) Cartwright," *NEHGR* 146 (1992):261-78. Evidence has been available for many years that the brothers Isaac and William Heath of Roxbury were in some way related to John Johnson of Roxbury, and to Edward Morris and his sister Elizabeth (Morris) Cartwright, and it is also known that the Heaths were from the area of Ware and Great Amwell, Hertfordshire, not far from the Essex border. Richardson provides extensive records from these two parishes which demonstrate convincingly that John Johnson also resided in these two parishes in Hertfordshire, and that his first wife, who died before the removal to New England, was Mary Heath, sister to Isaac and William. Furthermore, the Morris siblings of New England were children of Edward Morris and his wife Prudence Heath, also sister to Isaac and William. (In English records this family name was more frequently Morrison than Morris.)

John Plummer, "The Wives of Robert and John Bullard," *NEHGR* 146 (1992):279-80. Plummer points out that the recently published will of John Martyn of Barnham, co. Suffolk, identifies Martyn's daughter Anne as the wife of Robert Bullard who immigrated to Watertown about 1635 and died there in 1639. Anne married second Henry Thorpe, also of Watertown.

Gerald James Parsons, "Joseph and Benjamin Parsons and David Wilton," *NEHGR* 146 (1992):297-98. The author presents various items that have recently come to his attention, augmenting our knowledge of the Parsons, Wilton and Hoskins families.

Douglas Richardson, "Wells and Albright," *NEHGR* 146 (1992):298. Supplementing his earlier article (*NEHGR* 146 [1992]:28-34), Richardson offers some additional Wells and Albright entries from the Evesham, co. Worcester, parish registers.

Alfred A. Cave, "Who Killed John Stone? A Note on the Origins of the Pequot War," *The William and Mary Quarterly,* Third Series 49 (1992):509-21. Resisting current revisionist interpretations of the Pequot War, Cave first argues that it was indeed the Pequots, and not the West Niantics, who were responsible for the murder of Captain John Stone and his crew at the mouth of the Connecticut in 1634. He then uses this as a stepping-off point to further argue that the prosecution of the Pequot War itself was not a genocidal plot by the English against the Pequots. (Compare this article with that by Stephen Katz [*New England Quarterly* 64(1991):206-24], noticed earlier in this *Newsletter* [*GMN* 2(1991):31].)

Gwenn F. Epperson, "The True Identity of John Sales alias Jan Celes of Manhattan," *New York Genealogical and Biographical Record* 123 (1992):65-73. More than fifty years ago, George Andrews Moriarty proposed that the John Sayles who first appeared in Charlestown in 1630 was the same man who was later seen in Providence, Rhode Island. Epperson shows that the Charlestown man in fact went to New Netherland and died there in 1645, and that the Providence John Sales is another man entirely, not seen in New England records before 1645. The Charlestown and New Netherland man had lived in Little Waldingfield, Suffolk, in the late 1620s, before his immigration to New England.

Matthew Wood, "Jonas Wood 'Halifax,' of Huntington, Long Island," *New York Genealogical and Biographical Record* 123 (1992):79-82, 135-44. In the first installment of this article Wood discusses past work on the ancestry of Jonas Wood "Halifax" (to be distinguished from Jonas Wood "Oram"), of Halifax, Yorkshire, who had arrived at Watertown, Massachusetts, by 1635, and was later at Wethersfield, Connecticut, and at various towns on Long Island. He also adds information on the ancestry of this Jonas Wood which has not previously been in print, including brief accounts of the families of the immigrant's mother and maternal grandmother. In the second installment the author proceeds to discuss in great detail the career and the family of the immigrant; future installments will set forth the second and later generations of the family.

George Freeman Sanborn Jr. and Melinde Lutz Sanborn, *Vital Records of Hampton, New Hampshire, to the End of the Year 1900*, Volume One (Boston: New England Historic Genealogical Society 1992), pp. xii + 665, index. The authors have produced a meticulous, verbatim transcript of the vital records found in eleven volumes of Hampton town records, as well as vital events recorded in a variety of other places (such as census mortality schedules and Old Norfolk County records). The first book of town records contains a few entries from the 1630s and 1640s, but the bulk of the records do not begin until later in the seventeenth century. A second volume will include church and cemetery records.

Carlton A. Palmer, Jr., "The Palmer Families of New England, Revisited," *Mayflower Quarterly* 58 (1992):216-22. Palmer presents English baptisms which may pertain to Henry and John Palmer of Wethersfield, although proof is lacking. He then goes on to discuss the various William Palmers of Plymouth and sets forth a relationship which was disproven by Florence Barclay long ago. He claims that William Palmer Jr. married a daughter of Robert Paddock, when in fact Robert Paddock married the widow of William Palmer Sr., thus making William Jr. his stepson, and not son-in-law.

Great Migration Newsletter

Vol. 3   October-December 1992   No. 4

SAME NAME, SAME PERSON?

A common problem encountered by all genealogists, regardless of the time or place being researched, is deciding whether two records which include the same name apply to one person or to two. In the early stages of the Great Migration Study Project this problem arises very frequently in a specific form: a name appears in a record of, say, 1630, and then does not appear again for a decade or so, after which it is seen regularly. Aside from the general genealogical problem presented, this also determines who will make it into the early sketches of the Project, which apply only to people who had arrived by the end of 1633.

Several fairly simple examples of this sort of problem are seen in a single early record, the 28 September 1630 inquest into the death of Austen Bratcher "dying lately at Mr. Cradock's plantation" (*Records of ... Massachusetts Bay ...* 1:77-78). A jury of fifteen men (equivalent to a coroner's jury) was convened to "inquire concerning the death of Austen Bratcher." Fourteen of these men are attested in other records in 1630, and regularly in years thereafter. The fifteenth juror, however, William Bunell, presents a different pattern. There is no other record for him in 1630, whereas the other fourteen appear in the list of those asking to be made free on 19 October 1630, or the list of those admitted to freemanship on 18 May 1631, or both.

The next record for a man with the name of William Bunell is not until 7 October 1640, when the court "desires Watertown to grant Willi: Bunnell a lot, & if he do prove chargable, the country to bear it." There are no records in Watertown for this man, although a few further entries are found in the colony records. There is nothing in this sequence which demands that there were two different William Bunells, but there is equally nothing to demand that the man of the 1630 record was the same as the later man of the same name who begins to appear in 1640. (There was also a William *Burnell* of Boston, who is yet another man.)

A general principle guiding all decisions about inclusion in or exclusion from this first phase of the Great Migration Study Project is that we must have explicit grounds for stating that someone was here by the end of 1633. In this case we certainly have a record for a William Bunell in 1630, and so there will be an entry under this name. But we can not be certain that he is the same as the William Bunnell of 1640 or later. Certainty is not necessary, but here we do not even have circumstantial evidence which would connect the two records. The sketch for William Bunell will give the 1630 record, and then in a "Comment" section point out the later records, and the reason for not connecting them. We will never in such cases simply ignore such possible identifications. This has the merit of not including information that does not belong at this point; if newly-discovered evidence or better analysis proves that the 1630 and 1640 records apply to the same man, so much the better, and an appropriate emendation may be made at that time.

In addition to the jury of inquest, nine men were called as witnesses, because they had seen Austen Bratcher before he was buried. Three of these men were seen with some regularity in other records of 1630 and the years immediately following (William Barsham, Thomas Graves, Thomas Read) and do not present any great problem in this regard. Two are not seen again in any New England record and also are not difficult to deal with (James Crugott, Arthur Ellis). But the remaining four are similar to William Bunell in that about a decade passed before this name was seen again in New England (John Jarvis, Richard Linton, Thomas Painter, Thomas Ward). As with Bunell there is no evidence pointing strongly one way or another which would help answer the question of the identity of the man of the 1630 record with the later man of the same name. As a result, these four men will

(continued on page 26)

EDITOR'S EFFUSIONS

Research and writing has progressed to the point that the first book-form publication of the Great Migration Study Project is within sight. This will be a two-volume set, to be entitled *The Great Migration Begins: Immigrants to New England, 1620-1633*.

The bulk of the material in the set will be the sketches of families and individuals, a few examples of which have been published in past issues of the *Great Migration Newsletter*. There will be about nine hundred of these sketches, some of them a few lines long, and some three or four pages long, but most of them between one and two pages.

Ahead of the sketches, at the beginning of the first volume, will be an introductory essay, which will cover methods, sources, and some special topics. The methods sections will discuss the criteria for including a person or family in this set, and also for interpreting the evidence. The sources section will be organized by colony and then by town, and describe what records are available, and how they have been interpreted. The chapters on special topics will include such items as an annotated list of passenger ships from 1620 to 1633. The set will conclude with four indexes: by surname, by forename, by locality, and by ship (when known).

This publication is expected to be ready by the latter part of 1993, and pre-publication publicity will be circulated three or four months in advance of publication.

In the last issue of the *Newsletter* we promised that the Focus section would be on Wethersfield, but due to unforeseen difficulties Hartford has been substituted. Wethersfield will be covered sometime in 1993.

One of our subscribers, Danny D. Smith, has kindly pointed out an important addition to the bibliography on early Boston land records: Samuel C. Clough, "Remarks on the Compilation of the Boston Book of Possessions," *Publications of the Colonial Society of Massachusetts* 27 (1932):6-21.

Robert Charles Anderson, FASG   Editor
Margaret F. Costello   Production Assistant

The *Great Migration Newsletter* (ISSN 1049-8087) is published quarterly by the Great Migration Study Project, a project of the New England Historic Genealogical Society
101 Newbury Street, Boston MA 02116

The subscription rate is $8 for one year and $15 for two years. The subscription year is the same as the calendar year.

(*continued from page 25*)

be treated in the same way as William Bunell. (Of course if any reader has strong evidence which would help to resolve the status of any of these men, we would be glad to see it.)

A similar instance which arose a few years later is that of Thomas Brian, who appeared in Plymouth in 1633 as a servant of Samuel Eddy. The name is not found again in the records until 1642 when Thomas Briant, servant of Isaac Allerton, is brought before the Massachusetts Bay court. The connection back to Plymouth through Isaac Allerton is suggestive, but the gap of more than nine years between two records for a moderately common name should be reason for pause before saying that only one man is intended by these two records. Since there is no further record for a Thomas Brian or Briant, and since both records are mentioned in the sketch, the problem is slight.

Various mitigating factors do need to be taken into account, such as residence in a settlement with few records, and rarity of name. These two attributes combine in the case of Matthew Cannage, who is first seen as a fisherman at Richmond Island in Maine in 1633, and remained unrecorded for the next twenty years until he managed to get himself murdered under lurid circumstances in 1654, at that time a fishing master residing at Monhegan. Since the fishing communities Down East were very poorly documented, and since the name Matthew Cannage is quite unusual, we will treat these two records as applying to one individual.

A somewhat different example is that of "Morris Trowent" who was on 22 March 1630/1, along with two other men, presented at the Massachusetts Bay court and "whipped for stealing 3 pigs of Mr. Ralfe Glover's." On 16 October 1639 "Morris Truant" was married in Plymouth Colony, and thereafter appeared frequently in the records until his death in 1685. The three men who were punished in 1631 were apparently all young and single, and thus probably servants, so it is not surprising that "Morris Trowent" avoided being recorded for some years. This, combined with the unusual combination of forename and surname, leads to the conclusion that this is probably one man.

Finally, the case of Thomas Boreman of Plymouth provides a different version of the problem. In 1633 Thomas Boreman is taxed at Plymouth and later in the same year he appeared as a creditor in the estate of John Thorp of the same place. In this case there are several other records for a Thomas Boreman (or Bowman, or Boardman) in Plymouth in the late 1630s, but by 1643, at the time of the list of men able to bear arms, there were at least two men of this name in the colony, one in Barnstable and the other first in Sandwich and later in

(*continued on page 32*)

Focus on HARTFORD

SETTLEMENT OF HARTFORD

Cambridge was settled (as Newtown) in 1631, the Braintree Company arrived in 1632, and Thomas Hooker with more of his party came in 1633. But already by the winter of 1633-4 many of the inhabitants of the town wished to move elsewhere. At the General Court of 14 May 1634 leave was "granted to the inhabitants of Newe Towne to seek out some convenient place ...." They first looked to the north, along the Merrimack, but during the summer of 1634 an exploratory party was sent out to the Connecticut River, where a satisfactory site was located.

In late 1635 several families made the move from Massachusetts Bay, and began the building of the new settlement; in its first few years this location was considered part of Massachusetts Bay Colony, and was also called Newtown, a confusing state of affairs. (The situation was similar with the migrations from Dorchester and Watertown, the new settlements briefly retaining the old names, then being changed to Windsor and Wethersfield.)

Hooker and the majority of those associated with him remained in Massachusetts Bay for the winter of 1635-6, and then in the spring struck out for Connecticut. None of these settlers had lived in Cambridge for more than four years, and some for only one or two.

The only reason for the move explicitly stated was the alleged shortness and poor quality of the land, as set forth by John Pratt in a petition of 1635, which was interpreted by the General Court as nearly treasonous. But poor and insufficient land cannot have been the whole reason for wanting to remove, since the second wave of settlers at Cambridge managed well enough.

A more likely explanation for the move may be found in the mind of Thomas Hooker, the acknowledged leader of most of those who joined in the exodus. In the years just before 1636 the rapidly evolving New England church was erecting a new system of church admission, which involved a very detailed confession of faith, including a so-called "conversion narrative," an account of how one came to have saving grace.

Because admission to freemanship was dependent on church membership, the more difficult church membership requirements had the effect of erecting greater barriers to participation in politics and government. This was apparently disturbing to Hooker and others, since no such linkage or requirement was established in Connecticut.

FIRST CHURCH OF HARTFORD

In an earlier *Newsletter* we have already discussed the organization of the church at Cambridge, with the choice of Thomas Hooker as pastor and Samuel Stone as teacher on 11 October 1633, not long after their arrival (GMN 1:11). In a sense the church had existed for a year or more before its formal organization, since the so-called Braintree Company, the vanguard of Hooker and Stone, had arrived in 1632, clearly in the expectation that Hooker would soon come over.

Hooker and his church remained in Cambridge for less than three years. After the preparatory work done in 1635, Hooker and Stone left Cambridge in the spring of 1636 and made the move to their new home on the Connecticut River, which was briefly called Newtown before the name was changed to Hartford, presumably in honor of the birthplace of Samuel Stone.

With each of the migrations from Massachusetts Bay to Connecticut in 1635-6, the question arises of whether the church in Connecticut was newly founded after the move, or had a continuous existence with the church organized at Massachusetts Bay. With Dorchester we have seen that the church moved to Windsor, and a new church was formed at Dorchester in 1636 (GMN 1:29), and the situation was the same at Cambridge. In the first place, the depopulation of Cambridge was more complete than at any other town; Thomas Dudley may have been the only inhabitant of early 1635 who was still at Cambridge by the end of 1636. (The town was, however, quite crowded over the winter of 1635-6, for many who would buy the lots of those departing for Connecticut had arrived in 1635, and so co-existed in Cambridge with those who did not move to Hartford until 1636.)

The second reason for believing that the church founded at Cambridge in 1633 moved to Connecticut is the detailed description by Winthrop of the founding of a new church at Cambridge on 1 February 1635/6 by Thomas Shepard and those associated with him (*Winthrop's Journal* 1:214). Thus, for a few months in 1636 two churches existed simultaneously in Cambridge, a state of affairs which cannot have prevailed often, and almost never without a schism in a pre-existing church.

Little is known of the earliest years of the church at Hartford, because of the total loss of all church records prior to 1685. Some church matters, and various of Hooker's and Stone's church-related activities, are reflected in other records, such as Winthrop's letters and journal. There are, however, no lists of church admissions or baptisms, although a very few baptisms were for some reason included in the town's vital records, along with the births.

An era ended on 7 July 1647 when Thomas Hooker died. Samuel Stone carried on alone for thirteen years, and in 1660 was joined by John Whiting, a 1653 graduate of Harvard. A rift had developed in the Hartford church in the late 1650s, which led to the departure of a large part of the church and eventually the establishment of the town of Hadley in Massachusetts.

An excellent account of the careers of Thomas Hooker and Samuel Stone, and the history of the Hartford church from its beginnings in Cambridge, may be found in George Leon Walker's *History of the First Church in Hartford, 1633-1833* (Hartford 1884). Walker marshalls all the evidence available to him in 1884, and reports and interprets it with relatively little of the romanticism so common a century ago.

HARTFORD VITAL RECORDS

The vital records of Hartford before 1700 are scattered in three different places in the original records, and have been gathered and published in a variety of different forms. As a result, the researcher must examine a record carefully to be certain of the source, and of its validity.

Most genealogists first encounter the Hartford vital records, as they do most Connecticut vital records, in the Barbour collection. This set of records, organized early in this century by Lucius Barnes Barbour, exists in two different versions, a set of slips covering the entire state in one alphabetic sequence, and a set of typescript volumes arranged by town, and then alphabetically within each town.

The introduction to the Barbour volume for Hartford clearly states the original locations for the vital records. The actual Barbour "list was taken from a set of cards based on" these sources, but the "cards have not been compared with the original records and doubtless errors exist." The cards referred to here presumably constitute the slip index version of the Barbour index; even these were not taken directly from the original, but from a printed or manuscript copy.

The first of the three sources of seventeenth century vital records for Hartford may be found in a volume entitled "Original Distribution of the Lands in Hartford Among the Settlers, 1639." This book serves both as a book of proprietors' records for Hartford, inasmuch as it has entries for original grants from the town, but also as a

first volume of deeds, since many transactions of land between person and person prior to about 1675 are included in this volume as well. This "Book of Distribution" was first published in 1912 as Volume XIV of *Collections of the Connecticut Historical Society*, and was reissued in 1989 by Heritage Books. (We will examine the land record aspects of this volume one page hence.)

In the printed version of the "Book of Distribution," the vital records are found on pages 575 through 632, but in the original (we are told in the introduction to the published volume) these records are found on pages 1 through 33, reversed, at the end of the volume. These vital records had also been published in volumes 12 and 13 of the *New England Historical and Genealogical Register* (1858 and 1859), but with some errors which were corrected in the 1912 volume. Vital events as early as 1644 appear in this volume, and there are many entries well into the middle of the eighteenth century, so this volume was used for vital records long after it ceased to be used for land records. A microfilmed version of this volume may be seen at Hartford and Salt Lake City, but this is a nineteenth century copy; recent efforts to locate the original volume at the Connecticut State Library were unsuccessful, and it was suggested that the original, if it still exists, might be found with the Hartford City Clerk, or perhaps at the Connecticut Historical Society.

The second source which was used for the Barbour collection was *Births, Marriages and Deaths Returned from Hartford, Windsor and Fairfield and Entered in the Early Land Records of the Colony of Connecticut*, edited by Edwin Stanley Welles and published in 1898. Of the fifty-eight pages of records published in this slim volume, one page is from Fairfield and two from Hartford; the remaining fifty-five pages are vital records of Windsor. The thirty-one Hartford vital events in this volume were all recorded on a single page of Volume II of the colony land records, and are mostly from the early 1650s (pages 30-32 of the published records).

Of the thirty-one Hartford records published by Welles, twenty-nine are also found in the "Book of Distribution," although there are some discrepancies in dates between a few of the records. The only two records unique to this second source are the births of two children of William Andrews, Thomas in 1638 and Esther in 1641. This should not be surprising, since William Andrews was the clerk who maintained Volume II of the colony land records, and he took the opportunity to record retrospectively the earliest of his children to be born in Hartford; but since he was also Hartford town clerk during the 1650s, one wonders why he did not record these births in the "Book of Distribution" as well.

The last of the three sources exploited for the Barbour collection was "a copy of the Vital Records found in the Land Records and made by Mr. Frank Farnsworth Starr," which include copies of the two previous sources, as well as vital records found in the Hartford town deed books. Pages 39 through 56 of the Starr manuscript include the records from Volume One of the Hartford land records, beginning in the 1670s, when this volume was begun for land transaction purposes, and covering the rest of the seventeenth century.

To summarize what we have learned so far, the only source for Hartford vital records prior to about 1675 (except for the two Andrews births noted above) is the "Book of Distribution," the original of which seems to have sunk from sight. Nearly all of the records in the Welles volume, the colony copy, are duplicates of entries in the "Book of Distribution." (Since William Andrews apparently prepared a copy of the town records for a few years for submission to the colony, the "Book of Distribution" should be considered more reliable in those few cases where there are differences. This is the reverse of the guideline to be used for Windsor at this same time [TAG 61 (1985-86):95-96].)

A few additional remarks need to be made about the use of these records, and the relative validity of the various versions available. We have already seen that the vital records from the "Book of Distribution" as published in the *Register* in 1858 and 1859 were corrected, and therefore superseded, by the 1912 publication of the Connecticut Historical Society. Thus, the latter version should be preferred to the former.

In the Barbour version of the vital records, however, are found two different versions of the vital events from the "Book of Distribution." Thus, there are identical entries for the birth of Margrett Allyn, daughter of John Allyn, on 29 July 1660, with the citations "D:10" and "FFS:6." The first of these refers to the original page 10 of the "Book of Distribution," but is actually taken from the Barbour slip, which is in turn taken from the 1912 published version of the record. The second citation refers to the Frank Farnsworth Starr manuscript; the entry in the Barbour Hartford volume was taken from the Barbour slip, which in turn was taken from the Starr manuscript. Did Starr take his entries directly from the original volume, or did he also copy from the printed version? If the latter, then the "FFS" cited entries from the Barbour volume are three steps removed from the original. At best, all entries in the Barbour volume are two steps removed from the original, with all the potential for error which that entails.

At present (unless Starr worked from the original) our best source for these earliest Hartford vital records is the microfilm copy of the nineteenth century handwritten copy of the "Book of Distribution," the closest we now have to the original. Those interested in early Hartford should undertake a search for the original "Book of Distribution," and see that a microform copy is made.

EARLY HARTFORD LANDHOLDING

With limited exceptions, governmental records do not exist in Connecticut prior to 1639, whether at the town or colony level. The records of the Connecticut General Court do commence in 1636, but the Particular Court records (the Connecticut equivalent of Massachusetts Bay's quarter courts) begin in the summer of 1639, the book of Hartford "Town Votes" on 1 January 1638/9, and the "Original Distribution of the Lands in Hartford Among the Settlers" (which we will call here the "Book of Distribution") in February 1639/40.

Our knowledge of land granting and landholding in Hartford comes principally from the "Town Votes" (published as Volume VI of the *Collections of the Connecticut Historical Society* [Hartford 1897]) and the "Book of Distribution," and disproportionately from the latter. The volume of "Town Votes," really the minutes of the town meetings, actually begins with a brief document purportedly dated in 1635, but probably actually somewhat later. The regular series of meeting records begins in January 1638/9 and covers the usual gamut of town affairs, but with many orders about land granting and the conditions of holding the land.

On pages sixteen through twenty, undated but immediately after a meeting of 14 January 1639/40, are two lists. The first is "The names of [such inhabitants as have] Right in u[ndivided Lands]"; these would be the proprietors of Hartford. The second and shorter list comprises "The Names of such Inhabitants as were Granted lots, to have only at the Town's courtesy with liberty to fetch wood & keep swine or cows by proportion on the common"; these were probably late arrivals, or servants recently freed from servitude, or persons similarly disadvantaged.

The "Book of Distribution" was organized around this list of proprietors, although not in the same order. The clerk who set up the book apparently allocated one, two or four pages to each individual, probably based on the expected number of grants for a person of given wealth and social standing. For example, the listing of grants for William Goodwin begins on original page 19, and covers also pages 20, 21 and 22; then on original pages 23 through 26 are found grants to William Westwood, followed by Thomas Root on pages 27 and 28.

In his introduction to the published volume Albert C. Bates, the editor, discusses in detail the various town clerks of Hartford in the seventeenth century, and their dates of service. In the body of the transcribed text, Bates carefully annotated each entry to show which hand was used to write which individual grants, clearly indicating that the granting process was spread out over a number of years. Bates was unable to match the handwriting of the first two recorders with any of the known town clerks. (This is yet another reason for mounting a search for the original!)

Bates says of the first recorder that "[a]ll of the parcels of land recorded to Benjamin Munn, and the first part or earliest of those recorded to thirteen other owners, all entered on the early pages of the book, are written with blue ink in one distinctive handwriting, and are without question the earliest entries made in the volume." This does allow at least a suggestion of the identity of the first recorder. Wiiliam Spencer had been the town clerk at Cambridge for most of the 1630s, and certainly wrote with a distinctive hand. He moved to Hartford in 1639, and died there early in 1640, his nuncupative will being dated variously 4 March or 4 May of that year. His death at this date would explain the small number of records entered by the first recorder, and the need to bring in a second recorder so soon. Again, discovery of the original of the "Book of Distribution" would allow this suggestion to be confirmed or rejected, since the originals of the Cambridge records are available for comparison.

Returning to the grants themselves, a few sample holdings have been examined, ignoring for the most part the wealthier members of the community, and looking only at the grants recorded by the first and second recorders. This second condition ensures that we are only looking at the earliest grants, certainly all in the early 1640s, and perhaps all granted by the time of the first entries in February 1639/40, since the second recorder had to finish the work of the first.

THOMAS ROOT had five parcels granted in this early period, beginning with a houselot of two roods. He also was given four acres on the east side of the Great (i.e., Connecticut) River, one acre and two roods in the pine field, two acres in the west field, and one rood in soldier's field (original page 27).

JOHN MAINARD had nine pieces of land entered by the second recorder, the first of which was a two acre houselot. He also received one acre and eight perches on the east side of the Great River, one rood and two perches in the little meadow, two roods and twentyfive perches in the north meadow, six acres and thirtyeight perches of meadow and swamp in the north meadow, three acres and eleven perches in the cow pasture, six acres in the ox pasture, one acre and thirtythree perches in the neck of land, and another one acre, two roods and twentyone perches in the neck of land (original page 35).

RICHARD WEBB was also granted nine parcels during this period, and his houselot was the same size as John Mainard's. His remaining eight parcels were in much the same location as Mainard's, but a little larger. For example his holding on the east side of the Great River was two acres and sixteen perches, and his second holding in the north meadow, of meadow and swamp,

was fifteen acres, two roods and fifteen perches (original page 43).

NICHOLAS CLARK had by this same time received thirteen parcels and, like Webb and Mainard, his houselot was two acres. The remaining lots, however, were generally smaller than those of Mainard. His grant on the east side of the Great River was only two roods and four perches, and his allotment of meadow and swamp in the north meadow was three acres, one rood and seven perches (original page 46). (Nicholas Clark was known to have been one of the settlers of 1635, for he had been hired to build a house for John Talcott in advance of the latter's arrival in 1636.)

This brief survey of a few holdings already begins to show some patterns. Except for the very wealthy, the houselot was small and of uniform size, usually two acres, and for some only two roods. In most Massachusetts Bay towns there was a wider range of lot sizes, and all lots were generally larger, sometimes six and even ten acres.

Moving beyond the houselot, we see that just about everybody received a lot on the east side of the Great River. Then, depending on the total number of lots received, there were frequently holdings of two different sizes in the north meadow, and further parcels scattered around in other pastures and meadows.

On a broader scale three additional features are notable. First, all lot sizes were relatively small, with few outside of the elite receiving any lots greater than ten acres. Second, there were no large grants of plowland, upland or timberland; virtually everything in these earliest grants, aside from the houselot, was marsh, swamp, meadow, or pasture, all of which were oriented toward the raising of livestock.

The third notable feature flows from these: even several years after the settlement of the town, the proprietors of Hartford had distributed a relatively small proportion of the total acreage of the town. This is very much the pattern that we saw earlier in our study of landholding in Cambridge (GMN 1:13), and is unlike the Watertown pattern, in which most of the land had been given away in the first decade or so.

The distinction between Watertown and Cambridge demonstrated that two communities that were both largely of East Anglian origin could generate quite different patterns of granting land. We now learn, not surprisingly, that when Hooker and his adherents made the move from Massachusetts Bay to Connecticut, they carried along with them the same system of laying out land that they had already used. This stingy granting of land belies John Pratt's complaint about the shortness of land in Cambridge.

RECENT LITERATURE

Penny G. Douglass, "The English Origin of Robert[1] Blott of Charlestown and Boston, Mass.," *The American Genealogist* 67 (1992):65-67. Douglass presents records showing that Robert Blott married Susanna Selbee in 1609 at Harrold, Bedfordshire, where he had six children baptized. About 1621 he and his family moved to the adjoining parish of Puddington in Bedfordshire, where he had four more children before sailing for New England. This article brings us closer to understanding some of the ambiguities in the will of Robert Blott.

Robert Charles Anderson, "John Black of Charlestown Was Really Robert Blott," *The American Genealogist* 67 (1992):67-68. The author argues that all records for a John Black in the earliest years at Charlestown were scribal errors, and were intended for Robert Blott.

Pamelia Schwannecke Olson, "Two Priscillas and Three John Kirtlands of Saybrook, Conn., and Their Cousin Priscilla Kirtland of Lynn, Mass.," *The American Genealogist* 67 (1992):69-73. Olson surveys the first three generations of the descendants of Philip[1] Kirtland of Sherington, Buckinghamshire, and Lynn, Massachusetts, in order to sort out several persons of the same name.

Ruth Wilder Sherman, "A Chandler Note," *The American Genealogist* 67 (1992):96. Adds "one more reference to the daughters of Roger Chandler of Plymouth," a deed of 1692, supplementing an earlier article (TAG 27:1-6).

George Ely Russell, "John[1] and Jane Barcroft of Boston, Mass., and Virginia," *The American Genealogist* 67 (1992):112-13. Russell tracks John and Jane Barcroft (who were never Bancrofts of any kind) from Massachusetts Bay, where they resided in 1632 and 1633, to Virginia, where he died by 1636 without issue.

Dean Crawford Smith, "The English Origin of the Kempton Brothers of Plymouth Colony," *The American Genealogist* 67 (1992):132-35. Smith has discovered that the brothers Manasseh and Ephraim Kempton, early immigrants to Plymouth, were baptized at Berwick-upon-Tweed, Northumberland, and that both lived in London before removal to New England. Entries from the Merchant Taylors' School relating to the sons of Ephraim Kempton provide additional biographical interest.

Eleanor Cooley Rue, "Susanna Cooke, Wife of John Jenkins of Sandwich, Mass.," *The American Genealogist* 67 (1992):135. Entries from the records of the First Church of Boston identify the wife of John Jenkins as Susanna Cooke, servant of Atherton Hough.

Douglas Richardson, "The English Origin of Thomas[1] Gilbert of Braintree, Mass., and Wethersfield, Conn.: With a Note on Lydia Gilbert, Executed for Witchcraft in 1654," *The American Genealogist* 67 (1992):161-66. Richardson demonstrates that the immigrant Thomas Gilbert was from Yardley, Worcestershire, and argues that the Lydia Gilbert executed for witchcraft in 1654 was the second wife of Thomas, eldest son of the immigrant.

E. Brooks Holifield, "Peace, Conflict, and Ritual in Puritan Congregations," *Journal of Interdisciplinary History* 23 (1992):551-70. The current issue of this journal is devoted to the topic of "History and Religion: Interpretation and Illumination," and two of the articles impinge on the Great Migration. Holifield investigates the role of ritual in Puritan congregations in colonial New England. He notes that a major element in the Puritan view was a rejection of ritual as it existed in the established church in England early in the seventeenth century. But while the Puritan migrants to New England successfully shed these unwanted rituals, they inevitably took on newer, simpler rituals, appropriate to their goals of establishing harmony, and integrating the church with civil society. These rituals also led inevitably to conflict, and included ritualized ways of dealing with conflict.

Marilyn J. Westerkamp, "Puritan Patriarchy and the Problem of Revelation," *Journal of Interdisciplinary History* 23 (1992):571-95. Westerkamp uses the relatively new interpretive framework of "gender analysis" to examine the conflict between direct revelation from God (as experienced by women) and the religious and societal constraints of Puritan patriarchy. Among the specific examples investigated are the familiar cases of Anne Hutchinson and Mary Dyer, and the less-familiar church trial of Anne Hibbens in Boston in 1640.

Linda L. Mathew, "John Tefft and His Children: A Colonial Generation Gap?" *Rhode Island Roots* 18 (1992):76-80. William Tefft was in Boston by 1638, and his brother John was certainly in New England by 1646. Mathew describes the unorthodox lives of the children of John Tefft, and the estrangement between father and children; she then suggests some possible reasons for this state of affairs.

John B. Carney and Gale Ion Harris, "Thrice-Widowed Hannah Paine of Boston: The Widow Eliot, Fayerweather and Clark," *New England Historical and Genealogical Register* 146 (1992):377-82. The authors show that Hannah Paine, born at Boston 31 March 1662, daughter of John and Sarah (Parker) Paine, married successively Asaph Eliot (about 1682), Thomas Fayerweather (about 1689), and Samuel Clark (in 1698).

(continued from page 26)
Yarmouth. Which (if either) of these two men was the one who had arrived in Plymouth by 1633?

The records are, unfortunately, ambiguous in this matter. The early arrival was apparently a carpenter, as evidenced by a 1635 contract to work on the fort at Plymouth. The Yarmouth Thomas, usually spelled Boardman, was certainly a carpenter, but there is some evidence in the court records of 1638 that he had arrived from London very recently, perhaps in 1637 or 1638. On the other hand the Barnstable Thomas, usually spelled Boreman, was said by Otis to be a carpenter, but this has not yet been verified from contemporary sources. At the moment the allocation of the early records to either of the later men seems unresolvable.

There are dozens of examples of problems such as this among the 900 sketches now in preparation. Each one is approached on its own merits, but with a consistent set of standards, and in the larger context of all other similar cases. Sometimes the result is a brief essay which presents the single early record and the reasons for not including the later material, thought to be for a different man; and sometimes the result is a longer sketch with all relevant records, in which the decision has been that the records all apply to a single person. Whatever the final outcome, every potential connection of this sort receives some comment.

NEW BOOKS

Three new books have come to our attention which relate to the Great Migration, and may be of interest to our readers. Brief notices of these publications are given here; more detailed reports will appear in the future.

John Frederick Martin's *Profits in the Wilderness: Entrepreneurship and the Founding of New England Towns in the Seventeenth Century* (Chapel Hill NC 1991) is the most detailed discussion of the founding of new towns, and more particularly of the much-neglected topic of proprietorial systems, that we have ever had.

Jacob Price's *Perry of London: A Family and a Firm on the Seaborne Frontier, 1615-1753* (Cambridge 1992) tells the story of a prominent merchant family which had branches in London and in most of the English colonies on the Atlantic seacoast and in the Caribbean. The central figure in the story, Micajah Perry, was born at New Haven in 1641, his father Richard Perry having been one of the earliest settlers of that town.

David Underdown's *Fire From Heaven: Life in an English Town in the Seventeenth Century* (New Haven 1992) is a narrative history of Dorchester in Dorsetshire in the 1600s. Prominent in that history was the Puritan minister John White, the organizer of the voyage of the *Mary & John* in 1630.

Great Migration Newsletter

Vol. 4   January-March 1993   No. 1

EVEN IN THE BEST OF FAMILIES ...

One of the principal goals of the Great Migration Study Project has been to examine every date of birth, baptism, marriage, death and burial, with two questions in mind: Is the date accurate, and what is the primary source that supports that date? In the course of our work on the nine hundred families and individuals in New England by 1633, thousands of dates have been checked, and hundreds of errors and discrepancies have been found.

One might expect that problems with dates would be common among the less prominent families, but that when we come to examine the leading families, such as Winthrop, or Dudley, or Bradford, or Brewster, all would be in order. But this is not the case. Recently, in the preliminary work on the family of John Winthrop, a surprising number of errors, omissions, and discrepancies have been found. We will discuss here several of these chronological problems in the Winthrop family, not just for their intrinsic interest to Winthrop descendants, but as typical examples of the difficulties encountered with families at all social levels.

John Winthrop was born at Edwardstone, Suffolk, on 12 January 1587/8, son of Adam Winthrop, and married at Great Stambridge, Essex, on 16 April 1605 Mary Forth, daughter of John Forth. (The definitive genealogy of John Winthrop and his descendants is *The Winthrop Family in America* by Lawrence Shaw Mayo [Boston 1958], cited hereafter as *Mayo*. Much of our knowledge of the vital events for this family in England, aside from parish register entries, may be found in the various diaries of Adam Winthrop, father of the governor [*Winthrop Papers*, Volume One (Boston 1923)], cited hereafter as *WP* 1.)

The first two children of John and Mary (Forth) Winthrop, sons John and Henry, were born and baptized at Groton, Suffolk, in 1606 and 1608 (*Mayo* 32; *WP* 1:6, 159). The next two children are known to be son Forth and daughter Mary, but their baptisms are not found in the Groton register. On 10 October 1608 Adam Winthrop noted that "my soonne and his wyfe departed from Groton to dwell at Stambridge in Essex," and the editor informs us that this must be John and Mary (*WP*

1:94). Adam Winthrop entered in his diary under date of 30 December 1609 the news that "my sonnes third sonne [Forth] was borne at Stambridge in Essex" (*WP* 1:94), but he did not memorialize the birth of John's daughter Mary, which must have taken place about two years later.

John Winthrop and his wife may have moved to Great Stambridge in Essex partly to be near her family, but they were also able to benefit from the ministry of Ezekiel Culverwell, one of the leading Puritan ministers of the time and a man who would have a vast influence on John Winthrop's spiritual development. The Great Stambridge register survives for this period, and in it we find the baptisms of Forth, son of John Winthrop, on 10 January 1609/10, and Mary, daughter of John Winthrop, on 19 February 1611/2. Remarkably, these baptisms, whose location is so clearly pointed to by Adam Winthrop, do not appear in *Mayo*, or in any other published account of the Winthrop family so far encountered (although these entries are seen in the Great Stambridge register by many American tourists visiting this early Winthrop residence).

Not long after the birth and baptism of their daughter Mary, John Winthrop and his wife moved back to Groton (perhaps because Ezekiel Culverwell had in 1610 been silenced and removed from his ministerial post). The couple's fifth child was Anne, born, according to Adam Winthrop, at Groton on 3 August 1614, and died there on 17 August of the same year, aged fourteen days (*WP* 1:160). But Mayo tells us that she was born on the eighth of August, and buried on the twenty-sixth (*Mayo* 32). How can these dates be reconciled?

(continued on page 2)

EDITOR'S EFFUSIONS

The lead article in this issue examines a number of problems of chronology encountered in one family of the Great Migration, the family of John Winthrop, Governor of Massachusetts Bay. The reader might well wonder whether all this effort expended on seemingly minor details is justified. What difference does it make that William Winthrop, who died soon and left no descendants, was born on 20 August 1632 and not 14 August? Why should we care that 4 December 1647 could not be the marriage date for John Winthrop and the widow Martha Coytmore, when we know that they must have been married just a few weeks later?

Chronological analysis is one of the most powerful tools in the genealogist's kit. If two supposed siblings are recorded as born less than nine months apart, then we might suspect that one of the records is defective, or that we are dealing with two families and not one. If a marriage record is found for a man we are interested in, and the record appears to be reliable, and if three of his children were born before this date, then we suspect the existence of an earlier wife.

Because of the important consequences that may derive from the close analysis of dates, we must subject every family we study to this process. In many cases we will do no more than adjust a date by a few days. But in other instances our chronological investigations will lead to genealogically significant rearrangements. We may learn that a given child had a different mother than had been thought, or, as suggested above, that we have in hand records for two families rather than one.

Our presentation of the incorrect dates in the Winthrop family, then, has more than one lesson. First, we learn that even the most thoroughly studied families must be looked at again from time to time. Second, when multiplied by the hundreds of other families to be treated by the Great Migration Study Project, the four examples examined here provide some feel for the procedure used in preparing the sketches of these families for publication.

Robert Charles Anderson, FASG   Editor
Margaret F. Costello   Production Assistant

The *Great Migration Newsletter* (ISSN 1049-8087) is published quarterly by the Great Migration Study Project, a project of the New England Historic Genealogical Society
101 Newbury Street, Boston MA 02116

The subscription rate is $8 for one year and $15 for two years. The subscription year is the same as the calendar year.

(*continued from page 1*)

Examination of the original register of Groton, held at the West Suffolk Record Office at Bury St. Edmunds, showed that "Anna Winthrop daughter of John Winthrop Esq." was baptized 8 August 1614, and buried on 16 August immediately following. In the first instance, Mayo has mistakenly labelled the baptismal date as a birth date, but what about the burial? It might seem that he simply misread or mistranscribed the date, turning 16 into 26. But when we look a little deeper it would appear that Mayo did not examine the Groton register himself. In 1843 James Savage published in the Collections of the Massachusetts Historical Society extracts from the Groton register, provided to him by one Richard Almack, Esquire. In this version Anne's burial is given as 26 August, and it would appear from this and other examples that Mayo was relying on this transcript rather than the original in compiling the Winthrop genealogy.

We are left still with one discrepancy for this child. Adam Winthrop says she died on 17 August 1614, but the parish register claims she was buried on 16 August, the day before! One would think that Adam Winthrop, who was making entries in his 1614 almanac, would be the better authority, and that is the position that we will take; but there is very little to go by in making a decision here, and either date might be correct.

After having another short-lived daughter named Anne, Mary (Forth) Winthrop died, and John Winthrop married for the second time to Thomasine Clopton. This marriage lasted for only one year and two days, and after the death of Thomasine, Winthrop married for the third time to Margaret Tyndal, a marriage that would last for nearly three decades. When Winthrop sailed for New England in the spring of 1630, Margaret remained in Groton, and came to Boston in early November 1631.

Not quite ten months later, "Willyam the sonne of our brother John Winthrope Governor" was baptized at Boston on 26 August 1632. In his journal John Winthrop, at the end of a long list of events seemingly dated 14 August 1632, tells us that "The governor's wife was delivered of a son, who was baptized by the name of William." There is nothing surprising about this apparent twelve day gap between birth and baptism, for in the young colony the requirement to bring a child in for baptism on the next Sunday was soon relaxed.

Surprisingly, though, inspection of the original of Winthrop's journal (for another entry on the same page) revealed that Savage, usually a meticulously accurate transcriber, had omitted the day of the month for this entry. Thus, the correct reading is that William Winthrop was born on 20 August 1632, this record being the only item recorded by his father under that date. Even more surprisingly, Savage must have missed this date twice,

(*continued on page 8*)

Focus   *on*   *DEDHAM*

SETTLEMENT OF DEDHAM

With the increased rate of migration from England in 1634 and the years immediately after, the towns settled in 1630, at the coming of the Winthrop fleet, were becoming very overcrowded. By late 1635 the migrations from Massachusetts Bay to the Connecticut River Valley were under way, including the departure of many Watertown families for the settlement that would become Wethersfield. At about this same time Watertown, "in consideration there be too many inhabitants in the town & the town thereby in danger to be ruinated," ordered that no "foreigner coming into town" (i.e., no new settler) could share in the remaining undivided land.

Some of the new immigrants to Watertown in 1634, 1635 and 1636 were able to buy the commonage (or proprietorial) rights of those who were leaving for Wethersfield, but this still left many families who had no prospect of benefitting from future land divisions. A few of these families petitioned the General Court, and in 1636 were granted the large tract of land, running southwest from the Charles River nearly to the new settlement of Providence, that would become Dedham.

The recorded history of Dedham began when eighteen men gathered in Watertown on 18 August 1636 to hold a town meeting (Don Gleason Hill, *The Early Records of the Town of Dedham, Massachusetts. 1636-1659* [Dedham 1892], hereafter TR, 20). During the fall of 1636, and the winter of 1636-7, most of those intending to settle Dedham remained in Watertown, and seven more meetings were held there, the last being on 21 February 1636/7. A few men began to improve their Dedham lots during that first winter, and some may have resided there, but the settlement of Dedham did not begin in earnest until the spring of 1637.

Sometime during the winter of 1636-7 those attending the town meetings drafted and signed a town covenant, one of the earliest to survive in New England (TR 2-3). Appended to this document are 125 "names subscribed to the Covenant." In the past, many researchers have assumed that all these men signed the covenant at one sitting, in 1636. This was, however, a living document, and persons newly admitted to the town continued to sign for more than a decade. (More will be said on this point in our discussion of landholding.) In addition, several persons whose names appear on this list, and in the records of the first eight meetings, never settled in Dedham. Men such as Robert Feake and John Coolidge were willing to attend the meetings held in Watertown, and accept grants of land, but when it came time to actually make the commitment to leave Watertown, these and a few others did not move, and eventually relinquished their claims on Dedham land.

As Samuel Morse, John Gay, and other former Watertown residents were clearing land and erecting house frames in the spring of 1637, more new immigrants from England were arriving and moving directly to Dedham. Among these the most important was Reverend John Allin, who had been minister of Saxlingham-juxta-Mare in Norfolk for twelve years, but who had earlier connections along the Norfolk-Suffolk border. With him came several other families, including Eleazer Lusher, Robert Hinsdale, and various members of the Fisher family. These 1637 immigrants, and others to follow in 1638, soon changed the face of Dedham.

Within a very short time meetings were being held, organized and recorded by John Allin, looking toward the formation of a church in Dedham. Those in attendance expended much time and effort in choosing those who would be the "pillars," or founding members, of the church at Dedham. After much wrangling, it developed that almost all those so chosen were among the 1637 immigrants, or were later arrivals, such as John Hunting, who came in 1638. Of those who had attended meetings in Watertown during late 1636 and 1637, and had done the earliest work in settling Dedham, only Edward Alleyn was deemed fit to join with seven other later arrivals in organizing the church.

Although there is little direct evidence of dissension resulting from this development, the emigration from Dedham of several families in the next few years indicates that many were not pleased with this one-sided choice of the founders of the church. Ralph Shephard, Nicholas Phillips, John Rogers and the children of Abraham Shaw (who had died in 1638) had by 1641 moved to Weymouth. Philemon Dalton, his brother Timothy Dalton, Frances Austen and others had during the same period joined in the settlement of Hampton, New Hampshire.

As a result of all this movement, the immigrants of 1637 and 1638 soon attained a dominant position in civil as well as ecclesiastical affairs. The early Dedham settlers who had resided briefly in Watertown dwindled away to a small minority in the population. Those who had drafted and signed the town's civil covenant had little to do with the drafting and signing of the church covenant, and did not retain much power in the running of Dedham after 1640.

(In addition to copious surviving original records, Dedham has been blessed by the attention of many able historians. Kenneth Lockridge, in the heyday of the "new social history," prepared an interpretation of Dedham as a "closed, corporate, utopian commune" [*A New England Town: The First Hundred Years* (New York 1970)]; his presentation does not take into account this turmoil of the first five years or so of Dedham's history. A few years later Robert B. Hanson published a narrative history of Dedham down to the end of the nineteenth century, which supersedes the earlier histories of the town [*Dedham, Massachusetts: 1635-1890* (Dedham 1976)].)

DEDHAM CHURCH RECORDS

Prior to his arrival in New England, John Allin was rector of the parish of Saxlingham-juxta-mare, in north-central Norfolk, from early 1625 until early 1637. During this period of about twelve years he maintained, in his own hand, the register for that parish, in the standard manner, giving the bare particulars of baptisms, marriages and burials.

At Dedham he was minister for more than thirty years - from the organization of the church in 1639 until his death on 26 August 1671. Here also he maintained the church records, but with many differences from what he had done in England. (Don Gleason Hill, ed., *The Record of Baptisms, Marriages and Deaths... in the Town of Dedham, Massachusetts. 1638-1845* [Dedham 1888], hereafter CR, in which the records kept by Allin are printed in the first thirty-nine pages. There is then a gap in the records of the First Church at Dedham from 1671 to 1724, during the ministries of William Adams and Joseph Belcher. Robert Brand Hanson has partially filled this gap by publishing *The Deacon's Book: Records of the First Church, Dedham, Massachusetts, 1677-1737* [Bowie MD], which comprises for the most part the records of the financial affairs of the church.)

The one strand of continuity was in the recording of baptisms, carried out just as assiduously in the New World as in the Old. But there were very few burials or deaths noted, and these mostly at the end of the records. And there were, of course, no records of marriage kept by the minister, since the Puritans in New England conceived of marriage as a civil ceremony, and not one of the sacraments to be dispensed by the church.

John Allin included in his Dedham church records also the records of admission to church membership, along with dismissions to other churches as his members moved from town to town. There are also interpolated notes which provide additional information, such as the dates upon which some members of his congregation returned to England. For instance, on 20 July 1641 Ferdinando Adams applied for permission to return to England with the approbation of the church, and after considerable discussion this was granted. Allin then notes that Adams departed on 3 August 1641, which allows us to conclude that Adams sailed in the same ship with a number of the colony's luminaries who were returning to New England to participate in the Civil War on the Parliamentary side, as Winthrop tells us that John Winthrop Jr., Hugh Peter and Thomas Weld also departed on this day (*Winthrop's Journal* 2:37-38), and we have independent information that Thomas Lechford was on this ship as well.

As another example, Allin relates in detail the many comings and goings of Joshua Kent, who had been admitted to Dedham church in November 1644 (CR 28). Kent returned to England "with our testimonial" in January 1644[/5?], but was back in New England later in 1645, bringing with him two brothers. Joshua and his wife again sailed for England, in December 1647, "his reasons not well satisfying his friends or church here," but by October 1648 he had come back to Dedham "upon the troubles arising again in England & wars there" (CR 37). One wonders what he was trying to accomplish in these years, but after 1648 he remained in Dedham, where he died in 1664.

What makes this record truly distinctive is the long and detailed account in the first few pages of the complicated proceedings by which the founding members of the church were chosen. Nothing else like this survives from these early years in New England. Much of what is known about the procedure for organizing a New England church derives from John Allin's account.

We see here in excruciating detail the extreme lengths to which the congregation went in examining a potential church member, especially in this period so soon after the requirement of a conversion relation had been imposed as a part of the admission process. Joseph Kingsbury "remaining stiff & unhumbled & not clearing himself to satisfaction" was put off "to the judgment of the church when it should be gathered" (CR 7); three years later, "after diverse meetings in private & some experience of his spirit the church was so well persuaded of his repentance & faith as that he was received into the fellowship of the church" on 9 April 1641 (CR 24-25).

Third parties, even those not members of the church, were encouraged to raise objections against a potential pillar of the church. Edward Alleyn, in his long struggle to be accepted, had to respond to accusations made against him by "Mr. Daulton" (probably Rev. Timothy Dalton, but perhaps his brother Philemon) and "Francis Astye" (Austen) concerning "some offenses & distaste that had been" between them. Alleyn also had to suffer the indignity of waiting for persons to arrive from England who could speak in his behalf (CR 6, 8).

Since the ink and the handwriting in the original of this record are very consistent, despite the passage of more than thirty years from the earliest record to the last, the conclusion must be that Allin composed this record late in his life. This supposition is supported by the inclusion of many items out of chronological sequence, indicating that he was working from various notes which he had taken at an earlier date.

Where the dates can be checked, mostly by comparison of baptisms with the town records of birth, they are highly reliable. The same can not be said for John Allin's treatment of names. Francis Austen becomes Francis Astye, Mr. [Richard] Mather becomes Mr. Madden, and Edward Kemp becomes Robert Kemp (CR 8, 12, 14).

One other example of John Allin's problem with names indicates that the difficulty may have had a psychological component more profound than simple sloppiness. In the process of selecting the pillars of the church, early in 1638, Allin reported on Thomas Morse, who was deemed to be "so dark & unsatisfying in respect of the work of grace" that he could not be admitted at that point (CR 6). A short time later Thomas Morse was considered again, but was "left to the further trial of the church gathered" (CR 7). Finally, on 28 June 1640, more than a year after the church was organized, the congregation relented and Thomas Morse was admitted (CR 23). But there was no Thomas Morse.

On 8 October 1640 Samuel Morse was made a freeman of Massachusetts Bay. This was a little more than three months after the admission of "Thomas Morse" to Dedham church, but there was no record of the admission of Samuel Morse, and the church status of his sons is otherwise accounted for. Furthermore, on 24 December 1641 John Allin recorded the admission of "the wife of our brother Samuel Morse" (CR 26), implying that Samuel was a church member by that date. In other words, during the period of conflict, when Morse was being rejected as a church member, Allin referred to him as Thomas, but once the conflict was resolved and Morse was admitted, he was correctly called Samuel!

One possible explanation for this is that Samuel Morse was the son of a Reverend Thomas Morse, minister at Foxearth, Suffolk. But there is a more intriguing possibility. John Allin had married at Wrentham, Suffolk, in 1622 Margaret Morse, and it is likely that she was daughter of another Thomas Morse, who resided at Wrentham. Did the conflict with Samuel Morse at Dedham in 1638 and 1639 somehow recall an earlier conflict with his father-in-law?

Be that as it may, the church records of John Allin are among the most useful produced in early New England, from both the genealogical and the historical perspectives.

DEDHAM VITAL RECORDS

As with other types of records (church and town), Dedham is well endowed with surviving vital records, which were published by the town late in the last century (Don Gleason Hill, ed., *The Record of Births, Marriages and Deaths... in the Town of Dedham... 1635-1845* [Dedham 1886]). Unlike some of his colleagues, the earliest clerk did not limit himself to births and deaths, as apparently required by the colony. In consequence, the marriage records for Dedham begin in 1638.

Robert Brand Hanson, having used the Dedham records extensively in his detailed study of that town, had recognized the need for a new edition of this material, based on the detection of a number of errors and omissions in the Hill edition. As a result, he prepared a three-volume set, presenting in a new form the records of vital events from town, church and some private sources (Robert Brand Hanson, ed., *The Vital Records of Dedham, Massachusetts*, three volumes [Bowie MD 1989]). (While this new edition is welcome because of the corrections and the inclusion of previously unpublished material, the arrangement by alphabetic sequence rather than in the original order is not welcome, for it can lead to loss of information and to misinterpretations.)

In an earlier article in this publication we used the Dedham vital records, as published in 1886, to demonstrate some general points about the interpretation of New England vital records ("Early Vital Records," *Great Migration Newsletter* 2 [1991]:17-18, 24); some elaborations on this article, as it applies to Dedham, are in order.

One of the examples propounded in that earlier article dealt with the children of Austen Kalem, pointing out the difference between the two versions of the civil vital records (town and county), without coming to any resolution. Inexplicably, we did not examine the Dedham baptismal records. The county record gives a son Lot born 11 September 1640 and a daughter Sarah born 4 January 1641 (*NEHGR* 4 (1860):359), and the church records show "the son of our brother Kellam" baptized on 15 September 1640 and "Sarah the daughter of our brother Kellam" baptized 9 January 1641[/2] (CR 24, 26). The town records show only a son Lot born 11 September 1641, with no mention of a daughter Sarah (Hill 2; Hanson 1:193). In this instance, the county copy is clearly accurate, and superior to the town copy.

As noted in the previous article, there are some instances in which the town copy is more accurate than the county copy. Thus, the advice given in that article must be adjusted: with respect to the town of Dedham, discrepancies between the town and the county copies of the earliest records must be taken on a case-by-case basis - no preference should be given to either without reference to some third source.

EARLY DEDHAM LANDHOLDING

With most of the towns settled in 1630, we have found that the town records do not begin until some years later, and so we miss the earliest grants of home lots, and usually of some small parcels of meadow and arable land. Because the records of Dedham begin a month before the General Court had finally ratified the town's existence, one might expect that we would see here the process of land granting from the very beginning. Unfortunately, this is not the case.

At the first recorded town meeting, on 18 August 1636, seven men were granted lots of twelve acres each (TR 20). These might, on first examination, appear to be the home lots for these men, but this is probably not so. In the case of Samuel Morse, a separate, certified copy of this grant refers to the twelve-acre lot as his Gratification Lot (Hanson, *History of Dedham*, 30), which would not be his home lot, and would imply that the home lot had been granted earlier. (The Gratification Lot was an institution not seen in most other towns, whereby a man already admitted as a townsman was granted an additional lot to pass on to a friend, to entice that person to settle in Dedham and become a townsman also. This would suggest that Dedham was concerned about attracting enough suitable settlers in the early years.)

It would seem, though, that twelve acres was the standard size of home lot for a married man, for on 29 August 1636 the town ordered "that single men shall henceforth have eight acres for a house lot and no more."

No attempt will be made here to determine whether there was a standard sequence of grants made to each man, as we have seen with most of the other towns we have examined previously. This is partly because in the earliest years there are no comprehensive lists of grants in which all townsmen are included, and partly because the number of townsmen was not limited until the town was two decades old. (Also, the discussion in this section is based only on the published records of town meetings, and does not take into account an unpublished volume of proprietors' records.)

In several of the early Massachusetts Bay towns we have seen that the town at a very early date closed off access to the common, undivided land, and ordered that no new proprietary shares be created after that date; in Watertown, for example, this change of policy occurred in 1635, when there were well over one hundred proprietors. On 11 August 1637 it seemed that Dedham would take that route also, for the town ordered that "our proportion of allotments that we have formerly resolved upon are now fully complete" and "no more lots shalbe granted until a further view be made" (TR 34). But "a further view" must have been made very soon, as little time passed before Dedham again began to admit new townsmen, who would have full proprietorial rights.

For another nineteen years more townsmen were admitted, and as each came in he was required to sign the town covenant. Virtually all those who signed the covenant can be matched with an explicit record of admission, and the last person whose elevation to the status of townsman is on record is Thomas Metcalfe, on 5 January 1656/7 (TR 141). It took Dedham twenty years to get one-hundred-twenty-five townsmen, whereas Watertown and other early settlements had reached this number within five years or less. And by 1656 many of the earlier admissions had departed or died.

Most of the grants of land as presented in the published town volumes are piecemeal, with a piece of meadow granted to one man here and a parcel of arable to another man there. Not until 6 February 1642/3 do we get a grant in which all the proprietors receive a dividend at the same time; in this case the grant is of "upland ground fit for improvement with the plough," with most grantees obtaining about three to six acres, with some larger, such as John Allin with twenty-three (TR 94-96). Another grant to all proprietors was on 4 February 1644/5, when woodland lots of one to fourteen acres were given out (TR 109-11). But even after this date many smaller, individual grants were made as well.

Just a few weeks after the admission of Thomas Metcalfe to proprietorial privileges, the town finally decided to close out admissions, and on 20 February 1656/7 the town ordered that future divisions would be limited to those who were then townsmen (or their successors), and prepared a list of the seventy-nine remaining townsmen, setting out precisely the proportional share of each in the propriety. Interestingly, and by contrast with the older practice in other towns, absentee proprietors would be allowed to share in future divisions.

More than many other towns in Massachusetts Bay, Dedham continued to record transfers of land between person and person (after the initial grant from the town) in the town books. During most of the seventeenth century very few Dedham deeds will be found in the Suffolk County registry. The entries in the published town volumes are not in the form of proper deeds, but are given as one or two line abstracts of the particulars of the transaction. For example, in the selectmen's records for 23 February 1650/1 are abbreviated entries for more than two dozen grants and sales. A typical entry is "Joseph Morse sell Rich Ellice 2 acres upland abuts highway east swamp west Geo. Barber north Joseph Morse south" (TR 178). This might not satisfy a modern conveyancer, but other researchers will find such an entry highly satisfactory, in the absence of a recorded deed. When tracing land in Dedham in the seventeenth century, search for these brief entries is essential.

RECENT LITERATURE

Charles M. Hansen, "Mary Isaac's Descent from the Beauchamps: The Correct Lineage," *New England Historical and Genealogical Register* 147 (1993):3-10. Building on the work carried out by himself and Neil D. Thompson on the Beauchamp and Bodulsgate ancestry of Elizabeth Wydevill, Queen of Edward IV, King of England, Hansen has resolved a long-standing problem in the ancestry of Mary Isaac, mother of Samuel Appleton, immigrant to Ipswich, Massachusetts. Walter Goodwin Davis, in his study of the ancestry of Mary Isaac, was not certain whether William Haute, great-great-grandfather of Mary Isaac, was son of his father's first wife (Margaret Berwick) or second wife (Joan Wydevill). Hansen provides evidence which demonstrates that the line must have gone through the second wife, Joan Wydevill, making William Haute first cousin of Elizabeth Wydevill.

Douglas Richardson, "The English Ancestry of Edward Holyoke and of His Nephew, Thomas Morris of New Haven," *New England Historical and Genealogical Register* 147 (1993):11-34. Material is presented which expands on the known ancestry of Edward Holyoke, giving details on the father and grandfather of the immigrant. In presenting also the siblings of those two men, Richardson demonstrates that Thomas Morris of New Haven, Connecticut, and Mary, the wife of John Mansfield of Lynn, Massachusetts, known to be kinsmen of Holyoke, were in fact his nephew and niece, children of his sister Ann.

Leo H. Garman, "Early Woodmansees in America," *New England Historical and Genealogical Register* 147 (1993):35-48. Garman organizes the records of several early Woodmansee families in the colonies, including Robert Woodmansee, who was in Ipswich, Massachusetts, by 1635.

Jane Fletcher Fiske, "Matthew Grinnell's French Connection," *New England Historical and Genealogical Register* 147 (1993):71-72. The author presents parish register entries which show that Matthew Grinnell married Rose French at Lexden, Essex, in 1615, and that they had children baptized at that parish and at St. Botolph, Colchester, Essex. These records correspond with what is known of Matthew Grinnell in New England, and seriously damage the long-standing claims that Grinnell of was of French origin.

Richard J. Ross, "The Legal Past of Early New England: Notes for the Study of Law, Legal Culture, and Intellectual History," *The William and Mary Quarterly*, Third Series 50 (1993):28-41. The text of this review article describes in general terms the course of colonial legal scholarship of the last two decades. Genealogists will find great utility in the extensive bibliographic footnotes, which list many articles on detailed points of interpreation of legal documents.

Edwin G. Sanford, "'Judith at the Island': Judith (Smith) Fisher, the Wait Family of Massachusetts and Rhode Island, and Their English Origins," *The American Genealogist* 67 (1992):193-200. Sanford argues that the wife of Edward Fisher of Rhode Island was Judith Smith, who had come to Boston as a servant of Edward Hutchinson. Using this information and the association of Judith with Richard Wait, he uncovered the English origins of Judith Smith, and of Richard Wait and his brothers. Judith was baptized at Alford, Lincolnshire, while Richard Wait of Boston, Gamaliel Wait of Boston, Thomas Wait of Portsmouth, Rhode Island, and possibly Samuel Wait of Braintree were all baptized at Rigsby, Lincolnshire, sons of Richard and Margaret (Carter) Wait.

F.N. Craig, "The Well Beloved Mother-in-Law of Robert Marbury: Ancestor of Anne (Marbury) Hutchinson and Katherine (Marbury) Scott," *The American Genealogist* 67 (1992):201-10. The author fills in another blank in the extensively studied Marbury ancestry, providing evidence that the wife of Robert Marbury (greatgrandfather of the immigrant sisters) was Katherine Williamson, born late in the fifteenth century, daughter of John and Jane (Angevine) Williamson.

John Plummer, "The English Origin of Samuel[1] Bitfield of Boston, Massachusetts," *The American Genealogist* 67 (1992):236-42. Plummer demonstrates that Samuel Bitfield, immigrant to New England about 1639, was baptized at Wrington, Somersetshire, in 1602, and gives two generations of his paternal ancestry in that parish and in Bristol, Gloucestershire.

Douglas Richardson, "The Mother of Michael[1] Humphrey of Windsor, Connecticut," *The American Genealogist* 67 (1992):242. The author presents the marriage of a couple at Bridport, Dorsetshire, in 1615 who are probably the parents of Michael Humphrey, immigrant to Windsor, Connecticut.

Robert S. Wakefield and Alice H. Dreger, "The Wives and Children of James[2] Cole (circa 1625-1709) of Plymouth, Massachusetts," *The American Genealogist* 67 (1992):243-45. Wakefield and Dreger present a comprehensive sketch of the genealogical connections of James[2] Cole, son of James[1] of Plymouth. They demonstrate that Cole had three wives, of whom the first was undoubtedly a daughter of Edmund Tilson, who had arrived at Plymouth by 1638. They also differentiate James[2] Cole from contemporaries of the same name.

(continued from page 2)

for he omits it from both the first and second editions of the journal.

On 14 June 1647 Margaret (Tyndal) Winthrop died at Boston, and Winthrop soon married for a fourth and last time. His new wife was Martha, daughter of William Rainborough and widow of Thomas Coytmore. Some sources state simply that they married in December of 1647, but others, including Wyman's *Charlestown* and Pope's *Pioneers of Massachusetts*, give the date precisely as 4 December 1647.

Attempts to find a record for this marriage were fruitless. The vital records of Boston and Charlestown (the residence of the Coytmore family) do not include the marriage, nor does it appear in any other town. The resolution of the problem came about serendipitously during a search on another problem in the records of the Massachusetts Bay court. In March 1647/8, at a session of the General Court, the marriage contract between John Winthrop and "Martha Coytemore, the relict of Thom: Coytemore," dated 20 December 1647, was put into the record (*Mass. Bay Court Records* 2:234-35). With Martha Coytmore still a widow on 20 December, the marriage cannot have taken place on 4 December.

Wyman published his account of Charlestown families in 1879. What led him to propose 4 December 1647 as

the marriage date? Did he invent the date, or did he take it from some earlier secondary source? By following the sources backward in time, a likely answer has emerged. In 1864 William H. Whitmore prepared a brief article setting forth in abbreviated (and undocumented) form the early generations of the Winthrop family (*Register* 18[1864]:182-86). When he came to the fourth marriage of the Governor, he wrote "he married, fourthly, Dec., 1647, Martha Nowell [sic], widow of Thomas Coytmore." As a hypothesis, it would seem that Wyman (or some other genealogist between 1864 and 1879), reading too quickly, converted "fourthly" into "fourth" and thus arrived at a precise but totally incorrect date for this marriage. All that we can now say, in the absence of new evidence, is that John and Martha married on some date soon after 20 December 1647.

These four examples of missing or inaccurate dates in the family of John Winthrop (baptisms for third and fourth children; birth and burial dates for fifth child; birth date for first child born in New England; and date of fourth marriage) are typical of the problems found among families of all social levels. This process of checking dates carefully for internal consistency, and of looking in each case for the original source, is being repeated hundreds of times in the preparation of the sketches of all those persons who came to New England by the end of 1633, and is leading to many new interpretations.

Great Migration Newsletter

Vol. 4   April-June 1993   No. 2

LEADING LAYMEN IN ENGLAND

Three issues ago we discussed the role of the leading Puritan ministers, prior to their departure for New England, in linking Puritan congregations in various parts of England (*Great Migration Newsletter* 3 [1992]:17). We now wish to present evidence of similar connections between widely separated groups of Puritans, resulting from the movements of leading Puritan laymen who later made the migration to Massachusetts Bay.

Our first example will be William Coddington, who resided at Boston, Lincolnshire, before migration, and therefore was for some time under the influence of the Reverend John Cotton. William Coddington was in the Lincolnshire Boston in the 1620s, appearing there with a wife Mary (surname unknown) by whom he had two children baptized in that church. Coddington was one of the few who left Boston in 1630, joining with the Winthrop migration in that year, and preceding by three years or more most of the emigration from that place.

After his arrival in New England in 1630 he settled in the newly founded town of Boston, and joined the church during the first winter. During that same winter his wife Mary died, and in the spring of 1631 he returned to England, his main purpose apparently to find a new bride. It has been known that his second wife was Mary Mosley, and a recent search of the IGI under that name revealed the marriage at Terling, Essex, on 2 September 1631 of *John* Coddington and Mary Mosley. The minister at Terling at that time was Thomas Weld, who would leave for New England a year later, accompanied by several other Terling families, and who settled at Roxbury, where he joined with John Eliot in organizing the church. Although the marriage record gives the groom the wrong Christian name, the concurrence of the correct bride's name, at the right time, in a known Puritan town, suggests strongly that this is the record of William Coddington's second marriage.

In June of 1632, just nine months after this marriage, William Coddington, at that time in London, addressed a letter to John Cotton, still at Boston in Lincolnshire, in which he spoke of his desire to return to New England as quickly as possible, but noting that he would be delayed

in making that voyage until the spring of 1633, because his wife was with child, and her friends had persuaded her not to undertake the sea voyage at that time (Thomas Hutchinson, *The History of the Colony and Province of Massachusetts-Bay* [Cambridge 1936], 1:23).

If we have interpreted this marriage record correctly, then we have a case in which a man who had been long associated with John Cotton in Lincolnshire was married by Thomas Weld in Essex, at a time when neither Cotton nor Weld had made the move to New England. We may speculate as to whether Cotton provided the introduction to Weld, or whether Coddington had acquired a connection to Terling through some other channel; but the activities of Coddington do give some hint of the cross-fertilization taking place between widely separated Puritan congregations prior to departure for New England, and carried out by laymen.

We turn now to William Vassall, one of the most prominent among the men who travelled on the Winthrop Fleet in 1630, and one of those in whose name the charter for the Massachusetts Bay Company had been issued a year earlier. At the time of his marriage in 1613, Vassall was residing at Eastwood, in the southeastern corner of Essex. Some sources say that Vassall was from the parish of Rayleigh, which is quite possible, since Rayleigh and Eastwood are adjacent parishes. At Rayleigh he may have known Reverend Francis Bright, who was minister of that parish for some time, and who came to New England in 1629, only to return to England in 1630, never to return. Vassall's residence in this part of Essex also led to connections which would lead to fur-

(continued on page 10)

EDITOR'S EFFUSIONS

From the beginning, the Great Migration Study Project has had as one of its aims the preparation of data on the immigrants to New England that would be of value not just to the genealogical community, but to other scholars as well, including especially colonial historians. We have taken an important step in that direction with the recent publication of a note in the July 1993 issue of *The William & Mary Quarterly*. This short article describes for the readers of that journal the goals of the Great Migration Study Project, the accomplishments to date, and the plans for publication in the near future.

Conversely, the work of the Great Migration Study Project should also inform genealogists about relevant research being carried out by scholars in other disciplines. To some extent this is the purpose of the "Recent Literature" section in each issue of the *Newsletter*. The article on the final page of this issue, "A Note on Motivation," goes somewhat deeper into an issue raised by one small section in a recent interpretation of the reign of Charles I.

In an upcoming issue of the *Newsletter* we will move further in this direction, by devoting a major article to a group of recent monographs which are of importance to the study of the Great Migration. These books are certainly not written with the genealogist in mind, but they are of great value in understanding and interpreting the process of migration and the settlement of New England, and should be part of every researcher's background knowledge.

The towns to be explored in the "Focus" section of the remaining two issues this year are Hampton (in July-September) and Wethersfield (in October-December). In 1994 we will continue the effort to discuss towns from all of the New England colonies, and would be glad to have from our readers suggestions as to which settlements should be treated in the near future. We hope to cover one of the New England-oriented Long Island towns next year.

Robert Charles Anderson, FASG   Editor
Margaret F. Costello   Production Assistant

The *Great Migration Newsletter* (ISSN 1049-8087) is published quarterly by the Great Migration Study Project, a project of the New England Historic Genealogical Society 101 Newbury Street, Boston MA 02116

The subscription rate is $8 for one year and $15 for two years. The subscription year is the same as the calendar year.

(*continued from page 9*)

ther migration to New England. When Vassall made his second trip to New England in 1635, John Stockbridge and his family sailed on the same vessel, and it is now known that the Stockbridges were from Rayleigh. Vassall and Stockbridge soon settled together in Scituate, Massachusetts. Vassall's wife came from Cold Norton, a short distance north of Eastwood, and perhaps through this connection we find that a number of families from that vicinity came to New England as well.

William Vassall did not, however, reside only in the Rayleigh and Eastwood area. On 2 February 1626/7 his son William was baptized at Little Baddow in Essex, and on 20 April 1628 his daughter Anna was baptized there as well. Little Baddow was the location of the school run during these years by Thomas Hooker and John Eliot, and if we may deduce from this that Vassall was acquainted during these years with these two prominent ministers, then we have a solid connection between the Puritan congregations in the southeast of Essex, and the vast web which grew around Hooker and Eliot in the Braintree and Nazing areas of Essex.

A final example may fall into the same category, although further research is required. John Eddy was baptized in March of 1597 at Cranbrook, Kent, son of William Eddy, the vicar of that parish. As an adult John Eddy surfaced at Nayland, Suffolk, where he had three children baptized; he had married Amie Doggett, daughter of John Doggett of Groton, Suffolk. These latter connections would imply that Eddy was known to Winthrop nearly a decade before the migration to New England, and from the bishop's visitation of 1629 we know that there were several practicing Puritans in that parish. John Eddy's father was not known for Puritan activities during his tenure at Cranbrook, and his successor, Robert Abbot, was a Puritan of a very mild sort, not likely to be the focus of a group migrating to New England. But Cranbrook and several other parishes in the Weald of Kent provided many immigrants to New England, and it may well be that further research will demonstrate that John Eddy had some Puritan connection in Kent which led to his move to Suffolk.

As the exploration of the Great Migration continues, many more such connections between pockets of Puritan activity, as carried out by laymen, will be revealed. When these are added to the known connections through ministers, the full dimensions of the Puritan network become quite formidable.

An ultimate goal of the Great Migration Study Project is to display this network of Puritan connections at its fullest, and to be able to state just how large a proportion of the twenty thousand or so immigrants to New England in the 1620s and 1630s were tied to one another prior to migration.

Focus   on   PORTSMOUTH

SETTLEMENT OF PORTSMOUTH

The settlement of Portsmouth was a direct consequence of the so-called Antinomian Controversy of 1637. For their support of Anne Hutchinson and Reverend John Wheelwright, several dozen men, mostly from Boston, were disarmed in late 1637. Some of these people moved north with Wheelwright to found Exeter, and others moved south with the Hutchinsons to settle on the northern end of the island of Aquidneck, otherwise known as Rhode Island.

This group of about two dozen families that fled to the south included many strong-willed individuals in addition to Anne Hutchinson. Men such as William Codddington and John Coggeshall had held prominent positions in their towns of origin in England and in Boston, and they expected their views to have some influence wherever they were. As a result, at the end of the first year of the settlement of Pocasset (as Portsmouth was known in its earliest days) a split occurred in the town's political leadership, and about half the population moved to the southern end of Aquidneck and in early 1639 founded the town of Newport. (The island is only about fifteen miles long, and from 1639 until the creation of the town of Middletown in 1743, the two towns of Portsmouth and Newport covered the whole island. Many persons in both towns, and especially those close to the boundary line across the center of the island, would have business both in Portsmouth and Newport.)

The split that led to the founding of Newport arose from a dispute between William Coddington and the Hutchinsons. The Hutchinsonians took advantage of Coddington's absence in Massachusetts Bay in early 1639, and took over the government of Pocasset. While this was certainly the immediate cause of the settlement of Newport, we should also consider that during 1638 many more families moved into the settlement at the northern end of Aquidneck, and a division of some sort may have been necessary just to prevent overcrowding of grazing and planting land.

Both the manner of the keeping of the records in the first place, and the way in which some of them have been published over the last hundred years, have caused the records of Portsmouth and Newport to be intermingled in a confusing way. For this reason we will spend some time on the full range of documentary material for the first few decades of the island of Aquidneck, before moving on to those records applying solely to Portsmouth.

EARLY RHODE ISLAND RECORDS

In the first volume of *Records of the Colony of Rhode Island and Providence Plantations in New England* (Providence 1856), John Russell Bartlett began with "Records of the Settlements at Providence, Portsmouth, Newport and Warwick, from their Commencement to Their Union under the Colony Charter. 1636 to 1647." The records included in the Portsmouth section (pages 45 through 85) are drawn from as many as three different sources and are in various ways incomplete, incorrect and misleading (even though Bartlett does describe his sources briefly in his introduction).

The first few pages are copies of deeds (from more than one source) in which the island of Aquidneck is sold to the Englishmen by the Indians, there are the records of the first year of settlement at Pocasset, or Portsmouth. These begin on 7 March 1637/8, and continue through 28 April 1639 (pages 52 through 69). These pages actually come from a manuscript volume, held by the Rhode Island Archives, entitled "Records of the Island of Rhode Island: Mar. 7, 1638 - Mar. 12, 1644," which we will refer to here as "RI Records." Bartlett then continues with the early records of the town of Portsmouth itself (pages 70 through 85), running from April 1639 to December 1644. These same records, taken from the manuscript first volume of Portsmouth records, were published in 1901 as *The Early Records of the Town of Portsmouth,* and included the entirety of the original volume, containing deeds, wills, and other material as well as the town meeting minutes. (We will return to the Portsmouth town records later in this section and again in the next section.)

After his pages for Portsmouth, Bartlett then presents material on Newport, running from April 1639 through March 1644 (pages 87 through 128). This entire section is taken from "RI Records," and simply picks up where this material left off back on page 69. For the first year these records do pertain to Newport alone, but by November of 1639 the inhabitants of Portsmouth and Newport were already negotiating over a combination of their governments, and by 12 March 1639/40 this was an accomplished fact (Bartlett pp. 94, 100). The bulk of this section, therefore, designated by Bartlett as "Newport Records," is actually the record book of the combined government of Rhode Island (meaning the island of Aquidneck, and distinct from the Providence Plantations). The records of the town of Newport itself would have been kept separately and for this period are now mostly lost.

Because of this confusion in rearrangement and improper labelling of transcribed documents, researchers using Bartlett must be very careful as they try to interpret individual entries. We will use the various lists of those admitted as inhabitants or freemen to illustrate this point.

The beginning point is the list of those who organized the settlement at Pocasset on 7 March 1637/8 (Bartlett p. 52). Most of these men had been residents of Boston, and most had been disarmed at the peak of the Antinomian Controversy. As the year 1638 progressed many more men were admitted as freemen of Pocasset, and some were noted in the month-to-month meetings (Bartlett p. 58).

Most of the additions to membership, however, appear in a consolidated list, which in the published version appears much later, under the town of Newport (Bartlett pp. 91). This is properly dated by Bartlett in the margin as from 1638, but it is also appended without break to a Newport meeting of 1 October 1639. The latter meeting ends with the order regarding voting at Quarter Courts, and the 1638 list (which is on a separate page in the original) begins with the words "A Catalogue of such [persons]...." Note that this list does not include any of the men on the list of 7 March 1637/8, and that the month and day dates in the margin correspond with the dates of meetings at Pocasset in 1638. (The latter part of this list is headed "Inhabitants Admitted at the Towne of Nieu-Port since the 1° of the 3d [1 May], 1638." This is clearly an impossible date for admission to Newport; this section of the list apparently applies to Newport about 1640 or 1641.)

When the town split in early 1639, about half the families remained in Portsmouth and about half went on to Newport. The list compiled at the reorganization of Portsmouth (Bartlett p. 70) does not include most of the leading men of that community, such as William Baulston or William Aspinwall. Most of the names in this sequence are of those who joined the Pocasset settlement in 1638 after the original meeting, and chose to remain at the split of early 1639.

In Newport after the split, a list of nine men appears at the first meeting on 28 April 1639 (Bartlett p. 88), and then others are added from meeting to meeting (i.e., Bartlett p. 89). Then, when the two towns agreed to combine into one political unit, many of those who had stayed in Portsmouth were admitted as freemen of the new joint body (Bartlett p. 90).

A few specific examples may make this sequence of events more comprehensible. Robert Stanton was one of four men admitted as an inhabitant of Pocasset on 7 February 1638/9 (just before the town split up), and he appears at the appropriate place also in the full list of 1638 inhabitants (Bartlett pp. 66, 91). Immediately after the split he appears as one of those remaining in Portsmouth (Bartlett p. 70), but by December of 1639 (prior to the recombination of the governments) he had changed his allegiance and moved to Newport, where he was admitted as a freeman (Bartlett p. 95).

Philip Sherman presents a different profile. He was one of the founders of Pocasset on 7 March 1637/8 (Bartlett p. 52), and remained with that settlement at the split. He does not appear in the list of those reconstituting Portsmouth, but he is of record on the same day as one of the selectmen for the town (Bartlett p. 71). When the reamalgamation came early in 1640, he was among the first readmitted to that body (Bartlett p. 100). As a first settler of Portsmouth, and a loyal adherent of that government, his appearances in these lists have a different pattern than those of Robert Stanton.

Much of the material presented by Bartlett under Portsmouth and Newport was also printed by Howard M. Chapin in the second volume of his *Documentary History of Rhode Island* (Providence 1919). Chapin's technique was to print extensive verbatim extracts from the records, and stitch them together into a narrative with connecting sections of his own. His transcriptions and his citations to the original sources were better than those of Bartlett, but both versions have the effect of making it difficult for the modern reader to apprehend the original arrangement of the records.

Chapin presents in great detail the same sequence of events that we have described above. In his third chapter he describes the settlement of 1638, and begins with excerpts from the writings of John Clark and John Winthrop. He then prints the agreement of 7 March 1637/8 in which Portsmouth is organized, which Bartlett gave on his page 52; this is from the volume which we have called "RI Records," and which Chapin designates "I.R." Fifteen pages later Chapin transcribes the minutes of the meeting of 13 May 1638, which Bartlett gives on page 53, immediately after the above document.

"RI Records" ends in 1644, and for the ensuing period Bartlett and Chapin then draw on a volume, also in the custody of the Rhode Island Archives, entitled "Rhode Island Colony Records, 1646-1669." This fascinating volume has been mined for more than a century by Rhode Island researchers, and many parts of it have been published, but much remains unpublished. In his preface Chapin outlines its contents as "the minutes of the General Assembly, the minutes of the Aquidneck circuit courts, the minutes of the Colony Court of Trials, a large number of deeds [some as early as 1642], and a few vital records."

Bartlett published much of the General Assembly material, and Chapin included most of the Aquidneck circuit court records in his volume. The Court of Trials records from this volume were published independently in two slim volumes. The many deeds, mostly for Newport and Portsmouth, have not been published, and other materials remain buried in this omnibus record book (which has been microfilmed).

Yet another set of records which relates to Portsmouth was maintained at the colony level. These were the Rhode Island land evidences, the first volume of which has been published in abstract form (*Rhode Island Land Evidences, Volume I, 1648-1696* [Providence 1921; rpt. Baltimore 1970]). Unfortunately the abstracts are frequently so brief as to fail to convey the full meaning of the document, the index is not complete, and reference to the original is often necessary. Thus, a full search for land records for Portsmouth must include examination of this volume and the unpublished material in "Rhode Island Colony Records, 1646-1669," in addition to the volumes maintained by the town itself.

Returning to the two published versions of the Portsmouth town meeting records, we find that Bartlett's transcription is far inferior to that printed by the town of Portsmouth. Comparison with the original shows, for example, that in the meeting of 30 April 1639, when Portsmouth reorganized itself after the departure of the Coddington party to Newport, Bartlett misread many of the names: George Cleare is correct, and not George Chare; Wm. Heavens is correct and not W.T. Havenz; John More is correct and not John Mow.

In areas where the manuscript was damaged (which includes most of the earliest pages), Bartlett provides more than does the later version. This may be because more of the manuscript survived in 1856 than a half century later, but it may also be that Bartlett guessed at missing portions, but did not indicate them as such.

More serious is his claim on pages 78 and 79 that "An entire page is here obliterated." This would normally indicate that these pages were heavily stained or overwritten, and were no longer legible. But inspection of the original shows that these pages, and many others omitted by Bartlett, are quite easily read, and are included in the records as published by the town.

Research in Rhode Island is difficult enough without the addition of further obstacles during the process of publishing important documents. What Bartlett did was frequently quite acceptable in his day, and the efforts of Chapin are accurate and still very useful. Nevertheless, our investigation of Rhode Island families and history would be greatly facilitated by the publication of new versions of these early Rhode Island records, according to modern standards of historical editing. This would include verbatim transcripts of the documents, in their original order, with annotations discussing dating and other textual problems.

PORTSMOUTH TOWN RECORDS

In the preceding section we discussed some of the Portsmouth town records, mostly town meeting minutes, as they were published, and as they related to Newport records and other Rhode Island records. In the next section we will talk briefly about the vital records of the town. There are a few other records of Portsmouth which need to be described.

In addition to the minutes of the town meetings, the first volume of Portsmouth town records included many other things, such as ear marks, deeds, wills, marriages, and other miscellaneous items; these were part of the published volume of town records.

This system of mixing up all sorts of town business, common throughout New England, soon became too cumbersome, and by 1647 Portsmouth had begun a separate volume of Land Evidences, which ran through 1707, and included both deeds and probate matters. This volume had the peculiar title of "2nd Book - No. 1," signifying that it was the second book kept by the town which had records of land transactions, if one began the count with the first omnibus volume, but that it was the first volume dedicated solely to that purpose. This book was succeeded by "3rd Book - No. 2," and so on.

Near the end of the century the need was seen to separate deeds from probates and, as with other Rhode Island towns, a separate series of volumes, known in Portsmouth as "Town Council & Probate" volumes, was begun in 1697. This included other matters besides probates, such as records of the maintenance of the poor. As with the land evidence series, the first volume of Town Council records was called volume two.

Thus by 1697, some sixty years after the founding of Portsmouth, the town was maintaining four separate sets of records: town meetings, town council and probate, land evidences, and vital records, and this would continue to be the practice thenceforward.

In addition to these formally maintained records, there is at the Portsmouth Town Hall a bound volume called the "Portsmouth Scrapbook." This contains the originals of many documents, some as early as 1639, and continuing throughout the colonial period. Many of these items, but not all, are also recorded in the various books described above.

Finally, the Portsmouth Town Hall also holds a small collection of loose papers, covering the full range of town business, and ranging in date from the 1650s well into the nineteenth century. There are a few probate inventories from the middle of the seventeenth century, and a larger number of administrator's bonds from the beginning of the eighteenth century.

PORTSMOUTH VITAL RECORDS

Most of us have used the Portsmouth, Rhode Island, vital records in the form in which they were published by James N. Arnold a century ago. The fourth volume of *Vital Record of Rhode Island. 1636-1850* (Providence 1893) covered Newport County, comprising the towns of Portsmouth, Newport, Middletown, New Shoreham [Block Island (now included in Washington County)], Jamestown, Little Compton and Tiverton. (Little Compton and Tiverton were part of Massachusetts until 1746, and were attached to Newport County when they were transferred to Rhode Island.)

As with all of the material published by Arnold, the Portsmouth vital records are arranged alphabetically for the entire time period covered, with citations to the volume and page on which each record appeared. The marriages are presented in one alphabetic sequence, and the births and deaths in another.

The earliest volume of vital records for Portsmouth (like the early volumes of so many New England towns) was organized in family groups, with most entries beginning with the marriage of the couple at the head of the family, followed by the births of the couple's children in chronological order.

The Portsmouth volume seems to have been initiated about 1685, as many of the pages were apparently written all at one time, with all entries up to about 1685 in the same ink and in one consistent hand. A typical example would be that of George Lawton and Mary Wodell, who were married on 16 February 1680[/1], and had four children born between 1681/2 and 1695/6 (Original 1:16; Arnold 4:Portsmouth:29,81). The marriage record (which includes the names of the fathers of the bride and groom) and the birth records of the first two children (Mary, born 20 February 1681/2, and George, born 1 September 1685), appear to have been entered all at one sitting. The remaining two children (Elizabeth, born 12 September 1688, and Robert, born 5 January 1695/6) must have been entered individually, and probably shortly after the events themselves, for the handwriting of these two records is different from the earlier entries for this family, and differ also between themselves.

The process of collecting the material for this first volume must have taken some months, and perhaps even a year or so, if we assume that the work was begun in 1685. One family record appears in the form of an affidavit, given by Thomas Manchester and his wife Margaret Manchester. On 7 June 1686 they swore that they were present at the marriage of Ichabod Sheffield and Mary Parker, which must have taken place about 1660. This is then followed by the list of the children of this couple, born between 1661 and 1673 (Original 1:24; Arnold 4:Portsmouth:39,95).

As a result of this system of recording vital records, many of the items which appear in this volume were necessarily entered many years after the events themselves. This gives rise to the opportunity for many errors, depending on the source for these late-recorded entries. In addition, there is no guarantee that all these pre-1685 events took place in Portsmouth.

An example which demonstrates these latter points is the family of John Coggeshall. This record is unusual in that it presents three generations of the Coggeshall family on one page. It begins with the marriage of John Coggeshall, son of John of Newport, to Elizabeth Baulston, the daughter of William of Portsmouth. There follows then the birth on 12 February 1649 of John Coggeshall, son of this couple, and then the marriage of this John to Elizabeth Timberlake on 24 December 1669, and finally the births of twelve of their children (Original 1:32; Arnold 4:Portsmouth:14,64).

The first couple recorded in this entry, John and Elizabeth (Baulston) Coggeshall, were blessed with at least two additional children during the time of their marriage (they were divorced in 1655), and the absence of these other children, or of any other record of the two further marriages of this John Coggeshall, and the many children of those marriages, suggests that this page was entered by the younger John Coggeshall, and he merely took the opportunity to add his own birth date and the marriage record of his parents, something that the other residents of Portsmouth at that time did not bother to do. Since there is no record that the elder John Coggeshall ever resided in Portsmouth, it may be that the 1649 birth of the younger John actually took place in Newport and not Portsmouth.

As the first volume of vital records was laid out, a set of facing pages was assigned to each family. The left hand page was devoted to the marriage of the couple and the births of their children. In many cases, the family reached completion long before the page was filled, and so a later clerk could make use of blank portions of the book. The unused portion of the page that held the records for Robert Lawton was employed to list the children of Gideon Freeborn Jr. and his wife Ruth, beginning in 1727. Similarly, the page which began with the family of Ichabod Sheffield was filled out with the records of Lott Strange and his wife Mary, commencing in 1689; this was in the same hand as the Freeborn records noted just above, and so was probably entered many years after the events themselves.

The facing right-hand page was used sparingly to record later events. Note for example in the family of John and Elizabeth (Timberlake) Coggeshall that many of the children, whose births were recorded on original page 1:32, died soon, and their deaths were entered on original page 1:33.

RECENT LITERATURE

Gerald James Parsons, "John[1] Gallop/Gollop of Bridport, Dorsetshire, England, and Boston, Massachusetts," *The American Genealogist* 68 (1993):11-13. By examining carefully the original of the Bridport parish register, Parsons adds to what has been known about the English background of John Gallop and his family.

Frederick J. Nicholson, "The Family of Jonas[1] Humfrey of Dorchester, Massachusetts: With Notes on the Origin of Ralph[1] and Katherine (Foster) Tomkins of Dorchester and Thomas[1] Foster of Weymouth, Massachusetts," *The American Genealogist* 68 (1993):14-22. Although it has been known for many years that Jonas Humfrey was from Wendover, Buckinghamshire, Nicholson has now gone back to the English records and fleshed out Humfrey's family. In the process he has also found information on a related Foster family which sent settlers to New England.

Robert S. Wakefield, "George[1] and John[1] Lewis of Brenchley, Kent, England, and Scituate, Massachusetts," *The American Genealogist* 68 (1993):24-28. The author demonstrates that the brothers George and John Lewis were from Brenchley, Kent, and identifies their parents.

Janet Ireland Delorey and Dean Crawford Smith, "Mary[2] (Pratt) White of Weymouth, Massachusetts: Further Considerations," *The American Genealogist* 68 (1993):29-31. Building on earlier work by Frederick Nicholson, the authors conclude that "Macuth Pratt's 'daughter White' was the wife of Thomas[2] White, and not Thomas[1]."

Douglas Richardson, "The English Origin of John[1] Eaton (1590-1668) of Salisbury and Haverhill, Massachusetts," *The American Genealogist* 68 (1993):48-54. Richardson shows that John Eaton, immigrant to Salisbury, Massachusetts, was from Hatton, Warwickshire, and traces three generations of his paternal ancestry.

Alan D. Hodder, "In the Glasse of God's Word: Hooker's Pulpit Rhetoric and the Theater of Conversion," *The New England Quarterly* 66 (1993):67-109. Hodder notes the contradiction between the Puritan campaign against the Elizabethan and early Jacobean theater, and their use of theatrical metaphors in their sermons, and, after examining the rhetorical training received by the Puritans, and the theatrical elements in the Bible, concludes that the Puritan sermon "resides in the rhetorical space halfway between drama and the classical oration." He then applies these conclusions to the sermons of Reverend Thomas Hooker, and especially to the conversion process, which he presents as a dramatic confrontation between Christ and the Soul.

Barbara MacAllan, "More Thoughts on the Moulton Family," *New England Historical and Genealogical Register* 147 (1993):129-145. Drawing on her extensive knowledge of Ormsby, Norfolk, and vicinity, and on various land and court records not employed by earlier researchers, MacAllan has provided additional insights into the Moulton family, improving on the earlier articles on this family. MacAllan's work is an excellent example of the value of looking at material beyond the usual parish registers and probate records.

Robert Charles Anderson, "Elizabeth Moulton, Wife of Henry Skerry of Salem," *New England Historical and Genealogical Register* 147 (1993):146-47. As the result of a serendipitous discovery, the author identifies the wife of Henry Skerry of Salem, and suggests a place for her in the Moulton family of Ormsby, Norfolk.

Robert Charles Anderson, "The *Mary & John*: Developing Objective Criteria for a Synthetic Passenger List," *New England Historical and Genealogical Register* 147 (1993):148-61. Anderson defines some conditions which should be met before deciding that a person did or did not sail on the *Mary & John* in 1630, and then applies those criteria to the available evidence, resulting in a new and more objective synthetic passenger list for that ship.

Wayne Howard Miller Wilcox, "Further Notes on the English Home of the Cor(e)y Family of Rhode Island," *New England Historical and Genealogical Register* 147 (1993):162-63. The author demonstrates the Bristol origin of this Cory family. William Cory, baptized at Bristol in 1634, was certainly in Rhode Island by 1657, when he married Mary Earle. His father, John, may have died in England by 1636, but there remains a possibility that he lived beyond that date and was in New England in 1643.

Douglas Richardson, "The Stockton Family: Ancestry of Prudence (Stockton) Holyoke," *New England Historical and Genealogical Register* 147 (1993):164-73. Richardson sets forth three generations of the paternal ancestry of Prudence Stockton, wife of Edward Holyoke of Lynn, Massachusetts. The Stockton family was first in Shropshire and then moved to Warwickshire.

Jane Fletcher Fiske, "Edward Wilcox of Lincolnshire and Rhode Island," *New England Historical and Genealogical Register* 147 (1993):188-91. Fiske identifies the parents of Edward Wilcox, immigrant to Rhode Island by 1638, and shows that he was baptized at South Elkington, Lincolnshire, and resided in two other parishes in that county before moving to New England.

A NOTE ON MOTIVATION

A recently published history of the reign of Charles I demonstrates how a biased view on a historical point becomes embedded in the literature. Kevin Sharpe has written a 954-page tome on *The Personal Rule of Charles I* (New Haven 1992), of which seven pages (750-57) discuss the migration to New England and the motives of those who migrated.

Sharpe opens this section by stating that "the puritan migration ... is one of the triumphs of myth over evidence...." He then draws the majority of his supporting examples from the work of David Cressy, and specifically from that author's *Coming Over*. Despite the many good features of Cressy's book, on the question of migration he takes a narrow view of the records, and overemphasizes a few incidents in his interpretation.

This is not the place to refute Cressy in detail, but the following brief points may be made here:

1) The activities of a few criminals and malcontents who crept into the Winthrop Fleet are inflated;

2) The great difference between the small number of immigrants before 1633 and the much larger number after that date is not recognized;

3) The number of New Englanders who returned to England at the outbreak of the Civil War is overestimated; and

4) Evidence of persecution of Puritans in England is taken largely from well-known literary sources and the activities of the Court of High Commission, and so the true incidence of persecution, as reflected in the lower church courts, is missed.

Curiously, Sharpe undercuts his own argument in the last two pages of this section. He notes the various activities of the English church and state in attempting to stop or control the outflow of persons to New England. Since these attempts at border control included the requirements that shipboard services be conducted according to the Book of Common Prayer and that prospective emigrants swear an oath of conformity to the Church of England, we may conclude that the authorities thought that there was a Puritan migration.

The worst sin committed by Sharpe in this section of his book is to ignore totally the large body of recent literature on the motivations for migration to New England, other than that created by Cressy. A book published in 1992 should have taken into account the work of Virginia DeJohn Anderson as a counterpoint to that of Cressy. Few of the immigrants to New England made the voyage as the result of a single motivation, but the Puritan element was clearly very strong, thus making this movement quite distinct from the simultaneous migration to the Chesapeake or the Caribbean.

Great Migration Newsletter

Vol. 4   July-September 1993   No. 3

CITY STATES IN NEW ENGLAND

One immediate consequence of the increased pace of immigration in the years from 1634 to 1639 was overcrowding in the older towns, most of them settled in 1630 after the arrival of the Winthrop Fleet. The obvious solution to the problem was the rapid settlement of new towns, further into the hinterlands, and farther from Boston.

Many of these towns were formed within the bounds of Plymouth Colony and Massachusetts Bay Colony, each of which had a charter and therefore a constitutional basis for its government. These towns (such as Sudbury, Rowley, Taunton and Barnstable) immediately came under a higher government, and looked to Boston or Plymouth for authority in such acts as the laying out of land.

When settlers from Massachusetts Bay moved to the Connecticut river valley in 1635 and 1636, to form the towns of Wethersfield, Hartford, Windsor and Springfield, they drafted a compact for mutual government, initially intended to be a part of Massachusetts Bay, but soon set apart as Connecticut Colony. Even though this entity did not have a charter for many years, it did begin immediately functioning as a governmental body over the several towns.

Not all the towns formed in the late 1630s, though, fell within the bounds of Plymouth Colony or Massachusetts Bay Colony, and none chose at the beginning to associate themselves with Connecticut. The solution for many of the new towns was to enter into a civil covenant covering just the inhabitants of that one town. Each of these towns then became, for a year or several years, a tiny republic, answerable to no higher authority. Little city states were scattered all over the periphery of New England, as the new immigrants tried to establish themselves in settlements which had the right size, the right amount of land for the families present.

Although the records are not complete, many of these infant republics drafted their own constitutions, known variously as "combinations" or "covenants," obviously modelled on the similar documents drafted for the older

and larger colonies. A list of some of these towns is presented here.

EXETER: At the founding of Exeter in 1639 John Wheelwright and others entered into a Combination, in which they declared themselves directly subservient to King Charles. This Combination was revised and renewed in 1640 (Charles H. Bell, *History of the Town of Exeter, New Hampshire* [Exeter 1888], pp. 15-19).

DOVER: For its first several years the settlement at Hilton's Point had no organized government, but as the strength of Massachusetts Bay grew the settlers developed new arrangements, which culminated in the Dover Combination of 22 October 1640 (*NEHGR* 33 [1879]:91-101).

PORTSMOUTH: The families who were to settle in Portsmouth early in 1638, mostly from Boston, met in that town and established a government for themselves, before they actually moved to Aquidneck Island. Basing their pact on Biblical principles, their leader was to called a Judge, rather than President or Governor. When a portion of the population moved away to found Newport, they took the government with them, and those left behind in Portsmouth had to reform an independent government again (Howard M. Chapin, *Documentary History of Rhode Island*, Volume 2 [Providence 1919], Chapters III and VII).

NEWPORT: After one year at Portsmouth, William Coddington became dissatisfied with the new town, and went off with some of his supporters to the southern end

(continued on page 18)

EDITOR'S EFFUSIONS

In the Focus section of this issue, as part of our discussion of the town of Hampton, we include a brief tribute to Victor Channing Sanborn, an excellent but not very well known genealogist of a century ago. In the course of our work on the Great Migration Study Project we have encountered many similar researchers, some more prominent and some less, who have since about 1840 or so rooted around in the records of England and New England, trying to learn more about the ancestors of the first settlers of New England.

James Savage studied the records of Groton in the 1840s, for the Winthrops. At the turn of the century Henry FitzGilbert Waters scoured the wills at the Prerogative Court of Canterbury and other probate registries, and J. Gardner Bartlett and Elizabeth French looked everywhere for many families. A century and a half after Savage there is much work yet to be done, but without their efforts we could not be doing what we do today.

There is, of course, a well-known aphorism for this state of affairs: "If I have seen farther, it is by standing on the shoulders of giants." Those who would like to learn more about this form of television would benefit by putting genealogy aside for an evening and reading a truly remarkable and totally unclassifiable book by the sociologist Robert K. Merton, *On the Shoulders of Giants: A Shandean Postscript*, known affectionately to its devotees as OTSOG.

CORRECTION

Subscriber Raymond David Wheeler has pointed out an error in the last issue (*Great Migration Newsletter* 4 [1993]:14). The husband of Mary Wodell is given as George Lawton, when he was in fact Robert Lawton. Robert did have a father, a brother and a son named George, which may partially explain the blunder.

Robert Charles Anderson, FASG   Editor
Margaret F. Costello   Production Assistant

The *Great Migration Newsletter* (ISSN 1049-8087) is published quarterly by the Great Migration Study Project, a project of the New England Historic Genealogical Society
101 Newbury Street, Boston MA 02116

The subscription rate is $8 for one year and $15 for two years. The subscription year is the same as the calendar year.

(continued from page 17)

of Aquidneck Island, taking their one-year old government with them (Chapin, Chapter IX).

MILFORD: The settlers of Milford limited participation in town government to church members, and called their town meeting a General Court, the first meeting of which was on 20 November 1639 (*History of Milford, Connecticut, 1639-1939* [n.p., 1939], p. 7).

GUILFORD: Twenty-five men, led by Reverend Henry Whitfield, settled Guilford, and in June 1639 together signed a covenant for civil government, leaving the organization of the church until a later date; unlike some of the other city states, they did not declare allegiance to the king (Bernard C. Steiner, *A History of the... Original Town of Guilford, Connecicut...* [Baltimore 1897], pp. 24-25).

SOUTHAMPTON: In 1640 a number of the inhabitants of Lynn chose to move from that town to the eastern end of Long Island, where they founded the settlement that would become Southampton. By 1641 they were holding town meetings, which, as with some of the other little republics, were called General Courts (George R. Howell, *The Early History of Southampton...* [Albany 1887], pp. 50-51).

SAYBROOK: A fortified town was erected at the mouth of the Connecticut River in 1635 by a number of Puritan lords who had been trying for years to create a plantation of their own design. They had been frustrated in Massachusetts Bay, and again at Dover on the Piscataqua. They did not, however, devote much attention to Saybrook, for the greater part of their effort was directed to Providence Island in the Caribbean.

Note that these eight towns fall into three groups: those within the present bounds of New Hampshire, those within the present bounds of Rhode Island, and those along Long Island Sound and on the eastern tip of Long Island. The fates of these towns, the ways in which they lost their brief independence and were absorbed into larger sovereign bodies, were dependent on these locations.

Massachusetts Bay absorbed the towns north of the Merrimack very quickly. Dover, along with Strawberry Bank (later to become Portsmouth), submitted to Massachusetts government in 1641, and indeed many of the inhabitants had wanted this arrangement all along. Exeter held out a bit longer, but in May of 1643 some of the inhabitants of the town asked to join Massachusetts, and in September the petition was granted. The Massachusetts Bay General Court must have considered this a *fait accompli*, for they had included Exeter, along with

(continued on page 24)

Focus   on   HAMPTON

THE SETTLEMENT OF HAMPTON

The Massachusetts Bay General Court had in a sense begun the settlement of Hampton in 1636 when it allowed Richard Dummer and John Spencer to build a house there, probably a truck house for trade with the Indians. Massachusetts probably also had in mind the idea of staking out a claim in territory that they wanted, but which they weren't certain fell within the bounds of their patent.

Two years later Reverend Stephen Bachiler and a number of his associates, residing in Newbury, petitioned the Court that they be allowed this land for a new town, and on 6 September 1638 this request was granted.

Many historians have taken this action of the Court at face value and assumed that the settlement of Hampton took place in 1638. But this is immediately unlikely when one considers the time of year that the Court granted the petition; experienced New Englanders would not begin a new plantation that late in the year.

There are several lines of evidence which lead to the conclusion that the settlement of Hampton did not really get under way until the summer of 1639. First, this is the position of V.C. Sanborn (see below for more about this man), who noted that the few surviving baptismal records for these years make it virtually certain that Stephen Bachiler, and by implication most of his followers, remained in Newbury through the winter of 1638-9. This record began in Lynn in 1635, then moved to Newbury, where baptisms were performed as late as March of 1638/9; the first baptism identified as being in Hampton is undated, but probably took place in August of 1639, and others followed soon after.

Second, there is the evidence of a letter written by Bachiler to John Winthrop Jr. in October 1638, about a month after the General Court permitted the settlement of Hampton. He informed Winthrop that "we are resolved ... the second working day of the next week to set forward towards our plantation ... We were there & viewed it cursorily, & we found a reasonable meet place, which we shall shew you; but we concluded nothing" (*Winthrop Papers* 4:70). If they had still not made a final decision on the site for their settlement in October, there is little chance that any serious foundation work was done that fall.

Third is an undated list which contains the names of persons who came to Hampton in the first two years,

broken down into various categories, including those who came with Bachiler the first summer, and those who came in the second summer. This list exists as a loose sheet of paper in the files of the (Old) Norfolk County Court. Perhaps it was submitted to the court to assist in settling a dispute of some sort, but its association with other records has been lost.

The list has been printed more than once, appearing in the first volume of the *Provincial Papers of New Hampshire* (pp. 151-52) and in the *Genealogical Dictionary of Maine and New Hampshire* (where it is List 391a). The former of these two printed versions is highly unreliable, with rearrangements and omissions, while the latter is quite accurate.

We note immediately that Bachiler was said to have come to Hampton in the summer, which he could not have done in 1638, since summer was already past when the petition was granted, and from the letter cited above we know that in October of that year he and others were still engaged in exploratory visits to the site of what would become Hampton.

In addition, this undated list may be compared with other lists in the Hampton town records. The first recorded town meeting was held on 31 October 1639, and then at regular intervals thereafter. At a meeting on 30 June 1640, a summary list was entered of all those who had received grants of land.

The order of names in this list is similar to, but not the same as, the order in the undated list. Adjacent to some names in the town meeting list is a notation such as "if he come within 6 weeks" (this next to [_____] Jennery, who is undoubtedly Lambert Genere of Dedham, who did not settle in Hampton). Somewhat later in the list is "William Inglish (if he come within [_____] weeks)." This is evidence that on 30 June 1640 William English had not yet moved to Hampton, but that he was expected shortly. Since he is listed among those who came the second summer in the undated list, the second summer must be 1640.

The situation in Hampton may have been similar to that in Dedham, where the town was granted in 1636, and one or two families built houses in Dedham for that first winter, but the majority remained behind in Watertown, and made the move to the new town in 1637 (*Great Migration Newsletter* 4 [1993]:3). In like manner, we might suppose that a few hardy souls built rude dwellings at Hampton for the winter of 1638-9, but clearly the first large-scale settlement took place in 1639, when Stephen Bachiler came.

HAMPTON CHURCH

The story of the founding of the First Church at Hampton, and of its earliest years, comes across as just another typical episode in the long and stormy career of Stephen Bachiler. At the age of seventy-one Bachiler arrived in New England in 1632 as part of the Plough Company, a group of families which had banded together before leaving England, but whose exact religious goals are not known (V.C. Sanborn, "Stephen Bachiler and the Plough Company of 1630," *The Genealogist*, New Series, 19 [1903]:270-84).

Bachiler soon began the task of organizing a church at Saugus, with the families of the Plough Company as a basis. He quickly ran into trouble, and on 3 October 1632 the General Court ordered him to desist from organizing a church; on 4 March 1632/3 the Court relented and allowed Bachiler to proceed. Within two years Bachiler and his congregation were back before the Court, some claiming that the church was not properly organized. After an investigation a conference of church elders deemed that "they were a true church, though not constituted, at first, in due order, yet after consent and practice of a church estate supplied that defect." (For a somewhat more detailed version of the early history of the Saugus [Lynn] church, see *Great Migration Newsletter* 1 [1990]:20.)

Less than a year passed before controversy broke out again, Bachiler was ousted as minister, and the majority of the inhabitants of Saugus set about the business of organizing a new church. To their surprise Bachiler attempted immediately to reorganize his church around the few families that still adhered to him, thus raising the prospect of two churches in Saugus, something that the civil and ecclesiastical authorities in Massachusetts Bay were not ready to countenance. Bachiler and those with him did leave, with brief stops in Ipswich and Yarmouth before settling in Newbury.

Joseph Dow, in his *History of Hampton,* recounts some of this same history, and after discussing Bachiler's last actions at Saugus makes an interesting suggestion: "... here, in the renewal of the church covenant at Lynn, near the close of the year 1635 [by the old calendar, in which January and February come at the end of the year], we find the organization of the Hampton church" (p. 346). Dow apparently based his suggestion on nothing more than Winthrop's report of Bachiler's action, but if we follow Bachiler from 1636 to 1639, and listen to the later statements about him, we will see that Dow may very well be right.

There are at least three documents which suggest that Bachiler was minister of a congregation during his sojourn in Newbury. First, in a letter of 26 February 1643/4, after his ouster as minister at Hampton, and at a time when he was considering a call to the Exeter church, Bachiler described his situation for the church at Boston. After telling them of his arrival in 1632, he recounts "how the Lord shoved me thence by another calling to Sagust, then, from Sagust to Newbury, then from Newbury to Hampton" (*Winthrop Papers* 4:447). This is not a simple list of his removal from town to town, for we know from the town land grants that he resided in 1636 in Ipswich; by referring to callings he clearly implies that he led a church at Newbury.

Second, a few months later, in July of 1644, Winthrop enters in his journal an account of the upheavals in the Hampton church. In discussing the consequent call to Bachiler from the Exeter church, he points out that "Mr. Batchellor had been in three places before, and through his means, as was supposed, the churches fell to such divisions, as no peace could be till he was removed" (*Winthrop Journal* 2:216-17). Two of these three places were certainly Saugus and Hampton. By supposing that Newbury was the third Winthrop's account matches Bachiler's own in his February letter. Although this account does not tell us directly that Bachiler was minister of a church at Newbury, this would certainly complete the parallelism with Saugus and Hampton.

Third, a surviving page of baptisms, thought by V.C. Sanborn to be in the hand of Stephen Bachiler, spans the years from 1635 to 1641, and includes events occurring at Lynn, Newbury and Hampton (V.C. Sanborn, "The Grantees and Settlement of Hampton, N.H.," *Essex Institute Historical Collections* 53 [1917]:228-49, at 248; George Freeman Sanborn Jr. and Melinde Lutz Sanborn, *Vital Records of Hampton New Hampshire...,* Volume One [Boston 1992], pp. 3-4). While these might have been baptisms performed by other ministers, but preserved because they applied to families who later moved to Hampton, there is also the possibility that these were all baptisms performed by Bachiler during his peregrinations. On the other hand, he must have performed more baptisms than this over these years, and we would have to assume that he had retained records of only those in which the family followed him to Hampton.

Another suggestive record supports the hypothesis that Bachiler headed a church in Newbury. On 13 March 1638/9 forty-five men were made free at the Massachusetts Bay General Court. The last six of these were William Palmer, William Eastowe, Thomas Moulton, Richard Swayne, William Wakefield and Thomas Jones. All of these men were known to be in Newbury by 1638, but by 1639 had moved to Hampton. To be made free they had first to be members of a church, and the question arises: What church admitted them?

As we have seen in the previous section, the first large migration to Hampton took place in the summer of 1639, and not in the fall of 1638, so there would not have been a church at Hampton in March of 1638/9. There had been of course a church at Newbury since 1635, but the ministers of that church were Thomas Parker and James Noyes. Groupings of Newbury freemen are found on 25 May 1636 (John Knight to Anthony Mosse), 17 May 1637 (Henry Sewall Jr. to Thomas Coleman) and 2 May 1638 (Daniel Pierce to Henry Lunt), thus indicating regular admissions to this church.

We might expect that the six freemen of 13 March 1638/9 were just the next group of men admitted to Newbury church, except for one feature of this list: every one of the men went to Hampton. If this were just another batch of Newbury church admittees, we would expect perhaps to find some that stayed in Newbury and were never associated with Hampton and Bachiler, and some that did make the move to Hampton.

All of these records - Bachiler's letter, Winthrop's journal entry, the page of baptisms and the list of freemen - are consistent with the hypothesis that Stephen Bachiler was before 1644 minister of churches in three towns: Lynn, Newbury and Hampton. There can be no doubt about his ministry at Lynn and Hampton, but what are the further implications if we assume that he also led a church at Newbury?

As a first hypothesis, we might propose that Bachiler was one of the ministers at the known church at Newbury during these years. Our knowledge of the early years of the Newbury church is limited, and we do not have a contemporary list of ministers. But everything we do know points to Parker and Noyes as the ministers, in standard fashion for that time, with one as pastor and the other as teacher. There was not room for a third in the New England church government of that time. Furthermore Edward Johnson, although not the most reliable of sources, tells us in his *Wonder-Working Providence* that Noyes and Parker were the first ministers at Newbury; as a resident of Charlestown at the time Bachiler was in Newbury, Johnson should know what he is talking about here. And if Bachiler were minister at the Newbury church established in 1635, we would not expect to find a group of admissions, and therefore a group of freemen, none of whom stayed in Newbury.

The alternative hypothesis would be that Bachiler was minister of a second church at Newbury, independent of the Noyes/Parker church. This would be consistent with the four sources set forth above, and would support Dow's suggestion that the Hampton church had its birth in 1636 after the dissolution of the Saugus church. But this proposal runs into a different set of problems. Most importantly, the Massachusetts Bay authorities did not allow two churches in one town at this early date. Not until the founding of the second church in Boston, and then only after a long and difficult struggle, did the exist-

ence of two or more churches in one town become accepted practice.

If we are to accept the idea that Bachiler was running a second church at Newbury in 1638, then we must conclude that Winthrop and the other Massachusetts leaders treated Bachiler and his congregation as a special case. And we have some evidence for this position. The court orders relating to the difficulties of his stay at Saugus regularly distinguish between his general ministry to the population of the town, and his ministry to those that he brought with him. And clearly, in the agreement made at Bachiler's removal from Saugus, the General Court contemplated that he would continue to minister to those who stayed with him, without tying this congregation to any one town.

Bachiler throughout his nine-and-a-half decades went his own way, and frequently expected to be treated differently, or at least to get what he wanted. And perhaps, despite all his cantankerousness, he was held in special regard because, of all the ministers who came to New England in the 1630s, he was the only one who had actually been active at the peak of Elizabethan Puritanism in the 1580s.

While we cannot come to a definitive conclusion, we feel that a strong case can be made that for much of his time Stephen Bachiler carried his church around with him, and was not tied to one town as were all other churches. We can only hope for additional evidence to help us understand this unusual man and his many congregations.

THE DALTON-BACHILER CONTROVERSY

Wherever he went Stephen Bachiler became embroiled in controversy. As early as 1593 he was brought before Star Chamber for "very lewd speeches tending seditiously to the derogation of her Majesty's government," and in 1605 he was silenced for his outspoken Puritanism (*NEHGR* 74 [1920]:319-20). As we have seen above, he could not get along with his congregation in Saugus, and apparently not in Newbury either.

We should not be surprised therefore to find that he did not spend many years in Hampton before getting into trouble. Although our knowledge of the confrontation is fragmentary, we learn from Winthrop that by 1641, only two years into his ministry at Hampton, Bachiler was under attack from his colleague Reverend Timothy Dalton and from Dalton's many supporters in town. According to Winthrop, Bachiler "being about 80 years of age, and having a lusty comely woman to his wife, did solicit the chastity of his neighbor's wife" (*Winthrop's Journal* 2:53). After being censured, Bachiler was then excommunicated, and we hear no more of this matter for two years.

In the winter of 1643-4 Casco and then Exeter (or at least some families of Exeter) issued a call for Stephen Bachiler to become their minister, and at this time the differences between Bachiler and Dalton, and all the charges and countercharges of 1641, came into the open again. Bachiler wrote a long letter to the church at Boston describing his situation and asking for advice, and then another letter to Winthrop a few weeks later in a similar vein (*Winthrop Papers* 4:446-49, 457-59).

Winthrop discussed the call to the Exeter church in his journal, noting that the court stopped the action of Exeter "for they considered they were not in a fit condition for such a work." He noted further that at this court (apparently in May of 1644) "there came petition against petition both from Hampton and Exeter" (*Winthrop's Journal* 2:216-17). In other words, there were four petitions, two each from Hampton and Exeter, one supporting Bachiler and one opposing him. None of these petitions survive; if they did, we would have a wonderful insight into the factions that existed in these two towns at this early date.

Interestingly, at this same time the town of Hampton was beset by another controversy which made its way to the General Court. William Howard had been from the beginning of Hampton the leader of the town's train band, and in the process had developed a number of enemies. Petitions were sent to the General Court, and some of these survive (*Provincial Papers of New Hampshire* 1:165-67; *Winthrop Papers* 4:459-60).

During the course of these confrontations there are several entries in the records of the General Court in which commissioners were ordered to go to Hampton to "search and examine all differences" (Shurtleff, *Records of... Massachusetts Bay*, p. 147, this as late as 6 May 1646). Although it is not explicit, these commissioners were apparently investigating both the Bachiler dispute and the Howard controversy. It may be that these two conflicts were a reflection of some deeper schism in the Hampton population.

All the more do we regret the loss of the many petitions which flew back and forth in the fight between Dalton and Bachiler. If an exhaustive examination of these lost documents were possible, we might learn much about the inner dynamics of the Hampton population, about earlier patterns of migration, and about the fascinating character of Stephen Bachiler.

VICTOR CHANNING SANBORN

In our studies of the Great Migration we have frequently encountered such investigatory giants as James Savage, Henry FitzGilbert Waters and J. Gardner Bartlett. But there were others who were not so prominent, but who were just as skilled, and who made lesser, but still substantial, contributions to our knowledge of the early settlers of New England.

As a descendant of one of the three Sanborn brothers of Hampton, Victor Channing Sanborn (or, more commonly, V.C. Sanborn) was also a descendant of the Reverend Stephen Bachiler. As a consequence, he devoted such time as he could to research in English records of the Sanborns and the Bachilers.

In 1885, when he was only eighteen, Sanborn published in the Register "The Sambornes of England and America" (*NEHGR* 39 [1885]:245-55), which became the basis of his later book-length study of the family (*Genealogy of the Family of Samborne or Sanborn in England and America. 1194-1898* [n.p., 1899]), and indeed of all later research on the Sanborns.

His interest in Stephen Bachiler led V.C. Sanborn to undertake a careful study of the Company of the Plough, the religious group with which Bachiler was associated when he came to New England in 1632 ("Stephen Bachiler and the Plough Company of 1630," *The Genealogist,* New Series, 19 [1903]:270-84). This was only one of several articles which Sanborn chose to publish in England rather than in the United States.

In 1906 Sanborn helped to overturn the many-times printed fiction that Godfrey Dearborn had come from Exeter, or somewhere else in the West Country. He published wills which showed clearly the location of the family in Lincolnshire (*NEHGR* 60 [1906]:308-10).

One of the most interesting articles prepared by Sanborn was "The Grantees and Settlement of Hampton, N.H." (*Essex Institute Historical Collections* 53 [1917]:228-49), in which he examined the state of the knowledge at that time on each of the fifteen persons whose names are attached to the 1638 petition for the grant of the town of Hampton. In addition, he considered carefully the question of the date of the settling of Hampton, and arrived at a conclusion which is still seen to be substantially correct (see p. 19 above).

V.C. Sanborn stands out as a genealogist who approached his material objectively and systematically, unlike many of his contemporaries. Work like his, which survives the tests of time, is worthy of remembrance, and the modern reader of any of his articles will be well rewarded.

RECENT LITERATURE

David L. Greene, "The English Origin of Richard[1] North and His Daughter, Susanna[2] (North) Martin, Executed for Witchcraft in 1692," *The American Genealogist* 68 (1993):65-70. Greene demonstrates that Richard North, immigrant to Salisbury, Massachusetts, by 1641 was from Olney, Buckinghamshire, and was therefore part of the so-called "Olney cluster" delineated by Thomas Cooper. The baptismal record for Susanna (North) Martin is included.

Raymond David Wheeler, "The Father of Samuel[1] Stratton of Watertown, Massachusetts," *The American Genealogist* 68 (1993):84-86. The author confirms earlier suggestions that the immigrant Samuel Stratton was from Podington, Bedfordshire, and identifies his father and siblings.

Barbara J. Nichols, "Francis[1] Nichols of Stratford, Connecticut, Was Not a Brother of Deputy Governor Richard Nicolls of New York," *The American Genealogist* 68 (1993):113-14. Nichols provides additional information emphasizing and strengthening the conclusion that the origin and parentage of Francis Nichols of Stratford remain unknown.

David S. Lovejoy, "Roger Williams and George Fox: The Arrogance of Self-Righteousness," *The New England Quarterly* 66 (1993):199-225. Lovejoy examines the the points on which Williams and Fox agreed and disagreed, partly in the context of an attempt by Williams to engage Fox in debate when the latter was in Rhode Island in 1672. The confrontation between the two men is presented as a "battle between rational piety and unbridled enthusiasm," in which Williams came off second best.

Elizabeth French Bartlett, "The English Ancestry of Henry Ambrose of Hampton," *The New Hampshire Genealogical Record* 9 (1992):49-56. In a manuscript prepared more than fifty years ago (and now edited for publication by Melinde Lutz Sanborn) Bartlett identified Henry Ambrose, who settled in Hampton by 1640, as coming from Kersey, Suffolk, a parish immediately adjacent to Groton, the home of the Winthrops.

Oscar H. Kirkpatrick, "A Page Family Record," *The New Hampshire Genealogical Record* 9 (1992):58-62. The family record published here was prepared in 1807 by a man born in 1735, who was great-great-grandson of the immigrant Robert Page. Although some of the information about the earliest generations is incorrect, the document is an interesting example of a family record of this period. This private document does contain data on vital events not found in public records.

Robert Charles Anderson, "Philemon Dalton of Hampton, His Wife, and a Clue to His English Origin," *The New Hampshire Genealogical Record* 9 (1992):109. The author presents a marriage from Dennington, Suffolk, which is probably that of Philemon Dalton, immigrant to Dedham and then Hampton. His widow became the second wife of Christopher Hussey.

Douglas Richardson, "John Thompson of Weymouth and Mendon Was Not the Son of Mr. David Thomson of Thomson's Island," *The New Hampshire Genealogical Record* 9 (1992):110-16. Richardson argues, largely on the basis of difference in social standing, that John Thomson, the son of John Thomson, early settler on the Piscataqua, was not the same as John Thompson of Weymouth and Mendon. In the process the author provides much information on David Thomson.

Richard S. Wheeler, "More About the Partridge and Gaines Families of Olney, Bucks.," *The New Hampshire Genealogical Record* 9 (1992):180-81. Wheeler sets forth a few parish register entries which add to our knowledge of the Gaines and Partridge families of Olney, Buckinghamshire, part of the "Olney cluster" and settlers in Lynn, Massachusetts.

Stephen Baskerville, "The Family in Puritan Political Theology," *Journal of Family History* 18 (1993):157-77. Baskerville demonstrates how Puritan theologians utilized the images of everyday family life and relationships as metaphors of the believer's interactions with Christ and the church.

Robert Charles Anderson, "The Conant Connection: Part One, Thomas Horton, London Merchant, and Father-in-law of Roger Conant," *New England Historical and Genealogical Register* 147 (1993):234-39. The author identifies Sarah Horton, the wife of Roger Conant, as a daughter of Thomas Horton, a London merchant, and his second wife Catherine Satchfield. A second, earlier, marriage is found for Roger's brother Christopher, and adjustments are made to the birth order of the firt three children born to Roger in New England.

H. Clark Dean, " Eleanor Cogan, the Wife of Walter Deane of Taunton: An Evaluation of the Evidence," *New England Historical and Genealogical Register* 147 (1993):240-54. Based on the discovery of a relevant document from manorial records, combined with careful analysis, Dean argues strongly and convincingly that Eleanor, the wife of Walter Deane of Taunton, Massachusetts, was an elder daughter of William Cogan, by a first wife, and was not the sister of John Strong of Windsor.

(continued from page 17)

Dover, Hampton and Strawberry Bank, when they created Norfolk County on 10 May 1643. (See Charles E. Clark, *The Eastern Frontier* [New York 1970], pp. 37-47, for more detail on this process.)

The towns on Aquidneck Island took a different route to amalgamation. Portsmouth was founded in 1638, and Newport a year later, but only one year after that the two settlements had patched up their differences (mostly because of the efforts of William Coddington) to the point that they agreed to form a single government. This governmental entity of two towns continued in existence for seven years, holding General Courts from 1640 to 1647. In the latter year Portsmouth decided to join with Providence (which had obtained a charter in 1643), and Warwick and Newport soon followed, thus bringing Rhode Island as we now think of it into being. (See Charles M. Andrews, *The Colonial Period of American History,* Volume 2 [New Haven 1936], Chapter I, for a discussion of the stages in the creation of Rhode Island.)

Yet a third path was taken by the towns along Long Island Sound. A strong determinant here was the imminence of the organization of the New England Confederation in 1643, a combination of Massachusetts Bay, Plymouth, Connecticut and New Haven, largely for the purpose of common defense against the Indians. Only those four governments, and not any of the "city states," could join the confederation.

Milford and Guilford, which already had strong ties with New Haven, added themselves to that body. On Long Island, Southold went with New Haven, while Southampton chose to join Connecticut. With regard to Saybrook, Connecticut acted somewhat like Massachusetts Bay, using its superior strength to gain a foothold and then take over full control by 1644. Eventually, of course, New Haven, which never had a charter from England, was absorbed by Connecticut, when that colony recieved its own charter in 1662. (See Andrews, cited above, Chapters III, IV and V, for the story of Connecticut and New Haven.)

The heyday of the city state in New England lasted only a few years, as Massachusetts Bay Colony extended its reach into New Hampshire and the quasi-legal entities of Connecticut and New Haven took form. But during these years hundreds of immigrants to New England (or the adult male landowners, at least) had a chance to participate directly in the formation and running of independent governments. For that brief period they had closer contact with true democracy than they had ever had in old England, or than most of them would have in later years in New England.

Great Migration Newsletter

Vol. 4   October-December 1993   No. 4

DIARIES AND LETTERS

In previous issues of the *Newsletter* we have discussed a variety of sources, such as passenger lists, vital records and church records, which were generated by one official body or another. An important supplement to official records are the documents created by private individuals in the course of their everyday lives. We will examine here some of the diaries and letters written during the period of the Great Migration, and the way in which they interact with the official records to provide a more complete picture of the settlement of New England.

The most important diary is more than a diary - John Winthrop's *History of New England* (also known as Winthrop's Journal, and referred to hereinafter as WJ). This lengthy record includes private items, matters relating to the development of Massachusetts Bay and all the other early New England colonies, events at court which did not make it into the official court records, and much more. (In this *Newsletter*, and elsewhere in the work of the Great Migration Study Project, we use the 1853 edition prepared by James Savage. This is the most accurate edition yet to appear, and contains many useful annotations. The 1908 edition, part of the Original Narratives of Early American History series, was heavily bowdlerized, and should not be relied on. A modern edition would be most welcome.)

In one brief line Winthrop could provide a morsel of biographical detail available nowhere else, as, for example, under date of 7 April 1636 when he records that "Mr. Benjamin's house burnt, and £100 in goods lost" (WJ 1:220). This refers to John Benjamin of Watertown, and from this short entry we learn about his social status, the possibility that he was involved in trade, and a setback in his affairs.

Acting as magistrate, Winthrop recorded various misdemeanors in the back of his journal, such as the 20 July 1637 confession of John Hobby, apparently of Dorchester, that he had stolen some beaver skins from Samuel Cole of Boston (WJ 2:425-26). Entries of this sort are the equivalent of extracts from records of a magistrate's court, which otherwise do not exist this early.

Winthrop maintained his journal right up until his death in 1649, and so for the first two decades of Massachusetts Bay Colony this is an essential source for information about individuals and about the growth and change of New England communities and institutions.

At about the time of Winthrop's death John Hull, eventually mintmaster of the colony, began to keep his own diary, which was really two journals in one. First was an account of "Some Passages of God's Providence about Myself and in Relation to Myself," which, as one would expect from the title, confines itself to events within his own family (such as his marriage and the births of his children), and to the development of his own career (including his appointment to various colony offices) (*Transactions and Collections of the American Antiquarian Society*, Volume III [Worcester 1857], pp. 141-64). Parallel with this we find "Some Observable Passages of Providence Toward the Country" (ibid., pp. 167-250), which has some entries from the 1630s and 1640s, but begins in earnest in the 1650s and runs down to 1682.

This "public" portion of the John Hull Diary is especially useful for events in and around Boston, relating to the burgeoning merchant class, and including many of the pioneers of the 1630s who led long lives in New England. For example, it is Hull who supplies us with the information, not available in any other source, that Richard Davenport, who had arrived in New England in 1628 with Endicott, met his end on 15 July 1665 at the

(continued on page 26)

EDITOR'S EFFUSIONS

In an earlier issue we asked for suggestions for towns to be featured in the Focus section in the future. Several subscribers responded with specific requests, and some towns were mentioned more than once. As a result, the towns to be treated in 1994 will be Scituate, Weymouth, Southampton and Springfield.

We will attempt each year in the future to balance our coverage of towns in the Focus section, including at least one Connecticut town, one Massachusetts Bay town, and one Plymouth Colony town in each volume, with occasional forays into Rhode Island, New Hampshire and Maine.

Inasmuch as our cutoff date for the Great Migration Study Project is 1643, any settlement made by that year is eligible for inclusion in the Focus section. There were nearly eighty settlements made in New England by that year, including the New England towns on Long Island, a few of the Westchester County settlements, and the various fishing villages along the Maine coast. Consequently, there is enough material to keep the Focus section going for twenty years.

At about the time this issue of the Newsletter goes in the mail (mid-January) renewal notices will also be sent out. We are gratified that many subscribers have already sent in checks for renewal without being prompted, but everyone who has not resubscribed will receive timely notification.

Beginning with the July-September 1993 issue a new feature was added on the mailing label which should make it easier for you to determine the status of your subscription. In the upper left, immediately above your name, will be a two-digit number, which designates the last year for which you have paid. If the label on this issue reads "93" you should expect to receive a renewal notice. If it reads "94" or higher you need not worry at this time.

Robert Charles Anderson, FASG   Editor
Margaret F. Costello   Production Assistant

The *Great Migration Newsletter* (ISSN 1049-8087) is published quarterly by the Great Migration Study Project, a project of the New England Historic Genealogical Society
101 Newbury Street, Boston MA 02116

The subscription rate is $8 for one year and $15 for two years. The subscription year is the same as the calendar year.

(*continued from page 25*)

castle in Boston Harbor when he was "slain, with lightning, upon his bed" (p. 218).

Overlapping with John Hull's diary is that of Samuel Sewall, who began his entries in 1674 and continued until just before his death in 1729 (M. Halsey Thomas, ed., *The Diary of Samuel Sewall, 1674-1729*, 2 volumes [New York, 1973]). Sewall's diary also focusses on the Boston gentry, but is more inclusive and expansive than Hull's. Even though Sewall began his diary almost half a century after the arrival of Winthrop, there were still many immigrants from the 1630s living, the closing years of whose lives are documented by Sewall. On 18 December 1685, for example, Sewall reported that "Father John Odlin, one of the very first inhabitants of Boston, dies" (p. 88).

Just as John Winthrop's journal is the most important diary for the earliest years in Massachusetts, so the vast archive of correspondence collected by the Winthrop family is the largest collection of letters for the period. The Massachusetts Historical Society has published the papers of the Winthrop family from 1498 through 1654 in six volumes, with more to come (*Winthrop Papers*, 6 volumes [Boston, 1925-1992], hereinafter WP). (The Winthrop correspondence was also published much earlier in the *Massachusetts Historical Society Collections*, Fourth Series, Vol. 6 & 7, and Fifth Series, Vol. 1 & 8. In this version the letters were arranged by correspondent rather than chronologically, and so for some purposes may be a more convenient source.)

We have already made good use of the *Winthrop Papers* in previous issues of the Newsletter (e.g., GMN 3:10), and many extracts from the letters will appear in the sketches of individual immigrants. Frequently the Winthrop correspondence provides direct evidence of the English origin of an immigrant, especially of those who had lived in the neighborhood of Winthrop's old home in Groton. In a letter to John Winthrop of 17 January 1636/7, Robert Ryece described a dispute that had arisen in Lavenham, Suffolk, and had been carried over into New England. In support of his story Ryece stated that "the widow Onge, now of Waterton in N:E: but then of Lavenham," had witnessed one stage of the dispute in her own shop and could testify to the same (WP 3:347-48).

Many more letters have survived from other collections. Some years ago Everett Emerson gathered all letters he could find that had been sent from Massachusetts back home in the decade from 1629 to 1638 (Everett Emerson, ed., *Letters from New England: The Massachusetts Bay Colony, 1629-1638* [Amherst, 1976]).

(*continued on page 32*)

Focus   on   WETHERSFIELD

SETTLEMENT OF WETHERSFIELD

When the pace of migration to New England began to pick up in 1634 and thereafter, one of the Massachusetts Bay towns to feel the pinch of overpopulation was Watertown, a town which had been founded in 1630 at the coming of the Winthrop Fleet. The leading citizen in Watertown in that first year was Sir Richard Saltonstall, who brought with him many settlers from East Anglia, many with close associations with Winthrop and his part of Suffolk. These founders of Watertown were soon joined by immigrants from other parts of England, including especially a group from Yorkshire.

The standard history of Wethersfield is the massive two-volume set prepared by Henry R. Stiles, *The History of Ancient Wethersfield, Connecticut...*, 2 volumes (New York, 1904), hereafter Stiles. The first volume contains the historical material as such, and the second volume has the biographical and genealogical sketches of Wethersfield inhabitants. At the end of the second volume are several appendices which discuss various special topics, including the laying out of lands.

John Oldham, a man of considerable talent and great independence, who had settled at Watertown even though he had no close relationship with most of the early settlers of that town, made a prospecting tour to the Connecticut River in 1633, and reported back to his townsmen about the attractions of that region (Stiles 2:872-73).

Stiles argues, in one of the appendices (2:867-72), and in agreement with Charles M. Andrews, that a group of about eight men returned to the site of Wethersfield in 1634 and commenced the settlement there. Without desiring to enter into the debate over the priority of settlement as between Wethersfield and Windsor, a few cautionary comments should be made here.

The main evidence in favor of a 1634 settlement is the existence of a group of men known as adventurers, who received specific allotments of land by inclusion in this group (Stiles 1:24-29), and the likelihood that a crop of wheat was harvested in 1635, and therefore planted in 1634 (Stiles 2:868).

This all may be true, without requiring that the permanent settlement actually began in 1634. The adventurers may simply have invested financially in the move to the Connecticut at an early time, and this would seem very likely for such wealthy men as Nathaniel Foote and Leonard Chester. Others may have invested in the sense that they made a trip to the site of Wethersfield in 1634, examined the lands, and planted a crop to be harvested the next spring. Such people might well have received an additional grant of land, even if they did return to Watertown for the winter of 1634-5.

A small hint in favor of this latter interpretation is found in the Watertown land grants, where on 25 July 1636 Leonard Chester received a sizable tract of land in the Great Dividend. In Watertown at that time, one had to be a current resident in order to benefit from one's proprietary rights, and so it would seem that by that date Leonard Chester had not yet left Watertown.

Whatever the correct position on this point may be, we can say that, as with the emigrants from Cambridge (to Hartford) and Dorchester (to Windsor), a small group of the Watertown residents who were intending to move to the Connecticut did so in 1635, with a larger number following in 1636. When, on 3 March 1635/6, the Massachusetts Bay General Court granted a commission for the governance of the settlements on the Connecticut, the two men appointed for Wethersfield were Andrew Ward and William Swain, both of whom would receive "adventurer's land."

Within a few years Wethersfield itself began to feel the pinch of overpopulation, and at the same time dissensions were building in the church (see next page). As a result, emigrations from Wethersfield to even newer towns began when Wethersfield was itself only a few years old. A number of these departures from Wethersfield are discussed in Stiles (1:137ff.). There were contributions from Wethersfield to the settlement of Fairfield, Farmington, Milford, Branford and Guilford, among others.

We would like to take special note here of one exodus from Wethersfield which ties in with our earlier research on Watertown. One of the most important destinations for Wethersfield settlers who wished by 1640 to move on was the new town of Stamford. Reverend Richard Denton was a leading spirit in this migration.

When the early population of Watertown was studied, it was discovered that at least eight families which had settled early in that town decided in 1645 or 1646 to move directly to Stamford (*GMN* 1:8), including men such as Nicholas Knapp and Richard Ambler. In this way the earlier connection between Watertown and Wethersfield remained a powerful force ten years after the founding of the latter town.

WETHERSFIELD CHURCH

Very little is known of the early years of the church at Wethersfield, so little in fact that Sherman W. Adams, in his discussion of this subject in Stiles, was able to write only two pages (Stiles pp. 135-37). Wethersfield differed from its sister settlements, Hartford and Windsor, in that, whereas they had migrated with the churches that had been established in Massachusetts Bay, the Wethersfield settlers left the Watertown church behind, and therefore had to found a new church in their new town on the Connecticut River.

At the first recorded meeting of the Connecticut court, on 26 April 1636, it was noted that "a dismission was granted by the Church of Waterton in Masachusetts, dated 29th of Ma[rch] last, to Andrewe Warde, Jo: Sherman, Jo: Stickland, Rob'te Coo, Rob'te Reynold & Jonas Weede, with intent to form anew in a Church covenant in this River of Conectecott," which they have done "with the public allowance of the rest of the members of the said churches" (meaning presumably the churches at Hartford and Windsor). Thus, the founding of the Wethersfield church may be dated between 29 March and 26 April of 1636.

Among the many mysteries relating to the early history of this church is the identity of the early ministers. There was no shortage of qualified men in Wethersfield in the late 1640s, for during that period Richard Denton, John Sherman and Henry Smith would all settle in or pass through the town. Richard Denton was probably not in Wethersfield before 1640, as indicated by the terms of his first grant of land on 10 April 1640, which is worded as though he had just arrived in town (NYGBR 117:211). It is not likely that he was ever formally invited as pastor at Wethersfield, although he may well have preached at church meetings.

The list of the first six men dismissed from Watertown to form the new church at Wethersfield included John Sherman, but this was not necessarily the minister. The founders of a church in early New England would be all laymen, who would then unite in inviting a minister to lead their congregation. Thus, the John Sherman mentioned in the court order of 26 April 1636 may be Captain John Sherman, cousin of the minister. If so, he must have returned very soon to Watertown. Whichever John Sherman was in Wethersfield in 1636, he was sent to the colony court as deputy in May 1637, which would indicate that he was not serving as minister at the church at that time, as one man would not be allowed to hold civil and ecclesiastical posts simultaneously.

Homer W. Brainard makes a strong case that Henry Smith was already minister at Wethersfield by 1637, based in part on surviving family papers (TAG 10:7-14).

Smith was certainly in Wethersfield by the end of that year, and he was certainly pastor at Wethersfield in later years, but it is not clear that he had attained that position before 1640. Brainard's attempt to apply Edward Coke's "legal definition of a town" is not relevant, since English law and practice did not contemplate a church functioning on its own without a minister, as could be the New England way.

In July of 1639 John Winthrop took note of a schism in the Wethersfield church, where "of those seven which were the church, four fell off; so it was conceived, that thereby the church was dissolved, which occasioned the church of Watertown here (which had diverse of their members there, not yet dismissed) to send two of their church to look after their members" (Winthrop's Journal 1:367). Sherman Adams interprets this to mean that only one new church member had been added to the six who had formed the church three years earlier, and identifies this seventh member as Reverend Richard Denton. This may be true, but it is also possible that there had been some turnover in the church membership during these few years.

It may be, then, that the six founders of the church at Wethersfield were unable to attract a minister for these first few years (other than an occasional visiting preacher), and this would explain the failure of the number of church members to grow after 1636, and the retention by the early Wethersfield settlers of their membership in the Watertown church. The disappearance of all church records for both Watertown and Wethersfield until nearly 1700 makes the interpretation of these early years especially difficult.

WETHERSFIELD VITAL RECORDS

The earliest vital records for Wethersfield are in the volume labelled "Wethersfield Land Records - Vol. 1, 1640-1700." On the spine of this book, as it was bound in the late nineteenth century, there are the following dates for the vital records included: "Births 1635-1667/ Marriages 1648-1659/ Deaths 1649-1660."

Although the entries are not uniform in arrangement, most were entered census-style, taking up one family at a time. The earliest entries seem to have been made about 1650, or perhaps late in 1649. This is consistent with the beginning dates for marriages and deaths. The births dating as early as 1635 were clearly entered long after the fact, and there were very few after 1660, despite the indication that births as late as 1667 were included. In fact, as will be seen in the discussion of landholding, this book seems to have been little used after about 1660 for any purpose.

A typical family entry is that for Nathaniel Dickinson and his wife Ann. Five children are listed, the first being Sam[uel] who was born "about the middle of July 1638," and the last Azarias, born 10 October 1648. The vagueness of the date of birth of Samuel, and the uniformity of the ink and handwriting for all five children, indicate that this entry was made all at one time, no earlier than late 1648, and probably a year or two after that.

During the 1660s and 1670s some vital records were entered in the second volume of Wethersfield deeds. As we will see when discussing the next volume, however, not all of the births, marriages and deaths occurring in Wethersfield during these two decades can have made it into this book, since many additional items were entered after the fact at a later date in other places.

The first Wethersfield volume devoted principally to vital records is titled "Wethersfield Births Marriages Deaths, 1635-1843." At one end of the book are the vital records. When the book is reversed one finds a shorter section, containing Wethersfield ear marks, and orders of the colony court which applied to Wethersfield in particular or to town government in general.

Again, the inclusive dates for the vital records in this volume are misleading. A quick scan of the pages revealed many records from the 1660s and 1670s, a few from the 1650s, and none before. It may be that some Wethersfield antiquarian of the nineteenth or twentieth century saw that this was the first volume devoted solely to vital records, and thought that it must therefore have begun when the town was founded.

In fact, this second book of vital records was begun on 20 February 1678/9. A date is given in the upper left corner of each page, which appears to be the date on which the first entry on that page was made, and this is the earliest such date. As with the first volume, and more consistently, each page is initially devoted to one family, with several entries made at one time. These are frequently completed families, or families in which nearly all the children had already been born by the late 1670s or early 1680s. It is for this reason that so many of the entries have births from the 1660s and 1670s, even though these events occurred some years before the book was begun.

At the other end of the date range of this second volume, the year 1843 is also misleading. Regular use of the volume seems to have ended sometime in the 1730s or 1740s. Many of the entries were annotated, however, mostly with records of death for persons whose births are recorded here. Perhaps some of these annotations are as late as 1843.

One example, slightly atypical since it reaches back into the 1650s, is the family of Josiah Gilbert and his wife. This family group was entered as a unit on 18 March 1681/2, with a total of ten children, the first being Benjamin, born 22 September 1652, and the last Amy, born 12 April 1672. The first addition to this family entry was made just a few months after the original recording, when Elizabeth, wife of Josiah Gilbert, died on 17 October 1682. Among later annotations was the death record of son Josiah, ostensibly on 2 February 1765, although this would have made him 105 years old at death. This death entry was cross-referenced to another page in the volume where the record also appeared.

From the evidence in these volumes, births, deaths and marriages were not being actively recorded during the entirety of Wethersfield's existence in the seventeenth century. Because of the manner in which the entries were made we have records continuously, but certainly not completely, from 1635 to 1700. We need to be especially cautious, though, in using and interpreting those entries which include events from before 1650 or from the 1660s and 1670s. Some of this material may have been copied from earlier records of some variety, whether official or private. Part of the data, though, must rely solely on memory, and may be subject to greater error than the entries made contemporaneously with the events.

Apparently no vital records from Wethersfield were recorded at the colonial level during this period. Hartford and Windsor, but not Wethersfield, are represented in the records transcribed by Edwin Stanley Welles in 1898 as *Births, Marriages and Deaths Returned from Hartford, Windsor and Fairfield and Entered in the Early Land Records of the Colony of Connecticut.*

EARLY WETHERSFIELD LANDHOLDING

The first volume of Wethersfield town records is entitled "Wethersfield Land Records - Vol. 1, 1640-1700." As noted in the previous section this book also includes the earliest vital records of Wethersfield, but most of the volume is devoted to an inventory of the landholding in Wethersfield in 1641, with many records of transfers of title after that date.

At some point in the history of this book, the pages must have been reshuffled, since the earliest records now appear at the rear, with, for example, several pages from April 1640, in proper sequence, preceding a section for February 1640/1, again, within the few pages of this section, in proper sequence. This change in the arrangement of the pages sometimes makes it difficult to interpret the records, but usually the dates and relations of the individual entries are easily determined.

The earliest inventories of lands are dated 11 February 1640/1, with regular entries throughout the spring of 1641. Each page lists the holdings of one individual on that date, and apparently the recorder proceeded through the town, compiling the land records for several persons on any one day, and taking nearly half a year to complete his work. This procedure parallels what was done in Windsor at about the same time, and in Hartford a year earlier.

The actual grants of land on which these inventories are based had probably begun soon after settlement, in 1635 or 1636, but no lists of the grants of houselots, or of lots in the Wet Swamp, for example, have survived. Even though these inventories were gathered within a few years (five at most) after the grants, there are many indications of rapid turnover of the ownership of land.

On 27 April 1641, for example, were recorded the "lands of Jo: Robines Gent. which he bought of Jo: Clarke." This entry includes an extract from the actual deed of 10 October 1638 in which Clark sold the land to Robbins, a deed which does not exist elsewhere. Just a few pages later, on 28 April 1641, is the inventory of the "lands of William Comstock which he bought of Richard Mills."

There are, of course, landholdings which had been continuous from the founding of Wethersfield. The lands of Andrew Ward were recorded on 24 March 1640/1, and those of Robert Abbott on 5 April 1641. Both of these men had been among the earliest to move from Watertown to Wethersfield, and had not by 1641 relinquished any of their original grants.

What was a typical set of land grants? We will look at the inventories of three men who appear to have been typical of the Wethersfield population - neither very wealthy nor very poor. In his inventory of 24 March 1640/1, Andrew Ward is credited with eight parcels of land: houselot, four acres; Great Meadow, fourteen acres two rods; Great Meadow & Swamp, four acres three rods; Back Lots, two acres three rods; Dry Swamp, eight acres; Wet Swamp, six acres; West Field, fifty-four acres; and East Side of Connecticut River, two-hundred-sixty-four acres.

A few days later, on 5 April 1641, the holdings of Robert Abbott, seven parcels, were listed: houselot, three acres and a half; Great Meadow, three acres; Great Meadow & Swamp, eight acres and a half; Pennywise, four acres three rods; West Field, thirty-four acres; Wet Swamp, four acres; and Dry Swamp, eight acres.

Later in the same month, on 24 April, "Tho: Uffoatt," or Thomas Ufford, who had arrived in Wethersfield by way of Roxbury and Springfield, and not from Watertown, was shown as holding nine lots: houselot, four

acres; Great Meadow, four acres; Great Meadow, seven acres; Back Lots, five acres; Wet Swamp, ten acres; East Side of Connecticut River, one-hundred-seventeen acres; Pennywise, five acres three rods thirteen poles; West Field, sixteen acres; and West Field, sixteen acres and a half and five poles.

The sequence of grants is very familiar to us from our study of various Massachusetts Bay towns, although Cambridge may be a slightly better model here than Wethersfield's parent town of Watertown. The grant of a houselot, which presumably established proprietary rights, was followed by grants of a few acres of meadow and swamp land, which quickly becomes some of the most valuable land in town. These grants are then supplemented by somewhat larger grants of arable land, in this case the lots in the West Field. And then there are the grants of land on the East Side of the Connecticut River; given their size, these were apparently seen as lands of little value, which would not or could not be developed for many years to come, and may be likened to the Farms in Watertown. (For a verbatim transcript of one of these early inventories, see the estate of Edward Mason of Wethersfield, which was probated on 4 September 1640 [Charles William Manwaring, *A Digest of the Early Connecticut Probate Records*, 3 volumes (Hartford, 1904-1906), 1:23-24]. Mason apparently died shortly before these inventories were recorded, and so his record of landholdings appears as part of his inventory.)

As the many migrations away from Wethersfield in the early 1640s took place, land frequently changed hands, and this is reflected in the records in this volume. On 28 April 1644 four parcels were recorded to Thomas Ufford "which he bought of John Plum and Jo: Thompson." Not quite three years later, on 3 March 1646[/7], is the inventory of the "land of Will[iam] Goodrich which he bought of Tho: Uffoot lying in Wethersfield on Conecticot River." Sometime between the two dates Ufford had moved south to Milford.

We have examined above the grants made to Robert Abbott. On 2 June 1647 were entered the "lands of Tho: Olcott of Herford [Hartford] which he bought of Robt. Abbott of Totocat." Totoket was the native name for the town which soon became Branford, so Abbott had moved to this town by 1647, perhaps by way of New Haven.

In these early years there are no deeds as such for these transfers of land, and all we can say is that the sale must have taken place by the date on which the lands are entered to the new owner. Thus, even though we do not have deeds in the modern sense, we can frequently trace a continuous chain of title through these land inventories in this first volume of Wethersfield land records. Most entries in this first volume of land records (despite the dates in the title) end about 1660, when a second volume of deeds was begun.

RECENT LITERATURE

Clifford L. Stott, "English Origins of William and Judith (Tue) Knopp of Watertown, Massachusetts," *New England Historical and Genealogical Register* 147 (1993):313-28. The origin in Bures St. Mary, Suffolk, of William Knopp of Watertown, and of Thomas Philbrick who married Elizabeth Knopp, has been available in the genealogical literature for decades. Stott has identified the parents and wife of William Knopp, and has found baptisms for all the known children of this couple. Furthermore, the author has disentangled two contemporary William Knopps of Bures St. Mary, and has shown that the William Knopp who was brother-in-law of Thomas Philbrick was not the immigrant to Watertown, although there may have been a more distant relation. Finally, Stott found nothing to support the oft-stated claim of close kinship between William Knopp and Nicholas Knapp of Watertown.

Ralph Parmenter Bennett, "Further Notes on the English Background of John Parmenter of Sudbury and Roxbury, Massachusetts," *New England Historical and Genealogical Register* 147 (1993):377-82. Following up on the research of Elizabeth French earlier in this century, Bennett adds additional data to her Parmenter pedigree, and supports her conclusion on the placement of the immigrant to Sudbury in this family, noting at the same time that additional evidence in support of this identification would bo welcome.

Larry D. Gragg, "A Puritan in the West Indies. The Career of Samuel Winthrop," *The William and Mary Quarterly*, Third Series 50 (1993):768-86. Gragg narrates the life history of Samuel Winthrop, a younger son of Governor John Winthrop, as he established himself as a prominent planter on Antigua. The author then uses this material to reinterpret the accepted picture of the West Indian planter class, showing that not all were "rapacious entrepreneurs [who] lacked a sense of responsibility to family, church, and community." As an interesting sidelight, Gragg notes that Samuel Winthrop sent his sons back to New England for elementary schooling at Watertown under Ephraim Child, an old Winthrop family friend.

Robert Charles Anderson, "The Marriage Record for John[1] Shepard and Margaret Squire of Braintree, Massachusetts," *The American Genealogist* 68 (1993):145. That John Shepard of Braintree married Margaret Squire has been known for many years. The record of the marriage has been found in the 1630 Bishop's transcript for Kingweston, Somerset.

Robert Charles Anderson, "Notes on the Reverend Joseph[1] Hull of Weymouth and Barnstable, Mas-

sachusetts, and York, Maine," *The American Genealogist* 68 (1993):149. The author has found evidence that Joseph Hull was curate at Broadway, Somerset, for the two years prior to his emigration for New England in 1635. This note also includes the 1625 baptism for Temperance, daughter of Joseph Hull, from the Bishop's transcript for Northleigh, Devonshire. (She later married John Bickford of Dover, New Hampshire.)

Robert Charles Anderson, "The English Origin of Robert[1] Hinsdale of Dedham, Medfield, Hadley and Deerfield, Massachusetts," *The American Genealogist* 68 (1993):159. Baptisms for two children of Robert and Anne Hinsden of Pulham St. Mary the Virgin, Norfolk, are presented, and the argument is made that these are the two eldest children of Robert Hinsdale, immigrant to Dedham, Massachusetts, by 1637.

Melinde Lutz Sanborn, Robert Charles Anderson and Dean Crawford Smith, "The English Woltertons: Ancestors of the Waller and Brockway Families of Connecticut," *The American Genealogist* 68 (1993):160-75. The authors set forth records for the Wolterton family of Norfolk, including a compiled account of this family which included Gregory Wolterton, immigrant to Hartford, Connecticut. In addition, they further refine the analysis of Gregory Wolterton's will, and add new material on the connections between Wolterton and the Waller and Brockway families of New England.

John Plummer, "The English Origin of John[1] Holland of Dorchester, Massachusetts," *The American Genealogist* 68 (1993):176-81. Following up on leads derived from the New England connections of John Holland, Plummer presents data which locate the origin of Holland in Plymouth, Devonshire. The parents and wife of the immigrant are also identified, and baptismal records for the first three children of the immigrant couple are included.

Constance Post, "Old World Order in the New: John Eliot and 'Praying Indians' in Cotton Mather's *Magnalia Christi Americana*," *The New England Quarterly* 66 (1993):416-33. Post analyzes Cotton Mather's biography of Reverend John Eliot, emphasizing Eliot's missionary work among the Indians. The author points out that Mather dwells at length on the difference between the Puritan and the Catholic standards for allowing the Indians to be baptized and enter the church. Not surprisingly, Mather speaks approvingly of the high standards maintained by Eliot, equal to those employed in the churches run by the Puritans for themselves, and contrasts this with the relaxed standards of the Jesuits in New France.

(*continued from page 26*)

One of the most interesting items in this compendium is the long letter from Thomas Dudley to the Countess of Lincoln, written in the latter half of March 1630/1 (pp. 67-83). This letter, composed in a style similar to some of the published pamphlets of the period, provided much detail on the dispersal of the Winthrop Fleet around Massachusetts Bay, and even beyond, taking note of some immigrants who had removed to the Piscataqua or had even returned to England. Dudley also described the sequence of settlement of the Massachusetts Bay towns in 1630 and 1631.

Of more particular interest are the reports Dudley made of the deaths of various individuals. We are told that "about the beginning of September died Mr. [William] Gager, a right godly man, a skillful chirurgeon, and one of the deacons of our congregation" (p. 72). "Amongst those who died about the end of this January, there was a girl of eleven years old, the daughter of one John Ruggles, of whose family and kindred died so many that for some reason it was matter of observation amongst us..." (p. 77). Both Gager and Ruggles had been neighbors of Winthrop in England.

Also of interest from this volume is the December 1634 letter from James Cudworth of Scituate to his stepfather, Dr. John Stoughton (pp. 139-42). Cudworth re-lates much detail on the churches of Plymouth and Massachusetts Bay colonies which had been founded by that date (and their ministers), and on others that were in the process of being established. He also informs Stoughton that "my uncle Thomas is to be married shortly, to a widow that has good means and has five children." This would be the second marriage for both Thomas Stoughton (brother of Dr. John Stoughton), at that time of Dorchester, and Margaret (Baret) Huntington, the widow of Simon Huntington, who had come to New England in 1633.

The celebrated Roger Williams also left behind much corespondence (Glenn W. LaFantasie, ed., *The Correspondence of Roger Williams*, 2 volumes, 1629-1682 [Providence 1988]). The majority of these letters were to or from the Winthrops, and so much of this material had already been published in WP. But there are some items unique to this collection, such as a letter from George Ludlow to Williams written not long before 26 October 1637. Ludlow did not leave many traces during his brief stay in New England, and this letter is valuable in outlining his life.

Many more sources of early correspondence might be sampled, but these brief extracts should be sufficient to demonstrate that private sources are excellent places to look for details of historical and genealogical information omitted from the official records.

Great Migration Newsletter

Vol. 5   January-March 1994   No. 1

MIGRATION FROM COUNTY ESSEX

East Anglia, even if narrowly defined as just the three counties of Essex, Norfolk and Suffolk, made a larger contribution to the Great Migration than did any other region of England. What is perhaps not so well known is that immigrants from each of these three counties left England at different times and at different rates, and so the contributions of each of these three counties to the early development of New England were distinct.

Immigrants from Suffolk were disproportionately represented in the Winthrop Fleet of 1630. This should certainly not be surprising, since Winthrop recruited heavily in the area around Groton in southwestern Suffolk. The bulk of these Suffolk arrivals in Massachusetts Bay settled in Boston and Watertown. There were, of course, many more hundreds of Suffolk migrants in later years, from all parts of the county, but the pattern for this part of East Anglia was set early.

Norfolk differed in that relatively few came with Winthrop, or in the three years immediately following. Except for the beginnings in 1633 of the large migration from Hingham, most of the Norfolk contingent of the Great Migration came in the high migration years from 1634 to the end of the decade.

Essex occupied a position intermediate between Suffolk and Norfolk in the temporal unfolding of the settlement of Massachusetts Bay. From 1620 through the end of 1630, only a handful of persons who can be identified as from Essex appeared in New England. On the *Mayflower* were Christopher Martin, from Great Burstead, and his stepson Solomon Prower, but they both died soon after arrival.

In the Winthrop Fleet no more than half a dozen were certainly from Essex, including George Phillips of Boxted, and his parishioner Edward Howe, both of whom settled in Watertown, along with their neighbor in England, John Page of Dedham. William Colbron and Edward Converse, both from the parish of South Weald, were also substantial citizens, but they did not at the time bring many others from the same neighborhoods.

The pace of migration from Essex began to change in 1631. Perhaps the most important of these new immigrants was the Reverend John Eliot of Nazeing, Essex, who would become minister at Roxbury. As will be seen, he had developed a wide network of relatives and acquaintances consequent upon his ministerial activities in Nazeing, Chelmsford and Little Baddow, all in central and west Essex. He arrived on the *Lyon* on its second voyage of 1631, landing at Boston on 2 November. With him on that vessel were his brother, Philip Eliot, and his brother-in-law and sister, James and Lydia (Eliot) Penniman. Also in the same party was the large family of Richard Lyman, coming from High Ongar in Essex.

Not quite a year later, on 16 September 1632, the *Lyon* made yet another voyage, bringing one-hundred-twenty-three passengers, the majority from Essex. Many of these passengers were, or would become, attached to John Eliot and his church at Roxbury. These included John Cogswell (or Coggeshall), from Halstead, William Heath, from Nazeing (but before that from Ware in Hertfordshire), William Curtis from Nazeing, and Thomas Ufford from Nazeing. Many more would come to Roxbury from Nazeing and vicinity in later years, but these immigrants of 1631 and 1632, as well as some from 1633 whose passage is not recorded, formed the core of the Roxbury church.

On the same ship were several more families, also from Essex, but from a little further east. From Braintree came the prominent families of William Wadsworth and

(continued on page 2)

EDITOR'S EFFUSIONS

Some time has passed since we have discussed in this column the status of the main element of the first phase of the Great Migration Study Project, the preparation of the sketches of those nine hundred families and unconnected individuals who arrived in New England by the end of 1633. All but a few of the sketches have been drafted, some of them as short as five or six lines, and some as long as five or six pages. The process of revising the sketches and putting them into final form is well underway, and as each letter of the alphabet is completed, it is sent out for indexing and proofreading. In this way the volumes will be ready for the press soon after the writing process is completed.

One of the reasons that this set of books has taken longer than originally predicted is that the amount of material to be presented has expanded by almost fifty percent. Because we wish to correct as many errors as possible, and discuss all points in controversy, the average length of each sketch will be considerably longer than in the original plan. All of those who have read preliminary versions of some of these sketches have recommended maintaining this material, and not attempting to omit some items simply to attain some preconceived length.

Consequently, there will be three volumes covering these early years, rather than two, containing in excess of two thousand pages. We currently contemplate publication late in 1994 or early in 1995, and interested parties can expect to see pre-publication publicity in the mail by autumn, and further announcements in the July-September issue of this newsletter (which will be in the mails in less than six months from the arrival of this issue).

Suggestions for towns to be treated in the Focus section have continued to come in with renewals, for which we are grateful. We now have enough ideas for several years to come.

Robert Charles Anderson, FASG   Editor
Margaret F. Costello   Production Assistant

The *Great Migration Newsletter* (ISSN 1049-8087) is published quarterly by the Great Migration Study Project, a project of the New England Historic Genealogical Society
101 Newbury Street, Boston MA 02116

The subscription rate is $8 for one year and $15 for two years. The subscription year is the same as the calendar year.

(*continued from page 1*)

John Talcott. In August 1632 Governor John Winthrop noted that "The Braintree company, (which had begun to sit down at Mount Wollaston), by order of court, removed to Newtown. These were Mr. Hooker's company" (*Winthrop's Journal* 1:104-05). The families affected were Talcott, Wadsworth, and several others who had come on the *Lyon*. They were the vanguard of the large migration clustered around the Reverend Thomas Hooker, one of the most influential ministers of early New England. They removed to the nascent town of Newtown (later Cambridge) to await the arrival of Hooker. Many of them were admitted to freemanship on 6 November 1632; since there was no church at Cambridge at the time, they must first have been admitted to some other Massachusetts Bay church, presumably Watertown, whose early records no longer exist.

In 1633 both the Roxbury and Cambridge contingents were further augmented. This was more significant for Cambridge, since Thomas Hooker arrived on the *Griffin* on 4 September of that year, and so he and those who came with him, along with the families who had arrived in 1632, were soon able to organize a church. On the *Griffin* with Hooker was John Haynes, of Copford Hall, Essex, one of the wealthiest and most prominent of the early immigrants to New England.

In addition to these two strongly-associated groups of immigrants were arrivals from a third area of Essex, the market town of Saffron Walden, in the far northwest of the county, not far from the borders of Suffolk, Cambridgeshire and Hertfordshire. These half dozen or so families were not clustered around a charismatic minister, and they did not all settle in one Massachusetts Bay town. In this group were George Minot, who went to Dorchester, Samuel Bass and Cotton Flack, who settled in Boston, and Thomas Pidge, whose residence was Roxbury.

Although the numbers of immigrants in these three Essex groupings were not large, we need to remember that the total of immigration to New England in the years 1631, 1632 and 1633 was quite low. As a result this Essex contribution to New England immigration immediately after the arrival of the Winthrop Fleet was proportionally quite important.

The period between the arrival of the Winthrop Fleet in 1630 and the beginning of the heavy years of immigration in 1634 was a precarious one for New England. A number of persons not well-regarded by the Puritans had managed to get to Massachusetts Bay, and several of

(*continued on page 8*)

Focus on SOUTHAMPTON

PRELUDE TO SETTLEMENT

With the heavy migration of the latter years of the 1630s, all the older towns settled in Massachusetts Bay were becoming overcrowded. In 1637 Lynn had already sent off a sizable contingent to begin the town of Sandwich on Cape Cod, but even with these departures Lynn remained in 1640 too densely populated.

On 10 March 1639/40 several Lynn residents composed and signed a document known as the "Disposall of the Vessell," in which they allotted shares in their ship and contracted with Captain Daniel Howe of Lynn to assist them in settling on Long Island. (This document survives in the Southampton Town Hall and has been printed in the first volume of Southampton town records [hereafter STR] on pages one and two.)

At this time the Earl of Sterling laid claim to Long Island, and his agent James Forrett was in New England attempting to sell off portions of his master's property. (Of course the Dutch of New Netherland also felt that Long Island belonged to them.) The company of undertakers who had signed the "Disposall of the Vessell" then purchased from Forrett on 17 April 1640 "eight miles square of land," although the exact location on Long Island of this tract is not set forth in the deed. It is not clear whether the purchasers had an understanding with Forrett where they would set down, or whether they had free rein to choose a parcel of the appropriate size anywhere on Long Island. (This deed must have been executed at New Haven, since the witnesses were Theophilus Eaton and John Davenport.)

The tract of land they chose was on the Long Island Sound side of Long Island, in the vicinity of Manhasset Neck. When they began settlement there, in early May of 1640, most of the pioneers were apprehended by the Dutch and taken to New Amsterdam for questioning, since the Dutch believed this area to be part of their colony.

Those taken to Manhattan were Job Sayre, George Welby, John Farrington, Philip Kirtland, Nathaniel Kirtland and William Harker. The interrogatories to which these men were subjected survive and make very instructive reading. Each was asked the same series of questions, including name, place of birth, age and residence in New England. Inasmuch as these documents were first written in Dutch and then translated to English the place names and personal names are somewhat distorted, but can serve as strong clues to English origins, although in most cases the origins of these men are known from other sources.

For example, one of those questioned was "Jan Farington," aged twenty-four, from "Bockingamschier." This is of course John Farrington, who is known to have come from Olney, Buckinghamshire, where he was baptized in 1622 (TAG 65 [1990]:67). In these perilous circumstances, this young man had added six years to his age. (These interrogatories are in *New York Historical Manuscripts: Dutch, Volume IV, Council Minutes, 1638-1649*, trans. Arnold J.F. Van Laer [Baltimore, 1974], pp. 75-85; other documents pertaining to the same event may be found in B. Fernow, ed., *Documents Relating to the History of the Early Colonial Settlements Principally on Long Island ...* [Albany, 1883], 28-31.)

On 19 May 1640 the six prisoners were released, and the attempted settlement on Long Island Sound was abandoned. Some of the undertakers returned to Lynn, but others apparently remained on Long Island, in preparation for their second attempt shortly afterward.

SUGGESTED READING: There are two standard histories of Southampton, the earliest of which was prepared by George Rogers Howell (*The Early History of Southampton, L.I., New York, with Genealogies*, 2nd ed. [Albany 1887]). The historical portion is relatively brief and in the usual nineteenth century fashion arranged topically. The more valuable part contains the compiled genealogies, and is especially important for the nineteenth century material which may have been known only to the author and his contributors.

The second full-scale history was written by James Truslow Adams, one of the leading professional historians of the early twentieth century (*History of the Town of Southampton* [Bridgehampton 1918]). His history proceeds chronologically, with all aspects of Southampton life blended into the single narrative strand.

An excellent recent discussion of the settlement of Southampton and the events that led up to it was published by Thomas Cooper in *Suffolk County Historical Society Register* (15 [Spring 1990]:97-105, 16 [Summer 1990]:11-24). These two articles make many corrections to the earlier literature. Cooper focussed on the relation between the Pequot War and subsequent settlement along both sides of Long Island Sound, and on the leading role of Captain Daniel Howe in the settlement of Southampton. The author converted the New Style dates of the Dutch documents into the Old Style dates still in use in the Puritan colonies.

SETTLEMENT OF SOUTHAMPTON

After being ejected from their first chosen site on Long Island, the undertakers wasted little time making new plans. Back in Lynn, on 4 June 1640 the undertakers reaffirmed and made changes to their original agreement, in a document headed "A Declaration of the Company" (STR 1:6-7). At this same time they added at least one new undertaker, Mr. John Gosmer.

In a deed of 12 June 1640 James Forrett again granted a portion of the Earl of Sterling's lands to the men from Lynn, described this time as "all those lands lying and being bounded between Peacooeck and the easternmost point of Long Island with the whole breadth of the Island from sea to sea ..." (Adams, History of the Town of Southampton, pp. 263-64), with adjustments made on 7 July 1640.

Many of the families intending to move to Southampton remained in Lynn for some months more and, as will be noted in more detail below, organized a church in Lynn before the move. By December many of these persons had made the migration to Long Island, and on 13 December 1640 the inhabitants purchased the land from the Indians (STR 1:12-14).

From this date the town may be regarded as firmly established, as it had both a civil and a church covenant, and had, from the English point of view, clear title to the land. Like so many other New England settlements at this time, Southampton was a government unto itself, and not part of any of the established colonies (see GMN 4:17 for a discussion of other towns in similar circumstances). As such it held its own courts, and did not send representatives to the General Courts elsewhere.

These "city states" throughout New England were slowly absorbed by their larger and more powerful neighbors. As early as September of 1643 Southampton was contemplating amalgamation with New Haven Colony, for at that time the Commissioners for the United Colonies of New England gave permission for Milford and Southampton to take that step (Plymouth Colony Records 9:9). Milford did become part of New Haven, but Southampton reconsidered.

A year later, in September 1644, the same body granted to Connecticut the liberty to receive into their jurisdiction "Southhampton upon Long Iland" (PCR 9:21), and at the Connecticut General Court of 25 October 1644 Southampton took its place as the sixth town in that colony, represented by Mr. John Moore and Robert Bond (Colonial Records of Connecticut 1:112).

Between 1874 and 1925 William S. Pelletreau and others transcribed eight volumes of Southampton records, and these were published by the town. The bulk of the first published volume of records reproduces the first volume of town meeting records, from 1640 to 1660 (pp. 17-152). On page sixteen Pelletreau states that in 1862 he found "two rolls of paper ... which proved to be the leaves of a book, these I arranged in chronological order," which after binding became this first volume. Many entries in the book as published seem out of order, and deeper analysis might find that another sequence for these pages would be more acceptable. The index in the published volume is inaccurate and far from complete, and should be ignored.

The first fifteen pages of this first published volume are what might be called the town's "foundation documents," including the "Disposall of the Vessell" and the "Declaration of the Company." The originals of these are bound in a separate manuscript volume, along with some pages of court records for Southampton. The volume concludes with a few entries from a book of town accounts and an appendix with transcripts of other documents relating to the early history of the town. (The three succeeding published volumes are similarly arranged (for later dates), and the fifth volume includes more early documents, as well as some early deeds.)

The published version of the Southampton town records contains an amusing error which needs to be pointed out. At the outset of many town meetings, the clerk made a list of all freemen or townsmen (and those absent might be fined). The meeting of 8 March 1649[/50] is headed "A list of the perfect freemen inhabiting this Towne of Southampton" (STR 1:55). The term "perfect freemen" does not appear elsewhere, in Southampton or in all of New England, and some writers have tried to find an appropriate interpretation, thinking perhaps that it might have some specialized technical significance. But reference to the manuscript version of the town records shows that what was written was "A list of the present freemen ...," a standard formulation which does not require special interpretation.

In the Southampton town archives are several other unpublished volumes of seventeenth century records. Most important are two volumes of deeds, labelled D2 and D3, and covering the years 1678 to 1693 and 1698 to 1737 respectively. The numbering of these volumes does not necessarily imply that there was ever a volume D1, for, as with many other New England towns, the early volumes of Town Records also incorporate many deeds, so the town clerk may have thought of the first volume devoted solely to deeds as a continuation of the early material which had been mixed in with other town records, and therefore labelled it D2.

Beyond these volumes, the town vault also houses books of earmarks, court records, and other miscellaneous records.

EARLY SOUTHAMPTON LANDHOLDING

As with so many other New England towns, the Southampton town records, at least in the early years, do not record land grants in which all or even a large portion of the town's population participated. The houselots, and probably the meadow and arable lots as well, must have been granted to the earliest settlers during the winter of 1640-1, before the town records begin.

From the beginning there seem to have been irregularities and inconsistencies in the way that land was granted, leading to many controversies. Eventually the Connecticut magistrates had to intervene, and in 1647-8 a more clearly defined system was imposed on the town.

Before looking at this settlement we should examine those regularities which are discernible in the first seven or eight years of Southampton's existence. Our best evidence for this comes from those few examples in which a man newly arrived in town acquires a full complement of lots.

RICHARD ODELL: Before discussing this man's landholdings, one misunderstanding about his presence in Southampton must be resolved. On the agreement which immediately follows the "Disposall of the Vessell," and which was probably composed at Lynn early in 1640, the last name in the published version of this document is given as "the mark of Richard Odell," and this has been taken by many researchers to be the first appearance of Mr. Richard Odell, or Woodhull, anywhere in New England.

There are many problems with this, however, and this reading cannot be correct. First, Mr. Richard Odell of Southampton was one of the wealthiest inhabitants, and was frequently appointed to carry out the town's business. That such a man would not be able to sign his own name is highly unlikely.

Second, Howells in his history of the town reads the name as Richard Dyall. Examination of the manuscript of this document shows that the surname is most likely "Uzall," although the last few letters of the signature have been overwritten and can no longer be read with certainty. There was a Richard Uzell who appeared briefly at various places in New England in the late 1630s and 1640s, whose social status would more probably comport with an illiterate man appended to the end of such a record. If this document was in fact written at Lynn, then Richard Uzell most likely never went to Southampton.

The first record of Mr. Richard Odell in Southampton occurred on 7 March 1643/4, when he was assigned to the fourth ward of the town, for the purpose of benefitting from whales which might wash up on shore (STR 1:32).

A little more than a year later, on 7 July 1645, appears a very important record, in which it is "ordered that Mr. Richard Odell shall have given unto him the house lot that was formerly belonging unto Mr. Cole of Hartford, with the 8 acre lot belonging formerly unto the said Mr. Cole, with 48 acres of upland, and ten acres upon the plain with meadow and other appurtenances thereunto belonging upon condition that he possess the same three years and pay dues as are thereunto belonging" (STR 1:37).

There is no indication that Odell had bought or been granted any land prior to this, so apparently even so wealthy and prominent a man had to wait more than a year before being allowed all the privileges of proprietorship. He must have resided in Southampton for a year either as a renter, or as a guest in the home of some other inhabitant.

EDWARD JONES: On 22 October 1644 the Southampton General Court ordered that Mr. Jones should have "the lot granted unto him which was formerly granted unto John Budd of Yeanocock [Southold], viz: the house lot lying next unto Mr. Stanborough's to the north, and the ten acre lot that was Mr. Winthropp's, and eight acres which was appointed unto Mr. Cole of Hartford, and four acres of old ground upon the plain, if it can be found out, and 48 acres lying next to Mr. Cole's, provided that if he shall remove from this place with his family before 3 years shall be expired, that then he shall not sell more of the said allotment than he hath improved ..." (STR 1:33).

The elements that are common to these two collections of land are a house lot, an eight acre lot (probably "planting" or arable land) and 48 acres of upland, the least valuable land at this time. (The ten acre lot received by Jones is apparently another piece of arable land.) The "ten acres upon the plain with meadow" in Odell's collection of lots seems to be of mixed quality, but certainly includes the meadow land so important to the early settlers in maintaining their cattle. The "four acres of old ground upon the plain" would seem to be the meadow land obtained by Jones. In rough outlines, then, this "standard" collection of lots is much like what we have seen in towns in Massachusetts Bay.

On 11 June 1647 Edward Hopkins and John Haynes from Connecticut rendered an opinion as to the original intent of granting land, stating that "when the limits of the plantation were set out every man should have for quantity and quality within the bounds of the town & plantation alike according to their several proportions" (STR 1:45), again an arrangement well-attested in older New England towns. This opinion was accepted by the townsmen, and some pages further along in the town records, but probably on the same day (the date is given only as 11 June, without a year), "it is ordered by all the inhabitants of this town this day that this town is to be divided into forty house lots, some bigger some less, as men have put in a share, six thousand pounds to be divided into forty parts" (STR 1:50).

The consequence of this set of rulings is that from that date on each man's proportional share in the propriety was referred to as a lot of so many pounds. Thus one man might be entitled to a £150 share, while another might receive land in new dividends according to a £50 share. This only meant that the former man's acreage in a given dividend would be three times that of the latter proprietor. The "value" of the share in pounds had nothing to do with the actual value of the piece of land granted.

The forty house lots of the 11 June 1647 order corresponded to a £150 share, but of course there were more than forty households in Southampton. The £150 shares usually appeared in three pieces, each corresponding to a £50 share. Of course, some of the wealthier settlers would be entitled to a larger share. An interesting example is "Mr. Sticklin of Hempstead" [John Strickland] who "by his deputy his son-in-law Jonas Wood hath upon the second day of July in the year 1650 drawn for his meadow ground for his proportion of land being three hundred lb." (STR 1:47).

On 27 March 1648, apparently as part of the new arrangement, the town ordered that a £50 share would imply a three-acre house lot (STR 1:50-51). This had already been the practice in some cases, as for example on 17 February 1647/8, when the town ordered "that Mr. John Howell shall have 3 acres for a home lot" (STR 1:43). At a later date one finds further grants of three-acre house lots, such as those to Thomas Cooper on 3 September 1650 and to John Kelly on 10 April 1651 (STR 1:47, 48). On 5 March 1651[/2?] this order was repealed (STR 1:72), but three acres probably continued as the norm for house lots.

The references to shares of £100 or £50 continued to appear at many places in the town records, as for instance in the division of the Sagaponack lands in 1654 (STR 1:99-101). There were forty-one allotments, each designated as being at one or the other of these rates, and again they would correspond to the relative share of that grantee, and not the absolute value of the lot.

These few examples do not describe the full complexity of the system of granting land in early Southampton. Even so, this town clearly followed the basic New England pattern, already practiced in many Massachusetts Bay towns and known to many of the Southampton settlers, of a sequence of lots including a house lot, small parcels of meadow and marsh, a piece of arable land of modest size, and a larger tract of upland.

EARLY SOUTHAMPTON CHURCH

Once the undertakers had resolved on their second attempt at settlement on Long Island, at the eastern end, they wasted no time in organizing a church, even before most of them had left Lynn. Winthrop tells us that "being now about forty families, they proceeded in their plantation, and called one Mr. Pierson, a godly learned man, and a member of the church of Boston, to go with them, who with some seven or eight more of the company gathered (9) [i.e., November 1640] into a church body at Linne, (before they went), and the whole company entered into a civil combination (with the advice of some of our magistrates) to become a corporation" (*Winthrop's Journal* 2:7).

"Mr. Abraham Pierson a studient" was admitted to Boston church on 5 September 1640, and on 11 October 1640 "Our brother Mr. Abraham Peirson had leave granted by the Church to join in the gathering of a Church at the Long Isleland." As noted above he was within a month ordained minister of the new church intended for Southampton, and by December he was in Southampton, for on 13 December 1640 he was one of the witnesses to the purchase of the eastern part of Long Island from the Indians.

On 6 April 1641 "Mr. Abraham Pierson" was granted the second lot in a series of three on the Little Common (STR 1:22), apparently an addition to an earlier grant. Then on 7 March 1643/4 he was included in a list of those inhabitants allocated to the second ward (STR 1:32). His last appearance in Southampton town records was on 24 June 1647 when he and seven other of the town's leaders swore to an act of the whole town (STR 1:45).

Many writers have limited Peirson's ministry in Southampton to the years from 1640 to 1644, and claim that he removed to Branford in the latter year. But the document above makes it clear that he was in Southampton some years after 1644, and probably left not long before 1649 when his successor, Robert Fordham, was brought in. Pierson does not appear in Branford before 1650, when his daughter Grace was born there. In later years he moved again, to participate in the founding of Newark, New Jersey, where he again was minster, and where he died in 1678.

Records for these early years of the Southampton church do not survive.

(Abraham Pierson earned entries in both the *Dictionary of National Biography* and the *Dictionary of American Biography*. See also a brief account of his life in Samuel Eliot Morison, *The Founding of Harvard College* [Cambridge, 1935], p. 396.)

RECENT LITERATURE

William Thorndale, "A Clue to Richard Wollaston of Mount Wollaston," *The American Genealogist* 68 (1993):207. Using Virginia records, Thorndale has determined that Captain Richard Wollaston, briefly in New England in 1624, was nephew of Hugh Wollaston of Virginia.

Gale Ion Harris, "The Family of William[1] Kelsey of Hartford, Connecticut: With Notes on Hester[2] Kelsey, Wife of James[2] Eggleston, James[1] Eno, and John[1] Williams of Windsor, Connecticut," *The American Genealogist* 68 (1993):208-15. The author employs careful chronological analysis, including especially data from the Winthrop medical journals, to reinterpret the family of William Kelsey, immigrant to Cambridge, and then to Hartford. Most importantly, Harris determines that the older children of Kelsey were several years younger than had been thought. As noted in the subtitle of the article, much space is devoted to William's daughter Hester, and evidence for her three marriages.

Clifford L. Stott, "The English Ancestry of Humphrey[1] and Susan (Pakeman) Wythe of Ipswich, Massachusetts," *The American Genealogist* 68 (1993):216-24. Stott shows that Humphrey Wythe (or Wise), immigrant by 1636 to Ipswich, had resided in Nacton, Suffolk, and then in Woolverstone in the same county, the parish which had been ministered to by Reverend Timothy Dalton, who also came to New England. The author identifies the father of the immigrant, and possibly two additional generations in the Wythe line, as well as some of Humphrey's maternal ancestry.

Harry Macy, Jr., Addition to Gwenn F. Epperson, "The True Identity of John Sales Alias Jan Celes of Manhattan," *New York Genealogical and Biographical Record* 124 (1993):226-27. In the article here added to, Epperson demonstrated that the John Sales first in Charlestown moved to New Netherland, and was not the man of the same name who appeared in Rhode Island (*NYGBR* 123 [1992]:65-73, noted in *GMN* 3:24). Macy reanalyzes a New Amsterdam marriage of 21 August 1644, concluding that this entry records the second marriage of John Sales. This in turn leads to the conclusion that records found in the parish register of Little Waldingfield, Suffolk, belong to the same man.

Mark A. Peterson, "The Plymouth Church and the Evolution of Puritan Religious Culture," *New England Quarterly* 66 (1993):570-93. Although there has been significant recent research on church government in the early Plymouth church, little has been done with regard to the religious experience of the members of that church. Peterson undertakes a survey of that aspect of Plymouth

church during the period that Plymouth existed as a separate colony, examining first the early years when the church was frequently without a minister, and then the ministry of John Cotton, son of the famous minister of the same name at Boston. In the first decades of the Plymouth chuch, Peterson notes the following elements which made this church much different from those established in the Massachusetts Bay Colony: "the closed, lay-dominated character of the institution, the stagnant membership, the absence of sacraments, the limited and tentative spiritual guidance of the laity, [and] the shortage of preaching and catechism."

Gale Ion Harris, "John Blackleach, Merchant, of London and New England," *New England Historical and Genealogical Register* 148 (1994):7-44. The author has compiled a detailed account of the life and family of John Blackleach, a merchant who resided in several New England towns. He treats also the sons and grandsons of the immigrant, and in a separate section discusses Richard Blackleach of Stratford, Connecticut, who may be related to John Blackleach in some manner.

Douglas Richardson, "The English Ancestry of Edward[1] Porter of Roxbury, His Sister, Elizabeth (Porter) Johnson, and Their Cousin, Elizabeth (Dowell) Payson," *New England Historical and Genealogical Register* 148 (1994):45-60. Extending his earlier work on the Heath and Johnson families, Richardson provides evidence that Edward Porter of Roxbury, his sister Elizabeth (who married Isaac Johnson), and his cousin Elizabeth Dowell (who married Giles Payson) were from the parish of Ware in Hertfordshire, as were many of the other early immigrants to Roxbury.

Douglas Richardson, "The Gore Family of Roxbury: New Evidence and Suspected Connections," *New England Historical and Genealogical Register* 148 (1994):61-65. Building on the article immediately above, the author presents the baptismal records of the two eldest children of John and Rhoda (_____) Gore, from the parish of Ippolitts, Hertfordshire.

Clifford L. Stott, "English Background of George[1] and Margery (Hayward) Wathen of Salem and Their Nephew, William[1] Sargent of Gloucester, Massachusetts," *New England Historical and Genealogical Register* 148 (1994):67-78. Stott demonstrates that George Wathen, resident by 1640 at Salem, married at Trowbridge, Wiltshire, and then moved to Bristol before coming to New England. Furthermore, the sister of George Wathen married Andrew Sargent of Bristol, and they were parents of William Sargent who also came to New England and resided at Ipswich and Gloucester.

(*continued from page 2*)

them were punished and sent back to England, where they mounted a campaign among the enemies of the Puritans to have the charter of the Massachusetts Bay company revoked. In addition, some of the Puritans themselves were sending back gloomy reports, telling their friends back home that the land was not all that good, and that they lacked adequate provisions.

In this atmosphere the chance of the survival of the Puritan experiment would have been even more seriously threatened if there had been no new arrivals in New England, to at least replace those of the Winthrop Fleet who died or returned to old England. For this reason alone, Massachusetts Bay Colony owed much to the immigrants from Essex who made up such a large part of the new arrivals in the three years after Winthrop's landing. (Essex shares this honor with the West Country counties of Devon, Dorset and Somerset, for many of the immigrants from 1631 through 1633 were from this part of England, following along behind their countrymen who came to New England in 1630 in the *Mary & John*.)

Another feature of migration from Essex in the three years after the Winthrop Fleet is unique to that county. Insofar as the Great Migration as a whole was motivated by religious beliefs and principles, it may be argued that one of the crucial events was the elevation of William Laud from Bishop of London to Archbishop of Canterbury in August of 1633, and that this set off the high level of migration to New England beginning in 1634.

As a prelude to this argument, we should note that Laud was instituted as Bishop of London in July of 1628, and the entire county of Essex was in the Diocese of London. We do not have to look far to see the probable influence of Laud on the Puritans in Essex. Thomas Hooker and John Eliot had been running a school with strong Puritan leanings in Little Baddow, Essex, but not long after Laud became Bishop of London they closed down the school, and Hooker at that time left for the continent to escape persecution.

Under this interpretation, then, Laud's tenure in London was in all aspects preparation for his time as Archbishop of Canterbury, and his efforts immediately led to increased migration to New England from Essex. If the point made above is correct, that this Essex contingent was critical to the survival of New England in these transitional years, then Laud ironically contributed to the survival of his worst enemies.

A directed program of research in the surviving records of the Diocese of London could provide evidence to support this version of events, and in any event would add much to our knowledge of this episode in the Great Migration.

Great Migration Newsletter

Vol. 5   April-June 1994   No. 2

CHURCH MEMBERSHIP

Earlier articles in the *Great Migration Newsletter* have discussed the importance and the interpretation of lists of freemen, and in that context have pointed out that in Massachusetts Bay Colony, after 18 May 1631, church membership was a prerequisite for freemanship. As the New England church developed in the early years, the requirements for church membership changed, and soon it was necessary for each prospective member to relate a "conversion narrative," in which he or she described how it was that they had arrived at the condition of being certain of having saving faith, that is, being among the elect who, according to orthodox Calvinist doctrine were the only ones who would be saved.

The starting point for all research on this arcane subject is the work of Edmund S. Morgan, who elucidated much of the development of this procedure in New England (*Visible Saints: The History of a Puritan Idea* [Cornell University Press: Ithaca, 1965]). He pointed out that the Puritan churches in England and on the continent had for many years required that prospective church members demonstrate a knowledge of "historical faith," that is, that they should be able to respond to questions about their knowledge of reformed religion in the fashion of a catechism. There was also a requirement that the candidates demonstrate that they lived in a Godly manner. But all these things could be done by a "hypocrite," that is by someone who was only pretending to rebirth as a Christian. One strand of Puritanism demanded more, and the conversion narrative was the result.

The central point of Morgan's argument is that the conversion narrative did not exist in England or on the continent, but that it was an invention of those Puritans who came to Massachusetts Bay, as they created their new church in the 1630s. More particularly, Morgan argues that this step in being accepted as a member of a congregational church emerged about 1634, and that John Cotton, the teacher of the Boston church, was the leading figure in its development.

Very recently Michael J. Ditmore has come forth with a reinterpretation of some aspects of Morgan's thesis ("Preparation and Confession: Reconsidering Edmund S. Morgan's *Visible Saints*," *The New England Quarterly* 67 [1994]:298-319). While accepting Morgan's point that these relations of religious rebirth did develop in New England, he argues first that Thomas Shepard, rather than John Cotton, was the central figure in the creation of this requirement. Then, whereas Morgan had argued that the process began about 1634 and was fully developed early in 1636, Ditmore presents evidence that this procedure was not completely in place until 1638. He relates these activities to the period of reacting to and bringing under control the Antinomian activities of Anne Hutchinson and her followers, which reached their peak in 1637.

The largest and most important collection of conversion narratives to survive is that of Reverend Thomas Shepard of Cambridge. The bulk of these are contained in a notebook which Shepard entitled "The Confessions of Diverse Propounded To Be Received & Were Entertained As Members," which has been published as *Thomas Shepard's Confessions* (George Selement & Bruce Woolley, eds., [Boston 1981]). This volume contains fifty-one confessions, all of Cambridge residents, covering the years from about 1638 to 1645.

An additional group of narratives recorded by Shepard has been discovered more recently and published by Mary Rhinelander McCarl ("Thomas Shepard's Record of Relations of Religious Experience, 1648-1649," *William & Mary Quarterly*, Third Series, 48 [1991]:432-66).

(continued on page 2)

EDITOR'S EFFUSIONS

The lead article in this issue, on conversion relations, and the section on Scituate serve to remind us of the differences between Massachusetts Bay and Plymouth Colony, and beyond that of a larger theme of the first generation of settlment in New England.

When the Puritans were still in England, many of the differences which they had among themselves were submerged, or even went unnoticed, so long as they had common enemies such as Charles I and Archbishop Laud. But as soon as they reached New England, where the King and his agents could not easily reach, these differences became more important.

Thus, church membership became a prerequisite to freemanship in Massachusetts Bay, but not in Plymouth. Plymouth towns could wrangle over ministers for years without colony interference, but Massachusetts Bay towns could never do this. Charles Chauncy could argue for adult baptism more openly in Plymouth than he could in the Bay (although he was called to become President of Harvard College not long after the events related in these pages).

Similar differences may be found if we compare also Connecticut and New Haven colonies, and of course the disparities are even greater when we look at Rhode Island and the fishing communities north of Massachusetts.

Much of the history of New England in the 1630s and 1640s can be seen as the efforts of twenty thousand men and women of strong opinions to find a community of like-minded individuals, in a group of communities which differed very little one from another.

We regret the delay in the publication of this issue of the *Newsletter*. Our plan is to produce the next three issues at two-month intervals, which will put us back on schedule early next year.

Robert Charles Anderson, FASG   Editor
Margaret F. Costello   Production Assistant

The *Great Migration Newsletter* (ISSN 1049-8087) is published quarterly by the Great Migration Study Project, a project of the New England Historic Genealogical Society
101 Newbury Street, Boston MA 02116

The subscription rate is $8 for one year and $15 for two years. The subscription year is the same as the calendar year.

(*continued from page 9*)

This second and smaller Shepard notebook contains the relations of sixteen Cambridge residents, between May 1648 and August 1649.

The next largest collection of relations may be found in the notebook kept by Reverend John Fiske, most of which covers his ministry at Wenham. He maintained a record of all church business, whether disciplinary, sacramental or otherwise, and scattered through these pages are twenty-one conversion narratives (Robert G. Pope, ed., *The Notebook of the Reverend John Fiske, 1644-1675* [Boston 1974]).

Finally, a few conversion narratives recorded by Michael Wigglesworth have been preserved as part of his diary, and were edited and published by Edmund S. Morgan (*The Diary of Michael Wigglesworth, 1653-1657: The Conscience of a Puritan* [New York 1965]). Although Wigglesworth was minister at Malden at the time of this diary, three of the four narratives were for men from Cambridge, or with strong Cambridge association, and two of them showed extensive reliance on the writings and preaching of Reverend Thomas Shepard.

The surviving conversion narratives have been exploited extensively by scholars with a variety of interests. Patricia Caldwell studied them as a form of literature, and discussed their place in the development of American literature as a whole (*The Puritan Conversion Narrative: The Beginnings of American Expression* [Cambridge, England, 1983]). Three years later Charles Lloyd Cohen examined the same records from a religious perspective, exploring the importance of the conversion experience in the lives of the Puritans (*God's Caress: The Psychology of Puritan Religious Experience* [Oxford, 1986]).

More recently Michael McGiffert has come forth with a new edition of the autobiography of Thomas Shepard, with selections from his journal (*God's Plot: Puritan Spirituality in Thomas Shepard's Cambridge*, revised and expanded edition [Amherst MA, 1994]). This new edition incorporates a selection from the Cambridge conversion narratives already published. The volume concludes with an annotated bibliography on "The Cambridge Texts" and "On the Uses of the Cambridge Texts," which includes further detail on all of the items cited above, and many more as well.

The conversion narratives frequently contained bits of biographical information not found elsewhere, although the allusions can be quite obscure at times. Because most of these persons had already committed themselves

(*continued on page 16*)

Focus   on   *SCITUATE*

THE FOUNDING OF SCITUATE

Scituate was the third town organized in Plymouth Colony, preceded only by Plymouth itself and by Duxbury. One finds the claim in some secondary sources that Scituate was settled as early as 1628, but this appears to be based on a single incorrectly dated deed.

In the first volume of Plymouth Colony deeds (published as the twelfth volume of *Records of the Colony of New Plymouth in New England*, Nathaniel B. Shurtleff, ed. [Boston 1855-1861]) is a record whereby Henry Merritt of Scituate sold to Nathaniel Tilden of the same town a parcel of land in Scituate, dated 10 April 1628, but recorded 20 April 1644. This is one of a series of five deeds recorded the same day, all conveying Scituate land, the others being dated from 1636 to 1643. As there is no record of the parties involved in this deed being in New England before the mid-1630s, the date of this document should more likely be 1638, and the proposed settlement of Scituate by 1628 must be rejected.

The earliest volume of Scituate town records, as yet unpublished, includes some grants of land from the town of Scituate to various individuals dated as early as April 1633, which implies that some people were certainly present in that year, and probably in 1632. Three men received grants of land on 12 April 1633 "at the second cliff": Mr. William Gilson, Anthony Annable and Edward Foster. Anthony Annable had been in Plymouth Colony for a decade in 1633, but Gilson and Foster are not seen in records which would place them in the town of Plymouth before this date, so they may have only recently arrived. In any case, pending the discovery of additional evidence, these three men stand as the earliest settlers of Scituate.

At a General Court held at Plymouth on 1 January 1633/4 three constables were appointed - one for Plymouth, one "for the ward of [blank] bounded between Jones River & Green's Harbour," and a third "for the ward of Scituate." This record tells us many things. The area between the Jones River and Green's Harbor would become known as Duxbury, but apparently at this early date it had not yet been given this name, even though several families had been living there for some time.

Second, the designation of Duxbury and Scituate as "wards" at this time indicates that they were not yet viewed as separate towns, but as outlying parts of Plymouth. (The situation had been similar in Massachusetts Bay, where Winthrop and some of the other leaders apparently believed briefly that the settlement of several towns in 1630 was only temporary, and that the residents of these places would soon gather back into a single, compact settlement.)

Third, by comparison with later lists of town officers in the colony records, we see that the colony officials from the start maintained these lists in the order in which the towns were founded. Thus, three years later, at the General Court of 3 January 1636/7, the three constables were listed in the same order - New Plymouth, Ducksbury and Scituate. And on 5 March 1638/9 the constables were listed in the following order - Plymouth, Duxborrow, Scituate, Sandwich, Cohannet [Taunton], and Yarmouth.

In some other colonies antiquarians have argued for centuries as to whether this town was more ancient than that other neighboring town. For Plymouth Colony, these lists of officers have overriding importance, and obviate the need for such arguments.

The most prominent of the settlers of early Scituate was Mr. Timothy Hatherly, a wealthy merchant who had been at Plymouth in the early 1620s, but had returned to England several times. Next in importance was Mr. James Cudworth, who probably arrived in 1634. The original grants of land to these two men do not appear in the early records.

As noted in the next section, Reverend John Lathrop recorded the houses that existed in Scituate when he arrived, and those that were constructed in the years immediately after. His list is headed "The houses in the plant[ation of] Scituate at my coming hither, only these which was about end of Sept. 1634" (or more precisely, as he says elsewhere, 27 September 1634). At that point nine houses existed - Mr. [Timothy] Hatherly, Mr. [James] Cudworth, Mr. [William] Gilson, Goodman [Anthony] Annable, Goodman [Henry] Rowley, Goodman [Humphrey] Turner, Goodman [Henry] Cobb, Goodman [John] Hewes, and Edward Foster. (Note that this list includes the three men who had received the earliest recorded grants of land in the town [Gilson, Annable and Foster].)

In the two years between Lathrop's arrival and October 1636 fourteen more houses were built, and then another thirty-four in late 1636 and in 1637, after which Lathrop ceased recording this activity. His list frequently includes the information that one of the earlier settlers had built a second house within this short period, and sold the first house to a newcomer to town.

THE LATHROP CHURCH

Most of the ministers who came to New England during the Great Migration were English university graduates, and most had held a benefice in an English parish; they were, in other words, non-separating Puritans. The separatists in the Puritan movement were most definitely in the minority, the most famous of them being the Scrooby congregation which removed to Leyden and then came to Plymouth in 1620.

There was from the middle years of the reign of James I a separatist church which led a precarious existence in London, known as the Jacob church from the name of its first minister, Henry Jacob. Mr. Jacob was succeeded as the head of this church in 1624 by John Lathrop, who had been a minister in Kent for some years. In 1630 this church began to suffer differences within its own ranks, and then in 1632 a large part of the congregation was arrested, with the result that Lathrop spent two years in prison. After his release he came to New England, and it is not surprising that he chose to settle in Plymouth Colony, with its separatist traditon, rather than in Massachusetts Bay Colony. (The story of the Jacob-Lathrop church is told at great length by Murray Tolmie in *The Triumph of the Saints: The Separate Churches of London, 1616-1649* [Cambridge, England, 1977].)

When Lathrop arrived in Scituate he immediately began to keep records of events in town, in this case going beyond the normal categories of baptisms and burials. Of greater relevance to the growth of the town than the church, he took notice of the houses that had already been built before his arrival, and those which were built for some years after that time. Stiles, in the course of his antiquarian activities in the 1760s, saw the manuscript and made a transcript, but he could not always read Lathrop's hand. The person who appears in the Stiles transcript as "Christopher Cointer" can only be "Christopher Winter," for example. This transcript was published in 1855 and 1856, and undoubtedly additional errors were introduced at that time (*Register* 9:279-87, 10:37-43). The original of this document has apparently vanished from sight since Stiles saw it.

The Lathrop records as published begin with church admissions, starting with the organization of the church on 8 January 1634/5, with thirteen persons joining on that day. The admissions continue regularly until 11 November 1638, when there is a gap until the spring of 1643. In other words, no persons were admitted (assuming that what has come down to us is complete) from a year before the congregation moved to Barnstable until nearly four years after.

The records continue with baptisms and burials, in both cases beginning early in 1635 and ending in the mid-

dle of 1653, with a clear notation of when the events in Scituate stopped and those in Barnstable began.

This section of the records is followed by entries for many marriages of Scituate and Barnstable residents. This does not imply that Lathrop differed from the standard New England Puritan position that marriage was a civil contract, and should not be performed by a minister. In many cases Lathrop records the magistrate who performed the marriage, and several of these weddings took place in Plymouth or in some town in Massachusetts Bay, so this is most certainly not a record of marriages performed by Lathrop.

The next portion of the records as printed contains material relating to various church activities, such as days of humiliation and thanksgiving, as well as excommunications, disciplinary matters, and other miscellaneous matters. Finally, Lathrop included an accounting of the houses built in Scituate, as discussed above.

Among these miscellaneous categories of records kept by Lathrop was one not often seen - "Contraction." There were only three events under this heading, all of which took place after the church had moved to Barnstable. In one, "Our Sister Hull" renewed her covenant with Barnstable church; she had briefly joined the Yarmouth church, but soon repented. The other two entries were for marriage contracts - John Smith and Susanna Hinckley in 1643 and Henry Atkins and Elizabeth Wells in 1647.

When Lathrop left for Barnstable in 1639 with his many followers, many houses became available for purchase by newcomers, just as was the case in several Massachusetts Bay towns in 1635 and 1636, at the time of the removal to the Connecticut River by inhabitants of Watertown, Cambridge, Dorchester and Roxbury.

During Lathrop's ministry at Scituate thirty-six men and twenty-six women joined the church. Of these, nineteen, including Lathrop himself, left for Barnstable (although one or two, such as James Cudworth, soon returned to Scituate). A few others departed for other destinations in 1639 - Simon Hoyt to Windsor and Thomas Boyden to Watertown. Samuel House, Thomas Besbeech and George Kenrick had also left Scituate within another year or two, and William Gilson died in the winter of 1639/40.

As a result, there were only ten male members of Lathrop's church left behind in 1640 - Humphrey Turner, Edward Foster, Timothy Hatherly, Thomas Lapham, Isaac Stedman, William Vassall, Isaac Chittenden, John Winter, Richard Sillis and Thomas King. These were the men who would have to face the problem of gathering a new church.

CHAUNCY AND WETHERELL

After the departure of John Lathrop and much of his congregation for Barnstable in 1639, those church members who remained behind in Scituate had to decide how to proceed in a church manner. Our best evidence for this period of church history in Scituate has been printed by Samuel Deane in his history of the town, and constitutes the most important part of that history (Samuel Deane, *History of Scituate, Massachusetts, from its First Settlement to 1831* [Boston, 1831; rpt. 1975], pp. 59-90). The relevant documents which Deane prints were preserved by what later became known as the Second Church of Scituate, the church presided over by William Wetherell.

The first step taken by those who remained behind was to consult with Lathrop before his departure. The consensus was that the residue of the church which would still be in Scituate would be sufficient to constitute a church on their own.

Two ministers, apparently, briefly supplied the Scituate pulpit after the departure of Lathrop. Cotton Mather, in his account of the early ministers in New England, records one "----- Sexton" who was in Scituate after Lathrop, but who soon went back to England. Lechford in his *Plain Dealing*, a screed against the New England churches and governments published after his return to England in 1641, in listing the ministers of Plymouth Colony speaks of "Master Saxton also, who was coming away when we did." (Some secondary source think this was Giles Sexton, who was in Massachusetts Bay early in the 1630s, and did return to England as a minister during the Commonwealth period. But the Scituate man was Peter Saxton, who could only have been in New England for a very brief time [Samuel Eliot Morison, *The Founding of Harvard College* (Cambridge 1935), p. 399].)

The remnant of Scituate residents were also briefly served by a Mr. Christopher Blackwood "whom we had some thoughts to procure to be an officer for us. So we sent for him and he came to us and kept the day," but nothing further is heard of him in Scituate, and he apparently returned to England also (Deane, p. 74; Morison, p. 366).

The next move by the Scituate inhabitants (and a fateful one) was their invitation to Reverend Charles Chauncy, at that time residing at Plymouth, to come to Scituate and lead the church. Chauncy accepted the invitation, and immediately split the town into two more or less equal halves.

Chauncy was a staunch advocate of adult baptism, a position for which he was the strongest (and perhaps the only) promoter in New England at this early date.

Timothy Hatherly stood by Chauncy, but the only other man who could match Hatherly in wealth and social standing, William Vassall, was soon strongly opposed to the new minister. The split between the two factions may have been as much a power struggle between these two men as it was a theological dispute.

The correspondence, since it was preserved by the church that derived from Vassall's faction, tells us more about that side than it does about Chauncy. Nevertheless, we see endless detailed argumentation as to which of these two factions represents the legitimate successor to the Lathrop church. (From one perspective this was a sterile dispute, since the Lathrop church removed to Barnstable, just as the Dorchester church had removed to Windsor and the Cambridge church to Hartford some years before. Neither of the new churches in Scituate could rightly claim continuity with the Lathrop church.)

Such a split would not have been allowed at this date in Massachusetts Bay; the leading ministers and magistrates would have moved in and imposed a single church and a single minister on the town. In the more lenient Plymouth Colony, however, the two sides were permitted to continue their conflict for many years.

In one of the many letters he wrote during this dispute, William Vassall relates that at the time of Lathrop's departure eight men expressed a desire to form a new church (Deane 73; these men must all have been among the ten listed on the previous page). Two men from the Lathrop church - Thomas King and Thomas Lapham - joined with Vassall in his resistance to Chauncy. Only Hatherly is readily identified as a Chauncy supporter, but at least four more men from the Lathrop church must have joined with him.

Although the argument becomes highly muddled, the Chauncy church eventually won the title of First Church of Scituate. Vassall and his adherents finally settled on William Wetherell of Duxbury as their ministerial candidate. After much resistance from the town of Duxbury (and from Charles Chauncy) they were successful in installing Wetherell, and this group became the Second Church of Scituate.

The records of the Chauncy church, which still bears the name of the First Church of Scituate, have been lost for this early period. The records of the Second Church of Scituate, presided over by William Wetherell, later called the First Unitarian Church of Norwell, have been preserved. In addition to the documents referred to above, on the dispute between the two churches, the baptisms performed by Wetherell "since his election into office in September 1645" have been published (*New England Historical and Genealogical Register* 57 [1903]:82ff.).

EARLY SCITUATE VITAL RECORDS

The earliest vital records maintained in the town of Scituate were those kept by Reverend John Lathrop, discussed above. As noted there, he went beyond his ministerial duties and recorded marriages (performed by magistrates) and burials, in addition to the baptisms commonly recorded in church records of that time.

Once the Lathrop group had removed from Scituate to Barnstable, it would seem that vital records were not recorded on a regular basis for some years. In common with several other Plymouth Colony towns, Scituate did not send its vital statistics returns in to the colony for many years.

The first surviving instance of Scituate entries at the colony level occurs in 1653: "Names of those who were married, recorded by Leiftenant James Torrey, since he was chosen Town Clarke of the Town of Scituate, the 18th of July 1653" (Nathaniel B. Shurtleff, ed., *Records of the Colony of New Plymouth in New England*, Volume 8, Miscellaneous Records, 1633-1689 [Boston 1857], p. 17). This includes four marriages, four deaths and more than thirty births, mostly from the 1640s. In some cases, but not always, the births were grouped by family. For example, the section on births ends with records for six children of John Bryant, the first in 1644 and the last in 1653.

This submission to higher authority was an attempt to catch up after many years of delinquency, for over these two pages are entries covering more than a decade, going back to 1639. But even this record was not complete, for two pages later is "A Note of the Persons recorded since June last, per me, James Torrey, Town Clarke of Scituate, sent to March Court, 1654" (p. 19). This too had entries as early as 1639, and must have been added to after it was sent in, for there are entries from 1656 and 1657. These two sets of vital events were an attempt by Torrey to reach back to the time that the Lathrop group departed Scituate in 1639, and no farther. But even these records were not complete, for in later colony entries there are scattered Scituate events from the 1640s.

We find a similar picture if we look at the records as retained by the town of Scituate, rather than those sent on to the colony. The earliest volume of Scituate vital records (now called "Scituate Town Records - Vol. 6") has apparently been disbound and rebound a number of times, and so has several pages out of place. This book has separate sections for marriages, then births, and finally deaths. The earliest marriage record is for "Will[iam] Parker married to Mary the daughter of Tho: Rawlings in April 1639," which is on a page by itself, now numbered "10." Following this is a page numbered "1" which has a few marriage entries for 1640, and then one page

per year running into the 1660s; most of these pages have only a few marriages on them, and much unused space.

The page numbering begins anew in the section for births, with 1639 on page one, 1640 on page two, and so on to page 27 which covers 1665. Again, as with the marriages, there are only a few entries on each page. Much of the unused space has been filled with entries from after 1665, some as late as the early decades of the eighteenth century. (The section for deaths is less extensive, with only about thirty entries prior to 1675.)

What seems clear is that the town clerk must have started at some date well after 1639 an attempt to reconstruct the vital records for the years following the departure of Lathrop and his followers for Barnstable. The clerk apparently set aside a page for each year for marriages and births, and filled in entries as he obtained them from the families still in town. As with any such reconstruction, even when done just a few years after the events in question, there are likely to be errors in the records which would not be found had the entries been made contemporaneously with the events. (An article by Dean Smith and Melinde Sanborn examining this very point, with specific reference to the Kempton family, will appear in the *New England Historical and Genealogical Register* in the near future.)

By comparison with the colony entries, we can be sure that the town entries were not entered in simple chronological order as they happened. As noted above, the first marriage entry was for William Parker and Mary Rawlins in 1639. When we place this beside the colony record, we find this marriage not in the group of vital events sent in by James Torrey in July 1653, but among those submitted to the court in March 1654 (probably 1654/5). This could explain the circumstance noted above, that page one of marriages was allocated for 1640, and that the single marriage for 1639 was then placed on a page prior to this, which later was given the number ten. On this basis we may place the commencement of Torrey's reconstruction of the town's vital records no later than 1653.

After 1665 the records change form, abandoning the arrangement of one page per year for each type of event. The new system was like that found in many towns, with each page having the records of one or two families, sometimes with records from before the date when the family entry was begun on a given page. For example, "Mary the daughter of Steven Vinall was born November 29:1662" is found on page 24 of the annual series, along with other 1662 births. Then on page 34 is a list of the births of eight children of Steven Vinall, from 1662 to 1681, in three or four different hands. The entry for Mary is repeated here, in abbreviated form, and so this family entry was probably begun with the birth of one of the later children.

RECENT LITERATURE

Donna Valley Russell, "Roger[1] Toothaker of Plymouth, Massachusetts, and Some Descendants," *The American Genealogist* 69 (1994):1-8, 98-108. Roger Toothaker and his family sailed for New England in 1635 and soon settled at Plymouth, where Roger died in 1638. Russell presents a full genealogy of his descendants to the sixth generation in the male line, including a large branch which migrated to Maine.

Paul C. Reed, "Whitney Origins Revisited: John[1] Whitney of Watertown, Massachusetts, and Henry[1] Whitney of Long Island and Norwalk, Connecticut," *The American Genealogist* 69 (1994):9-14. Reed reanalyzes the problem of the English ancestry of John Whitney of Watertown, and finds additional evidence to support the earlier position of Jacobus, that the ancestry proposed in the 1896 Whitney genealogy is not correct. Comments are also made on the immigrant Henry Whitney.

Russell C. Farnham, "The English Origin of Ralph[1] Farnham of Ipswich, Massachusetts," *The American Genealogist* 69 (1994):32-36. Through the use of English probates and parish registers, the author demonstrates that Ralph Farnham, the immigrant to Ipswich, Massachusetts, derived from Rochester in county Kent.

Robert S. Wakefield, "The Tilson Family of Plymouth Colony," *The American Genealogist* 69 (1994):37-40.
Myrtle Stevens Hyde, "Edmund Tilson's English Origin Not Found," *The American Genealogist* 69 (1994):40-44. In the first of these two related articles, Wakefield presents a standard genealogical account of Edmund Tilson, who arrived in Plymouth by 1638, and of his children. Hyde follows this with a description of her search in English records for the origin of this family; although her search was ultimately unsuccessful, she clears away much underbrush, and paves the way for other researchers who may be interested in this problem.

Philip F. Gura, "Samuel Gorton's Commentary on the Lord's Prayer," *Rhode Island History* 51 (1993):121-27. Gura analyzes an unpublished treatise by Samuel Gorton, one of the more bumptious of the early Puritans, in order to gain greater insight into his character and into his place in the ranks of Puritan radicals. The author finds that Gorton, in his opposition to the emerging polity of the Congregational church in New England, was most closely allied ideologically with the Fifth Monarchists who were at their peak in England in the 1650s.

Robert Charles Anderson, "The Conant Connection: Part Two: Roger Conant, Two Culverwell Families, and the Puritan Network," *New England Historical and Genealogical Register* 148 (1994):107-29. The author explores two Culverwell families who were related to Roger Conant by marriage through his father-in-law Thomas Horton. Many members of these families were prominent in the Puritan movement in England, some as early as the 1560s, and the suggestion is made that Conant may have had closer ties with and more sympathy for the Puritans than has been thought.

Douglas Richardson, "The Ancestry of Dorothy Stapleton, First Wife of Thomas Nelson of Rowley, Massachusetts, With a Provisional Royal Line," *New England Historical and Genealogical Register* 148 (1994):130-40. Richardson produces evidence to show that Thomas Nelson of Rowley was from Cottingham, Yorkshire, in England, and that he married in the city of York Dorothy Stapleton. He then treats three generations of the Stapleton family, and proposes a line of descent from Edward III to Dorothy's father, Philip Stapleton.

F.N. Craig, "Note on the Chauncy Line," *New England Historical and Genealogical Register* 148 (1994):161-66. The author presents and discusses several documents relating to a number of men named John Chauncy in fifteenth century England, three of whom were ancestral to Charles Chauncy, second president of Harvard College.

Daniel R. Coquillette, "Radical Lawmakers in Colonial Massachusetts: The "Countenance of Authoritie" and the *Lawes and Liberties*," *The New England Quarterly* 67 (1994):179-211. Coquillette studies the earliest attempts at systematic lawmaking in Massachusetts Bay, and finds that these codes diverged greatly from what the New Englanders had left behind in England, both in substance and in the process of developing the codes. A proposed set of laws, not derived directly from the English common law, was published and circulated for comment, and then enacted some years later. The article concludes with an annotated bibliography of source material on early codification of laws in Massachusetts Bay.

Todd A. Farmerie, "The Probable Devonshire Origin of Ephraim Tinkham of Plymouth, Mass.," *The Mayflower Quarterly* 60 (1994):222-24. Because of Ephraim Tinkham's known association with Timothy Hatherley, and Hatherley's known connection with Barnstaple, Devonshire, the author has examined the registers of that parish, and has found a Tincombe family which includes an Ephraim baptized in 1618, who is very likely the immigrant to New England.

(*continued from page 10*)

to Puritanism while in England, many of the confessors referred to events which occurred prior to their migration to New England.

"Mr. Collins," for example, (Edward Collins of Cambridge) tells of his "mother going to Wethersfield [in Essex, England], and they there hearing of the ill family where I was, I was removed from thence under old Mr. Rogers of Wethersfield, where I stayed a year and got some good" (Shepard 82-83). Collins later went to [Earl's] Colne to hear a sermon, and also visited such places as Dedham, Essex, and Hoxne, Suffolk, to take advantage of the Puritan ministry in those places. Biographical details such as this are probably not available in any other surviving source.

Another interesting story was told by "Brother Crackbone's Wife" (Shepard 139-40). She was the wife of Gilbert Crackbone, who was almost certainly from Great Coggeshall in Essex. She tells us that her "brother sending for her to London in a good house, there I considered my course and ways especially of one sin." This is the opening line in her confession, and then some lines later she relates that "so being married and having poor means and having afflictions on my child and took from me and so troubled what became of my children.... And so came to New England."

This is not totally clear, but it would seem that this woman was sent to London before her marriage to Crackbone, and that she and her husband had at least one child who died young before they came to New England. This hints that "Brother Crackbone's Wife" may not have been from Essex, and this whole nexus of clues should eventually be of great value in working on the English origin of this family.

Beyond their intrinsic interest, these records can help in other ways, such as sorting out men of the same name. William Andrews made a confession in which he spoke of his apprenticeship in Ipswich in England, and hearing a sermon of the minister at Bramford, Suffolk. He then related details of his career as a mariner, before coming to Charlestown (Shepard 110-13). (This confession appears in the book in close proximity with those of John Stedman, John Trumbull, William Manning and Edward Collins.)

Three men by the name of William Andrews were admitted to freemanship in Massachusetts Bay between 1630 and 1649 - one each on 4 March 1633/4, 4 March 1634/5 and 13 May 1640. On this latter date William Andrews precedes a sequence of six men from Cambridge, including John Stedman, John Trumbull, William Manning and Edward Collins. Thus we are able to separate this William Andrews from the other two men of the same name.

Great Migration Newsletter

Vol. 5   July-September 1994   No. 3

PLYMOUTH FREEMEN

In Massachusetts Bay Colony freemen were admitted just before, or at the beginning, of a meeting of the General Court. The surviving lists are simply those generated at each court. In Plymouth Colony the clerks handled this same task differently. In the records of some courts there are entries for those admitted to freemanship, but these are not as complete as those for Massachusetts.

The Plymouth clerks also periodically compiled lists of those free as of a given date, and then annotated them. The first of these lists is at the beginning of the first volume of published Plymouth records, dated 1 January 1632/3. Inspection shows that this list also includes those made free in the years immediately after 1633, until a second comprehensive list was compiled for the court of 7 March 1636/7. This is the last such list in this volume of records, but there are other lists of freemen elsewhere in the Plymouth records.

In the eighth volume of the published Plymouth Colony records, which includes vital records and treasury accounts, is a series of lists (pages 173 through 210), including the 1643 list of men able to bear arms (pages 187 through 196). The section of interest to us here is the first fifteen pages (173 through 187) which ostensibly contains a list of freemen from 1633 and various lists of men who had taken the oath of fidelity, some dated 1657.

The list of freemen is headed by William Bradford, as governor, and the seven assistants, with the year date 1633 attached. We have already seen a list dated in January 1632/3 which is different from this one; comparison of the list of assistants shows that this list must have dated from 1639, a conclusion that others have reached at various times.

Note that in this list the names are arranged by town, and the towns are placed in their order of seniority (Plymouth, Duxbury, Scituate, Sandwich, Taunton, Yarmouth, Barnstable, Marshfield, Rehoboth and Nawsett [Eastham]). Some of these towns were settled after 1639, a point to which we shall return after looking at the lists of those who took the oath of fidelity.

At the top of page 178 we find "The Names of such as have taken the Oath of Fidelitie of the Towne of Marshfeild in the Yeare 1657," followed by similar lists for Rehoboth, Barnstable, Sandwich and Scituate. On page 181 is a list of seventeen names for Plymouth, undated, after which is a longer list of those who took the oath of fidelity in 1657. There are also undated lists for Duxbury, Scituate, Sandwich, Yarmouth and Cohannet [Taunton], 1657 lists for Duxbury, Eastham, Bridgewater, Yarmouth and Taunton, a Scituate list for 1644, and a few scattered entries for dates later than 1657. What date should be assigned to the undated lists?

We will begin by looking at the list for Duxbury, which contains forty names. About a third of the way through the list is Mr. William Kemp, who must have died by 1641, for the inventory on his estate was taken on 23 September of that year. Also in the list is Edmond Hunt, who resided in Cambridge and sold his land there in 1637, the same year he was granted land at Duxbury. The "undated" list of those taking the oath of fidelity at Duxbury may be dated between 1637 and 1641, and presumably this is the case for the other towns as well.

On 3 January 1636/7 Alexander Higgens, Humfrey Hewett and Thomas Whitney took the oath of fidelity. These are the first three names in the undated Plymouth list (page 181), so this is consistent with the earliest date derived from the Duxbury sequence.

At varying dates between 18 December 1638 and 7 February 1638/9 Mr. John Crow, Mr. Thomas Howes,

(continued on page 18)

EDITOR'S EFFUSIONS

In the six months since our last report, progress on *The Great Migration Begins,* the three-volume set which will cover all immigrants to New England to the end of 1633, has been substantial. Not long after you receive this issue of the *Newsletter*, the first volume of this set will be ready for the press, and the other two volumes will follow soon thereafter.

Two issues ago we stated that some of the sketches would be as long as five or six pages, but as they take final form, some are running longer. At the moment the longest, at ten full pages, is for Reverend Stephen Bachiler, the most intriguing of the early immigrants.

A brochure providing complete information on this set of books will be sent out in late January or early February, describing the volumes in much greater detail and offerring a special pre-publication price. Subscribers to this *Newsletter* will be the first to receive this mailing.

In addition, there will be a reception and a book-signing for this publication at the Boston Public Library on Wednesday, July 12, 1995, as one of the opening events of the Society's Sesquicentennial Conference to be held in Boston from the 13th to the 15th of July. A brochure describing this conference, including registration information, will be in the mail by the middle of January.

Aside from a program of more than a hundred lectures by leading authorities, there will be special talks by Pulitzer Prize winners David McCullough and Laurel Thatcher Ulrich. Also, the CD-ROM edition of the *Register* will be available for the first time.

The fourth issue of this volume of the *Newsletter,* which will focus on the town of Weymouth, will appear early in February. Plans for Volume Six, for 1995, are already being made; two of the towns to be examined next year are New Haven and Providence.

Robert Charles Anderson, FASG   Editor
Margaret F. Costello   Production Assistant

The *Great Migration Newsletter* (ISSN 1049-8087) is published quarterly by the Great Migration Study Project, a project of the New England Historic Genealogical Society
101 Newbury Street, Boston MA 02116

The subscription rate is $8 for one year and $15 for two years. The subscription year is the same as the calendar year.

(*continued from page 17*)

Mr. Anthony Thatcher and Mr. Marmaduke Mathews, all of Yarmouth, took the oath of fidelity, and they were the third through the sixth names in the list for that town (but not in their chronological order of admission) [page 185]. The court record for 7 January 1638/9 includes a list of nine "that are proposed to take up their freedom at Yarmouth," the first four of whom are the four men named immediately above. They were not made free immediately, since one of them took the oath of fidelity a month later; but they undoubtedly were admitted to freemanship late in 1639 (or at least the first six of them), since they are included in the list of freemen which is correctly dated in 1639 [page 176].

On 1 February 1638/9 twenty-one Scituate men, headed by Mr. William Vassall, took the oath of fidelity. In the undated Scituate list these men are entered in the same order, with the numeral "21" inserted after the last of these, John Stockbridge. There are twenty more names in this part of the Scituate list, and this is followed on the next page of the original by another section headed "At Scittuate, Januar[y] 15th, 1644." On 12 February 1638/9 "John Didcutt, of Sandwich, mariner," took the oath of fidelity, and in the undated Sandwich list John Didcutt is the twenty-eighth name, with the numeral "28" after his name.

We may draw a number of useful conclusions from the examples cited above. First, the "undated" lists of those taking the oath of fidelity were apparently drawn up early in 1639. In some of the towns some of those listed had taken the oath of allegiance as early as 1637, but in these cases the listed entries are not always in the chronological order in which the oaths were administered; but the long Scituate list for February 1638/9 is reproduced in the same order. The lists certainly incorporated earlier entries, but the compilation took place very close to February 1638/9.

Second, as with the earlier Plymouth compilations, clerks continued to make annotations for years after, so we may not say that everyone in these lists had taken the oath in 1639. In Scituate, for example, the first twenty-one names, were entered on page 21 of the original record book. On this same page are twenty additional names. On page 22 of the original volume is the heading "At Scituate, Januar[y] 15th 1644," with another thirty-two names. These may all have taken the oath on the same day, but an alternate interpretation would be that the first list, on original page 21, was augmented by new oath-takers from 1639 to 1644, that the page was then turned and given the heading of the current date, and further names were added in 1644 and thereafter.

(*continued on page 24*)

Focus *on* *SPRINGFIELD*

SETTLEMENT OF SPRINGFIELD

When many of the earliest residents of the Massachusetts Bay towns of Cambridge, Dorchester and Watertown were considering their move to the Connecticut River valley, to establish the towns of Hartford, Windsor and Wethersfield, the same activity, although on a smaller scale, was occuring in Roxbury. William Pynchon, the leading citizen of Roxbury and one of the half dozen or so most prominent men in the colony at the time, apparently wanted more scope for his many talents than was offerred him under the eye of John Winthrop, Thomas Dudley and the ministers of the Bay.

Accordingly he gathered about him a small group of associates, mostly from Roxbury, and in 1636 set out for a location on the Connecticut River north of the other English settlements, a site which gave him a dominant position for the fur trade further into the interior. On 15 July 1636 William Pynchon, Henry Smith and Jehu Burr purchased from the Indians the tract of land, then known as Agawam, which would become Springfield. (The name "Agawam" was attached to other localities in New England, such as the area that would become Ipswich. The word was not a specific name for a location, but was in Algonquian a generic term applied to large, flat, grassy places.)

The earliest records show that Pynchon had three principal colleagues in this venture, along with several others who made the move at the same time. These three were Henry Smith, Jehu Burr and John Cable. Smith was Pynchon's stepson, and had married Pynchon's daughter Ann, thus making him immediately the second most important man in the settlement. Burr certainly, and Cable probably, had also resided at Roxbury, and they were in some manner related to one another by marriage. In such matters as the contributions for building a house for Mr. Moxon, their minister, and for his yearly maintenance, these four men were always together at the top of the list, and contributed more money by far than any of the other early residents. Burr and Cable had removed by 1641 to participate in the founding of Fairfield, Connecticut, but Pynchon and Smith remained as the undisputed leaders of Springfield.

The early town records of Springfield are well-preserved and many have been printed. The first volume covers the years from 1636 to 1665, and includes the records of both the general town meetings and the selectmen's meetings. At the meeting of 30 December 1664 it was decided to maintain separate volumes for these two different meetings, and so volume two includes only the meetings of the selectmen, for the years from 1665 to 1682. These first two manuscript volumes were competently transcribed and published in 1898 by Henry M. Burt as Volume I of *The First Century of the History of Springfield[:] The Official Records from 1636 to 1736* ..., along with some valuable introductory material.

The third volume of town records contains the town meetings from 1664 to 1736, and this was published by Burt as the second volume in the above set, again with useful introductory essays, including excellent facsimiles of the handwriting of each of the early town clerks. The selectmen's records are continued in a manuscript volume now labelled "8A," covering the years from 1682 to 1713, but this and all succeeding volumes of town records remain unpublished. (Two other early record books, for vital records and land records, will be discussed on following pages.)

The jurisdictional status of Springfield was problematic for more than a quarter of a century. In the earliest years of settlement, before the relation of any of the Connecticut River towns with Massachusetts Bay was settled, Springfield was represented at the court which was usually held at Hartford. On 1 November 1636 "Mr. Pyncheon" was one of seven men who constituted the magistrates at such a court. On 5 April 1638 "Mr. [George] Moxa[m]" and "Mr. [Jehu] Burr" were "committees" (i.e., deputies) to a court held at Hartford. Early in 1639 Hartford, Windsor and Wethersfield adopted a new constitution, thereby declaring their independence from Massachusetts Bay. This was apparently the trigger which caused Springfield to drop away from the other river towns.

Ostensibly, then, Springfield reverted to subjugation to the Massachusetts government, but in fact, because of their distance from the Bay, as well as the independent strength of William Pynchon himself, the town became one of the free-standing "city states" which were so common in New England at that time (*Great Migration Newsletter* 4:17). When the four original counties of Massachusetts were formed in 1643 Springfield was not named, although one might have expected it to be included in Middlesex.

During the 1640s and 1650s the Massachusetts Bay General Court issued many orders regarding Springfield and the other new settlements in the Connecticut River valley, but these were not always effective. The relationship between Springfield and Massachusetts Bay is reflected by the court order of 14 October 1651 that "the inhabitants of Springfield ... shall be at their liberty whether they will send any deputy at the latter session of this Court, from year to year."

As the western part of Massachusetts expanded in the 1650s, with the settling of Northampton (1656) and Hadley (1661), the central government obviously wanted more control. In 1662, therefore, Hampshire County was organized to cover these towns, to which several more were soon added. There soon arose the peculiar arrangement whereby the Hampshire County probate records were maintained at Northampton, while the registry of deeds was at Springfield. When Hampshire County was divided late in the eighteenth century, the county name remained with Northampton, and Springfield and the other towns to the south became Hampden County. But all the early land records for Hampshire County are to be found in the Hampden courthouse in Springfield, and not at Northampton.

EARLY LANDHOLDING

At the Springfield town meeting for 2 January 1647/8 is the following order:

Whereas it is judged needful in sundry respects that each inhabitant should have the several parcels of their land recorded, therefore for prevention of future inconveniences it is ordered that every particular inhabitant of this township shall within six months after the date of this present order, repair to the Recorder who is chosen and appointed by the said inhabitants for that purpose, who upon information given him by each person of his several parcels of land, the number of acres, with the breadth & length of the said allotments, and who are adjoining on each side of them, shall by virtue of his office fairly record each parcel ...

The Recorder, at that time Henry Smith, soon began a volume which now bears the title "Records of Possessions, 1647-1709," and is labeled as volume 16. Given the town meeting order noted above, we should conclude that the book was begun no earlier than January 1647/8, and was probably compiled over the early months of 1648. Many other New England towns maintained similar volumes, but rarely do we find as explicit and informative a description of the process as we see above. The town was responding to an order of 11 November 1647 from the Massachusetts Bay General Court that they should "within twelve months ... bring in a transcript of their land, according to the law in that case provided...."

Smith allotted to each landholder of Springfield in 1648 a single right-hand page, on which he entered the landholding as of that date, in accordance with his in-

structions. The first entry, surprisingly, was for Mr. William Warrener, and not for William Pynchon, who appears as the second entry. The first few dozen of these entries were made at about the same time, but after a while there are entries in a different ink or different hand, indicating that as new landholders appeared, they were given their own page.

After these initial entries, Henry Smith and his successors heavily annotated them as later land transactions took place. Sometimes these additions and revisions filled the page, and further notes spilled over onto the reverse of the page or, just as often, onto the facing left-hand page. There are records here of hundreds, and perhaps thousands, of real estate deals, many of which are probably not recorded in the county deeds.

A typical entry might be that for Rice Bedortha, which appears on page ten. He had the following parcels:
- houselot with additions, four acres, by grant

- wet meadow, six acres

- on the other side of the river in the neck, two acres

- over Agawam River, five acres planting land

- in the Long Meadow, five acres of meadow land

- in the houselots, two acres

- in the back side of Long Meadow, two acres "in lieu of his third division lot over Agawam River resigned into the town's hands"

This straightforward listing of lands, which was probably what most of the inhabitants received, was then extensively augmented with further sales and purchases made by Bedortha in succeeding years. The form of the description of the first parcel of land, called the "houselot with additions," does not denote land added on immediately adjacent to the houselot, but is the local manner of stating that the houselot carries with it the proprietary right to shares in later divisions of land.

Since twelve years had elapsed between the settlement of the town and this compilation of landholding, there had been opportunity for many changes in possession of land before 1648, and this is frequently reflected in the initial entry. On page 23, for example, is the listing for Samuel Marshfield, which tells us that he is "possessed of a house lot with the additions by purchase from the widow Deeble...." She was the widow of John Dibble, who resided in Springfield as early as 1641. He died in September 1646 and his widow remarried in November 1647 William Graves of Stamford and presumably removed to that town not long before the compilation of this land inventory.

A straightforward example of an initial entry with later annotations may be found on page 15, which records the land of Roger Prichard. He had a houselot of two acres and a half, a parcel of eight acres "on the east side of the way leading to the mill," a seven and a half acre planting lot, four acres in the Long Meadow, and another two acres in the Long Meadow.

In the margin to the left of this listing are three later entries. The first two pieces of land are bracketed, with the comment "Sold to Thomas Bancroft 16 Feb. 1654." The third and fourth parcels are likewise bracketed, with the statement "Sold to son Nathaniel Pritchard [blank] April 1655." And finally next to the fifth tract of land is written "Sold to Alexander Edwards 8 Sept. 1656." Roger Prichard had moved to Milford in 1653, and within three years had divested himself of all his holdings in Springfield.

This volume of early Springfield land records has more information packed into it than most similar volumes, and should be examined by anyone with a genealogical problem in this town in the seventeenth century.

THE PYNCHON RECORDS

For most of the seventeenth century Springfield was in effect the private preserve of the Pynchon family - first, of William Pynchon, from the settlement of the town in 1636 until his departure for England in 1651, and then of his son, John Pynchon, until his death early in 1703. A recent economic history of early Springfield calls it "A Company Town" (Stephen Innes, *Labor in a New Land: Economy and Society in Seventeenth-Century Springfield* [Princeton 1983]). One result of this dominance by the Pynchons was a richness of private records, beyond the standard run of town records.

Because Springfield soon opted out of association with the Connecticut towns, and was so far from the Massachusetts Bay settlements, it enjoyed relative independence for most of this period. A court was established in 1639, and was dominated for years by the Pynchon family. The records for this court long remained in family hands, and have been published under the editorship of Joseph H. Smith, with the long but informative title *Colonial Justice in Western Massachusetts (1639-1702)[:] The Pynchon Court Record[:] An Original Judges' Diary of the Administration of Justice in the Springfield Courts in the Massachusetts Bay Colony* (Cambridge 1961).

As other towns were established in western Massachusetts, they also were covered by this court. Smith provides a lengthy introduction, including biographical material on William and John Pynchon, and on Elizur

Holyoke and Samuel Chapin, who also were active in court business. In addition, Smith writes extensively on the Massachusetts Bay court system, and on colonial legal procedure as exemplified in the Pynchon court; these sections have value far beyond their application to Springfield and Hampshire County.

One deficiency in these records as edited by Smith is that they omit marriages included in the court records, and some probate matters. This is a common failing of legal historical editing.

In their role as the leading and wealthiest citizens of Springfield, the Pynchons had financial dealings with almost all of the families in town, and, as other towns were settled, in neighboring areas as well. William Pynchon and his son John maintained careful records of all these transactions, in the so-called Pynchon account books.

Some of these records have been published as volume 61 of the Publications of the Colonial Society of Massachusetts, with the title *The Pynchon Papers[:] Volume II[:] Selections from the Account Books of John Pynchon, 1651-1697*, edited by Carl Bridenbaugh and Juliette Tomlinson (Boston 1985). The selections were made to illustrate specific points about the trading activities of the Pynchons, and so a published entry may be only a small part of what survives for a given person.

For example, on page 451 are two very brief extracts from the account of Walter Fyler (of Windsor) recording expenses he incurred in "running the line," presumably between Massachusetts and Connecticut. These two entries, taken from successive pages in the original, are intended to demonstrate the inclusion of public activities in private records, but there is obviously much more in the original books on Fyler. (Note also that many persons from towns in Connecticut are represented in these records.)

Not surprisingly, the Pynchons were also prolific correspondents, and many letters have survived, mostly written by John Pynchon. These have been collected in Volume 60 of the Publications of the Colonial Society of Massachusetts with the title *The Pynchon Papers[:] Volume I[:] Letters of John Pynchon, 1654-1700*, edited by Bridenbaugh and Tomlinson (Boston 1982).

These are copies of letters written by Pynchon; no incoming correspondence is included. As one might expect, much of the material relates to public affairs, but there are many private matters discussed as well. Many of the letters are to John Winthrop Jr., and are about medical matters. In these and other instances details of the lives of many Springfield residents are revealed. The largest number of letters are from 1675 in the aftermath of the raids at the beginning of King Philip's War.

EARLY VITAL RECORDS

The Springfield vital records as kept by the town begin in 1639, with a marriage recorded on 19 March 1638/9, while the first births and deaths recorded were from 1641. The town clerk kept a single book with separate sections for each category of event, and with the births, marriages and deaths entered in chronological order.

On a page facing the original first page of the records is evidence of the care taken with this volume by a nineteenth-century town clerk. On New Years Day of 1846 Joseph Ingraham carefully wrote "Preserve this book - it will be a curiosity to Generations that must follow us." We might wish that all towns had had recordkeepers who were this careful.

Another of the Pynchon records is the "Hampshire Records of Births Marriages Deaths," begun in 1651 by John Pynchon, just after his father had returned to England. Although apparently maintained privately, this volume is the equivalent of the county copies of vital records found elsewhere in Massachusetts Bay Colony. Records are included from Northampton (earliest date 1655), Hadley (1660), Westfield (1666), Suffield (1668), Hatfield (1670), Enfield (1682) and Brookfield (1690). Only Deerfield of the early Hampshire County towns is not included.

The Springfield entries in this book are advertised as beginning in 1639, but the volume was clearly started in 1651. Although there are variations in the hand from 1651 to the middle of 1693, the differences are minor, and were apparently all made by John Pynchon. In June of 1693 the hand changed drastically, and does not even appear to have been of a contemporary style. The Springfield records included in this book from 1639 through the early months of 1651 are on separate pages from the later records, and are all in this same post-1693 hand.

These records must, then, have been copied into the book no earlier than 1693. Comparison of the pre-1651 records in the town copy and in the Pynchon volume shows that the latter contains only those records included in the former. For this period the town copy should take precedence over the Pynchon record.

Comparison of the two volumes for the post-1651 period, however, tells a different story. Looking at the first four marriages in the Pynchon record, three are in the town record, but for one of these the Pynchon version is more informative. Each record has one marriage that the other omits.

Both have the marriage on "the 4th of the 4m[onth] 1651" (4 June 1651) of Richard Exell and Hannah Reeves. (This is reflected also in the inventory of landholdings, where Exell, upon marriage to the widow Reeves, takes over the parcels which had earlier been held by her first husband, Robert Reeves.)

The next entry in the Pynchon volume is "Jonathan Burt joined in marriage at Boston to Elizabeth Lobdell the 20th of the 8th mon: 1651" (20 October 1651). Not only is this vital event not recorded in the Springfield town records, it is also omitted from the Boston records!

The third marriage in the Pynchon book is "Mr. John Allin of Hartford joined in marriage to Mrs. Hannah Smith the 19th of the 9th month 1651" (19 November 1651). The town volume also has this entry, but without the useful information that the groom was of Hartford.

At this point the town volume includes a marriage not noted by Pynchon: "Nathaniell Pridget [i.e., Prichard] joined in marriage to Hannah Lanckton the 4 day of the 12mo. 1651" (4 February 1651/2).

Finally in this small sample, the two sources agree that "Samuel Marshfield joined in marriage to Hester Wright the 18th of the twelfth month 1651" (18 February 1651/2).

Two more examples will allow us to draw some conclusions about those features of the Pynchon volume of vital records which distinguish it from the town records. Pynchon includes the marriage of David Chapin and Lydia Crump on 29 August 1654 in Boston. As with the marriage of Jonathan Burt and Elizabeth Lobdell, this item is in neither the Springfield nor the Boston records.

The first death recorded by Pynchon was that of "Samuell Kitcherell son-in-law to Anthony Dorchester died and was buried the 9th of 4th mo. 1651" (9 June 1651). This level of detail is not always maintained in the records kept by town clerks.

"Mrs. Hannah Smith" who married John Allin of Hartford was daughter of Henry and Anna (Pynchon) Smith, and therefore niece of John Pynchon. Jonathan Burt and David Chapin, whose Boston marriages Pynchon took note of, were sons of Henry Burt and Samuel Chapin, both of whom were closely associated with Pynchon in running the town of Springfield.

The Pynchon Record of vital statistics is, then, something of a hybrid. For the second half of the seventeenth century it served the same purpose as the county-recorded vital records of other Massachusetts Bay counties. But it was also a very personal expression of the social and dynastic position of John Pynchon, in which he could record events of special importance to him and those around him.

RECENT LITERATURE

Neill DePaoli, "Beaver, Blankets, Liquor, and Politics: Pemaquid's Fur Trade, 1614-1760," *Maine Historical Society Quarterly* 33 (1993-4):166-201. Combining archaeological evidence with research in historical documents, DePaoli surveys a century and a half of fur trade in the Pemaquid region. The activities of Abraham Shurt and other early residents of the area are examined.

Doris Jones-Baker, "'The rest left no posterity here...' in Plymouth Colony: The 'Lost Descendants' of the Mayflower Pilgrims of 1620 in England and Holland," *Genealogists' Magazine* 24 (1994):489-95. The author, noting that many descendants of *Mayflower* passengers remained in or returned to England or Holland, summarizes what is known in this regard about five *Mayflower* families: Gilbert Winslow, Isaac Allerton, John Tilley, William Brewster and Moses Fletcher. With the exception of the unlikely suggestions of additional sons for William Brewster, most of this material has already appeared in journals in the United States.

Gerald James Parsons, "Parsons Families of the Connecticut Valley: Part One," *New England Historical and Genealogical Register* 148 (1994):215-38. Parsons commences a systematic and comprehensive survey of early Parsons families in western Connecticut and Massachusetts, treating in this first installment three brothers, Joseph Parsons of Springfield and Northampton, Benjamin Parsons of Springfield, and Thomas Parsons of Windsor, sons of William and Margaret (Hoskins) Parsons of Beaminster in Dorsetshire.

Douglas Richardson, "Evidence for Four Generations of a Matrilineal Line," and "A Royal Line for Mary (Cooke) Talcott," *New England Historical and Genealogical Register* 148 (1994):240-58. Taking note of neglected clues, Richardson shows that the second wife of John[2] Talcott was Mary Cooke, daughter of Joseph1 Cooke of Cambridge. This then leads to evidence proving that Cooke's wife was Elizabeth, daughter of Governor John[1] Haynes, and that the first wife of Haynes was Mary Thornton, daughter of Robert and Anne (Smith) Thornton of Hingham, Norfolk, England. A line of ascent to Edward I leads through Robert Thornton.

Virginia DeJohn Anderson, "King Philip's Herds: Indians, Colonists, and the Problem of Livestock in Early New England," *William and Mary Quarterly*, Third Series 51 (1994):601-24. After studying the records relating to the care of livestock during the first two generations of New England settlement, Anderson concludes that "no problem vexed relations between settlers and Indians more frequently in the years before the war than the control of livestock," and that this was a major factor in the onset of King Philip's War. Several of the examples cited involve the immigrant generation.

Gale Ion Harris, "William[1] Williams, Cooper, of Hartford, Connecticut, and his Sons-in-law, William Buckland and William Biggs," *The American Genealogist* 69 (1994):87-94, 174-83. William Williams apparently arrived in New England at the very end of the Great Migration, first appearing of record in Hartford in 1646. This article treats the immigrant and his children, including his eldest daughter Elizabeth who married William Buckland. Harris argues convincingly that he was a previously unknown son of William Buckland of Hingham and Rehoboth.

James L. Hansen, "The Ancestry of Joan Legard, Grandmother of the Rev. William[1] Skepper/Skipper of Boston, Massachusetts," *The American Genealogist* 69 (1994):129-39. Hansen builds on an earlier article by Mary Lovering Holman and provides solid evidence for the identity of the wife of Richard Skepper, grandfather of the immigrant William Skepper, as Joan Legard, daughter of Ralph Legard of Yorkshire, and provides for her lines of ascent to Edward I and Edward III.

Norman W. Ingham, "A Gosse-Nichols-Bull-Jones Connection," *The American Genealogist* 69 (1994):140-41. The author presents additional evidence which supports the conclusion that Phebe, the widow of John Gosse, married Robert Nichols of Southold and Saybrook, and that Phebe, daughter of John and Phebe Gosse, married Robert Bull of Saybrook.

Robert S. Wakefield, "The Family of Isaac[1] Stedman of Scituate and Muddy River, Massachusetts," *The American Genealogist* 69 (1994):155-59. Wakefield organizes what is known about Isaac Stedman, immigrant to Scituate, and then summarizes the evidence on each of his children.

Raymond D. Irwin, "Cast Out from the 'City upon a Hill': Antinomian Exiles in Rhode Island, 1638-1650," *Rhode Island History* 52 (1994):3-19. After presenting a brief introduction to the Antinomian controversy of 1637, Irwin examines the later activities of eighty-six families which left Massachusetts Bay because of that episode. He concludes that as a group they were not as "radical" as they have been portrayed, either by Winthrop and other contemporaries, or by later historians. The author notes that many of them returned to Massachusetts Bay, and that those who supported later "radical" groups, such as the Quakers or Gortonists, were a minority of the exiled families.

(*continued from page 18*)

Third, the list of freemen which is advertised as for 1633, but which is really for 1639, was presumably compiled at the same time, or perhaps a few months later. This list was certainly augmented and altered very soon after compilation. In early 1639 Barnstable was not yet recognized as a Plymouth Colony town, as it did not send deputies to the General Court, or have a constable appointed. But on 3 December 1639 Rev. Joseph Hull and several others were admitted as freemen, and they would be joined at Barnstable by Lathrop and his followers. None of these could have been listed in February 1638/9, but the entries for Yarmouth are followed by those for Barnstable in the "1639" list, with the Hull and Lathrop parties intermixed. Entries for Marshfield, Rehoboth and "Nawsett" [Eastham] follow, and these must have been added some years later.

Adding all this up, then, we may identify a "1639" group of lists of freemen and those taking the oath of fidelity. The freemen for the six oldest towns (Plymouth, Duxbury, Scituate, Sandwich, Taunton and Yarmouth - all those legally recognized in 1639) are on pages 173 through 176 of the published volume, with records for four later towns carrying over onto page 177. Lists of those taking the oath in or about 1639 in the same six towns may be found on pages 181 through 186 (ignoring the lists explicitly attributed to 1657 or other dates).

Viewed in this light, the 1639 compilation becomes the third in a series of periodic updates of the records of freemen, the first being in January 1632/3 and the second in January 1636/7. Inevitably, as the clerks edited these lists, they would become difficult to interpret, and it may be this steady deterioration in utility that caused the clerks to begin afresh, in 1633, 1637 and 1639.

If this interpretation is correct, and if the surviving records are reasonably complete, the clerks apparently did not need to clean the slates again until 1657. We have already seen the lists of those taking the oath of fidelity in 1657 salted in among those taken in 1639. On pages 197 through 202 are lists with the modern editorial comment "The following appears to be a lists of Freemen, and to have been taken about the year 1658." Preliminary superficial analysis indicates that this date is reasonably accurate, suggesting that these lists should be linked with the oath of fidelity lists for 1657. And this fourth complete revision of the lists was apparently followed by only one more during the life of Plymouth Colony, represented on pages 202 through 209 of the published volume by lists (this time of freemen only) for each of the towns. The date is given as "the first [blank] 1683/4," and some later additions were made to this list as well. Apparently, though, the clerks made no attempt to compile another comprehensive list prior to the absorption of Plymouth Colony by Massachusetts Bay in 1692, under the Second Charter.

Great Migration Newsletter

Vol. 5   October-December 1994   No. 4

EARLY MASSACHUSETTS PROBATE

When the participants in the Great Migration made the decision to leave for New England, most probate matters in England were handled by the ecclesiastical courts, and so when we are researching in England we look in such places as the Episcopal Consistory Court of Hereford, the Archdeaconry Court of Norwich or the Peculiars in the Consistory Court of the Dean and Chapter of Exeter.

When these migrants arrived in New England no such courts existed, nor did the settlers desire to have ecclesiastical courts, for probate or for any other matters. The ecclesiastical courts had constantly pestered those with Puritan inclinations, and although few experienced the punishments doled out by Star Chamber or the Court of High Commission, hundreds of those who later came to New England had been presented at the Bishops' Visitations for infractions such as refusing to kneel at communion or travelling to other parishes on Sundays to hear a favorite Puritan minister preach.

As a result of these changes, the settlers of Massachusetts Bay had to find a way to carry out probate business in the civil courts which they established upon their arrival in New England. Because of the history of the Massachusetts Bay Company, these courts developed from what were in essence the regular business meetings of a chartered company, and so the earliest probate matters in Massachusetts Bay appear in the published records of Massachusetts Bay (cited herein as MBCR).

The first item in these records that concerned itself with probate matters was an order of 16 August 1631 "that the executors of Richard Garrett shall pay unto Henry Harwood the sum of 20 nobles, according to the proportion that the goods of the said Richard Garrett shall amount unto" [MBCR 1:91]. This was not the administration of an estate, but an order resulting from the claim of Henry Harwood against the estate. The order speaks of "executors" already in place; these may have been appointed by the court in a record that no longer exists, or this action may have been taken outside court. (Note that the distinction between executors [for testate proceedings] and administrators [for intestates] was not always observed in early colonial records.)

The next recognizable probate action is more straightforward: on 4 March 1632/3 "There is administration granted to Roger Ludlowe, Esq., of the goods and chattels of John Knight, who deceased in November last" [MBCR 1:103]. We may deduce from this that John Knight probably lived in Dorchester, which was Ludlow's home at this time. Knight and Ludlow may have been related in some way, or it may be that these two men had known one another in England.

In these developing probate records we can trace the fate of one woman who lost two husbands in the space of just a few years. On 6 October 1634 it was "ordered that Lieutenant Feakes, Mr. Richard Browne, Mr. Pendelton & Epharim Childe shall take an inventory of the goods & chattels of Mr. [blank] Craford, lately deceased, & return the same into the next Court" [MBCR 1:132]. These four men were all of Watertown, and so we assume that Crawford was as well. (From Winthrop we learn that on 12 August 1634 "[a]bout midnight, one Craford [who came this summer], with his brother and servant, having put much goods in a small boat in Charles River, over against Richard Brown his house, overset the boat with the weight of some hogsheads [as was supposed], so as they were all three drowned" [WJ 1:165].)

Four years later, on 5 June 1638, the Court appointed three prominent men "to examine all things concerning

(continued on page 26)

EDITOR'S EFFUSIONS

By now, many of you have received the first volume of *The Great Migration Begins* and have had a chance to study it carefully. As this editorial is being written, the second volume is at the printer, for shipment in late November of 1995, and the final editorial work on the third volume is under way.

Several aspects of the final preparation of these volumes have consumed more time than was expected. One of the most time-consuming aspects of the research has been my determination to find a contemporary source for every statement made. This has been possible in most cases, but the quest for such evidence sometimes takes many hours for one item.

The secondary literature of genealogy is littered with claims of marriages and affiliations for which no evidence is given. These claims are then repeated again and again so that they take on a life of their own. Thousands of such claims have been encountered in the compilation of the sketches in *The Great Migration Begins*. Sometimes the desired evidence may be found in just a few minutes, and in some cases hours of research are necessary.

Future issues of this *Newsletter* will provide accounts of how some of these problems have been solved. In most cases the claims of the secondary literature turn out to be true, but in other instances the statements are found to be quite imaginary. Perhaps the most frustrating are those in which a stated marriage turns out to be correct, but some modern writer has imagined an exact date of marriage, when no such record exists.

As work on the third volume of *The Great Migration Begins* approaches an end, this Newsletter will appear on a more regular schedule, and we will be back on course as early as possible in 1996. Thank you all for your patience.

Robert Charles Anderson, FASG   Editor
Margaret F. Costello   Production Assistant

The *Great Migration Newsletter* (ISSN 1049-8087) is published quarterly by the Great Migration Study Project, a project of the New England Historic Genealogical Society
101 Newbury Street, Boston MA 02116

The subscription rate is $8 for one year and $15 for two years. The subscription year is the same as the calendar year.

(*continued from page 25*)

Mr. White & Mr. Woolcote, & to do it within 14 days, & Mrs. Woolcot is to bring in a perfect inventory, & distinguish the goods inventoried between his and the children's" [MBCR 1:232, 311]. The widow of [blank] Crawford and John Woolcott was Winifred, who within a few years found a more enduring marital partner in Thomas Allyn of Barnstable.

In England the highest probate court, the Prerogative Court of Canterbury, recorded the wills and administrations of English men and women who had died at sea or "in parts beyond the seas." Some of those who set sail for New England died aboard ship and never reached their new home. We find in the Massachusetts Bay Court records cases in which probate was instituted on the estates of such persons.

On 3 March 1634/5 the Court noted that John Stanley had "died intestate, in the way to New England, & left three children undisposed of, the youngest whereof is since deceased, having also left an estate of £116, in goods & chattels" [MBCR 1:134]. The Court then went on to divide the estate equally, and to designate Thomas and Timothy Stanley, brothers of the deceased, each to take under their care one of the children, son John and daughter Ruth.

On another occasion the Court dealt more briefly with a similar situation. On 4 September 1638 the "will of Silvester Bauldwin was presented into the Court, & his wife Sarah & son Richard were allowed executors according to his will" [MBCR 1:235]. Baldwin had died at sea in June [Savage 1:105]. We see here several differences by comparison with the Stanley case. Baldwin left a will, whereas Stanley was intestate. In the case of Stanley no mention was made of a widow, and the surviving children were clearly quite young, whereas Baldwin left a widow, as well as a son old enough to participate in the settlement of the estate. These differences presumably explain the brevity of the Baldwin entry.

Other entries just as brief could provide important genealogical information. On the same day as the Baldwin probate, "John Knowles (having married the widow of Ephraim Davies, who was sister to Robert Bills) was granted administration of the estate of Robert Bills" [MBCR 1:235]. More genealogical meat could hardly have been packed into twenty-four words.

On occasion the Court would be faced with a situation in which someone had departed from Massachusetts Bay, leaving behind both debts and assets. In these instances the Court frequently employed language very similar to

(*continued on page 32*)

Focus on WEYMOUTH

SETTLEMENT OF WEYMOUTH

The early history of Weymouth is more convoluted and more obscure than that of most other Massachusetts Bay settlements. From 1622 until 1635 the location was inhabited more or less continuously, but Weymouth (then called Wessagusset or Wessaguscus) was not during these years a "settled" plantation.

The first to arrive were the vanguard of Thomas Weston's projected colony, who made it to New England in the summer of 1622. This group was ill-provisioned, and included Phineas Pratt, whose narrative of his adventures during the winter of 1622-3 tells us much of what we know of this first attempt.

Weston himself arrived in 1623, as did Robert Gorges, who had his own plans for the same territory. Both of these men soon abandoned their efforts to settle the south shore of Massachusetts Bay, and most of the men they had brought with them soon dispersed, to Maine, to Virginia, or back to England.

A remnant of the companions of Weston and Gorges remained, the most prominent being William Jeffreys and John Bursley. They were among the persons who contributed in 1628 to the fund, organized by Bradford, which was collected for the purpose of returning Thomas Morton to England.

Only one or two of these earliest settlers remained in Weymouth after 1635. In the earliest compilation of vital records (see below), carried out early in 1644, and covering only families still resident in Weymouth in that year, only Richard Silvester and Clement Briggs had children recorded as born before 1635.

The best account of these early years in Weymouth was published more than a century ago by Charles Francis Adams, as the first of his *Three Episodes of Massachusetts History* [2 volumes; Boston 1892]. Adams studies each of the early settlers carefully, including the evidence for their early presence in this community.

In 1923 the Weymouth Historical Society published a four-volume *History of Weymouth, Massachusetts*, the first two of which are historical and provide much detail on the early period, although not with as much authority as Adams. (The third and fourth volumes, containing genealogies of the early families, were prepared by George Walter Chamberlain.)

EARLY VITAL RECORDS

For the first generation of its existence, the only vital records we have for Weymouth are those which were submitted to the county or colony clerk. These records survive as part of the compilation made in early 1644 of the vital records of most of the towns of the newly formed Suffolk and Middlesex counties.

As with the other towns included in this document, records were collected only for those families still resident in Weymouth at the time of compilation. (For more discussion on this set of records, see GMN 2:17-18, 24, 4:5.) Weymouth differs, though, in that two different versions of the pre-1644 vital records were sent in to the county clerk. The reason for this duplication does not appear, but an examination of the differences between the two versions is instructive.

What we will call the "earlier version" appears as the last in the sequence of towns to submit their first batch of records [*Register* 8:348-49]. This submission contains eighty-one entries, most of them births, with a few deaths or burials included. This set of entries is followed by the second group of records for Boston, beginning in 1644, after which are similar records for several of the other towns.

At a later point, where one would expect to find the Weymouth records from the period beginning in 1644, we find instead entries from the same period as those already submitted [*Register* 9:171-72]. This grouping of records, which lists fifty-six events, we will call the "later version."

Comparing the two versions, we find that fifty-one of the entries are common to both. This includes a few instances in which the two entries differ somewhat in the details of the date or the spelling of the name. (The existence of the two sets of these records was pointed out to me by Eugene C. Zubrinsky, who has analyzed the differences in the entries for the Carpenter family in his article on the family of William Carpenter of Rehoboth, which will appear in the October 1995 issue of TAG.)

On both occasions when the Weymouth records were submitted to the county, the same time period was covered. The earliest record in each is the birth of Thomas, son of Clement Briggs, on 14 June 1633, and the latest was the birth of Jacob, son of Nicholas Norton, on 1 March 1643[/4]. (The evidence that allows us to interpret the otherwise ambiguous date of this last entry will appear as we examine other aspects of the vital events.)

Looking first at the "later version" of the Weymouth vital records, we see only five entries not included in the "earlier version." The earliest of these entries is the 6 July 1641 birth of Mary, daughter of Thomas Dyer. The other four events are deaths or burials in 1642 or 1643. Perhaps the Weymouth town clerk, or someone else in town, noticed deficiencies in the records of 1642 and 1643, felt the need to "correct" the official record, and rather than simply send in the missing items, instead resubmitted the entire body of records with the five additions.

If this is the case, however, why are there thirty-one entries which are in the "earlier version" but not in the "later version"? The answer to this question tells us much about how the records were originally arranged, and about the record-keeping techniques of the county clerk.

Of the thirty-one items which are unique to the "earlier version," twenty-nine (and perhaps all thirty-one) fall within a narrow range of dates, from June 1639 to March 1640/1. Furthermore, the "later version" contains no records from this time period. (There is some slight overlap at the beginning of this span of time, for the "later version" does include the birth of Mary, daughter of John King, on 15 June 1639, whereas it does not have the birth of Prudence, daughter of Edward Bates, on 11 June 1639.)

The two events which are outside the time period stated above, but which were omitted from the "later version," were the births of Joseph, son of Mathew [Macuth] Pratt, on 10 June 1637, and Nehemiah, son of Richard Webb, on 19 October 1641. In the former instance, there is substantial evidence that the birth actually took place on 10 June 1639, and so fell within the omitted period [TAG 65:36, 91]. The absence of Webb the second time around may have a similar explanation, or it may be a simple scribal error unconnected to the other thirty omissions.

We have shown earlier that the Dedham vital records were entered by the town clerk in chronological order, and then rearranged alphabetically by the county clerk [GMN 2:24]. The same explanation would seem to be the case for Weymouth, for otherwise we would have to hypothesize that the county clerk went systematically through the alphabetical list and omitted only records for certain dates. This tells us also that the second submission from Weymouth must have been quite independent from the first, and that the county clerk for a second time undertook the alphabetic rearrangement. Presumably he misplaced a sheet or two the second time around.

The difference between the two versions of the Weymouth records also allows us to determine the date used in this town for the beginning of the year. Among the entries omitted on the second occasion were the births of John, son of John Osborne, on 2 February 1639, of Martha, daughter of Geofrey Staple on 17 February 1639, of Thomas, son of Thomas Clapp, on 15 March 1639, and of Sarah, daughter of Robert Tucker, on 17 March 1639. To fall within the omitted time period of June 1639 to March 1640/1, these events must all be given the double-dating of 1639/40. This is an instructive, if extreme, example of the frequent need to examine and analyze a source in its entirety in order to interpret one record within that source.

Apparently Weymouth town clerks did not return any vital records to the county clerk for the next twelve years. Records for many of the other Massachusetts Bay towns for these years were collected, but the next items for Weymouth were submitted in 1658, covering the previous two and a half years, from June of 1655 until February of 1657/8 [Register 12:349-50]. This set of entries included births, marriages and deaths. Another batch of records for the town was submitted in 1659, covering 1658 and part of 1659, and including only births and a few deaths [Register 20:44].

The regular run of Weymouth vital records, as maintained by the town, apparently begins in 1655, corresponding roughly with the records submitted to the county in 1658. A series of births (with a few deaths) dating from 1655 to 1699 was published in 1849, the description of which consisted of a single sentence: "These records are said to have been copied from an old quarto book which is now lost" [Register 3:71-72, 166, 269-70, 4:57-60, 171-72].

The Weymouth town clerk does currently hold a volume entitled "Births, Marriages and Deaths: Weymouth: 1655-1790." This may be the "old quarto book which is now [1849] lost." On page 100 of this volume we find this statement: "The following births were taken out of one of the town's old books that were gotten too old and torn that many of the names were gone, others partly gone, which makes this record so imperfect as it is." This volume was created in the late seventeenth century, and the older book referred to therein was probably discarded not much later.

The births on this page begin in 1655 with Edward Bate, son of Edward & Susan Bate, and continue through page 122 with entries down to 1699. This apparently corresponds to the material published in 1849. There is another section for births from 1699 to 1725, and a third section for the period after 1725. The earliest marriages appear to be about 1700, and the death records begin in 1727.

EARLY MINISTERS

Although several university-educated ministers passed through Weymouth in the late 1620s, the settlement was attached ecclesiastically to Dorchester in the early 1630s, before any attempt was made to organize a church. This arrangement is similar to the one that Roxbury had for a much shorter time with Dorchester.

The Massachusetts Bay list of freemen for 1 April 1634 included as the last six names Bernard Lumbert, Henry Wulcott, Rich[ard] Hull, John Gallop, Richard Silvester and Will[ia]m Horseford. Five of the men were known to be of Dorchester at this time, but Silvester was connected only with Weymouth. The much longer list of freemen of 14 May 1634 includes a sequence of ten names (from Philip Randall to Steven French), nine of whom were Dorchester men. Imbedded in this sequence was James Parker, at that time a resident of Weymouth. These arrangements of names indicate that Silvester and Parker had joined the Dorchester church in order to attain freemanship at a time when there was no organized church in Weymouth.

Wessaguscus graduated from an unorganized habitation to a settled town in 1635, with the arrival of the Reverend Joseph Hull and his party. On 8 July 1635 Winthrop reported that "[a]t this court Wessaguscus was made a plantation, and Mr. Hull, a minister in England, and twenty-one families with him, allowed to sit down there - after called Weymouth" [WJ 1:194]. Hull had arrived just a few weeks before, with a number of families from Batcombe and Broadway in Somersetshire [Hotten 283 86], the latter of these parishes being the last church at which Hull officiated in England [TAG 68:149].

Although the official organization of the church is said to have occurred in 1639, there is good evidence that Joseph Hull and his party had established a church soon after arrival. In the 2 September 1635 list of Massachusetts Bay freemen are the following six consecutive names: Joseph Hull, Will[ia]m Reade, Richard Adams, John Upham, Rob[er]te Lovell and Will[ia]m Smyth. In contrast to the earlier Weymouth men admitted to freemanship, there are in this instance no Dorchester men mixed in with those of Weymouth. Again on 3 March 1635/6 Henry Kingman, Thomas White and Angel Hollard, known to have been living in Weymouth at that time, appear together in the list of freemen. Of these nine men, seven (including Joseph Hull) had sailed on the same vessel earlier in the year.

The sequence of events described in the last three paragraphs is reminiscent of what happened at Lynn a few years earlier [GMN 1:20]. There a few men had been admitted as freemen before the establishment of any church, perhaps having been admitted at Salem. When Reverend Stephen Bachiler arrived he organized a church and he and several of his congregation became freemen on 6 May 1635. There was much dissension, and the Lynn church soon broke up (or at least ceased to function in Lynn). In 1636 a new church was founded, on a sounder basis, and Winthrop took notice of the Lynn events in much the same way he did later for Weymouth.

We may say, then, that the first Weymouth church was organized in 1635 with Joseph Hull as first minister. At least in its early days this church must have been considered a properly covenanted church, since the colony accepted freemen who had been admitted there.

Joseph Hull left Weymouth about 1638, and an attempt was made late in 1637 and early in 1638 to institute Reverend Thomas Jenner as Hull's replacement. On 9 January 1637/8 Winthrop tells us that "[d]iverse of the elders went to Weymouth, to reconcile the differences between the people and Mr. Jenner, whom they had called thither with intent to have him their pastor. They had good success of their prayers" [WJ 1:301].

The success must not have been as good as Winthrop thought, for Edward Johnson tells us that "not liking the place, [Jenner] repaired to the Eastern English," meaning Maine, where he was seen in Saco as early as 1641, although he had probably been there some years already at that date [Morison 384-85].

Finally, on 30 January 1638/9 Weymouth was convenanted anew. On that date Winthrop reports that a "church was gathered at Weymouth with the approbation of the magistrates and elders. It is observable, this church, having been gathered before, and so that of Lynn, could not hold together, nor could have any elders join or hold with them. The reason appeared to be, because they did not begin according to the rule of gospel, which when Lynn had found and humbled themselves for it, and began again upon a new foundation, they went on with a blessing" [WJ 1:346].

Accompanying this paragraph is a much longer section on the attempt to install Mr. Robert Lenthall as minister at this time. However, "he was found to have drank in some of Mrs. Hutchinson's opinions, as of justification before faith, etc.," and so he was admonished, forced to repent, and not permitted to become minister at this church. He moved soon to Newport, and a number of other Weymouth residents accompanied him at this time.

The man who became the Weymouth minister in 1639 was Reverend Samuel Newman, who served for about five years before his removal to Rehoboth. Newman was succeeded by Thomas Thatcher, who continued in office until 1669, thus providing the Weymouth church with some stability at last.

EARLY LANDHOLDING

The surviving seventeenth century records of the town of Weymouth apparently do not include a separate proprietors' volume or, as exists in some towns, a "Book of Possessions." A number of grants of land, however, are included in the first volume of town meeting records. Most of these records have been published as part of the history of the town published in 1623 by the Weymouth Historical Society [1:183-202], but many of the entries have been misread.

The earliest of these records dates from 1636, but appears in the original volume just after the grants of 2 February 1651/2. This latter grant was in fact an order to lay out the Great Lots which had been "named in the old town book." This would indicate that the 1636 list of grants of Great Lots was copied out of this older book, which is apparently now lost (and may be the same as the "old book" from which the vital records were copied some years later).

The 1636 list of grants of Great Lots contains only sixteen names, at a time when there were more families than that in town. We know from the colony records that twenty-one families were allowed to move to Weymouth in the fall of 1635, and there were already a few families resident in town before that date, so one might expect to find twice as many persons in this list. Perhaps a portion of the list was omitted when it was copied early in 1652; on the other hand, the inventory of landholding compiled about 1643 (see below) does not contain any grants of Great Lots which cannot be accounted for by this short list.

Although there is not a separate "Book of Possessions" as such, there is a brief equivalent inventory of landholding included in the volume of town meeting minutes (and published along with the other lists discussed here). The editor of this inventory suggests that this record "must have been compiled not earlier than Oct. 26, 1642, the date of the death of William Fry, whose daughters are named among the property owners, and [not later than] May 21, 1644, the date of the deed of Thomas Dyer to Thomas Bayley, conveying a grant of the property described as belonging to him."

This editor goes on to say that "[t]here is reason to believe that the original record was made by Rev. Samuel Newman." This opinion must be based on the last item in the inventory entry for Newman, "[t]wo acres of wood in a great swamp near my house," and assumes that the inventory was compiled all at one time. This document would, therefore, represent the situation in Weymouth at just about the time that several inhabitants were making the move to Rehoboth.

Because this listing of possessions was created nearly a decade after the town was formally organized, and twenty years after the earliest settlement, there are many internal indications of lands held by persons no longer in Weymouth. The two leading citizens of the town for several years in the late 1620s and early 1630s were John Bursley and William Jeffreys. Both men had left for other locations by the time of this record, but we learn something of the grants of land to them. Edward Bate, for example, held "four acres of swamp, 2 acres of it first given to Mr. William Jeffereyes and 2 acres to Richard Silvester." William Torrey had "an acre of salt marsh first given to Mr. John Buslem," Henry Kingman had "three acres in the Easterneck of salt marsh first given to Mr. Buslem" and Nathaniel Adams held "eighteen acres in the East Field first given to Mr. Buslem." We even learn, from the holdings of William Torrey, that "Capt. Silanova" briefly held land in Weymouth, one of the few records of this man's brief presence in New England.

Because we have only the short list of 1636 grants of Great Lots, and because so much of the land had changed hands by 1643, a parcel-by-parcel analysis would be necessary to determine what a typical series of grants would have looked like. Most of the landholders had a piece of marsh or meadow, and one or more larger pieces of land, sometimes described as upland. There are no entries which identify homelots, and unless the inhabitants were living on one of their larger parcels of land as included in this record, we conclude that the homelots were omitted from this compilation.

A typical holding might be that of Angel Hollard who held five parcels: five acres in the East Field first granted to him; eight acres in the East Field first granted to Widow Streame; three acres granted first to Joane Richards; two acres and a half of meadow at Hocklie first granted to Clement Briggs; and twenty-three acres in the Great Lots.

The town history also includes a number of later grants of land which were recorded in the town meeting volume. We have referred to two of these above, for the 1636 grant of Great Lots was actually entered in 1651, to accompany the order of 2 and 3 February 1651/2 in which these lots, and others granted in the same area, were actually laid out.

These lists must be used with care, as there are many errors in the printed versions. In the entries for 2 February "John Worster" should actually be "John Bester" and "William Chard" should be "William Richards." In the list of 3 February "Robert Harlow" is correctly "Mr. Robert Luntome [Lenthall]," and entries for Nicholas Norton and Samuel Butterworth, crossed out in the original, are omitted altogether.

RECENT LITERATURE

Clifford L. Stott, "The Finney Family of Lenton, Nottinghamshire, and Plymouth, Massachusetts," *New England Historical and Genealogical Register* 148 (1994):315-27. Stott has discovered the English home of the Finney family which arrived in Plymouth Colony late in the 1630s. The family consisted of two brothers (John and Robert), two sisters (Katherine, who married Gabriel Fallowell, and Anne, who married Samuel King), and the widowed mother of these four siblings. Robert Finney, the head of this family, may have died at sea on the way to New England, or soon after arrival in Plymouth.

Dean Crawford Smith and Melinde Lutz Sanborn, "Seeing Double: The Children of Ephraim[2] and Joanna (Rawlings) Kempton," *New England Historical and Genealogical Register* 148 (1994):342-44. Smith and Sanborn resolve an interesting problem regarding the children of Ephraim Kempton. If one were to take the town and church records of this family at face value, there would be eleven children of Ephraim and his wife, born usually at intervals of about eleven months. Closer examination of the two sources shows that in this case the baptismal records are far more reliable than the entries in the town book, and that there were in fact only five children in the family.

Gerald James Parsons, "The Early Parsons Families of the Connecticut River Valley," Part Two, *New England Historical and Genealogical Register* 148 (1994):345-60. In this second installment of his treatment of early Parsons families, the author concludes the presentation of the sons of Thomas Parsons of Windsor. This installment also includes an important correction to Part One.

Rosalie Eggleston and Linda Eggleston McBroom, "The Mother of Bygod[1] Eggleston of Windsor, Connecticut," *The American Genealogist* 69 (1994):193-201. The authors have resolved a number of discrepancies in the records of the Eggleston family by identifying the two wives of James Eggleston, father of Bygod. They show that the first wife of James (and the mother of Bygod) was almost certainly Margaret Harker, daughter of Miles Harker (thus explaining why James Eggleston called Ralph Harker "my brother"). The second wife of James Eggleston was Juliana Frear.

Patricia Law Hatcher, "Mary[2] Hale, Wife of Deacon Edward[3] Putnam, Accuser in the Salem Witchcraft Trials," *The American Genealogist* 69 (1994):212-18. In seeking the identity of the wife of Edward Putnam, Hatcher explores many possibilities, and discusses at length the family of Thomas Hale of Newbury. She concludes that Edward Putnam's wife was very likely Mary Hale, born in 1660, granddaughter of the immigrant.

Norman W. Ingham, "The End of William[1] Kelsey," *The American Genealogist* 69 (1994):218. Ingham has found an entry in the New London County Court Records which narrows the range of dates within which William Kelsey must have died.

Richard W. Cogley, "Two Approaches to Indian Conversion in Puritan New England: The Missions of Thomas Mayhew Jr. and John Eliot," *Historical Journal of Massachusetts* 23 (Winter 1995):44-60. Cogley contrasts the approaches of Mayhew and Eliot to proselytizing the Indians, beginning in the 1640s. He points out that Mayhew placed greater emphasis on destroying the power of the powwows, who were both the medical and religious leaders of the natives, whereas Eliot put more effort into overcoming the influence of the sachems. In the end, although Eliot has had the greater historical reputation in these endeavors, Mayhew (and his kinsmen who succeeded him) obtained better results.

David C. Brown, "The Keys of the Kingdom: Excommunication in Colonial Massachusetts," *The New England Quarterly* 67 (1994):531-66. Brown first notes that the practice of excommunication in the early Congregational Church has to be understood in the context of its earlier usage in the Roman Catholic Church and in the Church of England. He then discusses the problems of excommunication in a Calvinist setting, in which humans should not be able to influence God's choice of the elect. Furthermore, given the rejection by the Puritans of the ecclesiastical courts which they had been subject to in England, excommunication in New England was no longer accompanied by penalties imposed by the courts, thus diminishing the impact of this form of punishment. The use of excommunication continued to decline, and was virtually extinct by the middle of the eighteenth century. In addition to reasons stated above, this decline was the result of the widespread adoption of the Halfway Covenant (which overburdened the churches with persons who were not in full communion, but who were supposed to be under church discipline) and of the rise of religious toleration.

LeRoy W. Sowl, "Thoughts on the Two Mary Fifields of Early Hampton," *The New Hampshire Genealogical Record* 10 (1993):32-34. Sowl suggests some lines of further research into the identity of Mary, the wife of William[1] Fifield, and of an older Mary Fifield of Hampton.

Robert Charles Anderson, "Dalton Addendum," *The New Hampshire Genealogical Record* 10 (1993):81. The author reports on correspondence resulting from an earlier article on the Dalton origin; the full date of marriage for Philemon Dalton is included.

(*continued from page 26*)

that found in early probate matters, and so the unwary might be led to believe that these absconders had died, when they had merely moved away.

An example may be found on 2 July 1633 when the Court had to face both problems on the same day. In the first action "Mr. Woolridge & Mr. Gibbons are appointed to join with Mr. Graves & Mr. Geneson to inventory the goods & chattels of Alex[ander] Wignall." After taking up three other matters of a different nature, the Court then recorded that "[a]dministration is granted to Mr. Mayhewe of the goods & chattels of Mr. Ralfe Glover, deceased, &c." [MBCR 1:106].

In both cases there is an order to take an inventory of the goods and chattels of the person in question, which is why some have interpreted both of these as probate entries. But in the case of Mr. Ralph Glover there is an explicit grant of administration, and an explicit statement that he is deceased; neither of these words is used for Alexander Wignall, so we should not assume that he was deceased on the date of this order. We know in this case that Wignall had not died, for on 3 September 1633 he was "fined £10 for drunkenness, quarrelling, breach of an order of Court, & contempt of authority" [MBCR 1:108]. Perhaps he had returned from an absence. On the other hand, the order of 2 July 1633 may have been in the nature of a bankruptcy proceeding.

On 3 March 1635/6 the General Court, recognizing the great increase in business coming before it, established four subordinate courts called Quarter Courts, to be held four times a year, one based at Ipswich, one at Salem, one at Cambridge and the fourth at Boston [MBCR 1:169]. Most of the probate business soon went to these courts. The records for the Ipswich and Salem courts have been published for most of the seventeenth century, and many probate entries may be found there.

In 1643 the General Court took the next logical step and established four counties to handle a wider range of court business: (Old) Norfolk, Essex, Middlesex and Suffolk [MBCR 2:38]. Middlesex, however, remained for some years a concept found only on paper, and until 1649 all deeds, probates and other court matters for Middlesex County towns will be found in the Suffolk records.

The discussion above pertains to Massachusetts Bay Colony only. Plymouth Colony court records include many entries for probate matters resulting from the epidemic of 1633, during which more than twenty persons died. Plymouth Colony at about this same time began a separate volume of probate proceedings, although probate matters continued to appear in the colony court records.

Great Migration Newsletter

Vol. 6   January-March 1997   No. 1

DOCUMENTING MARRIAGES

One of the most time-consuming tasks in preparing the sketches for *The Great Migration Begins* was the identification of the spouse or spouses of the children of the immigrants. With half or more of the nine hundred immigrants treated in these three volumes marrying and having children, and with many of these children marrying more than once, there were a few thousand marriages to be investigated, involving several hundred surnames.

The easiest to work with, obviously, were those with a recorded marriage, and there were many hundred of these. But even here there could be problems. The date, for example, might be difficult to interpret. Sometimes the bride or groom was just a name, and could not be placed in his or her family. In most cases, no extensive effort was made to identify the parents of this spouse.

There are, of course, thousands of instances among the children of our immigrants in which there is no record of the marriage, but the identity of the spouse, and of the spouse's parents, is known. In many cases an earlier genealogist has written authoritatively on such marriages, and we have documented the liaison by citing the appropriate secondary publication, generally an article in one of the leading genealogical journals.

This may seem an abandonment of our stated goal of providing documentation of original sources for all statements. Were we citing secondary sources that were themselves undocumented, this would be true. But the secondary publications to which we are directing our readers are entered here precisely because they are well-documented and well-argued. Frequently the line of reasoning which the author follows in proving the marriage is long and complicated, and more than could be included in the limited space of the sketches in *The Great Migration Begins*. We include these citations here after examining carefully the author's arguments and in most cases looking at the contemporary sources cited, and because, finally, we agree with the assessment of the earlier genealogist, and wish to direct the interested reader to that genealogist's work, rather than try

to digest it, with the attendant opportunity for misrepresentation, in the pages of *The Great Migration Begins*.

As an example, William Spencer settled first in Cambridge, having arrived in New England by 1631, and then moved on to Hartford where he died in 1640 [*GMB* 3:1721-25]. He left two daughters and one son. The two daughters were born in the early 1630s, and so did not marry until many years after the death of their father. No marriage record has been found for either of these daughters. Research by George McCracken has, however, set forth the identities of the men who married these two daughters of William Spencer. In 1958 McCracken studied several Case immigrants of Connecticut, one of whom was John Case of Milford [*TAG* 34:66-69]. In 1961 he published a study of William Wellman, who married Spencer's daughter Elizabeth [*TAG* 37:7-9]. In both of these cases McCracken discussed the evidence for these marriages, in each instance involving several documents.

Unfortunately, we do not always find a well-crafted and fully documented article which we may cite in support of all the marriages of interest to us. In the majority of cases, the identity of the spouse has long been known, but all too often this identity is simply stated in the secondary sources, without the supporting evidence being supplied. The task of the Great Migration Study Project has been to find this evi-

(continued on page 8)

EDITOR'S EFFUSIONS

As this column is being written, Volume Three of *The Great Migration Begins* has been shipped. This brings to an end Phase One of the Great Migration Study Project, and work on Phase Two has already begun.

There have been many favorable and welcome comments on the three volumes of *The Great Migration Begins*, and we thank you for the response. As would be expected, some errors and omissions have already been detected. Please send these along. They are being collected and will be published at some future date in an appropriate format. (The three-volume set may be ordered from NEHGS, Sales Dept., 160 N. Washington St., Boston MA 02114-2120. The price is $112.50 for NEHGS members and $125.00 for non-members; a postage and handling charge of $5.00 should be added for each set.)

You will notice that the last newsletter published was Volume Five, Number Four, dated October-December 1994, and that this issue, Volume Six, Number One, has been dated January-March 1997. You have not missed anything, and your subscription remains valid for the number of years for which you have already paid. Thus, if at the end of Volume Five you had another year of the newsletter coming to you, you will receive all of Volume Six; if you had paid for two additional years of the newsletter, you will receive Volumes Six and Seven. Renewal notices will not go out until the end of Volume Six.

Since the newsletter was not published during 1995 and 1996, there has been much in the way of new books and articles published during those years which must be covered in the Recent Literature section, along with the material that will appear in 1997 and ensuing years. We will discuss and summarize all these publications in this and in upcoming issues of the newsletter.

In many ways Phase Two of the Great Migration Study Project will look just like Phase One. The format of the

sketches will remain the same, and the sources used to produce them will include the previous ones as well as some new augmentations.

Whereas Phase One covered the fourteen years from 1620 through 1633, Phase Two will cover only two years, 1634 and 1635. Nevertheless, there will be close to 1500 sketches for these two years, as opposed to about 900 for the earlier period. This great difference derives from the greatly accelerated pace of immigration beginning in 1634. (As this rate of immigration continued until 1640, the reader will be able to get some idea of the eventual magnitude of the entire Great Migration Study Project.)

A number of things, however, will be done differently. Most importantly, I will no longer be working alone, as I was until last year. Since early September of 1996, Melinde Sanborn (who worked extensively with me in the latter stages of Phase One) and George Sanborn have been working with me regularly, for a substantial part of each week.

Having compiled the list of sketches to be included in Phase Two, George, Melinde and I have divided up the list, each of us taking responsibility for a portion of them.

A major difference in the way we will work in the future is that one volume will be issued at a time, rather than waiting for the full set to be completed for all 1500 sketches. For now, this means that we contemplate a first volume with about 300 sketches, covering the first three letters of the alphabet. Since these volumes, probably four or five for Phase Two, will be published over a period of years, we will be including the appropriate indexes in each volume, rather than in the last volume of the set.

On the technical side there have been some changes as well. The first three volumes were composed using XyWrite 3.0, which served us well. We have moved on to XyWrite 4.0 for Phase Two. This change will probably not be visible to the reader, as no major alterations to the sketch format are contemplated. Many users of *The Great Migration Begins* have been very complimentary about the arrangement of the sketches and the appearance and readability of the text.

The newsletter, which had been laid out using Ventura, is now being formatted in Word for Windows. Although the two programs are quite different, the format of the newsletter will not be changed during 1997, although some design features may change in the near future.

The database for keeping track of the sketches was prepared in Access this time, and we are now able to print out in seconds a list of persons who lived at any time in any given community, so that if we are going to research in western Massachusetts we can have a list of anyone who lived in Springfield, Northampton and Hadley, for instance.

Robert Charles Anderson, FASG   Editor
Shawna Grimm Hansen   Production Assistant

The Great Migration Newsletter is published quarterly by the Great Migration Study Project, a project of the New England Historic Genealogical Society, 101 Newbury Street, Boston MA 02116

The subscription rate is $12 for one year and $20 for two years.

Focus   on   NEW HAVEN

THE SETTLEMENT OF NEW HAVEN

The spring of 1634 brought many changes to the nature of the migration process. Two of these changes are important for the story of the settlement of New Haven. First, the pace of migration accelerated greatly, so that rather than two or three hundred new arrivals per year, as had been the case since 1628, there were now two or three thousand immigrants each year from 1634 until the end of the decade. Among the many effects of these increased numbers was the overcrowding of the old towns in Massachusetts Bay. Already in 1635 and 1636 large numbers of families had set out for the new plantations on the Connecticut River.

Second, the "clerical companies" became a much more important and prominent part of the Great Migration. A "clerical company" was a grouping of a few dozen families, from a small number of neighboring parishes in England, who had gathered around a strongly charismatic Puritan preacher, and chose to come to New England in his company. Early examples of such groups were the Braintree company from eastern Essex, centered on Reverend Thomas Hooker, and the Nazeing company, on the Essex-Hertfordshire border, adhering to Reverend John Eliot.

Beginning in 1624 Reverend John Davenport had begun to gather around him a group of followers in his parish of St. Stephen's, Coleman Street, London. Given its location, this parish attracted some quite wealthy merchants, including most importantly Theophilus Eaton. Davenport did not hide his Puritan inclinations, and when William Laud was elevated to the Archbishopric of Canterbury in late 1633, Davenport, like so many other Puritan ministers, fled for the Low Countries.

Finally, in the spring of 1637, Davenport, Eaton, and others of the congregation boarded the *Hector* and sailed for New England. Like most other clerical companies which arrived in the mid-1630s, Davenport and his group did not have a place already selected where they would reside. Most immigrants spent the first year living in an already-settled town, perhaps with a friend who had arrived some years earlier. In most cases we do not know much about this process, but because of the prominence of Davenport and Eaton, their first year in New England is well-recorded.

Many towns tried to lure this powerful minister for their church, and presumably Davenport was tempted, but in the end he chose to move to Long Island sound, west of the settlement that had been begun in 1635 at Saybrook. Also during 1637 another clerical company, led by Reverend Peter Prudden, had arrived in New England, and, after also rejecting offers from Dedham and elsewhere, threw in their lot with Davenport.

Thus in the spring of 1638 the combined clerical companies of Davenport and Prudden sailed from Boston to Quillipiac, where they began the settlement that would become New Haven. Shortly after arrival the settlers agreed upon a civil covenant to govern their colony; no copy of this covenant survives (it is only referred to in a document from late in 1639), and this agreement seems in any case to have been an interim arrangement, pending the organization of the church.

The New Haven church was established, with seven founding members, Davenport included, on 21 or 22 April 1639, and on the latter day Peter Prudden and his following organized the Milford church. On 4 June 1639 a new covenant for civil government was drawn up, and on 25 October 1639 the first court under this new government was held.

Davenport and Eaton clearly admired the system of civil and church government adopted in the Bay, in which one had to be a church member to be a freeman, and a freeman to vote in colony affairs. But the New Haven settlers seem to have taken matters a step further, and although they did not adopt a full-fledged theocracy, they did swing the balance between church and state a bit further in the direction of the church than had Winthrop, Cotton and Shepard in Massachusetts Bay. This would seem to be the reason that a permanent civil covenant was not enacted until after the arduous process of forming the church was complete.

As a result, New Haven, both town and colony, was a more stringent Puritan society than was Massachusetts Bay, whereas the towns on the Connecticut River were somewhat less stern than those of the Bay.

(The discussion above derives from Isabel Calder's history of the colony and from the first volume of colony records; see page six below.)

AN EARLY LIST OF ESTATES

The first volume of the published records of New Haven Colony contains, on pages 91, 92 and 93, a list of the "Names of the Planters," which includes information for each name on the list of "Persons Numbered," "Estates," acreage received in four different divisions of land, and "Rates yearly paid for land." This list is undated, but falls immediately after a 5 July 1643 meeting of the New Haven court, and before a General Court of 6 July 1643.

In his 1967 study of the family of Henry Peck of New Haven, Donald Lines Jacobus stated that "the list of planters and estates ... was clearly drawn up as early as 1640-1, though copied into the records in 1643" [NEHGR 121:81]. Jacobus does not provide evidence for this conclusion in the Peck article, and no discussion of his dating of the list has been encountered elsewhere in Jacobus's writings.

We will attempt here to arrive at a reasonably precise dating of this list, and in doing so we are no doubt following in the footsteps of Jacobus and taking much the same approach that he did to this problem. Because the list includes a column for "Persons numbered," we will examine as many as possible of the families for which we have strong evidence for family size independent of this list. This should allow us to establish a range of dates for each of these families, within which the household size given in the list would be correct for that family. Once we have obtained a substantial number of these individual ranges of dates, we can merge the data and, if there are no serious inconsistencies, arrive at a date for the document as a whole.

Let us first look at the family of Thomas Kimberly, an immigrant studied carefully by Jacobus himself. The listing shows that he had a household of seven. Thomas Kimberly and his wife had a child baptized at New Haven on 17 November 1639, at a time when there were already four surviving children in the family, making by that date a household of seven. The next child was baptized on 19 December 1641.

On this basis alone, then, we can say that the list was compiled not later than 19 December 1641 and no earlier than 17 November 1639. One possible complication would arise if Kimberly had one or more children born in England, beyond the list known to us, alive in 1639 but dead by 1641, and not recorded in New Haven records. We have no reason to believe that such a situation existed and, as we shall see, this would be inconsistent with our knowledge of other families.

As a second example let us take the family of William Tuttle, who, like Kimberly, appears in the list with a household

of seven. He had a child baptized at New Haven on 7 April 1639 and another on 22 November 1640. From various studies of this family we know that the child baptized early in 1639 was the fifth surviving child, who thus, with his parents, made up a household of seven. So on this evidence we place the making of the list after 7 April 1639 and before 22 November 1640.

Some slightly different examples are found among less mature families. Jarvis Boykin (or Boykett) who had migrated to New Haven from Charlestown, is credited with a household of two. The earliest record of a child born in New Haven (and the oldest known child for this immigrant) is a son Nathaniel baptized in September 1641. Thus the household of two would be Jarvis and his wife, prior to the arrival of their first child in September of 1641.

Henry Rutherford is credited with a household of two. The first child recorded to him in New Haven is a daughter Sarah, born on 31 July 1641, but not baptized until 1 October 1643. This would seem to date the list before 31 July 1641.

A somewhat less informative case is that of John Brockett, with a household of but one, clearly himself. His first child was a son John, baptized at New Haven on 31 December 1642. Assuming that this baptism took place soon after birth, and at the end of a full-term pregnancy, Brockett must have married no later than the end of March 1642, after which time he would have been shown with a household of two. The marriage may, of course, have taken place some months earlier.

Information which will help us date this document also comes from the records of land grants. On 29 October 1640 a Court of Elections at New Haven ordered that "Jer[emiah] Dixon [be] allowed to add to his estate formerly given in, so much as will make it three hundred pounds, so as he pay all rates for that estate backward and forward" [NHCR 1:44]. The entry for Jeremiah Dixon shows him with an estate of £300, indicating that the list was made after 29 October 1640.

On the same day another court order was made, that "Tymo[thy] Baldwin's lot shall have land laid to it for 6 heads & £500, and reserved for an elder" [NHCR 1:44]. In the list we find two entries for "An Elder," and none for Timothy Baldwin. The second entry for "An Elder" immediately follows that of Widow Baldwin, and is for 6 heads and £500, supporting the same conclusion as the Jeremiah Dixon entry, that the list was created after 29 October 1640.

The list includes entries for several widows, which causes us to search out the dates of death of their husbands. The will of "old father Sherman" [Edmund Sherman] was presented at court in May 1641, indicating that his wife was already a widow by that date, as indicated in the list. Edmund Sherman is almost certainly the "Goodman Sherman" who was admitted a member of New Haven Court on 29 October 1640 [NHCR 1:44], so again the list must have been made after this date.

Taken together these records provide a very narrow range of dates within which this document would have been produced - between 29 October 1640 and 22 November 1640. Since we have not examined all families and all records which bear on this problem, this great precision may be illusory, but for the moment we will proceed on the assumption that the list was prepared within this period of slightly more than three weeks.

As noted above, some of our information for determining the date of this document comes from a Court of Elections held at New Haven on 29 October 1640, the earliest date on which we think the drafting of the list might have taken place. Nothing in the record of that court refers directly to such a list, but a number of the actions taken at that court made adjustments to the estates of individuals, and those adjustments are accounted for in the list.

The next meeting of the court was on 4 November 1640, but nothing relating to individual landholding or to the preparation of a list was included. Two further court sessions on 2 December 1640 and 6 January 1640/1 were very brief and handled only minor criminal and probate matters.

Looking back a bit further, a General Court was held on 23 October 1640 at which many orders regarding the division of land were made, including detailed provisions for the paying of taxes. While these various observations do not prove that the list of estates was prepared during late October and early November 1640, they are certainly consistent with that conclusion, and no contrary evidence has been found.

Having obtained a date for the compilation of this list, in agreement with the conclusion of Jacobus, we can now use this information to help in our interpretation of some of the entries in the list.

One interesting case is that of Thomas Fugill, a prominent citizen of early New Haven, who soon went back to England to stay. At the time we think this list was produced, Thomas Fugill was secretary of the colony, and may well have been the compiler of the document.

He appears in the list with a household of two, but on 2 August 1640 had a daughter Mercy baptized, indicating that the family size was at least three before October 1640, thus seemingly violating the conclusion which we have already made. The likely solution may be found in the baptism of a second child, a son John on 13 July 1641. The lapse of less than a year between the first and second baptisms strongly suggests that the first child had died soon after birth, thus reducing the family size to two again by October of 1640. Since the Fugill family returned to England in 1646 we do not know the later history of the children of Thomas and his wife, but if future research in England does trace this family, evidence might be found to confirm or confute this scenario.

Another family worth considering in this context is that of Timothy Ford, who is given a household of two in this list. In at least one account he and his unnamed wife are given five children, the third of whom, a son Samuel, is said to be born about 1640 [TAG 3:611]. This would make the household size either four or five in late 1640, depending on when Samuel might have been born.

There are, however, no dates of birth or baptism for these five children (aside from an adult baptism for son Matthew). Samuel was married in 1673, which certainly does not require that he be born as early as 1640; a birth about 1648 would be more likely. Timothy Ford's daughter Mary was the first of his children to be married, in 1662, suggesting a birth about 1642. The evidence seems to be consistent, then, with the birth of five children to Timothy Ford in the 1640s, all after the estimated date for the list of estates. The household of Timothy Ford in this document would therefore consist of himself and his wife, to whom he had presumably been married only recently.

There are many more entries in which the household size is given as two. Some of these are for men who married, but who never had children, or who had only one child, at a date much later than 1640.. Presumably, then, many of these households consist of husband and wife, who were throughout all or most of their married lives childless. This suggests, but does not prove, that these men were married by October or November of 1640. They might, of course, have been married years earlier.

One also must consider the possibility that the households enumerated in this list were not limited to the nuclear family. The family might include siblings of the head of household or his wife, or possibly servants, or any number of other combinations. As a result, we can say only that the household size gives us an upper limit for the number of children in the family. A household of seven, for example, should have no more than five children (assuming husband and wife were both alive at the time), but there might be fewer.

NEW HAVEN HISTORIOGRAPHY

As the first settlement in what would become New Haven Colony, the town of New Haven has attracted much attention from historians and genealogists over the last two centuries. Because the town was briefly coterminous with the colony, we will discuss here records and writings on both.

Many records were created by New Haven, both town and colony, before absorption into Connecticut in 1665. The colony records were published in 1857 and 1858, in two volumes (Charles J. Hoadly, ed., *Records of the Colony and Plantation of New Haven, from 1638 to 1649* [Hartford 1857], and *Records of the Colony or Jurisdiction of New Haven, from May, 1653, to the Union ...* [Hartford 1858]). As can be deduced from the inclusive dates of these two volumes, there is a gap in the records from 1649 to 1653.

The seventeenth-century records of the town of New Haven have been published in three volumes (Franklin Bowditch Dexter, ed., *Ancient Town Records, Volume I, New Haven Town Records, 1649-1662* and *Volume II, New Haven Town Records, 1662-1684* [New Haven 1917, 1919]; Zara Jones Powers, ed., *Volume III, New Haven Town Records, 1684-1769* [New Haven 1962]). The first half of Volume I helps fill the gap which was noted above in the colony record, from 1649 to 1653. There remain unprinted the records of the selectmen, from 1665 to 1714.

In 1972 Richard Hegel published a slim volume entitled *Nineteenth-Century Historians of New Haven*, in which he discussed five writers of the last century. Three of these - Leonard Bacon, John Warner Barber and Edward Rodolphus Lambert - published the bulk of their work in the 1830s. These men worked in a period before the professionalization of the historical community, and at a time when there was not much reliance on original documents.

The remaining two authors - Edward Elias Atwater and Charles Herbert Levermore - produced their work a half century later, in the 1880s, when the standards of the historical craft had evolved greatly, as a result of which their volumes are still useful to the modern researcher.

Edward E. Atwater published his *History of The Colony of New Haven to Its Absorption into Connecticut* in 1881, a tome of more than six hundred pages. The first few chapters provide a chronological treatment of the early years of New Haven, but the later chapters take up a topical approach to the subject. Many original documents, including letters and court records, are quoted fully and at length.

Charles H. Levermore's *The Republic of New Haven: A History of Municipal Evolution*, issued only five years after Atwater's history, was a very different production. Covering the whole range of New Haven's history, Levermore focussed on the growth and development of town and then city government, reflecting one of the prominent strands of academic historical investigation at the end of the nineteenth century.

A half century more would pass before another book-length treatment of New Haven was attempted, until in 1934 Isabel MacBeath Calder completed *The New Haven Colony*. Calder corrected many mistakes and misinterpretations made by her predecessors.

She provided an important service by summarizing the origins, as known to her, of the earliest settlers. Some she connected with their immigration groups, as those who came with Davenport and with Prudden. Others did not come directly from England, but had resided elsewhere in New England for some years (see page 47). Her lists should be used with caution, however. For example, recent research has shown that Edmund Tapp did not come in 1637.

Most importantly she made extensive use of the records of the parish of St. Stephen's, Coleman Street, London, to demonstrate the activities of some of the men who would become leaders in the settlement of New Haven, in the years just before they departed for New England. Frederick C. Hart Jr. has recently shown, in his study of the family of Reverend John Jones of Fairfield, that much of value remains to be elicited from the records of this parish [*TAG* 71:52-54].

We would be remiss, of course, if we did not also mention in this section the work of Donald Lines Jacobus on his native New Haven. In July of 1922 appeared the first issue of his quarterly publication, the *New Haven Genealogical Magazine*, the bulk of which was devoted to his comprehensive compilation of the "Families of Ancient New Haven."

His march through the alphabet filled eight volumes and 2068 pages, ending in April 1932. The entries in this compendium were highly abbreviated, with brief citations to the original documents, but with no extended discussion of difficult problems.

After the completion of his New Haven project Jacobus chose to continue his periodical, changing the title at first to *The American Genealogist and New Haven Genealogical Magazine*, and then finally to *The American Genealogist* (known to all as *TAG*). The scope of this journal soon moved well beyond New Haven families, but over the years detailed studies of aspects of New Haven genealogy have appeared in the journal.

RECENT LITERATURE

Alice H. Dreger, "William[1] Perry of Scituate and Marshfield, Massachusetts," *The American Genealogist* 70 (1995):42-48. The author outlines the life of William Perry, landowner of Scituate by 1638, and delineates his children and grandchildren. (Some corrections to and comments on this article were published in TAG 70:84.)

David T. Robertson, "Some Savin Hill (Dorchester) Families," *New England Historical and Genealogical Register* 149 (1995):28-40. Robertson studies three families who were early residents of what is now the Savin Hill section of Dorchester: John Gurnell, John Mason and Hezekiah Mero. John Gurnell had arrived in Dorchester by 1639, and perhaps a few years earlier. John Mason was a son of Sampson Mason, who came to New England about 1649, and Hezekiah Mero appeared in Dorchester about 1700.

Gale Ion Harris and Anthony Hale Burke, "Hannah Edwards, First Wife of Joseph[2] Hills of Glastonbury, Connecticut," *New England Historical and Genealogical Register* 149 (1995):41-45. The authors demonstrate that Joseph Hills, son of William Hills of Hartford (an immigrant to New England in 1632), took as his first of three wives Hannah Edwards, daughter of John Edwards, and, through her mother, Dorothy (Moulton) (Finch) Edwards, granddaughter of Robert Moulton [GMB 1:668, 2:944, 1305].

Clifford L. Stott, "John[1] Plumb of Connecticut and His Cousin, Deputy Governor Samuel[1] Symonds of Massachusetts," *The American Genealogist* 70 (1995):65-74, 149-55. Stott has extended and expanded our knowledge of the ancestry of John Plumb in several directions. First, he provides additional information on the father and grandfather of the immigrant, whose identities were known from previous research. Stott then extends the family of Grace Crackbone, mother of the immigrant, by identifying Grace's mother and adding a generation, and perhaps two, to the Crackbone line. In addition to the summaries for the Plumb and Crackbone families, there is a section on Purcas of Great Yeldham, Essex, the family of the wife of John Plumb's paternal grandfather. The immigrants John Plumb and Samuel Symonds were first cousins, both being grandsons of Robert[B] and Elizabeth (Purcas) Plumb.

Clifford L. Stott, "William[1] Shepard, Father of John[2] Shepard of Westfield, Massachusetts," *The American Genealogist* 70 (1995):82-83. The author strengthens earlier research by Donald Lines Jacobus, presenting two documents which increase the likelihood that Experience Hart, one of the eight daughters of Edmund Hart of Westfield, married William Shepard and had by him a son, John Shepard of Westfield.

Dean Crawford Smith and Paul C. Reed, "Four Generations of English Ancestry for the Noyes Families of New England," *The New England Historical and Genealogical Register* 149 (1995):105-21. Smith and Reed have established the English ancestry of James[1] Noyes and Nicholas[1] Noyes of Newbury, Massachusetts, and have delineated four generations of that ancestry. This discovery arose in the course of researching Peter[1] Noyes of Sudbury, who was distantly related to the Noyes brothers of Newbury.

Douglas Richardson, "Heath-Johnson-Morris Update: The Ancestry of Agnes (Cheney) Heath," *The New England Historical and Genealogical Register* 149 (1995):173-86. Following up on his own earlier research on several early Roxbury families, Richardson has found records which identify the wife of William[A] Heath of Ware, Hertfordshire (father of the immigrant brothers William and Isaac Heath), as Agnes Cheney, daughter of Robert and Joan (Harrison) Cheney. He goes on to trace the Cheney line for two additional generations, and also to identify the father and siblings of Joan Harrison.

Margaret E. Newell, "Robert Child and the Entrepreneurial Vision: Economy and Ideology in Early New England," *The New England Quarterly* 68 (1995):223-56. Robert Child is remembered for his Remonstrance of 1646, in which he challenged many of the political foundations of the Massachusetts Bay Colony. His opposition, and that of the equally prominent men who associated with him, has largely been interpreted in political and religious terms. Newell examines the economic and entrepreneurial activities of Child, in England, New England and elsewhere, mostly involving the establishment of mining and manufacturing operations, and revises the traditional position by showing that dissatisfaction with the development of these enterprises in the setting of Massachusetts Bay was an important underpinning of the Remonstrance.

Michael Freeman, "Puritans and Pequots: The Question of Genocide," *The New England Quarterly* 68 (1995):278-93. Continuing the long-running argument over the origins of the Pequot War and the motivations of the Puritans during that conflict, Freeman addresses the question of whether the Pequot War was an instance of genocide. After a brief review of earlier conflicts between Englishmen and Indians, not just in New England but also further south and long before the Great Migration, he looks closely at the evidence for the Pequot War and concludes that it was genocide. (Freeman misidentifies the two Oldham boys who sailed with John Oldham as his sons, when they were certainly more distant kinsmen, perhaps nephews [GMN 2:1351-55].)

dence, even though most of it had already been located by previous researchers who chose not to pass these details on to their readers.

For those marriages in which the identity of the spouse is known, even though no marriage record exists, two different items had to be documented - the approximate date of the marriage, and the identity of the parents of the spouse. On some occasions these two points might be proved by the same evidence, but more frequently different sources provided the desired result.

Benjamin Silvester, son of Richard Silvester, married by 1687 Mary Standlake, daughter of Richard Standlake [*GMB* 3:1680-81]. The estimate of the date of marriage derives from the birthdate of the couple's earliest known child, on 26 December 1687. But the identity of the bride's father is found in two deeds dated in 1701, in which the heirs of Richard Standlake redistributed the land they had received from him.

Similarly, John Stearns, son of Isaac Stearns, married by 1654 Sarah Mixer, daughter of Isaac Mixer [*GMB* 3:1749]. The date of the marriage is approximated from the birth of the only child of this couple in "the second week of May 1654." In his will of 8 May 1655 Isaac Mixer made a bequest to "my daughter Sarah the wife of Jno. Sternes." Even though only a year elapsed between these two records, both must be cited in order to document the marriage as best we can in the absence of a marriage record.

The family of Reverend Samuel Stone of Hartford offers several examples of the sort of evidence needed in such cases [*GMB* 3:1771]. In his will Stone named four daughters, three of whom were already married, but did not give their married surnames. Nearly twenty years later, in 1681, his widow died and in her will named her stepdaughters [i.e., daughters-in-law] Rebecca Nash, Mary Fitch and Sarah Butler, and her own daughter Elizabeth Sedgwick.

The will provides the evidence for the marriage and the identity of the spouse, but does little to estimate the date of the marriage. In the case of Rebecca, the first child was born on 12 March 1657/8, so the marriage presumably took place by about 1657. We estimate the dates of marriage of Sarah Stone to Thomas Butler and of Elizabeth Stone to William Sedgwick from entries in John Winthrop Jr.'s medical journal, relating both to the date of treatment of these women, and the ages of their children.

There were hundreds of marriages which were proved by evidence of this sort, and a regular way of expressing the evidence was developed, in which a single parenthetic statement follows the marriage. This statement includes a very brief extract from the record pointing to the date of the marriage, with the citation to the source appended in square brackets. This first part of the statement is ended by a semicolon, after which a very brief extract of the document proving the parentage is presented, again followed by the source citation in square brackets, after which the parenthetical statement is closed.

Great Migration Study Project
101 Newbury Street
Boston, MA 02116

Great Migration Newsletter

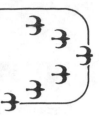

Vol. 6   April-June 1997   No. 2

PASSENGER SHIPS OF 1634 - Part I

In the first fourteen years of the Great Migration, from 1620 through 1633, the year in which the most immigrants arrived was 1630, when the Winthrop Fleet and a few other vessels brought about a thousand passengers, and perhaps not even that many. In the remaining years of this period anywhere from a handful to a few hundred people came to New England.

The first inklings that this would change came in late 1633, when two vessels arrived with Thomas Hooker and several hundred other passengers, the first of those to leave England after the translation of William Laud from Bishop of London to Archbishop of Canterbury. Although the increase in the persecution of the Puritans resulting from this move was not the only reason for the increase in the desire of the Puritans to leave England, it was certainly an important factor.

So, in 1634 the pace of the Great Migration ratcheted itself up, by a factor of about five to ten times what it had been earlier. The purpose of this article, which will appear in two parts in this issue and the next, is primarily to inventory the ships that came from England to New England in that year. A secondary purpose is to begin to establish the data which will allow us to state with greater assurance how many new settlers appeared in New England in 1634 and the later years of the decade of the 1630s.

Prior to 1634 John Winthrop noted in his journal the arrival of each ship, usually giving the name of the ship and its master, the tunnage, the number of passengers, and sometimes other information, such as the number of cattle or the time of passage across the North Atlantic. But in 1634 he was unable to continue this practice, partly because of the increased number of ships, but also because of changes in the way he kept his journal.

His first mention of ships was in an undated entry, apparently from late February or early March, in which he noted that "[b]y this time 17 fishing ships were come to Riches [Richmond] Isle & the Isles of Shoals" [WJ

1:148]. There was an annual competition among the fishing vessels, most of them from the West Country, to get to the fishing banks in the Gulf of Maine early enough in the year to get their share of the catch. These vessels were based for a few months of the year not only at Richmond Island and the Isles of Shoals, but at such places as Monhegan and Pemaquid Islands. Most of those coming on these ships were mariners and fishermen, who were only transients in New England. Occasionally some of these men made a permanent residence Down East.

There might be passengers on these fishing boats who were bound for one of the Puritan colonies further south, but these were relatively rare. The fishing ships were, however, frequently used by Puritans in both old and New England to carry letters back and forth.

On 2 or 3 May 1634 Winthrop reports "the arrival of the ship at Pemaquid, which brought 30 passengers for this place" [WJ 1:155]. The ship is not named, nor are any of its passengers, but these are the first arrivals in Massachusetts Bay we see in this year. Note that this was less than two weeks prior to the sitting of the Court of Elections for 1634, at which 104 men were admitted to freemanship. Unless special exceptions were made, there would not have been time for any of these immigrants to have gone through the procedure of being admitted to a Massachusetts Bay church, a prerequisite to freemanship.

(continued on page 10)

EDITOR'S EFFUSIONS

Research and writing of the next volume in the Great Migration series is well under way. The approximately fifty sketches for the letter A have been drafted and will soon be in final form. There are more than a hundred and fifty sketches for the letter B, and we are well along in the research and drafting process for these. The letter C, which will complete this new volume, has about one hundred sketches, to which we will turn our attention in late summer or early fall.

The title for the first three volumes in the series, *The Great Migration Begins*, expresses the time period and the subject matter well. We have, however, painted ourselves into something of a corner. How should we title the next series? *The Great Migration Continues* or *The Great Migration Carries On* won't do. So we issue this challenge: send in your suggestion for the series title for the four or five volumes that will cover the years 1634 or 1635. If your proposed title is the one we decide to use, you will be rewarded with a two-year extension to your subscription to this newsletter.

In this column in the last issue we stated that your mailing label should contain a number which would tell when your subscription expires. Unfortunately, this was not true, but this should be corrected for this issue.

The current issue does something which we have not done before: the lead article was too large to be contained in one issue, and so will be carried over and continue in the next. In this first installment a list is compiled of ships known to have arrived in 1634. The second installment builds on this list to attempt to derive a general picture of the migration process in that year. In a later issue this year, we hope to present another innovation - a lengthy article (in this case a FOCUS section which takes a closer look at a town previously treated here) not written by this editor.

Robert Charles Anderson, FASG   Editor
Shawna Grimm Hansen   Production Assistant

The Great Migration Newsletter is published quarterly by the Great Migration Study Project, a project of the New England Historic Genealogical Society, 101 Newbury Street, Boston MA 02116

The subscription rate is $12 for one year and $20 for two years.

(continued from page 9)

This is the basis for the rule which is generally followed in the Great Migration Study Project, that all those admitted as freemen at the Court of Elections in May of each year are assumed to have arrived in the previous year. This assumption may occasionally be erroneous, but only in rare and exceptional cases.

The floodgates burst in May, during the sitting of the Court of Elections, when Winthrop noted that "The week the court was there came in 6 ships with store of passengers and cattle. Mr. Parker a minister & a company with him being about 100 went to sit down at Agawam & diverse other of the newcomers" [WJ 1:158]. (In a postscript to a letter dated 22 May 1634 Winthrop gives a different version of this same note: "Here are 6 ships lately arrived with passengers and cattle, most of them came in 6 weeks space. We have settled a plantation 20 miles to the northward, near Merimacke. Mr. Parker is to be minister there" [WP 3:168].)

This increased rate of arrival of passenger ships is reflected in an order of the Privy Council dated "the last of February 1633[/4]," stating that "Whereas by a warrant bearing date 22nd of this present the several ships following bound for New England & now lying in the River of Thames were made stay of until further order from their Lordships vizt: *The Clement & Job, The Reformation, The True Love, The Elizabeth Bonadventure, The Sea Flower, The Mary & John, The Planter, The Elizabeth & Dorcas, The Hercules & The Neptune.*" The Privy Council permitted the ships to proceed, with a number of provisos, including the need for the passengers to take the Oath of Allegiance and Supremacy, and the requirement that the ship masters on their return submit "the names of all such persons as they shall transport" [NEHGR 9:265-66]. The masters may have submitted these lists, but, as we shall see, only three such lists survive. Many of the ships listed by the Privy Council are seen making voyages to New England with passengers in other years, so we may presume that most, if not all, of these ships did come to New England in 1634, and that some of these ships were among the six that arrived in early May.

(On 24 May Winthrop also speaks of "Mr. Fleming, master of a ship of Barnstable, [who] went eastward to cut masts there, and so to return to England" [WJ 1:158]. As this entry comes on the same page as the reference to the arrival of the six ships, and is followed immediately

(continued on page 16)

Focus   *on*   **DOVER**

EARLY POLITICAL HISTORY

We examined Dover briefly in an earlier *Newsletter* [GMN 2:29], but this settlement deserves to be studied in greater detail, which we do in the next four pages.

Some treatments of early New Hampshire history claim that the region that became Dover was settled in 1623, at the same time that David Thomson, as agent for Sir Ferdinando Gorges and John Mason, planted at the mouth of the Piscataqua. This statement is based on the writings of William Hubbard, compiled in 1680, which linked Edward and William Hilton to David Thomson, having them all arrive in 1623 [Hubbard 214]. This was picked up a century later by Jeremy Belknap, and has been repeated many times since. Noyes, Libby and Davis pointed out that this could not be correct, partly based on the report from 1624 by Christopher Levett, which gave no indication of settlement on the Piscataqua above Strawbery Bank [*The Great Migration Begins* 2:950, citing GDMNH 331, 334].

The land which would become Dover and parts of some of the neighboring towns remained in dispute for many years, and a deposition dating from about 1654 sets forth a reasonably precise chronology, which we may test against other documents. The declaration was made to the Massachusetts Bay General Court by John Allen, Nicholas Shapleigh and Thomas Lake "of their right in the two patents, Swampscot and Dover" [NHPP 1:157-58]. We shall introduce one at a time the first five points made in this deposition, and then comment on each. (Throughout the following discussion the reader should be aware that there is much confusion over these grants, and the Squamscott Patent may have covered a larger area than that described by modern writers.)

Point 1: "That Mr. Edward Hilton was possessed of this land about the year 1628, which is about 26 years ago."

We do know that Edward Hilton had settled by 1628 on the point of land which would be called Hilton's Point, for in that year he contributed toward the fund which was raised to send Thomas Morton back to England. As noted above, there is no reliable evidence that Hilton was in New England any earlier. (In 1660 William Hilton, Edward's nephew, made a deposition which has been used to claim arrival of Edward Hilton by 1623, but this document only states that William Hilton came to Plymouth in 1621, his wife and children came in 1623, "and in a little time following settled ourselves upon the River of Pischataq[ua], with Mr. Edw[ard] Hilton" [SJC Case #362; NEHGR 36:41-42; GMB 2:955], not a very precise indication of the date of removal.)

Edward Hilton returned to England in 1629 to secure a proper grant of land from the Council for New England, and on 12 March 1629/30 he successfully obtained a patent which allowed him "all that part of the River Pascataquack, called or known by the name of Wecanacohunt, or Hilton's Point, with the south side of said River, up to the fall of the river, and three miles into the mainland by all the breadth aforesaid" [NHPP 10:698]. (This grant has been published as the "Squamscott Patent," but it may be the Dover Patent.)

Point 2: "Mr. Hilton sold the land to some merchants of Bristol, who had it in possession for about 2 years."

This is maddeningly uninformative. We don't know when the two-year period began or ended (although points 4 and 5 below will help us firm up the chronology) and we don't know who the Bristol merchants were (although we note that Bristol merchants were active further to the east, and some had received a patent for Pemaquid).

Point 3: "The Lord Say, the Lord Brook, Sir Richard Saltonstall, ... and others bought the said land of Bristol merchants...."

These were the so-called "Puritan lords," very wealthy men of Puritan leanings who undertook a number of colonizing activities in the New World, including the settlement of Providence Island and Saybrook. Had they succeeded in any of their endeavors, they would have installed a feudal system much like that proposed by Gorges and Mason, but with a Puritan ecclesiastic government rather than under the Church of England.

Point 4: "The lords and gentlemen engaged the said land (so purchased) about 9 years, and placed more inhabitants at Dover, some of which came over at their cost and charges, and had their several letters set forth unto them."

The first evidence of this seen in New England was the receipt by Winthrop of a letter from London, dated 25 March 1633, which informed him that "There are honest men about to buy out the Bristoll men's plantation in Pascataque, and do purpose to plant there 500 good people before Michaelmas next. C[aptain] Wiggin is the chief Agent therein" [WP 3:114-15]. This soon came to pass (although with a much reduced contingent of immigrants), for on 10 October 1633 Winthrop reported the arrival at Salem of the *James* which "brought Capt. Wiggen & about thirty with one Mr. Leveridge a godly minister to Paskataquack (which the Lord Say & the Lord Brook had purchased of the Bristol men)" [WJ 1:137].

Point 5: "The 14th of the 4 mo. [June] 1641, Mr. Wyllys, Mr. Saltonstall, Mr. Holyoke and Mr. Makepeace, for themselves and partners, put the said patent under the government of the Massachusetts, reserving 1/3 of Dover patent, and the whole of the south part of the river, to the lords and gentlemen...."

Now we can begin to put the chronology together. If the "lords and gentlemen engaged the said land ... about 9 years," and relinquished their control in June of 1641, then they would have acquired it about 1632. As we have seen above, they had not yet purchased the patent on 25 March 1633, but were soon to do so, implying that "about 9 years" in this case simply means more than eight years.

There are two more steps backward. The Bristol men were "in possession for about 2 years," so they would have purchased the patent from Hilton about 1631. And since he had received the patent in March of 1630, Hilton's term of possession of the patent would have been just about a year.

Having established this sequence of events, we need to examine a few other happenings in Dover in the late 1630s. Massachusetts Bay began to take a serious interest in the settlements north of the Merrimack in 1638, after many of the Hutchinson and Wheelwright exiles had removed to that area. (We will see more evidence of these exiles when we study in the next section some of the early settlers of Dover.)

At about this same time the Puritan lords were losing interest in this settlement, as they were far more concerned with their plantation on Providence Island, off the coast of Nicaragua. By 1640 the inhabitants of the area that would become Dover were beginning to act for themselves, and on 20 October 1640 they entered into the so-called Dover Combination, in which they "voluntarily agreed to combine ourselves into a Body Politic," complaining that "his Gracious Majesty [had] hitherto settled no order for us to our knowledge" [NHPP 10:700].

Massachusetts Bay continued to press these settlers to come under the Bay government, but on 4 March 1640/1 most of those who had signed the combination also put their names to a petition in which they exhibited a willingness to submit, but did not wish to do so "until such time as the owners come over to us, which we suppose will be about three months hence" [NHPP 1:127]. Three months passed, and on 2 June 1641 the General Court noted that "the lords and gentlemen patentees of Dover & other tracts of land upon the river of Pascataque have passed a grant of the same to this Court" [MBCR 1:332].

Not surprisingly, the leaders at the Bay quickly took steps to absorb Dover, setting up courts and arranging for the town to send a deputy to the meetings of the General Court, even though Dover had no freemen in the sense that was accepted by Massachusetts. Dover was independent no longer.

EARLY SETTLERS

The first document that provides the names of most, if not all, of the adult male residents of Dover is the Combination of 2 October 1640. We will return to that list, and to the associated Petition of 4 March 1640/1, later in this section, but by the time of these two documents Dover had been settled for twelve years or more, and we need to study a number of other documents in an attempt to identify the earliest settlers of the town.

Before we deal with original records, we should mention one list of early Dover residents that was concocted sometime in the nineteenth century. In the first volume of the Provincial Papers of New Hampshire, in the section on Dover, is a list prepared by Rev. A.H. Quint of the "names of families in Dover ... between 1623 and 1641 (most of whom probably came in 1633)"; there are thirty names in this list [NHPP 1:118-19].

Quint believed in the now-discredited assertion that Edward Hilton had arrived by 1623, and he was also working without the benefit of the list of those who had signed the Dover Combination in 1640. As a result this list omits a number of men now known to have been in Dover by 1641, and includes some others who cannot be shown to be present that early. This list should be ignored.

We must begin, of course, with Edward Hilton and his family, soon to be joined by his brother William, who had been living for some years at Plymouth, and perhaps briefly had some other intermediate residence.

In the patent issued to Edward Hilton in 1630 by the Council for New England we learn that "Edward Hilton & his Associates hath already at his and their own proper costs and charges transported sundry servants to plant in New England aforesaid at a place there called by the natives Wecanacohunt otherwise Hilton's Point" [NHPP 10:697-98]. Although this is standard language encountered in most of these patents, we must accept this as a reasonable account, for very few of these early immigrants came as loners, such people as William Blackstone being the rare exceptions.

Who were these servants? We don't have direct evidence of the names of any of them, but it is likely that some of those we see appearing in the records on this part of the Piscataqua a few years later were among these servants. This is one of the frustrations in working in early New England records north of the Merrimack. The records are very few, and regular runs of town records usually don't begin until later in the century. As a result we must frequently come to this same conclusion, that there were certainly people there, and some of them are probably the people we see there ten years later. But there must also be many who came and went, or who came and died, and whose names we will never recover.

The next person to appear on the Dover stage was Thomas Wiggin, whom we have already met above. He had arrived in New England by 1630, when he witnessed the delivery of the Vines patent. He returned to England in 1632, married in July of 1633 Catherine Whiting, the daughter of one of the "lords and gentlemen" who had just bought the Squamscott Patent, and was back in New England by the fall of 1633 [GMB 3:1982-85].

While in England Wiggin had taken a number of steps which defended Winthrop and the other leaders of Massachusetts Bay against the attacks by Gorges, Mason, Thomas Morton and others. In this way the settlement on the west side of the upper reaches of the Piscataqua was for these middle years of the 1630s firmly distinguished from the other settlements (at the locations that would become Portsmouth, Kittery and Berwick), all of which were under the influence of Gorges and Mason.

The only other resident of Dover before 1633 whose name has been recovered is the unfortunate John Hocking, who was present at least as early as 1632, when he had dealings with William Hilton. Hocking trapped and traded on the Kennebec, as agent for the Puritan lords, and in 1634 he confronted a group from Plymouth Colony, who had a stronger claim to the Kennebec area. During the dispute, in the space of just a few minutes, Hocking shot and killed Moses Talbot of the Plymouth party, and was himself gunned down [GMB 2:960-62]. Only by involvement in such sensational events were some of these early settlers on the Piscataqua preserved for history.

Accompanying Wiggin on his return in 1633 were a number of new immigrants, among whom we can identify with certainty only Mr. William Leverich, the first of a string of ministers we shall encounter who were unable to establish a stable church at Dover. Leverich lasted only a couple of years at Dover, moving on briefly to Boston, then to Plymouth Colony, and finally to various of the English settlements on Long Island [GMB 2:1178-80].

There are several signers of the Dover Combination in 1640 who had arrived in New England by 1633, but did not settle immediately in Dover. Philip Swaddon was in Watertown as early as 1631, as a servant of Robert Seeley. Disliking his servitude, he decamped for the Piscataqua, where for some time he had a wigwam at Braveboat Harbor (now part of Kittery). When he moved further up the river is uncertain, but by 1640 he was in Dover [GMB 3:1787-89].

James Rawlins was in Massachusetts Bay by 1633, for on 14 May 1634 he was admitted to freemanship in that colony. Where he resided immediately after his arrival in New England is unknown, but he was soon a resident of Newbury, and then made his way further north, appearing in Dover no later than 1640 [GMB 3:1552-55].

The Stephen Tedder who signed the Dover Combination, and was in Dover for some time thereafter, may be the Stephen Kidder earlier seen elsewhere on the Piscataqua in the company of Ambrose Gibbons, but these may be two different men [GMB 2:1131, 3:2102].

Henry Langstaff, who was apparently, despite his own testimony, resident on the Piscataqua as early as 1631, did not come immediately to Dover, and is almost certainly the "Henry Lahorn" seen on the Dover Combination [GMB 2:1156-60; GDMNH 49].

Notice that neither Thomas Wiggin nor either of the Hiltons signed the Dover Combination in 1640. Scanning the forty-two names that are on the list, we find that there are none who can be proven to be resident in Dover in 1633 or earlier. We have seen above that some of them had lived elsewhere on the Piscataqua, and had drifted into Dover sometime before 1640. (As we shall see later, some of these may well have resided at Bloody Point, a piece of land in contention between Dover and Portsmouth. A few of these men may never have moved, but only became incorporated into Dover through a resolution of this boundary dispute.)

Returning to settlers whom we can identify and whose time of arrival is reasonably certain, we come next to 1638, and the aftermath of the Antinomian Controversy in Massachusetts Bay. As a result of this conflict, many Bay residents were either exiled or chose to depart from that colony. Some, of course, like the Hutchinsons, removed to Rhode Island, founding the towns of Portsmouth in 1638 and Newport in 1639. Others moved north, including the earliest settlers of Exeter.

Among these exiles few were more prominent than John Underhill. He had been a soldier in the wars in the Low Countries, and had signed on as one of the military contingent that was to protect the settlers of the Winthrop Fleet. He was not a typical Puritan, and was constantly at odds with Winthrop and other leaders in the Bay.

Underhill may have briefly accompanied Wheelwright to Exeter, but by the latter part of 1638 he was at Dover, engaged in activities that were not to Winthrop's liking. In a journal entry of March 1639, Winthrop referred to events that had happened the previous fall, in which he complains of the settlers at Dover because they did "encourage and advance such as we had cast out from us for their offenses [i.e., Wheelwright and his supporters]" and "they had aided Mr. Wheelwright to begin a plantation there [Exeter], and intended to make Capt. Underhill their governor in the room of Mr. Burdett, who had thrust out Capt. Wiggin, set in there by the lords" [WJ 1:350; GMB 3:1859-65].

In this confrontation we also meet Mr. George Burdett, a fascinating man who had already had a career as a prominent Puritan preacher in England, and who had arrived in

New England in 1635, residing first at Salem. Not finding Massachusetts Bay to his liking, he moved to Dover about 1638. We pick up an outline of his activities again from Winthrop, in the latter's description of events at Dover: "One Mr. Hanserd Knolles, a minster in England, who came over the last summer ... was denied residence in the Massachusetts; whereupon he went to Pascataquack, where he began to preach; but Mr. Burdett, being then their governor and preacher, inhibited him. But, he being after removed to Acomenticus, the people called Mr. Knolles, and in short time he gathered some of the best minded into a church body, and became their pastor, and Capt. Underhill being their governor, they called their town Dover" [WJ 1:392].

One of Burdett's first acts as governor of Dover was to reverse the settlement's "foreign policy," by writing to Archbishop Laud (a man who would certainly not be favorably disposed toward Burdett) asking Laud for protection against the designs of Massachusetts Bay [NHPP 17:497-98].

Winthrop filled several pages of his journal with accounts of his long-distance disputes with Burdett, in which each managed to intercept and read the other's mail. Nothing came of Burdett's machinations, and shortly thereafter he made his move to Acomenticus [York].

And so, with the departure of Burdett, one boisterous minister was replaced by another, but the sequence does not end there. By early 1641 another disruptive minister, Thomas Larkham, had appeared, and managed to lure most of the Dover residents away from Knolles. But, again in the words of Winthrop, he "did soon discover himself. He received into the church all that offered themselves, men notoriously scandalous and ignorant ... so as there soon grew sharp contention between him and Mr. Knolles" [WJ 2:33]. These two ministers then began excommunicating one another, John Underhill became involved (on the side of Knolles), and the confrontation became violent.

Underhill, Knolles and Larkham all signed the Dover Combination in October of 1640 [NHPP 10:701]. A few months later, on 4 March 1640/1, Thomas Larkham and twenty-four of his adherents petitioned Massachusetts Bay, complaining of Underhill's actions [NHPP 1:126-28]. In a very short time, however, all three of these main combatants had left Dover. Underhill was in Stamford, Connecticut, by 1642, Knolles returned to England in 1641 or 1642, and Larkham did the same a year or two later.

With the departure of these men, and the submission of Dover to Massachusetts Bay authority, the town became for a while a quieter and less interesting place. The remaining inhabitants of Dover had arrived in town from here and there, and not as part of any organized group, as was the case with so many other New England towns. In 1642 they had to begin almost from scratch, finding new leaders and molding themselves into a community.

DOVER NEIGHBORHOODS

The earliest settlement in the area that became Dover was on Hilton's Point, or Dover Point, the narrow strip of land between the Piscataqua River and the Bellamy River. As the population increased the inhabitants spilled out in all directions, giving rise to a number of different neighborhoods within Dover.

Eventually these various neighborhoods were split off as independent towns, but for some decades they remained part of Dover, and were separated in the annual town tax lists. The three principal settlements that we will take notice of are Dover Neck and Cocheco, Bloody Point and Oyster River. A clear example of this division may be found in the tax list of 23 July 1677, as published by Noyes, Libby and Davis [GDMNH 51].

Dover Neck was the extension of Dover Point, as it widened to the north between the Piscataqua and the Bellamy Rivers, to the Cocheco River. Moving up the Cocheco River one came to the settlement known as Cocheco, which corresponds to the present city center. These are the only ancient Dover neighborhoods which remain within the modern boundaries. (In their lists of place names, Noyes, Libby and Davis include entries for these and many other Dover localities; for Dover Neck they say "site of the pioneer town of Dover, now a farming district.")

Bloody Point was the northern extension of Strawbery Bank, and was separated from Hilton Point by the opening from the Piscataqua River into Little Bay and then on into Great Bay. As we have seen above, Henry Langstaff resided at Bloody Point, and his is one of the twelve names on the so-called Bloody Point Petiton, a plea that they be allowed to remain as part of Dover, and not be attached to Portsmouth for purposes of taxation. This petition is undated, and was published by the editors of the Provincial Papers as if dated in 1644; Noyes, Libby and Davis estimate that this document was created after 1663 [NHPP 1:176-77; GDMNH 48]. In 1714 Bloody Point was set off as Newington.

The remaining neighborhood represented in the tax lists is Oyster River. This setttlement was, as the name indicates, up the Oyster River, and was some distance from Cocheco, and quite distinct from it. By the time of the 1677 tax list Oyster River was nearly as large as Dover Neck and Cocheco combined. In 1732 this part of Dover was set off as Durham.

Another town which was never part of Dover as such, but which should be mentioned here is Stratham. Although considered to be part of Exeter before being established as a town, Stratham was a part of the Squamscott Patent, in the area where the four original towns of Portsmouth, Dover, Exeter and Hampton came together.

RECENT LITERATURE

Eugene Cole Zubrinsky, "The Hammonds of Rehoboth and Swansea, Massachusetts," and "Elizabeth Bartram, Wife of (1) William Hammond Sr. of Rehoboth and Swansea and (2) Joseph[2] Fiske of Lynn and Swansea, Mass.," *New England Historical and Genealogical Register* 149 (1995):211-29, 230-43. Zubrinsky systematically and convincingly delineates the life of William Hammond of Rehoboth and Swansea and of his wife Elizabeth (Bartram) (Hammond) Fiske, and along the way clears up many errors and confusing statements in the secondary literature, and in primary records as well.

Douglas Richardson, "The English Ancestry of the Merwin and Tinker Families of New England," *New England Historical and Genealogical Register* 149 (1995):295-311, 401-32. Richardson sets forth the evidence that Miles Merwin derived from Clewer, Berkshire, and provides him with four generations of ancestors in the paternal line. He then shows that John Tinker, of Boston and Lancaster, was a younger half-brother of Miles Merwin's mother. Other connections to early immigrants are noted.

Ethel Farrington Smith, "John Jenkins of Barnstable, Massachusetts," *New England Historical and Genealogical Register* 149 (1995):339-59, 150 (1996):74-90. John Jenkins arrived in New England in 1635, eventually settling in Barnstable. Smith has produced the first reliable genealogical account of him and of the early generations of his descendants.

Robert Charles Anderson and Melinde Lutz Sanborn, "Betty Baulston and John Coggeshall: An Early Rhode Island Divorce," *New England Historical and Genealogical Register* 149 (1995):361-73. Stimulated by two newly-discovered depositions, the authors examine the divorce of John[2] Coggeshall and Elizabeth[2] Baulston. They also discuss the paternity of the children of this marriage.

Matthew J. Grow, "A Belated Reply: The English Origins of John and William Pratt of Connecticut," *New England Historical and Genealogical Register* 149 (1995):374-78. By carefully examining the original parish register, Grow has relieved a chronological difficulty in the proposed origin of John and William Pratt, as being from Stevenage, Hertfordshire, though the proof remains incomplete.

Robert S. Wakefield, "Elizabeth[3] Thomas, Wife of Joshua[2] Matson and Sampson Moor of Boston," *The American Genealogist* 70 (1995):138-41. Wakefield has identified the wife of Joshua Matson (son of the immigrant Thomas Matson), and in the process has demonstrated that a Nathaniel Matson claimed to be of the same generation did not exist.

Douglas Richardson, "The English Origin of the Lakin Family of Reading and Groton, Massachusetts," *The American Genealogist* 70 (1995):142-48. The author presents evidence showing that William and John Lakin were from Ruddington, Nottingham.

Gale Ion Harris, "Sarah[2] Risley, Wife of Samuel[1] Crooke of East Hartford, Connecticut, and John[3] Payne of Southold, Long Island," *The American Genealogist* 70 (1995):162-70. Using the Winthrop medical records and other evidence, Harris reconstructs the life of Sarah Risley (daughter of immigrant Richard Risley), including her two marriages.

Dean Crawford Smith and Melinde Lutz Sanborn, "The English Origins of the Howe and Treadway Families of Watertown, Massachusetts," *The American Genealogist* 70 (1995):171-80, 71 (1996):86. Smith and Sanborn resolve a long-standing genealogical puzzle by proving the identity of one, and possibly both, of the previously unconnected legatees of Edward Howe of Watertown and his widow.

Eugene Cole Zubrinsky, "The Family of William[2] Carpenter of Rehoboth, Massachusetts: With the English Origin of the Rehoboth Carpenters," *The American Genealogist* 70 (1995):193-204. The author locates the Carpenter family of Rehoboth in Shalbourne, Berkshire, and details the life of William the son of the immigrant.

Ian Watson, "Three Mary Peases of Salem, Massachusetts," *The American Genealogist* 70 (1995):205-8. Watson sorts out three Mary Peases of Salem, and allocates them to their proper husbands.

John Plummer, "The Possible English Origin of Richard[1] Mann of Scituate, Massachusetts," *The American Genealogist* 70 (1995):220-22. The author provides clues that may lead to establishing the origin of Richard Mann of Scituate.

Clifford L. Stott, "Lothrop and House Entries in the Parish Registers of Eastwell, Kent," *The American Genealogist* 70 (1995):250-52. Stott presents a number of parish register entries that add to our knowledge of the families of Rev. John Lothrop and his brother-in-law Samuel House.

(continued from page 10)

by "These ships, by reason of their short passage ...," clearly referring to the six ships which arrived in early May, it is likely that this Barnstable ship was one of the six.)

At the beginning of July Winthrop first noted that "The *Hercules* of Dover returned by St. George's to cut masts to carry to England" [WJ 1:160]. His next entry states that "The last month arrived here fourteen great ships, and one at Salem," and one suspects that the *Hercules* was one of these. In a later entry, still in July, he reports as follows: "For the success of the passengers and cattle in the ships: Diverse of the ships lost many cattle; but the two which came from Ipswich, of more than one hundred and twenty, lost but seven. None of the ships lost any passengers, but the *Elizabeth Dorcas*, which, having a long passage, and being hurt upon a rock at Scilly, and very ill victualled, she lost six passengers at sea, and diverse came sick on shore, who all recovered ..." [WJ 1:161-62]. The *Hercules* and the *Elizabeth Dorcas* were in the list of ships detained briefly by the Privy Council in England, and some of the other ships in that list must have been among the June arrivals as well.

On 9 July 1634 Winthrop learned that "Sir Ferdinando Gorges and Capt. Mason sent [blank] to Pascataquack and Aquamenticus, with two sawmills, to be erected, in each place one" [WJ 1:163]. This was the *Pied Cow*, which Ambrose Gibbins reported as having arrived on 8 July [NHPP 1:92]. Among the passengers on this vessel were such settlers as William Chadbourne and James Wall.

Two more passenger ships appeared in Boston Harbor during the September sitting of the General Court, noted by Winthrop on the 18th of that month: "... the *Griffin* and another ship now arriving with about two hundred passengers and one hundred cattle (Mr. Lothrop and Mr. Simmes, two godly ministers, coming in the same ship)" [WJ 1:170]. The second of these two ships was very likely the *Philip*, for the London port book for 1634 has two entries in July for ships bound for New England: on 19 July the *Philip*, Richard Hussey master, and on 21 July the *Griffin*, Thomas Babb master [WP 3:170, 171]. (This ship was making something of a specialty of off-season voyages with prominent ministers, for the previous year it had arrived at about the same time with John Cotton, Thomas Hooker and Samuel Stone.)

The final passenger ship arrival recorded for this year was "The *Regard*, a ship of Barnstable, of about two hundred tons, [which] arrived with twenty passengers and about fifty cattle," by the thirteenth of November [WJ 1:178].

In the second installment of this article, we will explore these same records in more depth, looking into such matters as the surviving passenger lists, synthetic lists for some of these ships compiled in later years, and an estimate of the total number of immigrants that arrived in this year.

(to be continued in Volume 6, No. 3)

Great Migration Study Project
101 Newbury Street
Boston, MA 02116_

Great Migration Newsletter

Vol. 6   July-September 1997   No. 3

PASSENGER SHIPS OF 1634 - Part II

In the first installment of this article we catalogued the passenger ships known to have come to New England in 1634. There are records of twenty-six vessels, arriving from May through November, known to have carried migrants to New England. Our task now is to draw some conclusions from this list of ships, about the number of individuals who made the passage in 1634, and about the value of the published passenger lists.

First, of these twenty-six ships, contemporaneous lists of passengers survive for only three. The two ships from Ipswich, mentioned in passing in the previous installment, and certainly among the fifteen ships reported by Winthrop to have arrived in June, were the *Francis* and the *Elizabeth*.

As with the ships sailing from London, these two ships were apparently stopped briefly, and then sent on with the instruction that they would submit a list of passengers upon their return. In November of 1634 these lists were entered at the Ipswich Custom House. (If the ships sailing from London carried out their instructions, then we would have full lists for another eighteen ships or so. But these lists have not been found, and have presumably been destroyed.) There were 84 men, women and children on the *Francis*, and 102 on the *Elizabeth* [Hotten 277-82].

The only other ship whose list of passengers has come down to us is the *Mary & John* (probably not the same ship as the famous one from the West Country in 1630). This document was entered at Southampton, recording passengers who had embarked there. In this record the ship is called "the *Mary & John* of London," so this is presumably the same vessel which was in the list of those stopped at London earlier in the year. We do not know whether any passengers had boarded the ship in London, but, given the number who came on at Southampton, there were probably few or none [Drake's Founders 68-71].

The list consists of the names of 54 males, apparently all adult (omitting two names of men who are marked as "left behind"). If this ship also carried women and children in the same proportions as the two Ipswich vessels, then the

Mary & John must have carried somewhere between 170 and 190 passengers in all.

Now, armed with this information, we can attempt an estimate of the total number of passengers who came in 1634. Harking back to the first part of this article, we saw that the first and last of the ships coming in this year were relatively small. The unnamed ship that came to Pemaquid in May had 30 on board, and the *Regard*, arriving in November, had 20. The *Pied Cow*, coming to Piscataqua, was of unknown size, but was probably relatively small also, and so we will guess that it was carrying 25 immigrants. For these three ships, then, there were about 75 passengers.

When the *Griffin* and her sister ship (perhaps the *Philip*) landed in September, Winthrop noted that they had "about two hundred passengers," or about one hundred apiece. Aside from what it tells us specifically about these two vessels, we may combine this figure with what we have learned about the three ships with passenger lists, and use as a very rough figure for the capacity of the remaining "great ships" about one hundred apiece.

The rest of the passengers came on the twenty-one ships that came in May (six) and June (fifteen). Of these, we have the names of the ten which were stopped at London early in the year (including the *Mary & John*, which also stopped at Southampton), and the two from Ipswich. We

(continued on page 18)

EDITOR'S EFFUSIONS

As hinted in the last Newsletter, we present for the first time in this issue an article written by someone other than the Editor. Patricia Law Hatcher has taken another look at the Roxbury church records, which were examined here in 1991 (*GMN* 2:13). Her analysis has penetrated deeper than did ours, and has come up with some interesting new discoveries.

Her most important new finding is the concept of "joinings," in which on a given day several people are admitted to the church, and in the list as created by Eliot are entered according to family status. This allows us to learn things about the people on the list that cannot be discovered simply by looking at the name in isolation.

This provides us with another opportunity to expand on what we have referred to elsewhere as "list analysis." In our research we are constantly confronted with lists of one kind or another - tax lists, church membership registers, lists of proprietors, signers of covenants, and so on. Many times, in our rush to gather information and solve a problem, we just grab the name of interest to us off the list, and move on to the next source.

If some other researcher has already studied that list in detail, and provided for us a way to interpret a single entry in that list, then nothing has been lost. But if no one has done this work for us, we may be missing much information by moving on so quickly.

The entire solution to a problem may rest in that little tidbit of information which can only be uncovered by studying in detail the way a list is constructed. We should be prepared, then, to devote as much time as necessary to the study of such lists, even if the ultimate prize is not immediately obvious. Pat Hatcher's article on Roxbury should serve both as a source of useful new information on the early settlers of Roxbury, and as a model for the analysis of lists.

We also include in this issue those additions and corrections to *The Great Migration Begins* that have appeared since Volume III was sent to the printer.

Robert Charles Anderson, FASG   Editor
Christina A. Olson   Production Assistant

The Great Migration Newsletter is published quarterly by the Great Migration Study Project, a project of the New England Historic Genealogical Society, 101 Newbury Street, Boston MA 02116

The subscription rate is $12 for one year and $20 for two years.

(continued from page 17)

will estimate, then, that these ships carried about 2100 passengers.

Taken all together, then, a first estimate of the number of arrivals in New England in 1634 would be about 2375. We should remember that the total of all immigrants to New England from 1620 to 1633 was about 2500. In 1634, in other words, the European population of New England nearly doubled.

In fact, since most of the ships came in within a few weeks in the late spring, the residents of New England were confronted with a doubling of their numbers in the space of less than two months. The consequences of this demographic invasion would have been enormous for the polity and economy of Massachusetts Bay Colony.

As noted above, passenger lists for only three of the 1634 ships have survived, accounting for about 350 of the immigrants, or about seventeen percent. What do we know of the passengers who arrived on the remaining ships?

There are some clues which can allow us to construct partial lists for one or two of the other ships. This is what Colonel Banks attempted to do in his *Planters of the Commonwealth*, published in 1930. We will evaluate the work done by Banks as we study the clues available about other passengers.

Banks presents the results of his research for 1634 on pages 107 through 125. This includes the three known lists, for the *Francis*, the *Elizabeth*, and the *Mary & John*. He has also picked up the various references given by Winthrop and others about the remaining ships, but he has interpreted some of this information differently than have we, and he has also added material that is incorrect and made suppositions that are unwarranted.

He includes two ships named the *Hercules*, one of which left Southampton on 18 April 1634, and the other of which was from Sandwich [pp. 107-8, 114-17]. The first of these was associated with the *Mary & John*, the passenger list of which has the annotation that "These six passengers took their oaths of Supremacy & Allegiance the 24th of March and were left behind … as intended to pass in the *Hercules*." To this were appended an additional six names, also "to pass in the *Hercules*," but apparently not left behind by the *Mary & John*. Of the first six, none are of record in New England, while of the second six most are. Banks included all twelve names, and only these twelve names, in his entry for this ship. We cannot argue with this decision, but there is at least a suspicion that the first six of these names were left behind twice.

(continued on page 28)

Focus   *on*   **ROXBURY**

Members of the
First Church of Roxbury

by Patricia Law Hatcher, C.G.

In articles and lectures relating to the Great Migration Study Project, Robert Charles Anderson has often remarked on the valuable information to be gleaned simply by studying lists. See, for example, his discussion of using the frequent pattern of men from the same town being named together on the list of freemen in order to separate two or more men of the same name (*GMN* 1:17, 24).

This study looks at another list—the first 200 members (through 1638) of the First Church of Roxbury as identified in "The Rev. John Eliot's Record of Church Members," published in part in 1881 in the *Register* (35:21–24, 241–247) and at greater length in *Roxbury Land and Church Records,* Sixth Report of the Boston Record Commissioners (Boston, 1884).

THE LIST

When, how, why, and by whom was this record created? Anderson has suggested (*GMN* 2:13) that this book was begun by Eliot when he took over the church from Thomas Weld in 1641. However, several pre-1641 entries have information dated after that time. For example, the entry for Philip Eliot begins a lengthy paragraph with the statement that he died in 1657; the entry for Joane Atkins ends with the phrase "had letters of Dismission to Maldon this 13th 2m 1669."

The list is headed, "A recorde of such as adjoyned themselves unto the fellowship of this Church of Christ at Roxborough : as also of such children as they had when they joyned, & of such as were borne unto them under the holy Covenant of this Church who are most p[ro]perly the seed of this Church." This wording suggests that the list was prepared in response to the adoption of the Half-Way Covenant by the Synod of 1662, which provided for the baptism of the children of those who had themselves been baptized, but were not yet full members.

Without examining the handwriting on the original, we can merely speculate as to when the list was written. William Trask's description in the *Register* states that the records were deposited with NEHGS, but someone has written in the margin of the copy imaged on the *Register* CD-ROM "Ms. volume is in possession of the church & kept in a

bank vault. (1962)." The volume has since been removed from the vault to the church, and was purportedly destroyed in a fire. (A photostatic copy was apparently made in 1965, the location of which is currently being investigated.)

It appears that Eliot may have created the record by copying the names in order from the original membership list (now lost), allowing space for comments, and annotating as he went, leaving blanks where he thought he might later recall a specific detail. If the main impetus to preparing the list was the Half-Way Covenant of 1662, then there were also later annotations, such as that of Joane Atkins noted above.

One gets the impression that Eliot sensed the historic importance of the Puritan experiment and felt that he should record certain details for posterity. About one third of these 200 entries have significant annotations, but there are twice as many annotations in the first 100 entries as in the second 100 entries. He was considerably concerned with the moral strengths or transgressions of some of the brethren, especially those who followed Ann Hutchinson.

There may be other reasons for the brevity or lack of annotations in some cases. We know, for example, that the Victorian-era editors of this record bowdlerized many of the entries, and so we may be lacking evidence of the social misbehavior of some of Eliot's congregation.

Analysis of the list began by creating a chart-style database, incorporating data from the church records and from other sources. Sequential membership numbers were assigned, which match those used in *The Great Migration Begins*. Over the course of the study, columns were added, deleted, changed, merged, and split as factors appeared more or less significant and the picture became clearer (pages 24 and 25 below).

JOININGS

Studying the list in this format highlighted some apparent patterns. When focusing on the single women, it was noted that about half the time their names preceded those of a couple. Several times they were preceded by the names of single men.

Closer examination of marital status showed a hierarchy forming a pattern (albeit with some anomalies). Couples joining together are listed first; then widowed and married men; then widowed and married women; then single men; and, lastly, single women. The implication is that the concept of "rank" for the Roxbury church was most closely related not to wealth or age, but, surprisingly, to domestic union.

This is therefore not *a simple list*, but rather *a chronological series of short lists*—lists of those becoming members on specific days. The hypothesis followed in this article is that people joined the church in groups. In this article, this group event is called a "joining."

Dates. Once the joining divisions were made, work began on dating the joinings. Because of the small number of individuals and the lack of sufficient information about many, this must be considered a tentative rather than definitive division.

The church was founded sometime between July 1632 (when John Winthrop indicated that Thomas Weld intended to be their minister) and November 1632 (when the established church called Eliot to be their teacher). That there were 7 other groups joining before the next spring's General Court points to a date in late summer. Several sources for dates were used as delimiters to determine other joining dates (see end of article).

For genealogists the joining pattern is useful information. If you have no dated arrival information about your ancestor, but he or she joined with another individual who, say, became a freeman on 4 September 1634, then you can say your ancestor probably arrived by summer 1634. If further analysis of a later joining shows someone who became freeman on 14 May 1634, then you can now say that this ancestor probably arrived by the fall of 1633. Note that the new information on the later joining affects the dating of all earlier joinings. Thus, you can determine an "arrived-by" date for an ancestor for whom no such specific information exists. Several examples below point out the potential of this type of analysis.

Table of annual joinings

year	member #	total	joinings
founders	1–21	21	1
1632	22–63	42	7
1633	64–102	39	10
1634	103–119	17	5
1635	120–143	24	8
1636	144–156	13	4
1637	157–173	17	3
1638	174–200	27	6

CHURCH MEMBERSHIP

To become a church member one had to demonstrate knowledge and understanding of doctrine, profess faith, be of good behavior and character, and accept the covenant with the church. Depending on the congregation and the individual, these may have been done before the congregation, before a smaller group of members, with the minister, or in writing (women were less likely to have to appear before the entire congregation). Then the church was allowed several weeks to determine if there were concerns about the fulfillment of any of these requirements before full membership was granted.

Another requirement, that of a narration of saving grace, was begun by some churches about 1633 or 1634 and legislated as a requirement for newly formed churches in 1636. This was not a requirement in England, and it must have been something of a shock for newly arrived Puritans, some of whom may have been unable to identify and narrate such an event (or, actually, series of events) in their lives. This likely lengthened the time span between arrival and joining for some and may also explain several instances in which spouses did not join together or one spouse never joined.

Similarly, the dip in membership in 1634 or in 1636 and 1637 may indicate the time at which the narration of saving grace was implemented in Roxbury. See Anderson's discussion of church membership and of modern theories about when the conversion narrative became a requirement (*GMN* 5:9-10, 16).

FAMILY MIGRATION

The chart-like presentation of this study quickly highlighted the likelihood that the Winthrop fleet may have contained fewer *family groups* than has been supposed. Of the first 200 Roxbury members, 41% joined as couples, yet of the 18 founders of the Roxbury church who joined in the first group, only three joined with their wives. The wives of nine of these joined later, as did the wives of the next three men who joined. The most likely reason that so many wives did not join with their husbands is that they weren't yet in New England. Apparently many of the wives (and presumably children) did not arrive until late summer or early fall 1632. The ships of 1632 brought not only ten couples to the Roxbury church, but also ten wives of members.

In later years, however, only 15 couples joined in separate years, possibly indicating that New England was no longer considered an unknown, unsettled wilderness.

SERVANTS

Eliot identified most of the single men and women on the list as "servants." But these were not the indentured servants of, say, Maryland or Virginia. The servants of Roxbury were not necessarily poor or unconnected. Puritan families often placed their children in the homes of other Puritans as servants. In many ways, the "masters" were more like sponsors or foster parents. Many of these young people had relatives living in Roxbury or elsewhere in New England, married soon after arrival, and took their places as established members of the community.

To find origins for a single person, one might do well to look at potential sponsors (couples who joined the church earlier) and at the future spouse (because the friendship may have begun before sailing).

There appears no clear pattern as to when the servant relationship was established, nor who paid for the passage. Grace and Fayth Newell (aged 13 and 14), oldest children of Abraham and Francis Newell, sailed on the same ship as their parents and three siblings. [Fayth appears as Ruth in the published version of Eliot's list.] But on the port list, Grace is accounted (along with John Lea and, possibly, Clare Draper) as part of the household of William and Bridget Westwood; Fayth is accounted with John and Mary Bernard (along with Henry Haward).

William and Bridget were married in Glemsford, Suffolk, in 1630; Clare was born in Lexden, Essex, in 1595. Origins for the Newells aren't known. Perhaps the Newells temporarily placed the girls with the other families in Ipswich for the duration of the voyage, since Eliot treats them as a family unit and the Westwoods went on to Hartford.

INDIVIDUAL EXAMPLES

As the chart developed, several anomalies were noticed that demonstrate the potential gained by individual researchers studying the list. For example, based on information in *The Great Migration Begins*, John Carman (24) and William Parke (6) initially were listed as single men at the time of joining. This seemingly broke the hierarchical pattern described above.

John and Florence Carman. Anderson argues quite reasonably that since Florence Carman did not join with her husband, "it is likely that she arrived in that year [1632] and married Carman very soon." The first part of the statement is true—they had a child born 8 July 1633, so she must have been in New England by October 1632. But the chart suggests that John Carman was a married man at the time of joining in the second group of members. Since Florence did not join with John, she possibly was still in England —where she and John likely married. Descendants perhaps would do better to look there for a marriage.

William Parke and Martha Holgrave. Eliot says of William Parke, "he came . . . a single man, . . . he afterwards married Martha Holgrave." Note that Eliot does not state that he *joined* as a single man.

Anderson states that Martha Holgrave married William Parke "by 1637," based on the birth of their first child (and possibly on the membership for "Martha Parke wife of [blank]" who joined in 1638 as member 200). From this estimate, he derives for Martha a likely birth date (1617) and order of birth (2nd), plus a probable marriage date (1615) and birth date (1590) for her father John Holgrave of Salem.

"Martha Parke, the wife of Willia[m] Parke," joined as member 87 in the midst of the 1633 joinings, which shows that William and Martha definitely were married by then. However, the list hierarchy indicates that they were already married in July 1632 when William joined. Why Martha did not join then with William is unknown, but the possibility exists that, like several other wives, she was not yet in New England. Why there are no known children before 1637 is unclear.

The second church admission for a Martha Parke, as member 200, must have been for Martha (Chaplin) Parke, first wife of Robert Parke, and mother of this William Parke.

Information about the Holgrave family doesn't add much. All that can be said definitively of John Holgrave's arrival is that it preceded his freemanship on 5 November 1633. If the family came as a unit, then he was more likely in New England by the spring of 1632. Given that the young couple also needed an opportunity to meet, it may be that the Holgraves came on the same ship as William Parke in "12th month, 1630 [i.e., 1630/1]," or that they were from the same area of England. Possibly the couple had married before William's emigration.

In any event, moving up the marriage date has a ripple effect, changing Martha's estimated birth date (1612), birth order (1st), parents' marriage (1612) and father's birth date (1587). It also changes the mix of Holgrave family members for the Salem land grant in December 1637.

John Perrie. Although less clear-cut than the above examples, John Perrie's (17) information may also require revision. His name occurs amid three other married men whose wives never joined the church. The wife of Gregory Baxter (15) had recently given birth, which may explain her absence at this time, although not later. Francis Smith (16) was married by 1627, but his wife may still have been in England. The wife of John Leavens (18) was, according to Eliot, "bedrid divers years."

John Perrie's position before Leavens implies that he, too, was married. This in turn implies that the Sawbridgeworth marriage for John Perrie and Ann Newman in 1629 likely does apply to the immigrant, but that Ann died before coming, on the voyage, or after arrival, but before his marriage to the Elizabeth who was probably the mother of his children, who were born after 1637.

RETURN TRIPS

The chart shows another anomaly. George Alcock (50) joined immediately after John Eliot and his wife Ann, around November 1632. Eliot said of Alcock:

> . . . when the people of Rocksbrough joyned to the church at Dorchester (untill such time as God should give them oportunity to be a church among themselves) he was by the church chosen to be a Deakon esp'c to regard the brethren at Rocksbrough : And after he adjoyned himselfe to this church at Rocksbrough, he was ordained a Deakon of this church :

Clearly, Alcock was a pillar of the church at Roxbury. Why is he not in the group of founding members? Possibly for the same reason that many of the wives were not there—he was not in New England in July 1632. Eliot also says of Alcock:

> he maide two voyages to England upon just calling thereunto ; wherein he had much experiens of Gods p[re]servation & blessing. he brought over his son[n] John Alcock. he also brought over a wife by whom he had his 2d son Samuel borne in the year.

Perhaps genealogists jump quickly to the genealogical information, neglecting Eliot's intriguing statement, "upon just calling thereunto ; wherein he had much experiens of Gods p[re]servation & blessing." The statements with which Eliot augmented his church book were almost always related to the spiritual life of the individual. Even narrations of physical illnesses and vital events were given as part of the place of the individual in the religious community. Thus, one wonders if Alcock's "just calling" was for the purpose of visiting Puritan followers of John Eliot and Thomas Hooker in East Anglia, and if the experience of God's preservation and blessing was related to his success in encouraging and assisting their migration to New England.

Several ships arrived in the summer and fall of 1632. Alcock's position on the church list in 1632 places him amid a group of East Anglian families presumed to have arrived on the *Lyon* in September, including several Eliot family members. It seems possible that serving as a connection between the Roxbury Church and East Anglian congregations was a significant purpose of his trip. Perhaps we have given insufficient attention to the idea that some of the churches may have been sending members back to England to encourage and facilitate Puritan migration.

Eliot mentioned two trips to England. A careful study of the chronology for George Alcock clearly points to a trip between his appearances as Deputy to the General Court on 14 May 1634 and 2 September 1635, a span of about 15 months (there being no other sufficient time interval). This would have been his second trip, when "he also brought over a wife by whom he had his 2d son Samuel borne in the

year." This might be interpreted to imply that Samuel was born within one year after Alcock's return, and so by the end of 1636, which would be in conflict with the date of birth for this child entered in town records: 16 April 1637. If, however, this is one of the instances where Eliot left a blank for the year of birth of Samuel, but never went back to fill it in, then there is no discrepancy. The nineteenth-century editors then failed to note the blank space and completed the sentence with a full stop after the word "year," thus misleading twentieth-century genealogists.

The port lists and the church membership list show another group of East Anglian families sailing in the spring of 1635. Is this merely an interesting coincidence—or perhaps a clue to the origins of Alcock's second wife?

INCLUSIVENESS

The church membership list was compared to two other records to determine what proportion of Roxbury residents were church members. A high percentage presumably reflects the importance of membership, and by inference would indicate that most new arrivals sought church membership in a fairly timely manner. A low percentage would indicate the opposite.

In the early years of Roxbury, residency and church membership seem very strongly coordinated. Early Roxbury vital records (*NEHGR* 5:334, 6:183–84, 377–78) covering this time period are far from complete, but only two names prior to 1639 are not reflected in the church list: the wife of Robert Mason and widow Jane Wise were buried 1637. Possibly these are mother and daughter—Jane being in error for Elizabeth, member 121, mother-in-law of Joseph Weld (*TAG* 55:149–50). Perhaps Mary (Wise) Mason died before completing the membership process.

Sometime between May 1638 (when James Astwood arrived) and December 1640 (when George Alcock died), there was recorded a "note of the estates and persons of the Inhabitants of Rocksbury" (*NEHGR* 2:52–54). It contains 70 names, only 5 of whom (7%) are not on the church rolls: John Corteis, Thomas Waterman, Widow Iggulden, John Pettit and John Crane.

Clearly the vast majority of the earliest residents of Roxbury, whether male or female, married or single, master or servant, sought membership in the church.

Since church membership was a prerequisite for freemanship, the next question to ask is how many of the male church members became freemen. Of the first 200 members of the church, 104 were men, of whom 101 took up their freedom. The three exceptions were William Cornwall, Thomas Hills (who was probably still a servant when he died a year and a half after joining the church) and [Thomas] Griggs.

ORIGINS

The membership of the Roxbury church was strongly East Anglian (here defined restrictively as eastern Hertfordshire, Essex and southwestern Suffolk). At least three-fifths of the members had roots in parishes no further than 70 miles apart. In addition to those with known East Anglian origins, the passengers who sailed from London and a significant proportion of those classified as "unknown" are likely East Anglian, based on associations in New England and on surname.

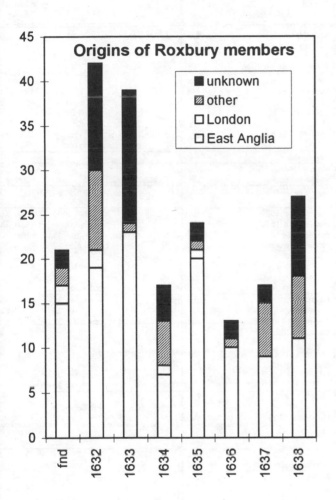

Especially in its earliest years, Roxbury was not only fairly homogeneous, it was very connected, more so than many other New England congregations.

Roxbury included several family clusters, such as the Eliots (37, 38, 49, 50, 118, 133, 153) and the Heaths (9, 17, 35, 36, 90, 95, 131, 164, 165). When one adds those persons from parishes with which the Eliots and Heaths had connections, such as Nazeing (7, 47, 39, 40, 100, 129, 130, 132, 135, 147, 166, 167, 182), Bishop's Stortford (3, 33, 183, 184), Chelmsford (52, 53), and Little Baddow (127), the continuing effect over time of this network is obvious.

Those looking for origins of Roxbury's earliest settlers should probably look first at East Anglia. However, new members beginning in 1634 may be from other parts of England as Archbishop Laud's policies were applied to the entire country (*GMN* 5:1-2, 8). The most significant new influence was seven members from Kent between 1634 and 1638.

ABOUT THE CHART

Double horizontal lines separate the years of admission, beginning with the founders (*fndr*).
Single horizontal lines separate the joinings.

Col. 1: (year) Year of church membership.

Col. 2–4: (name) Names of members. In order to conserve space, husbands and wives are entered on the same line of the chart when they joined together, even though they are separate entries in the Eliot list.

Col. 5, 6: (m/f) Assigned sequential membership number.

Col. 7, 8: (m/f) Married church members.
C = joined as a couple.
L = wife joined later.
E = husband joined earlier.
w = widow or widower.
x = spouse never joined.
m = married a church member.

Col. 9, 10: (m/f) Single church members.

Col. 11, 12: (last English record) Location of last known residence in England. Based on variety of sources, including *GMB*, Roger Thompson's *Mobility and Migration*, family histories, IGI entries, and traditional "said to be" origins. Undoubtedly, some of the information is inaccurate. (Abbreviations: b = born; ch = child born; r = resided; m = married)

Col. 13: (port lists) The port lists in Coldham's *Complete Book of Emigrants* and early issues of the *Register* provided approximate departure dates for some individuals between 1632 and 1635.

Col. 14: (Eliot et al.) Eliot's annotations were a primary source of arrival or first-New-England-event dates, but occasionally appear to be in error. A few miscellaneous dates from sources such as the Roxbury vital records were used. (Abbreviations: *arr* = date-arrived-by; *ch* = record of birth of a child; *ct* = court appearance; *jn* = joined church)

Col. 15: (freeman) For men, church membership was a prerequisite for freemanship.

				m	f	m	f	m	f	last Eng record		port lists	Eliot et al	freeman
fndr	Pinchon	William		1		w				Springfield b 1590	Es		arr 30	8 May 1642
	Welde	Thomas		2		C				Terling ch 1631	Es			6 Nov 32
	Dennison	William		3		L				Bishop's Stortford ch 1620	Ht			3 Jul 32
	Lambe	Thomas		4		C				Barnardiston ch 1628	Su		arr 30	19 Oct 30
	Wakeman	Samuell		5		L				Bewdley b 1603	Wo		arr 31 9	7 Aug 32
	Parke	William		6		L				Bildeston r 1621	Su		arr 30 12	18 May 31
	Rawlins	Thomas		7		L				Nazeing	Es		arr 30	19 Oct 30
	Cole	Robert		8		L							arr 30	19 Oct 30
	Johnson	John		9		L				Ware ch 1628	Ht			19 Oct 30
	Gamlin	Robert senr		10		w				sailed fr London	Lo	7 Mar 32		14 May 34
	Lyman	Robert [sic]		11		C				Navestock ch 1621	Es		arr 31 9	11 Jun 33
	Burr	Jehu		12		L				Roxwell	Es			19 Oct 30
	Chase	William		13		L				Wivenhoe	Es		arr 30	19 Oct 30
	Bugby	Richard		14		L				Boreham ?	Es			19 Oct 30
	Baxter	Gregorie		15		x				Sporle	Nr			6 Mar 31/2
	Smith	Francis		16		x								18 May 31
	Perrie	John		17		x				Sawbridgeworth	Ht			4 Mar 32/3
	Leavens	John		18		x				sailed fr London	Lo	7 Mar 32	arr 32	4 Mar 33/4
	Welde		Margaret		19		C			Terling ch 1631	Es			
	Lyman		Sarah		20		C			Navestock ch 1621	Es		arr 9m31	
	Lambe		Elizabeth		21		C			Barnardiston ch 1628	Su		arr 30	
1632	Dummer	Richard		22		L				Odiham m 1632	Ha			6 Nov 32
	Talmage	William		23		L				Barton Stacey	Ha			14 May 34
	Carman	John		24		L							arr 31	4 Mar 32/3
	Wakeman		Elizabeth		25		E						arr 9m31	
	Bur		—		26		E			Roxwell	Es			
	Woodforde	Thomas		27				s		sailed fr London	Lo	7 Mar 32	arr 32 jn half yr	4 Mar 34/5
	Hammond		Marjery		28				s				arr 32 jn half yr	
	Chase		Mary		29		E			Wivenhoe	Es			
	Coggeshall	John	Mary	30	31	C	C			Castle Hed ch 1630	Es			6 Nov 32
	Watson	John		32				s		sailed fr London	Lo	7 Mar 32		5 Nov 33
	Dennison		Margaret		33		E			Bishop's Stortford ch 1620	Ht		jn 32	
	Cole		Mary		34		E							
	Heath	William	Mary	35	36	C	C			Nazeing ch 1629	Es		arr 32 jn soon	4 Mar 32/3
	Curtis	William	Sarah	37	38	C	C			Nazeing ch 1632	Es		arr 32 jn soon	4 Mar 32/3
	Offitt	Thomas	Isabel	39	40	C	C			Nazeing ch 1626	Es		arr 32	4 Mar 32/3
	Morrell	Isaac	Sarah	41	42	C	C			Hatfield Broadoak	Es		ch: 26 Nov 32	4 Mar 32/3
	Brewer	Daniel	Joanna	43	44	C	C							14 May 34
	Crofts	Griffin	Alice	45	46	C	C						ch: 5m30 (R)	18 May 31
	Rawlins		Mary		47		E			Nazeing	Es			
	Gouldthwaight	Thomas		48				s					ct: 14 Jun 31	14 May 34
	Eliot	John	Ann	49	50	C	C			Nazeing	Es		arr 9m 31	6 Mar 31/2
	Alcock	George		51		w				Leicester r 1628	Le		arr 30	19 Oct 30
	Prentise	Valentine	Alice	52	53	C	C			Chelmsford m 1626	Es		arr 31 jn 32	7 Aug 32
	Pratt	Abraham	Johanna	54	55	C	C			London r 1629	Lo			19 Oct 30
	Pinchon		Francis		56			m						
	Dummer		Mary		57		E			Odiham m 1632	Ha			
	Talmage		[Elizabeth]		58		E			Barton Stacey	Ha			
	Shelly		Ann		59				s				arr 32	
	Short		Rebeckah		60				s				arr 32	
	Bugby		Judith		61		E			Boreham ?	Es			
	Carman		Florenc		62		E						ch: 8d5m33	
	Blott		Mary		63				s		Harrold b 1609	Be		arr 32	
1633	Hills	William		64				s		High Ongar	Es	7 Mar 32		14 May 34
	Gamlin		Mary		65				s					
	Gamlin	Robert jr	Elizabeth	66	67	C	C						arr 20d3m	3 Sep 34
	Lyman		Phylis		68				s		Navestock ch 1621	Es		arr 31	
	Moody	John	Sarah	69	70	C	C			Moulton ch 1632	Su		arr 33	5 Nov 33
	Walker	John		71		L								14 May 34
	Hinds		Elizabeth		72				s					arr 33	
	Ballard		Elizabeth		73				s					arr 33	
	Porter	John	Margaret	74	75	C	C			Messing	Es			5 Nov 33
	Cornwall	William	Joane	76	77	C	C			Fairstead m 1632	Es			none
	Bass	Samuel	Ann	78	79	C	C			Saffron Walden ch 1632	Es			14 May 34
	Parker	Nicholas	Ann	80	81	C	C						arr 33	4 Mar 33/4
	Sherman	Philip		82				s		Dedham b 1610	Es		arr 33	14 May 34
	Huntington		Margaret		83		w			Norwich ch 1631	Nr		arr 33	
	Pigge	Thomas	Mary	84	85	C	C			Saffron Walden ch 1632	Es			14 May 34
	Finch	Samuel		86		x								14 May 34
	Parke		Martha		87		E							
	Tatman	John		88		L								2 May 38
	Wilson	Thomas		89		C				Bocking	Es		arr 4m 33	14 May 34
	Johnson		Margery		90		E			Ware ?	Ht			
	Wilson		Ann		91		C			Bocking	Es			
	Rawlings	Jasper	Jeane	92	93	C	C			Ingatestone ch 1608	Es			3 Sep 34
	Hewes	Joshua		94				s		Royston	Ht		arr 7m33 jn 6mo	4 Mar 33/4
	Johnson	Isaac		95				s		Ware r 1628	Ht			4 Mar 34/5
	Hemingway	Ralph		96				s					ch: 30d2m35	3 Sep 34
	Odding		Sarah		97				s		Messing	Es			
	Hills	Thomas		98				s					arr 33	[d 11m 34]
	Hale	Thomas		99				s						14 May 34
	Riggs	Edward		100		x				Nazeing ch 1632	Es			14 May 34
	Walker		[Katherine]		101		E						ch d Aug 33	
	Hues		[Elizabeth]		102				s		Royston	Ht			

	m	f	m	f	m	f	last English record		port lists	Eliot	freeman
1634 Stow	John	Elizabeth	103	104	C	C		Biddenden b 1582	Ke		arr 17d3m34	3 Sep 34
Cumpton	John		105					s	Cranbrook ?	Ke			3 Sep 34
Newell	Abraham		106		L				sailed fr Ipswich	Su	30 Apr 34	arr 34	4 Mar 34/5
Freeborn	[William]		107		x				sailed fr Ipswich	Su	30 Apr 34		3 Sep 34
Burrell	{John}	Sarah		108		x			Norwich ?	Nr		ch: Jul 34	
Potter	Robert	Isabell	109	110	C	C							3 Sep 34
Howard		Elizabeth		111				s					
Pepper	Richard	Mary	112	113	C	C			Terling ch 1630	Es	30 Apr 34		4 Mar 34/5
Perkins	William		114		x				sailed fr London	Lo	7 Mar 32		3 Sep 34
Sever	Robert		115		x				Earles Colne	Es			18 Apr 37
Disborough	{Walter}	[Phebe]		116		x			Saffron Walden	Es			
Peake	Christopher		117					s					4 Mar 34/5
Paison	Edward		118					s	Nazeing	Es			13 May 40
Baker	Nicholas		119					s	ed Cambridge	Ca			3 Mar 35/6
1635 Weld	Joseph		120		w				Sudbury	Su			3 Mar 35/6
Wise		Elizabeth		121		w			Sudbury	Su			
Bell	Thomas		122		L				Bury St Edmund m 1631	Su			25 May 36
Webb	William		123		L				Rattlesden	Su			25 May 36
Mott	Adam	Sarah	124	125	C	C			Saffron Walden m 1616	Es	18 Jul 35		25 May 36
Carder	Richard		126		x								25 May 36
Vassaile		Anna		127		x			Little Baddow ch 1628	Es	13 Jul 35		
Whittamore	Lawrence		128					s	Stanstead Abbott r 1635	Ht	6 Apr 35		18 Apr 37
Ruggles	John	Barbara	129	130	C	C			Nazeing r 1635	Es	6 Apr 35	arr 30	18 Apr 37
Heath	Isaac		131		x				Bishops Stortford m 1629	Ht	11 Sep 35		25 May 36
Astwood	John		132		L				Nazeing r 1635	Es	6 Apr 35		3 Mar 35/6
Eliot	Philip		133		L				Nazeing m 1624	Es			25 May 36
Bowis		Elizabeth		134				s	Nazeing r 1635	Es			
Astwood		Martha		135		E			Nazeing r 1635	Es			
Gunn	Jasper		136		x				Great Bursted b 1607	Es	18 Jul 35		26 May 36
Bircharde	Thomas		137		L				Fairsted m 1620	Es	19 Sep 35		17 May 37
Cheney	John	Martha	138	139	C	C			Langford m 1631	Es		arr 35	17 May 37
Norrice		Mary		140				s	Horsely	Gl			
Bull	Henry		141					s	sailed fr London	Lo	13 Jul 35		17 May 37
Jenner	Thomas		142					s	Fordham	Es			8 Dec 36
Bell		[Susanna]		143		E			Bury St Edmund m 1631	Su			
1636 How	James	—	144	145	C	C			Hatfield Broadoak	Es			17 May 37
Bircharde		Mary		146		E			Fairsted m 1620	Es	19 Sep 35		
Graves	John		147		L				Nazeing	Es		arr 3m33	18 Apr 37
Gore	John		148		L				Ippollitts ch 1634	Ht			18 Apr 37
Swaine		Mary		149				s	Biddenden	Ke			
Lorde		Jane		150				s					
Paison	Giles		151					s	Nazeing r 1635	Es	6 Apr 35		18 Apr 37
Porter	Edward		152		L				Chelmsford m 1624	Es		arr 36	17 May 37
Eliot		Elizabeth		153		E			Nazeing m 1624	Es	6 Apr 35		
Newell		[Francis]		154		E			sailed fr Ipswich	Su	30 Apr 34		
Dowell		Elizabeth		155				s	Ware b 1609	Ht			
Pepper		Phillis		156				s					
1637 Williams	Robert		157		C				Great Yarmouth	Nr			2 May 38
Welde		Judith		158		m							
Hagbourne	Samuel		159		C				Gloucester b 1014	Gl			2 May 38
Williams		Elizabeth		160				C	Great Yarmouth	Nr			
Hagbourne		Katteren		161				C	Gloucester b 1614	Gl			
How	Abraham	—	162	163	C	C			Hatfield Broadoak	Es			2 May 38
Geary	Arthur	[Francis]	164	165	C	C			Little Haddam ch 1628	Ht			14 Mar 38/9
Ruggles	Thomas	Mary	166	167	C	C			Nazeing	Es		arr 37	22 May 39
Bridges	Edward		168		x				Great Bursted m 1614	Es			22 May 39
Johnson		Elizabeth		169				m	Ware	Ht			
Spisor		Christian		170				s	Eastwell	Ke	11 May 37		
Gore		Rhoda		171		E			Ippollitts ch 1634	Ht			
Write		Rachel		172				s					
Boyse		Johanna		173				s	Boughton und Bleam b 1618	Ke			
1638 Mihill	[Thomas]	[Ellen?]	174	175	C	C							13 May 40
Boyse	Mathew	—	176	177	C	C			Boughton und Bleam ch 1621	Ke			22 May 39
Greene		widdow [Mary?]		178		w							
Porter		Anna		179		E			Chelmsford m 1624	Es			
Miller	John	Lidea	180	181	C	C			Cambridge ed 1627	Ca			22 May 39
Holmes	George		182		L				Nazeing b 1594	Es			22 May 39
Chandler	William	Hannah	183	184	C	C			Bishop's Stortford	Ht		arr 37	13 May 40
Webb	{William}	—		185		E			Rattlesden	Su			
Robbinson	{Thomas}	Selene		186		x			Ingatestone	Es			
Sheafe		—, widdow		187		w			Cranbrook ?	Ke			
Blackburn	Mr [Walter]	Mrs	188	189	C	C							22 May 39
Chapin	Samuel	[Cecily]	190		L				Paignton ?	De			2 Jun 41
Griggs	[Thomas]		191					s					none
Peacock	Richard	Jane	192	193	C	C			Stansted Abbey	Ht			22 May 39
Roberts	John		194		L					Wa		arr 36	22 May 39
Astwood	James	Sarah	195	196	C	C			Kings Walden m 1633	Ht		arr 38	22 May 39
Kilborne	George		197					s					13 May 40
Harbettle		Dorothy		198				s					
Wallis	Ann			199				s					
Parks		Martha		200		x							

ADDITIONS AND CORRECTIONS TO
THE GREAT MIGRATION BEGINS

Volume I, page xxv, paragraph one, line three: "describe" in place of "described."

Volume I, page xxv, paragraph six, line three: "1930" in place of "1630."

Volume I, page xxxiii, paragraph two, line five: "everything" in place of "everthing."

Key to Titles, HarVR: "Records" in place of "Reocrds."

Key to Titles, Pynchon Court: "Record" in place of "Reocrd."

JEREMY ADAMS, page 9, CHILDREN: i JOHN: The marriage certificate, dated 1 September 1657, of "John Addams and Abigaill Smith" is accompanied by a letter of consent from the two fathers, "Rich[ard] Smith" and "Jer[emy] Addams"; the place of marriage is not stated [RPCC 182].

JOHN BAKER, page 76, COMMENTS: A different version of the testimony of Robert Johnston includes the statement that John Baker was "a member of Cotton's church in New England" [CSP America and West Indies, 1661-1668, p. 117]. This confirms the identification of John Baker of Boston with the man hanged in London in 1663.

ABRAHAM BROWN, pages 245, 2087, CHILDREN: A third child, Mary, was baptized at Childerditch on 8 February 1623/4; Hannah, baptized at Childerditch on 25 August 1622, was buried at South Weald on 10 October 1628 [Kempton Anc, Part I, pp. 184-85].

GRIFFIN CRAFTS, page 490, COMMENTS, last word on page: "Stephen" in place of "Samuel."

EDMUND GROVER, pages 824-26: Janet Ireland Delorey found at St. Nicholas Acons, London, the baptism on 16 April 1628 of John, son of Edmund and Prudence Grover [TG 10:129-30], which fits the immigrant nicely.

EDMUND HART, page 867, ESTATE: paragraph five, "Edmund Hart *lately* of Waymouth, planter."

WILLIAM HILTON, page 955, line 23: "(documentary evidence no*t* seen)."

JOHN HOWLAND, page 1022, MARRIAGE: "baptized Henlow, *Bedfordshire*."

WILLIAM HUDSON, page 1036, CHILDREN: iv NATHANIEL: Delete "no further record." Add "m. Boston 1 December 1659 'Elizabeth Alford, daughter of William Alford of Boston' [BVR 72]."

WILLIAM KNOPP, page 1146, BIBLIOGRAPHIC NOTE, line 5: NEHGR 147:315-28.

THOMAS LAMB, pages 1154-55: The last item in ESTATE should be dated 2 July 1677 (*not* 1697). As a result, we only know that daughter Mary married James Bayley before 3 March 1697/8, but not how much earlier the marriage might have taken place.

JOHN LEGGE, page 1167, CHILDREN: i SAMUEL: "b. about 1642 *(deposed 1 November 1666 "aged about twenty-four" [EQC 3:344]*; deposed aged 37 years, 1 August 1679 [SJC #1789])."

JOHN MASON, page 1227, DEATH: "Under date of 30 January 1671/2 Simon Bradstreet records that 'Major Jno. Mason who had several times been Deputy Governor of Connecticot Colony, died. He was aged about 70. He lived the 2 or 3 last years of his life in extreme misery with the stone or strangury or some such disease. He died with much comfort and assurance it should be well with him' [NEHGR 9:46]."

THOMAS PRENCE, page 1522, BIRTH: "Lechdale" should be "Lechlade."

WILLIAM SPRAGUE, page 1736, line 4 of will: "one *horse*" instead of "one house."

WILLIAM VASSALL, page 1872, CHILDREN: ii JUDITH; and WILLIAM WHITE, page 1980, CHILDREN: i RESOLVED: The colony record of their marriage, 8 April 1640 [PCR 8:19], differs from the Scituate record, which has 5 November 1640.

CHRISTOPHER WADSWORTH, page 1891, last word: "virtue" in place of "virture."

RECENT LITERATURE

Clifford L. Stott, "The English Origin of James[1] Penniman of Boston and Braintree, Massachusetts," *The American Genealogist* 71 (1996):12-18. By searching systematically in thirty-two parish registers, Stott discovered that the immigrant James Penniman was baptized in Chipping Ongar, Essex.

Robert L.V. French and Melinde Lutz Sanborn, "The Rev. William[1] Worcester of Salisbury, Massachusetts," *The American Genealogist* 71 (1996):50-51. The authors have found Olney, Buckinghamshire, baptisms for four children of Rev. William Worcester.

Frederick C. Hart Jr., "The Rev. John[1] Jones of Fairfield, Connecticut," *The American Genealogist* 71 (1996):52-54. Hart publishes baptisms at Abbot's Ripton, Huntingdonshire, for five children of Rev. John Jones, prior to 1630, as well as baptisms for three additional children, from 1631 to 1635, at St. Stephens Coleman Street, London.

Myrtle Stevens Hyde, "The Ancestry of Prudence Bird, Wife of Martin Kellogg of Braintree, Essex, England (Who Had Descendants in New England)," *The American Genealogist* 71 (1996):87-92. Hyde documents three generations of paternal ancestry for Prudence (Bird) Kellogg, three of whose sons came to New England.

Gale Ion Harris, "Daniel[1] Garrett and His Family of Hartford, Connecticut," *The American Genealogist* 71 (1996):93-104. Harris provides a full treatment of Daniel Garrett, immigrant to Hartford by 1640, and of his children.

Donald S. Barber, "The English Origin of Thomas[1] Barber of Windsor, Connecticut," *The American Genealogist* 71 (1996):111-12. Barber demonstrates that Thomas Barber, immigrant to Windsor in 1635, was baptized in Uffington, Lincolnshire.

Robert Charles Anderson, "Alice (Frost) (Blower) Tilly," *The American Genealogist* 71 (1996):113. The author argues that Alice Frost was wife successively of Thomas Blower and William Tilly.

Barbara Lambert Merrick, "Doty and Churchill of Plymouth Colony: The Two Claimed Wives of Thomas[2] Doty," *The American Genealogist* 71 (1996):114-20. Merrick demonstrates that Thomas Doty had only one wife, Mary Churchill, daughter of John Churchill, and that this wife married as her second husband Henry Churchill, whose parentage is unknown.

Lois Ware Thurston, "The English Ancestry of Leonard[1] Harriman of Rowley, Massachusetts[,] and John[1] Harriman of New Haven, Connecticut," *New England Historical and Genealogical Register* 150 (1996):29-47. Thurston argues that Leonard and John Harriman were probably sons of Matthew Harriman of Uldale, Cumberland.

Gale Ion Harris, "George Chappell of Windsor, Wethersfield, and New London, Connecticut," *New England Historical and Genealogical Register* 150 (1996):48-73. The author presents a comprehensive treatment of George Chappell (who arrived in New England in 1635) and of his four sons.

Paul C. Reed and Dean Crawford Smith, "Dorothy _____, The Key in Our Search for Shadrack Hapgood," *New England Historical and Genealogical Register* 150 (1996):141-56. Reed and Smith have determined that a Dorothy of unknown parentage married first Nicholas Blake and second Thomas Noyes. Her first child, Mary Blake, married Shadrack Scullard, and their daughter Joan married Thomas Hapgood and became the mother of the immigrant Shadrack. Dorothy's first son with Thomas Noyes was Peter, the immigrant to Sudbury, and greatuncle of Shadrack Hapgood.

David A. Macdonald, "A New Look at the Corwin and Shatswell Families," *New England Historical and Genealogical Register* 150 (1996):180-89. The author has found Chancery documents which show that there were five Shatswell siblings, of whom at least four came to New England: John; Margaret (m. Matthias Corwin); Sibyl (fate unknown); Theophilus; and Mary (m. George Webster). The evidence also increases the likelihood that George and Matthias Corwin were brothers, leaves William Shatswell unconnected, and provides no Shatswell wife for William Sargent.

Craig Partridge, "Elizabeth Herbert, Wife of (1) John White and (2) George Corwin," *New England Historical and Genealogical Register* 150 (1996):190-97. Partridge shows that Elizabeth Herbert who married first, in England, John White, and second, in New England, George Corwin, was baptized at All Saints, Northampton, Northamptonshire, daughter of John Herbert. He also discusses the family of her first husband, John White.

(continued from page 18)

The second *Hercules*, from Sandwich, does not belong in this section at all, for it sailed in 1635 and not 1634 [NEHGR 75:217-26, 79-107-9]. Banks may have been misled by the fact that most of the passengers took their oaths before the calendar change in the early part of the year, and so the dates are given as 1634. Furthermore, there is a clerical error, in which Thomas Gardner is entered as taking his oath on 26 March 1634, which should be correctly 26 March 1635. Nevertheless, the ship arrived in New England in 1635, and is misplaced in Banks.

Another 1634 ship for which Banks attempted a synthetic list is the *Griffin*. Winthrop tells us only that "Mr. Lothrop and Mr. Simmes, two godly ministers," were on this ship [WJ 1:170]. These were Rev. John Lathrop and Rev. Zachariah Symmes; Banks then assumed that each of these men was accompanied by his wife and children, and so their names are entered into the synthetic list.

Also on the *Griffin* was the notorious Anne Hutchinson, as we learn from the transcript of her examination in November 1637. Zachariah Symmes and William Bartholomew both recall incriminating statements that she had made when they were aboard ship on their way to New England. On this basis, Banks has included in his list the families of both William Hutchinson and William Bartholomew.

Finally, Banks includes the families of Nathaniel Heaton, Thomas Lynde, Richard Haines and William Haines. Heaton may have been included because it was known that he, like the Hutchinsons, had come from Alford, Lincolnshire, and it was therefore assumed that they had travelled together, but there is no more evidence than that. The remaining three families were said to be from Dunstable, Bedfordshire, and it is not known whether there is evidence for the presence on the *Griffin*.

In general the attempts made by Colonel Banks to generate synthetic lists of passengers were unsuccessful. We should look to the few reliable surviving contemporaneous lists, and continue to look for clues embedded in later documents which might point to the ship on which a given immigrant came. But for the most part we will never know who came on which ship in 1634.

Great Migration Study Project
101 Newbury Street
Boston, MA 02116

NON-PROFIT ORG.
U.S. POSTAGE PAID
Burlington, VERMONT
Permit No. 579

Great Migration Newsletter

Vol. 6   October-December 1997   No. 4

CHARLESTOWN INHABITANTS OF 1635

In writing the sketches of Charlestown residents, we have been making frequent use of a list of persons said to have been inhabitants of Charlestown in "January 1635." When we meet a date like this, out of context, there is always difficulty in deciding whether this should be 1634/5 or 1635/6. Most, but not all, colonial New England record-keepers used 1 March or 25 March as the first day of the new year, and so we are correct more often than not if we assume that a date in January or February of, let us say, 1635, if given without double-dating, should be interpeted as 1635/6.

This is what we have done to this point in the Great Migration Study Project with this list, and so there are a number of sketches in the volumes already published which contain an entry based on this assumption. In the sketch of Ralph Sprague, for example, is the following, under COMMENTS:

"Admitted as an inhabitant of Charlestown in 1629 [ChTR 2], and included in lists of 9 January 1633/4 and January 1635/6 [ChTR 10, 15]."

The list of interest here is the one cited above as "ChTR 15," that is, page 15 of the "original" Charlestown town records. As with so many early records, the meaning of "original" is a very slippery thing. Although some fragments of what was the earliest town book survive, what we generally use is the compilation prepared by John Greene, town clerk in the 1660s. He took what were then the oldest records, and combined them with extracts from the colony records and, apparently, memories of some of the oldest settlers, to produce a hybrid record which must be used carefully.

One detail of this record which must be examined closely is the pagination. Over the years, two different sets of numbers have been placed on the pages - a folio number and a page number. The folio number is given on the upper right corner of each leaf in the volume, and then a page number is entered on the front and back of each leaf. Thus, the first sheet of paper in the volume is Folio 1, the front of which is Page One and the back of which is Page Two.

This works fine up through Folio 7, which has Page 13 and Page 14. But the next Folio is 8*, with Pages 15 and 16, and the Folio after that is 8, with Pages 17 and 18. Examination of the actual items entered on these pages shows that the chronological sequence is continuous from the end of Page 14 to the beginning of Page 17; in fact, the town meeting of 11 July 1635 begins at the bottom of Page 14 and continues at the top of Page 17.

Folio 8*, then, is intrusive, and not in its proper chronological sequence. Page 15, the "front" side of this Folio, begins with three brief, undated town orders. This is followed by a list of "The names of those that are to have planting ground Januar[y] [blank] 1635," and then the item of direct interest to us here, "A list of the names of the inhabitants of this town record[ed?] this month of January 1635."

Page 16 begins with a meeting dated "The 9 of the xij month [i.e., 9 February]." At the end of material under this date it is stated that "the orders above written were fully agreed upon the 9 day of the xij month 1635," to which ten men signed their names. Nine of these men were among the ten who were elected Charlestown select-men on 10 February 1634/5 [ChTR 13]. The tenth select-man, Robert Moulton, was known to have moved to Salem sometime in late 1635 or early 1636 [GMB 2:1304]; he is replaced in the list under consideration by John Woolrich. Thus we conclude that this record on Page 16 should be

(continued on page 30)

EDITOR'S EFFUSIONS

Just before work began on this issue of the Great Migration Newsletter, we sent out to our reviewers the drafts of the sketches for the last half of the letter C for those immigrants who arrived in 1634 and 1635. This completes this stage of the work on the next Great Migration volume to be published. As soon as this newsletter is off to the printer, we will put the finishing touches on the sketches for the letter A, and send them off for proofreading and indexing.

Our efforts in the opening months of the New Year will be to do the final research and revisions on the letters B and C. As usual, B is a letter with many sketches, in this case more than 150, so there is still work to be done.

One of the great lessons we learned in completing the three volumes of the first phase of the Great Migration Study Project is that the work necessary to convert the first draft of a sketch into the finished product is often greater than anticipated. There may be many reasons for this added effort. Sometimes this may be the need to collect the evidence for the marriage of one of the children of an immigrant, even when the identity of the spouse has been correctly stated in some respected secondary source. At other times it is the desire to track down a more reliable version of some important source, a version closer to the original, which one can use with greater confidence than a printed or modern copy of the source. A third possibility is the irresistible urge to follow up on a promising lead that arises late in the research process, perhaps a clue to the English origin, or to the identity of a spouse.

As the Great Migration Study Project has advanced we find ourselves trying to squeeze more and more into each sketch. This may mean it takes a little longer to finish a sketch, but we think you will be pleased with the result.

By the time of the next Great Migration Newsletter, we should be able to tell you when this next volume will be coming off the presses.

Robert Charles Anderson, FASG   Editor
Aileen M. Novick   Production Assistant

The Great Migration Newsletter is published quarterly by the Great Migration Study Project, a project of the New England Historic Genealogical Society, 101 Newbury Street, Boston MA 02116

The subscription rate is $12 for one year and $20 for two years.

(continued from page 29)

dated 9 February 1635/6. (With respect to Robert Moulton, this analysis also tells us that he had departed for Salem by this date, and had been replaced as selectman by John Woolrich.)

Page 16 continues with a meeting of "the 13 of the xij month," which we take to be 13 February 1635/6, at which a new slate of selectmen was elected (nine men this time instead of ten). The page concludes with a copy of a record made "At a General Court holden at New Towne the 3d of March 1635," which is easily identifed as being from the court of 3 March 1635/6 [MBCR 1:168].

Folio 9 (Pages 19 and 20) is devoted solely to a grant of hayground on 9 February 1635 (seemingly connected to the 9 February 1635/6 records discussed above), and Folio 10 (Pages 21 and 22) has town records dated from 22 March 1635/6 to 1 July 1636.

Based on this analysis, it would seem that Folio 8* should be shifted to come after Folio 8 and before Folio 9. Thus Folio 8 would end with a meeting of 6 December 1635, to be followed by Folio 8* with records of January 1635, which would now be interpreted as January 1635/6.

And so it would be if our analysis ended here. But now let us look at the people who are included in the list of inhabitants of "January 1635." There are seventy-two names on the list, mostly men, but also including two women, both widows: Prudence Wilkinson and Ann Higginson.

We are looking for names of persons who moved into or out of Charlestown between January 1634/5 and January 1635/6. Many of the seventy-two are inhabitants who had lived in Charlestown since 1629, 1630 or 1631, and would continue to reside there for many years - men such as Increase Nowell, William Dady, and Ralph Sprague.

Another useful list of Charlestown inhabitants contains "The names of such as were admitted inhabitants of this town Anno 1634," which comprises twenty-five names. Of these, twenty-three are in the list of inhabitants of "January 1635" (including "Mrs. Sarah Oakly," who married in 1634 Edmund Hobart, and "Mrs. Crowe," whose husband John came soon after). Only Matthew Mitchell appears among those admitted in 1634, but not in the list of "January 1635."

An interesting group of names on the list are those families which first settled in Charlestown, but departed for Hingham, where they received grants of houselots in the summer of 1635. These were Edmund Hobart Sr., Edmund Hobart Jr., Joshua Hobart, Anthony Eames and Thomas Chubbock.

(continued on page 36)

Focus on **RICHMOND ISLAND**

BRIEF HISTORY OF EARLY RICHMOND ISLAND

For most of the early fishing communities of the Maine coast the surviving evidence is vanishing to nonexistent. Occasionally one of these fishermen would impinge on one of the better-recorded settlements to the south, or would become involved in some incident that came to the attention of the Puritan authorities in Massachusetts Bay. But for the most part these men (and a few women) labored in relative obscurity, and are very poorly documented.

There is, however, one exception. Robert Trelawny, a merchant of Plymouth, Devonshire, financed a fishing operation in New England for many years, and extensive correspondence and financial records for this settlement have survived, affording us the best picture we have of one of these communities. (For further details on the Trelawny Papers, see below, page 34; in the remainder of this article, citations to page numbers only are to these papers.)

Fishing vessels out of Plymouth were apparently active in the area of Casco Bay as early as 1626, for we have depositions dated in 1640, such as those of Peter Garland, mariner, and John Cosens, sailor, which include claims of "having known and frequented [the River of Casco] for fourteen years or thereabouts" [239].

Whether these fishing expeditions were underwritten by Trelawny we do not know, but we do have evidence that Trelawny had sent agents to the Maine coast by 1631. On 1 December 1631 the Council for New England issued a patent to "Robert Trelawny, Moyses Goodyeare, and their Associates," stating that these men had "adventured and expended great sums of money in the discovery of the coasts and harbors of those parts, and are minded to undergo a further charge in settling a plantation in the mainland hereafter mentioned" [3].

The land granted in this patent was described as "being along the seacoast eastward, between the land before mentioned to be granted to the said Captain Thomas Camock ... and the bay and river of Cascoe, extending and to be extended northwards into the mainland so far as the limits and bounds of the land granted to the said Captain Thomas Camock as aforesaid do or ought to extend towards the north," along "with free liberty ... to fowl and fish, and stages, quays, and places for taking, saving, and preserving of fish to erect, make, maintain, and use in, upon, and near the island commonly called Richmonds Island" [4-5].

As with so many of these early grants of land in New England, the boundaries were very vague, and in later years

Trelawny and his agents tried to take advantage of this by claiming more land than fell within their patent. (See the map prepared in 1884 by James Phinney Baxter, giving his interpretation of the correct extent of the various grants in this part of Maine [between pages 62 and 63].)

On 18 January 1631/2, Trelawny and Goodyear designated "John Wynter and Thomas Pomery of Plymouth ..., mariners," as their agents to take possession of their patent [15-17]. Winter must have sailed for New England soon after this, for Thomas Cammock later reported to Robert Trelawny that "Mr. Winter ... came into Richmonds Isle before our ship about five days; for we had a tedious and dangerous passage, and on the 22th of April it pleased God that we safely arrived at Rich[monds] Isle" [18].

On 21 July 1632, John Winter, exercising his power of attorney for Trelawny and Goodyear, took possession of the lands granted in the patent of 1 December 1631 [17]. Shortly thereafter he returned to England, presumably to report to Trelawny and to organize additional men and provisions for the fishing operation at Richmond Island. (On 23 July 1632 Thomas Cammock wrote as if Winter had already departed for England [18-22], but he may still have been in New England as late as 30 July, when Richard Vines placed more lands into Winter's hands [17].)

One of the first problems confronted by John Winter was the presence within the patent of George Cleeve, one of the most cantankerous immigrants to New England in the first generation. Cleeve had a house on the mainland just opposite Richmond Island, from which Winter had ejected him by the fall of 1633 [208-9]. For years afterward Winter and Cleeve were at one another's throats in the various Maine courts.

After spending the winter in England, John Winter returned to Richmond Island in the *Welcome*. He reported to Trelawny that "We arrived here the second of March [1632/3], finding our men here in health, ... but there came in a ship of Barnestable some three weeks before us, the master's name is William Garland, and took away our stage from our men and kept it all the year" [22]. Several fishermen came to Richmond Island with Winter on this voyage. (A synthetic list of the passengers on this voyage is supplied by Noyes, Libby and Davis [GDMNH 4]; this list has not been analyzed for the purposes of this article.)

At this point, by the summer of 1633, the Trelawny Plantation at Richmond Island was firmly established. We are now ready to examine the ships and immigrants which arrived in 1634 and 1635.

ARRIVALS OF 1634 AND 1635

Since the Great Migration Study Project is currently working on the years 1634 and 1635, we will take a close look at the synthetic passenger lists for those years proposed by Noyes, Libby and Davis. Their analysis of the material from the Trelawny Papers is found in List 21, on pages 4 and 5 of the *Genealogical Dictionary of Maine and New Hampshire*. This list tells us that the *Hunter* and the *James* arrived in 1634 and the *Speedwell* in 1635. For each of these vessels the master is named, and in each case one or more passengers is also listed - nine for the *Hunter*, one for the *James* and fifteen for the *Speedwell*.

The surviving records of the Trelawny Plantation do not include lists of these passengers, nor do the lists appear in any of the surviving English port books. These passenger lists are synthetic creations of the twentieth century, brought together by Noyes, Libby and Davis in the process of compiling the *Genealogical Dictionary of Maine and New Hampshire*. Our task here is to examine the records of the seventeenth century to see if these synthetic lists are well supported.

On 18 June 1634 John Winter reported that the *Hunter* had arrived at Richmond Island on 2 February 1633/4, with Mr. Owen Pomeroy as master [25-26, 39]. After a season of fishing and trading, the *Hunter* departed Richmond Island on 3 July 1634 [44]. Then, on 18 September of the same year, Winter wrote that the *James* had arrived on 29 August, with Mr. Bowes as master [49]. In the following year, on 11 June 1635, Winter informed Trelawny that the *Speedwell*, Mr. Narias Hawkins master, had arrived on 26 April [55].

We will first examine the second of the three ships, the *James*, as it differs from the other two. First, the *Hunter* and the *Speedwell* appear to be the annual supply ships sent to the plantation early in the season, whereas the *James* arrived much later in the year, long after the good fishing was over, and at a time when the needs of the Richmond Island settlers were not so great. Second, only one passenger, George Dearing, is suggested for the *James*.

As with so many of these early settlers of the Maine coast, the evidence for their date of arrival is indirect, deriving from records created many years after their migration. In his report of 10 July 1637, John Winter noted that "Georg[e] Dearing, the house carpenter, takes the time of the beginning of his 3 years' service to begin the first day he came to your house, & will stay no longer to make out his 3 years' service" [113]. On the 29th of July, Winter added the information that "George Dearinge, the house carpenter, is gone from us, & says his time is out; he went from the plantation the 10th of this month" [119].

Clearly George Dearing considered his service to have begun on or about 10 July 1634, "the first day he came to

[Trelawny's] house." If this house is meant to be the building erected by Trelawny's agents on Richmond Island, then Dearing could not have come on the *James*, for that ship did not arrive until 29 August. But if Dearing had come on the earlier vessel that year, the *Hunter*, what was he doing between 2 February 1633/4 and 10 July 1634?

It would seem, then, that the event relied upon by Dearing was a visit to Trelawny's house in Plymouth, where he would have signed his three-year contract to work at Richmond Island. This would be about seven weeks before the arrival of the *James* in New England, an appropriate time for a westward crossing at that time of year. On this basis, then, George Dearing can be accepted as a passenger on the *James*.

Let us go back now to the *Hunter*, which had arrived at Richmond Island on 2 February 1633/4. Noyes, Libby and Davis assign to this vessel "A fishing company including apparently: Richard Downing, Richard Corber, Robert Waymouth, Jos[eph] Crase, William Helborne, Tho[mas] Arrowsmith, William Tucker, John Sanders, [and] ship's carpenter Tho[ma]s Treleage" [GDMNH 4].

Of these nine men, eight appear in a single list on page 38 of the Trelawny Papers. This list is part of a much longer group of documents comprising the financial accounts of the plantation for the fishing season of 1634 [34-43], drawn up at the time of the departure of the *Hunter* in early July of 1634, and in order to understand the list with these eight names, we must get a better grasp on the full range and import of these accounts.

This set of accounts consists of at least five separate documents: 1) an invoice of supplies and trading goods sent to Richmond Island in the *Hunter* [34-36]; 2) an account of what the plantation owes [36-38]; 3) "an account of our fish made out of the *Hunter*, 1634" [39]; 4) "an account [of] what third part of the money of the fish and train and pease ... to be divided among our Company, being 13 shares here in New England for this year's work" [40-42]; and 5) an account of fish and furs loaded on the *Hunter* to be taken to England [42-43].

The first, third and fifth of these accounts contain very few names, and these appear in all cases to be the names of ship's masters and crew, and so not to be considered as immigrants to New England. (This matter of discriminating between transient mariners and those who actually made a home in New England, however brief, is one of the most difficult decisions to be made in deciding whether or not a person is to be included in the Great Migration Study Project, and unfortunately this decision sometimes has a subjective component to it.)

The fourth list is very carefully drawn up, and sets forth the wages due to a number of men who appear to have been at

INDEX TO PERSONS IN VOLUME SIX
Compiled by Aileen M. Novick

Richmond Island for a full year at least. The heading on the document states that it is "for this year's work," which might be interpreted to mean only for the fishing season of 1634, and so not extending back into 1633. But in the body of the document is an entry "for my [i.e., Winter's] wages for the year," and an allowance to "Thomas Kinge our carpenter" of a full year's wages.

Thus all the men named in this list should be accounted as having arrived no later than 1633, and on this basis they are included in the synthetic list for the *Welcome* compiled by Noyes, Libby and Davis [GDMNH 4]. (Unfortunately, this analysis was not performed during the compilation of the three volumes of *The Great Migration Begins*, and so some of these men were omitted from those volumes; this error will be corrected in future publications of the Project.)

We come now to the second of the five lists, the list headed "The Plantation Owes," which contains much of what we know about those who would have come on the *Hunter* in 1634. This is the most disorganized of the five lists, and consequently the most difficult to interpret. It seems to consist of at least four sections: 1) an account of money owed for goods supplied to the plantation [36-37]; 2) a section headed "Advent'" (meaning "adventures" or "adventurers") [38]; 3) another account similar to the first [39]; and 4) "hiredmen's wages" [39].

The first and third sections of this second list are akin to the first, third and fifth lists, in that the men (and in this case a few women) named were not all clearly residents at Richmond Island, even for a single fishing season. Some were certainly members of the crew of the *Hunter*, and others may have been merchants who never left England. Noyes, Libby and Davis deemed some of the persons in this list to be arrivals in 1633 (i.e., Edward Fishcock, Henry Roberts and Richard Pynne). We do not attempt in this article to fully analyze these two sections of the second list.

The second section of the list is presented in three columns, the first containing odds and ends of trading goods, the second a money amount, and the third a man's name. None of these names appears in any other New England record, and the best interpretation is that these were minor merchants, probably mostly from Plymouth, who had placed trading goods aboard the *Hunter* in hopes of profiting at a distance from the trading activities of Trelawny's plantation. They were adventurers in the mercantile sense of the term, and not travellers on the high seas.

This leaves us with the fourth section of the second list, the "hiredmen's wages." This is where we find eight of the nine names that are included in the synthetic passenger list of the *Hunter*. That they are thus set off and distinguished from the men in the fourth list, the known arrivals of 1633, indicates that these men had arrived in 1634, and were being paid for their labors during the 1634 fishing season only.

The puzzling aspect is that twenty names appear in this section of the list, and the eight who were included by Noyes, Libby and Davis in the passenger list are in no way distinguished from the other twelve. The amount owing to these men ranged from £4 16s. 8d. (Richard Corber) to 17s. (Geo[rge] Perden), indicating that they had worked for widely differing amounts of time; but the eight men placed on the synthetic list were at all levels of payment, and not the most highly paid, who would presumably have been longest at Richmond Island.

It would seem, then, that all of these twenty names should be accounted as passengers on the *Hunter*, or none should. And likewise, all should be included as settlers at Richmond Island (and therefore eligible to have a Great Migration Study Project sketch) or none should. Because they are all being paid for work at Richmond Island, they will all be considered residents there, and will all be accorded a sketch, however brief it may be.

There remains the ninth passenger on the *Hunter*, the "ship's carpenter, Tho[mas] Treleage." His name is found in the fourth list among these accounts [41], imbedded in the account for "Thomas Kinge our carpenter," a 1633 arrival and servant to Mr. Nicholas Langworthy. King is instructed to "pay the carpenter of the *Hunter*, Thomas Treleage, 3s. for tools bought of him." Treleage certainly sailed on the *Hunter*, but he appears only in his role as a crew member, and will not be considered a settler at Richmond Island.

Finally, we wish to examine the synthetic passenger list for the *Speedwell* of 1635. Noyes, Libby and Davis here supply us with fifteen proposed names (in addition to the captain, Mr. Narias Hawkins): Mr. Edward Trelawny, George Rogers, Richard Cummings, Roger Willing, Alexander Freethy, William Freethy, Roger Bucknall, Peter Hill, John Lander, William Ham, John Billin, Oliver Clark, John Symons, John Vivion and Peter Cobb [GDMNH 4].

Mr. Edward Trelawny was Robert Trelawny's brother, and he was certainly in New England by 1635 [66-76]. In his letter of 11 June 1635, reporting the arrival of the *Speedwell*, John Winter announced that he planned to return to England, and that he will "be forced to leave the whole business here unto Mr. Haukin, hoping your brother will be assistance unto him" [56], a clear indication that Edward Trelawny had sailed with Narias Hawkins.

Six more of the *Speedwell* passengers are identified by their participation in a rebellion against their master at Richmond Island. Upon his return to Richmond Island in 1636, Winter found that "The Company fell into a mutiny with me because I would not give them bills for the last year's for the money which they were to have above their shares, which I know not whether it be paid or no; but they taking such distaste at it, some of them fell into such a mutiny, & they are gone away from the plantation, & do purpose to fish for themselves" [92-93]. Winter then identified "The parties which are gone is [John] Lander, which I doubt is the leader of them all, & William Ham, Oliver Clarke, John Bellin, William Freythey, & John Simmons" [93].

Another man in the synthetic list, Alexander Freethy, was brother of William Freethy. He is not seen in New England until 1637, and in their account of Alexander Freethy, Noyes, Libby and Davis argue that Alexander probably "came with Mr. Winter in the *Agnes* [in] 1636, as he went home in 1638 before his 3 years were up" [GDMNH 245].

As an aside, this raises two interessting points about the mechanics of creating large genealogical compilations. The *Genealogical Dictionary of Maine and New Hampshire* was issued in parts, over a period of more than a decade. The "Lists" section, which includes the synthetic passenger lists we are discussing here, was in the first part, whereas the Freethy section was included in one of the later parts. Presumably, then, when compiling the lists the authors made the assumption that the two brothers had come together, even though there was evidence for only one coming in 1635. Then, upon closer examination, they found the evidence that Alexander probably arrived a year after his brother, and by this time it was too late to correct the "Lists."

This leads to the second point, which was taken into account in the preparation of *The Great Migration Begins*. It has been very common in genealogical publications to make the assumption that if one member of a family came to New England in a certain year, then the entire family came in that same year. The Freethy example is only one of many cases where closer examination of the evidence, or evidence found at a later date, shows clearly that brothers, or uncles and nephews, or fathers and sons, came in different years. For this reason, the Great Migration Study Project has adopted a specific set of rules, somewhat arbitrary, but explicit and consistent, on the question of family migration [GMB 1:xvi].

The evidence for the remaining seven men is found for the most part in the accounts of the plantation compiled in 1639 [181-98]. Evidence for length of service, and therefore presumably for date of migration, is frequently buried in these accounts. For example, the entries for John Hempson and Thomas Sheppherd tell us that they are being paid "for 2 years' service" [184, 185]. But not all of the entries contain information which would allow us to pinpoint the date of arrival.

We are confronted again with a situation similar to that seen with the fourth section of the second list for 1634, the accounting of "hiredmen's wages." Noyes, Libby and Davis have again in the case of these 1639 accounts included some of the men in their 1635 synthetic passenger list, but have excluded most, without giving us their reasoning.

For our present purposes we will look at just two of these seven, Richard Cummings and John Vivion. Richard Cummings first appears in this account of 1639 [187]. There is no explicit statement of his length of service. The two items which do help us in this regard are in the credit column: "for his share this year [1639]" and "for his share of fish taken with Narias Hawkins his company."

Noyes, Libby and Davis have apparently taken the second of these two items to prove that Cummings came with Hawkins in 1635. But examination of the career of Narias Hawkins in New England shows that this inference is not inevitable. After the defection of John Lander and his five partners, Hawkins apparently reorganized his efforts, and clearly was working with a different group of men in his fishing activities in 1638 [135-37]. It is more economical, then, to assume that the account for Richard Cummings represents two years of fishing, 1638 with Narias Hawkins and 1639 with John Winter. On this interpretation of the account, Cummings need not have arrived before 1638.

John Vivion does appear in the Richmond Island records prior to the 1639 accounts. In a letter of 29 July 1637, John Winter tells Robert Trelawny that "Your man Vyvion is run away from the plantation, & I do believe he will get to the westward in the Bay, & will get into some of the ships of London that are bound for the Straits" [119]. The 1639 account for "John Vivion" states explicitly that it covers the period from 24 May 1636 to 5 June 1639 [192]. Nothing shows his presence in New England before 1636.

Careful examination of the 1639 accounts, and of the remainder of the Trelawny Papers, might reveal additional arrivals in 1635 (and in 1634), but the complete analysis of the 1639 financial records is beyond the scope of this article. For the moment, the passenger list of the *Speedwell* in 1635 must be limited to Mr. Edward Trelawny and to John Lander and his five comrades.

TRELAWNY PAPERS

The collection of documents known as the Trelawny Papers was lost to history for more than two centuries. In 1872, John Wingate Thornton noticed a clue which led to the Rev. C.T. Collins Trelawny of Ham in England, who held the family muniments, and was persuaded to donate the papers to the Maine Historical Society [vii-viii]. James Phinney Baxter then prepared the papers for publication, as Volume III of the *Documentary History of the State of Maine* [Portland, 1884].

The bulk of the documents in the Trelawny Papers cover the earliest years of the settlement of Richmond Island, from 1631 to 1648; most were prepared by John Winter, who had died by 1648. The few remaining items are spread out over a century and a half, the last being dated 4 April 1809.

RECENT LITERATURE

Robert Leigh Ward, "The English Origin and First Marriage of Deacon John[1] Dunham of Plymouth, Massachusetts," *The American Genealogist* 71 (1996):130-33, 250. Ward shows that John Dunham was married in Clophill, Bedfordshire, and his eldest son was baptized in Henlow, Bedfordshire.

Barbara Lambert Merrick, "Rebecca[2] Lapham, Wife of John[3] Washburn of Bridgewater, Massachusetts," *The American Genealogist* 71 (1996):134-36. Merrick demonstrates that Rebecca Lapham, daughter of the immigrant Thomas Lapham, married John[3] Washburn and not Samuel[3] White, as some sources have claimed.

Henry B. Hoff, "Elizabeth (Foote) Jennings of County Essex, England: Sister of Nathaniel[1] Foote of Wethersfield, Connecticut, and Joshua[1] Foote of Providence, Rhode Island," *The American Genealogist* 71 (1996):149-50. The author has found the will of Elizabeth (Foote) Jennings, sister of two immigrants to New England, thus extending our knowledge of this family.

John C. Brandon and Janet Ireland Delorey, "Lawrence[1] and Cassandra (Burnell) Southwick of Salem, Massachusetts: Their English Antecedents, With Notes on Ananias[1] Conklin and William[1] Burnell," *The American Genealogist* 71 (1996):193-97. Brandon and Delorey set forth new data which extend our knowledge of the English background of Lawrence Southwick and his wife Cassandra Burnell and her family, including her brother William Burnell, who had come to Boston by 1640. The authors also include additional information on the immigrant Ananias Conklin.

Robert Charles Anderson, "Samuel[2] Cole, Son of Job[1] Cole, of Eastham, Massachusetts," *The American Genealogist* 71 (1996):198-99. The author presents evidence that the immigrant Job Cole had a son Samuel, who married and had three children.

Helen S. Ullmann, "Isaac[2] and Mary (Root) Bronson of Waterbury, Connecticut," *The American Genealogist* 71 (1996):206-14. Ullmann has prepared an account of the family of Isaac[2] Brunson (John[1]) and his wife Mary Root, correcting a number of errors about this family that have appeared in print.

Lloyd DeWitt Bockstruck, "The Identity and Origin of Elizabeth Felkin, Wife of Thomas[1] Page of Saco, Maine," *The American Genealogist* 71 (1996):216-19. Bockstruck has identified the wife of Thomas Page of Saco as Elizabeth Felkin, daughter of Christopher Felkin of London, a member of the Drapers' Company. In the process, he has clarified the English background of Thomas Page himself.

Gale Ion Harris, "Sarah[2] Salmon of Southold, Long Island, Probable Wife of Joseph[2] Edwards and Samuel[2] Curtis of Wethersfield, Connecticut," *The American Genealogist* 71 (1996):235-41. Harris sets forth an intricate web of evidence that strongly suggests that the Sarah who was successively wife of Joseph Edwards and Samuel Curtis was daughter of William[1] Salmon of Southold, Long Island.

Robert S. Wakefield, "The Probable English Origin of Mr. John[1] Coombs of Plymouth Colony," *The American Genealogist* 71 (1996):247-50. The author examines the family of Francis Combe of Hemel Hempstead, Hertfordshire, who may be the father of John Coombs, immigrant to Plymouth Colony.

Alan A. Wickham and James W. Petty, "Thomas Wickham of Chichester, Sussex, England, and Wethersfield, Connecticut," *New England Historical and Genealogical Register* 150 (1996):260-76. Wickham and Petty demonstrate that Thomas Wickham, who arrived in New England by 1648, was from Chichester, Sussex, and his father was an elder halfbrother of the three Chatfield brothers who had earlier settled in Guilford.

Robert Charles Anderson, "The English Origin of John Livermore of Watertown and New Haven," *New England Historical and Genealogical Register* 150 (1996):433-35. The author shows that John Livermore of Watertown and New Haven was from Wethersfield, Essex, and his mother was a sister of William Hammond, early settler in Watertown.

Myrtle Stevens Hyde, "Corrected Ancestry for Nathan Aldus of Early Dedham, Massachusetts," *New England Historical and Genealogical Register* 150 (1996):473-94. Hyde presents extensive data on the English ancestry of Nathan Aldus, correcting previously published information on his great-great-grandfather.

Rebecca J. Tannenbaum, "'What Is Best to Be Done for These Fevers': Elizabeth Davenport's Medical Practice in New Haven Colony," *The New England Quarterly* 70 (1997):265-84. Relying mostly on correspondence between Rev. John Davenport and John Winthrop Jr. and on the latter's medical journals, Tannenbaum explores the role of women in the practice of medicine in seventeenth-century New England.

Michael P. Winship, "Contesting Control of Orthodoxy among the Godly: William Pynchon Reexamined," *William and Mary Quarterly* 54 (1997):795-822. Winship describes the sources of the strand of Puritanism adopted by William Pynchon, which eventually resulted in his estrangement from the leaders of Massachusetts Bay Colony.

(continued from page 30)

These names at least should not be on the list if the date was meant for January 1635/6.

The list includes persons who arrived in 1634, and does not include persons who departed during 1635. The next step is to ask about those who arrived in Charlestown in 1635. Unfortunately, there is no consolidated list of 1635 arrivals as there is for 1634. We do, however, have the church records and town meeting records to assist us.

Seven men were admitted to Charlestown church in January and February 1634/5: Robert Blott, William Bachelor, Thomas Lynde, William Johnson, Thomas Pierce, George Bunker and John Sibley [ChChR 8]. All are in the list of 1634 arrivals, and all are in the list of "January 1635." No more men were admitted in the next five months; then, from August 1635 through January 1635/6 five more men were admitted: Peter Hobart, James Hayden, Michael Barstow, Thomas Brigden and Thomas Ewer [ChChR 8]. None of these made it into the list of "January 1635/6."

From the town meetings in 1635 six additional men are seen, being granted houselots or other parcels of land: Robert Rand, Robert Hawkins, Henry Lawrence, Faintnot Wines,

Thomas Bonney and Isaac Cole. Again, none of these men are in the list of "January 1635."

The argument might be made that only proprietors were included in this list (since that is the meaning at that time of "inhabitant"), and that none of the eleven men listed above as 1635 arrivals were proprietors (claiming, perhaps, that the grants of land excluded a proprietary share). But nine of the eleven appear in the 1638 Charlestown land inventory, with collections of land that indicate they were proprietors at that time. To accept this argument, we would have to assume that all nine resided in Charlestown in 1635 but did not become proprietors until 1636 or later, an unlikely assumption.

We seem to be left with a contradiction: the placement of this list in the town records (as corrected in the discussion above) points toward a date of January 1635/6, whereas the analysis of individuals would lead us to an interpretation of January 1634/5.

We should remember, however, that the town records as we have received them were reworked and rewritten by John Greene, and he himself may have misinterpreted the date of this list. The evidence from the analysis of individuals is very strong, and so in future sketches this list [ChTR 15] will be reported as January 1634/5. All sketches already published which make use of this record should be corrected accordingly.

Great Migration Study Project
101 Newbury Street
Boston, MA 02116

Great Migration Newsletter

Vol. 7   January-March 1998   No. 1

PASSENGER SHIPS OF 1635 - Part I

In the last volume of the *Great Migration Newsletter*, we studied and identified the ships that brought passengers to New England in 1634, the first of the two years to be covered in the second phase of the Great Migration Study Project [*GMN* 6:9-10, 16-18, 28]. In this issue and the next two, we will take a close look at the passenger vessels that came to New England in 1635.

We have more information on the ships and their passengers for 1635 than for any other year, largely because of the survival of the London Port Book for that year, but also because several other passenger lists survive for some of the outports. Given this wealth of detail, our examination of the passenger traffic for this year will have to serve as the model for what must have happened in each of the remaining years in the decade, inasmuch as migration continued at the same pace through 1640, but the records for 1636 and later have not survived so extensively.

Although the London Port Book will be the principal source of information for this series of articles, we will, as we did with the year 1634, proceed chronologically in discussing the arrivals of ships.

As was usually the case, the first ships to arrive in New England were the smaller fishing and trading vessels, connected in some way with "the Eastern parts." In January, Governor Winthrop reported that "[a]bout the middle of this month, Mr. Allerton's pinnace came from the French about Port Royal" [WJ 184]. This vessel was the *White Angel* of Bristol, which Allerton had recently acquired from the London merchants who were involved with the plantation at Plymouth [Bradford 226-45 *et passim*].

The *White Angel* may not have been returning from England on this voyage, but only from a coasting expedition to Port Royal, and so there were probably no passengers from England on board. By June the *White Angel* was at Richmond Island, taking on freight and about to return to England [Trelawny Papers 56, 58, 60].

The supply vessel for Richmond Island in 1635 was the *Speedwell,* which arrived on 26 April, with Narias Hawkins as master. There were at least seven passengers on this vessel, and perhaps more [GMN 6:33-34].

The arrival of the *Speedwell* was the occasion of concern among the settlers at Massachusetts Bay, indicating the fears of the English settlers about attacks by the French and by pirates. On 26 April 1635, Winthrop tells us that

> An alarm was raised in all our towns, and the governor and assistants met at Boston, and sent forth a shallop to Cape Ann, to discover what ships were there. For the fishermen had brought in word to Marblehead, that two ships had been hovering upon the coast all day, one of about four hundred tons, and the other three hundred and fifty, and were gone in to Cape Ann. But it proved to be only one ship of eight tons, bound for Richman's Isle, and the other a small pinnace of ten tons [WJ 188].

The larger ship was the *Speedwell*, but the smaller is unidentified.

One of the most interesting arrivals of 1635 was the unnamed vessel from Weymouth in Dorsetshire. The list is date "the 20th of March 1635," which has been

(continued on page 2)

EDITOR'S EFFUSIONS

As this issue of the *Great Migration Newsletter* goes to the printer, we are also putting the finishing touches on a book which will reprint the first five volumes of the *Newsletter*. In the early years of the *Newsletter*, there were far fewer subscribers than we now have, and we know that there are many people who would like to have a complete set of the back issues. The reprint volume will make that possible.

Also, having all the issues in one place, with a consolidated name index, as well as indexes of the principal subjects and places covered, will make it much easier for those interested in the Great Migration to make use of this material.

In the first five years of the *Great Migration Newsletter,* we covered in detail all of the towns which were settled from 1620 to 1633, the period covered by the three volumes of *The Great Migration Begins*. We also treated many of the types of records which were used in creating the sketches in those volumes, such sources as lists of freemen and proprietors' records. The *Newsletter* in those years, then, may be considered an extension of the essay on sources which appears in the first volume of *The Great Migration Begins*.

We will soon be sending out a brochure giving more details on this reprint volume, along with ordering information.

The next Great Migration Study Project publication to go to press after the *Newsletter* reprint will be the first in the next series of volumes, covering the first part of the alphabet for the years 1634 and 1635. The first half of this book, which will be about the size of one of the volumes in the first series, is now ready for the printer. An advanced draft of the second half of the book is done, so all that remains is the polishing and revising of this section, and then the proofreading and indexing. (This work will not occupy the time of the entire Great Migration team, so work is already under way on the second volume of Series II, for the letters D through H.)

This work will consume most of the summer, and by the time of the next issue of this *Newsletter*, we will be ready to announce a firm date for the first volume of Series II.

Robert Charles Anderson, FASG   Editor
Aileen Novick   Production Assistant

The Great Migration Newsletter is published quarterly by the Great Migration Study Project, a project of the New England Historic Genealogical Society, 101 Newbury Street, Boston MA 02116

The subscription rate is $12 for one year and $20 for two years.

(continued from page 1)

interpreted as 20 March 1635/6 by both Hotten and Coldham [Hotten 283-86; Coldham 175-76]. Convincing evidence, however, shows that this vessel must have sailed in the spring of 1635. The list is headed by "Joseph Hall of Somerset a minister aged 40 years," who is Reverend Joseph Hull. On 2 September 1635 Joseph Hull, William Reade, Richard Adams, John Upham and Robert Lovell, all of whom are on this passenger list, were admitted freemen of Massachusetts Bay [MBCR 1:371], implying that they had been admitted to some church, in this case the newly established church at Weymouth [GMN 6:29].

Banks and others claim that this unnamed vessel arrived on 5 May 1635 (the day before the meeting of the General Court). This is not impossible, inasmuch as many of the other vessels crossed the Atlantic in six weeks in the spring of 1635, and if this vessel left Weymouth on 20 March 1634/5, an arrival in the first week of May could have been accomplished, and so, pending further evidence, we will accept this as the date of arrival. However, the earliest evidence we have for the presence of these passengers in New England is an order at the court of 8 July of that year, in which "There is leave granted to 21 families to sit down at Wessaguscus" [MBCR 1:149]. Winthrop also relates this story, and further states that "Mr. Hull, a minister in England," was part of this group [WJ 1:194]. It may be, then, that this vessel did not arrive in New England until early June, along with a number of other ships, including, as we shall soon see, several from London.

On 25 March 1635, Emmanuel Downing wrote, probably from London, to John Winthrop Jr., who was then at Groton in Suffolk, to discuss some family matters. He then closed the letter with a passage which explains much about the organization of the London Port Book, and the procedure for organizing the passenger vessels [WP 3:195]:

> I do hear there will go at least 20 ships this year to the plantation [i.e, New England]. There is one at the Custom House appointed to received Certificates and give discharges to all such as shall go to the plantation. Some that are going to N.E. went to him to know what they should do. He bade them bring him any Certificate from minister, churchwardens or justice that they were honest men and he would give them their pass. They asked him what subsidy men should do. He answered that he could not tell who were subsidy men, and would discharge them upon their Certificates.

The dockside official was telling those who wished to sail for New England, but who were not sure that they met the government's requirements for passage, that he would take

(continued on page 8)

Focus on BOSTON FIRST CHURCH

Reverend James Allen's
Church Census of 1688

by Melinde Lutz Sanborn, F.A.S.G.

On 9 January 1687/8, pastor James Allen set about making a list of the living members of his Boston First Church. With over a half century of admissions to cover, he employed the early book of records to methodically consider the names in their original order. His twelve-page list, with subsequent annotations, is reprinted in the three-volume *Records of the First Church of Boston*, in *Publications of The Colonial Society of Massachusetts*, Vols. 39-41, pp. 84-95, from which the following discussion is drawn.

Reverend Allen's list comprised a number of useful features. It consisted of two columns per page, the men on the left and the women on the right. To the left of each of these columns were 1) a chronological column of dates, being the year the person became a church member, and 2) a short column added at an indeterminate later date in which the surviving members are counted. The regular numbering stops in the men's list after James Burgess, #33, although a #40 appears eight living members later, suggesting perhaps that #33 properly belongs to Jeremiah Dummer, in the place immediately before James Burgess in the list. The regular numbering stops in the women's list after Deborah Faire #80, although a #120 and a #140 appear against living women members #122 and #139, respectively.

Following each name in both main columns, a later annotation of "dead" may occur. In the great majority of cases, members annotated as dead were not numbered, but in ten cases, the dead were numbered. Of these ten, five can be demonstrated to have died in the year 1698, three have unknown death dates, one died in 1693 and one in 1694.

At first glance, this might seem to indicate that the numbering was done just prior to the earliest numbered death date, 1693, to make a count of the living persons at that time. However, the known death dates of a significant number of *un*numbered persons fall after 1693, invalidating that interpretation.

A total of living men church members was made between the dates of 28 August 1692 and 23 April 1693: "In all alive, 95." A total of living women church members was made between 17 and 30 October 1692: "220," yet six en-

tries later, another total is given next to the date 19 March 169[2/]3: "260," which cannot be accounted for by any plausible explanation. A total of living women church members was made in late 1696 between the dates 25 October 1696 and 8 November 1696: "294 Alive 1696." An actual count of the list, omitting those indicated as "dead," comes to within three of this number.

To the end of his list, Mr. Allen appended the names of persons who were cast out, or excommunicated, from the church. It is somewhat ironic that the surviving man of greatest membership seniority was the excommunicate John Hurd, who joined the Boston church with his wife, Mary, on 7 July 1639, but was cast out several times "for drunkenness, having had often warning thereof," between 1649 and 1666.

We learn something of the motivations for the list as we look at it more closely. We see from the pages immediately preceding that for some time prior to June 1681, Elder John Wiswall kept the list of admissions, but toward the end of his life, it was evidently incomplete. In 1687/8, James Allen set about reconstructing the list, giving at least an approximate year of admission from 22 May 1681 through 1686. His list beginning on 28 August 1687 is once again contemporary. "Phalti Mansfield" appears in this reconstructed list, against a 1685 date, but her name, along with others, has been crossed out, suggesting that Allen's memory was faulty.

For every apparent rule, there is an exception, however. The second woman member, Katherine Douse, appears out of her original chronological order, but the list is fairly uniform thereafter. The count also contains errors, including two number "5"s in the women's list, and the inclusion of at least one person who must have been dead when the numbering was done (James Burgess, who died 27 November 1690, assuming the #33 is correctly assigned to him).

We can detect at least one error in the names themselves. Allen calls his fifth surviving woman member "Mary Woodward now Harwood," while it is clear from other records that her first name was actually Rachel. This was probably a simple transposition, since a Mary Woodward joined the church less than a year before Rachel, in 1641.

By 1687/8, all but two of the original members who joined in the 1630s were dead. These two were Margaret (_____) Cooke, who joined in 1630-1, and Mary (_____) Hurd, who joined in 1639.

Thanks to Mr. Allen's systematic approach, by process of elimination, we learn many details regarding the lives of the early church members, particularly of the deaths of many for whom we have no other death record. New maiden and married names are discovered through his practice of indicating first a woman member's name when she joined the church, followed by "now _____," giving a new surname. The residence of the living members is assumed to be Boston, except in those cases where Allen specified differently.

In the period from the founding of the church until 1641, there are many instances of single women, maidservants to some prominent family or other, about whom we know nothing more. The further career of Ann Nidds, for instance, who joined the church "maid servant to our brother Willyam Brenton" on the original list, can now be asserted to have ended in the fifty-four years between her admission in 1634 and 1687/8. It can be said that Martha Blackett "maid servant to our teacher John Cotton," who joined in 1634, Mary Hudd, " maid servant to our brother John Winthropp the Elder," and Rebecca Dixon "our brother Richard Bellingham's maidservant," also died before 1687/8. Efforts to identify these women, and any others who were early members of the Boston church but failed to make the 1687/8 list, must pass this muster as a further test of their identities.

The entire original Wheelwright contingent, dismissed on 6 February 1638/9 to "the Falls of Paschataqua" [Exeter], had died by 1687/8. So, too, it was with the cluster of members who came from the church at Dorchester on 23 March 1643/4.

IDENTIFYING WIVES

We are also told the 1687/8 whereabouts of each living member and the current surname of women who had married since their admission. Along with many who had properly recorded marriage records, we discover 16 without recorded marriages: Martha Stanbury "now Cozens," [Katherine] Naney "now Naylor," Elizabeth Brooking "now Groves," Hannah Ballantine "now Long," Hannah Hull "now Knight," Elizabeth Stevens "now Bligh," Deborah Waite "now Paddy," Elizabeth Lawson "now Twing," Elizabeth Clesby "now Goodwin," Elizabeth Eldridge "now Parris," Elizabeth Pounding "now Bridgham," Hannah

Harrison "now Marrion," Ruth Marshall "now Fairfield," Mercy Bozworth "now Rolestone," Ann Manning "now Gerish," and Judeth Beers "now Allin." While the identities of each of the foregoing women were suspected, this list constitutes proof. (Several of the members named above had joined the church as married women, so their earlier surnames were not maiden names.)

Nine Marriages

A search of the literature suggests that in nine more instances we have new evidence bearing upon the unsuspected identities of the following women: "Goody Shurwood now Nicholson," "Temperance Willis now Barnes," "Hester Loxton now Buckley," "Elizabeth Davie now Taylor," "Palty Mansfield now Dorrel," "Rebecca Price now Gibson," "Hannah Pease now Prouse," "Abigall Porter now Wyer" and "Mary Arnold formerly Clough."

1. The "Goody Sheerod" who joined the church 15 December 1666 was Hannah Bumstead, who married at Boston 18 April 1659 Thomas Shearer [BVR 1:71]. This is supported by the fact that "the wife of Ambrose Dawes" was admitted to the church the same day, she being Mary Bumstead, sister of Hannah. Perhaps Hannah was the "child of one Bumstead, a member of the church ... that fell from a gallery in the [Roxbury] meeting house about eighteen feet high, and brake the arm and shoulder ... and it pleased the Lord also that this child was soon perfectly recovered" [WJ 2:203].

Hannah and Mary's father, Thomas Bumstead, named them in his will of 25 May 1677, calling Hannah the wife of Thomas Sherwood [SPR 6:530]. Thomas Sherwood/Shearer had died by 29 January 1677/8, when Hannah, his relict, took administration of his estate [SPR 12:357]. She was thus available to remarry to a Nicholson before 1687/8. She was still "Hannah Sherrard, widow," on 10 May 1682, when her land bounded property sold by the executors of John Morse [SLR 12:203].

While there were four Nicholsons in Boston in the early 1680s, only George Nicholson had a wife Hannah. George never became a member of the Boston church, but he died before 4 April 1693, when widow Hannah married at Boston to Samuel Ruck. She was called "Hannah Ruck late Nicholson" when she took administration on George's estate [SPR 14:162]. Because George had no children, his property was divided between widow Hannah and his siblings, who included Edward Nicholson, Citizen and gunmaker of London, Robert Nicholson of Brough near Stainmore, Westmoreland, and deceased sister Annas Kidd. His childless status is also probably the reason why Torrey found no literature on him and did not include him in his *New England Marriages Prior to 1700*. When Hannah died in 1703, her son from her first marriage, Alexander Shearrer, cooper, was granted letters of administration on the "estate of his mother Hannah Ruck, deceased...with the consent of your father-in-law Samuell Ruck" [SPR 15:220].

2. "Temparance Wills" was admitted a member 23 May 1669 and became the second wife of James Barnes by 28 September 1680 when they recorded the birth of a son [BVR 151]. She is very probably the Temperance, daughter of Michael Wills "member of Ch. of Dorchester," who was baptized at Boston 9 April 1648 [BVR 28].

3. "Ester Lockstone" was both admitted and baptized 21 August 1670; her baptismal record calls her "aged 20 years" [BVR 117], so Luxton was probably her maiden name. Her subsequent marriage may well have been to Thomas Bulkely, with whom she had children recorded in Boston, beginning with Eleanor on 16 September 1685 [BVR 164].

4. "Elizabeth Davey" was admitted 5 March 1671/2. A candidate for her husband is Richard Taylor of Boston who died in 1673 and had a second wife Elizabeth.

5. "Palti Mainsffeild" was admitted 16 May 1675 and married John Dorrell, with whom she had a first recorded child, Margaret, born at Boston 21 July 1680 [BVR 151].

6. "Rebecca Prince" was admitted 9 March 1678/9, very likely soon after her marriage to Job Prince. *NE Marriages Before 1700* indexes her as Rebecca (Phippen) (Baldwin) (Prince) Clark, wife and widow successively of Samuel Baldwin, Job Prince and George Clark. The 1687 list would add a Gibson marriage between Prince and Clark.

7. "Goody Pease," admitted 11 April 1680, was probably the wife of John Pease, who, with wife Hannah recorded children in Boston starting with Elizabeth, born 15 January 1677[/8?] [BVR 142]. After Pease's will was probated in 1683 [SPR 6:440], a Roger Prouse appeared with wife Hannah in Boston, recording a child, Peter Prouse, born 1 May 1686 [BVR 170].

8. No contemporary record of admission survives for Abigail Porter or Mary Arnold. Both Abigail and Mary probably joined the church between June 1681 and August 1687/8, the period of the imperfect list. Abigail was the daughter of "our brother Abell Porter," and was baptized in the church 13 December 1646. The 1687 list solves the mystery of the identity of Abigail's husband. Her father, Abel Porter Sr. of Boston, left a will dated 15 September 1685 in which he made a bequest to "my daughter Abigail and her children after her," but never mentioned her married name [SPR 6:527]. Peter Weare and Abigail had been married since about 1683, and had recorded one child by the time her father wrote his will [BVR 164]. Since Abigail was almost forty at this time, unless her father was being unduly optimistic, Abigail had by this time probably had

children with an earlier, also unrecorded, husband, thus suggesting an avenue for further research.

9. Mary (Clough) Arnold was a special case. While she had no record of admission, she was "cast out for receiving stolen goods, filthiness in speech and carriage, [and] impenitence" by unanimous consent on 19 April 1691, and evidently brought back into the church again on 26 April 1691 [BChR 91].

MOBILITY IN RESIDENCY

We do not learn as much from the mentions of residency. As expected, the great majority of living members remained in Boston. By a curious twist of fate, two of the most senior surviving church members were no longer living in New England; Nehemiah and Hannah Bourne, who joined in 1642, were in London in 1687/8. Nathaniel Rennolds was in "N: Bristall" [Bristol, then in Plymouth Colony, now in Rhode Island]. Henry Allin, merchant was "in old Engl." as were Mistress Norman, Stephen Mason, Mistress Usher, and John Squire.

ANNOTATIONS OF THE DEAD

Probably over a span of many years, but perhaps no later than 1698, more notations were made to the list. This time, the original list was amended to show which of the 1687/8 survivors were "dead, dismissed, excommunicated or gone." Bartholomew Tippin was "gone" as was Samuel Parris. In this short span of years, a staggering 89 members had died, truly marking the end of the Great Migration generation.

Deaths Supported By Vital Records

Of these 89 members who died between January 1687/8 and say 1698, very few had recorded death records. No such records survive for Boston for the year 1688, but of the 1689-1698 era deaths, only 26 appeared in the Boston or Charlestown vital records. Certainly some of these people may have died somewhere else, but since they were still members of the Boston church at their deaths, that number was likely very small.

Of the 50 dead men, only 20 had Boston or Charlestown death records. Of the 39 dead women, only 6 had Boston or Charlestown death records. These 40% and 15% ratios may be representative of, or higher than, the wider population in Boston as a whole. Since church members, especially Boston First Church members, were frequently people of means, and had already displayed their abilities to follow procedure by taking the necessary steps to become members, their families may have been more likely to properly report deaths and pay the fee for recording.

Deaths Supported By Probate Records

These annotations can be checked for death dates in other records. Quite a few of the men left probates, a few of the women, also. Of the 50 dead men, twenty-three had Suffolk probates between 1687/8 and 1698, or 46%: Henry Allen, Edward Ashley, Nicholas Baxter, Jonathan Bridgham, James Burges, Bartholomew Cheevers, Thomas Dewer, Hugh Drury, John Dyer, John Glover, Joseph How, Richard Knight, John Lowell, Samuel Mason, Samuel Peirse, Ephraim Sale, Robert Sanderson, John Search, James Townsend, John Tuttle, John Twing, Joseph Webb and Robert Williams.

Of the 39 dead women, only five left Suffolk probates in the same period, or roughly 13%: Mistress Elizabeth Sanderson, Ann Gerish, Hester Houchin, Mistress Susannah Oxenbridge and Sarah Franks. Not considered in these figures are those who may have left testamentary deeds, which might be another source of approximate death dates.

Deaths Mentioned By Sewall

There are other sources to be used to support the deaths found in this list. Samuel Sewall mentioned thirteen of them in his diaries, nine men and four women. For some he provided details of their demise. Perhaps the most interesting was the excommunicate John Hurd, about whose death Sewall gives substantial detail, naming the many people who came to pray with him, and concludes with "Sept. 22 [1690]. His former carriage was very startling and amazing to us. About One at night he died..." [Sewall 1:267].

Tuesday, Feb. 7. [1688] My Aunt Gerrish dies between 7. and 8.... Had the Measles lately, and now by Flux, vapours and others inconveniences, expires before I had so much as heard of her being ill [Sewall 1:159].

Wednesday, Apr. 4. [1688] At night Sam. Marion's wife hangs herself in the Chamber, fastening a Cord to the Rafter-Joist. Two or three swore she was distracted, and had been for some time, and so she was buried in the burying place [Sewall 1:163].

Dec. 3. [1690] Brother Needham dies and Goodw. Deacon [Sewall 1:271].

Feb. 12, 1691/2 Joshua Atwater dies, falling off the outward Wharf; he was drowned about 2. or 3. in the morning, intangled in the wood as the Jury brought it in; was going on board the Sloop Mary. Was excommunicated [Sewall 1:289].

March 23, 1691/2 ...About 5. P.M. Moses Bradford, essaying to draw a youth out of the Water at Capt. Wing's Con-duit, fell in himself and was drown'd, many people round about trying to save him. Boy was taken out alive [Sewall 1:289].

Augt. 25. [1695] Robt Williams the Bell-Ringer, Publisher and Grave-digger died this morn. He was suddenly stricken the fifth-day before, just after his ringing the five-a-clock Bell; fell down as essayed to go up his own stairs, and I think so continued speechless till death [Sewall 1:337-38].

Oct. 5, 1694 ...Cous. Mary Dummer dies about break of day... [Sewall 1:321].

In other cases Sewall merely mentions the death or burial: Lieut. Ephraim Sale [2 Dec 1690], Mr. Robert Saunderson [7 Oct 1693], Bartholomew Cheever [18 Dec 1693], Mr. Joseph Webb [11 Oct 1698] and Mr. John Glover [25 Sept 1696] [Sewall 1:271, 314, 316, 356, 399].

With his social connections, it is not surprising that Sewall mentioned a fair number of the persons who had vital records and/or probates. His lifelong interest in wealthy widows is seen in the disproportionate numbers of them he memorialized. In fact, 12% of the women were mentioned in Sewall, as compared to 18% of the men, the closest margin between the sexes from any source.

Of the 58% of men who had some formal identification of death date from the three sources mentioned above, 46% left probates, 40% left recorded deaths in the town records, and 18% were mentioned by Sewall. 12% of the men appeared in all three sources, and 45% had both recorded deaths and probates.

Of the 31% of women members who had some formal identification of death date as discussed above, 15% left recorded deaths, 13% left probates, and 12% were mentioned by Sewall. None of the women appeared in all three sources, and only about 2% had both recorded deaths and probates.

The 20 unrecorded men and 26 unrecorded women may be found in the records of other towns, may have moved away without being noted, or may have left testamentary deeds. Identification of several of the women members was hampered by the omission of their given names. Although each woman was checked in Torrey for a possible remarriage after 1687/8, no new marriages were found. It may be representative of the Boston population as a whole in this time frame that 42% of men and 69% of women are missing from the most frequently used sources for death records.

Pastor Allen merely wanted to keep tabs on the number of members in his congregation, but for us, his annotated list brings reliable insight into an era of very erratic record-keeping.

RECENT LITERATURE

John Bradley Arthaud, "The Sallows-Solas-Sollis-Sollace Family: Mariners of Salem and Beverly, Massachusetts," *The American Genealogist* 72 (1997):1-14, 115-34. Arthaud presents an account of Michael Sallows, immigrant to Salem by 1635, and seven generations of his descendants.

Gale Ion Harris, "John[1] and Mary (Hart) Greet of Westfield, Massachusetts, Southold, Long Island, and Wethersfield, Connecticut: With Notes on the Family of Edmund[1] Hart and on Charity[2] Hart, Wife of Thomas[2] Loveland of Glastonbury, Connecticut," *TAG* 72 (1997):42-48. Harris identifies two more daughters of the immigrant Edmund Hart: Mary, who married John Greet, and Charity, who married Thomas Loveland.

Gordon L. Remington, "The Two Daniel Footes of Cambridge, England: Brother and Nephew of Nathaniel[1] Foote of Wethersfield, Connecticut, and Joshua[1] Foote of Providence, Rhode Island," *TAG* 72 (1997):49-55. Following in the footsteps of several distinguished predecessors, the author has explored and clarified more ramifications of the Foote family.

Craig Partridge, "The English Origin of Edmund[1] Tapp of New Haven and Milford, Connecticut," *TAG* 72 (1997):65-80, 73 (1998):65-73. Partridge presents extensive evidence demonstrating that Edmund Tapp derived from Bennington and Felmersham in Bedfordshire.

Gordon L. Remington, "Alice Brotherton, Wife of John[1] Doggett of Martha's Vineyard," *TAG* 72 (1997):89-100. Remington shows that the first wife of this John Doggett was Alice Brotherton of Husborne Crawley, Bedfordshire.

Robert Charles Anderson, "William Ballard Is Really William Bullard," *TAG* 72 (1997):135-36. The author argues that two published records which have been ascribed to William Ballard of Lynn in fact pertain to William Bullard of Dedham.

Eugene Cole Zubrinsky, "'To Say It Doesn't Make It So': Clues to the Probable Identity of the Wife of Jonathan[2] Bliss of Rehoboth, Massachusetts," *The New England Historical and Genealogical Register* 151 (1997):31-37. While discussing the identity of the wife of Jonathan Bliss, Zubrinsky has much to say about the family of his father, the immigrant Thomas Bliss of Braintree, and also about the family of George Puffer of Braintree.

Marya Myers and Donald W. James, Jr., "A New Look at the Family of Francis and Philip James of Hingham: Immigrant Ancestors," *NEHGR* 151 (1997):61-86. The authors present a full treatment of Francis James and Philip James, immigrants to Hingham in 1638. Francis James "apparently had no children"; the first few generations of the posterity of Philip are included in the article.

Gale Ion Harris, "William[1] and Mary Briggs of Boston and the Connecticut Valley with Notes on their Sons-in-Law John Harris and Wolston Brockway," *NEHGR* 151 (1997):87-101. Harris sets forth a complete account of William and Mary Briggs, who first appeared in Boston in 1642; they later resided in Wethersfield, Middletown and Lyme, Connecticut. Special attention is paid to their daughter Hannah, who married first John Harris and second Wolston Brockway.

David L. Greene, "The English Origin (and Spiritual Turmoil) of John[1] Ingersoll of Westfield, Massachusetts," *NEHGR* 151 (1997):153-65. Although John Ingersoll did not arrive in New England until more than a decade after the end of the Great Migration, this article is important to the Great Migration in its discussion of the alleged connection, now shown definitively to be false, to Richard Ingersoll, 1629 immigrant to Salem.

Richard H. Benson, "Probable English Origins of James and Alice Nash of Boston and Weymouth," *NEHGR* 151 (1997):166-70. Benson provides evidence to show that James Nash and his wife Alice of Boston and Weymouth were from Great Missenden, Buckinghamshire.

Myrtle Stevens Hyde and John Plummer, "The English Ancestry of New England Settlers Joshua and Anthony Fisher [Fisher and Bert]," *NEHGR* 151 (1997):171-91. The authors have traced four generations of the paternal ancestry of the brothers Joshua and Anthony Fisher, with additional information on the ancestry of Margerie Bert, their paternal grandmother.

Wayne H.M. Wilcox, "Capt. Thomas Hawkins, Shipwright, of London and Dorchester, Massachusetts, and Three Generations of His Descendants," *NEHGR* 151 (1997):192-216. Wilcox provides a detailed account of the family of Thomas Hawkins, resident of Dorchester by 1636, along with his descendants to the fourth generation.

(continued from page 2)

whatever documents they presented at face value, and would not make further inquiries. This passage provides further evidence for the argument that these statements of loyalty to the government and to the established church should not be taken seriously. Presumably, most of the passengers of Puritan leanings sought out a minister or justice of the peace who was of their same persuasion to provide the certificate which they could carry to the Custom House official.

The London Port Book of 1635 included lists of persons desiring licenses for passage not just to New England, but also the the English colonies in the Chesapeake and the Caribbean, and also to a number of locations in the Netherlands. A number of partial transcripts of this document have been published, but none include the names of those going to the Low Countries.

Of the various published versions which include the New England-bound ships, the best remains that prepared by Hotten more than a century ago. His readings are accurate, and also adhere most closely to the original arrangement of the material. Coldham's version is also accurate in the readings, but not so assiduous in maintaining the original order. The volume prepared by Colonel Banks, *The Planters of the Commonwealth*, is the worst, as he made many

unwarranted assumptions in his listings, and it is not always easy to determine what came from the Port Book and what was added by Banks.

The first persons to arrive at the London docks ready to go to New England were "Peter Howson xxxj years & his wife Ellin Howson 39 years old," who brought in their certificates on 11 March 1634/5, from the minister of St Giles Cripplegate, London. Also on this day "Thomas Stares," aged 31, and "Suzan Johnson," aged 12, presented their certificates from "Turris London[ensis]" [i.e., the Tower of London, presumably meaning the parish of St Peter in the Tower]. These four passengers were not assigned to any vessel, which may have been a simple clerical oversight, or may have meant that no ship bound for New England was yet available at London [Hotten 42].

The next entry pertaining to New England was on 16 March 1634/5, the only entry for the *Christian* [Hotten 42-43]. Twenty-seven names appeared in this list, most of them unattached males in their late teens, twenties, or early thirties, along with the family of Francis Stiles. As we shall see, the makeup of this vessel was unlike that of others to New England in 1635, and as such it was the last manifestation of the "old" way of organizing migration to New England.

(to be continued in Volume 7, No. 2)

Great Migration Study Project
101 Newbury Street
Boston, MA 02116

Great Migration Newsletter

| Vol. 7 | April-June 1998 | No. 2 |

PASSENGER SHIPS OF 1635 - Part II

In the last issue of the *Newsletter*, we began our discussion of the arrival of passenger vessels in New England in 1635. After listing some of the smaller ships which arrived relatively early in the year, we began to describe the ships and passengers recorded in the London Port Book for that year.

At the end of the first installment, we learned that the *Christian* took on twenty-seven passengers on 16 March 1634/5. This voyage was organized by Sir Richard Saltonstall (now back in England after a brief residence in Watertown) and some of his associates, who were hoping to establish a settlement to their own liking, not under the influence of John Winthrop and like-minded men. The passengers on the *Christian* were mostly carpenters, under the management of Francis Stiles, sent ahead to build a town up the Connecticut River, on the site of what would become Windsor. On 16 June 1635 Governor Winthrop reported that a "bark of forty tons arrived, set forth with twenty servants, by Sir Richard Saltonstall, to go plant at Connecticut" [WJ 1:192].

Before Stiles and his work party could make much progress, the advance party of the settlers from Dorchester had arrived and interfered with the plans set in motion by Saltonstall. In the end, Saltonstall's proposed settlement failed, most of the passengers of the *Christian* were absorbed by Wethersfield and the other river towns, and Saltonstall and his associates moved on to other fields [WJ 1:204; WP 3:217-9, 229-30].

Soon after the small complement of the *Christian* came to the London docks, several other ships also began to take on passengers. The *Planter* received its first passengers on 22 March, and continued to accept them until 11 April. Other vessels which were taking on passengers at about this time (with their beginning and ending dates) were the *Hopewell* (1 April to 6 April), the *Rebecca* (6 April to 9 April), the *Elizabeth* (8 April to 17 April) and the *Increase* (15 April to 18 April) [Hotten 43-68].

At about this same time, ships in at least three other ports were taking on passengers. Throughout the month of

March passengers in the Weald region of Kent were obtaining certificates of conformity and appearing in Sandwich to sign up for passage on the *Hercules*. About twenty families or individuals appeared, comprising just over a hundred passengers [Drake's Founders 82-84; NEHGR 75:217-26].

At Weymouth in Dorset, the *Marygould*, Edward Cuttance master, was taking on goods and passengers on 30 March 1635; the only passengers known for certain are "Thomas Holbrook, his wife and children" [NGSQ 71:173]. Given this date and the presence of Thomas Holbrook and his family, this vessel is almost certainly the one with passenger list dated at Weymouth 20 March 1635 that carried the Reverend Joseph Hull and his company of more than twenty families from Broadway and Batcombe in Somerset, a total of 106 passengers [Hotten 283-86].

Then, on 5 April 1635, a number of persons "shipped themselves at the town of [South]Hampton, in the *James* of London, 300 tons, William Cooper Master," for New England [Drake's Founders 55-57]. "The total number of these men, youths, and boys are 53 persons, besides the wives and children of diverse of these" [Drake's Founders 57]. Based on this statement, this ship probably carried between 150 and 200 passengers.

We have, therefore, evidence of at least eight passenger vessels preparing for departure to New England in late

(continued on page 10)

EDITOR'S EFFUSIONS

When the *Great Migration Newsletter* began, the *Focus* section was conceived as a place to discuss in detail an early New England community, with inquiry into the settlement of the town and the early records of the town. Beginning with Volume Six, the focus of the *Focus* section has begun to change somewhat.

First, Pat Hatcher and Melinde Sanborn investigated in great detail an aspect of the church records of Roxbury and Boston. Then, in this issue appears a study of an important event in early Cambridge history, the almost total turnover in population in late 1635 and early 1636.

These *Focus* installments have maintained the emphasis on individual towns, but have been more narrowly defined than were earlier efforts. In the next issue of the *Newsletter*, we will move in a different direction, examining the early records generated by the Middlesex county court. The *Focus* section will continue to have installments of the older variety, but will at the same time continue to evolve by looking at a wider range of topics.

Most of you have received a brochure describing the volume which reprints all issues from the first five years of the *Great Migration Newsletter*. This volume also includes a consolidated index of names, places and subjects for all these issues, and may be purchased for $19.50 ($17.55 for NEHGS members), plus $3.50 for shipping; orders should be sent to NEHGS Sales, 160 N. Washington St., Boston MA 02114-2120.

The sales of this volume have been very gratifying, and the first printing is nearly gone, with a second printing to be made in the near future. An unfortunate error has been discovered in the name index, from which all entries for the surnames between Bates and Bush were omitted. This problem will be corrected for the second printing. Those who have already purchased the volume may obtain a copy of this section of the index by sending a stamped, self-addressed envelop to *Index Insert, Great Migration Newsletter*, 101 Newbury St., Boston MA 02116.

Robert Charles Anderson, FASG   Editor
Aileen Novick   Production Assistant

The Great Migration Newsletter is published quarterly by the Great Migration Study Project, a project of the New England Historic Genealogical Society, 101 Newbury Street, Boston MA 02116

The subscription rate is $12 for one year and $20 for two years.

(continued from page 9)

March or early April 1635. What evidence do we have that these vessels actually made the voyage? In early June Winthrop reported a number of ship arrivals. On the 3rd, he noted that "Here arrived two Dutch ships," which brought cattle, and there "arrived also, the same day, the *James*, a ship of three hundred tons, with cattle and passengers, which came all safe from Southampton within the same time [i.e., "five weeks three days"]. Mr. Graves was master, who had come every year for these seven years" [WJ 1:191-92]. This accounts for one of the eight ships, although the master must have been changed at the last minute.

Then, on 7 June, Winthrop noted that the "Lord's day there came in seven other ships, and one to Salem, and four more to the mouth of the bay, with store of passengers and cattle. They came all within six weeks" [WJ 1:192]. Here are twelve ships, apparently all with passengers, and we have knowledge of only seven ships (the eight described above, less the *James* of Southampton) which could have arrived this early. Six weeks back from 7 June would place us in the third week of April, which corresponds closely with the last date on which the London ships listed above were closing down their passenger lists. Thus, seven of the twelve ships would have been the *Planter*, the *Hopewell*, the *Rebecca*, the *Elizabeth* and the *Increase* (all from London), the *Marygould* of Weymouth (see below) and the *Hercules* of Sandwich.

In 1666, in the course of a Weymouth land dispute, Thomas Holbrooke, who had sailed on the *Marygould*, deposed that "in the year 1635 this deponent came to New England with Mr. Hull & that company, we came ashore at Dorchester the seventh of June & Mr. Hull & company went to the place that is now called Waymoth" [SJC Case #815]. If we accept this thirty-year old memory at face value, then the *Marygould* was one of the ships that Winthrop reported as arriving on 7 June 1635.

We are left, then, with six vessels which departed England in late April, apparently with passengers, and arrived in New England on 7 June 1635, for which we have no record.

While these ships were crossing the north Atlantic, at least three more ships still in England were preparing for departure. Two of these ships were at the London docks, the *Susan & Ellen* accepting passengers from 13 April to 9 May, and the *Elizabeth & Anne* from 17 April to 14 May [Hotten 54-78]. The port book for Weymouth includes a list of passengers for the *Hopewell* (clearly a different ship from the one that sailed from London), dated 8 May 1635 [NEHGR 71:173-74].

If these ships all left England in mid-May, and also crossed in the space of six weeks, then they should have arrived in

(continued on page 16)

Focus on CAMBRIDGE

"STRAITNESS FOR WANT OF LAND"

With the rapid rate of increase in immigration beginning in 1634, the Massachusetts Bay towns that had been settled at the time of the arrival of the Winthrop Fleet were becoming more and more crowded. On 14 May 1634 the General Court granted leave "to the inhabitants of Newe Towne [Cambridge] to seek out some convenient place for them, with promise that it shall be confirmed unto them, to which they may remove their habitations, or have as an addition to that which already they have, provided they do not take it in any place to prejudice a plantation already settled" [MBCR 1:119]. Governor Winthrop reported at this time that "[t]hose of Newtown [Cambridge] complained of straitness for want of land, especially meadow, and desired leave of the court to look out either for enlargement or removal, which was granted; whereupon they sent men to see Agawam and Merimack, and gave out they would remove, etc." [WJ 1:157].

The most detailed evidence we have for this problem derives from a letter written in late 1634 or early 1635 by John Pratt, a Cambridge resident [GMB 3:1507]. The letter itself does not survive, but Winthrop reports that at a Court of Assistants held on 3 November 1635, "John Pratt of Newtown was questioned about the letter he wrote into England, wherein he asserted diverse things, which were untrue and of ill report, for the state of the country, as that here was nothing but rocks, and sands, and salt marshes, etc." [WJ 1:206-7]. Pratt managed to save himself by writing a letter in defense, which the Assistants found satisfactory [MBCR 1:358-60], but even in his defense he made a number of points about the constraints on growth in the older settlements in Massachusetts Bay. (Ironically, on 3 March 1635/6, just a few months after this confrontation, and very shortly before his departure from Cambridge, John Pratt was appointed to a colony committee to lay out land in Watertown [MBCR 1:167].)

Watertown, Dorchester and Roxbury also felt the pinch, and made similar requests. One response to this problem, as noted by Winthrop, was to look for more land close to the towns already settled. As a result, Concord, Newbury, Hingham and Weymouth were added to the list of "authorized" plantations in 1635.

Another way of attempting to solve the problem was to look further afield for good agricultural land. A number of expeditions had explored the Connecticut River Valley, and found several sites suitable for settlement. As we shall see, Cambridge joined in this movement, creating in 1635 and 1636 the new town of Hartford.

1635 CAMBRIDGE LAND INVENTORY

On 1 April 1634 the Massachusetts Bay General Court ordered that each town should compile an inventory of individual landholdings and submit it to the Court within six months [MBCR 1:116]. This order was not immediately successful, and was renewed by the Court on 4 March 1634/5 [MBCR 1:137].

On 3 February 1634/5, the town of Cambridge responded to the earlier directive by issuing an order of its own, "that four men should be chosen … to join with the constable to [prose]cute the same about ensuring of land…. These five or the major part of them shall [meet] every first Monday in the morning at [the ringing] of a bell that those which desire to have their lands entered may repair thither to the constable's house" [CaTR 11-12; CaBOP 2].

The town then began a separate book of records for this purpose, and entered on the first leaf the various colony and town orders referred to above. The survey was then begun on 1 May 1635, the first Tuesday in that month. Nine men's estates were surveyed on that date, commencing with the most prominent men in town – Thomas Dudley, John Haynes, Thomas Hooker and Samuel Stone [CaBOP 2-7].

The next group of entries was dated 4 June 1635, the first Thursday in June. Twelve men were surveyed on that date. There was then a hiatus, and no surveys were carried out on the first Mondays of July and August. The work resumed on 20 August 1635, when four more estates were summarized.

On 5 September 1635, the first Saturday in the month, an additional seven men had their entries compiled, and on 5 October 1635 (at last a Monday), fourteen more were done. Finally, on 10 October 1635, the work was completed in a rush when forty estates were surveyed. In all, eighty-six estates were registered.

We can already see in this sequence of dates some of the dynamics of migration of the summer of 1635. Once set in motion, the process of recording landholdings worked correctly for two months, May and June, during which approximately one-quarter of the landholders in Cambridge had their real property surveyed.

The failure to survey estates early in July and August may be related to the great influx of new settlers to the town in those months, leading to uncertainty as to who would be holding land in the near future. Also, all involved may have been simply too busy to attend to this largely bureaucratic duty.

The return to surveying in late August, which was most certainly not the first Monday of the month, may be related to the handful of alienations of land which are embedded in the records at this point. As noted above four men (William Goodwin, John Steele, William Lewis and Richard Webb) entered their lands on 20 August 1635.

These entries are immediately followed by four deeds. Three of these are dated 25 August 1635, when "Symond Willard," John Bridge and "Dollerd Davis" each sold a piece of land to Richard Girling [CaBOP 15]. The lands of these three men had been surveyed together on 4 June 1635 [CaBOP 10]. Willard and Davis, having just arrived in New England in 1635, were ending their brief sojourn in Cambridge and were moving on to participate in founding the new settlement of Concord in early September [MBCR 1:157; WJ 1:199-200].

In the fourth intrusive deed, dated 28 August 1635, John Steele sold all his land in Cambridge to Robert Bradish. This is the first explicit evidence we have for the departure of one of the men who would settle Hartford. We know that a number of them went to the Connecticut in the latter part of 1635, and this action by Steele would indicate that he was one of those first settlers.

A few other sales in late 1635 were recorded a few pages later. On 5 October 1635, Thomas Scott sold to John Russell one of his two parcels of land [CaBOP 17]. Two days later "Steaven Harte of Newtowne" sold to Joseph and George Cooke "my dwelling house in Newtowne with the yards & all the several parcels of land & meadow" he held in town [CaBOP 42]. Two sales occurred on 20 October 1635: "John White of the Newtowne" sold to Nicholas Danforth "all the right, title and interest which he hath in those several parcels of land as they are recorded in this book in folio 3" [CaBOP 36], and "John Bridge of Newtowne" sold to Roger Harlackenden, Joseph Cooke and George Cooke "my dwelling house in Newtowne ... with the yard & all the several parcels of land & marsh thereunto belonging" [CaBOP 41].

1636 LIST OF HOUSES

On 8 February 1635/6, the Cambridge selectmen included in their records a listing of "The names of those men who have houses in the town at this present as only are to be accounted as houses of the town" [CaTR 18-19]. This list is not easy to interpret. The heading, just quoted above, implies that there may be houses which are not "to be accounted as houses of the town." Does this mean that "houses of the town" is another way of defining a proprietary share? Perhaps.

Not all of the houses listed were strictly "in the town." The eighty-five names in the list are subdivided under five headings: "In the town," 51; "In Cowyard Row," 2; "In

Westend," 24; "By the Pine Swamp," 1; "On the south side of the River," 2; and "By the Fresh Pond," 5. Furthermore, many of the people listed were credited with more than one house, some with as many as six, so that about 125 houses are represented. Are these all physical houses, or do they, again, represent proprietary shares? Some of the new residents did buy the estate of two or more departing families.

Leaving these questions aside, we can extract useful information from this list of houses by comparing it with the 1635 land inventory. Of the eighty-five entires in the 1635 inventory, seventy explicitly included houses. Of these seventy names, twenty-two did not appear in the 1636 list of houses. Had all of these families left Cambridge by the time of this list? If so, Cambridge had lost a quarter of its population in just a few months.

All of these families did move out of Cambridge at this time, but not all of them went to Hartford. Dolor Davis removed to Duxbury (although he would later join Simon Willard in Concord). Two families, those of Thomas Hett and Jonathan Bosworth, are next found in Hingham. And four men went next to Ipswich: Daniel Denison, Samuel Dudley, Edmund Garner and Thomas Scott.

Fifteen of the twenty-two resided next in Hartford, and we may assume that they all made the move late in 1635 or early in 1636: Samuel Stone, John White, William Westwood, William Butler, Andrew Warner, Nathaniel Ely, William Goodwin, John Steele, William Pantry, Samuel Greenhill, Stephen Hart, William Kelsey, Stephen Post, George Stocking and John Barnard.

In the months immediately after the "inventory of houses," sales of land in Cambridge continued. On 17 March 1635/6, "William Wetherell of the Newtowne" sold to John Benjamin "one house & twelve acres of land lying on the south side of Charles River" [CaBOP 35-36]. On 24 March 1635/6, "William Ruskew now husband of the late widow Hester Must" sold to John Benjamin "one acre of ground ... lying in Shipmarsh" [CaBOP 36]. On 1 April 1636, "William Spencer of the New Towne" sold to Nicholas Danforth "three acres and a half of land ... in the neck of land" [CaBOP 37-38].

Continuing with this series of sales, on 19 April 1636, "William Kelsey of the New Towne" sold to Thomas Fisher a parcel of meadow [CaBOP 42]. On 1 May 1636, "John Taylcott of the Newtowne" sold to Nicholas Danforth nine parcels of land [CaBOP 36-37], apparently comprising all the land credited to him in the inventory on 5 October 1635 [CaBOP 23]. The next day "Thomas Hooker of the New Towne" sold to Nicholas Danforth "one acre of land being the lot of Edward Hopkins" and "Edward Stebinge of the New Towne" sold to Nicholas Danforth six parcels of land [CaBOP 38-39], again corresponding closely to his holdings in the inventory on 5 October 1635 [CaBOP 21-22].

Again, not all of these men made the move to Hartford in 1636, but several of them did. As noted below, William Spencer did not go to Hartford until 1639, and William Wetherell is next seen in Duxbury. But William Ruscoe, William Kelsey, John Talcott, Thomas Hooker and Edward Stebbing were all among the 1636 migrants to the Connecticut.

Additional sales were recorded in 1636 and 1637, some of them by men who had moved to Connecticut a year or more earlier [CaBOP 36, 40-44]. Even with all these recorded sales, however, there must have been far more which were never recorded.

This is a reminder of the evolving system of land transferral which was developing in the New England colonies. In England, the centuries-old customs were changing, but were still followed in many areas. But in the New World there were no institutions, and no experience of dividing up lands which had not as yet been possessed by any Europeans.

The system of proprietors developed to handle the initial distribution of land among deserving settlers, but almost immediately there came into existence an "after-market," as the original grantees wanted to sell their land and move on, or for some other reason wished to dispose of their holdings.

The county system would not come into being in Massachusetts Bay until 1643, and so in these earliest years, by default presumably, such alienations of land as were recorded were entered in the town books. Even after the county courts came into existence, many towns continued to record deeds.

The recording of land transactions in town books spread throughout New England, and only in Massachusetts and the states and colonies directly deriving from Massachusetts (New Hampshire and Maine) was there a move to recording at the county level. In Rhode Island and Connecticut, and in Vermont, which largely followed the Connecticut model, deed recording has always been at the town level.

To modern eyes the system followed by Rhode Island, Conencticut and Vermont seems to be an aberration, but it was in fact the original norm, away from which all the other states have moved.

Getting back to conditions in Cambridge in the spring of 1636, we know from many other records, both in Massachusetts Bay and in Connecticut, that the migration to Hartford continued steadily during 1636, and more slowly in following years. Rather than examining these individual moves in great detail, we will jump ahead to 1639, the next year for which we have a pertinent survey record.

During 1639 the selectmen of Cambridge carried out another inventory of landholdings in the town [CaBOP 45-70]. This listing is more difficult to interpret than the parallel record of 1635, for a number of reasons. The beginning and end of the record are not so clearly delineated, there are multiple entries for some individuals, and some of the entries are interrupted by other material.

Nevertheless, without subjecting this document to extensive analysis, we can draw from it some useful conclusions. There are entries for about sixty-five individuals, as compared with eighty-five for the 1635 list. The number is smaller partly because some of the new residents had bought the estates of two or more of the departing families. Also, there are clearly a few omissions, at least. Atherton Hough, who does appear in the 1635 inventory, is absent from the list of 1639. This is undoubtedly because he lived in the area that became East Cambridge, far from all the other settlers of Cambridge.

Of these sixty-five, only eight were included in the 1635 list: John Bridge, Abraham Morrill, Bartholomew Greene, John Masters, Samuel Greene, Edward Winship, William Mann and Guy Banbridge. Some of these (Samuel Greene and Edward Winship, for example) are found at the very end of the 1635 list, and represent the beginning of the turnover in population; they are not part of the core of earlier residents who were closely associated with Hooker. None of the eight were among the town's leaders, either before or after 1635.

In the space of just over a year, then, we see a replacement of ninety perecent or more of the population of Cambridge, including all of the lay and religious leaders. The new residents of Cambridge were, like the earlier residents, mostly East Anglians, and so the English folkways transferred to Cambridge in these two different time periods were much the same. But the new settlers, led by Rev. Thomas Shepard, were much more closely allied with John Winthrop, Rev. John Cotton and the other Massachusetts Bay leaders than Rev. Thomas Hooker and his associates had been.

A useful summary of many of the changes of ownership which occurred in Cambridge in 1635 and 1636 may be found in an unlikely place. In the course of preparing his monumental Tercentenary History of Harvard College, Samuel Eliot Morison studied early landholding in Cambridge in great detail, and produced a number of excellent maps showing the development of the town [*The Founding of Harvard College* (Cambridge 1935)].

In a set of maps placed between pages 192 and 193 of this volume, with the assistance of Albert P. Norris, Morison has included a map of the central settlement of Cambridge, with each of the houselots numbered. This is accompanied by a translucent overlay showing the modern streets and some of the modern buildings. The key to this map identifies the succession of the earliest owners of each of the houselots. This key was prepared with great care, obviously based largely on the various early land inventories.

DORCHESTER, WATERTOWN AND ROXBURY

While all of this was going on in Cambridge, there was similar activity in at least three other Massachusetts Bay towns: Dorchester, Watertown and Roxbury.

In Dorchester, one of the lay leaders, Edward Rossiter, had died in 1630, soon after arrival, and Rev. John Maverick, one of the two ministers who had come on the *Mary & John*, died during the winter of 1635-6. But the two remaining leaders of the 1630 immigration, Roger Ludlow and Rev. John Warham, and presumably others as well, made the decision in 1635 to move to Connecticut.

Evidence for this move is found in the Dorchester town records, although not so abundantly as with Cambridge. On 12 August 1635, for example, two Dorchester residents, Thomas Holcombe and Thomas Dewey, sold to Richard Jones all of their landholdings in Dorchester [DTR 12], clearly in preparation for the move to the new settlement.

The turnover of properties in Dorchester was quite extensive, but not so complete as in Cambridge. The majority of the migrants to Connecticut were from the West Country component of the town's population, which had been the greater part since 1630, but was being rapidly diluted by the newer immigration of 1634 and 1635. As with Cambridge, the church founded in 1630 by Warham and Maverick was moved to Connecticut, and a new church was founded in 1636, with Rev. Richard Mather as the first minister.

Population pressure was also being felt in Watertown, and this Massachusetts Bay settlement also gave rise to a Connecticut River town: Wethersfield. The records of Watertown do not show the transfers of land so explicitly as do the records of Cambridge and Watertown; there are no deeds of sale by those emigrating from Watertown.

We can, however, trace the departure of many early Watertown residents by careful analysis of the land grants and land inventories which were maintained in the proprietors' records. For example, Thurston Rayner arrived in New England in 1634 on the *Elizabeth*, joining many other families which had come from southern Suffolk and northern Essex in England. He was granted a homestall, apparently in 1634, but did not participate in any later divisions of land in Watertown. Rayner's proprietary share was acquired by Gregory Stone, who was the grantee of some small parcels of land which were given out in late 1635 or early 1636 [GMN 1:4-6].

Rayner would thus appear to be one of those who left Watertown in 1635 and became one of the first settlers of Wethersfield. This same pattern, or a similar one, can be traced for many other Watertown settlers in these same records.

The emigration from Watertown was substantial, and provided most of the early population of Wethersfield, but it did not have quite as drastic an effect on Watertown as did the emigration from Cambridge and Dorchester. First, the number of families which remained in Watertown was somewhat greater than in the other two towns. Second, unlike the situation in Cambridge and Dorchester, the church founded in Watertown in 1630, and its minister, Rev. George Phillips, remained in Watertown, and the Wethersfield settlers founded a new church of their own.

A fourth town was founded on the Connecticut River, well north of the other three. William Pynchon of Roxbury in 1636 settled the town that would become Springfield. Unlike the other three Massachusetts Bay towns, however, Roxbury was very lightly affected. Not many of the residents went along with Pynchon, and some of the Springfield settlers came from other towns. The movement to Springfield was largely a personal statement by Pynchon. While Springfield was briefly allied with the other three River Towns, and might under different circumstances have become a part of the colony of Connecticut, Pynchon soon chose to ally himself more closely with Massachusetts Bay, and Springfield eventually became the nucleus of Hampshire County.

A curious feature of the first year or so of settlement in the three southerly towns deserves mention. When the settlers first arrived in 1635, and well into 1636, rather than making the effort to assign distinctive names to these towns, they simply reused the names of the towns they had come from. Thus, the town that would become Hartford started life as Newtown, at a time when the town in Massachusetts Bay that would become Cambridge was still called Newtown. The same situation prevailed for Dorchester and Watertown.

This failure of imagination could obviously result in confusion, both among the New Englanders of 1635 and 1636, and among modern interpreters of these records. Examination of the sales of Cambridge lands reveals a minor variation in the use of the name "Newtown." In some cases, the residence of the grantor is given as "of the New Town," while in others it is given simply as "of New Town."

One might postulate that the use of the definite article pointed to the new settlement on the Connecticut, while the simpler usage was intended for the older and more familiar settlement. But examination of the individual instances does not support this hypothesis. William Spencer, for example, on 1 April 1636 calls himself "of the New Town," but he did not make the move to Hartford until 1639. We cannot even suggest that he moved briefly to the Connecticut in 1636, returned to Cambridge, and then went back to Hartford in 1639, since he is recorded as active in Massachusetts Bay on 28 March 1636 and 13 April 1636 [GMB 3:1721]. The minor difference in usage of the town name is, unfortunately, meaningless.

RECENT LITERATURE

Jonathan A. Shaw, "John Shaw of Plymouth Colony, Purchaser and Canal Builder," *New England Historical and Genealogical Register* 151 (1997):259-85, 417-37. The author provides a comprehensive biography of the immigrant and an account of his descendants to the fourth generation in all lines.

Vernon Dow Turner, "Lydia Gamer, the Wife of Humphrey Turner of Scituate," *New England Historical and Genealogical Register* 151 (1997):286-90. Turner presents evidence which confirms conclusively the long-proposed identity of the wife of Humphrey Turner.

Clifford L. Stott, "William Crispe of Laxfield, Suffolk: Great-grandfather of Anthony[1] and Joshua[1] Fisher of Dedham, Massachusetts," *New England Historical and Genealogical Register* 151 (1997):291-99, and Myrtle Stevens Hyde, "The Godbold Ancestry of New England Settlers Joshua and Anthony Fisher," *New England Historical and Genealogical Register* 151 (1997):300-7. Stott and Hyde extend the known English ancestry of these two early immigrants to Dedham.

Douglas Richardson, "The Tenney Family of Lincolnshire and Rowley, Massachusetts," *New England Historical and Genealogical Register* 151 (1997):329-41. Richards provides evidence that Thomas and William Tenney, who were among the earliest settlers of Rowley, were from Great Limber, Lincolnshire.

Johan Winsser, "Walter Blackborne, a London Milliner Briefly in New England," *New England Historical and Genealogical Record* 151 (1997):408-16. Winsser shows that Walter Blackborne, who arrived in Roxbury in 1638, soon moved to Boston, and then returned to England, was a milliner of London.

Jeremy D. Bangs, "Cornet Robert Stetson's Arrival in Scituate and the Birth Date of His Son Joseph," *New England Historical and Genealogical Register* 151 (1997):438-41. Bangs argues that Robert Stetson had arrived in Scituate by 1642, without any firm evidence for earlier residence there. Bangs also discusses the birth dates for Stetson's sons Joseph, Benjamin and Thomas.

Harry Macy, Jr., "Captain John Underhill Revised," *New York Genealogical and Biographical Record* 127 (1996):22-23. Macy reinterprets the life of John Underhill, based on a newly-discovered deposition.

Gale Ion Harris, "The Earlier Career of Hannah (Wakeman) Hackleton, Edward Whittaker's Wife in the Esopus," *New York Genealogical and Biographical Record* 127 (1996):65-75, 227. Harris documents the tumultuous life of Hannah

(Wakeman) (Hackleton) Whittaker, daughter of Samuel Wakeman, early settler of Roxbury, Cambridge and Hartford [GMB 3:1899-1901]. She had children with three men, two of whom became her husbands.

Frederick C. Hart, Jr., "A Proposed Family for Thomas[1] Jones of Fairfield, Connecticut, and Huntington, Long Island," *New York Genealogical and Biographical Record* 128 (1997):100-9, 167-76. Hart provides an excellent synthesis of what is known about this immigrant and his children. This Thomas Jones was certainly in Fairfield by 1649, and may have arrived in New England some years earlier than that.

Francis J. Bremer, "The Heritage of John Winthrop: Religion along the Stour Valley, 1548-1630," *The New England Quarterly* 70 (1997):515-47. Bremer explores the immediate familial background of John Winthrop's Puritanism. William Winthrop, John's uncle, was in the 1560s and 1570s active in Protestant circles in London. Adam Winthrop, John's father, was prominent in Puritan circles in western Suffolk for several decades, and through these connections John Winthrop was influenced by such prominent clergymen as John Knewstub and Henry Sandes.

Arne Delfs, "Anxieties of Influence: Perry Miller and Sacvan Bercovitch," *The New England Quarterly* 70 (1997):601-15. The author investigates the manner in which the criticisms made by Sacvan Bercovitch of the work of Perry Miller on Puritan intellectual history have resulted in a reaffirmation of much of Miller's work.

Michael P. Winship, "William Pynchon's *The Jewes Synagogue*," *The New England Quarterly* 71 (1998):290-97. Winship discusses a relatively obscure pamphlet, in which Pynchon argues that the primitive synagogue of the Old Testament should be the model for reformed church government. This recommendation of Pynchon's was at odds with the congregationalism of early New England, and closer to the Presbyterian model. In particular, Pynchon was opposed to the "conversion narrative" as a prerequisite for church membership.

Mary Beth Norton, "'The Ablest Midwife That Wee Know in the Land': Mistress Alice Tilley and the Women of Boston and Dorchester, 1649-1650," *The William and Mary Quarterly,* Third Series 55 (1998):105-34. Norton publishes and describes the several petitions from Boston and Dorchester women supporting an early New England midwife. This political action by a group of women stands out as a unique event in the British North American colonies. Alice (Frost) (Blower) Tilly and her two husbands, Thomas Blower and William Tilly, had all immigrated to New England in 1635.

(continued from page 10)

early July. These ships certainly did arrive in New England in 1635, for most of the passengers soon appear in New England records in one way or another. Winthrop did not take note of their arrival, however, nor did any other source.

The next passenger ship of which we have record had a very curious and troubled history. On 16 August 1635, Winthrop described a severe storm, certainly a nor'easter and possibly a hurricane, which inflicted heavy damage throughout eastern Massachusetts Bay. He tells us that the "*Great Hope*, of Ipswich, being about four hundred tons, was driven on ground at Mr. Hoffe's Point, and brought back again presently by a N.W. wind, and ran on shore at Charlestown" [WJ 1:196]. The adventures of this vessel can be followed, with difficulty, in a number of cases in the High Court of Admiralty [English Adventurers 67-69, 105]. In one of the depositions (not all of which agree with one another), Christopher Vennard tells us that "Richard Gurling was Master of the *Hope* of Ipswich from June 1634 until his death on 14 May 1636." Robert Lea deposes that he was purser of the *Hope*, and that "[h]er passengers were carried to New England."

On 25 August 1635, "Richard Girling, mariner," bought land in Cambridge from Simon Willard, John Bridge and Dolor Davis [CaBOP 15; CaTR 19]. Apparently Girling planned to settle in Cambridge, perhaps after completing the present voyage and returning to England, but, as we learn from other depositions in the Admiralty case, he died in Barbados in 1636. In a series of actions beginning in 1637 and ending in 1639, the Cambridge estate of Girling was liquidated and the meager proceeds returned to the widow, apparently in England [MBCR 1:203, 219, 232, 238, 268].

Since the *Great Hope* sailed from Ipswich, and Richard Girling contemplated settling in Cambridge, we may hypothesize that his passengers were from East Anglia and that many of them would also have settled in Cambridge. The *Great Hope* would thus be the 1635 equivalent of the *Francis* and the *Elizabeth* in 1634 [GMN 6:9-10]. Investigation of families of East Anglian origin which appear in Cambridge in the summer of 1635 might permit partial reconstruction of the passenger list of this ship.

This same storm destroyed or endangered a number of other ships, including some that were working along the New England coast, as well as other passenger ships from England. Rev. Joseph Avery and his family and several others, sailing from Ipswich in Massachusetts Bay to Marblehead, were overtaken off Cape Ann and almost all on board died [WJ 1:196-97; Young's First Planters 485-95].

The *Angel Gabriel* and the *James*, both from Bristol, were also caught in the storm. We will tell their story in the next issue.

(to be continued in Volume 7, No. 3)

Great Migration Study Project
101 Newbury Street
Boston, MA 02116

Great Migration Newsletter

| Vol. 7 | July-September 1998 | No. 3 |

PASSENGER SHIPS OF 1635 - Part III

At the end of the last installment of this article, we had reached the point when the *James* and the *Angel Gabriel* were ready to set sail from Bristol. We have an unusual wealth of information on these two vessels for two reasons: Rev. Richard Mather sailed on the *James* and kept a journal of the voyage, and the *Angel Gabriel* was lost in a storm on the New England coast, an event which Winthrop took note of in his journal.

Mather tells us that he left Warrington, Lancashire, on 16 April 1635 and arrived in Bristol on 23 April, where "we found diverse of the company come before us; but some came not till after us" [Young's Planters 448]. The party did not board the *James* until 23 May, on which day "there came aboard the ship two of the searchers, and viewed a list of all our names, ministered the Oath of Allegiance to all at full age, viewed our certificates from the ministers in the parishes from whence we came, approved well thereof, and gave us tickets, that is licenses under their hands and seals to pass the seas, and cleared the ship" [Young's Planters 448-49].

On 26 May another ship bound for New England, the *Angel Gabriel*, appeared, and on the 27th "our master, Captain Taylor, went aboard the *Angel Gabriel*, Mr. [Daniel] Maud, Nathaniel Wales, Barnabas Fower, Thomas Armitage and myself accompanying him" [Young's Planters 450]. (Mather later named Matthew Mitchell, George Kenrick and John Smith as other passengers.

The *James* (described as being a ship of 220 tons) and the *Angel Gabriel* (240 tons) finally left harbor on 4 June, in company with three other vessels bound for Newfoundland. Due to contrary winds, they were detained in Bristol Channel until 22 June, on which day "about noon [we] lost all sight of land." The next day the two New England bound ships were left behind by the other three, and on 4 July those on the *James* "lost sight of the *Angel Gabriel*, sailing slowly behind us, and we never saw her again any more" [Young's Planters 461].

On 8 August the *James* finally made landfall, off Monhegan Island. For the next week the ship worked its way down the New England coast, anchoring at the Isles of Shoals on the evening of the 14th. They expected to arrive at Cape Ann the next day, but were caught in the terrible storm of 15 August, and barely avoided shipwreck at the mouth of the Piscataqua [Young's Planters 473-75].

Winthrop, misdating the storm as having happened on the 16th, reported that "[I]n this tempest, the James of Bristol, having one hundred passengers, honest people of Yorkshire, being put into the Isle of Shoals, lost there three anchors, and, setting sail, no canvas nor ropes would hold, but she was driven within a cable's length of the rocks at Pascataquack, when suddenly the wind, comng to N.W., put them back to the Isle of Shoals and, being there ready to strike upon the rocks, they let out a piece of their mainsail, and weathered the rocks" [WJ 1:196].

Late in the day they were able to continue on their way, and finally on the 17th they were able to come to anchor at Boston. No lives were lost among the "hundred passengers, ... twenty-three seamen, and twenty-three cows and heifers, three sucking calves, and eght mares" [Young's Planters 476].

This same storm of 15 August 1635 did much damage throughout New England, blowing over large trees, knocking down houses, and causing at least two memorable shipwrecks. One of these involved a vessel sailing southward from Ipswich, carrying the families of Rev.

(continued on page 18)

EDITOR'S EFFUSIONS

Both the lead article and the *Focus* section in this issue provide examples of a documentation problem frequently encountered during the Great Migration Study Project: the publication in secondary sources of depositions for which no citation is given. Many times we find reference to depositions which would seem to have been generated by the Middlesex court, but which can no longer be found in the surviving file papers. Now we have a better idea of what has happened to many of these documents, which were clearly available to our genealogical predecessors, but which no longer exist. And in the case of the Cogswell depositions relating to the *Angel Gabriel*, printed in the Cogswell genealogy, they would seem to be generated in the probate process in Essex County, but these documents are not represented in the published Essex probate records.

When we are confronted with this situation, we first attempt to locate the deposition among surviving documents. This is not always possible, as in the case of some of the Middlesex documents, but in other cases, such as the many depositions cited by Noyes, Libby and Davis in the *Genealogical Dictionary of Maine and New Hampshire*, we believe that a body of documents exists which we have not yet located.

If we can not locate the original, we must then decide whether the version of the document given in the secondary source seems to be reliable. Blatant forgeries are rare, but do exist, and must be guarded against. More subtle are the inaccuracies in reading or transcription by earlier workers. When we decide that such a document is genuine, we will include it, with a citation of the following form: "[Cogswell Gen 11, citing an unknown source]."

In the first issue of this volume of the *Great Migration Newsletter*, we predicted that the lead article on ship passenger lists would appear in three installments. This issue contains the third installment, and obviously we are not done; there is material for two additional installments. Because so much more is known about passenger vessels in 1635 than in any other Great Migration year, we feel that an investigation of this length is warranted.

Robert Charles Anderson, FASG   Editor
Aileen Novick   Production Assistant

The Great Migration Newsletter is published quarterly by the Great Migration Study Project, a project of the New England Historic Genealogical Society, 101 Newbury Street, Boston MA 02116

The subscription rate is $12 for one year and $20 for two years.

(continued from page 17)

Joseph Avery and Thomas Thatcher, a total of twenty-three persons, all but two of whom perished when the ship was destroyed on the rocks off Cape Ann [Young's Planters 485-95].

The other ship that foundered on 15 August 1635 was the *Angel Gabriel*, the companion of the *James* on part of the voyage from Bristol. As noted above, these two ships parted company on 4 July, and the distance between them must have become considerable over the next month, as the *James* had reached Monhegan by 8 August, and the Angel Gabriel was only as far as *Pemaquid* by the 15th.

Both Mather and Winthrop dispose of this part of the story in a few words, but the consequences for the passengers were great indeed. Mather tells us that "the *Angel Gabriel*, being then at anchor at Pemmaquid, was burst in pieces and cast away in this storm, and most of the cattle and other goods, with one seaman and three or four passengers, did also perish therein, beside two of the passengers that died by the way, the rest having their lives given them for a prey" [Young's Planters 478]. Winthrop was terse in the extreme: "*Gabriel* lost at Pemaquid" [WJ 1:197].

After these two entries, our only certain evidence for this ship came more than forty years later, in a probate dispute among the heirs of John Cogswell of Ipswich. On 1 December 1676, "Samuel Haines, now aged sixty-five years or thereabouts," deposed "that I lived with Mr. John Cogswell, Sen., in Old England about three years, a servant with him, and came over along with him to New England in the ship called the *Angel Gabriel*, and was present with him when my Master Cogswell suffered shipwreck at Pemaquid, which was about forty years ago last August when the ship was cast away" [Cogswell Gen 11].

Haines went on to testify at length about the goods of Cogswell that were saved, with great emphasis on a Turkey-work carpet that was in contention. He also remembered "that my master had two mares and two cows, which were shipped aboard a ship at South Hampton in Old England, and came safe ashore to New England that same summer as we came here." Haines concluded by reporting that Cogswell was accompanied by three sons: William, "who was about fourteen years of age then"; John, about twelve; and Edward, about six [Cogswell Gen 12].

A similar deposition was given the same day by "William Tarbox, Sen., aged sixty-two or thereabouts," who was also a passenger on the *Angel Gabriel*, and who soon joined Haines as a servant of John Cogswell [Cogswell Gen 11].

Another deposition, dated 5 April 1677, tells much the same story, but adds a very important genealogical detail

(continued on page 24)

Focus on MIDDLESEX COUNTY

Middlesex County Court Papers
By Melinde Lutz Sanborn

Research in published and manuscript sources demonstrates that the collection of original file papers associated with the early Middlesex County Court has been steadily shrinking since before the middle of the last century. Eight separate sources, representing different portions of the court records, have been identified that shed light on these losses.

On 3 March 1635/6, the Massachusetts Bay General Court ordered that four courts, one at Ipswich, one at Salem, one at Newe Towne (Cambridge) and one at Boston, were to meet quarterly to dispense justice in their respective jurisdictions [MBCR 1:11]. While Ipswich and Salem met separately, it is evident from the business that came before the Boston and Cambridge courts that the division between these two was not observed. The last merged court session to be held at Cambridge for which we have minutes commenced on 6 March 1637/8 [MBCR 1:219], while the last merged court session to be held at Boston for which we have minutes commenced on 7 September 1641 [MBCR 1:334]. Regardless of the town in which the court met, business from both Cambridge and Boston jurisdictions was heard by one court.

Not until 10 May 1643 was the plantation of Massachusetts Bay formally divided into four "shires": Essex, Middlesex, Suffolk and Norfolk [MBCR 2:38]. The two counties, Middlesex and Suffolk, continued to maintain a merged quarter court, as well as a single set of deeds and probates. These deeds and probates are now known only as Suffolk County records.

A gap appears between the last merged Quarter Court minutes of 7 September 1641 and the first distinct Middlesex Court records dated in October of 1649. The gap in Suffolk County records is even greater, with no minutes surviving until the 31 October 1671 session. It is probably no coincidence that the earliest separate Middlesex deeds and probates commence in March of 1648/9, when Increase Nowell recorded a Brian Pendleton deed. This deed was followed by the May 1649 will of Mathew Day, recorded 2 November 1649, and the 14 June 1649 power of attorney of David Yale. At this early period, Nowell did not consistently mention when he recorded each document, a feature that soon became standard practice in every Massachusetts court.

On 17 October 1649, it was ordered that the Middlesex Quarter Court should meet on the first third day of the second month and the first third day of the eighth month each year [MBCR 2:284]. While it had been customary for the courts to convene quarterly, the new order called for only two courts per year, with the Governor allowed to call a special court at his discretion for the trial of persons charged with capital offenses. This October 1649 order is the first evidence we have of a separate Middlesex Court.

RECORD BOOKS

Thus it was that in late 1649, not many months after the death of Gov. Winthrop, Middlesex County began to keep its own separate records. In the case of the Middlesex County court, original records included not only the individual papers presented during the court, but a court minute book which typically described the principals in the case and any action taken. In the early period, the minute book for Middlesex also included brief abstracts of individual depositions, reflecting a practice of taking evidence by shorthand in the court rather than writing out the testimony for the deponent to sign and enter into evidence as was done later. Theoretically, court minutes were taken by the Clerk in a wastebook and later transcribed carefully into the official court minute book. Unfortunately, none of these wastebooks are known to survive for Middlesex.

To get an accurate picture of what file papers are actually missing and not merely rearranged, it is necessary to include in our examination the original court minute books for the period. The surviving separate court minute books for Middlesex County begin in the hand of Thomas Danforth for a county court held at Cambridge 30 October 1649 and entitled by him "liber. 1." Based on the cases being heard in the October 1649 court, it is evident that many matters were being resumed from the previous merged courts in the eight year gap described above.

The first minute book begins with Mr. Increase Nowell's suit against John Martine for breach of covenant, Edward Hurst vs. Richard Dexter for detaining a heifer, Mr. Atherton Haugh vs. Mr. Henry Dunster, Mr. Nathaniel Bisco against William Kerley Sr. for loss of a cow, Rafe Hall vs. Widow Cole and others, Samuel Stratton and wife for speaking evil of the magistrates, and administration granted to Jane Guy of Watertown. The next court, held in April 1650, saw Increase Nowell suing Thomas Martine, Richard Temple suing Thomas Goble and family for trespass and defamation, John Bridge and Gregory Stone for the town of Cambridge suing Atherton Haugh for money due to the ministry, and the infamous Phebe Page against John Flemming for slander.

This final case is a perfect example of the inclusion of depositions in the court minute book. While no original file papers survive for Phebe's unsuccessful suit, the minute book provides extensive detail and includes depositions by Goody Hawkins, George Bullard, Bartholomew Person, James Knop, John Lawrence, Ephraim Child, Ellis Barron, Nathaniel Bisco, Joshua Stubbs, Joseph Tainter, John Spring, William Priest, Richard Blois, John Brabrick, John Stratton, Samuel Saltonstall, Anthony White, Goody Parks, William Parker, Goodman Pierce and Goody Mixture. It seems that everyone in Watertown had an opinion or a piece of gossip regarding Phebe Page. The court must have been full that day. In fact, it may have been the intense note-taking required by this case that convinced recorder Thomas Danforth to change his method of entering testimony into the court minute books. He never again attempted to include depositions to this extent in the minutes, and within a year had abandoned the inclusion of testimony altogether, contenting himself for the most part merely with principals and results.

These early minute book entries will be compared to surviving file papers, below.

Pulsifer Transcript - 1851

A very accurate and satisfactory copy of the surviving original court minute books was completed in 1851 by David Pulsifer. As in the originals, Volume 1 covered "1649" through 16 October 1663. Volume 2 may be the records mentioned in a surviving file paper dated 4 October 1671 when the court commented that

> After the burning of the Court House, wherein was also burnt the Court Book of Records for trials, and several deeds, wills and inventories, that have been delivered into Court before the fire was kindled... [Paige's *History of Cambridge,* 212],

and again in court on 3 April 1677,

> Upon information that several records belonging to this county were casually burnt in the burning of the house where the court was usually kept, this court doth order that the recorder take care that out of the foul copies and other scripts in his custody he fairly draw forth the said records into a book and present the same to the county court when finished and that the treasurer of the county do allow him for the same [Pulsifer 3:171].

If these were the records from the eight year gap in court minutes from 16 October 1663 to 4 October 1671, no new copy as authorized by the court survives. (Volume 2 as transcribed by Pulsifer contained no court records but was devoted exclusively to vital records "1672-1745.") Volume 3 contained minutes from the courts of 4 October 1671 through 24 (11) 1680 and Volume 4 contained April 1681

through October 1686 courts. The binding of an unnumbered volume labelled "SESSIONS 1686-1688 and 1692-1723" left a gap between from 1688 to 1692. A short transcript at the end of the first volume contains "Thomas Danforth's record of Commissioners for ending small cases" dated 14th (4) 58.

Given these spotty records, it is quite amusing to discover that Recorder Lawrence Hammond registered "A List of such Bookes and Files belonging to the Courts & County of Midd^x as did remaine in ye Custody of me Laurence Hammond, late Clerk and Record^r there after my House and Office was broken open, and the greatest part of the Records of the said Courts and County by Violence taken away, on or about the 6th day of February Anno Domini 1690." This yellowed document, now kept in a "Mixed Records" collection at the Massachusetts Archives, details twenty books and eleven files that survived the "burglary." The records taken were not lost, but merely seized following the fall of the Andros administration, and the entire collection was reunited just a few years later.

FILE PAPERS

Wyman's notes – pre-1879

A more serious and more permanent attrition is illustrated by a comparison with surviving records of the item-by-item abstracting done by Thomas B. Wyman, begun possibly as early as 1849, but probably decades later, and ending sometime before his death in 1879. These abstracts are the earliest known description of the original papers and provide a key to their early organization. Two volumes of Wyman's manuscript abstracts, carefully dated and described, covering the years 1649 through 1671, are held in the NEHGS manuscript collection.

While it is now impossible to tell, it would appear that Wyman made an abstract of every piece of paper he encountered. He mentions illegible papers of "no purport" that would surely have been ignored had he been looking only for significant items. Evidently he could read the dates in these instances, however, for they are uniformly calendared. Despite the 1649 starting date of the court minute book, Wyman's first abstracts date to 1651 and later. The list begins with a description of goods related to Michael Spenser, a summons to widow Cole on the complaint of Rafe Hall and the matter of Ralph Woorey vs. William Broughton. These are followed by the presentment of Thomas Arnold concerning baptism, the presentment of Cambridge *re* Sudbury and a difference among Samuel, Benjamin and Ephraim Child. The first testimonies on his list belonged to Isaac Sterns, John Fiske, John Benjamin, Robert Genison, Martin Underwood, Edward Winship and Robert Bancroft. All in all, only widow Cole's case is familiar from the original minute books.

In addition to giving precise dates to each piece of paper, Wyman indicates the beginning of new "Files," such as "The Second File," "The Third File," and so on. It may be speculated that Wyman's "Files" are identical with the "Boxes" described by Alice Busiel, below. These Wyman abstracts reflect the organization of the original papers in, let us say, the 1870s.

Busiel Volume – 1917

In 1917, Middlesex County Probate clerk Alice E. Busiel finished the compilation of a volume of records containing "copies of papers and records and some abstracts from paper [dated] prior to the appointment of a Judge of Probate in 1692." She further described the records she had dealt with: "Volumes 1, 3, 4 and 6 are in the safe in said [Probate] Office. Copies of Volumes 1, 3 and 4 and also the Boxes referred to are in the cases on the corridor in the said Office." The copies in the cases were undoubtedly Pulsifer's transcripts. Busiel's handwritten volume was microfilmed by the LDS Church in November of 1964.

It is possible that some of the Middlesex County Court files pertaining to probate matters and now deemed missing were retrieved from these boxes in the cases in the corridor by Miss Busiel and not returned.

Holman Abstracts – 1932

In 1932, in volume 85 of the *Register*, Mary Lovering Holman, F.A.S.G., supplied a list of persons whose ages could be found on Middlesex county court depositions given between 1675 and 1695. She remarked that it was by no means an exhaustive list, but that some might find it useful. A comparison of this list with a list made by the present writer, which *does* attempt to be exhaustive, made the attrition rate terribly apparent. Of the 214 names on Holman's list, 36 cannot now be found.

A close examination of the missing names shows little pattern in the losses. Of the years represented, 1691 is responsible for 15 missing depositions, and the others are truly random. While it is possible to imagine political reasons why fewer depositions were taken in 1691, that is not what is happening here. These records were readily available as late as 1932, although Holman's attention to them suggests that she found them in a distinct grouping, not usually accessed. As it is, we may never know what Roger Buck, Sarah Burnap, William Butterick, Samuel Cattell, Daniel Cheever, Elizabeth Clarke, James Converse, Richard Cutter, Thomas Fillebrown, David Fiske, Samuel Foster, Steven Gay, Nathaniel Gilbert, Samuel Hastings, Samuel Hide, Judith Hussey, Edward Johnson, Matthew Johnson, George Lawrence, William Locke, Sarah Lyne, Theophilus Marsh, John Maynard, George Moore, Jeremiah Morse, John Parks, Thomas Prentice, Edward Rawson, Israel Reed, Josiah Richardson, John Stedman, William Stetson, John Swan,

James Turner, John Warren, Joseph Wellington, Richard Whitney and Josiah Wood had to say to the court. The oldest of these deponents was 85-year-old Stetson, the youngest, 16-year-old Sarah Lyne.

While it is to be hoped that a 16% rate of loss is not representative of the collection as a whole, it may be close to the truth.

Newspaper Coverage - 1936

In the decades after Wyman and Busiel worked with them, the original papers languished at the court house, where they grew musty with exposure to insects and mold.

Speaking to a Cambridge journalist in 1936, Harvard professor Eldon R. James noted that many records had gone missing. In an article by Lester G. Ainley in the *Cambridge Chronicle* of 10 May 1936, James claimed that "There is no doubt that this condition is the result of looting, the work of genealogists, antiquarians and autograph hunters."

Prof. James was quite familiar with the original records. In about 1935, he was part of a coalition of Harvard Law School professors and Cambridge Historical Society members who sponsored a petition for a W.P.A. appropriation to preserve and arrange the surviving court papers. The Middlesex Registrar of Probate Loring P. Jordan provided photostating equipment, and a team of "skilled young women" flattened and packed the papers for shipment to Harvard, having applied numbers to each document. These numbers were stamped on a small piece of paper and then glued to the document, usually to the upper right hand corner; the last document contained in the first volume of photostats was numbered 1113 and dated about 1664.

A graduate seminar at the Harvard Law School undertook to catalog and sort the papers, employing seven graduate students, whose ability to read the old handwriting may be called into question, and the resulting arrangement was gathered into large yellow envelopes, with descriptive inventories on the outside and scraps of paper with individual captions on the inside. This folio system attempted to collect related papers under each quarter court date, but usually clumped several years' worth of documents together.

Photostats - 1937

Photostats of the original papers, processed in the Probate court, were bound, catalogued under Harvard Law School Library MS 5575 v. 1, and ultimately received by the library on July 21, 1937. The records are clear and sharp, for the most part easy to read, and mercifully lack the erratically inaccurate captions that plague the microfilms.

Unlike Wyman's abstracts, this arrangment of papers began with a summons to Samuel Stratton Sr. & wife dated 3 9mo

1649, a summons to widow Cole dated 2 8mo 1649, an Atherton Haughe bond of 17 6mo 1649, a summons of Raph Woorey dated 23 1mo 1649, a list of presentments and three pages of documents relating to Radulphus Woorey. As compared to the methodical abstracts done by Wyman more than 50 years earlier, this order of items reflects considerable shuffling, evidently according to date.

Microfilms – 1972 and 1974

A sixth set of records invaluable for documenting the loss of papers is the microfilming done by the Church of Jesus Christ of Latter-day Saints, dated 25 February 1974 – 1 May 1974. (An abortive attempt to film the originals in 1972 produced an inferior film, which is generally unavailable due to the superiority of the later filming.)

The greatest disadvantage to the 1974 filming is the retention of the captions created in the W.P.A. period. These small scraps of paper are frequently included many frames away from the document they describe and it is sometimes impossible to identify where they actually belong. In some instances the old stamped numbers glued on prior to photostating in the 1930s still cling to the papers, but in most instances they have been lost, and these numbers are not used in the folio inventories. Many documents were filmed upside down and paper clips are often visible. The paper items are grouped in as many as four Roman-numeralled sections, but they are not individually numbered, and only a rough span of dates is imposed as organization.

The folio listings were not included in the photostats bound at Harvard, but the full extent of the W.P.A. rearrangement is more evident in this filming than anywhere else. Either the W.P.A. workers or the Harvard graduate students attempted to date cases that had undated original papers by looking at Pulsifer's transcript. This was often a useful approach, but its reliability can be questioned. A particular problem with this tactic is that a case could be appealed and heard years, even decades later, and old documents could be copied and brought to the new case, or even removed from the old cases and included with records of a much more recent date. While such anachronisms can sometimes be detected through a familiarity with certain handwriting, this is not always reliable.

The 1974 microfilm version begins with widow Cole's summons of 22 8mo 1649, a request to keep an ordinary in Malden dated 22 1mo 1651, John Parish being sued by Richard Russell on 4 7mo 1652, an attachment of Michael Spencer dated 22 12mo 1649, Cambridge suing Dedham over town lines, Edmund Goodenow being appointed lieutenant for Sudbury on 1 2mo 1651, a call for Sudbury men to choose a jury dated 1 1mo 1651/2, and a Michael Spencer bond. Once again, there are among these documents only a few overlaps with the court minute books and the earliest Wyman transcripts.

Original File Papers

Perhaps it is more important to know what kind of records have been lost over the years, rather than how many. The results of the comparisons above would indicate that depositions have been lost at a higher rate than other kinds of records. Summonses and routine paperwork appear to survive best of all. Part of the reason for this could be that depositions occasionally contain autographs of more than just the court personnel. Depositions also often contain detailed and valuable information, rarely found in other documents. Their desirability and rate of disappearance both point to the "looting" alluded to by Professor James over fifty years ago.

It is known that folios 47, 48, 53, 30X, 79X and 65A have been missing since 1991, but were present in 1974 when the second microfilming was done. Dr. Roger Thompson used folios 33-57 extensively in the work related to his *Sex in Middlesex*, published in 1986. Presumably the 1986 book was based on research done over a span of years prior to that date, when folios 47, 48 and 53 were clearly among the other surviving original records.

The original court records are currently arranged in roughly chronological order and by case, and stored in Hollinger boxes at the Massachusetts Archives. The pencilled descriptions used to label each paper during the Harvard Law School seminar are retained. In some instances, the Pulsifer transcript pagination or court date has been pencilled onto the original documents. An incomplete card index to some names is available at the Massachusetts Archives and on microfilm.

In tackling *The Great Migration Begins* and the current *Great Migration Second Series* volumes, it became noticeable that many documents cited by previous researchers, such as Charles Thornton Libby, Sybil Noyes and Walter Goodwin Davis, were not to be found despite diligent search. This has required the unfortunate use of citations to the secondary sources, with a further indication that the location of the original is no longer known.

In some instances, we have been able to locate the missing documents in the Harvard photostats, and barring that, in the brief abstracts done in the last century by Thomas B. Wyman. Many records still remain undiscovered, unfortunately, and may have fallen prey to the "looting" described by Prof. James.

Most researchers will attempt to access the Middlesex County court papers through the microfilmed version, as that is the most accessible version. When the researcher is attempting to locate and confirm a document referred to elsewhere in the literature, and the document cannot be found on the microfilm, the researcher should make the effort to look in addition in some of the other places described above.

RECENT LITERATURE

Frederick C. Warner and Donald Lines Jacobus, "Mr. William[1] Clarke of Salem, Massachusetts: An Exchange of Letters," *The American Genealogist* 72 (1997):183-86. In 1963 Frederick C. Warner and Frances Davis McTeer published a carefully reasoned article about the children of William[1] Clarke of Salem, to which Jacobus appended an "Editorial Note." Warner disagreed with Jacobus with regard to some points in this note, as a result of which Warner wrote a letter to Jacobus, which is published here along with the reply by Jacobus.

Robert Charles Anderson, "Congregations in Flight: The Beginning of the Laudian Migration to New England," *The American Genealogist* 72 (1997):257-62. Anderson discusses the differences between migration to New England up to 1633, and migration after that date, with emphasis on the influence of Archbishop William Laud on the later migration.

John C. Brandon, "The English Origin of Elder Hatevil[1] Nutter of Dover, New Hampshire: With an Account of His Uncle, the Reverend Anthony Nutter, Puritan Minister of Fenny Drayton, Leicestershire, and Woodkirk, Yorkshire," *The American Genealogist* 72 (1997):263-84. Brandon marshals extensive evidence to demonstrate that Hatevil Nutter, immigrant to Dover by 1635, was son of Edmund Nutter of Fillongley and elsewhere in Warwickshire. A brother of Edmund Nutter, Rev. Anthony Nutter, was a prominent Puritan minister at Fenny Drayton, Leicestershire, and Woodkirk, Yorkshire. Rev. Anthony Nutter almost certainly was acquainted in England with Rev. John Reyner, who was later the minister at Dover.

Jane Fletcher Fiske, "A New England Immigrant Kinship Network: Notes on the English Origins of the Scudders of Salem and Barnstable, Massachusetts, Bridget (-----) (Verry) Giles of Salem, and Joanna (Chamberlain) Betts of Long Island," *The American Genealogist* 72 (1997):285-300. The author has delineated a very extensive and interesting network of immigrants to New England, centering on the brothers Thomas and John Scudder, and deriving from Horton Kirby, Kent. Thomas Scudder, his wife and five children settled at Salem in 1637, and he died there twenty years later. John Scudder, brother of Thomas, died in 1625 or 1626, and his widow, who was a sister of Thomas and Israel Stoughton of Dorchester, married as her second husband Robert Chamberlain. This second husband died in 1639, after which the widow, her surviving Scudder daughter and her two surviving Chamberlain children came to New England. Her eldest surviving Scudder child, John, had come to New England in 1635. Another member of this extensive kinship network who came to Salem was Bridget (_____) (Verry) Giles, who was probably a niece of Thomas and John Scudder

Neil D. Thompson, "The Origin and Parentage of Francis[1] Eaton of the *Mayflower*," *The American Genealogist* 72 (1997):301-4. Following up on a clue from Bristol apprenticeship records, which has long been in print, Thompson has unearthed additional English records which indicate that Francis Eaton was baptized at St. Thomas parish in that city in 1596, son of John and Dorothy (Smith) Eaton. Thompson also shows that the given name of Francis Eaton's second wife was Dorothy.

David L. Greene, "Notes on Francis[1] Eaton of Plymouth," *The American Genealogist* 72 (1997):305-9. Greene elaborates on the findings in Thompson's article, discussing three points: a potential, but unlikely, connection with the small settlement at Cape Ann; the likelihood that Isaac Allerton, while in England on business for himself and the settlement at Plymouth, had arranged the apprentice for Francis Eaton; and some details regarding the wives and children of Francis Eaton.

Gordon Lewis Remington, "Old Wine into New Bottles: The Case of George[1] Lewis of Brenchley, Kent, and Scituate, Massachusetts," *The American Genealogist* 72 (1997):311-20. Remington examines in detail the history of research into the English origin of George[1] Lewis of Scituate, adding considerably to what is already known. As he points out, the basic facts of the origin have been in print in this country since 1942, but in an obscure location and without proper documentation. Over the years this knowledge has been passed along, but with various layers of misinformation added. Remington points a number of lessons drawn from his research on this problem.

Gordon Lewis Remington, "Mary Doggett, Wife of George[1] Lewis of Brenchley, Kent, and Scituate, Massachusetts," *The American Genealogist* 72 (1997):321-28. While doing the research described immediately above, Remington discovered that the wife of George Lewis was not Sarah Jenkins, as many sources had claimed, but was Mary Doggett, daughter of Thomas Doggett of Horsmonden, Kent. This leads to a potential connection with Simon Willard and Dolor Davis, also from Horsmonden.

Robert S. Wakefield, "Joseph[2] Taber of Bristol County, Massachusetts: Additions to Anderson's *Great Migration Begins* and Torrey's *New England Marriages*," *The American Genealogist* 72 (1997):329-32. Wakefield shows that Joseph[2] Taber, son of Philip[1] Taber (or Tabor) did marry, and by wife Hannah (surname unknown) had at least five children [cf. GMB 3:1793]. Wakefield also provides the evidence for the marriage of Joseph's sister Lydia to Pardon Tillinghast, a deed in which Joseph refers to Lydia's son Joseph Tillinghast as cousin [i.e., nephew]. Also, a son of Joseph married a daughter of Elizabeth.

(continued from page 18)

which neither Haines nor Tarbox deemed relevant: "Mary Armitage, daughter of John Cogswell, Sen., deceased, aged about fifty-eight years," had also sailed on the *Angel Gabriel*, and was able to corroborate the testimony of her father's servants [Cogswell Gen 12]. Given the presence aboard ship of this daughter, we assume that John Cogswell was accompanied also by his wife and probably one more daughter.

From these depositions we can begin to construct the passenger list of the *Angel Gabriel*: John Cogswell, his wife, three sons and two daughters; Samuel Haines; and William Tarbox – a total of nine.

The *Angel Gabriel* was clearly one of those vessels, like the *Mayflower* and the *Mary & John*, which nineteenth-century descendants wanted their ancestors to have come on, for there are several bogus claims for other immigrants.

William Hubbard claimed that the Rev. Joseph Avery was on the *Angel Gabriel* [Hubbard 200], but Savage pointed out his error. Hubbard conflated the wreck of the *Angel Gabriel* and the wreck of the coasting vessel carrying Avery around Cape Ann, disasters which occurred on the same day in the same storm.

The claim that Robert Andrews of Ipswich was an *Angel Gabriel* passenger probably derives from the false claim about Avery, since Andrews was one of Avery's creditors. But we can easily show that Andrews was in New England when the *Angel Gabriel* was still in England; Andrews was made a freeman on 6 May 1635, an event which required his presence in New England.

And Joshua Coffin's claim that Henry Beck of Dover was on this ship is easily refuted, since Beck is known to have sailed for New England on the *Blessing* from London.

Banks was especially perverse in his attempt to construct a passenger list for the *Angel Gabriel*, as he does not include the Cogswell family and its servants, nor does he include the others whose false claims are given above. His only two candidates are Ralph Blaisdell and Henry Simpson, both of York. For Blaisdell, Banks tells us that "a family tradition has been furnished" that he came on the *Angel Gabriel* [York Hist 1:99]. Banks had found the names Ralph Blaisdell and Henry Simpson associated in Lancashire records about 1590, and on this basis suggests this as their origin, and apparently also uses this as justification for placing them on the same ship. While none of this is impossible, it is far from proven, and we do not even accept them as 1635 immigrants.

Finally, noting that John Cogswell was from Westbury, Wiltshire, and that he shipped his livestock on a vessel sailing from Southampton, we would suggest that the *Angel Gabriel* passengers need not have been from Lancashire and vicinity, as were the passengers on the *James* associated with Rev. Richard Mather.

(to be concluded in Volume 7, No. 4)

Great Migration Study Project
101 Newbury Street
Boston, MA 02116

Great Migration Newsletter

Vol. 7   October-December 1998   No. 4

PASSENGER SHIPS OF 1635 - Part IV

In our last installment, we described the travails of two ships, the *James* and the *Angel Gabriel*. In mid-June, when these two vessels were just preparing to leave from the Bristol roadstead, six other ships were taking on passengers at the London docks, and by mid-July, when the *James* and *Angel Gabriel* were halfway through their voyage, and still in sight of one another, these six ships had taken on all their passengers.

The first of these vessels to take on passengers was the *Abigail*, which registered eight emigrants on 4 May 1635. This ship was still at dockside on 10 July when the last of the recorded passengers appeared. Among this latter group were John Winthrop Jr., his wife and his younger brother Deane Winthrop. Perhaps the vessel had been contracted to delay passage until the arrival of this eminent person, returning to New England after a brief visit in England.

The other five ships were the *Blessing* (which took on passengers from 17 June until 13 July), the *James* (19 June to 13 July), the *Defence* (20 June to 18 July), the *Love* (13 July only, eight passengers) and the *Pied Cow* (18 July to 23 July, four passengers).

Our information on the sailing and arrival of these six ships may be divided into three groups of two each. First, we are informed by Governor Winthrop on 6 October that

> Here arrived two great ships, the *Defence* and the *Abigail*, with Mr. Wilson, pastor of Boston, Mr. Shepard, Mr. Jones, and other ministers; amongst others, Mr. Peter, pastor of the English church in Rotterdam, who, being persecuted by the English ambassador … and not having had his health these many years, intended to advise with the ministers here about his removal.

> The special goodness of the Lord appeared in this, that the passengers came safe and hale in all the ships, though some of them long passages – the *Abigail* ten weeks from Plimouth, with two hundred and twenty persons, and many cattle, infected also with the small-pox [WJ 1:201-2].

Winthrop went on at length to describe two additional passengers on these ships – his son, "John Winthrop, the younger," and "one Mr. Henry Vane, son and heir to Sir Henry Vane, comptroller of the king's house" [WJ 1:202-3]. This latter arrival would within one year become governor of the colony.

We note first the discrepancy between the number of passengers claimed for the *Abigail* by Winthrop (220) and the number who had registered at dockside in London (180). We cannot be sure of the explanation for these additional forty immigrants. Perhaps Winthrop just had the number wrong, or else it may be that the London lists are incomplete. As we will see shortly in the case of the *Defence*, there were a number of passengers who boarded in disguise, sometimes illegally.

In 1646 or shortly thereafter, Rev. Thomas Shepard composed a "Memoir of Himself," a substantial portion of which described the preparations for this voyage to New England, and the voyage itself [Young's First Planters 499-558]. Shepard and a number of his followers made an attempt to sail for New England late in 1634, but after many difficulties they turned back.

Having spent the winter in London, Shepard and others "set forward about the 10th of August 1635…. In our coming we were refreshed with the society of Mr. Wilson, and Mr. Jones, by their faith, and prayers, and preaching."

(continued on page 26)

EDITOR'S EFFUSIONS

One of the guiding principles of our work on the Great Migration Study Project is that we attempt as often as possible to examine the original, or at least the earliest surviving copy, of as many documents as we can, especially probate records and the sources related to English origin. In order to assist us in this work, and to do our job more efficiently, we have over the years acquired many of these records on microfilm, so that we can examine these records without spending large amounts of time travelling to distant repositories. (Of course, in those cases where we have not yet obtained microfilm, we continue to travel to courthouses, archives and Salt Lake City.)

In order to make our work even more efficient, we have recently obtained a microfilm reader-printer. Prior to this, when examining records on microfilm, we were obliged to create a transcript or abstract by hand, then take this to our computer station and key in the details. (The layout of the equipment at our two main worksites made it difficult to read from the microfilm screen and enter text directly into the computer.) This had the dual disadvantages of taking extra time and also possibly introducing errors in the copying process.

With our new equipment, we can simply make a photocopy of the desired documents, take them to our computer work stations, read them there, and make entries directly into the sketch in progress. An additional advantage to this approach is that we also create something that we can add to the physical file for that sketch. Thus, when it is necessary to reexamine a document at a later date, no time is wasted in cranking through the microfilm a second or third time.

Robert Charles Anderson, FASG   Editor
Aileen Novick   Production Assistant

The Great Migration Newsletter is published quarterly by the Great Migration Study Project, a project of the New England Historic Genealogical Society, 101 Newbury Street, Boston MA 02116

The subscription rate is $12 for one year and $20 for two years.

(continued from page 25)

Shepard then reported that "upon October the 3d, we arrived, with my wife, child, brother Samuel, Mr. Harlakenden, Mr. Cookes, &c. at Boston."

The passenger list for the *Defence* does not include the name of Thomas Shepard, but there is an entry for "Husb[andman] John Sheppard," with wife Margaret and son Thomas, aged three months [Hotten 99], which corresponds with what we know of Rev. Thomas Shepard and his family. Thus, he altered both his given name and his occupation in order to mislead the port officials. Roger Harlakenden also appears on the passenger list, along with Samuel Shepard (listed as his servant), and both Joseph and George Cooke [Hotten 100].

There are, however, no entries in the London port book for anyone that can now be identified as Rev. John Wilson or Rev. John Jones, so they managed to get on the *Defence* without the knowledge of the dockside authorities. Rev. Hugh Peter was more likely on the *Abigail*, but he also does not appear in the official lists. Thus, the discrepancy between the number of passengers according to the port book and the number according to Winthrop is partially explained.

One further problem with regard to the published passenger list for the *Defence* remains to be discussed. Col. Banks includes in one of his compilations an entry for the ship *Desire*, with twelve passengers [Planters 130]. Comparison with other versions of the London port books quickly reveals that Banks invented a ship out of thin air, and that these passengers in fact came on the *Defence* [Hotten 89, 91].

The arrival dates of the remaining four ships in this grouping of six are unknown, but we can say something about their passage. First we will take up the two ships with the larger complements of passengers, the *James* and the *Blessing*. These two vessels did not have as many passengers as many of the other ships did; there were 67 on the list for the *Blessing* and 50 on the *James*.

Given the dates that these ships took on passengers, one would expect that they left London about the same time as the *Abigail* and the *Defence*, and therefore also arrived in New England about the same time. Perhaps Winthrop did not mention them at the same time because there were fewer passengers, and certainly fewer prominent passengers. Or perhaps they arrived at a different time than the *Abigail* and the *Defence*. At any rate, we can be certain that these ships did arrive in New England, since most of the persons named in the port book appear in New England late in 1635 or early in 1636.

(continued on page 32)

Focus   *on*   **HINGHAM**

SETTLEMENT OF HINGHAM

Hingham first appears in the records on 25 September 1634, when the settlement, then named Barecove (or Bear Cove), was assessed £4, in a year when the entire colony paid taxes of £600, and the three largest towns, Boston, Dorchester and Cambridge, paid £80 apiece [MBCR 1:129]. (Some modern sources claim that Hingham was settled as early as 1633, but this appears to be a misinterpretation of the Cushing Record, to be discussed below.)

In its first year or so of existence Barecove should probably be thought of as an extension of its neighbor immediately to the west, Wessaguscus (soon to be known as Weymouth). At this time Wessaguscus itself was an offshoot of Dorchester, and the majority of the residents of these latter two places were from the West Country of England. (This relationship among the three communities was still evident on 20 November 1637, when the General Court ordered that "Mr. [Nathaniel] Duncan [of Dorchester] should train at Waymoth, … & to see if Hingham be provided of officers, & if not, he to supply" [MBCR 1:210].)

The first two names that we can associate with Barecove are John Alderman and Joseph Andrews. On 30 September 1634, Governor Winthrop tells us of "one Alderman, of Bear Cove, being about fifty years old, [who] lost his way between Dorchester and Wessaguscus, and wandered in the swamps three days and two nights, without taking any food, and, being near, spent, God brought him to Scituate" [WJ 1:171-72]. Then, on 8 July 1635, "Joseph Andrewes [was] sworn constable of Barecove" [MBCR 1:149].

"John Elderman" and "Joseph Androes" were two of the passengers who sailed from Weymouth in old England early in 1634 [NGSQ 71:171-2, 77:251]. The passengers on this vessel were from the West Country, and many of them settled at Dorchester, but several others settled at Hingham.

On 2 September 1635, the General Court declared that "[t]he name of Barecove is changed, & hereafter to be called Hingham" [MBCR 1:156]. This order is somewhat unusual, since in almost all other instances in these earliest years of Massachusetts Bay, the "pre-incorporation" name of a settlement was of Algonkian origin, as for example in the order of the same day that "Wessaguscus is also changed, & hereafter to be called Waymothe." This may suggest that the tract of land between Wessaguscus and Nantasket was of no great use or interest to the indigenous population.

The new name for the town arose because of the great influx of settlers who had their origin in the parish of Hingham in

Norfolk in old England. At some point in his life Daniel Cushing, who was about fifteen years old in the mid-1630s, compiled "A list of the names of such persons as came out of the town of Hingham, and towns adjacent in the County of Norfolk, in the Kingdom of England, into New England, and settled in Hingham, in New England" [NEHGR 15:25-27]. Cushing listed the immigrants family by family, in chronological order of arrival. The earliest came in 1633, with a few more in 1634, 1635 and 1637. The bulk of the passengers (133) came on the *Diligent* in 1638 . More than two hundred persons are enumerated by Cushing.

As noted above, because this list begins with several members of the Hobart family, along with a few others, who arrived in 1633, this has been taken by some as the date of settlement of Hingham. But all those who came in 1633 and 1634, as well as Rev. Peter Hobart, who came in 1635, settled first in Charlestown. Records for all these persons are complete and continuous in Charlestown until the summer of 1635, when many of them made the move to Hingham. We are left, then, with the first appearance of Dorchester-connected settlers in 1634, followed by the great influx in 1635 of immigrants from old Hingham, some coming over from Charlestown and some directly from England.

Returning to the development of the standard town institutions, we find that Hingham was grouped with Boston, Roxbury, Dorchester and Weymouth when the system of Quarter Courts was established on 3 March 1635/6 [MBCR 1:169], although when the magistrates were named for that court there was no representative from Weymouth or Hingham [MBCR 1:175]. On 13 December 1636, Hingham was grouped with the same four towns when the three military regiments were organized [MBCR 1:186]. These groupings were the basis on which Suffolk County was organized seven years later.

Although other newly settled towns were granted a brief moratorium from paying taxes to the colony, Hingham was not so lucky. On 3 September 1636 and again on 3 March 1635/6, the town was assessed £6; of the thirteen towns rated, only Weymouth was smaller [MBCR 1:158, 166]. Hingham was assessed £8 10s. on 1 August 1637, £24 on 15 November 1637 and £36 on 12 March 1637/8 [MBCR 1:201, 209, 225]. The increase in the size of the tax payment did not reflect an increase in the wealth of the town, but a fixed proportional share of a larger colony levy; Hingham continued during this period to be ahead only of Weymouth in the tax tables.

On the day that Weymouth and Hingham were both given their formal English names, Weymouth was allowed immediately to have a deputy at the General Court, but Hingham did not have this privilege so soon. The first recorded appearance of a deputy from Hingham was on 25 May 1636, when Joseph Andrews and Nicholas Baker were sent [MBCR 1:174]. And finally, the town reached full maturity when on 12 March 1637/8 Thomas Loring was "allowed to sell wine & strong water" [MBCR 1:221].

EARLY HINGHAM LANDGRANTING

Hingham began granting lands in 1635, the records of which survive in three different forms. Although all were compiled at about the same time, we can make some suggestions as to the order in which they were created. The first was probably the volume in which the grants are arranged by the type of lots which were granted, generally on a given day. (These may be found on fiches numbered 41 through 45 in the microform version of the records, with a modern transcript on fiches 6 through 11.)

As it now exists, this volume begins with houselots granted on 18 September 1635, the first to Thomas Wakeley. This page is mutilated, but even so enough survives to tell us that a page or more has been lost at the beginning. This entry for Thomas Wakely says "It is likewise agreed upon, that Thomas Wakelie shall have his House Lot, five acres next to Richard Betscombe, upon the same [neck]." The words "likewise" and "same," and the reference to Richard Betscombe as a neighbor to the westward, tell us that this entry follows one for Richard Betscombe on a previous page, now not in existence. In one of the later volumes, we find the entry for the houselot of Richard Betscombe, which tells us that his neighbor in one direction is Thomas Wakeley and in the other is William Walton, from which we may deduce that William Walton's was the next-to-last entry on this lost page. Further tracing of neighbors of Walton, and so on, should allow substantial reconstruction of this lost material.

On separate pages there are grants of planting ground, Broad Cove Meadows, Great Lots and other types of parcels.

The remaining two sets of records are rearrangements of this first volume, with the various lots grouped together according to grantee. One of these volumes is relatively brief (original on fiche 5; modern copy on fiche 4). This volume begins with the entry for Thomas Wakeley, and tells us that he had been granted a five-acre houselot, six acres of planting ground, a small planting lot of one acre and a half, three acres of meadow, and a Great Lot of sixteen acres.

The last volume is arranged in a similar way, but is more extensive, partly because it contains later transfers of land beyond the original grants from the town (original on fiches 13 through 18; no modern copy found). That this volume was created after the first volume mentioned above, and

probably after the second, is indicated by the details given in some of the entries. In the first two volumes noted above, for example, in the entry for Andrew Lane we find that his houselot is described as being "next to Nathaniel Baker, his brother-in-law, to the westward," whereas in the last volume described the information about the marital relationship has been omitted. Similar information on several other early settlers appears in other entries in the first two volumes, but has also been omitted from the third. As we see so frequently, we are never safe in examining just one version of a set of records, when two or more versions exist. We also conclude that the early Hingham town clerks were very busy men, frequently copying and recopying their earliest records.

Despite these omissions, however, the third volume described is in many ways the most useful. First, it is easily the most legible of the three sets of originals. Second, it groups together all the land granted to an individual, along with the dates of the grants, information that is not included in the second volume.

This third volume also allows us to see at a glance what constituted a typical set of parcels granted to one person. Joseph Andrews, for instance, was given a houselot of five acres, a Great Lot of twenty-four acres, a planting lot of three acres, four acres of planting land, eight acres at Rocky Neck, five more acres of planting land, two acres for a small planting lot, eight acres of salt marsh, and two acres of fresh meadow. The last of these lots was granted in 1637, and all the rest in 1635. We are not surprised to find that the assortment of types of parcels is very much like what we find in other Massachusetts Bay towns.

HINGHAM CHURCH

Worthley, in his compilation of information on the early Congregational churches of New England, gives 18 September 1635 as the date of organization of the Hingham church [*An Inventory of the Records of the Particular (Congregational) Churches of Massachusetts Gathered 1620-1805* (Cambridge 1970), p. 286]. No source is given for this date. The early church records do not exist, and Winthrop failed to mention the organization of this church in his journal (perhaps because of his concentration on the ecclesiatical problems being created during this same period by Rev. Roger Williams at Salem and Rev. Stephen Bachiler at Lynn).

It may be that Worthley was misled by the essay on "Ecclesiastical History" written by Francis H. Lincoln [*History of the Town of Hingham, Massachusetts* in Three Volumes (Hingham 1893), Volume I, Part II, page one]: "The first church in Hingham was formed in September 1635.... On the second of September, 1635, the name of Bare Cove was changed to Hingham; and on the eighteenth of the same month Mr. Hobart and twenty-nine others drew for houselots. Here Mr. Hobart gathered the church which was the twelfth in order of time in Massachusetts proper."

Here we have the story of the founding of the church and the date of 18 September 1635 in close juxtaposition, but not the claim that the first happened on the second. There is good reason to believe that the church was in fact founded somewhat later.

In the brief list of those men who were admitted to freemanship on 2 September 1635 is found "Peter Hubbert," in a context which does not allow us to assigne him to a town [MBCR 1:371]. But the church records of Charlestown tell us that "Mr. Peeter Hubberd" was admitted to that church on 30 August 1635 [ChChR 8]. In early September, then, Rev. Peter Hobart was still a resident of Charlestown. Just over two weeks later he and several others were drawing houselots at Hingham. This places the removal of Hobart and several others from Charlestown to Hingham in a very narrow time frame. It is unlikely, however, given the example of other New England towns, that a church was also organized within this brief period.

Our first solid evidence that the church had been formed is the list of freemen of 3 March 1635/6, where we find a grouping of eleven men who were known to be residents of Hingham: William Walton, Thomas Loring, Clement Bates, Thomas Wakely, William Norton, George Ludkin, George Marsh, John Otis, Nicholas Baker, Nicholas Jacob and David Phippen [MBCR 1:371]. The church was founded, then, no later than 3 March 1635/6; we may never be able to narrow the date more closely than that. This list almost certainly does not include all the founders of Hingham church, since a number of the earliest residents, including Edmund Hobart, father of Rev. Peter, had earlier been admitted to Charlestown church, and already made freemen before the removal to Hingham. Two additional groups of Hingham freemen, and therefore recent church members, were recorded on 9 January 1636/7 (Richard Betscombe, Anthony Eames, Samuel Ward, Thomas Hammond and Thomas Underwood [MBCR 1:372]) and on 13 January 1638/9 (Mr. Joseph Peck, Henry Smith, Edward Gilman, Thomas Cooper, John Beal, Henry Chamberlain, Thomas Clapp, John Palmer and John Tower [MBCR 1:375]).

Whatever the date of founding of Hingham church, Hobart served alone as pastor for more than two years, until 28 November 1638 when "Mr. [Robert] Peck was ordained teacher of the church" [NEHGR 121:11]. Then, on 29 January 1639/40, "Henry Smith and Ralph Wodward [were] chosen deacons," and on 2 February following they were ordained [NEHGR 121:12].

Rev. Peter Hobart (and therefore the Hingham church) stood out in the earliest years in New England as one of the few ministers who favored and actually implemented the Presbyterian rather than the Congregational form of church membership (the other similarly inclined ministers being Rev. Thomas Parker and Rev. James Noyes at Newbury). William Hubbard, writing just a few years after the death of Peter Hobart, in a brief gem of understatement which borders on humor, described him as "a man well qualified with ministerial abilities, though not so fully persuaded of the congregational discipline as some others were" [Hubbard 192].

Although Winthrop and the other orthodox Massachusetts Bay leaders may have been distracted at the time the Hingham and Newbury churches were organized, these Presbyterian leaders eventually came into conflict with the Congregationalists, especially in the case of the Remonstrance of 1646 [Robert Emmet Wall, Jr., *Massachusetts Bay: The Crucial Decade, 1640-1650* (New Haven 1972), *passim*].

EARLY VITAL RECORDS

There is no complete set of vital records for the earliest years of Hingham. We have to look in at least three different places to uncover the vital events of the first and second generations of settlers.

The earliest of the three sets of records is the journal of Rev. Peter Hobart, which commences with an entry for 1635. The original of this journal does not survive, and we now have available to us a copy made probably late in the seventeenth century by Peter's son David. The document was published in full by C. Edward Egan Jr. in 1967, with careful annotations[NEHGR 121:3-25, 102-27, 191-216, 269-94]. There are on occasion problems in assigning an exact date to an event recorded by Hobart, sometimes because of the arrangement of the records, and sometimes because of damage to the journal itself; these difficulties are discussed by Egan in his introduction to the published transcript.

The records are a mix between a private record and the records of the church at Hingham. The first entry is for the arrival of Hobart, his wife and four children in New England in 1635, followed by an entry for the birth of his fifth child, in Charlestown. There is then a gap of nearly two years, at which time we learn that "Hannah Hobart my daughter" was born on 30 April 1637, was baptized on 7 May, and died soon after.

In early 1638 the journal expands to include a regular stream of baptismal and marriage records for Hingham residents. The baptismal entries are evidence of Rev. Peter Hobart's pastoral activities in Hingham, but the marriage records are not, as marriage was a civil function at this time. In fact, the first marriage recorded is that of Joshua Hobart and Ellen Ibrook, which took place at Cambridge.

Hobart also took notice of a wider variety of events as well. On 8 November 1638, for example, he reported "a church gathered at Dedham," and on 28 November of the same year he noted that "Mr. Peck [was] ordained teacher of the church."

Peter Hobart continued to make regular entries in his journal, about thirty a year at the beginning, slowly rising to about fifty a year, until his death on 20 January 1678/9 [NEHGR 121:202-3]; most of the items were baptisms, marriages and deaths.

Despite the careful work done by Egan, there are a few misreadings in his transcription and, as always, if there is some doubt about the published entry, recourse should be had to the original of the journal. In December of 1645 there appears the baptism of "Sarah Boston," a surname not noticed in Hingham, or elsewhere in New England at this early period [NEHGR 121:18]. About two years later, on 5 March 1647/8, is found the baptism of "Rebeckah Beerstow" [NEHGR 121:20]. Examination of the original journal reveals that "Boston" should be "Bestow," and these two baptisms are the principal evidence for the residence of William Barstow and his family in Hingham during these years.

The next set of Hingham vital records is contained in the misnamed "Early Records of Boston," which were published a century and a half ago in the Register, and which are really the copies of the town vital records submitted to the county recorder. The earliest surviving records for Hingham are a small grouping for the years 1645 through 1650, containing six births and five deaths [NEHGR 9:172]. For this same period, Hobart in his journal listed more than one hundred baptisms and about thirty deaths.

Even given the small number of entries in the county copy for these years as compared to the Hobart journal, some of the county copy entries do not appear in the Hobart journal. The baptism of Hannah, daughter of Simon Burr, in 1646 and the death of Esther Burr in 1645 were missed by Hobart. On the other hand, the county copy clearly has some errors, such as the death of Thomas Collier, given as 6 April 1646, when Hobart places this event exactly one year later.

More of these county copies of Hingham events are also included in the "Early Records of Boston," covering the years 1651 through 1657. This time the submission was more complete, comprising seventy-eight births, thirteen marriages and eleven deaths [NEHGR 13:213-15]. Although no item-by-item comparison has been made of this group of records with the Hobart copy, it is evident that the overlap is much greater. It should be noted that this set of entries was submitted by "John Fearing, Clerk of the Writs."

The third set of early Hingham vital records was compiled by Daniel Cushing, the same who had compiled the list of emigrants from Hingham in England, discussed above. The first page of this book is headed "Hingham Register Book of the Births, Deaths and Marriages in the said town begun and

kept by Daniell Cushing Senior chosen thereto by the town 15 August 1665." The significance of this date is seen on page four of the volume, where we find that "John Fearing Clerk of the Writs deceased on the 14 day of May 1665." Combining this item with our previous investigations of the earlier county copies tells us that Fearing must have been town clerk for at least twenty years. Given the reference to his office in his death record, we may conclude that he had recorded vital events for all of this twenty years. What became of the vast majority of these records?

Daniel Cushing did not simply begin to enter the records of vital events that occurred after his date of appointment. He began by reaching back twenty years, to his own marriage to Lydia Gilman, after which he entered in chronological order the births of his seven children born between 1645 and 1660.

A few other entries were made out of sequence. Immediately after the family of Daniel Cushing are two other entries, not in the hand of Daniel Cushing, but of the same era, one for a daughter of Joshua Hobart baptized in 1639 and the second for a son of Joseph Grafton baptized in 1663. Next comes the marriage of John Jacob and Margery Eames in 1653, the births of three of their children, the death of Margery, the remarriage of John Jacob in 1661 and the birth of two more of his children, the last being in 1664. This sequence is followed by a birth from 1664 and a marriage from 1664.

The regular sequence of records commences with the death of John Fearing on 14 May 1665. Only two more intrusive groupings are found after this date – the 1657 marriage of Joseph Grafton (again not in Daniel Cushing's hand), and seven children of John Lassell, born between 1652 and 1664, placed in the 1667 records. Cushing regularly noted when he submitted the year's records "to Boston," meaning to the county recorder.

In the period before 1665, the surviving vital records are certainly not complete. For the small group of records submitted by John Fearing, we find some not recorded by Peter Hobart, and so we may assume that the same omissions existed in the years for which we do not have the Fearing records. On the other hand, there are a number of instances for which we have two or even three independent records for the same event. For example, John Fearing recorded the birth of Deborah Cushing, daughter of Daniel Cushing on 18 November 1651 [NEHGR 13:213]. Daniel Cushing himself noted his daughter's baptism on 23 November 1651 on the first page of his record, and Rev. Peter Hobart also included the baptism in his list for November 1651 [NEHGR 121:24]. (In the published version of this latter entry, the date has been reconstructed as 13 November, which is clearly incorrect. This further implies that the following entry made by Hobart, the death of "Mr. Ibrook," should be read as 24 November rather than the reconstructed 14 November.)

RECENT LITERATURE

Christopher Gleason Clark, "The English Ancestry of Joseph Clark (1613-1683) of Dedham and Medfield, Massachusetts," *The New England Historical and Genealogical Register* 152 (1998):3-23. Clark demonstrates that Joseph Clark of Dedham was baptized at Banham, Norfolk, and that he had sisters Rebecca (who married Ralph Wheelock) and Elizabeth (who married George Barber). Joseph Clark also had siblings Rowland and Mary who may have come to Dedham, and if so, the latter married Benjamin Smith. Priscilla Clark who married Nathaniel Colebourne may also have been a member of this family.

Clifford L. Stott, "The Correct Origins of Nathaniel Dickinson and William Gull of Wethersfield and Hadley," *The New England Historical and Genealogical Register* 152 (1998):159-78. Stott shows that Nathaniel Dickinson dervied from Billingborough, Lincolnshire, and that his wife was the widow Ann (_____) Gull, mother of William Gull. Who also came to New England.

James Raywalt, "The Identity of Sarah, Wife of Daniel Scofield and Miles Merwin – Still a Mystery," *The New England Historical and Genealogical Register* 152 (1998):179-83. The author argues that, despite many claims in the literature, Sarah, wife of Daniel Scofield and Miles Merwin, was not the daughter of Rev. John Youngs.

Gordon L. Remington, "The English Origin of William[1] Mead of Stamford, Connecticut," *The American Genealogist* 73 (1998):1-10. Remington presents evidence that William Mead of Stamford was baptized in Watford, Hertfordshire. This research also demonstrates that Gabriel Mead of Dorchester was not a brother of William.

Eugene Cole Zubrinsky," Deacon John[1] Warfield and His Family of Medfield and Mendon, Massachusetts: With Proof of the Paternity of Deacon Samuel[2] Warfield," *The American Genealogist* 73 (1998):11-21. Zubrinsky treats in detail the family of John Warfield, who does not appear in New England until the early 1650s, but whose three wives were daughters of three Great Migration immigrants: John Shepard, Ralph Wheelock and Robert Randall.

John C. Brandon and Janet Ireland Delorey, "Terms of Endearment: The Puzzling Will of Rebecca Bacon, With the English Origins of Rebecca Potter, Wife of William[1] Bacon, Ann Potter, Wife of Anthony[1] Needham, and Joseph[1] and Eleanor (Plover) Boyce of Salem, Massachusetts," *The American Genealogist* 73 (1998):23-32. The authors show that Rebecca (Potter) Bacon was baptized at Holy Trinity, Coventry, Warwickshire, and that her niece, Ann Potter, also came to New England, where she married Anthony Needham. In addition, Joseph Boyce of Salem probably derived from Burford, Oxfordshire.

Douglas Richardson, "New Light on the English Ancestry of William[1] Chandler and of His Cousin, Margaret Chandler, Wife of William[1] Dennison, Both of Roxbury, Massachusetts," *The American Genealogist* 73 (1998):50-57. Richardson argues cogently that William Chandler and Margaret (Chandler) (Monk) Dennison, wife of William Dennison, were first cousins, and not second cousins, as had been earlier supposed.

Clifford L. Stott, "The Gloucestershire T(h)ayer Ancestry: The Ancestry of Cicely Tayer, Wife of James[1] Davis of Haverhill, Massachusetts, and Probable Cousin of Thomas[1] and Richard[1] T(h)ayer of Braintree, Massachusetts," *The American Genealogist* 73 (1998):81-90, 209-19. Stott presents extensive evidence on the Tayer family of Thornbury, Gloucestershire, which included Cicely Tayer who married in 1618 at Thornbury James Davis. Thomas and Richard Thayer of Braintree also derived from this parish, but their connection to the family is uncertain, largely because at the critical time the Thornbury parish register did not identify the parents of children being baptized.

William B. Saxbe, Jr., "Thomas[2] Walling and His Way With Women: Seventeenth-Century Misconduct as an Aid to Identification," *The American Genealogist* 73 (1998):91-100. The author delineates the life of Thomas Walling of Providence, and argues that he was a son of Ralph[1] Wallen of Plymouth and Barnstable. This identification is based largely on a pattern of antisocial behavior, including association with Margaret (White) (Colwell) (Walling) Abbott, who was unkind to all of her husbands.

Paul C. Reed, "The Fraudulent Ancestry of Deacon John[1] Dunham of Plymouth," *The American Genealogist* 73 (1998):101-4. Reed carefully and systematically dissects and destroys four generations of ancestry supposed to attach to John Dunham of Plymouth. He shows that the alleged grandfather of the immigrant, Ralph Dunham, did not exist, having been created out of a misreading of a record for a Ralph Denman. As Reed points out, what we can now rely on for our knowledge of the ancestry of this immigrant is found in an earlier article by Robert Leigh Ward [TAG 71 (1996):130-33].

Dean Crawford Smith, "Some Olney Cluster Corrections: Newhall, Farrington, Worcester, Fuller," *The American Genealogist* 73 (1998):119-22. The author supplements the earlier work of the late Thomas Cooper on a number of families of Olney, Buckinghamshire. By re-examining the parish registers and Bishops' transcripts of Sherington, Olney and Clifton Reynes, Smith has added to our understanding of the immigrant families of Anthony and Thomas Newhall, Edmund Farrington, Rev. William Worcester and John Fuller.

(continued from page 26)

A few comments about the various ships named the *James* are in order. We have firm evidence of three different ships of this name bringing passengers to New England in 1635. The *James* of London sailed from Southampton in April, with passengers from Wiltshire and Hampshire, and arrived in New England on 3 June [GMN 7:9-10]. The *James* of Bristol, carrying passengers from Yorkshire, left the west of England in June and arrived in New England in August [GMN 7:17]. And, as we have seen just above, another *James* began to take on passengers at London in mid-June and probably arrived in New England in October.

The first and last of these, although both connected with London, cannot be the same vessel, as the first of them was at Boston on 3 June, and the third was dockside at London on 19 June. Banks claims that the third of these vessels "arrived at Boston the last week in September" [Planters 151]; no support for this statement has been found in contemporary records, and perhaps Banks was confused by the multiplicity of ships named *James*.

Finally, we take up the last pair of these six ships which were taking on passengers at the London docks in July, the *Love* and the *Pied Cow*, each of which was credited with a very small group of passengers. On the *Love* there were only eight entered by the port official: William and Ursula Cherrall; Francis, John and Sarah Harman; Walter Parker; and William and Mary Browne [Hotten 109]. Interestingly, of these eight only William Browne and his wife can be identified as having arrived in New England (and even that identification is not totally certain).

The *Pied Cow* had an even shorter passenger list than did the *Love*, with just four persons recorded: William Harrison, John Baldin, William Baldin and Robert Bills [Hotten 106, 110]. Only one of these, Robert Bills, is known to have arrived in New England (and he died within months of landing).

It would appear, then, that only three of the twelve passengers on these two ships actually made it to New England. Although it is possible that the other nine died during the passage, or chose at the last minute not to make the crossing, such a high proportion of "no-shows" is not seen on the other vessels. There is not sufficient evidence to be certain, but perhaps William Browne and wife and Robert Bills took passage in one of the other ships leaving at that time, and the *Pied Cow* and *Love* never did sail for New England.

In the final installment of this essay, we will look at five more ships which arrived late in the year, and then summarize what we know about passenger arrivals in 1635.

(to be concluded in Volume 8, No. 1)

Great Migration Study Project
101 Newbury Street
Boston, MA 02116

Great Migration Newsletter

Vol. 8   January-March 1999   No. 1

PASSENGER SHIPS OF 1635 - Part V

The year ended with five more ships arriving in New England in November. The *Hopewell*, Thomas Babb master, began to take on passengers at London on 28 July, and by 11 September had on board a complement of sixty-three migrants [Hotten 110, 123, 130, 144].

According to depositions taken before the High Court of Admiralty, the *Hopewell* "arrived off Plymouth, New England, in November 1635 when the pilot taken on board to guide her into harbor ran her aground and weakened her to such an extent that her Master, Richard French, gave her up for lost and told Thomas Babb to save what he could. Her passengers for Virginia had to be sent in other ships" [English Adventurers 63]. "Mr. Bentley, a passenger in the gun room, had 10 servants on board to be delivered to Virginia who were obliged to leave the ship in New England and go on by other vessels" [English Adventurers 64].

There is no one by the name of Bentley in the London port book entries for this ship, and none of the passengers are designated for Virginia. This is additional evidence that the London port book did not capture the names of all the passengers that would eventually sail on a given ship.

Two other ships which were taking on passengers at London in September were at least in part involved in the efforts of a number of the Puritan lords to establish a new settlement to be made at the mouth of the Connecticut River, the town which would become Saybrook. On 16 August 1635, Edward Hopkins wrote from London to John Winthrop Jr., who would be leading the settlers at Saybrook, giving details of goods that were sent on "the North Sea boat," referring to the same ship later as "this bark, the *Bachler*" [WP 3:201-5]. In the same letter, Hopkins stated that some goods would also be sent "per the *True Love*, Mr. Gibbs, who will be ready I hope to set sail within 14 or 20 days in whom such servants as are provided by the gentlemen are to be shipped" [WP 3:202-3].

The London port book entry for the *Batcheler*, Mr. Tho[mas] Webb master, on 11 August was quite brief: "Lyon Gardner 36 years & his wife Mary 34 years, & Eliza[beth] Coles 23 years, their maid servant, & Mr.

W[illia]m Jope 40 years" [Hotten 118]. Hopkins describes the passenger contingent as "Sergeant Gardener and W[iilia]m Job his workmaster with the Sergeant's wife and his maid" [WP 3:203]. On 28 November 1635, Governor John Winthrop reported "Here arrived a small Norsey [North Sea] bark, of twenty-five tons, sent by the Lords Say, etc., with one Gardiner, an expert engineer or work base, and provisions of all sorts, to begin a fort at the mouth of the Connecticut. She came through many great tempests; yet, through the Lord's great providence, her passengers, twelve men, two women and goods, all safe" [WJ 1:207-8]. (Here again, we see that there were ten passengers beyond those listed in the London port book.)

The *Truelove*, John Gibbs master, took on sixty-seven passengers, all on 19 September [Hotten 131-32]. As noted above, some goods were shipped on this vessel for use at the new settlement at Saybrook, and an inventory of those goods, dated 15 September 1635, survives in the Winthrop papers [WP 3:208-9]. The *Batcheler* must have departed before the *Truelove*, for on 21 September 1635 Edward Hopkins again wrote from London, including "a copy of my letter sent per the *Bachler*, whereby you may perceive what was laden aboard this ship the *True Love*, together with a bill of lading for the same" [WP 3:209-10]. As late as 24 September, Edward Hopkins was still preparing letters to be sent on this vessel. Unless the *Truelove* avoided the bad weather, she may have arrived in New England as

(continued on page 2)

EDITOR'S EFFUSIONS

As we work on new sketches, we have frequently been asked, by interested readers of the Great Migration volumes, if we have made any major discoveries lately. Such discoveries are made from time to time, such as newly-found English origins for some immigrants, or long-sought spouses for others. But more frequent, and in the overall perspective of the Project, just as important, are the many, many small changes and adjustments made in almost every sketch.

In an earlier issue of the *Newsletter*, we presented details of several such corrections that had to be made in the family of Governor John Winthrop [GMN 4:1-2, 8]. Another such example has recently been encountered in the final work on the next Great Migration volume to appear. The family of Thomas Bull of Hartford has not received much attention in the secondary literature, and in those accounts which do exist, the dates of birth and the birth order for his children are ill-defined.

Traditionally, Thomas Bull is credited with seven children, and he has said to have married at Hartford in 1643, his wife's name being Susanna. No record for such a marriage is found in Hartford records or elsewhere.

The corrective for this situation is found in the medical records kept by John Winthrop Jr. Over the period of a decade and more he treated several members of Thomas Bull's family. Examining all these entries, we find that there were at least eight children in this family, and Winthrop gave ages for all of them. In the case of the two children for whom we have baptismal records, the ages given by Winthrop are in good agreement.

In the end, we find that the earliest child was born about 1638, so, unless Thomas had two wives, his marriage could not have taken place in 1643. And the newly calculated years of birth for the children rearrange the sequence. Such changes as these are the core of what is being done by the Great Migration Study Project, and when taken all together will give us a much better picture of early New England.

Robert Charles Anderson, FASG   Editor
Aileen Novick   Production Assistant

The Great Migration Newsletter is published quarterly by the Great Migration Study Project, a project of the New England Historic Genealogical Society, 101 Newbury Street, Boston MA 02116
www.nehgs.org

The subscription rate is $12 for one year and $20 for two years.

(continued from page 1)
late as early December.

While these three ships were preparing for their voyage at London, at least two more ships in lesser ports were also making ready. On 12 September 1635, the *Unity*, John Taylor master, took on board nine men with their families at Weymouth, Dorsetshire [NGSQ 71:175]. Assuming each man was accompanied by a wife, two children and a servant, then there were upwards of forty passengers on this vessel, which probably arrived in New England sometime in November.

John Hull, writing many years after the events, related that when "I was ten years old, my father removed to New England, with whom I came, by way of Bristol, in the ship *George*, Mr. Nicholas Shapley master. We set sail from Kingrode [Kingsroad], in Bristol, upon the 28th of September, 1635; and by the 7th of November (being the seventh day of the week) we arrived at Boston in New England" [Hull 142]. Hull spoke of "many passengers" being on this ship.

Having worked our way chronologically through the ships that are known to have come to New England in 1635 with passengers, a number of questions remain. There are cases where we know of families which arrived in New England in 1635, but not the ship on which they arrived. For example, Daniel Cushing, in his accounting of the early families of Hingham, listed five families from Hingham in England who came to New England in 1635 [NEHGR 15:25].

Passengers from this part of England might have sailed from Yarmouth or Ipswich, but we do not have records from either of these outports for 1635. From other records we do know that the Great Hope sailed from Ipswich in the summer of 1635 [GMN 7:16], but we do not have a list of the passengers. These Hingham passengers might have come on this vessel, but there may well have been an unrecorded ship from Ipswich or Yarmouth that brought them.

A different sort of story is that of the Rev. John Norton. In a December 1635 entry in his journal, Winthrop tells us that "Mr. Norton, a godly man, and a preacher in England, coming with his family to the Massachusetts, the ship, wherein he was, was by contrary winds put into Plimouth, where he continued preaching to them all the winter" [WJ 1:209].

John Norton does not appear in any of the surviving passenger lists from 1635. The story of a ship being forced into Plymouth has some similarities with the fate of the *Hopewell*, described above, and there was a William Norton, aged 25, on that ship. This was the brother of Rev. John, who was presumably on the *Hopewell* also. In this case, no additional vessel need be hypothesized.

(continued on page 8)

Focus   *on*   **EXETER**

FORCES FOR SETTLEMENT

The beginnings of the settlement of Exeter may be found in the Antinomian Controversy of 1637, in which Mrs. Anne Hutchinson and Rev. John Wheelwright were the leaders of a number of people in Boston, and some elsewhere in Massachusetts Bay, who believed that they were experiencing continuing personal revelations from God. This belief was unacceptable to the "orthodox" ministers who were in the process of building what became the Congregational Church.

During the early stages of the Antinomian Controversy, the General Court was intent on excluding all people who might support Wheelwright's ideas. In May 1637, the Court had ordered that only people allowed by the magistrates might inhabit the Massachusetts Bay. This served to deny permanent homes to many passengers of a ship which arrived in July 1637, bearing families from Lincolnshire, including friends of Wheelwright. "Here came over a brother of Mrs. Hutchinson, and some other of Mr. Wheelwright's friends, whom the governor thought not fit to allow, as others, to sit down among us, without some trial of them. Therefore, to save others from the danger of the law in receiving of them, he allowed them for four months. This was taken very ill by those of the other party, and many hot speeches given forth about it, and about their removal, etc." [WJ 1:278].

In late 1637, as a result of the Antinomian Controversy, fifty-eight Boston men, five men from Salem, three from Newbury, five from Roxbury, two from Ipswich, and two from Charlestown, were ordered disarmed and disenfranchised. In November 1637, Samuel Cole, John Button, Isaac Gross, John Biggs, Thomas Wardell, Henry Elkins, Robert Hull, Hugh Gundison, George Burden, William Wardell, Richard Gridley, William Townsend, Thomas Oliver, Oliver Mellowes, Richard Fairbanks, John Oliver, Thomas Matson, John Davis, William Dineley, Richard Cooke, Zaccheus Bosworth, Mathias Fance, James Johnson, Robert Royss, Edward Rainsford, Jacob Eliot, John Odlin, John Clarke, Nicholas Parker, James Penniman, Richard Waite, James Brown, Ralph Hudson, William Pell, and Thomas Savage hastily recanted, signing undated apologies, but many continued to hold their views in private [WP 3:513-16]. Some of these disarmed and disenfranchised men remained in Massachusetts Bay, but many others soon removed to Portsmouth or Exeter.

During a winter of discontent, these supporters of Anne Hutchinson and Rev. John Wheelwright split into two groups; the one led by Hutchinson went to Rhode Island and settled the town of Portsmouth, the other followed Wheel-wright into the northern wilderness to found Exeter. As a result, about twenty families arrived between November 1637 and May 1638, to find the land between the Lamprell and Squamscot rivers occupied by the sagamore Wehanownowit. As Wheelwright deposed in 1668, "when I with others first came to sit down at Exeter, we purchased of the Indians to whom (so far as we could learn) the right did belong, a certain tract of land about thirty miles square to run from Merrimack River eastward and so up into the country" [MA Arch 112:186b]. Samuel Dudley deposed that he had seen the deed, dated 3 April 1638, by which the sagamore released his rights. In November of 1936, the Exeter Historical Society raised $2500 and purchased this original deed at auction when part of the William Randolph Hearst collection was sold in New York.

There were in fact two Indian deeds of 3 April 1638, the first of which was signed by "Wehanownowit Sagamore of Piskatoquake" in the presence of James Wall, William Cole and Lawrence Copeland. It granted all his lands "from Merimack River to the patents of Piscatoquake ... to go into the country northwest thirty miles as far as Oyster River" to "John Whelewright of Piscatoquake, Samuel Hutchinson & Augustine Stor of Boston, Edward Calcord & Darby Field of Piscatoquake & John Compton of Roxbury and Nicholas Needome of Mount Walliston." A more specific deed, dated the same day, gave rights to Wheelwright and Storre in a thirty-mile square area of land between the Falls of "Pischataqua" and Oyster River. This deed was witnessed by Edward Colcord, Nicholas Needham and William Furber. Wehanownowit was joined by his son, Pummadockyon, in this second deed. The major difference between these two deeds was the description of the southern boundary, the first deed making it the Merrimack and the second deed a line three miles north of the Merrimack, which was in accord with the Massachusetts Bay charter. It is clear from the language used here and that used by the General Court later, that none of the principals involved had an accurate idea of what the land they were claiming encompassed.

(A fraudulent deed from several sagamores to Wheelwright, alleging a purchase on 17 May 1629, was presented in the 1707 trial of Allen vs. Waldron, long after all the principals in the 1638 deeds were dead. Used in a court proceeding over title to most of New Hampshire, this forged document is best discussed by James Savage [WJ 1:486-514].)

Winthrop took exception to this settlement, saying that the Bay had claim to "Winicowett" [Hampton] having built a house there "above two years since," and that some of the lands claimed by Exeter were first visited by men sent by the Bay to "discover Merrimack" [WJ 1:349, 363].

THE EXETER COMBINATION

Some months after their dismissal from the Boston church, the men of Exeter made a pact. The Exeter Combination, dated 4 July 1639, acknowledged the right granted by the King to plant "in the western parts of America" [NHPP 9:250-51] and made no mention of control by the Massachusetts Bay. The pact was an agreement to erect a government according to the liberties of "our English colony of the Massachusetts" and to obey the Christian laws in England and "all other such laws which shall upon good grounds be made and enacted amongst us according to God, that we may live quietly & peaceably together in all godliness and honesty." As printed in the Provincial Papers, the Combination is heavily edited, with spelling of the names of the signers quite different from the way they actually appear.

Examination of a microfilmed copy of the original Combination (page 15 of volume 1, Exeter town records, 1636-1693 [LDS microfilm #15783]) demonstrates that the signers of the Combination were (those who signed by mark indicated with an asterisk): "John Whelewright, Augustine Storre, Thomas Wight, William Wentworth, Henrey Elkins, George Walton*, Samuell Walker, Thomas Pettit, Henry Roby, William Wenbourne, [Thom]as Crawley*, Chr: Helme, Darby Field*, Robert Read*, Edward Rishworth, Francis Mathews*, Rallf Halle, Robert Soward*, Richard Bullger, Christopher Lawson, George Barlow*, Richard Moris, Nicholas Needham, Thomas Willson, George Rawbone*, William Coole*, James Walles*, Thomas Levitt*, Edmund Littlefeeld, John Crame*, Godferye Dearebarne*, Philemon Pormort, Thomas Wardwell*, William Wardwell*."

A nearly contemporary copy of the Combination, appearing in an early copy of Exeter town records, being "volume 2, pp. 13-14" [LDS microfilm #15135], alters the spelling of many of these names, and adds the name of Robert Smith, who did not appear in the original. Why Smith was included in this later copy is a matter for speculation. The two Combinations were both written in an old hand, probably no more than twenty years apart, although clearly not by the same person. It is possible that the copyist was certain that Robert Smith was present and inserted the name on his own authority.

Notable among the men who failed to sign the Combination, were John Compton, who was of Roxbury as early as 1634 and had been disarmed with Wheelwright, and Lawrence Copeland of Braintree. Both figured in the Indian deeds, but soon returned to Boston and Braintree, respectively. Isaac Gross had also been disarmed, having been in Boston as early as 1635, and had been dismissed from the Boston church, but did not sign the Combination and returned to Boston in a few years. Christopher Marshall was of Boston in 1634, and was dismissed with the others from Boston church, but did not sign the Combination, nor receive property in the first divisions. William Moore was a stranger in Boston in 1636, received lands in Exeter in December 1639, and married Henry Roby's daughter, yet did not sign.

Of the men who did sign the Combination, Wheelwright, Elkins, Bulgar, Morris, the Wardwells and Pormort had been dismissed from the Boston church. Wilson and Hall were purported to have preceded the Wheelwright party, and Leavitt is said to have come in the July 1637 ship and gone immediately to Exeter, thus arriving in advance of the Wheelwright party, if only by a few months (although the evidence for these claims is not seen). Pettit was disarmed with the rest. While not disarmed, Cole was in Boston as early as 1636 and witnessed one of the Indian deeds for Wheelwright, as did the "Irishman," Field. Cram, Read, Winborn and Needham were originally of Boston. Seward did not figure in the division of Exeter lands until 1640, which may suggest that all these men did not sign the Combination at the same time. Helme was undoubtedly of the July 1637 ship passengers, but also received no allotment in the first division of lands. Wall came on the *Pied Cow* and worked for Mason, and Walton had been in the country since 1635.

This left twelve families as potential passengers on the July 1637 ship of Wheelwright supporters: Storre, Wight, Wentworth, Walker, Roby, Rishworth, Matthews, Dearborn, Lawson, Crawley, Barlow, Rawbone and Littlefield. Leavitt and Helme were almost certainly on that ship as well.

Of these likely passengers, several are clearly connected to Wheelwright or Hutchinson by ties of kinship. Augustine Storre had married in Alford, Lincolnshire, Susannah Hutchinson; William Wentworth was a kinsman of Wheelwright's; Edward Rishworth was the son of Esther Hutchinson of Laceby, Lincolnshire; Christopher Lawson was the son of Ann Wentworth; and Christopher Helme was the son of Priscilla Wentworth.

In late 1639, the inhabitants of Exeter proposed that they become annexed to the Massachusetts Bay government, and sent their proposal to the court, but seeing Dover accepted on terms that they did not like, withdrew their request [WJ 1:385]. For nearly four years more they remained independent, like several other "city states" erected in New England about this time [GMN 4:17-18, 24].

On 10 May 1643, Massachusetts Bay General Court noted that "Excetter peition was answered, being it fell within our patent; the Court took it ill they should capitulate with them" [MBCR 2:37]. And on 7 September 1643, "Whereas Excetter is found to be within our patent, upon their petition they were received under our government" [MBCR 2:43]. A fragment of this petition survives and earlier researchers have transcribed the legible names, but clearly many more names were to be found on the cramped page [MA Arch 112:8].

EXETER CHURCH

Sometime in mid-1638, some of the Wheelwright men believed themselves to be sufficiently established to request dismissal from the Boston church, which request was denied a hearing. This actual petition does not survive.

In mid-December 1638 Governor John Winthrop, summarizing the aftermath of the Antinomian Controversy, stated that "Those who went to the falls at Pascataquack, gathered a church, and wrote to our church to desire us to dismiss Mr. Wheelwright to them for an officer; but, because he desired it not himself, the elders did not propound it. Soon after came his own letter, with theirs, for his dismission, which thereupon was granted. Others likewise (upon their request) were also dismissed thither" [WJ 1:338].

When Rev. Wheelwright joined Richard Morris, Richard Bulgar, Philemon Pormort, Isaac Gross, Christopher Marshall, George Bates, and Thomas and William Wardell in requesting dismissal a second time, it was granted on 6 January 1638/9, provided the church "at the Falls of Paschataqua…be rightly gathered and ordered" [BChR 1:23]. The families of some of these men and a few others were dismissed on 3 March 1638/9: Susannah Hutchinson, widow; Mary, the wife of Mr. Wheelwright; Lenora, the wife of Richard Morris; Henry Elkins; and Mary Elkins, his wife [BChR 1:23].

On 10 May 1643, at the same time that the town of Exeter was negotiating to come under Massachusetts Bay authority, "Mr. Wheelwright had a safe conduct granted, & liberty to stay 14 days, so it be within 3 months next ensuing" [MBCR 2:37] Winthrop also reports on this incident, adding the information that "he came and spake with diverse of the elders, and gave them such satisfaction as they intended to intercede with the court for the release of his banishment" [WJ 2:144].

By the end of 1643 he and many of his congregation moved on to settle the town of Wells, Maine. Wheelwright explained himself further to the Bay authorities in letters written in the winter of 1643-44, and his banishment was lifted [WJ 2:195-98]. He ended his days as minister at Salisbury, after spending several years, ironically, as minister of Hampton.

After a brief interlude when Thomas Rashleigh preached at Exeter, in May 1644 Rev. Stephen Bachiler of Hampton was called to the church at Exeter following the great fire that destroyed his entire library. However, on 29 May 1644, the General Court stepped in and denied his settlement, due to the "divisions and contentions" in Exeter [WP 4:458; MBCR 2:67-68]. In 1650 the town found a more lasting solution in the Rev. Samuel Dudley, who presided until his death more than thirty years later. No church records survive from these early years.

TOWN RECORDS

The original Exeter town records are currently being inventoried by Peter Parker of Inlook Group, and are inaccessible. A WPA handwritten copy was prepared from some of the surviving records, but unlike other New Hampshire towns, these records are not included in the WPA index to names in town records at the New Hampshire State Library and on microfilm elsewhere. No original Exeter town records in the holdings of the New Hampshire Archives, New Hampshire State Library or New Hampshire Historical Society date to the Great Migration period.

Microfilms of the original first town record book show that it was an ancient book originally used as an account book, and contains several pages dating to 1636 of Roxbury accounts, and several pages of the same date for Dorchester accounts. The original owner of this book is not known. These early records, which combined town records and the sitting of the Exeter "Court," are further evidence that the settlement considered itself an independent city-state. The chief man in the town was called the "Ruler," and the town passed its own legislation, including laws against treason [NHPP 1:140].

Some of these early records have been published in two places, with, however, differences between the two. Charles H. Bell, in his *History of Exeter* [Exeter 1888; reprint Bowie, Maryland, 1979] included as Appendix II (pp. 435-47) "Transcripts of the Exeter Records, 1639 to 1644." The first volume of New Hampshire Provincial Papers includes some pages from the "Exeter First Book of Records," transcribed by Hon. S.D. Bell, containing material from 1639 to 1645 [NHPP 1:137-45]. Without comparison with the originals, we cannot tell which of these is more complete, but in the absence of further evidence the version given by Charles H. Bell is probably the more reliable.

TOWN BOUNDARIES

Beyond the records mentioned above, much of what we know about the early settlement and inhabitants of Exeter stems from a series of petitions and their attendant supporting depositions regarding the boundaries of the town.

On 24 May 1652, the inhabitants of Exeter petitioned that due to the "poor and mean estate and condition of our present plantation, by reason of the straitness of our bounds which at our first coming to set there was a large tract of land from Oyster River to the Falls between Salisbury and Hampton with good [quantity] of meadow and meet enlargements, fit to make of [a] town for subsistence, and all the said tract of land then lying vacant, and no patent or persons then laying claim to it, as we could hear of but the Indians only, we … settled ourselves at Exeter Falls for the conveniency of the river, and gave [a] … farm to Mr. Whelwrite

… after which purchase of ours, this honored court saw it meet to grant out a township to Mr. Bacheler and the inhabitants of Hampton which Township of theirs cut off almost all our meadows." This grant, combined with the encroachment of Dover, was enough to put the town in dire straits, threatening their access to Lamprey River and depriving them of a place to graze cattle. Edward Hilton, John Legat , Tho[mas] Pettit, Nicolas Lissen, Thom[as] Cornish, Edward Gilman Senior and Edward Gilman Junior, on behalf of the rest, signed this petition and awaited an answer [MA Arch 112:41]. In June of 1652 the commisioners invited the petitioners to try again at the next session, where the Dover deputies would also be heard.

Seeing that there would be no favorable outcome, on 24 June 1652, the inhabitants tried another tack, explaining that since they had insufficient meadows, "the Indians have informed us that there are three or four spots of meadow … about seven or eight miles from town" to the northwest far from any other plantations, that could fill their need, if the court would only grant them permission to acquire them. The court granted this request [MA Arch 112:39]. This 1652 grant demonstrated just how little the General Court knew about the geography of the area they claimed.

The matter of the bounds shared with Dover would not go away, however. In the 1660s, Exeter tried again, saying that Capt. Wiggins's farm appeared to actually lie within the bounds of Exeter and that the tiny quantity of meadow at Lamprey River that Exeter had purchased and quietly possessed for years was now being encroached upon by Dover. They also asked that three men be appointed to end controversies, Anthony Stanyan, Samuel Greenfield and James Wall, and that John Hoyt be clerk of the writs [MA Arch 112:8]. A large number of Exeter residents signed this undated petition, showing that more than twenty years after the Combination, many original settlers were still present and a sizable number of new settlers had arrived: Robt [ ], Abraham Drake, Anthony Stanyan, Balthazar Willix, Francis Swaine, Henry Roby, Humphrey Wilson, James Wall, John Bursley, John Davis, John Legat, John Smart, John Tedd, Nathaniel Boulter, Nicholas Swaine, Ralph Hall, Richard Carter, Robert Hethersay, Samuel Greenfield, Thom[as] Joanes, Thomas King, Thomas Wight, William Mooer, Tho[mas] Bigges, Abraham Drake, Christopher Lawson, John Cram, Nathaniel Boulter, Rich[ard] Bulgar, Robert Smith, Rob[er]t Seward, Samuel Walker, Tho[mas] Rashleyghe, Thomas Pettit, Thomas Wardwell, William Cole, William Moore, and William Winborn. The General Court could not grant their petition, however, without tinkering with all their requests, and authorized other men to settle controversies and serve as clerk.

On 3 April 1668, John Gilman wrote the last of his "humble petitions" to the Massachusetts Bay General Court asking that they be taken care of as a town, having had very unsatisfactory results from earlier efforts (including a decision

reached and immediately repealed [MA Arch 112:52]). He reminded the court that "we humbly conceive to be our just right in a township our reasons are (1) our purchase of ye Native [and (]2) our paying rates & all charges here as also our willing … submission to the Massachusetts government" [MA Arch 112:186].

On 12 May 1668, the court replied, "In answer to the desire of John Gylman in behalf of the town of Exetter for settling the bounds of their town the magistrates consent that Exeter bounds be stated & settled according to a return of Mr. Richard Walderne, Mr. Samuel Dalton & Capt. Robert Pike, who were a committee appointed by the General Court bearing date the eighth of the 8th month 1667, provided that all pine trees fit for masts which are twenty four inches diameter & upwards within three foot of the ground, that grow above three miles from their meeting house where it now stands in any place within the bounds of the said Town, are hereby reserved for the public and if any p[er]son or persons shall p[re]sume to fall down any such pine tree fit for masts he or they shall forfeit ten pounds for every tree, the one half to [be paid to] the informer & the other half to the public treasury of the country provided also that this grant unto the Town of Exeter shall not infringe Mr. Samuel Symondes in his grant of two hundred & fifty acres of land formerly granted" [MA Arch 112:186].

The most interesting document among the papers supporting the 1668 Exeter petitions to the General Court was a deposition by John Begod, who evidently was an accomplished traveller, familiar with the lands in eastern New Hampshire. He testified that he had often travelled between Lamprey River and Newichewannock Falls, that it was ten miles overland and sixteen to twenty miles by water. He described the rivers that went down to the ocean "where they have set up their mills," and stated that Exeter had only two rivers that ran to the tide, while Dover had four. He further deposed that Dover's lands greatly exceeded those of Exeter, the latter "encompassed with such swamps as is very unsuitable for raising of Cattle" and that Mr. Hilton lived within two or three miles of Lamprey River and raised cattle nearby, further restricting the available pasturage [MA Arch 112:43].

Born of opposition to the Massachusetts Bay government, Exeter lost all battles over boundaries with their more orthodox neighbors before the General Court. As early as 1639, they had sought to become part of the Bay, but desired to retain the lands they had purchased through the Indian deed, a 30 mile by 30 mile tract that the General Court refused to acknowledge. Exeter very unwillingly witnessed the carving up of large portions of their perceived territory into the towns of Dover, Hampton, Salisbury, and Haverhill. Later daughter towns split off in the usual fashion were Brentwood (from which was later formed Fremont), Epping, and Newmarket (from which was later formed South Newmarket [now Newfields]).

RECENT LITERATURE

Caleb Johnson, "The True Origins of Stephen[1] Hopkins of the *Mayflower*: With Evidence of His Earlier Presence in Virginia," *The American Genealogist* 73 (1998):161-71. Johnson demonstrates that Stephen Hopkins resided at Hursley, Hampshire, in the first decade of the seventeenth century. Additional evidence supports the claim that Stephen Hopkins of the *Mayflower* was the man of that name who was earlier in Bermuda and Virginia.

Patricia Law Hatcher, "Reconstructing Sarah (Odding) Sherman, Wife of Philip[1] Sherman of Portsmouth, Rhode Island," *The American Genealogist* 73 (1998):176-80. The author shows that Sarah Odding, who came to Roxbury in 1633 with her mother and stepfather was the daughter of William Odding of Braintree, Essex.

Gordon L. Remington, "Rebecca Revisited: The Unidentified Wives of Angell[2] Husted and Jonathan[2] Reynolds of Greenwich, Connecticut," *The American Genealogist* 73 (1998):201-6. Remington argues convincingly that Rebecca, the widow of Angell Husted, was Angell's second wife, that she had earlier been wife of Jonathan Reynolds, that she was not mother of any of Angell's children, and that she was not Rebecca Sherwood.

John C. Brandon, "Four Early Immigrants to Maine and New Hampshire: Hercules Hunking, Arthur Gill, Sampson Penley, and Thomas Stanford," *The American Genealogist* 73 (1998):223-27. Brandon has found documents in published English records that provide additional information about four immigrants to northern New England. Depositons by "Hercules Hunkyn" and Arthur Gill place them in Stonehouse, Devonshire, in 1635. A 1651 letter from William Hingston to Robert Jordan refers to the immigration of Sampson Penley and Thomas Stanford.

Robert E. Bowman, "Ensigns Revisited: The Origin of the Given Name *Ensign* in the Cole, Mann, and Otis Families of Scituate, Massachusetts, with Notes on the English Origin of the Ensigns of Scituate," *The American Genealogist* 73 (1998):241-55. The author has found additional records for the Ensign family in Cranbrook and Biddenden, Kent.

Leslie Mahler, "English Baptisms for Two Children of John1 Pike of Newbury, Massachusetts," *The American Genealogist* 73 (1998):256-57. Mahler has found the baptisms of two children of John Pike in Landford, Wiltshire.

Paul C. Reed and Dean Crawford Smith, "The English Ancestry of Peter[1] Noyes," *The New England Historical and Genealogical Register* 152 (1998):259-85, 491. Reed and Smith provide extensive documentation for five generations of the paternal ancestry of Peter Noyes of Sudbury, showing that the Noyes family resided in and near Andover, Hampshire, from the middle of the fifteeth century.

Christopher Gleason Clark, "Mr. Wheelock's Cure," *The New England Historical and Genealogical Register* 152 (1998):311-2. Clark has found records which show that Rev. Ralph Wheelock was curate of Eccles, Norfolk, from about 1632 to 1635, and that two of his children, Gershom and Rebecca, were baptized there.

George Freeman Sanborn Jr., "Thomas[1] and Mary (Healy) Brown of Newbury, Massachusetts, and Their Family," *The New England Historical and Genealogical Register* 152 (1998):347-52. Following up on a lead in the passenger list, Sanborn has confirmed that Thomas Brown of Newbury derived from Christian Malford, Wiltshire, finding in that parish the record of Brown's marriage to Mary Healy and the baptism of their eldest child, Francis. The author then goes on to summarize in standard form the family of the immigrant, including the evidence for placing Nicholas Brown of Newbury as a son of this couple.

Helen S. Ullmann, "The Three Messengers: Henry, Andrew, and Edward: Clearing the Decks," *The New England Historical and Genealogical Register* 152 (1998):353-72. The author reviews the evidence about the three Messenger immigrants, and concludes that there is no firm evidence that they were brothers, or related at all, although the possibility remains. She then summarizes carefully what is known about Andrew and Edward Messenger.

Dean Crawford Smith and Douglas Richardson, "English Ancestry of Nathaniel[1] Heaton of Boston, Mass., and His Nephew, James[2] Heaton of New Haven, Conn.," *The New England Historical and Genealogical Register* 152 (1998):430-52. The authors present information on the immigrant Nathaniel Heaton, showing that he was baptized at Habrough, Lincolnshire, and carrying back his paternal ancestry for three generations. They also include material on Nathaniel's sister-in-law, Elizabeth (Tenney) Heaton, and nephew, James Heaton, who came to New Haven.

Richard Evans, "Jeffrey Howland, Citizen and Grocer of London," *The New England Historical and Genealogical Register* 152 (1998):453-64. In the last century, the Howlands of Plymouth Colony were thought to be descended from the Howlands of Essex in England. This has been shown to be false, but interest in the Howlands of Essex continues. Evans clarifies what is known about Jeffrey Howland, opening the way to placing him properly.

(continued from page 2)

In summary, we have identified twenty-eight ships by name which brought passengers to New England in 1635, in addition to which Winthrop indicates that at least another five, whose names we do not know, arrived in June of that year. Of these, records for eighteen are found in the London port book, and we can count 1180 passengers recorded on these vessels. And on the *Marygould* of Weymouth we know that another 104 came. If we allow conservatively 60 passengers on each of the remaining nine ships, and on each of the five referred to by Winthrop, then there were another 840 arrivals, giving us a minimum of just over 2100 passengers.

However, as we have noted in several places above, there were certainly unrecorded passengers on many of these vessels, and perhaps other vessels of which we have no knowledge whatsoever. Making allowance for these probable additional immigrants, we can estimate that somewhere between 2500 and 3000 people arrived in New England in 1635.

We do not have records as good as these for any of the ensuing years. We do, however, have evidence that a number of vessels arrived in each of the years from 1636 to 1640, and we also have the evidence of many new immigrants arriving each year through the rest of the decade of the 1630s. Winthrop did take special note when the immigration dropped off abruptly at the beginning of the English Civil War, and so we would expect that he would also have taken note if there were major variations in the numbers of arrivals in the preceding years. On this basis, we conclude that the rate of immigration from 1634 to 1640 proceeded at a steady rate year by year, in the range of 2000 or so a year.

CORRECTIONS

Alert readers have pointed out two errors in recent issues of the *Great Migration Newsletter*, both involving names of passengers discussed in the ongoing series on ship passenger lists of 1635.

In the third installment, as part of the discussion of the vessel which was shipwrecked off Cape Ann during the storm of August 15, we gave the name of one of the few survivors as Thomas Thatcher [GMN 7:18], but the correct name was Anthony Thatcher.

Later in the same installment, in the discussion of the *Angel Gabriel*, we referred to a deposition of William Tarbox, giving as a citation a genealogy of the Cogswell family. Unfortunately, the Cogswell genealogist misread this deposition, and the name should have been William Furber. The depositions in this case can be found in Volume 39 of the Massachusetts Archives.

We thank the several readers who pointed out each of these blunders.

Great Migration Study Project
101 Newbury Street
Boston, MA 02116

Great Migration Newsletter

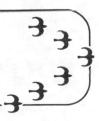

Vol. 8   April-June 1999   No. 2

NEW ENGLAND IN NEW JERSEY

Prior to 1664 European settlement of the region which came to be East Jersey was limited to the Dutch town of Bergen, and a few scattered Dutch farms. Bergen was located in the northeasternmost corner of New Jersey, between the Hudson and Hackensack rivers, and was organized in 1660, based on a number of earlier small settlements.

With the conquest of New Amsterdam by the English in 1664, the population and settlement of East Jersey changed rapidly. Many of the New England villages, especially on the eastern end of Long Island, were overcrowded, and exploratory visits to East Jersey had already been made before 1664.

In rapid succession three large land patents were issued to immigrants from New England, and within less than a decade these three settlements had spawned three more, so that by 1669 East Jersey consisted of Elizabeth, Woodbridge, Piscataway, Middletown, Shrewsbury and Newark, along with Bergen and a few other scattered small habitations.

In October 1664 the grant of Elizabethtown was signed, with the formal grant being made on 1 December 1664 to John Baker of New York, John Ogden of Southampton, and John Bayly and Luke Watson of Jamaica. The Elizabettown grant was a large tract of land west of Staten Island and north of the Piscataway River.

John Ogden typifies the majority of the earliest inhabitants of Elizabeth. Before residing in Southampton, he had lived in Stamford and Hempstead. Most of those who first came to Elizabeth were from Southampton or Southold on the eastern tip of Long Island, or from Hempstead, Huntington or Jamaica farther west. (Tracing the migration steps further backward, we note that much of the migration to these western Long Island towns came from Stamford and Fairfield on the mainalnd, from which we can trace back to Wethersfield on the Connecticut River and ultimately to Watertown in Massachusetts Bay. Not all of the Elizabeth settlers followed this strand of migratio, of course, but many did.)

In May of 1666 the owners of the Elizabethtown patent sold the southern half of their land to a group of men from Newbury, Massachusetts, headed by Daniel Pierce, John Pike and Andrew Tappan; this became the town of Woodbridge. The confirmatory deed for Woodbridge was signed by nine men: Daniel Pierce, Joshua Pierce, John Pike, John Bishop, Henry Jacques and Hugh March of Newbury, Stephen Kent of Haverhill, Robert Dennis of Yarmouth and John Smith of Barnstable.

The last two names on the Woodbridge deed are the leading edge of a number of immigrants to this town (and to Piscataway) from the Cape Cod towns. And this also demonstrates a feature of migration within New England which we have encountered before, but which deserves emphasis. The settlement of new towns was neither totally random nor totally from one source. Most often a new settlement would attract settlers from two or three older locations. These older locations would not necessarily be connected in any way. There were no strong connections between the Cape Cod towns and the Merrimack River towns which sent settlers to Woodbridge.

Just a few months later, in December 1666, the owners of the Woodbridge lands sold one-third of their holdings to four New Hampshire men – John Martin, Charles Gilman, Hugh Dunn and Hopewell Hull – who called their new settlement Piscataway.

(continued on page 10)

EDITOR'S EFFUSIONS

We are pleased to announce the completion of the first volume in the second series of Great Migration volumes. Because the rate of migration to New England increased dramatically in 1634, from a few hundred a year to two or three thousand, and would continue at that pace for the remainder of the decade, this next series will cover only the years 1634 and 1635.

When we began work on this volume, our intention was to include the first three letters of the alphabet, and we worked toward that goal for some time. But as the date for publication neared, we realized that this would produce a volume of about a thousand pages, which is on the cumbersome side. Consequently, this volume will cover only A and B, and C will be pushed over into the second volume in the series. The full title for the current volume, then, is *The Great Migration: Immigrants to New England, 1634-1635, Volume I, A-B.*

As a result of the decisions outlined above, the second volume of the second series will cover the letters C through F, and there will be six volumes altogether for the years 1634 and 1635. The increased number of volumes in this series is a direct consequence of the number of sketches, with about 900 in the first series and more than 1300 in this second series. In addition, we are attempting to use a wider range of sources as we learn more about the records, particularly the unpublished town records.

Choosing to produce volumes of this size has the added advantage of helping the Great Migration team to pace its work better, and to shorten the interval between the publication of one volume and the next. The second volume of this series is already well-advanced, with a preliminary or intermediate draft of most of the sketches already done.

You may order the newly published volume for $45 (or $40.50 for NEHGS members) plus $3.50 for shipping, from New England Historic Genealogical Society, 160 North Washington Street, Boston MA 02114.

Robert Charles Anderson, FASG   Editor
Aileen Novick   Production Assistant

The Great Migration Newsletter is published quarterly by the Great Migration Study Project, a project of the New England Historic Genealogical Society, 101 Newbury Street, Boston MA 02116
www.nehgs.org

The subscription rate is $12 for one year and $20 for two years.

(continued from page 9)

The name Piscataway obviously derives from the Piscataqua River in New Hampshire, along which lived these four earliest purchasers, and many of those who followed to this new settlement. But, just as with Woodbridge, there were also many who came from Cape Cod. In *The Great Migration Begins*, we have already encountered two of them. Richard Higgins and John Smalley both settled first in Plymouth by 1632, and in 1645 they were among the first settlers of Eastham on the Cape. By 1670 they had left Plymouth Colony and were residing in Piscataway.

The second patent to be issued was in April 1665, for the area that would become Monmouth County. The grantees of this patent were from Gravesend on Long Island (John Bowne, James Grover, Richard Stout, Samuel Spicer, Richard Gibbins, John Tilton and William Goulding), Shelter Island at the eastern end of Long Island (Nathaniel Sylvester) and Newport, Rhode Island (Obadiah Holmes Jr., William Reape, Nicholas Davis and Walter Clarke). Again we see the theme of immigrants from two different sections of New England coming together to form a new community in New Jersey.

The immigrants to the Monmouth Patent created a number of nuclei of settlement, and within a very short time there were regions within the patent known as Middletown, Shrewsbury and Portland Point, each with its own deputies to the assembly. By the end of the 1660s, Middletown and Shrewsbury were recognized as separate towns.

The third major patent was for Newark, north of Elizabethtown, given in May 1666 to a group of settlers from Branford, Milford and Guilford, from that part of Connecticutt which had until recently been a part of New Haven Colony.

A leading force behind this migration was Rev. Abraham Pierson, minister at Branford, and among the lay leaders were Jasper Crane of Branford and Robert Treat of Milford. New Haven Colony was the strictest and most extreme of the Puritan colonies, and when New Haven Colony was incorporated into Connecticut, men such as Pierson no longer had the governmental support to practice their in the way they liked.

In general, East Jersey provided a place where New Englanders of all stripes could practice their particular form of Protestantism without as much hindrance as at home. Many of the immigrants from Rhode Island and Cape Cod were Baptists and Quakers. In addition, partly because of the Dutch influence, there were settlers who belonged to denominations not familiar to the New Englanders.

(continued on page 16)

Focus on TAUNTON

SETTLEMENT OF TAUNTON

The organization of towns in Plymouth Colony proceeded in distinct stages. For the first dozen or so years of the Colony's existence there was only the town of Plymouth itself. Then, about 1632 or 1633, two additional towns, Duxbury and Scituate, were formed.

A third burst of town formation took place in 1637 and 1638, when four towns were founded: the three Cape Cod settlements of Sandwich, Yarmouth and Barnstable, and the first inland settlement of the Colony, Taunton.

At the beginning of his entries for 1638, Winthrop reported the settlement of two towns, Taunton and Sandwich [WJ 1:302-3]. He described the beginnings of Taunton thus:

> This year a plantation was begun at Tecticutt by a gentle-woman, an ancient maid, one Mrs. Poole. She went late thither, and endured much hardship, and lost much cattle. Called, after, Taunton.

The first references to Taunton in the Plymouth Colony records were not directly to the settlement itself, but to a marriage that took place there, and to the administration of the oath of allegiance, giving the residence of principals under another of the Indian names used for the region that would become Taunton [PCR 1:103]:

> Richard Paul and Margery Turner, of Cohannett, were married the viijth of November, 1638.

> Mr. Richard Smyth, of Cohannatt, tooke the oath of allegiance to the King, & fidelitie to the colony [8 November 1638].

Soon after, on 4 December 1638, seven men (Mr. William Poole, Mr. John Gilbert Sr., Mr. Henry Andrews, John Strong, John Deane, Walter Deane and Edward Case) were admitted freemen, and John Strong was "sworn constable of Cohannett until June next" [PCR 1:105].

Captain William Poole and Henry Andrews, the first deputies to the General Court for Cohannet, attended the court of 4 June 1639, but Poole was at some point replaced by Mr. John Gilbert [PCR 1:126].

TAUNTON CHURCH

In *Plain Dealing; or News from New England*, Thomas Lechford describes the organization of the church at Taunton [Plain Dealing 95-96]:

> *Cohannet*, alias *Taunton*, is in *Plymouth* Patent. There is a Church gathered of late, and some ten or twenty of the Church, the rest excluded. Master *Hooke* Pastor, master *Streate* Teacher. Master *Hooke* received ordination from the hands of one master *Bishop* a School-master, and one *Parker* an Husbandman, and then master *Hooke* joined in ordaining master *Streate*. One master *Doughty*, a Minister, opposed the gathering of the Church there, alleging that according to the Covenant of *Abraham*, all men's children that were of baptized parents, and so *Abraham's* children ought to be baptized; and spake so in public, or to that effect, which was held a disturbance, and the Ministers spake to the Magistrate to order him. The Magistrate commanded the Constable, who dragged master *Doughty* out of the Assembly. He was forced to go away from thence, with his wife and children.

Since Thomas Lechford left New England in early August 1641, the church at Taunton was founded no later than that date, and if we take "gathered of late" to mean within the last year, we must conclude that the church was organized in late 1640 or early 1641, and not in 1637, as some have claimed.

On 23 July 1640, "William Hooke, Minister of God's Word; sometimes of Axmouth in Devonshire, now of Taunton, in New England," delivered a sermon which was published in London in 1641. The church was apparently organized by this date, and the sermon may even have been given at the founding of the church.

Support for this chronology may be found in the peripatetic career of Rev. Francis Doughty. As late as 29 July 1639 he was residing in Dorchester [Lechford 137], but by 2 March 1640/1 he had removed to Taunton, when "Mr. Francis Doughty, of Taunton, for selling a pound of gunpowder to the natives, … is fined 30s." [PCR 2:8].

EARLY TAUNTON VITAL RECORDS

The earliest vital records for the town of Taunton are a few marriages which are entered directly into the Plymouth Colony court records. The first of these is reproduced earlier on this page. The second is for "William Harvey & Joane Hucker of Cohannett, married the second of April, 1639" [PCR 1:120], and a few more follow.

William Harvey was the first town clerk of Taunton, and if he maintained a register for vital records, it has been lost. The same applies to the second town clerk, Oliver Purchase.

The earliest surviving group of Taunton vital records was kept by the next town clerk, Shadrach Wilbore, who took office about 1665. Close examination of his records tells us many interesting things, including the likelihood that when he took office, no earlier vital records existed.

In the back of the first volume of Taunton proprietors' records are fifty-two pages of vital records. Although there are many events recorded here that predate 1665, we can demonstrate that Wilbore began this register in 1665. Records continue in his hand until the late 1690s, just before his death, and in the latter pages of this record are some vital events from the early eighteenth century, entered in another hand.

At the same time that he began to maintain the register of vital events, Wilbore began to submit to the colony an annual account of births, deaths and marriages for Taunton. This had been done for many of the other Plymouth Colony towns from the early 1640s, but not for Taunton, so this is one of the indications that Taunton vital records were not maintained by earlier clerks. Much of what we can say about the records in the proprietors' volume is derived from careful entry-by-entry comparison with this colony copy of some of these records.

Fifteen of these annual submissions survive: 28 February 1665/6, 1 March 1667/8, 1 March 1668/9, 6 March 1670/1, 3 March 1671/2, 1 March 1672/3, 2 March 1673/4, 1 March 1674/5, 5 March 1676/7, 4 March 1677/8, [March 1678/9], [March 1679/80], 28 February 1680/1, [March 1681/2], 5 June 1683 [PCR 8:30, 36-38, 35-36, 39-40, 54-55, 59-60, 58-59, 55, 65-66, 69-70, 68-69, 82-83, 81-82, 79-80, 85-86].

The first submission to the colony, on 28 February 1665/6, contained only four entries - two marriages, a death and a birth [PCR 8:30]. This submission was something of an anomaly, as all four entries were included in the next list sent to the colony.

Two years and a day later, on 1 March 1667/8, Wilbore sent a second, much longer list to the colony. The sixty-three entries of this list are found spread across the first five pages of the proprietors' record section of vital records, and comprise only a fraction of the entries found on each of those pages.

The first page of the proprietors' record is unlike all the others, in that it contains only marriages and deaths, arranged chronologically rather than by family. Sixteen of the entries from the 1 March 1667/8 submission are from this page, and constitute about one-third of the entries on this page.

The remaining pages of the proprietors' records are arranged by family, with two, three or four families to a page. The second page is also somewhat anomalous, inasmuch as the first "family" is actually two, the records of the families of John Bundy and Samuel Smith being intermixed. The other families on this page are Thomas Caswell, Shadrach Wilbore himself, and Samuel Hall.

Shadrach Wilbore's own sequence of entries may be taken as a typical example. In the completed section, there are ten birth records, for children born from 1659 to 1683. The first five of these were in the list submitted to the colony on 1 March 1667/8, the last of these five being the birth of his daughter Hannah on 24 February 1667[/8], just a few days before the submission to the colony.

Although the handwriting on all these early pages is unmistakably that of Shadrach Wilbore, slight differences in the hand and clear differences in the intensity of the ink indicate that these entries were made over a period of time, and this set of records must constitute the original register maintained by Wilbore.

Other families commenced by the time of this submission were George Shove, John Smith, Samuel Hollway and William Briggs on page three, Jared Talbot, John Eddy, Richard Briggs and John Dean on page four, and Samuel Lincoln Sr., Robert Crossman and Jonah Austin Jr. on page five. (In the published colony records based on this submission, the items for Jonah Austin Jr. are given as if for "Jonah Allin Juni[o]r." The original of the proprietors' record version represents the head of family as "Jonah Asten Junior," with the "st" of the surname written in such a way that it could be misread as "ll.")

The next submission to the colony was dated exactly a year later, on 1 March 1668/9 [PCR 8:35:36], and contained twenty-three entries. None of these entries comes from the first page of the vital records section of the proprietors' records.

The first six items were births of children in families which already had entries in the vital records (a daughter of John Bundy, three children of Thomas Caswell, a son of Richard Briggs and a daughter of John Dean). The remaining seventeen events were for children of families which had not previously had an entry (John Lincoln [2], Daniel Fisher [2], Jabez Hacket [6] and John Richmond [7]).

We can now add to our description of how Shadrach Wilbore maintained the vital records by looking at what happened in the space of the year between the second and third submissions to the colony. First, he added new births to families which had already been begun in his register, but he did not record on the first page of his register any marriages or deaths during this period.

Second, he added four new families to the register. All four of these families had children born prior to the second submission, and all resided in Taunton prior to that date as well, so he was not adding the families at this time because they were recently married or had recently moved to Taunton. Presumably, then, he was slowly building his records of the families of Taunton, either as he had time or as the families chose to come to him.

Let us examine one more annual submission, the fourth one, on 6 March 1670/1 [PCR 8:39-40]. This submission contains fifty-three entries, the first three of which are from the first page of the vital records in the proprietors' volume, and the next ten from families with previous entries in the book. The remaining forty records are for ten families who were first entered in the record volume after the previous submission [Hezekiah Hoare (7), Joseph Gray (1), Jonathan Briggs (2), Thomas Lincoln Junior (8), James Leonard Junior (2), Edward Bobbitt (7), James Phillips (4), Joseph Williams (1), James Bell (7) and Joseph Staples (1)].

Notice that two years passed between the third submission and the fourth. Is there a missing submission? Examination of the register shows that there were no new families entered between the third and fourth submissions, and for those families which were already entered at the time of the third submission, there are no new entries which were not included in the fourth submission. Shadrach Wilbore simply skipped a year in reporting to the colony, and this would happen again.

We have already determined that the records as they appear in the proprietors' volume are the source for the material submitted to the colony. Whenever records are copied there is always the chance for error to creep in, and this is certainly the case with these entries.

First, there are several straightforward copying errors. In his fifth submission, Wilbore reports the birth of Mary Armsbee, daughter of Thomas Armsbee, on 3 October 1671 [PCR 8:54], but in the vital records register this was earlier written as 3 October 1670. As the former date was created from the latter, 1670 should be taken as the correct year of birth, and this will generally be the case in discrepancies of this sort. Furthermore, comparison with other birthdates in the Armsbee family points to 1670 as the correct year of birth.

There are other examples of such copying errors. Shadrach Wilbore reported the birth of his own son Shadrach as 5 December 1672 [PCR 8:59], which was apparently what he had originally entered in the proprietors' volume, but he later rewrote December as September, which is presumably correct, as the emendation is in Wilbore's hand.

As an aside, we note that the compiler of the published Taunton vital records expended much energy on making these item by item comparisons as well. As published, the birthdate for the younger Shadrach Wilbore is given as 5 September 1672, indicating that the compiler relied primarily on the proprietors' volume. However, there is also included the annotation"[Shadrah Wilbore, Dec. 5, P.C.R.]," thus indicating the discrepancy.

A second type of error is omission. In the second submission to the colony Wilbore included the first seven children of Thomas Caswell as entered in the vital records register

[PCR 8:36-37], and in his third submission he included three more children [PCR 8:35-36]. There was, in addition, a daughter Hannah, born after the first seven and before the other three, who is recorded in her proper place in the register, but was not included in any submission to the colony.

There are no markings in the proprietors' volume to indicate where a given family entry stood with respect to the submissions, so the only way Wilbore could know what to send in to the colony would be by comparison with earlier submissions. Obviously, he was not completely accurate in this part of his procedure. On a few occasions, he reported the same event twice, as with the death of Hopestill, the wife of George Shove, on 7 March 1673/4 in his eighth and ninth submissions [PCR 8:55, 65].

A third type of error was more complicated, being the conflation of two register entries into one submission entry. The family of Samuel Hall as entered in the proprietors' volume includes births of a son Nicholas on 23 January 1668 and a daughter Elizabeth on 28 October 1670, whereas the colony submission has only "Nicholas Hall, the son of Samuell Hall, was borne the 28th of October 1670" [PCR 8:39]. In a scriptorial error known as haplography, Wilbore has jumped from the middle of one line to the middle of the next, fusing the first half of one entry onto the second half of the next, thus creating a new and totally erroneous record. The compiler of the published Taunton vital records has also noticed and marked these errors.

Finally, we should note that not all of the events recorded by Wilbore occurred in Taunton. In some cases this is stated explicitly, as with the family of James Leonard Junior, where the record shows that some of the earlier births took place at Braintree. Since Wilbore frequently collected vital records ten or twenty years after the events themselves took place, we should always be alert for this possibility even where not explicitly stated.

All in all, the vital records register maintained by Shadrach Wilbore is a splendid and reliable source, and should be preferred to the colony submissions when there is a discrepancy.

The vital records from this register were also published separately in 1862 and 1863 by Edgar H. Reed [NEHGR 16:324-28, 17:34-37, 232-36]. This transcription is reasonably accurate (except for the family of Richard Godfrey [NEHGR 17:235]), but the order of the pages and of the families has been altered.

One other set of seventeenth-century Taunton vital records survives, the record of marriages performed by Major Thomas Leonard as local magistrate. This record runs from 1684 to 1713, and contains more than two hundred entries. Some, but not all, of these marriages were also recorded by Shadrach Wilbore.

EARLY TAUNTON LANDHOLDING

Because of the loss by fire of most of the early Taunton town records, we have only a fragmentary record of the granting of lands to the early inhabitants of the town. We can, however, recover from some of the later proprietors' records an outline of the types and numbers of parcels that were granted.

One of the earliest surviving documents is a slender volume that was maintained by Oliver Purchase in his few years as town clerk. Several of the pages in this little book have a heading of the form "The Record of the Lands belonging unto Richard Williams." In this instance, the remainder of the page is blank.

In a few cases, though, some of the actual land entries were included. A page dated 16 July 1649 gives the lands of William Parker: "his home ground," being about six acres; a parcel of land, of unstated type, "on the other side of the great river," also about six acres; "forty acres of arable land lying & being on the far side of the great river"; ten acres of land, of unstated type, "on the north side of the great river"; and "a certain quantity of meadow & meadowish land lying & being on the north side of the great river."

The next set of records in point of age is Volume One of the Proprietors' Records, begun in 1661. This book also has a few compilations of the landholdings of individuals. An example, compiled in 1661, is that of Francis Smith: home lot of six acres; six acres "on the farther side of the great river"; thirty acres and a half "on this side of the great river in the home reach socalled"; and a parcel of meadow.

This was followed by a volume compiled by Shadrach Wilbore in the 1680s. One entry is for Thomas Gilbert, beginning with the lands "derived from the purchase right of his father Thomas Gilbert (deceased) he being one of the first purchasers and inhabitants of said Taunton": home lot of twelve acres; twelve acres "on the east side of the great river"; a parcel of meadow; two acres of "swamp and meadow and meadowish land"; and fifty-nine acres of land. (Some of this land may have been acquired by the second generation Thomas Gilbert.)

The picture we obtain from these records is much like that we have seen in other early New England towns: a homelot (to which is attached the proprietary right); a parcel or two of planting (or arable) land; a parcel or two of meadow land; and perhaps a larger parcel of outlying land, of little agricultural value.

The three different volumes noted above do not contain the records for all the early inhabitants of Taunton. However, the use of these records, in conjunction with probates and deeds, should allow, with some effort, a nearly complete reconstruction of early Taunton landgranting.

ORDER OF TOWN FORMATION

Arguments arise from time to time over the priority in time of the formation of New England towns, and, given the loss of records, and the silence of those records that do survive, we frequently have difficulty in adjudicating these disputes.

For the early Plymouth Colony towns, we are assisted by a feature of the recordkeeping of the Colony clerks. Examining several entries in the early records, most of them lists, we see that the towns are usually listed in the same sequence. Furthermore, where we do have specific information, this sequence conforms with what we know about the order of formation of the towns, so we may assume that this sequence represents the contemporaneous understanding of the order in which the towns were established.

The earliest example of such a sequenced list occurs on 1 January 1633/4, when the constables were chosen, Joshua Pratt for Plymouth, Christopher Wadsworth for "the ward of [blank] bounded between Jones River & Greens Harbour" [Duxbury], and Anthony Annable for Scituate [PCR 1:21]. Lists of constables for 3 January 1636/7 and 7 March 1636/7 maintain the same sequence [PCR 1:48, 54], as do all later and longer lists.

The next list of constables, dated 6 March 1637/8, replicates the earlier sequence for the three older towns, and adds for the first time a fourth, Sandwich [PCR 1:80]. "Ten men of Saugus" had on 3 April 1637 been given permission "to view a place to sit down" [PCR 1:59], but no other reference to this settlement is seen in Plymouth Colony records until this list of constables, indicating that actual settlement did not take place until late in 1637, or even early in 1638.

A year later, on 5 March 1638/9, the list of constables was expanded to six, in the following order: Plymouth, Duxbury, Scituate, Sandwich, Cohannet and Yarmouth [PCR 1:116]. On 3 September 1638, the court gave permission to Gregory Armstrong and Gabriel Wheldon "to go dwell at Mattacheese [Yarmouth], with the leave of the committees for that place" [PCR 1:95]. If this represents an "official" recognition of the formation of Yarmouth, then Taunton must have existed "officially" at an earlier date, even though we see no records of the town until November of 1638.

A few months later, on 4 June 1639, the list of constables runs to seven towns, with Barnstable now appended to the end of the list; on the same day, the deputies to the General Court are also listed, with the same towns in the same order, but with a note that the Barnstable deputies were "made in December Court, 1639" [PCR 1:125-26].

The next town to appear in the lists was Rexham [name soon changed to Marshfield] on 2 March 1640/1 [PCR 2:9], followed by Rehoboth on 4 June 1645 [PCR 2:84] and Nauset [Eastham] on 2 June 1646 [PCR 2:102].

RECENT LITERATURE

Jeremy Dupertuis Bangs, "Towards a Revision of the Pilgrims: Three New Pictures," *The New England Historical and Genealogical Register* 153 (1999):3-28. Bangs draws interesting conclusions from examination of three seventeenth century pictures. The first, by Adam Willaerts, dated 1620, he identifies as a view of the Pilgrims as they are leaving Delfshaven, and the second, also by Willaerts, dated 1638, he argues to be an early view of Plymouth in New England. The third item, an engraving of 1654 of those assembled for the Treaty of Westminster, apparently includes a depiction of Edward Winslow not long before his death in the Caribbean in 1655.

Abbott Lowell Cummings, "John Comins (c. 1668-1751) of Woburn and Oxford, Massachusetts, and Windham County, Connecticut: Exploring His Origins and Connections," *The New England Historical and Genealogical Register* 153 (1999):52-72. As a prelude to his discussion of John Comins, who first appears in New England in 1689, Cummings surveys all seventeenth-century immigrants to New England of that surname, including some who came during the Great Migration.

Douglas Richardson, "The English Origin and Ancestry of the Parker Brothers of Massachusetts and of their Probable Aunt, Sarah Parker, Wife of Edward Converse," *The New England Historical and Genealogical Register* 153 (1999):81-96. The author has determined that the five Parker brothers of Woburn (John, James, Abraham, Joseph and Jacob), at least two of whom had arrived in New England by the early 1640s, derived from Great Burstead, Essex. Furthermore, Sarah Parker, first wife of Edward Converse, was probably their sister.

Paul C. Reed, "Two Somerby Frauds," *The American Genealogist* 74 (1999):15-30. Reed investigates two cases in which Horatio Gates Somerby embellished the truth in claims of English origin of early New England immigrants. In the first case, the Blakes of Dorchester, the author notes that "the immediate connection was disproved as long ago as 1891" (by Francis E. Blake), and then goes on to demonstrate errors and fabrications at several other points in Somerby's pedigree. In the second instance, Reed shows that the published ancestry for Roger and William Billings is based on an invented will, and the "origin of the Billing(s) family of Dorchester … is unknown."

Gale Ion Harris, "Thomas[1] and Anna (Wright?) Burnham of Hartford, Connecticut: A Note on Dubious Dates," *The American Genealogist* 74 (1999):33-37. The author demonstrates that many of the dates given in a nineteenth-century genealogy of the Burnham family are demonstrably false, thus throwing doubt on all dates in that genealogy which are not supported by contemporary records.

Clifford L. Stott, "The English Origin of Thomas[1] Faxon of Braintree, Massachusetts," *The American Genealogist* 74 (1999):41-49. Stott has found in the parish registers of Swalcliffe, Oxfordshire, the marriage record and the baptisms for the three known children of Thomas Faxon, who appeared in Braintree by the early 1640s.

Dean Crawford Smith, "When Did Thomas[1] Newhall of Lynn, Massachusetts, Really Immigrate to America," *The American Genealogist* 74 (1999):50-52. Smith shows that Thomas Newhall came to New England late in 1637 or early in 1638, thus disproving claims in the earlier secondary literature that this immigrant had settled in Lynn by 1630.

Leslie Mahler, "The English Ancestry of Richard[1] Dole of Newbury, Massachusetts, With a Note on Francis[1] Doughty, Minister of Long Island," *The American Genealogist* 74 (1999):53-57. The author has found the baptism of Richard Dole, resident of Newbury by 1639, in Rangeworthy, Gloucestershire, and from that starting point has identified the immigrant's father and grandfather. In addition, Francis Doughty, immigrant to Dorchester, was curate of this parish in 1632.

Myrtle Stevens Hyde, "The English Origin of 'Farmer' George[1] Clark(e) of Milford, Connecticut," *The American Genealogist* 74 (1999):72-73. Hyde has found a will which shows that "Farmer" George Clarke of Milford derived from the vicinity of Watton-at-Stone, Hertfordshire.

Peter S. Leavenworth, "'The Best Title That Indians Can Claime': Native Agency and Consent in the Transferal of Penacook-Pawtucket Land in the Seventeenth Century," *The New England Quarterly* 72 (1999):275-300. Drawing on "a database of over 110 deeds culled from provincial records and county deed registries," the author examines the transfer of land along the Merrimack from the Penacook-Pawtucket Indians to the English, and concludes that it was not always a one-sided dispossession of the Indians by the English.

Gordon L. Remington, "Robert[2] Huestis of Westchester County: His Ancestry and Descendants," *The New York Genealogical and Biographical Record* 129 (1998):1-12, 97-108, 191-206, 276-284, 130 (1999):54-60. Remington poses a number of problems pertaining to Robert Huestis and his family and presents his resolution of those problems. He then sets forth records for the family in Bridport, Dorsetshire, and compiles four generations of agnate descent from Robert[2].

(continued from page 10)

The immigrants from New England did not just bring with them their religious practices. They also attempted, as well as they could, to carry over the principles of town government to which they had become accustomed.

The earliest town records of Newark were published in 1864, and provide us with evidence of this continuity (*Collections of the New Jersey Historical Society*, Volume VI). Having obtained their grant, the founders signed an agreement on 24 May 1666, and declared that they would meet again in October.

On 30 October 1666, a meeting was held "touching the intended design of many of the inhabitants of Branford." This document was similar to the town covenants which had been the norm in New England since the 1630s. As good citizens of the former New Haven Colony, those who created the document made provision for both ecclesiastical and civil government. They began the important work of granting and laying out land, and also attended to lesser matters such as fencing and defense against wolves. At a meeting on 10 September 1668 they "agreed to build a meetinghouse as soon as may be," as good an indication as one might wish that this was still a New England community.

In summary, the six New England towns erected in East Jersey in the second half of the 1660s derived their inhabitants from towns at both ends of Long Island, from along Long Island Sound and around Narragansett Bay, from Cape Cod towns in Plymouth Colony, from towns on the north shore of Massachusetts Bay, and from towns along the Piscataqua River in New Hampshire. The settlers came, therefore, from jurisdictions which varied greatly in their governmental organization and in the way in which church and state interacted. What was common to all these places of origin is that they were on the seacoast. Very few of the early migrants of East Jersey came from the inland towns of New England.

BIBLIOGRAPHIC NOTE: The best modern history of East Jersey is that published by John E. Pomfret in 1962, *The Province of East New Jersey, 1609-1702: The Rebellious Proprietary*; we have relied on this volume heavily in the narrative above. In 1949 the Board of Proprietors of the Eastern Division of New Jersey issued *The Minutes of The Board of Proprietors of the Eastern Division of New Jersey from 1685 to 1705*.

A number of county and town histories were also consulted in writing this newsletter article, but we will take special notice only of the remarkable set of volumes by Orra Eugene Monnette, *First Settlers of Ye Plantations of Piscataway and Woodbridge, Olde East New Jersey, 1664-1714*. Monnette was one of the worst genealogists of any generation, and his genealogical conclusions should be ignored, but there is also much valuable source material included in this publication.

Great Migration Study Project
101 Newbury Street
Boston, MA 02116

Great Migration Newsletter

| Vol. 8 | July-September 1999 | No. 3 |

TOWN OFFICES: SELECTMAN - PART I

The office of selectman is a quintessentially New England institution. For centuries New England towns have been governed by a panel of three men (and more recently women) who carried out much of the town's business between one annual town General Meeting and another.

This office did not exist in England, where most of the local affairs were handled by the church vestry or the remnants of the manorial system. We will begin a series of articles on officeholding with a two-part article on the growth of the office of selectman. We start by looking at the development of this office in half a dozen of the earliest Massachusetts Bay towns.

At the first Boston meeting on record, on 1 September 1634 [BTR 1:1], we find ten men running the meeting and making decisions. These men are not given any title, and they may well have been appointed on an *ad hoc* basis, because for more than a year thereafter we see only general meetings of the town.

On 14 March 1635/6, at a general meeting of the town, twelve men were appointed to "oversee, look into and set order for all allotments within us, and for all comers unto us, as also for all other the occasions and businesses of this town, excepting matters of election for the General Court – and so from time to time to be agreed upon and ordered by them, or the greater part of them, for these next six months" [BTR 1:8-9].

On the one hand, we do not have a name for this group of officers, but, on the other hand, in their appointment we have a charter for their activities. The tasks which they are to carry out are enumerated, and the one piece of business which they cannot fulfill on their own ("matters of election for the General Court") is also explicitly stated. Their manner of voting and term of office are also set forth. As we shall see, this group will evolve into the selectmen.

On 16 September 1636, again at a general town meeting, the charter was renewed, when ten men were "chosen for these next six months to oversee and set order for all allotments belonging to this town, and for all other occasions and busi-nesses of the same (excepting matters of election for the General Court)" [BTR 1:11]. Six months later, on 20 March 1636/7, eleven men were appointed, and again on 16 October 1637 [BTR 1:16, 20].

Toward the end of the six-month term of this group of officers, attendance started to fall off, with only five or six men appearing [BTR 1:32-33]. Then, on 23 April 1638, only seven men were "chosen, as formerly for the Town's occasions, for these next six months, to be ordered by them or by five of them at least" [BTR 1:34]. There was no discussion of the reasons behind this decrease from eleven to seven.

On 5 November 1638, seven men were again chosen, but, on 13 May 1639, the number was increased to nine [BTR 1:35-36, 41]. On nine more occasions, nine men were chosen to "order the town's affairs for these six months next ensuing," although the interval between elections often stretched to nine months or more [BTR 1:44, 55, 61, 65, 70, 72, 75, 79, 84].

The change came with the election of 26 December 1645, at which nine men were "chosen for this year the Select Men" [BTR 1:86]. Three months later, at a "general town's meeting" on 23 March 1645/6, "it is agreed that on the second day of the first month is appointed to meet at eight of clock in the morning to choose Deputies for the General Court and townsmen for that year and Constables and Surveyors for the Highways, every year" [BTR 1:87].

(continued on page 18)

EDITOR'S EFFUSIONS

Recently the Great Migration Study Project has won two awards, one from the General Society of Mayflower Descendants and one from the National Society Women Descendants of the Ancient & Honorable Artillery Company. In each instance the editor has been asked to deliver a short talk as part of the award ceremony.

Our plan on each occasion has been to speak briefly about the origin and progress of the Project, and then to finish with some comments which are particularly relevant to the honoring body. In the case of the Mayflower Society, the English origin of three of the *Mayflower* passengers had been discovered since the publication of *The Great Migration Begins*, and so the speech was an opportunity to speak of the vigor of *Mayflower* studies and of the opportunities for even more discoveries.

More interestingly, the preparation for the Artillery Company talk led to some small but very useful improvements in the Great Migration Study Project. First, to this point in our research we have been relying on the published history of the Artillery Company by Oliver Roberts for our information on those early immigrants who were members of the Artillery Company. Prior to this speech we visited the curator of the Artillery Company at Faneuil Hall. Unfortunately there are no surviving seventeenth-century records for this institution, so we will continue to rely on the Roberts history. But now we know.

Second, we have been ignoring the evidence in probate inventories of the possession of various weapons by many men, in support of their activities in the local train band. Henceforth, we shall take note of these items and record them in that section of the sketch on *OFFICEHOLDING* where information on military service is recorded. This will be similar to our practice in the *EDUCATION* section where we include information from probate inventories on book ownership, and on rare occasion the possession of spectacles. The stimuli to improving the Great Migration sketches come in unexpected ways.

Robert Charles Anderson, FASG   Editor
Aileen Novick   Production Assistant

The Great Migration Newsletter is published quarterly by the Great Migration Study Project, a project of the New England Historic Genealogical Society, 101 Newbury Street, Boston MA 02116
www.nehgs.org

The subscription rate is $12 for one year and $20 for two years.

(continued from page 17)

The officers elected on 26 December 1645 remained in place for fifteen months, and then on 18 March 1646/7 seven men "are chosen this year the Selectmen" under the new order [BTR 1:90]. And so in the first month [March] of each year seven men were elected, to be called "townsmen" on 13 March 1647/8, but "select men" or "Selectmen for the Town's affairs" in most years thereafter [BTR 1:92, 94, 99].

In Cambridge, on 3 February 1634/5, "At a General Meeting of the whole town, it was agreed upon by a joint consent that 7 men should be chosen to do the whole business of the town" [CaTR 11]. On 4 September 1637, "there are chosen for townsmen to order the town affairs this year following only" seven men [CaTR 29]. On 26 October 1638, "there were chosen for townsmen to order the town affairs for the year following" seven men, two of whom were the constables [CaTR 34].

This pattern continued until 1645, when the Cambridge town records make reference to "more chosen by the town to join with seven select men that were then in place for the ordering of some special affairs of the town" [CaTR 67]. Even with this reference to the "selectmen," on 10 November 1651 the town records mention "townsmen for the prudential affairs of the town" [CaTR 93].

In Salem, at a meeting of 22 February 1635/6, mention was made of the "town representative" [STR 1:15]. This might be thought to refer to the town's designated deputies to the Massachusetts Bay General Court, but just a month later, on 28 March 1636, the town records speak of the "town representative viz: 13 men deputed" [STR 1:15]. The view of the town of Salem, then, was apparently that they had chosen thirteen of their number to "represent" the entire town in those affairs relating specifically to the town.

Within a year, the number of men so chosen had shrunk to ten, and then to eight, but on 20 June 1637 it was again twelve [STR 1:34, 38, 44, 45, 48, 50]. On 30 March 1640, a Salem town record tells of a "former order that the seven men which were chosen for the ordering of the affairs of the town" [STR 1:99]. On 10 August 1642, there was "a particular meeting of the 7 men," and on 13 March 1648/9, we find a reference to the "selectmen" [STR 1:113, 157]. A series of three meetings in the space of less than a year shows that the terminology was in flux at that time: 17 December 1649, "a meeting of the select men"; 12 August 1650, "a meeting of the 7 men"; and 22 August 1650, "a meeting of the select men" [STR 1:162, 165]. Thereafter, these officers were referred to regularly as selectmen.

The town of Dedham was formed half a decade after the arrival of the Winthrop Fleet, and so had before it several years of experience by the other towns of Massachusetts Bay. Its earliest meetings, held in Watertown in late 1636

(continued on page 24)

Focus   *on*   *PROVIDENCE*

EARLY TOWN RECORDS

In most early New England towns, the earliest town records were a mixture of everything that related to the activities of the town. Town meeting records might be mixed in with land grants, vital records, earmarks, notices of stray live-stock, and so on. This condition was exacerbated in Rhode Island, where the town was also responsible for probate matters. Only when the town was a few decades old did the clerks see fit to establish separate series of records for different town activities.

In Westerly, Rhode Island, for example, the first volume of records, from 1661 to 1707, contains every type of record generated by the town during those years. In 1699 the town began a separate volume for probate records, and then in 1707 separated the town meeting and vital records in a third series of volumes [RIRoots 7:25-27].

Providence was an older and larger town, and the early records are consequently more voluminous and more complicated than those of Westerly.

The city of Providence published the early town records in twenty-one volumes over a span of years from 1892 to 1915, and in the introduction to each volume included a brief assessment of the place of each volume in the overall collection of town records. As the series proceeded and the editors learned more and more about the records, their evaluations of some of the earlier volumes changed.

According to the editors of these volumes, "The first volume of records selected for perpetuation in print is the earliest in date of the existing public records of the city, and has at different times been referred to in town documents as the 'First Book of the Town of Providence,' and 'The Long Old Book with Parchment Cover'" [PrTR 1:iii-iv].

Close examination of this volume indicates that this may not, in fact, be the "earliest in date." The first three pages (of the original) contain an undated town agreement (apparently from 1636) and the "agreements & orders the second year of the plantation" [PrTR 1:1-5]. The fourth page is a deed of 12 October 1663, and pages five and six have births for three families, and a land grant recorded 27 January 1670/1 [PrTR 1:5-9].

The remaining seventy-six pages of the volume record deeds, land grants and a few probates from about 1659 to 1671. In analyzing the second published volume, the editors noted that the volume at some time in its history had come apart and had then been rebound incorrectly, with the bulk

of the material running from back to front chronologically [PrTR 2:ix]. Although they don't say so, a similar fate seems to have befallen this first printed volume as well. The last item in the regular series of deeds, on pages 109-111, was recorded on 27 July 1659. As one works backwards through the volume, toward page six (as printed), the dates of recording become later and later, reaching 27 January 1670/1.

There are no records in this first published volume of general town meetings from any date. The first three pages, although they clearly relate to the earliest years of settlement of the town, are of a very general nature, and have the appearance of a retrospective attempt to capitulate the founding documents of Providence. We will make a further assessment of this "earliest" volume of town records after we have examined several more of the published volumes.

The next volume we will consider, the second in the series as published, bears on the title page the following entertaining description: "The Second Book of the Town of Providence Otherwise Called the Old Town Book, the Short Old Town Book, the Old Burnt Book and Sometimes Called the Book with Brass Clasps." In the introduction we are told that "The volume which is now reproduced in print was commenced after the 'First Book Town of Providence' ..." [PrTR 2:iv]. This conclusion is presumably based on the records dated to 1636 in the "first" volume.

In this "second" volume we find first what appear to be excerpts from town meetings from the early 1640s through the late 1650s, consisting, with one exception, of land grants and land transactions [PrTR 2:1-39].

In the prefatory matter to this volume is a "Table showing the dates of the meetings for town purposes which are referred to in the book now reproduced in print" [PrTR 2:xv-xviii]. The first seven entries in this table are spread over the years from 1642 to 1659, and occur within the first twenty-two pages of the volume as printed. The remainder of the table is a long string of dated meetings, from 27 April 1649 to 25 March 1661, with several meetings for each year.

These two sections of the table represent very different sorts of records. The first seven items in the list of "meetings for town purposes which are referred to" are not records of town meetings as such, but are extracts of one or two land transactions from meetings of those dates.

The dates in the second and much larger part of the table do denote a regular sequence of full town meetings. The record of each meeting generally opens with the appointment of a moderator (still a feature of New England town meetings). The meetings might record land transactions, elections to town and colony offices, town ordinances, lawsuits, and many other items.

The June meeting was usually called the Court of Elections, for a wide range of town and colony officers were elected at that time. Four additional meetings, in January, April, July and October, were designated Quarter Courts (later called Quarter Meetings), and other meetings were called Town Meetings. Despite these divergent names, any type of business might be transacted at any of these meetings.

The next volume of Providence records undertaken by these editors was called, among other things, the "Third Book Town of Providence," and was sufficiently large that it had to be published in three parts, comprising Volumes 3, 4 and 5 of the printed series.

This book begins with a town meeting (actually a Quarter Court) of 27 April 1661, and proceeds steadily to a Town Meeting of 11 March 1675/6 [PrTR 3:1-250, 4:1-53]. Presumably the regular keeping of the records was interrupted at this point by King Philip's War. These Town Meeting records continued to include recorded deeds.

When recordkeeping resumed, Town Meeting records were entered in a different book, and the present volume was used mostly for deeds, although a substantial portion included vital records, the first place in the Providence town records where more than one or two families had their vital statistics entered. The deeds from this original book cover the rest of Volume 4 as published [PrTR 4:53-260] and more than half of Volume 5 [PrTR 5:1-252]. Vital records consume most of the rest of Volume 5 [PrTR 5:252-332], although even in this range a number of deeds are interspersed.

The sixth and seventh published volumes contain "The First Book for Providence Town Council Particular Use" (although there seems to have been an older volume, in existence in 1677 but lost before 1755, called "A small paper book containing the enrollments of wills" [PrTR 6:iii]).

This first Town Council book commences with the record of a meeting on 25 March 1678, and contains a regular sequence of such meetings until 14 September 1686 [PrTR 6:4-155]. These meetings are dominated by probate proceedings, with the acts of the council in accepting and examinging documents interspersed with transcripts of the documents themselves.

The Town Council considered other matters as well, such as the disposition of persons who had moved to Providence from other towns and might become a burden to the town, licenses for inns, and marital problems (most notably the bigamous marriage of Lawrence Clinton to Mary Wooden [PrTR 6:26-27; TAG 64:150]).

This volume continues with papers of the estate of Silas Carpenter, probated in 1701 [PrTR 6:156-59], then a series of probate documents presented to the Town Council from 1714 to 1721 [PrTR 6:159-93]. Next comes a long section, spanning the two published volumes, consisting of probate documents from 1699 to 1716 [PrTR 6:194-290, 7:1-182]. Finally, the last group of pages presents the probate papers from a few estates in 1694, 1698, 1701, 1705 and 1708 [PrTR 7:182-217].

Published Volumes 8 and 9 transcribe a book with the legend "Town Meetings No. 3 1677-1750." Volume 8 actually begins with transcripts of a few loose sheets of paper which record meetings of late 1676 and early 1677, when the town was recovering from the depredations of King Philip's War [PrTR 8:11-17].

The bound volume of town meeting records begins with the annual election meeting on 4 June 1677 and continues steadily until 21 May 1688 [PrTR 8:17-176], when many of the governmental institutions in Rhode Island, and throughout New England, were shut down by Gov. Andros and his Dominion of New England. This long sequence of town meetings is supplemented by the transcript of a loose sheet of paper which records town meetings of 1691 [PrTR 8:177-79]. The records of these town meetings include copies of a few surveys of land grants from the town, but no deeds from person to person.

Volume 9 continues the publication of this same volume of records, but the remainder of the material pertains to miscellaneous matters of a later date, including coroner's inquests, stray livestock, highway surveys and apprenticeship agreements.

The tenth volume in the series includes the material in a book with the name "Town Council No. 1 1692 to 1714." The precise range of dates covered is 31 August 1692 through 25 June 1714. The acts of the Town Council are recorded, but the actual probate documents are not included in this volume.

Volume 11 bears the title "Town Meeting No. 1 1692-1715." The exact dates of town meetings included runs from 6 June 1692 to 27 October 1715, covering the final years of the long run of Thomas Olney as Town Clerk. In this volume there begin to appear separate meetings of "The Purchasers and Proprietors of Providence."

The twelfth published volume is referred to as "Town Council Record No. 2, 1715-1732" and contains the proceedings of that body from 1715 to early 1725, with a few additional entries for the years from 1728 to 1734 pertaining only to the granting of tavern licenses.

The thirteenth published volume is known as "Town Meeting No 2 1716 1721." The editors here resume their practice of including a table of meeting dates [PrTR 13:iv-v], which, despite the title of the volume, actually runs to 1725. They also note that this may have been a waste book, rather than the "official" copy of the town meeting records for these years. It should be noted, though, that this span of years follows immediately the four decades of service of Thomas Olney as Town Clerk, and the seemingly unusual arrangement may merely reflect the new practices of town clerks who did not have Olney's skills and experience.

The fourteenth published volume is called "Deed Book No. 1." There were of course several earlier volumes which included deeds, but this was the first devoted totally to that type of record.

The first two deeds were recorded on 1 April 1678, with several more recorded later that month. The deeds as recorded (or at least as printed) were not entered in strict chronological sequence, with, for instance, a jump from mid-1679 to mid-1683, and then back to 1679.

Most of the documents are sales of land from one landholder to another, but there are also many records of land laid out to persons by the town, including crude plats of some of the parcels. No other type of document appears in this volume. As is usually the case with deed registers, many of the instruments, although recorded in 1678 or later, were actually executed at an earlier date, with a number from the early 1660s, and even earlier.

The last recording date in this "first" deed book was 22 May 1705, although there seems to have been a gap from about 1699 to 1704 when no deeds were recorded in this volume.

Volumes 15 and 17 as printed contain several hundred loose papers held by the City of Providence, presented in chronological order. Volume 15 covers the years 1639 through 1682, while Volume 17 picks up the sequence in 1682 and carries on to 1722. The documents cover a large range of subject matter, such as petitions, accounts, extracts from town records (some of which do not survive in book form), depositions, tax lists and letters.

The sixteenth published volume bears the title "Will &c. No. 2, From Sept 12 1716 to Jan 7 1728/9," and contains the various probate documents processed by the Town Council over that range of dates.

(Volumes 18 and 19 of the published series will not be considered here, as they contain the tombstone inscriptions of the North Burial Ground.)

Finally, Volumes 20 and 21 contain the records of "Deed Book No. 2," beginning with deeds recorded on 22 June 1705. Volume 20 covers about half of this deed book, through deeds recorded on 6 November 1711. Volume 21 is quite slender, picking up where Volume 20 left off, but not completing the transcript of "Deed Book No. 2." The whole project of publishing Providence town records apparently ran out of steam at this time.

Having completed our survey of the twenty-one published volumes of Providence town records, we return to the question of the antiquity of Volume 1. Almost all of Volume 1 consists of deeds and other land records dated from 1659 to 1671. By contrast, Volume 2 includes a complete series of town meetings from 1649 to 1661, and deeds and other land records from 1642 to 1659.

In other words, nearly all of Volume 2 is of earlier date than Volume 1. Volume 1 does begin with only three pages of original material that comes from the 1630s. This may truly be a fragment of the first volume of town records, the bulk of which is now lost. Or it may simply be a few extracts from the earliest lost records, at attempt to preserve the foundation documents of the settlement of Providence.

Whatever the case may be, the material published as Volume 2 deserves the name of oldest surviving book of Providence town records.

We now proceed to a broad summary of the material in the published volumes, and a few conclusions about the evolution of recordkeeping in this town.

Presumably a record volume was maintained from the earliest years of Providence's existence, but all or most of it has been lost, and we are left with a fairly complete set of records beginning in the late 1640s. As with many other New England towns, the first few volumes contain a melange of all sorts of records, with town meetings, deeds, wills, vital records and other materials all mixed together in one volume.

With the possible exception of a book of wills and other probate matter begun before King Philip's War, the first attempt to separate out different categories of records into separate volumes took place in 1678, in the aftermath of King Philip's War, when a system of three series of volumes was begun. The town meeting volumes were continued, and new books were begun at the same time for deeds and for Town Council business. For a time, some deeds were also recorded in one of the old town meeting books, and the Town Council volumes contained acts of the Council along with the probate documents themselves.

A second separation of records into separate volumes occurred in 1692, again in the aftermath of a serious disruption, this time the discontinuation of local recordkeeping during the Dominion of New England in the later 1680s. When the full town functions resumed in 1692, a new town meeting volume was begun, and two sets of books were instituted for the Town Council, one for the acts of that body and another for the various papers generated by each estate.

We conclude this section by bringing together the volume and page ranges for each of the record categories. (In those cases where only a volume number is given, and no range of pages, either the entire volume is devoted to that category of records, or the records are scattered throughout the volume.)

Town Meetings

1649-1661	2:40-145
1661-1675	3:1-250, 4:1-53
1676-1691	8
1692-1715	11
1716-1725	13

Deeds

1642-1659	2:1-39
1659-1671	1:8-111
1662-1704	3,4,5
1678-1705	14
1705-1713	20-21

Town Council

1678-1686	6
1692-1714	10
1715-1725	12

Wills

1694-1708	7:182-217
1699-1716	6:156-159, 194-290, 7:1-182
1714-1721	6:159-193
1716-1729	16

EARLY PROVIDENCE VITAL RECORDS

Although there is no early volume devoted entirely to vital records, there are entries for births, marriages, marriage intentions and deaths scattered through a number of these published volumes.

Volume 1 contains a page and a half of birth records for four families, arranged by family, the earliest date being 1633 (Roger Williams's daughter Mary, actually born in Plymouth) and the latest being in 1658, so they may not have been entered until the latter date [PrTR 1:7-8].

Volume 2 also contains some scattered entries, some being entered by family [PrTR 2:18, 35], and some being marriage intentions included in town meeting records [PrTR 2:83, 121, 122, 123, 125, 126, 128, 133, 135].

In the large original book published in Volumes 3, 4 and 5, scattered entries by family become somewhat more frequent in Volumes 3 and 4, and then in Volume 5 we reach the first

occurrence of what appears to be dedicated reporting of these events [PrTR 5:254-332], although even here there are some deeds and other records intruding upon the vital records, and, as the entries are made mostly by family, we cannot tell without examination of the original whether the entries were made contemporaneously with the events, or were recorded later in census style.

Finally, in Volume 8 there are a few very important records of vital events for late 1676 and early 1677, when the town was recovering from King Philip's War [PrTR 8:14-16].

Most of the vital records in these early volumes have been published in two other places: Edwin M. Snow, *Alphabetical Index of the Births, Marriages and Deaths, Recorded in Providence From 1636 to 1850 Inclusive* [Providence 1879], and James M. Arnold, *Vital Record of Rhode Island. 1636-1850. First Series. Births, Marriages and Deaths ... Vol. 2. Providence County* [Providence 1892].

Comparing entries in these three sources provides some useful information. One of the births in Volume 1 is that of Stephen Dexter, son of Gregory, born 1 November 1647 [PrTR 1:7]. Arnold [Arnold 2:Providence:220, citing 1:4] and Snow [1:20, citing 5:337] both reproduce this entry. Snow is certainly citing a transcript. The citation in Arnold is close to that in the published town records, but examination of other records in Volume 1 shows that he was not working from the original. There must, therefore, be at least two transcripts of these entries from Volume 1.

Comparison of entries from Volumes 2 and 3,4,5 tells a similar story. Volume 2 prints the 2 June 1655 marriage intention of Thomas Slow and Elizabeth Paumer (Palmer) [PrTR 2:83]. Again, Arnold and Snow both print these records, again from later transcripts [Arnold 2:Providence:171, citing 1:123; Snow 1:323, citing 5:339].

Volume 4 has the 1 January 1702 marriage of John Barnes and Mercy Allen [PrTR 4:96]; this marriage is printed by Arnold and Snow, again from transcripts [Arnold 2:Providence:13, citing 1:319; Snow 1:89, citing 5:345 and 1:14].

A most interesting situation arises with the entries in Volume 8. Two examples are the burial on 7 September 1676 of Henry Wright, son of Samuel Wright, and the marriage on 2 January 1676/7 of Samuel Winsor and Mercy Waterman [PrTR 8:14, 15]. Interestingly, neither Arnold nor Snow reports either of these entries, and apparently they omit all the entries from Volume 8.

Clearly Arnold and Snow worked entirely from transcripts, and did not look at the originals. Not surprisingly, we should prefer the records from the published town records to the versions given by Arnold and Snow, and for the entries in Volume 8 we have only that one source.

RECENT LITERATURE

F.N. Craig, "The Marbury Ancestry: Gernon and Rycote Lines," *The New England Historical and Genealogical Register* 153 (1999):164-72. The author provides additional ancestral lines, extending back to the twelfth century, for Grace (Chetwode) Bulkeley, Anne (Marbury) Hutchinson and Katherine (Marbury) Scott.

Christopher Gleason Clark, "Colborne Origins and Clark Revelations," *The New England Historical and Genealogical Register* 153 (1999):180-82. Clark demonstrates that the Priscilla Clark who married Nathaniel[1] Colborn, immigrant to Dedham, was not a daughter of Thomas Clark of Banham, Norfolk, and argues that Nathaniel Colborn was baptized at Woolverstone, Suffolk, in 1611, son of Leonard Colborn.

Helen Schatvet Ullmann, "Notes on a Line from Henry[1] Adams" and "Some Notes on John[1] Bent of Sudbury, Massachusetts, and His Grandfather, John[B] Bent of Weyhill, Hampshire, England," *The New England Historical and Genealogical Register* 153 (1999):213-20. The author discusses some difficult points revolving around the immigrants Henry Adams and John Bent.

John C. Brandon, "Bennett-Conant Connection," *The New England Historical and Genealogical Register* 153 (1999):221. Brandon has solved a longstanding puzzle by demonstrating that Jane, the wife of William[1] Bennett of Salem was Jane Knowles, daughter of Thomas and Jane (Conant) Knowles of East Budleigh, Devonshire, and thus also niece of Roger Conant of Salem.

Patricia Law Hatcher, "Research and Red Herrings: The Wives of William[1] Luddington and Matthew[1] Moulthrop of New Haven, Connecticut, with Their English Origins," *The American Genealogist* 74 (1999):81-96, 209-24. Hatcher demonstrates conclusively that William Luddington derived from North Kelsey in Lincolnshire, that Mathew Moulthrop was baptized at Bridlington in Lincolnshire, and that these two men married at Wrawby, Lincolnshire, the sisters Ellen and Jane Nicholl, daughters of Thomas and Dorothy (George) Nicholl of Wrawby.

Gale Ion Harris, "The Skinner Wives of Robert[1] Reeve and John[1] Colt of Hartford and Windsor, Connecticut: An Old Mix-up," *The American Genealogist* 74 (1999):97-100. Using the Winthrop Medical Journal, Harris shows which of two daughters of John Skinner, a resident of Hartford by 1639, married Robert Reeve, and which married John Colt.

Leslie Mahler, "The English Origin of James[1] Thomson of Charlestown and Woburn, Massachusetts," *The American Genealogist* 74 (1999):101-4. Mahler presents evidence that James Thomson of Charlestown had lived in Frieston and Fishtoft in Lincolnshire before coming to New England.

Myrtle Stevens Hyde, "The Probable English Origin of Mark[1] Symonds of Ipswich, Massachusetts," *The American Genealogist* 74 (1999):114-16. The author has found some records which suggest that Mark Symonds of Ipswich had resided in Great Birch, Essex, before migrating to New England.

"The Will of Humphrey Fenn of Coventry, Co. Warwick, England," *The American Genealogist* 74 (1999):117-21. Humphrey Fenn was ancestor of a number of early residents of Salem (see TAG 73:23-32), and his will provides interesting context to the motivations for migration to New England in the mid-1630s.

Neil D. Thompson and Harry Macy, Jr., "Enigmas #11: The Connection Between John Latting of Oyster Bay, Long Island, and the Pratts," *The American Genealogist* 74 (1999):122-27. Land which had belonged to John[2] Pratt, son of Phineas[1] Pratt, was in 1751 sold by Jonathan[4] Pratt, grandson of John, and by John Latting of Oyster Bay. Thompson and Macy present different accounts of the possibility that Latting might be a Pratt relation.

David L. Greene, "A Note on Thomas[1] Marshfield of Windsor, Connecticut," *The American Genealogist* 74 (1999):127. Greene discusses a document from the Wyllys Papers that adds to our knowledge of the financial difficulties of Thomas Marshfield.

Gale Ion Harris, "Hannah (Osborn) (Ashcraft), Wife of Deliverance[2] Blackman of Stratford and Stonington, Connecticut," *The American Genealogist* 74 (1999):128-30. Harris identifies the wife of Deliverance[2] Blackman, son of Adam[1] Blakeman, resident of Guilford by 1638.

Timothy L. Wood, "Worlds Apart: Puritan Perceptions of the Native American during the Pequot War," *Rhode Island History* 56 (1998):63-75. Wood reexamines the causes and motivations of the Pequot War, and concludes that a principal driving force was the desire of the Puritans to convert the Indians. Their misunderstanding of Indian religious beliefs, and their failure to convert the Pequots, led the Puritans to determine that the Pequots were in a pact with the devil, and as such should be suppressed.

Jennifer Reid, "Roger Williams's *Key*: Ethnography or Mythology?" *Rhode Island History* 56 (1998):76-86. The author argues that Roger Williams's treatise on the Narragansett Indians is not the accurate ethnographic study that many historians have claimed it to be, but represents his conception of the Noble Savage as applied to his indigenous neighbors (although it does not present some of the more negative evaluations made by some of his Puritan contemporaries).

(continued from page 18)

and early 1637, were general town meetings, attended by all those who intended to make the move from Watertown to the new settlement at Dedham in the spring of 1637.

The first town meeting actually to be held in Dedham took place on 23 March 1636/7, and similar general town meetings continued on a frequent basis until 17 May 1639 [DeTR 1:28-53]. Even with the prior experience of thousands of other inhabitants of Massachusetts Bay, the men of Dedham did not immediately institute an office in which some small number of the heads of family would do the business of the whole town. About forty men attended these meetings, comprising as many of the landholders as were in town and able to attend on that date.

At the town meeting on 17 May 1639, those assembled noted that "Whereas it hath been found [by long experience] that the general meeting of so many men in one [some words lost] of the common affairs thereof, have wasted much time to no small damage & business [is] thereby nothing furthered, it is therefore now agreed by general consent, that these 7 men hereunder named we do make choice of & give them full power to contrive, execute & perform all the business & affairs of this our whole town to continue unto the first of the tenth month next: Edw: Alleyn, John Kingsbery, John Luson, Elea: Lusher, John Dwite, Robte Hinsdall, John Bacheler" [DeTR 1:53].

The new system was inaugurated on 29 June 1639 with a meeting of those "deputed for ordering of town affairs" [DeTR 1:54]. Meetings of these seven men continued at regular intervals during the rest of 1639, and then on 31 December 1639 "the whole town were warned to meet together this day to make choice of new men for the ordering of town affairs according unto a town order in that behalf" [DeTR 1:62].

This pattern then continued for many years thereafter. On 29 December 1640 the "7 men were chosen" [DeTR 1:75]. It soon became the custom to hold the annual general town meeting on 1 January or a day or two thereafter. On 1 January 1646/7, the formula changed slightly, with the choice of seven men to "act in town affairs for the ensuing year having the same power their predecessors had" [DeTR 1:114]. A year later, on 3 January 1647/8, the men were "chosen to order the prudential affairs of our town for the year next ensuing," and then a year later (the precise date not recorded) the seven men were "chosen for the select men for the year next ensuing" [DeTR 1:117, 124].

On 1 January 1650/1 the town reverted to an older formula, in which the seven men were "authorized to act in the behalf of the town as their predecessors were" [DeTR 1:134], but this was apparently the last gasp of the old system, as the next several annual general meetings saw the choice of the seven men as "select men" [DeTR 1:135, 138, 139, 140].

(to be continued)

Great Migration Study Project
101 Newbury Street
Boston, MA 02116

Great Migration Newsletter

Vol. 8   October-December 1999   No. 4

TOWN OFFICES: SELECTMAN - PART II

In the first installment of this article, we began our examination of the office of selectman by looking at the records of Boston, Cambridge, Salem and Dedham, looking closely at the names used in each town for the office, and the numbers of men chosen. We will now look at a few more towns, then at the colony records, and finally summarize what we have found and arrive at some conclusions.

At the beginning, Dorchester did things differently. On the first surviving page of the town records, at the end of a meeting dated 21 January 1632/3, are the signatures of John Maverick, John Warham, William Gaylord and William Rockwell [DTR 1]. These were the pastor and teacher of the church, and the two deacons.

This pattern continued through 1633 and into 1634, with two, three or all four of these men signing the various town orders [DTR 1-7]. This may be an indication that the settlers of Dorchester, who were, after all, initially separate from the rest of the Winthrop Fleet, intended a community in which the church and town government were more closely melded than in the other Massachusetts Bay towns.

On 8 October 1633, there was "An agreement made by the whole consent and vote of the plantation," a long and complicated order which envisioned a regular sequence of meetings of the whole town, coupled with meetings of "twelve men, selected out of the company, that may or the greatest part of them meet as aforesaid to determine as aforesaid, yet so as it is desired that the most of the plantation will keep the meeting constantly … and that the greater voice both of the 12 and the other shall be of force and efficcacy as aforesaid" [DTR 3]. This cumbersome arrangement, almost like a miniature bicameral legislature, was fraught with internal inconsistencies, and was apparently never put into full effect, as the ministers and deacons continued for another year to sign the town orders.

At the end of 1634 Dorchester fell into line with the rest of the colony. On 28 October 1634, the town "agreed that there shall be ten men chosen to order all the affairs of the plantation, to continue for one year, & to meet monthly according to the order Oct: 8. 1633, in the page 15, and no or-der to be established without seven of them at least and concluded by the major part of these seven of them and all the inhabitants to stand bound by the orders so made as aforesaid according to the scope of a former order in May 11th 1631" [DTR 7]. The first ten men chosen were Thomas Newbury, Israel Stoughton, Henry Woolcot, Nathaniel Duncan, George Phelps, William Hathorne, Roger Williams, George Minot, Giles Gibbs and Henry Smith.

[As an aside, note that this extract tells us much about the lost Dorchester records. The order of 8 October 1633 is said to be on page fifteen, but as found by the editors in 1880, this page was assigned the number six (the first surviving page being numbered five). And there is also reference to an order dated 11 May 1631, less than a year after the arrival of the *Mary & John*, a clear indication that in Dorchester at least written records were maintained from the beginning of settlement.]

On 2 November 1635, nine men were "chosen for ordering the affairs of the plantation, November 1635, to continue for half a year" [DTR 13]. Despite the appointment of only nine men, the group were referred to in the next paraagraph, under the same date, as "the ten men." Then on 27 June 1636 there is record of "a meeting of twelve men formerly chosen by the plantation for ordering the affairs thereof," followed by a list of thirteen names, with a place for a fourteenth [DTR 16].

(continued on page 26)

EDITOR'S EFFUSIONS

To this point, all publications of the Great Migration Study Project have been in traditional print form, but it has long been our desire to issue our publications in electronic form as well. Recently the New England Historic Genealogical Society concluded a group of agreements with Ancestry.com, to produce various NEHGS material on CD, on the Web, or both.

The agreement with regard to the Great Migration Study Project will first produce a CD version of the three volumes of *The Great Migration Begins*, and will then place this same material online, on the Ancestry.com website. In this and the next issue we will describe the CD product, and then in a later issue the online version of this material.

Miraculously, we were able to find a complete set of the disks with the text of *The Great Migration Begins*, disks which had been gathering dust for five years. The text of these volumes was prepared in XyWrite 3, an obsolete dialect of a nearly extinct wordprocessing program. This data had to be converted into Folio Infobases, the format used by Ancestry.com for its CD publications. A technician in Utah wrote a conversion program, which was more than 95 percent successful, but which still left hundreds of problems in the text, mostly in formatting.

At first approach, the work needed to clean up the formatting seemed to promise hours of mindless drudgery. There was some of this of course, but these many hours of work permitted a reacquaintance with the sketches which provided many useful insights about the evolution of how sketches have been written.

For example, two sketches were found in which there was a single category for *OFFICES AND EDUCATION*, rather than two separate categories, as in all other sketches. This is a remnant of a very early version of the sketch format, which was quickly revised. The result of all this review is that the sketches on the CD have a more consistent format than those in the printed volumes.

Robert Charles Anderson, FASG   Editor
Debra MacEachern   Production Assistant

The Great Migration Newsletter is published quarterly by the Great Migration Study Project, a project of the New England Historic Genealogical Society, 101 Newbury Street, Boston MA 02116
www.newenglandancestors.org

The subscription rate is $12 for one year and $20 for two years.

(continued from page25)

On 2 October 1636, twelve men were chosen for six months, but the next record for choice of officers was nearly a year later, on 10 September 1637, when ten men were chosen, although only nine names appear [DTR 19, 24]. Again a year passed, and on 30 October 1638/9 ten men were chosen for six months [DTR 35]. The next choice of officers did occur in six months, when on 13 February 1638/9 seven men were chosen for six months [DTR 38]. Seven men became the standard number elected thereafter, and the term of office was changed to a year rather than six months. A typical record of election is as follows: "The 24th of the 7th month 1644 at a town meeting the 7 men underwritten were chosen to order the affairs of the town till the 1st of the 9th month which shall be in the year 1645, and to have full power to make orders to bind the town as former 7 men have had except in giving and disposing of lands" [DTR 52].

The records of Dorchester unfortunately become sparse for the late 1640s and early 1650s, but on 8 May 1648 there is a reference to "4 of the Roxbury selectmen being with us," and on 9 December 1650 we find the report of a committee appointed by "the select men of Dorchester" [DTR 58-59].

In the very first entry in the first surviving page of the Watertown town records, on 23 August 1634, it was "agreed by the consent of the freemen, that there shall be chosen three persons to be [worn] the ordering of the civil affairs in the town, one of them to serve as town clerk, and shall keep the records and acts of the town. The three chosen are William Jennison, Briam Pembleton, John Eddie" [WaTR 1].

The chronology of the Watertown records becomes a bit jumbled at this point, but at a meeting which seems to be 30 November (or December) 1635 it was "agreed by the consent of the freemen that these 11 freemen shall order all the civil affairs for the town for this year following, & to divide lands," and on 10 October 1636 a similar order was entered [WaTR 2].

Elections of these officers continued on a regular basis, with eleven men chosen on 30 December 1637 and 10 December 1638 [WaTR 3, 4]. On 6 December 1639 the number was bumped up to twelve, with no reason given in the records [WaTR 5], and the size of the body of officers continued at this level for two more years [WaTR 6, 7]. On 21 November 1642 "9 freemen [were] chosen to order the town affairs for this year," and the same again on 28 November 1643 [WaTR 8, 9], after which there is a gap of nearly four years in the Watertown records.

When the records resume in 1647, we find on 8 November that "to order the prudential affairs of the town Mr. Brisco,

(continued on page 32)

Focus   on   SALISBURY

By George F. Sanborn Jr., F.A.S.G., and Melinde Lutz Sanborn, F.A.S.G.

SETTLEMENT OF SALISBURY

On 4 September 1639, at the same time that Sudbury, Hampton and Rowley were named, it was announced at the General Court that "The other plantation beyond Merrimack shall be called Colechester" [MBCR 1:271]. At that same court, a petition from the freemen of Colchester was referred to the magistrates in Salem, it being a minor matter not suited to the General Court [MBCR 1:272]. It was so minor that it is not of record in the Quarterly Courts in Salem, and if pursued at all, was perhaps decided by two magistrates rather informally.

This petition may, however, have been the "petition of the inhabitants of Colechester" addressed by the General Court on 9 November 1639, when it was "granted for Mr. Samuell Dudley, Mr. [William] Worster, Christo[pher] Batt, Samuell Winsley, John Saunders and Henry Monday to order all businesses of the town ... that such as have indirectly obtained greater lots than of due belongs to them, the same should be reformed, and that care be taken for preventing such inconveniences hereafter" [MBCR 1:277]. This order in effect established a board of selectmen, and is unusual in including the town's minister as one of these officers. This "reforming" is not evident in the town books, however.

The maturation of the town, including the establishment of the usual governmental institutions, was completed in just over a year. On 13 May 1640 the first deputy, Christopher Batt, was sent to the General Court, and he appeared again in that capacity on 7 October 1640 [MBCR1:288, 301]. Then, on 7 October 1640, the Court announced that "Colechester is henceforward to be called Salsbury" [MBCR 1:305]. This renaming was the standard sign that the town had completed its development process, but was unusual in that the first name, the name replaced, was of English rather than Algonquian origin. This relatively rapid maturation, and the difference in naming practices, may represent an evolution in the way in which Massachusetts Bay towns were being developed after a decade of the colony's existence.

Several other orders affecting Colchester were entered on 13 May 1640. The town was assessed £15 in a colony rate of £1200 [MBCR1:294]. "Mr. Christo[pher] Batt is desired to train the company at Colchester" [MBCR1:291]. "Goodman Mundie, Antho[ny] Colebie & Mr. Winslo" were appointed as Colchester representatives to a colony committee on the regulation of livestock [MBCR 1:295]. And on 1 September 1640 "Mr. Samuel Winslow" was appointed surveyor of arms [MBCR1:300].

Salisbury was in the following months further integrated into the legal and political network. On 2 June 1641 "Salsberry & Hampton are joined to the jurisdiction of Ipswich, & each of them to send a grandjuryman once a year to Ipswich" [MBCR 1:326]. (When the first four Massachusetts counties were established in 1643, Salisbury was separated from Ipswich, and included in Norfolk County.) Also on 2 June 1641 "for Salsberry, Mr. Batt, Mr. Dudley, & Mr. Winslow [i.e., Winsley]" were appointed commissioners to end small causes, "and one of them to see people join in marriage, & keep records" [MBCR 1:329].

Winthrop attempted to confuse matters, stating apparently under date of March 1638/9 that "Another plantation was begun upon the north side of Merrimack, called Sarisbury, [now Colchester]," and went on to discuss the land troubles at Hampton and Exeter [WJ 1:348]. (None of the early settlers of Salisbury were as troublesome to Winthrop as Wheelwright [then a resident of Exeter, Salisbury's neighbor to the north] on whom Winthrop focussed much attention.)

This statement is clearly anachronistic, since, as noted above, the change of name did not come until late in 1640, and, in any case, Winthrop has the naming sequence backwards. This must be one of those later entries which Winthrop placed in his journal long after the events which they recorded.

Winthrop includes a more accurate, and presumably more contemporaneous, entry in his journal in June, when he reports that "There were also diverse new plantations begun this summer here and at Plimouth, as Colchester upon Merrimack ..." [WJ 1:368]. This statement is consistent with the General Court records, making it clear that Colchester, which would become Salisbury, was settled in the summer of 1639.

Like other early Massachusetts Bay towns, particularly those to the north of Boston, Salisbury was embroiled in lengthy controversies over the town boundaries. On 13 May 1640, Mr. Edward Woodman, Mr. William Paine, and Mr. Thomas Nelson were appointed to view and settle the bounds between Hampton and Colchester, and to make return to the Court [MBCR 1:289]. Presumably these were prominent and "indifferent" men, who could come to a negotiated agreement on the lines. None of them were Salisbury men. Their report was heard by the Court on 7 October 1640 and immediately there was conflict [MBCR 1:303].

The review and revision of the town lines would continue for decades. In 1668 a section of Salisbury was set off as Amesbury; and a portion of the town was also incorporated into Seabrook, New Hampshire.

EARLY SETTLERS

Various petitions from Salisbury inhabitants, directed to the General Court, provide reference lists that complement the first lists of taxpayers and land grantees, enabling us to determine who was early in the town.

Two lists of the recipients of the first division of land in "Colchester" on 7 November 1639 exist. One is found in the front of the town's earliest book of land records, and a shorter list, evidently of a later date, although it is undated, is found in the Massachusetts Archives [MA Arch 112:2]. The longer list included *Samuel Dudley, *William Worcester, *Francis Dove, *Henry Biley, John Eaton, Edward French, Richard Wells, *John Rolfe, *John Sanders, Isaac Buswell, *John Severance, *Thomas Bradbury, John Hodges, *Josiah Cobbit, Jarret Haddon, John Bailey, Henry Brown, *Anthony Sadler, *Roger Eastman, *John Stevens, Robert Fitts, Samuel Hall, John Hoyt, William Holdred, *Robert Ringe, Thomas Barnet, John Elsley, William Allen, William Barnes, Richard North, *Abraham Morrell, William Osgood, *William Hooke, John Hall, *Samuel Winsley, *Christopher Batt, *Robert Pike, William Partridge, *Thomas Dummer, Henry Munday, *George Carr, Samuel Fellows, William Sargent, *John Harrison, *Philip Watson-Challis, *Luke Heard, *Anthony Colby, *Christian Browne, *Richard Singletary, *Thomas Hauxworth, John Ayers, *Thomas Rowell, John Dickison, John Clough, Daniel Ladd, *John Fuller, Thomas Carter, Enoch Greenleaf, Richard Goodale, Richard Courier, Joseph Moyce, Andrew Greeley, Ralph Blaisdale, Robert Codman, John Wheeler, *Thomas Macy, Joseph Parker, John Coles and *John Clifford. (The shorter list contained only the names denoted by an asterisk. No satisfactory explanation for the many discrepancies between the two lists has been suggested.)

Like many other grantees receiving land at the first settlement of a town, some of these men never actually lived in Salisbury or stayed only a very short time before moving on. A fair number were first in neighboring towns, particularly Lynn and Ipswich, before coming to the new settlement. A few are known to have been associated together in England before their arrival in Salisbury. Of those whose English homes are known, the majority appear to have come from Buckinghamshire, Wiltshire and Essex.

Many followers of the Rev. William Worcester, once Puritan vicar of Olney, Buckinghamshire, came to New England, including John Fuller and William Partridge, who first resided in Lynn, before coming to Salisbury. It is noteworthy that a number of Rev. Worcester's parishioners in England immigrated to New England, many before he did, but did not resettle in Salisbury with him. Although his English origin remains unknown, Edward French was in some way a "brother" to Rev. Worcester, and certainly moved in Worcester's orbit, and so may also have been from the same part of England.

Henry Biley and John Hall were not only both from Sarum (Salisbury), Wiltshire, but were successively married to the same woman, Rebecca Swaine. Twice widowed, Rebecca went on to marry Rev. Worcester and then Deputy Governor Samuel Symonds. Christopher Batt (who named Salisbury), John Wheeler, and Francis Dove were also from Salisbury in Wiltshire. John Bailey was from Chippenham, Wiltshire. John Sanders is said to have come from Wiltshire.

Samuel Hall returned to his home near Malden, Essex, and died there leaving a 1679 will that generously remembered his New England neighbors. He called Rebecca Swaine's son, John Hall of Islington, "my adopted cousin," and proceeded to leave "unto Boston in New England and other towns in that Colony that hath most suffered by the wars and by that late great happening in Boston [fire] one hundred pounds" [Commissary Court of London L:375]. His executor, that same John Hall, who had gone from Salisbury to London and become a goldsmith, distributed money to several old friends from Salisbury, including Moses Worcester, son of Rev. William Worcester. The remarkable correspondence of John Hall from England back to his mother, Rebecca (Swaine) (Hall) (Biley) (Worcester) Symonds of Salisbury (and elsewhere), survives in the manuscript collections of the American Antiquarian Society in Worcester, Massachusetts, and has seen short abstracts in print.

Samuel Hall's widow, Sarah, of Langford, Essex, who died the next year, also left a will that remembered the friends who had once lived in Salisbury, bequeathing cloth "for the use of the poor of Newbury, Hampton and Amesbury in New England" [Commissary Court of London L:483].

Thomas Bradbury came from Wicken Bonhunt, Essex, and Robert Pike was of Longford, Essex.

Aside from the above three groups, a number of early Salisbury settlers are known to have come from other English counties. Anthony Colby was from Horbling, Lincolnshire. Samuel Dudley was of Yardley Hastings, Northhamptonshire. Thomas Rowell was of Mancetter, Warwickshire. Enoch Greenleaf was of St Mary-le-Tower, Ipswich, Suffolk. Richard Goodale was of Downham Market, Norfolk. William Holdred was of St Alphage, Cripplegate, London, and John Hodges was also of London.

Robert Ringe, John Sanders, John Cole, Roger Eastman, William Osgood, and John Rolfe all came in the 1638 voyage of the *Confidence*. Samuel Fellows may have been of Lincolnshire.

Thomas Dummer returned home to Chicknell, North Stoneham, Hampshire. William Hooke ended up in Bristol, England. Initially a settler of York, Ralph Blaisdell was possibly among the Lancashire families that sailed from Bristol in 1635 accompanying Rev. Richard Mather.

SALISBURY CHURCH

Rev. William Worcester, the first Salisbury minister, came to New England in 1639, settled in Salisbury and became a freeman on 13 May 1640. Also accepted as freemen that day were other Salisbury men, presumably members of his church, including John Saunders, Thomas Bradbury, Thomas Dummer, and perhaps John Hall, although this last man may have been from another town since his name was near the end of the list and not close to any of the other Salisbury men. This sequence of events indicates that Salisbury church was organized in late 1639 or possibly early 1640.

Evidence for continued admissions to membership in Salisbury church is found in additional appearances of Salisbury men in the lists of freeman admissions. Samuel Dudley and Josiah Cobbit were accepted as freemen on 7 October 1640 (the same day the General Court proclaimed that "Colechester" would henceforth be called Salisbury), and William Hooke was accepted 12 October 1640.

William Worcester died in 1662 and was succeeded by Rev. John Wheelwright, who was just returning from a sojourn in England after having been minister at Exeter, Wells and Hampton. Wheelwright died in 1679, after which their was a hiatus of eight years during which Salisbury church had no settled minister.

The earliest surviving Salisbury church records date from 1687, with the arrival of Rev. John Alling. Any records which may have been kept by Worcester and Wheelwright were apparently not passed on to Alling, and were reported missing as early as 1865.

TOWN RECORDS

A fair assessment of early Salisbury records is contained in the opening pages of David W. Hoyt's *The Old Families of Salisbury and Amesbury, Massachusetts*, first printed in 1897. The surviving original town books are to be found in a vault at the Salisbury Town Clerk's office. Copies made in the 19th century of selected books are kept with the originals. As one of the towns in which the Quarterly Courts met, several interesting record series pertaining to court minutes are also to be found in the vault.

A modest proportion of Salisbury-related deeds are to be found in the Ipswich deed series and the Old Norfolk County deeds rather than in the Essex County deeds. As early as November of 1642, William Osgood of Salisbury was mortgaging his interest in the town's most important mill to a Newbury man [Ipswich Deeds 1:3]. Other, apparently random, deeds from Salisbury inhabitants appear in the Ipswich and Old Norfolk County series.

The early town meetings must have been quite unruly. In May 1639 Anthony Colby was fined for being "dissored" (disorderly) in the meeting and Mr. William Hooke was fined for getting up and leaving the meeting without liberty [Salisbury Town Book 1:1]. By 1640 a unique set of rules was laid out in the minutes, including the requirement that "Every freeman shall speak by turn and not otherwise and shall signify when he is to speak by rising up or putting off his hat, and his speech being ended, shall signify it by putting on his hat or sitting down, and in case he be interrupted by the moderator and shall refuse to cease, shall forfeit for every such offense 1 shilling" [Salisbury Town Book 1:17].

Granting of Land

In the reverse [backwards and upside-down] of the earliest book of Salisbury town records, each page was devoted to the grants received by the earliest proprietors. The grants were usually dated, or described as, for example, "According to the first division of the Town of Salisbury...." The lists usually included as many as six grants, as follows:

First Division – usually contained four acres intended for a houselot; the near meadow grant to be allotted at 4 acres per 100 pounds value; the upland planting lots which were to be allotted at a rate of 4 acres to each family valued at less than 100 pounds, six acres for each valued between 100 and 150 pounds, and 4 acres per 100 pounds value over 150 pounds. A grant of 3 August 1640, a grant of 26 October 1640, a grant of 29 November 1640, a planting lot granted 7 January 1640/1, a grant of 16 April 1642 and a grant of 20 February 1642/3.

These grants were not always recorded in chronological order, however, and the grant of 20 February 1642/3 frequently is found inserted before the 26 October 1640 grant. This suggests that the records were created in early 1643 from a yet earlier source or sources. These entries used only one side of the page, and a century later, the town clerk kept minutes of later meetings on the opposite pages and in the empty spaces on the land grant pages, as well.

The following two examples show the difference between the very first allotments to men of varying family size and wealth, but also demonstrate how many exceptions there were to the rules cited above:

1) "According unto the 1st division of the town of Salisbury there was granted unto Edward French a house lot containing per estimation two acres more or less lying between the house lots of Robert Pike on the west & Thomas Macy on the east, the one end abutting upon Mr. Sam. Dudley's planting lot & the other end upon the highway leading to the Great Neck; also there was granted him a planting lot upon the hoghouse neck containing per estimation six acres more or less, lying between the lands of Robert Pike the upland upon three sides of it & his meadow on the other side; Also there was granted unto him a meadow lot containing per estimation four acres more or less lying between the meadow lots of Mr. Sam[ue]l Hall to the west & Abraham Morrill's to the east, the one end, butting upon the Little River & the other end upon the neck; Also there was granted unto him a great planting lot upon the west of the Pawwaus River containing per estimation twenty acres more or less lying between the great lots of Jno Eyres Senr & Daniel Ladd, one end butting upon the River Merrimack the other upon the common; Also at a meeting of the freemen it was ordered that Edward French should have ten acres upon the east side of the Pawwaws River, in lieu of his twenty acre lot granted him, upon the west side of the Pawwaw River, in the range of lots butting upon the River Merrimack. The said ten acres more or less lying between the ten gore lots of the Widow Hauxworths & William Allen, the one end butting upon the Pawwaus River & the other end upon the common" [Salisbury Town Book 1:3].

2) "According unto the first division of the town of Salisbury there was granted unto Philip Challice one acre more or less of upland for a house lot, lying between the house lots of Josiah Cobham on the west & John Hodges on the east, butting with the end upon the south side of the street; also there was granted him two acres more or less of meadow lying between the lots of John Hodges on the north, E[ast] & John Severance on the south; W[est] butting with one end upon the great creeke and the other end upon the south side of Mr. Hodges house lot" [Salisbury Town Book 1:12].

Edward French was a married man of some means, who was closely affliated with the town's first minister. Philip Challis was a very young, unmarried man, who had come from Ipswich and began humbly in the new settlement. Consequently, Edward French received twenty-two acres in the early grants, and Philip Challis only three acres.

It is rare to find such a concise explanation for the allotting of lands as is found in the 24 February 1662/3 Salisbury town meeting records [Salisbury Town Meeting Book, 1:71 (reverse)]. Land "above the Mill" was to be granted to:

"… all the townsmen inhabiting the old town of Salisbury according to the rule of two four six and eight.
The Rules to w[hi]ch they had an eye in dividing of the land:
    1st The charge or disbursem[en]t that men have been generally at

    2ly The service that men have been put upon generally
    3ly The number of the persons in a family
    4ly The necessity that men have and theirs
    5ly The antiquity of the inhabitants and the legality of their rights."

By October of 1640, the houselots of men who had failed to take up their land and settle families on it were already being reassigned, as when Henry Brown received "that house lot that Tho: Macy should have had."

Vital Records

The earliest book of Salisbury vital records is a tall slim volume containing records commencing with the birth of Wymond, son of Mr. Thomas Bradbury and Mary his wife, in 1637. The records, for the most part, are kept chronologically, with births beginning in 1637, deaths in 1641 and marriages in 1660. Rarely are there any family groupings of births that interrupt the chronology.

When Wymond Bradbury was born (and also when Judith, the second child of Thomas Bradbury, also recorded at Salisbury, was born), Salisbury had not yet been settled, and Bradbury was living in York (or perhaps Ipswich). As early as 10 December 1641, Bradbury was clerk of the writs at Salisbury [MBCR1:345], and he clearly took advantage of this position to include in the Salisbury records the earlier births of his own children.

As the shire town for old Norfolk County, Salisbury was the place where town vital records were returned, per the General Court's order of 9 September 1639 calling for deaths, births and marriages to be recorded on penalty of a fine.

Quarterly Courts

In the Salisbury town clerk's vault, in the center of a 19th century copy of 18th century records, we find a fifty-two page transcript of "certain deeds and other instruments copied from the old record books of this Town by Joseph M. Eaton and completed this day, Salisbury October 5th 1874." These items are headed "A book of records for the remain of the County of Norfolk upon the north side of Merimack River" and cover items as early as a late recorded deed of 1666, and extend until 1692.

The appearance of Salisbury men in the other quarterly courts in Ipswich, Salem and Hampton was a regular occurrence. The first matter of major controversy regarding Salisbury men seems to have been the way George Carr ran the ferry across the Merrimack. The complaints of many unhappy travellers brought the court's attention to how often he was willing to cross, how much he charged for passengers, and whether he would let cattle swim alongside his ferry.

RECENT LITERATURE

Kenneth W. Kirkpatrick, "Loose Ends in the Bradbury *Ahnentafel*," *The New England Historical and Genealogical Register* 153 (1999):259-77. The author tackles a number of difficult, longstanding problems in the fifteenth- and sixteenth-century ancestry of Thomas Bradbury, resolving some and presenting interesting conjectures about others.

Neil D. Thompson, "The English Ancestry of Thomasine (Clench) Frost, First Wife of Edmund[1] Frost of Cambridge, Massachusetts," *The New England Historical and Genealogical Register* 153 (1999):278-90. Thompson argues that Thomasine Clench, wife of Edmund Frost of Cambridge, was daughter of Robert and Joan (Webb) Clench of Bottisham, Cambridgeshire, and then proceeds to provide two additional generations of Clench ancestry for Thomasine.

Edwin M. Puckett, "The English Background of Dorothy Daye, Wife of John Pike of Newbury, Massachusetts," *The New England Historical and Genealogical Register* 153 (1999):319-22. The author has found the wills of Thomas Daye and Joane (Morris) Daye of Boscombe, Wiltshire, the parents of Dorothy Daye, wife of Great Migration immigrant John Pike.

Mary Banning Friedlander, "Block Island Settlers of Joshua's Town, Lyme, Connecticut, 1701-1800: Banning, Niles, and Tiffany Families," *The New England Historical and Genealogical Register* 153 (1999):323-43, 453-65. In the course of studying some early eighteenth-century families of Lyme, Connecticut, Friedlander has compiled the first three generations of descent from John Niles, who had settled in Dorchester by 1634.

Gary Boyd Roberts, "A Genealogical Bibliography of Middlesex County, Massachusetts, Testators, 1649-1660," *The New England Historical and Genealogical Register* 153 (1999):344-58. Roberts has compiled citations to secondary sources (including the three volumes of *The Great Migration Begins*) which treat individuals whose estate papers are included in the recently published first volume of Middlesex County probate records

Myrtle Stevens Hyde, "A Study of the Downing Family in England, with Connections in Early New England: Emanuel[1] Downing and Abigail[1] (Goade) Moulton of Salem, Massachusetts, and Abigail[1] (Downing) Montague of Hadley, Massachusetts," *The American Genealogist* 74 (1999):161-74, 299-308. With the immediate goal of identifying the wife of Richard Montague of Hadley, the author has undertaken a comprehensive treatment of the Downing family. In addition to adding to our knowledge of Emanuel Downing and his ancestry, Hyde has shown that Abigail (Downing) Montague was daughter of Joseph Downing (and therefore niece of Emanuel Downing), and that Abigail (Goade)

Moulton, wife of Robert[2] Moulton of Salem, was daughter of Abigail (Downing) Goade (and therefore another niece of Emanuel Downing).

Leslie Mahler, "English Baptisms for the Green(a)way Family of Dorchester, Massachusetts," *The American Genealogist* 74 (1999):193-95. Mahler shows that John Greenway, who arrived at Dorchester in 1630, resided in Mildenhall, Wiltshire, from 1603 to 1609. The residence of this family from 1610 to 1630 remains unknown.

Robert Charles Anderson, "A Further Note on Thomas[1] Marshfield of Windsor, Connecticut," *The American Genealogist* 74 (1999):225. Anderson interprets an entry in Winthrop's Journal to apply to Thomas Marshfield, thus providing additional information about his financial problems.

Doris J. Woodward and Patricia Law Hatcher, "The English Origin of Nathaniel Woodward, Early Settler of Boston, Massachusetts, and Ancestor of Beamsley Woodward of Maine," *The Maine Genealogist* 20 (1998):147-68. Woodward and Hatcher confirm and extend earlier work of John B. Threlfall, placing the immigrant Nathaniel Woodward in Puddington, Bedfordshire, from 1621 to 1630. They then go on to show that the family had earlier resided in Rushden, Northamptonshire, where Woodward married Margaret Lawrence in 1608, and where some earlier Woodwards were found. Among the children of this couple baptized in Rushden was Lambert Woodward, not previously known to be part of this family.

Alison Games, *Migration and the Origins of the English Atlantic World* (Cambridge: Harvard University Press, 1999). Professor Games bases her book on an exhaustive analysis of the 1635 London Port Book, followed up by a detailed study of the lives of hundreds of the passeengers. She uses this material to conduct a study of the early colonization process in New England, the Chesapeake, Bermuda and a number of Caribbean islands.

Her main thesis is that the migration process itself, and the environment in which the "travelers" found themselves at the end of the migration, were the overriding factors in the ongoing integration of the new settlements in the Atlantic world.

This work is an excellent balance between the older literature, which focusses on the differences between the English colonies, and some of the newer scholarship which overreacts in the opposite direction, giving more emphasis to the similarities.

Games has been very successful in ferreting out details of the lives of many of these immigrants, and some of her discoveries will add to what we already know of some of these people. This volume is highly recommended for anyone interested in the period of the Great Migration.

(continued from page 26)

Joseph Bemis, Willyam Hammant, John Sherman, John Whetny Se[nior], Lt. Mason, [and] Roger Porter were chosen" [WaTR 10]. On 30 November 1647 is the record of "a meeting of the seven men" [WaTR 10]. Sometime in the four-year interval, then, there was a change in the number of men chosen, and a change in the name used to describe them.

The pattern continues in this way, with the election of seven men in late 1648, and many references to meetings of "the seven men." On 7 December 1649 we find "a meeting of the select men," followed just three days later by a general town meeting at which seven men were "chosen to order the town affairs for the year ensuing" [WaTR 18-19]. Meetings of "the seven men" continue through 1651, but on 19 January 1651/2 we find again "a meeting of the select men" [WaTR 30], and that usage continues thereafter.

The records of the General Court of Massachusetts Bay Colony do not have many references to these town officers in the early years, but there are a few passing mentions which help with our investigation. On 20 May 1642 there is a reference to "the selected townsmen," and on 14 June 1642 a mention of "the chosen men appointed for managing the prudential affairs of [every town]" [MBCR 2:4, 6, 9]. Four years later, on 7 October 1646, we hear of "the 5 or 7 or more men in every such town, which are selected for prudential affairs" [MBCR 2:162-63]. On 11 November 1647 is a more concise reference to "all constables, selectmen, &

commissioners for towns," and in May 1656 to "the selectmen in every town" [MBCR 2:225, 397].

In summary, then, when the office which came to be known as selectman came into being, each town struck out on its own. The number of such officers in each town might be, at one time or another, any number from three to thirteen. In most towns these officers were chosen annually, but in Boston and Dorchester the term of office was at first only six months.

The variety was equally great in the name used for this office, with some being called townsmen (although this term could be confused with, and eventually referred only to, the proprietors), or the chosen men, or the seven men, or nine men, or the men deputed.

As the years passed, the particulars of the office became more standardized. Boston and Dorchester soon abandoned their six month terms, so that by the mid-1640s all towns had one-year terms. The number of men chosen converged in all towns on seven, which was the norm by the late 1640s.

Finally, the name "select men," which eventually evolved into the single word "selectmen," came into use, first appearing in Boston and Cambridge in 1645, and in all the towns studied here by 1649. In each town there was a transitional period of a year or two or three in which the old terminology continued, but by 1652 the office was everywhere referred to by its modern name.

Great Migration Study Project
101 Newbury Street
Boston, MA 02116

Great Migration Newsletter

Vol. 9   January-March 2000   No. 1

WINTHROP MEDICAL JOURNAL

The medical journal of John Winthrop the Younger is one of the most important seventeenth-century documents which remains unpublished. This record has become an increasingly important source in the compilation of sketches for the Great Migration Study Project, especially for those immigrants who settled in Hartford and elsewhere in Connecticut.

The surviving medical journal of John Winthrop Junior consists of nearly a thousand pages, each of which has about ten entries. A typical entry consists of three parts: an identifier, including the name and sometimes brief biographical information; a description of the symptoms; and the prescription. A few sample entries follow (many of the entries are much longer than those selected here; the symbols $, ^ and G are employed here as crude representations of apothecary symbols used by Winthrop):

> 17 March 1656/7: "Jonathan Sacket almost 2 yeares old 2 gr: ½ $: for wormes" [p. 7].

> [3] July 1663: "Baldin Sarah daughter of Sam: Baldin of Norwotuck eates durt 3 dos. 1¼ g. $ & 2 dos. ½ g. addit:" [p. 512].

The first entry in Winthrop's records is dated 10 March 1656/7 and the last 26 July 1669 (although a handful of miscellaneous, undated pages may include a few prescriptions made at a later date). The opening date most certainly does not indicate the beginning of Winthrop's medical practice, since there are many items in his correspondence which indicate that he was giving medical advice as early as 1640. Furthermore, there are explicit indications in the earliest surviving pages that Winthrop had been maintaining records of his medical practice prior to 10 March 1656/7. On page 7 of the surviving manuscript, Winthrop prescribes for Hester Clerke of New Haven, and notes that "she had several times for breaking out of hir eares $ as in the other booke." On page 10, in two successive entries of 20 March 1656/7, Winthrop includes the following note: "vide the other booke." He used similar references to pages within the remaining material, and so these references to "the other book" clearly indicate at least one earlier journal in which he kept similar notes.

The first entry was made toward the end of Winthrop's brief residence in New Haven, and this section continues for fifty-four pages, ending on 10 July 1657. There follows a hiatus of about four months, and then in mid-November 1657, soon after settling in Hartford, Winthrop resumed seeing patients, entering his notes in a section called "The Loose Sheets" [pp. 55-62].

Beginning on 30 November 1657, Winthrop instituted a new arrangement of his records, starting a separate "book" for each of the major towns in Connecticut. Most of his patients were, of course, from Hartford, and a section of 204 pages covers this town from 30 November 1657 until 30 June 1661. Other "books" commenced at this time were for Windsor, Wethersfield, Middletown and Farmington. For those towns which supplied him with few patients, Winthrop maintained additional pages, on which he would make entries for Springfield, New London, and other more distant settlements. As late as the summer of 1660 he was beginning new sections for Southampton, Branford and Stratford.

By August of 1660, however, he was apparently having second thoughts about this arrangement, for on the 23rd of that month he began a new "book" which brought back together Windsor and Wethersfield in one grouping, along with a number of other lesser towns, leaving Hartford, Farmington and Middletown with their own sections.

These various separate groupings by town came to an end on various dates in June 1661, with the latest definitely dated

(continued on page 2)

EDITOR'S EFFUSIONS

As this issue of the *Great Migration Newsletter* is being written (late February 2001), the next Great Migration volume, the second in the second series, is at the printer. This volume covers the letter C through F, for the years 1634 and 1635. Work on the next volume, covering the letters G through J, will soon begin.

As we move along in the Great Migration Study Project, the question arises as to how these volumes should be cited. Our recommendation is to use GMB (for *The Great Migration Begins*) for the first series, and GM 2 for the second series. Since the volumes in the second series are separately paginated, an additional element is needed for citations. The citation to the sketch of Alice Ashby, in the first volume in the second series, would be GM 2:1:92, while the citation to the sketch of James Cudworth, in the second volume, would be GM 2:2:249-58.

For the entire history of the Great Migration Study Project, more than twelve years now, we have used XyWrite, a venerable word-processing program, to write all our sketches. In its heyday this was one of the most popular programs among professional writers, and still has a loyal following.

Working with this program has become increasingly difficult, however, as other computer technologies have changed more rapidly over the last decade, and the time has come to make a change. One solution would be to move to one of the few word-processing programs which are at this time being widely used. Or we could move to one of the more complicated desktop publishing programs.

Either of these choices would produce an excellent product. Our path will be different, however. We have embarked on an effort to configure an XML editor to allow us to create Great Migration sketches directly in XML (eXtensible Markup Language). In a future issue of the Newsletter we will report on this effort at greater length, and explain how this will expedite the work of the Project, and make it easier to publish our sketches in different media.

Robert Charles Anderson, FASG   Editor
Debra M. MacEachern   Production Assistant

The Great Migration Newsletter is published quarterly by the Great Migration Study Project, a project of the New England Historic Genealogical Society, 101 Newbury Street, Boston MA 02116
www.nehgs.org

The subscription rate is $12 for one year and $20 for two years.

(continued from page1)

entry being in the Hartford section on 30 June 1661 [p. 266]. This was, of course, just a few days before he left Hartford, on his last and most important trip to England.

After a gap of almost exactly two years, the medical journal resumed, on or about 25 June 1663, just a few days after Winthrop had arrived again in Hartford, at the end of his voyage to England. With this new beginning, he abandoned altogether the earlier arrangement by town, and for the remainder of the surviving material maintained a single chronological sequence, for another six years, until 26 July 1669 [pp. 511-940, excepting 559-60 and 883-89].

As if the ink damage, cramped handwriting, abbreviations and apothecary symbols did not already make the decipherment of the manuscript difficult enough, Winthrop occasionally added additional obstacles. For three types of entries, he resorted to Latin for the presentation of the symptomatology, sometimes in abbreviated form. The most common reason for adding this extra layer of obscurity arose when a female patient complained of obstetrical or gynecological problems. The other two types of entries in which Winthrop reverted to Latin were for bad breath, and for his own children. In the latter case he threw in yet another slight obstruction, a primitive cipher attempting to hide the name of the child.

> 11 July 1658 (Hartford section): "Eltulclyo twait-notrharmonpu obstruentur menses post quam fluebant partum diei …" [p. 118].

> 17 February 1665/6: "Twaitnotihorpolpaflintosi 8 g $ aurati …" [p. 626].

The first of these entries is for his daughter Lucy and the second for his son Fitz[john], reading alternate letters in the encoded names. Winthrop clearly attempted to make these encoded names pronounceable, and also seems to have inserted an element of humor, since each instance contains the sequence "waitnot," and his other son was named Waitstill.

In adddition to its obvious value for colonial medical history, the Winthrop medical journal also contains much evidence bearing on genealogical problems.

> 27 January 1663/4: "Case Richard his wife of Winsor she was Elis: Purchas Nic: Parker his wifes daughter feares dropsy being sometimes swelled 4 menses nupta …" [p. 530].

The form of this entry is a very common one, Winthrop identifying the patient by her maiden name, and further indicating that the patient's mother had remarried, her first husband having been John Purchase and her second husband

(continued on page 7)

Focus on STAMFORD

SETTLEMENT OF STAMFORD

The settlement of Stamford was one stage in a process which had begun in Watertown in Massachusetts Bay in 1634, moved on to Wethersfield in Connecticut in 1635 and 1636, and had many more ramifications in the years after the first move to Stamford. This process was generated by a combination of population pressure, the search for better agricultural land, and differences of expression within the Puritan community. In this first section of our examination of Stamford we will look at the larger questions of the chronology of the settlement and the immediate political consequences. In the second section we will look more closely at the first twenty men who committed themselves to the building of this plantation.

The land which would become the town of Stamford lay within the area governed by the newly established colony of New Haven, and had been purchased by New Haven men [NHCR 1:199]. On 4 November 1640, when New Haven was not yet two years old, the colony responded to "Andrew Warde and Rob[er]t Coe of Weathersfield [who] were deputed by Weathersfield men, the 30[th] of the 8[th] month commonly called October 1640, to treat with the court at Newhaven about the plantation (lately purchased by the said town) called Toquams" [NHCR 1:45]. New Haven court agreed to the purchase, and imposed upon the purchasers the same conditions as had been set forth earlier for the settlers of Totokett (later Branford).

This region which the Wethersfield men had purchased was also called Rippowams, and on 27 October 1641 "Andrew Warde and Francis Bell of Rippowams [are] admitted members of this court and received the charge of freemen" [NHCR 1:58]. At this same court, "Thurston Rayner [was] chosen constable for Rippowams ... but is not to be established in his office till he have received his charge from this Court and testified his acceptance thereof to this Court" [NHCR 1:58].

On 6 April 1642, "Mr. Mitchell and John Whitmore of Rippowams was also admitted members of this Court, and accepted the charge of freemen," and the "plantation of Rippowams is named Stamforde" [NHCR 1:69]. The "deputies for Stamforde" immediately complained "that their plantation are at some difference with the Indians, and therefore require help of advice from this Court," which the Court acceded to [NHCR 1:69-70].

Just who these deputies were is not clear, inasmuch as Stamford was the first new town to be given full legal status in the colony after New Haven, and the distinction between town and colony had not yet been clearly established. Perhaps Andrew Ward and Francis Bell held this office, as they were the first from Rippowams to be made freemen of the colony. And it may be that in this context "deputy" meant the town officers, the selectmen, and not the representatives to the colony government, which was not yet fully operational.

On 26 October 1642, "Goodman Warde of Stamforde, is chosen constable this ensuing year" [NHCR 1:78]. On 3 April 1643, Ward, writing "in the name and by the consent of the free burgesses there," informed the court that Stamford had appointed "Captain John Underhill and Richard Geldersleeve for their deputies at this General Court, and desire a magistrate may be chosen for the better carrying on of their affairs in that place, and do nominate Mr. Mitchell and Thirton Rayner for that place," to which the court assented, naming Rayner as the magistrate [NHCR 1:85].

During the spring and summer of 1643, the governments of Massachusetts Bay, Plymouth, Connecticut and New Haven negotiated the establishment of the New England Confederation. In the words of Isabel Calder, the "formation of the New England Confederation forced the plantations of Guilford and Milford to the east and west of New Haven, each with its independent plantation government, to cast in their lot with New Haven, for only in this way could they gain the protection afforded by the confederation" [Calder 116].

As a result, on 27 October 1643, a General Court met at New Haven, firmly establishing the new order of New Haven Colony, with deputies from New Haven, Milford, Guilford and Stamford; Richard Gildersleeve and John Whitmore represented the latter town [NHCR 1:112]. (On the previous day, "Mr. Rayner" had been chosen magistrate for Stamford [NHCR 1:112].) From this point on, New Haven Colony and the town of Stamford were fully and firmly established.

Skipping ahead two decades, when New Haven Colony was absorbed into Connecticut Colony, an explicit Connecticut order reflected Stamford's change of jurisdictional allegiance. On 9 October 1662, "[t]his Court doth hereby declare their acceptance of the Plantations of Stanford and Greenwich under this government upon the same terms and provisions as are directed and declared to the inhabitants of Guilford. And that each of these Plantations have a constable chosen and sworn" [CCCR 1:388].

[Bibliographic Note: The classic history of Stamford was published in 1868 by E.B. Huntington [*History of Stamford, Connecticut, 1641-1868, including Darien until 1820*

(Stamford 1868; rpt. Harrison, New York, 1979)].
Huntington included brief biographical sketches of the earliest settlers, although he is too generous in ascribing earlier Wethersfield residence to some of them [pp. 27-47].

In the course of her comprehensive history of New Haven Colony, Isabel MacBeath Calder touched frequently on the development of the town of Stamford [*The New Haven Colony* (New Haven 1934)], especially pp. 61-63, 76-77, 108-10.

In 1991 Jeanne Majdalany published an account of Stamford in the seventeenth century, describing activities in the town decade-by-decade [Jeanne Majdalany, *The Early Settlement of Stamford, Connecticut, 1641-1700* (Bowie, Maryland, 1991)]. Majdalany was joined by Edith M. Wicks in the compilation of an appendix containing "Genealogies of the Stamford Families of the Seventeenth Century"; this appendix is undocumented and is less successful than the earlier part of the book.]

EARLY STAMFORD SETTLERS

When Daniel Finch arrived in New England in 1630 and settled at Watertown, he was among the founders of the town, and built his house on land previously untouched by Europeans. Four years later, when Robert Coe and Andrew Ward and Thurston Rainer arrived, the town was crowded, and there was not enough land available to satisfy all the new arrivals.

In its earliest years Watertown was a settlement of East Anglians, and all four of these men were, or are thought to have been, from that part of England. Robert Coe was from Boxford, Suffolk, and Thurston Rainer was from Elmsett, Suffolk, only a few miles away. These four men, and many others from Watertown, chose to make the move from Watertown to Wethersfield in 1635.

In 1634 and 1635 also, a number of immigrants from Halifax, Yorkshire, were coming to New England. Among these were Matthew Mitchell and his brother-in-law Edmund Wood. Mitchell flitted about for his first two years in New England, residing briefly at Charlestown, Concord, Springfield and Saybrook, before settling for a somewhat longer period in Wethersfield in 1637. Edmund Wood also resided at Springfield, and made the move to Wethersfield, with his sons Jeremiah and Jonas (called Jonas Wood "Owram" to distinguish him from Jonas Wood "Halifax", another immigrant from the same part of England, of no known relationship, but also an immigrant to New England about this time). (See Matthew Wood's excellent article, "English Origins of the Mitchell, Wood, Lum and Halstead Families," for an account of the interrelations among these immigrants,

both in England and after arrival in New England [NYGBR 120:1-9, 98-101, 142-47, 229-36, 121:96-101].)

Rev. Richard Denton, who was also from Halifax, arrived in New England sometime between 1635 and 1640, and joined some of his former parishioners at Wethersfield [NYGBR 117:163-66, 211-18, 120:10-12].

During the stay in Wethersfield, some intermarriages took place between these two groups of settlers. Most importantly, perhaps, about 1638 Thurston Rainer married, as his second wife, Martha, the eldest daughter of Edmund Wood [TAG 37:11-16; NYGBR 120:9].

These ten men (Daniel Finch, Robert Coe, Andrew Ward, Thurston Rainer, Richard Denton, Matthew Mitchell, Edmund Wood, Jeremiah Wood, Jonas Wood "Owram" and Jonas Wood "Halifax") all appear on the list of those who in 1640 pledged to make the new settlement at Stamford [TAG 10:40, abstracting Stamford Town Records 1:5]. In fact, this grouping of four East Anglians and six Yorkshiremen made up exactly half of this initial group.

Of the remaining ten men, less is known about their English origins, but several of them resided briefly at Wethersfield as well (Samuel Clark, Richard Gildersleeve, Jeremiah Jagger, John Jessup, Samuel Sherman [Wethersfield Hist 238, 355-56, 459, 461, 625]).

When a religious dispute broke out in Wethersfield in 1640, the faction led by Rev. Richard Denton chose to leave town, and, as noted above, approached the New Haven authorities with the idea of purchasing a tract of land along Long Island Sound forty miles west of New Haven.

A brief summary of the events that led to the settlement of Stamford goes as follows: A number of East Anglian families which had settled in Watertown in the earliest years of Massachusetts Bay Colony chose to leave Watertown in 1635 because of population pressures, participating in the establishment of Wethersfield, Connecticut. A number of Yorkshire families, arriving in New England during this same turbulent phase of the Great Migration, also found their way to Wethersfield. Some of the East Anglians became associated with the Yorkshiremen, both genealogically and religiously, and this group, led by Rev. Richard Denton, formed the core of the new settlement of Stamford.

Interestingly, most of this group of twenty first settlers of Stamford had moved on within a decade or so. Several were among the original proprietors of Hempstead, and moved there in 1644. The list of original proprietors of that town includes nearly half the names from the list of the original twenty of Stamford: Jeremiah Wood, Richard Gildersleeve, Thurston Rainer, Robert Coe, Jonas Wood "Halifax," John Seaman, Edmond Wood, Jonas Wood "Owram," and Samuel

Clark [*The Nassau County Historical Society Journal* 29 (1969):31-32].

The fate of the Rev. Richard Denton during this period is not certain, but he was probably at Hempstead as well, although perhaps not as early as 1644 [NYGBR 214-16]. Matthew Mitchell died at Stamford in 1645 [NYGBR 120:99]. Andrew Ward, and a few of the others, had by the end of the 1640s moved on to Fairfield. By 1650, then, all of the original leaders of the move from Wethersfield to Stamford had died or moved on, and the government of the town was in the hands of later arrivals (although, of course, some of these "later arrivals," such as Francis Bell and John Whitmore, had settled in Stamford only a few months after the original twenty).

EARLY STAMFORD TOWN RECORDS

In 1933, 1934 and 1935, Donald Lines Jacobus published extensive abstracts from the first volume of Stamford records [TAG 10:40-45, 110-18, 174-83, 11:32-41, 87-98, 157-166, 220-29]. This volume contained a very wide range of types of records, including such usual town records as land grants, elections of officers, and vital records. As one of the earliest outposts of New Haven Colony, the town of Stamford also operated its own court, handling probate and other court proceedings. As a result, this volume goes beyond what is normally found in town records volumes.

The first two pages which were abstracted (pages 5 and 6) contain what might be called the foundation documents of the town: a list of the twenty men who agreed to settle Stamford (used as the basis for the previous section of this article), a damaged list of thirty men who had contributed to the purchase price for the town, and a list of twenty-nine men granted marsh and upland (along with a few other items) [TAG 10:41-42; see Majdalany, p.6, for a facsimile of original page 5].

The volume then continues with a miscellany of probate documents and court proceedings, both civil and criminal. The first probate document recorded was the "[i]nventory of the estate of Matthew Mitchell presented 16 June 1646," along with the undated will [TAG 10:42].

By the eighteenth page of the original volume we begin to encounter vital records, the first being the marriage of "Stephen Cloyson" and "Elizabeth Periment" on 11.11. 1654 (probably 11 January 1654/5), followed by other records for this family [TAG 10:43-44]. The next two pages of the original volume, after the entry of an undated probate inventory, contain a more or less chronological sequence of births, marriages and deaths in Stamford in 1656, 1657 and 1658 (with one item from 1652) [TAG 10:44-45]. These pages conclude the first installment of the abstracts.

The second installment of these records begins with an editorial comment: "Pages twenty-one to seventy-three [of the original] are devoted mainly to land, probate and other entries, with but a few vital entries. Below is a brief digest, not complete, of the most important entries in these pages, including such vital records as occur. Following this is a complete copy of the vital records from page seventy-four onwards" [TAG 10:110].

Nothing from pages twenty-one through twenty-four was deemed worthy of publication, and for several of the other pages in this range Jacobus abstracted only "[Page 25] Lands of Daniel Scofield, 1650," for example [TAG 10:110]. This would most likely indicate that the entire page was taken up with an inventory of all the lands held by Daniel Schofield in 1650.

The very brief abstracts printed for this range of pages include further probate and court entries, and, as noted by Jacobus, a few vital records. On page 64 of the original, for example, are the death records for Jeremiah Jagger, in 1658, and for David Pettet, son of John, in 1657 [TAG 10:111].

On page seventy-four of the original, as stated in the editorial note, the full chronological sequence of vital records picks up again, with many entries from 1657, 1658 and 1659, apparently continuous with the entries on the original pages nineteen and twenty [TAG 10:112-13]. From that point on, the vital records as published are extensive and apparently quite complete for the remainder of the seventeenth century and well into the eighteenth.

Jacobus promised, however, that the abstracts from the section containing original pages twenty-one through seventy-three included "such vital records as occur." Our work on the sketch of Jeffrey Ferris demonstrated, though, that this was not correct. From the Barbour Index we learn that Peter Ferris (son of Jeffrey) married Elizabeth Reynolds at Stamford on 15 July 1654, the source being given as page 55 of this first volume of records.

Examination of the nineteenth-century transcript of this page showed that it began, as did so many others in this section of the book, with the land inventory of one of the early settlers. But, tucked into the blank space at the bottom of the page were six vital records entries from 1654 and 1655, including "Petter Ferris & Elizabeth Renealls joined the 15 July 1654" (original p. 55; transcript p. 67).

We have not done a complete comparison of the original volume with the Jacobus abstract, so we cannot say whether other records are buried in this way, but the possibility is there. There do not appear, however, to be any vital records from the 1640s, the first decade of the existence of Stamford. A complete published transcript of this earliest volume of Stamford town records would be a welcome addition to the literature.

RECENT LITERATURE

Joy Forster, "The Lost Children of Bedfordshire's Pilgrim Fathers: The Tilley Family of the Mayflower," *The Mayflower Quarterly* 65 (1999):322-25. The author has traced a line of descent from Robert Tilley, a son of Mayflower passengers John and Joan (Hurst) Tilley who remained in England.

Michael R. Paulick, "The 1609-1610 Excommunications of Mayflower Pilgrims Mrs. Chilton and Moses Fletcher," *The New England Historical and Genealogical Register* 153 (1999):407-12. From an examination of the records of the ecclesiastical courts of the Diocese of Canterbury, the author has found that in 1609 Moses Fletcher and the wife of James Chilton were both excommunicated, for participation in the private burial of a child. Pailick then goes on to discuss other, earlier, English records relating to Moses Fletcher and James Chilton. Finally, he also sets forth some records from Canterbury which probably pertain to John Ellis and Richard Masterson, two other names which also appear in Leiden.

D. Alden Smith, "The Descendants of Stephen Bryant of Plymouth, and of His Son-In-Law, Lt. John Bryant of Plympton," *The New England Historical and Genealogical Register* 153 (1999):413-34, 154 (2000):41-60, 227-43, 370-74, 477-994. Stephen Bryant had arrived in Plymouth by 1643, and soon married Abigail Shaw, daughter of John Shaw, who had arrived by 1627. Smith has prepared a detailed account of this immigrant and of his Bryant descendants for four generations (including the descendants of his daughter Abigail, who married a John Bryant of no other known relationship).

Craig Partridge, "John[1] Herbert and His Son, Captain John Herbert," *The New England Historical and Genealogical Register* 153 (1999):448-52. Building on his earlier work on Elizabeth (Herbert) (White) Corwin, wife successively of John White and of George Corwin, who had arrived in Salem by 1638 [NEHGR 150:190-97], Partridge now examines more closely her brother John Herbert, who came to New England in 1635 and also settled in Salem and then moved to Southold by 1652. The article concludes with a study of John Herbert, son of this immigrant.

Patricia L. Haslam, "Captain Daniel Patrick of The 1630 Winthrop Fleet and Some of His Descendants," *The New England Historical and Genealogical Register* 153 (1999):466-84. Haslam has prepared a detailed study of the life of Captain Daniel Patrick, one of the more interesting immigrants of the earliest years of the Great Migration to Massachusetts Bay. The author also provides additional material on the children of the immigrant, and especially on the son Daniel, also known as Daniel KirkPatrick.

Richard C. Bingham, "Fenton Records in Sheffield, Yorkshire," *The New England Historical and Genealogical Register* 153 (1999):499. Bingham provides additional evidence that Anne, the wife successively of Thomas Bingham (in England) and of William Backus of Norwich, Connecticut, was Anne Fenton, and not Anne Stenton. In her will of 1642, Alice Fenton of Sheffield makes a bequest to "my eldest daughter Anne wife of Thomas Bingham."

Clifford L. Stott, "The English Origin of Richard[1] Swaine of Hampton, New Hampshire, and Nantucket," *The American Genealogist* 74 (1999):241-49. Stott has demonstrated that Richard Swaine, who first appears at Newbury in 1638 but who probably came to New England as early as 1635, was baptized at Binfield, Berkshire, and later resided in Easthamstead in the same county before migrating. The author also sets forth three generations of paternal ancestry for the immigrant.

Gordon L. Remington, "Corrections: George[1] and Mary (Doggett) Lewis of Brenchley, Kent, and Scituate, Massachusetts," *The American Genealogist* 74 (1999):258. The author presents a handful of corrections to his earlier articles on the family of George Lewis of Scituate. Most of this material continues the author's efforts to trace the history of research on this immigrant.

Leslie Mahler, "The English Origin of Anne[1] Motley/Matley/Mattle, Wife of William[1] Douglas of New London, Connecticut," *The American Genealogist* 74 (1999):275-80. Mahler, following up on clues which have long been in print, presents evidence showing that Anne Mattle, who would become wife of William Douglas of New London, was baptized in 1601 at Denford, Northamptonshire, daughter of Thomas Mattle, who later resided at Ringstead.

Gale Ion Harris, "Thomas[1] Bell, Boston Executioner, and His Son Thomas[2] Bell of Stonington, Connecticut," *The American Genealogist* 74 (1999):281-91. Thomas Bell had arrived in Boston by 1637; the author treats fully his family and the family of his son of the same name. Harris proposes that the immigrant may have married Anne Essex, a single woman who had been admitted to Boston church in 1633.

Marsha Hoffman Rising, "Enigmas #12: Was Elizabeth, Wife of Richard[1] Cutter of Cambridge, Massachusetts, a Daughter of Robert[1] Williams of Roxbury?" *The American Genealogist* 74 (1999):292-98. Attempting to explain an item in the will of Robert Williams which refers to a granddaughter Elizabeth Robinson, Rising demonstrates that chronological problems make it highly unlikely that she was that daughter of Richard Cutter who married William Robinson, and therefore unlikely that Cutter's wife was the daughter of Williams. The author also shows that Thomas Robinson of Roxbury did not marry a daughter of Robert Williams.

(continued from page 2)

Nicholas Parker. These relationships have already been worked out in the genealogical literature, but there is no marriage record for Richard Case and Elisabeth Purchase, and so this record allows us to estimate that event as having occurred in late September 1663.

Gale Ion Harris, especially, has made much use of these records in his studies of East Hartford families. In 1995, for example, a number of Winthrop entries for the adolescent Jeremiah Diggins opened Harris's discussion of that man and his family, and provided the earliest records for Jeremiah [TAG 70 (1995):18-26]. In 1996 Harris used several items from the Winthrop medical journal to estimate many dates of birth for the children of Daniel Garrett, and thereby establish a solid foundation for the treatment of this family [TAG 71 (1996):93-104].

The Winthrop medical journal is also being employed with increasing frequency in the construction of sketches for the Great Migration Study Project. In the sketch of Stephen Hart, from the first set of Great Migration volumes, a series of entries from 1657 through 1664 provided the principal evidence that Stephen's daughter Rachel married John Cole [GMB 2:873].

Over the years, John Winthrop Jr. treated eight children of Thomas Bull of Hartford, some of them more than once, each time giving the age of the child. One of these children was previously unknown to writers on this family, and the many dates permitted a confident reconstruction of the birth sequence of these children, leading to other adjustments in the chronology for this family [GM 2:1:473-75].

A similar result has been obtained in the most recent Great Migration volume, with the family of James Ensign, also of Hartford. Winthrop medical journal entries again helped to structure the birth order of the children, and again provided evidence for another child not previously known [GM 2:2:456-57]. In this case, the knowledge of the additional child provided additional evidence for the English origin of this immigrant.

Winthrop treated patients from every ethnic group known to exist in New England at the time. In some cases, there were in New England very few representatives of a given ethnicity, so the fact that they made their way into the medical journal at all is another indication of the range of coverage of Winthrop's practice.

> 31 July 1664: "Hetfield Mathias an high duchman of Dantsick now lives at New Haven hath paine in knee & swelled ..." [p. 567].

> 5 May 1665: "[blank] Edmond Irishma[n] at Mr. Wadsworth 8 g $" [p. 593].

> 30 May 1666: "Bullieere Julian (a Frenchma[n]) his wife of Saybrook she was Elis: Brooks hath menses superfluos ..." [p. 657].

There were other entries for patients from these countries, as well as a number of Scotsmen, and at least one person described as "a Cornish man." As in other records of this period, the Irishmen and Scotsmen frequently appeared without surname, indicative of their social status as perceived by the English population.

After the English, the most common ethnic group represented is the Native Americans, for whom there are perhaps a few hundred entries.

> 7 August 1664: "Ahostuck Indian his wife of Hartford very ill can scarse speak having had ague ..." [p. 570].

> 22 April 1665: "Wahasatux an Indian his squa Jone of Podunk paine in joints & sore eyes 8 g $ 2 dos. & agua G of ye eyewater a quart" [p. 591].

> 20 February 1665/6: "Indian Girle 13 y: daught[er] of Weahapotan of Wethersfeild a nanganset ma[n] but married a wethersfeild Squa ..." [p. 627].

Not surprisingly, given Winthrop's residence, the majority of these entries were for Podunk Indians, living in a settlement quite close to Hartford. There may be enough records to give an estimate of the demographic structure of this group of Indians.

There are also several dozen entries for African Americans in the medical journal. When combined with material from probate records and other sources, these will give some indication of family structure at that time.

> 25 June 1665: "Negro Girle Sarah 2 y: daught[er] of Philip who was Mr. Crowe's Negro ...
>   Negro Domingo son of Philip ½ y: ..." [p. 597].

> 2 April 1664: "Negro Maria Mr. Blackleech servant paine in stomack 6 g $: 1 vomit & many stooles" [p. 551].

Many of the Irishmen, Scotsmen, African Americans and Native Americans represented in the journal were servants to the English, but many of the English were themselves servants.

> 13 July 1660 (Windsor): "Barnet Deborah 20 y: servant to Mr. Woolcot she came ashore out of Engl[and] but 3 weekes since, hath great paine in stomack" [p. 470].

> 11 March 1666/7: "Adams Beniamin about 16y: servant to J. Richards of Hartford hath some breaking out 6 g $" [p. 710].

Winthrop undoubtedly provided real assistance to many of his patients. Sometimes, though, for all his knowledge and assurance, he appeared to be adrift in his diagnoses and prescriptions.

> 20 October 1663: "Gailer Hanna 16 y: she hath ulcer in one nostrill below it healeth soone with Mrs. Russell's oyntment, but healeth again soone after if it be left to heal of itselfe, then it continueth well longe &c. 4 dos. of 5 g. $ & 3 dos. 2 g. addit. & unguent de ^ or Mrs. Russell's" [p. 517].

> June 1663: "Gilbert Gilbert 4 y: had wormes many, & cough etc. & lung ague like hectick ½ g: Dr. Hobson's extraction he tooke at 3

tymes every night through mistake for he should have taken all at once. But they found was better by it. This day I gave more 2 dos. of ½ g: to take at 2 several nights leaving a night or 2 between &c." [p. 511].

Finally, on some occasions Winthrop was confronted with situations which weren't covered by any of the books in his vast chemical, alchemical and medical library.

> 25 January 1665/6: "Burna[m] Anne 3 y: daught[er] of Tho: of Podunck had a pea up high in the right nostrill, had been in it about 3 weekes. Jan: 27: I blew it out by stopping the mouth close & with an hollow elder cane blew in the other nostrill & blew it out. The elder wall kept close & full to the nostrill a little looseness being about the end" [p. 619].

(Many years ago Col. Charles E. Banks abstracted a large number of entries from the Winthrop journal, and after his death these were published [TAG 9:54-61, 64, 23:62-64, 124-28, 231-34, 24:41-47, 108-15]. These abstracts represent only a fraction of all the entries, and seem to have been selected haphazardly. More importantly, many of them were misread. No reliance should be placed on these abstracts.)

Great Migration Newsletter

| Vol. 9 | April-June 2000 | No. 2 |

PROBATE INVENTORIES - PART I

Every genealogist hopes to find that the ancestor he or she is researching left a will, naming spouse and children and grandchildren, thus solving several difficult problems all at once. Other probate documents are useful as well, such as the distribution to the heirs of an intestate estate, or an administrator's account. In this issue of the *Great Migration Newsletter* and the next, we will examine in detail one type of probate document, the inventory.

Because of the obvious value of a will in illuminating genealogical problems, the probate inventory is not always scrutinized as closely as it should be. In some abstracts of probate documents, the inventory is represented by nothing more than a notation of the date of appraisal and the total value of the estate. An example of this sort of abbreviated and incomplete publishing of probate inventories which we encounter in Great Migration work is the set of abstracts produced by Charles Manwaring for the early records of the Hartford Probate District [Charles William Manwaring, comp., *A Digest of Early Connecticut Probate Records*, Vol. 1, Hartford District, 1635-1700 (Hartford 1904)]. Even when we might be inclined to rely upon the published version of a will, we must still go to the original to learn anything useful about the inventory.

As is the case with so many categories of records, modern standards for transcribing or abstracting are more exacting. An excellent example is the recent publication of the first volume of the Middlesex County, Massachusetts, probate records, prepared by Robert Rodgers, in which very accurate and full transcripts of all documents are included [Robert H. Rodgers, *Middlesex County in the Colony of the Massachusetts Bay in New England: Records of Probate and Administration, October 1649-December 1660* (Boston 1999)]. Rodgers has been especially assiduous in tracking down documents from all available sources.

Probate inventories have been a favorite source for social historians, primarily for estimating wealth and economic status. But many other investigators have found these documents useful as well. Architectural historians make excellent use of those inventories in which the moveable items are listed room by room.

Genealogists also frequently focus on the total valuation of the estate, and thereby sometimes miss all sorts of detail on many aspects of the life of the deceased. We will later in this article examine the indicators of wealth, but before we get to the body of a probate inventory, we need to examine the information which is buried away in the usually brief sections at the beginning and end of the inventory.

An inventory usually begins with a few lines which state at a minimum the name of the deceased, but can give other information as well. A typical, simple heading is that for Christopher Cane of Cambridge [Rodgers 131]:

An inventory of the estate of Christopher Cane lately deceased at Cambridge

Prized the 15th - 1 - 54

The residence of the deceased at the time of death frequently appears in this part of the inventory, but sometimes it is not stated at all. The date of appraisal sometimes appears at the end of the inventory, and sometimes not at all.

When the estate of John Ball was appraised, additional data were added [Rodgers 213]:

The 6 of 8 month 1655
An Inventore of the Estate of John Ball of Concord lately deceased
Berued the First of the 8 month 1655

(continued on page 16)

EDITOR'S EFFUSIONS

In the last issue of the *Great Migration Newsletter* we noted that we are shifting from XyWrite to XML as an environment for drafting and publishing Great Migration sketches. We would like to take some space in this issue to explain what that means, and how it will affect the work of the Great Migration Study Project.

XyWrite is a venerable word-processing program, once very popular among professional writers, but now largely eclipsed by Word and WordPerfect. All five of the Great Migration volumes published to date have been prepared using XyWrite, which has also been used for more than a decade to produce the *New England Historical and Genealogical Register*. Time marches on, however, and there have been no upgrades or new versions of XyWrite for years.

More importantly, now that we are publishing the Great Migration volumes in three media (print, CD-ROM and web), the conversion process from the print version to the other two has become a serious consideration. Last year, when we worked with Ancestry.com to produce the CD-ROM version of *The Great Migration Begins*, the old electronic files of those first three volumes were converted from XyWrite to Infobases, a format used for many Ancestry.com products. After that, the Infobases version was converted again, this time to HTML for the web version.

The Great Migration editor expended more than one hundred hours in the process of making the conversion to Infobases, and Ancestry.com staff an equivalent amount. A better process was needed. Using Word or WordPerfect, with their web utilities, would be a partial solution to this problem. But a better solution is available.

XML, which stands for eXtensible Markup Langauge, is similar to, but more flexible and more powerful than, HTML, the lingua franca of the web. HTML began as a tool for controlling the structure of documents (paragraphs, headers and so on), and then began to take on a second function, the control of style (fonts, colors and so on).

Robert Charles Anderson, FASG   Editor
Debra M. MacEachern   Production Assistant

The Great Migration Newsletter is published quarterly by the Great Migration Study Project, a project of the New England Historic Genealogical Society, 101 Newbury Street, Boston MA 02116 www.newenglandancestors.org

The subscription rate is $12 for one year and $20 for two years.

HTML was not flexible (additions to the standard had to be made by a committee, or were created by software companies for their own products), and it also did not address the problem of describing the data itself.

XML was developed for the specific purpose of describing data, leaving the areas of document structure and style to other, related, technologies. XML is flexible, in that the user creates and defines his own markup tags, and is not limited to those created by an official body. And XML can be prepared in a simple text editor, such as Notepad, and contains no proprietary markup which would prevent easy transport from one user to another.

An XML document, aside from some preliminary administrative commands, consists of a set of nested pairs of markup tags. In the case of the Great Migration work, each sketch will open with a "<sketch>" tag and close with a "</sketch>" tag. Building on the familiar structure of a Great Migration sketch, this so-called document tag will contain a sequence of five other pairs of tags corresponding to the major subdivisions of a sketch:"<migration> … </migration>," "<biographical> … </biographical>," and so on. Each of these, in turn, will contain an appropriate sequence of tags. Thus, the "<genealogical> … </genealogical>" tag will contain "<birth> … </birth," "<death> … </death>," and so on.

The tags described in the previous paragraph are known as elements, and each element can contain other elements only, or text only, or a combination of text and other elements. This allows a very fine subdivision of the data, as for example in the following abstract of a deed:

<deed>On <date>24 May 1644</date>, <name>John Cotton</name> sold to <name>John Wheelwright</name> forty acres of upland in <place>Braintree</place> <citation> <source>SLR</source> <detail>1:44</detail> </citation>.
</deed>

This all looks very clumsy, and would not be at all pleasant to read if presented in just this way. The solution to this apparent problem comes from another related technology, called XSL, for eXtensible Stylesheet Language. Using XSL, we create a stylesheet, which is used to transform the text above into ordinary English, suppressing the element tags, and at the same time applying such style features as we might like, such as italics or bolding.

The features that makes XML and its related markup languages so powerful, and so appropriate to the needs of the Great Migration Study Project, is that more than one stylesheet can be applied to the underlying XML document. Thus, working with the same XML file, representing one Great Migration sketch, we can create three different

(continued on page 14)

Focus on CAMBRIDGE

In 1990, in the second issue of the *Great Migration Newsletter*, we devoted the Focus section to the town of Cambridge, and within that section discussed the early church records [GMN 1:14]. All that survives from the years before 1700 are a handful of conversion narratives recorded by Rev. Thomas Shepard, and a census of members compiled by Rev. Jonathan Mitchell in January 1658/9 and the years immediately following.

In more recent issues of the Newsletter we have on two occasion revisited towns which had been earlier featured in a Focus section, for the specific purpose of looking more closely at church memberships lists. In 1997 Patricia Law Hatcher examined the first seven years of the Roxbury church records kept by Rev. John Eliot, and made important discoveries about the sequence in which new members were entered in the records [GMN 6:19-25]. In 1998 Melinde Lutz Sanborn investigated a late seventeenth century list of Boston church members, which included only surviving members from the earliest days of the church [GMN 7:3-6]. In both of these instances, the careful study of these lists has provided insights into the records which allow us to mine more information from these lists than cursory inspection might suggest.

The census of church members maintained by Rev. Jonathan Mitchell has some similarities with the Roxbury and Boston records noted above, and in other ways is very different. We will take a detailed look at this short document, to see what we may learn about early Cambridge settlers, and also about the conduct of church affairs in the first two genera tions in New England.

JONATHAN MITCHELL'S REGISTER

We do not know whether the Rev. Thomas Hooker maintained church records during his three years of residence at Cambridge; if he did, he certainly took them with him when he removed to Hartford in 1636.

Likewise, we do not know whether the Rev. Thomas Shepard kept records of membership and baptism while he was Cambridge minister, but he certainly took careful note of many of the conversion narratives which were required of prospective church members.

Thomas Shepard died on 25 August 1649, and for nearly a year the church at Cambridge was without a minister, until Jonathan Mitchell, a Harvard graduate of 1647 [Sibley 1:141-57], was ordained over that church on 21 August 1650.

There was apparently not yet a tradition of leaving church records in the hands of the church in these early years, and, if Shepard had kept such records, they might well have been part of his estate. But, inasmuch as Mitchell soon married Shepard's widow, we would expect that any records kept by Shepard would have come into the possession of Mitchell, along with the rest of his estate.

The records compiled by Rev. Jonathan Mitchell do not commence until January 1658/9, suggesting that he did not inherit any records form Shepard, which further implies that Shepard probably did not keep records of membership and baptism.

Mitchell's register was acquired at some point by the antiquarian Thomas Prince, and were then "recovered from the Prince Collection by Dr. [Abiel] Holmes," minister at Cambridge from 1792. The Mitchell record was then published in 1906, along with other, later Cambridge church records [Stephen Paschall Sharples, ed., *Records of the Church of Christ at Cambridge in New England, 1632-1830* (Boston 1906)].

ARRANGEMENT OF THE REGISTER

The records as published cover twenty-seven pages. The original pagination is also indicated, the manuscript having thirty-six pages, and we will use the manuscript page numbers in our citations below.

The title to the document, apparently added by a later editor, states that it is "in the hand-writing of Rev. Mr. Jonathan Mitchell," and internal evidence makes it clear that this was a "living" document, with additions made to an initial base of entries.

Mitchell himself began the register with a brief explanatory preamble:

The Church of Christ at Cambridge in N[ew] E[ngland] or the names of all the members thereof that are in full communion; together with their children who were either baptized in this Church, or (coming from other churches) were in their minority at their parents joining, taken and registered in the 11 month 1658.

Mitchell then entered the data in family groups, the first three, on the first page, being Thomas Shepard, Mitchell himself, and Richard Champney, one of the ruling elders. The second page was left blank, and the third page also had three family entries, for Edmund Frost, the other ruling elder, Captain Daniel Gookin and Charles Chauncy, at that time president of Harvard College.

Mitchell's intent seems to have been to enter three families on each odd-numbered (recto) page, and to leave each even-numbered (verso) page blank, beginning, as was typical of the time, with the church officers and other leading citizens of the town. But his system soon broke down, and by page five his entry for Nathaniel Sparrowhawk spilled over onto page six, and thereafter only page eight was blank.

For the remainder of the document, most pages have three family entries, although some have only two and others have four or more, the total being about one hundred and twelve family groups. (The exact number is uncertain, because one family group is sometimes followed immediately by another headed by a son of the couple in the first, and it is not clear whether this was intended for one entry or two. Examination of the original, which has not been attempted for this article, might clarify some of these doubtful entries.)

DATING THE REGISTER

Although Mitchell states that these families were "registered in the 11 month 1658 [i.e., January 1658/9]," it is evident that Mitchell began his record in December 1658, and the January date may indicate the conclusion of the complete census of members and their families as of that date. Several members are recorded as having been admitted on 10 or 15 December 1658, and the death of Edward Goffe on 26 December 1658 is also noticed. There are only four records dated prior to December 1658: two dates in the family of Thomas Shepard, and the admission to membership of two persons who had been dismissed from some other New England church (Charles Chauncy and Elizabeth (Periman) Moore [pages 3, 16], second wife of Francis Moore).

The first twenty-six pages of the manuscript are devoted totally to families in which at least one adult was already a member of Cambridge church in January 1658/9. Beginning with Mary Paddlefoot in the middle of page thirty-two, and running to the end of page thirty-six, all families were admitted after January 1658/9, with the entries for the remainder of the record appearing more or less in chronological order from November 1659 to May 1667.

The entries on page twenty-nine seem to be intrusive, with Abraham Errington said to admitted on 27 March 1663, and John Adams on 18 May 1666. But in both these instances the wives appear to have been members in full communion in January 1658/9, and so we conclude that these two families were included as part of Mitchell's initial census, with the husbands bing admitted later, and so noted by Mitchell.

Only two other families seem to be out of place, Deborah Wilson, admitted on 5 March 1665/6 [page 27], and Hannah Holmes, admitted on 31 May 1667 [page 31]. These entries are both at the bottom of the page in question, and are toward the end of the sequence of admissions, and so were

probably squeezed into these empty spots after page thirty-six had been filled. As with so many other points of interest in this record, examination of the original could well settle this point.

So we can now summarize Mitchell's methods in compiling this record. Having apparently failed to keep any church records for the first nine years of his ministry, he decided late in 1658 to make amends, and, beginning probably in mid-December 1658, he began registering data about the families in his congregation, attempting to place three families to a page, and leaving room at the end of each family for future events. By the end of January 1658/9, he had completed this census, and had filled thirty-one pages and had begun a thirty-second, reaching the end of this first stage of his efforts with the family of Samuel Stone.

Beginning in February 1658/9, he began entering individual events as they occurred, with a number of baptisms dating from that month (e.g., Nathaniel Healy, son of William and Grace, baptized 6 February 1658[/9] [page 17] and Samuel Champney, son of Samuel and Sarah, baptized 13 February 1658[/9] [page 30]). As new members were admitted from families not already represented in the register, he appended new family entries to his record, eventually filling thirty-six pages, and finally going back and squeezing a few final entries into blank spaces earlier in the book. He continued updating his register for the remainder of his life, with a baptism dated on 24 May 1668 [page 17], and his death occurring on 9 July 1668. (A baptism dated 17 July 1668 poses a problem [page 35], as there would have been no minister at Cambridge on this date.)

INTERPRETING THE ENTRIES

A simple tyoe of entry has two living parents as members, and takes note of the baptisms of their children [page 9]:

Mr. Elijah Corlet, schoolmaster, & Barbara his wife both in full communion.

           Their children

Rebeccah   }

Hephzibah   }   all baptized here

Ammi Ruhamah   }

The lack of dates tells us that these three children were baptized prior to 1659, but not whether they were baptized by Shepard, or by Mitchell, or by both. The lack of any additional information for the children suggests that they were still minors at the time Mitchell compiled his record. We have, then, a family which was complete by January 1658/9. (Some other family entries which share these same properties are those of Edward Mitchelson and William Manning [pages 12, 13].)

When we turn to the published Cambridge births, we find entries for all three of these daughters. For Hephzibah and

Ammi Ruhammah, however, there are no dates, and the citation is to the Mitchell record, so we have no independent corroboration of this record. For Rebecca, there is a complete date of birth, 14 August 1644, which clearly comes from the town civil records.

Mitchell consistently listed children in correct birth order, so we can state that Rebecca was the eldest child (or at least the eldest child to survive), and based on her date of birth, she would have been baptized by Rev. Thomas Shepard. If the other two daughters were born at the usual two-year intervals, we would estimate their dates of birth as 1646 and 1648 respectively, and they also would both have been baptized by Shepard. But there may have been intervening children who died young, and further investigation of the later lives of these two daughters (not undertaken here) would be necessary to better estimate their dates of birth.

Many entries are more complicated, giving some additional genealogical information, and showing baptismal dates for children born after January 1658/9 [page 14]:

Sarah Longhorn the wife of Thomas Longhorne & daughter of Elizabeth Green aforesaid is member in full communion.
       Her children
Sarah   }
Elizabeth   } all baptized here
Mary   }
Samuel, baptized December 9 [16]60
Mercy baptized May 11 1662
Patience Longhorn baptized April 3d 1664

First, the clear implication is that Thomas Longhorn is not a member of Cambridge church, and he was probably not a member of any New England church. Second, "Elizabeth Green aforesaid" appears earlier on the same page, as "Elizabeth Green the wife of Bartholmew deceased," so these two entries together prvide sufficient evidence to identify the wife of Thomas Longhorn. Bartholomew Green died intestate, very soon after arrival in New England, and his widow Elizabeth did not mention any of her daughters in her will, so we might not be able to make this identification without Mitchell's record.

Turning to the children of Thomas and Sarah, and looking only at the records given above, we would estimate that the children born and baptized before Mitchell compiled his register were born about 1654 (Sarah), 1656 (Elizabeth) and 1658 (Mary). This is the normal procedure, employing standard Great Migration guidelines. If we had no other evidence to go on, this is the way the sketch would be prepared.

In this case, however, we would be in error. In the published Cambridge vital records under "Langhorne" are the births to this couple of Thomas on 26 August 1647 and of Sarah on 26 February 1648[/9], and the death of the son Thomas on 5 April 1648. Under "Longhorn" are records derived from the baptismal entries above, as well as the birth of a daughter Mary on 5 September 1653 (or 1 March 1653), and the death of daughter Mary on 27 March 1654.

These two children who died young both lived long enough to be baptized. Since Thomas does not appear in Mitchell's list, we conclude that the Mary who is included by Mitchell was a second daughter of that name, born after 1654. So Mitchell does not take notice of children who had died young prior to 1659.

The daughters Elizabeth and Mary listed by Mitchell could have been born about the time estimated above, but Sarah was certainly born several years before.

Mitchell also includes records of families in which some of the children were born and baptized in England, before the migration to New England [page 25]:

Johanna Sill a member in full Communion as was also her husband (John)
       Their children
Joseph Sill but 3 years old at his mother's joining with this church
Elizabeth Sill now Hicks not 2 years old at the same time: both of them baptized in England

The ages given for the children, when correlated with other records, will allow an estimate of the date of migration and of other events in this family. Joseph Sill died at Lyme, Connecticut, on 6 August 1696 "in 60 year" [TAG 10:223, citing LymeTR 1:102], and so he was born in late 1636 or early 1637. This would place his mother's admission to Cambridge church about 1639 or 1640, and his sister's birth about 1638. This would further place the family's migration at about 1639, give or take a year.

John Sill was admitted to freemanship on 2 May 1638 [MBCR 1:374], implying that he had arrived in New England no later than 1637. One resolution of this slight discrepancy would be that Joanna was pregnant at her husband's departure for New England and remained behind to bear her second child before coming to New England a year or two later. Or perhaps, and probably more likely, Mitchell is simply off by a year or so in his calculations.

The emphasis upon including all individuals in the family structure, an important feature of Puritan New England society, is seen in several entries, as for example [page 7]:

John Bridge also deacon of the church & Elizabeth his wife both in full Communion
   Under his care also is Joseph Lampson the son of Barnabas Lampson deceased sometimes a member of this Church
   Also Dorcas Bridge the daughter of Dorcas (the wife of Thomas Bridge) deceased sometimes in full Communion with us

Dorcas was granddaughter of John Bridge, but Joseph Lampson was not related to Bridge in any known manner.

Barnabas Lampson died about 1640, and left his son Joseph in the care of "my brother Bridge" (meaning brother in the church). By the date of Mitchell's register Joseph was probably already twenty-one years old, or nearly so, and would soon marry Elizabeth Rice, but was still considered a part of this family.

There were, however, a few individuals who did not fit into any of the families. Some of these were widows all of whose children were adult and on there own, but there were a very few like "Robert Browne member of this Church in full Communion" [page 30] who was not associated with anyone else, although he may have been married at the time.

Other entries provide interesting information about church practices of the time. Members who moved away but did not request dismission were still considered members. "Mr. Samuel Shepard & his wife now living in Ireland do yet stand in memberly relation to us" [page 9]. "Hannah Thatcher (the wife of Samuel Thatcher) living in Water-towne is a member in full Communion with this Church" [page 25]. Hannah, whose parentage is unknown, had married Samuel Thatcher by 1645, and had presumably been living in Watertown for a decade and a half when Mitchell entered her in his register.

In his preamble, Mitchell promised that he would include all children "(coming from other churches) [who] were in their minority at their parents joining".[page 1]. A number of family entries include such children, from which we learn the age at which a person might become a church member, something not usually stated explicitly.

The entry for "Richard Robins & Rebecca his wife both members in full Communion formerly dismissed to us from the Church at Charlestowne" listed four children, "all baptized here save the eldest who was baptized at Charlestowne & yet under 14 years of age at his parents joining with us" [page 15]. Elizabeth, the second wife of Francis Moore, was not from Cambridge, and in the entry for Francis Moore we are told that "Elizabeth now wife of Francis aforesaid hath 3 children but they were all above the age of 14 years (the youngest viz: Rebecca being above 15) at the time of her joining with this church" [page 16].

The clear implication of these entries, and of several others, is that fourteen is the age of minority for church purposes, which further implies that a boy or girl of that age would be eligible for church membership. This conforms with the legal principle that a person of fourteen could choose his or her own guardian, and could witness a legal document.

The church register created by Rev. Jonathan Mitchell is unlike any other record we have for this period, and will continue to provide important information on Cambridge residents to be studied by the Great Migration Study Project in the future.

(continued from page 10)

stylesheets, one to produce as output camera-ready pages for the print version of the sketch, another to produce the appropriate electronic file for the CD-ROM version, and a third to produce a different electronic file for the web version.

Beyond this, the same set of stylesheets may be applied to any number of documents structured in the same way. Thus, once the three stylesheets described above have been created, they can be used over and over again, as more sketches are created. A sketch, therefore, has to be written and edited only once, to provide three (or more) different outputs. The conversion from one format to another, or from one medium to another, is no longer a time-consuming, labor-intensive activity.

XSL can do more than just apply different output styles to a fixed document structure. XSL can also perform transformations of an XML document, in which the data can be output in a different sequence, or in which only selected data items are included in the output. At some future date, we might wish to prepare a different type of publication, something like Banks's *Topographical Dictionary*, in which we include only the basic data on the English origin and first New England residence for each immigrant. To do these, we would need only create a new stylesheet and apply it to the existing sketch documents to have a new publication.

And this is not all. The tagging of names, places and other data may also at a future date permit the direct creation of indexes.

As noted above, XML documents, including stylesheets, are strictly ASCII files and may be created directly in a simple word-processor, such as Notepad or Wordpad. But the repeated typing of all the tags, with their angle brackets, would soon become very tedious. Fortunately, the growing popularity of XML has stimulated the development of many XML editors and other advanced tools.

With the assistance of Bob Velke, creator of *The Master Genealogist*, we have chosen a product called *xmlspy*, and have begun to configure this product specifically for Great Migration work. This authoring tool automates much of the process of creating XML documents, with time-saving tricks such as allowing elements which have already been defined to be dropped into a document at any place by clicking on a context-sensitive list of choices.

Very soon we will be drafting and editing all Great Migration sketches as XML documents. The final product will not look any different to the reader's eye, but the use of XML will make the production of sketches much more efficient, and the output, in whatever medium, will be more useful to the genealogical researcher.

RECENT LITERATURE

Gale Ion Harris, "James and Sarah (Eliot?) Harris of Boston and New London," *The New England Historical and Genealogical Register* 154 (2000):3-32. James Harris was probably born about 1642 and first appeared in Boston in the late 1660s, but his parentage remains unknown. Harris argues that the wife of James Harris was probably Sarah Eliot, daughter of Jacob Eliot, a resident of Boston by 1631.

Robert Charles Anderson, "The English Origin of Isaac Gross of Boston and Exeter," *The New England Historical and Genealogical Register* 154 (2000):33-34. The author presents parish register entries which demonstrate that Isaac Gross resided from 1615 to 1630 at King's Lynn, Norfolk.

John B. Carney, "Was Simon Gross of Hingham a Descendant of Isaac Gross of Boston?" *The New England Historical and Genealogical Register* 154 (2000):35-40. Carney argues persuasively that Simon Gross, who first appears in Hingham in 1675, was not a son or grandson of Isaac Gross, immigrant to Boston by 1635.

Anita A. Lustenberger, "Rosemorgie, Rosemorgan, Morgan: A Name in Transition," *The New England Historical and Genealogical Register* 154 (2000):63-77. Although Richard Rosemorgie did not appear in New England until 1664, his wife was Hopestill Merrick, daughter of John Merrick, who settled in Charlestown by 1641.

Kenneth W. Kirkpatrick, "The 'Loving Cosens': Herbert Pelham, Sir Arthur Hesilrige, and Gov. Edward[1] Winslow," *The New England Historical and Genealogical Register* 154 (2000):78-108. The author examines in detail the question of the relationship among the three men named in the title of the article, and proposes that "Winslow was second cousin to both Dorothy (Greville) Hesilrige and Elizabeth (Bosvile) (Harlakenden) Pelham ... by way of a triply shared descent from ... Fulke and Elizabeth (Willoughby) Greville."

Jeremy Dupertuis Bangs, "Another Look at the Identity of Edward Winslow's Wife, Susanna (?Fuller) White," *The New England Historical and Genealogical Register* 154 (2000):109-18. Bangs takes up the long-vexed question of the identity of the wife of William White of the *Mayflower*. A William White did marry in Leiden Ann Fuller, sister of Samuel Fuller of the *Mayflower*, and Bangs argues that she could well have been the Susanna who came to New England as wife of William White and then married Edward Winslow. As Bangs notes, the "Leiden documents by themselves do not provide a decisive answer," but he clearly leans toward the solution that identifies these two men named William White.

Paul C. Reed, "The English Ensigns: Ancestral to Thomas[1] Ensign of Scituate, Massachusetts, and James[1] Ensign of Hartford, Connecticut," *The American Genealogist* 75 (2000):1-15, 130-44, 229-40. Building on the research of previous writers, Reed provides extensive documentation on the father of the immigrant brothers Thomas and James Ensign, as well as on their mother and her ancestry, and on the ancestry of the wife of Thomas.

Anne McKee Niles, "Jane Littlefield, a New Wife for Nathaniel[3] Niles of East and West Greenwich, Rhode Island," *The American Genealogist* 75 (2000):16-25. The author identifies a husband and wife who were married in 1700 by detailed examination of the early generations of descent from two Great Migration immigrants, Edmund Littlefield of Wells and John Niles of Braintree.

Myrtle Stevens Hyde, "Phelps Corrections," *The American Genealogist* 75 (2000):26. Hyde corrects some dates in an earlier article she had written on William Phelps, who settled at Dorchester in 1630 and then moved to Windsor in 1635.

Gale Ion Harris, "James[2] Bradish of Cambridge, Massachusetts, and Newtown, Long Island, New York," *The American Genealogist* 75 (2000):47-50. The author traces the life of James Bradish, son of Robert Bradish, who had settled at Cambridge by 1635.

S. Allyn Peck, "William Eyre, a Probable Great-grandfather of Richard[1] Miles of New Haven, Connecticut," *The American Genealogist* 75 (2000):72-73. Peck presents evidence which identifies the wife of Thomas Miles, grandfather of Richard Miles who had settled in New Haven in 1639.

Roger Thompson, "Enough of Thorough: Watertown as a Case Study of Early Massachusetts Town Government," *The New England Quarterly* 73 (2000):560-582. Thompson commences with a brief overview of recent writing on the subject of early Massachusetts town government, noting that "during the 1960s and 1970s, analysts almost invariably concluded that early Massachusetts town governments were run by their elites.... Men of wealth and standing in the community could expect to be elected selectmen as a mere matter of right" (p. 561).

Using Watertown as a case study, Thompson finds that most of the men chosen for selectmen were indeed from the top strata both socially and economically. But, he argues, these men did not continue to serve year after year "as a mere matter of right." He argues that the body of townsmen acted as a powerful check on the actions of this elite, and that "the most important predictor of survivability in office ... was a selectman's ability and readiness to reflect the will of the town" (p. 579).

Most of the selectmen studied by Thompson were immigrants during the Great Migration, and this article frequently cites the published Great Migration volumes.

(continued from page 9)

We see here that the inventory was taken just five days after the burial of John Ball. The death of John Ball does not appear in the published Concord vital records, so the probate inventory in this case provides an excellent substitute for the death record.

Probate inventories in some jurisdictions frequently give a date of death, more often than a date of burial, for the person whose estate is being appraised. The researcher needs to be careful, however, since the language of these preambles is sometimes vague, and it is not always certain whether the date given is the date of death or the date of appraisal.

Even when no date of death or burial is given, the probate inventory is often our best evidence for a date by which the person must have died, since the probate inventory is generally the first document created in the settlement of the estate. Thus, in many Great Migration sketches, when a range of dates is given for the death of an individual, the closing end of the range will be from the inventory.

Turning to the end of the probate inventory, various expected and unexpected items may be found there as well.

As noted above, the date of appraisal will sometimes be placed at the end of the document rather than the beginning.

There will frequently be a sentence giving the date that the inventory was presented at court, and who presented it, usually the administrator of the estate. This will often be the widow of the deceased, and may give us the only evidence we have that she survived her husband. For example, on 3 October 1654, at the end of the lengthy inventory of Thomas Brigham,

Mercy Brigham executrix of the last will and testament of the within named Thomas Brigham deceased, attested upon oath that this above and within written is to her best knowledge a true inventory of the whole estate of her husband Thomas Brigham deceased [Rodgers 191]

Other information that does not fit in the body of the inventory may be tucked in at the end. A note at the end of the inventory of the estate of John Bachelor of Reading tells us that the "household goods by the providence of God were the most of them taken away by fire" [GM 2:1:119, citing MPR Case #594].

(to be continued)

Great Migration Newsletter

Vol. 9   **July-September 2000**   **No. 3**

PROBATE INVENTORIES - PART II

In the last issue of the *Great Migration Newsletter*, we discussed in general terms the genealogical importance of probate inventories, and then presented some examples of useful information that may be found at the beginning or at the end of the inventory, outside the main body of the document. In this second installment, we will explore the central part of the probate inventory, the listing of the property of the deceased.

A probate inventory can be a very brief and simple document, if the deceased had relatively few goods, or if the appraisers chose to be concise in their enumerations. Or the inventory can be very long, especially if every item in the household is enumerated separately.

The main division in an inventory is between the real estate and the personal estate. These two parts of the inventory are not necessarily set off by explicit headings, but the real estate is generally gathered together in one section of the document. (Although most jurisdictions in New England included real estate in the probate inventory, this was not always the case. In Plymouth Colony especially the real estate was rarely included, suggesting that this portion of the estate was handled differently in Plymouth Colony than elsewhere.)

A relatively simple example is that of Gabriel Wheldon of Malden, compiled early in 1654. The total value of the estate was £40 11s. 8d., encompassed in eighteen one-line entries [Rodgers 147]. Nearly a quarter of the value of the estate is to be found in the first two lines, which list "an house lot" and "an house-frame," this being all the real estate. The next line takes note of a debt owed to the estate, and then nearly half of the value of the estate is contained in a further three lines, enumerating the livestock ("three cows and one calf," £14; "one heifer and one yearling," £4; and "one sow with three suckling pigs," 15s.). The remainder of the entries cover clothing, furniture and other household goods. As is typical for such brief versions of probate inventories, little detail is given; for example, we learn merely that Wheldon owned "wearing clothes" valued at 15s., without being told how extensive Weldon's wardrobe was.

Some of the most interesting and informative probate inventories are those in which the appraisers proceed systematically, room by room, and enumerate each item in great detail. A relatively simple example of this type of inventory is that of Christopher Cane of Cambridge, taken on 15 March 1653/4 [Rodgers 131-33]. First comes "the chamber above the parlor," which contains clothing, listed item by item (suits, coats, shirts and a hat) as well as a chest, two chairs and "a little flockbed and bolster." Next comes "the parlor," which also contains several beds, along with the associated bedding, as well as "one cupboard table" and "three joined stools."

The third room is "the kitchen" which contains, as one might expect, the usual assortment of platters and dishes and cooking implements, "one small table cupboard and two forms," and the weapons that the deceased would have used as a member of the trainband. The last room in the house was "the kitchen chamber," which contained such odds and ends as an old cradle, a short ladder, two old scythes, three-and-a-half bushels of wheat and one bushel of rye. Finally, the inventory lists the land, the livestock, and some farm implements.

This describes the standard early New England "starter" house, with two rooms over two rooms, undoubtedly arranged on either side of a central hearth and chimney. The "chamber above the parlor" would have been the master bedroom, where Christopher Cane and his wife slept.

(continued on page 18)

EDITOR'S EFFUSIONS

In the last installment of this column, we filled more than the usual amount of space discussing our use of XML and associated technologies in drafting and editing Great Migration sketches. Although the actual effects of XML are invisible to the reader, the decision to use XML has enforced a complete review of the way in which we do sketches, and has led us, for the first time in twelve years, to make some adjustments in the formatting of sketches.

We have been using two different formats for sketches. The bulk of the sketches have included the usual list of section headings (ORIGIN, OCCUPATION, BIRTH, DEATH and so on). But for a substantial minority of the sketches, when there are relatively few records for the individual, the sketch has had only a free-form section for the records themselves, followed by a COMMENTS section for discussion of the records.

Henceforth we will use the first of these formats for all sketches. For the immigrants who are represented in very few records, many of the section headings will not have any content, and so those sections will be omitted. The same information will be presented; it will just be arranged in a slightly different manner. From the XML point of view, this will permit the work to be accomplished with a single template and a single stylesheet.

A second change will be instituted at the beginning of each sketch, in the first grouping of sections which relate directly to migration. In the past we have made these entries (for ORIGIN through RETURN TRIPS) very short, and without citations (the evidence for these statements appearing elsewhere in the sketch).

As we create sketches in the future, we will include the evidence and the citations to that evidence directly in these sections. This will have the immediate benefit of relieving the reader of the task of searching through a long sketch looking for the support for the statements made. It will also give the XML processor the ability to manipulate this data directly, which will make the sketches more like a database.

Robert Charles Anderson, FASG   Editor
Debra M. MacEachern   Production Assistant

The Great Migration Newsletter is published quarterly by the Great Migration Study Project, a project of the New England Historic Genealogical Society, 101 Newbury Street, Boston MA 02116
www.newenglandancestors.org

The subscription rate is $15 for one year and $28 for two years.

(continued from page 17)

The room immediately below, the "parlor," was an all-purpose room, used during the day as a sitting room, and at night as the bedroom for the children, of whom there were five aged fourteen or younger in 1654 [GM 2:2:5].

On the other side of the chimney was the kitchen, which also would have been heavily used during the daytime. Both the kitchen and the parlor contained tables and chairs, so meals might have been taken in either room. The "kitchen chamber," although it contains an "old cradle," seems to have been used solely as a storeroom. (The description of the cradle as old indicates that it was no longer in use, and the youngest child was by this time about five years old.)

A more complicated version of the room by room inventory is that of William Andrews of Cambridge, a more wealthy man than Christopher Cane. Taken in 1652, this inventory surveyed the goods in two houses, "the farm" and "the house at the Town" [Rodgers 74-77]. The farm house apparently had only two rooms, "the parlor" and "the new room," and the listing of real estate and debts followed the appraisal of these two rooms. The town house was a much grander building, with a hall, parlor, parlor chamber, hall chamber, kitchen chamber, shop and kitchen. The inventory concluded with a detailed listing of the linen.

Probate inventories may also be helpful in determing occupations. William Wright arrived in Plymouth in 1621, and died there in 1633, having left relatively few records. But his probate inventory included "many tools consistent with the trade of joiner, and seemingly in excess of what would be owned by an ordinary yeoman or husbandman" [GMB 3:2075]. James Deetz and Patricia Scott Deetz have analyzed the probate inventories of William Wright, John Rickard and Judith Smith in great detail [*The Times of Their Lives: Life, Love, and Death in Plymouth Colony* (New York 2000), pp. 188-210].

We also use probate inventories in the Great Migration Study Project to help in documenting the education and military service of the immigrants. Returning to the inventory of Christopher Cane, we find an entry for "four old books," valued at 4s. Such entries are very common, and just as often a listing for a Bible or two is also found. In some cases, the inventories include the titles of the books. In a few instances the inventory may show that the deceased owned spectacles.

Also in the inventory of Christopher Cane, we saw that the kitchen held, in addition to the expected kitchen utensils, such items as "one sword and bandoliers," and "one bill hook and old iron." All able-bodied men between sixteen and sixty were required to turn out regularly to exercise with the local trainband, and Cane was about forty years old at the time of his death.

Focus   on   SUDBURY

SETTLEMENT OF SUDBURY

We first hear of the town which would become Sudbury in the Massachusetts Bay General Court records on 6 September 1638:

The petitioners, Mr. Pendleton, Mr. Noyse, Mr. Brown, & Company, are allowed to go on in their plantation, & such as are associated to them; & Lt. Willard, Thomas Bro[wn], & Mr. John Oliver are to set out the bounds of the said plantation, & they are allowed 4s. a day, each of them, & Mr. John Oliver 5s. a day, to be borne by the new plantation. And the petitioners are to take care that in their allotments of lands they have respect as well to men's estates & abilities to improve their land, as to their number of persons; & if any difference fall out, the Court or the council shall order it [MBCR 1:238].

More than a year passed before the affairs of Sudbury came before the General Court. On 4 September 1639,

It was ordered, that the new plantation by Concord shall be called Sudbury [MBCR 1:271].

Three other new towns were assigned their names on the same date: "Winnacunnet shall be called Hampton," "Mr. Ezechi[el] Rogers plantation shall be called Rowley," and "The other plantation beyond Merrimack shall be called Colchester." Note especially that Court was no longer recognizing all new towns first by the Indian name associated with the location, a feature of nearly all earlier town naming patterns.

At this same meeting of the General Court,

The order of the Court, upon the petition of the inhabitants of Sudberry, is, that Peter Noyes, Bryan Pendleton, J[ohn] Parmm[enter], Edmond B[rown], Walter Hayne, George Moning, & Edmond Rise have commission to lay out lands to the present inhabitants, according to their estates & persons, & that Capt. Jeanison, Mr. Mayhewe, Mr. Flint, Mr. Samuel Sheopard, & John Bridge, or any 3 of them, shall, in convenient time, repair to the said town, & set out such land & accommodations, both for houselots & otherwise, both for Mr. Pelham & Mr. Walgrave, as they shall think suitable to their estates, to be reserved for them if they shall come to inhabit there in convenient time, as the Court shall think [fit] [MBCR 1:271].

The reference to "inhabitants of Sudberry" indicates that a number of families had already made the move to the new plantation in late 1638 and early 1639. They had presumably already settled on their homelots, and had begun to mow grass and plant crops, so this court order, like so many others, just legitimizes actions already taken, in this case by the group of men who would become the proprietors of Sudbury.

The General Court did not issue an explicit order permitting Sudbury to send a deputy to the General Court, but the town was first represented at the General Court on 13 May 1640, by Peter Noyes, one of the principal petitioners for the founding of the town [MBCR 1:288]. Other early deputies from Sudbury were Edmond Rice, Walter Haynes, and the office rotated among these three men in the early years.

It will be noted that Sudbury only sent one deputy to the General Court at this time, while most towns were sending two. This presumably reflected a court order of 8 September 1636, which stated that

no town in the plantation that hath not 10 freemen resident in it shall send any deputy to the General Courts; those that have above 10, & under 20, not above one; betwixt 20 & 40, not above two; & those that have above 40, three if they will, but not above [MBCR 1:178].

If the town of Sudbury followed this edict strictly, we can conclude that the number of freemen in Sudbury (and therefore also, we assume, the number of male church members) did not grow greatly in the early years.

On 13 May 1640, at the same General Court at which Sudbury was first represented by a deputy, the General Court filled some other important town offices. "Mr. Brian Pendleton is desired to train the company at Sudberry, & Mr. Peter Nois is appointed surveyor of the arms at Sudberry" [MBCR 1:291], and "Edward Goodner [Goodenow] was chosen, & sworn constable of Sudberry" [MBCR 1:296].

Even so, Sudbury was not yet considered a mature town, for a week later "Sudberry is for one year exempted from rates from this day, being the 20th of the 3th month 1640," and in the colony rate made at the same court Sudbury was excluded [MBCR 1:292, 294, 295].

The political development of the town continued later in the year when, on 7 October 1640, the General Court ordered that "Mr. Peter Noyse, Walter Hayne, & John Parmiter are authorized to end small businesses at Sudbury under twenty shillings" [MBCR 1:306]. "Mr. Peter Noise" was appointed to "take caption or cognizance, & to take replevies," and "Mr. Thom[as] Flinte is also allowed to marry at Concord & Sudberry" [MBCR 1:307].

One other token of the maturity of an early New England town was the appointment of a keeper of the ordinary, but we do not find such an order for Sudbury in these earliest years. Sudbury was a small town on the frontier, and probably did not have to entertain many travellers.

SUMNER CHILTON POWELL'S *PURITAN VILLAGE*

In 1963 Sumner Chilton Powell published his remarkable study, *Puritan Village: The Formation of A New England Town*. Although not perhaps recognized as such at the time, this was the first entry in an important development in colonial historiography, the so-called "new social history," the first American effort in the English tradition begun by Lewis Namier.

Powell examined in detail the genealogical sources available to him at the time, and compiled a list of the English origins of "*Sudbury Settlers, 1639-1641*" [Appendix 1, pp. 165-72]. Unfortunately, Powell emulated many other investigators in relying too heavily on Banks's *Topographical Dictionary* and N.C. Tyack's dissertation on "Emigration from East Anglia to New England, 1600-1660."

Powell demonstrated that many of the original petitioners for the settlement of Sudbury had earlier resided at Watertown in Massachusetts Bay. Some of them had become proprietors there, largely by purchase, but most of these petitioners were unable to obtain lands in Watertown, and this hunger for land was undoubtedly the driving force in the settlement of Sudbury, and of many other towns opened up in New England in these years of heavy migration, just before the coming of the English Civil War.

Powell's main concern was to examine landholding in Sudbury, and how this might have been affected by the English experiences of the earliest settlers. To do this, he carefully selected a handful of the Sudbury petitioners, mostly from among the leaders, where he had exceptionally strong evidence of their English origin.

He made his choices well, and wrote separate chapters on Peter Noyes, from Weyhill, Hampshire, Edmund Rice, from Berkhamsted, Hertfordshire, and Edmund Brown from Sudbury, Suffolk. He also examined some of the early Sudbury residents who had come from East Anglia, such as John Parmenter and Thomas Cakebread.

Despite the caveat expressed above regarding the English origin stated for some of the settlers in Appendix I, Powell's work is truly extraordinary, and should be consulted by anyone interested in the early history of this town. The extent of the work he did in English records, exhuming many detailed local records on these immigrants, would be difficult today, forty years after Powell carried out his research.

The results of this research are laid out in Appendices II, III and IV, as well as in the particular chapters on the selected immigrants. The bibliography lists a staggering number of archival materials examined in England, and for the counties listed, can still serve as a thumbnail guide to researchers today.

EARLY LANDGRANTING

The first order of the General Court regarding Sudbury, quoted in full at the beginning of this section, included instructions on setting out the bounds of the plantation. In 1638 the town of Watertown included what are now the towns of Waltham and Weston. The western boundary of Watertown, corresponding now to the western boundary of Weston, at that time abutted in part on the somewhat younger town of Concord. The grant of land to the Sudbury petitioners covered a tract of land abutting Watertown on the west and Concord on the south (see map in Bond's Watertown, between pages 984 and 985).

When the plantation was less than two years old, the inhabitants petitioned for "the addition of a mile in length upon the southeast & southwest sides of the plantation," which was granted, "provided it may not hinder a new plantation" [MBCR 1:289].

Every New England town wished to attract a great man or two, as only such men would be made magistrates, and a magistrate in residence added importance to a town. On 4 September 1639, when Sudbury received its permanent name, and the laying out of lots was confirmed, the General Court also ordered the appointed committee to set out "land & accommodations, both for houselots & otherwise, both for Mr. Pelham & Mr. Walgrave, as they shall think suitable to their estates, to be reserved for them if they shall come to inhabit there in convenient time" [MBCR 1:271].

On 13 May 1640, "Mr. Pelham & Mr. Walgrave are granted their lots at Sudbury absolutely, without condition of dwelling there, only Mr. Pelham promised to build a house there, & settle a family there, & to be there as much as he could in the summer time" [MBCR 1:292]. "Mr. Pelham" was Herbert Pelham, who resided for a few years in Cambridge, and probably did spend some time in Sudbury. William Pelham, Herbert's younger brother, did reside for some time in Sudbury, but was not as "important" a man as Herbert. "Mr. Walgrave" was undoubtedly Thomas Waldegrave, father of Herbert Pelham's first wife, Jemima Waldegrave. Thomas died in England in 1642, and never came to New England.

Returning to the first court order, of 6 September 1638, we see that the Sudbury settlers were ordered "to take care that in their allotments of lands they have respect as well to men's estates & abilities to improve their land, as to their number of persons" [MBCR 1:238]. Thus did the General Court attempt to ensure that the social and economic differences within the population of Sudbury would be maintained, and in fact accentuated.

Aside from the volume of town meeting records, one of the earliest volumes of Sudbury records is an inventory of landholding, with the following title page (with some parts illegible on the microfilm):

A true record of the names of the Inhabitants [of] Sudbury with the quantity of the several parcels [worn] them granted of the first settling in the plantation [worn] record of all such lands which have been by them sold [worn] to any others who now hold the same in possession [worn] every several parcel of land doth bound one upon [worn] and commonly called or known by such names and [bounds?] as hereafter followeth

This volume had apparently been first used in England for the accounts of a cloth merchant, with many entries for 1632 and 1633. Upon being brought to New England, it was turned around and the land records were entered from the other end.

As with so many other similar volumes which we have encountered in other towns studied in this Newsletter, a separate recto page was set aside for each proprietor, and in this case a blank leaf was left between each of these early entries. For some of the more prominent men, all or most of the space allotted was used for original grants and for resales. But for many of the ordinary settlers only a portion of the space available was used.

In later years, other town clerks filled the unused spaces with other, frequently unrelated records, some as late as the Revolutionary period, and so the volume includes a wide range of material, spread out over a century and a half. Sumner Chilton Powell was apparently unaware of this volume during his research, for he would certainly have made extensive use of it had he known of it.

The first entry in the book is for "The lands of Mr. William Pelham":

His houselot containing by estimation fifty acres or thereabout the same more or less lying on the northeast end of the [field?] near to the lands of William Ward.

Also a parcel of meadow containing by estimation sixteen acres and a half be the same more or less lying in the great river meadow next adjoining to the meadow of John Stone.

Also a parcel of meadow containing by estimation thirty-three acres and a half be the same more or less lying in the great river meadow between the meadow of the widow Wright and Thomas Browne.

Granted to Mr. William Pelham eight acres of meadow lying towards Concord [line?] in the way that leads from Concord to Sudbury joining to the lands of William Ward which parcel of meadow Mr. William Pelham sold to the said William Ward. Also granted to Mr. William Pelham 17 acres of meadow lying [in a?] parcel of meadow that goes out of the gulf towards Concord bounds & lyeth next adjoining to Concord bounds , which two parcels are his 3d division of meadow. Also 5 acres of meadow for allowance to Mr. William Pelham's 3d [worn] of meadow lying on the west brook between the meadows of John [worn] & John Goodenow.

Also granted and laid out to Mr. William Pelham in the year 1658 one hundred & thirty acres of land be it more or less in the two miles last granted the town of Sudbury being the eight and fortieth

lot and lieth in fourth and southwest squadron having the land of Mr. Peter Noyes on the north and the lands of John Parmenter Senior on the south, the said lot of Mr. Pelham being bounded at the west by the wilderness and bounded at the east end by the middle highway joining to our first squadron of lots.

The first three of these items are in the same ink and in the same formula, and represent the earliest set of grants in the town. The fourth, longer entry was clearly made at a later date, and there is an erased item in the margin which may have been the year of this grant (probably in 1645 or 1646). The fifth and final item is explicitly stated to be made in 1658.

Given the prominence of William Pelham, the size of the granted lots is certainly greater than the average, but, as we shall see, William Pelham did not receive the full round of grants. Furthermore, the 1658 grant was made to persons who had already sold out their Sudbury land (see, for example, the entry for Solomon Johnson), so this was a division of land based on rights held at an earlier date.

Again we see in this entry a feature found in many early New England town records. William Pelham sold one of these lots to William Ward, and the transfer is very briefly entered here in the records of the proprietors. Many parcels of land were sold and resold several times before one of the transactions was entered in the county records, and these volumes always need to be part of the title search.

An entry toward the middle of the spectrum is that for Solomon Johnson. His initial grants are as follows:

His houselot containing six acres more or less lying in the northwest row adjoining to the west side of William Ward's houselot.

Also seven acres of upland lying between the houselot of William Ward by the lands of William Pellam.

Also seven acres of meadow lying on the north side of the meadow of Edmund Rice towards Concord line.

Also eight acres of upland lying on the north side of the river towards Concord line lying between William Ward and John Freeman a little brook running through the midst of it.

The grants made to Johnson were smaller than those made to Pelham, but Johnson received upland as well as meadow, whereas Pelham received only meadow. Perhaps in Pelham's case the meadow was included in the large houselot. The next item in this entry shows William Ward, who abutted to a number of these parcels, consolidating his holdings:

All which said lands with all right thereto belonging the said Solomon Johnson sold unto William Ward and now is in the possession of the said William Ward.

Solomon Johnson had moved on to help settle Marlborough, but still received his share in the 1658 grant.

More typical entries might be those of Robert Beast [Best] and John Parmenter Senior. In the first series of grants, Best received a houselot of four acres, nine acres of upland, three-and-a-half acres of meadow and seven-and-a-half acres of meadow. Parmenter received a houselot of five acres, eleven acres of upland, and three parcels of meadow, of five, twelve and ten acres. Note that both these men received upland, which was not in the list of grants to William Pelham.

On 24 October 1643, the two men exchanged parcels of meadow, and the text of this agreement is entered twice, on each man's page.

In 1645 Best received three parcels of land, one of upland, twelve acres, and two of meadow, five-and-a-half acres and one acre. In 1646 Parmenter similarly received twenty-one acres of upland and eight acres and three-quarters of meadow. Finally, both men participated in the division of 1658 "in the two miles last granted the town of Sudbury."

We can attempt to widen our knowledge of the landholding patterns by examining probate records for these early Sudbury settlers. Unfortunately, these inventories do not always provide as detailed a list of the parcels of land as we might like.

For example, Robert Best, whose list of land grants we have looked at above, died in 1655. In his will he bequeathed "My land and house at Sudbury with all the appurtenances thereto belonging, as common[,] meadows, wood, etc." [Rodgers 174]. At this time, "appurtenances" referred to the undivided proprietorial share which attached to that particular houselot.

The inventory was equally uninformative, providing a single entry for "his house and land in Sudbury" [Rodgers 175]. In this instance, we do not get very far in trying to compare the lands granted to Robert Best with those he held at his death. Note, however, that he did receive his share in the 1658 division, even though he had been dead for three years, the grant being made to "the heirs of Robert Best."

EARLY VITAL RECORDS

The earliest vital records of Sudbury are in the same volume as the land records discussed above (or at least that is the way the pages are now bound). The handwriting of these early vital records is the same as that of the land records. Note also the use of the phrase "A True Record" at the head of each section. (We might wish that more records were so conveniently labelled as "true." Our analytical efforts would be greatly simplified.)

The first page of these records contains "A true record of the marriages," with thirteen entries, dated from 1639 through

1647, filling less than half the page. The second page, although not provided with a heading, lists deaths and burials, with eleven entries from 1640 through 1647, again filling less than half the page. In this instance, a later town clerk took advantage of the empty space to enter the records of several stray horses from the 1690s.

The next page has the heading "A true record of the birth of the children borne in Sudbury." These birth records cover the same period from 1639 through 1648, and were entered during at least four sessions, with different intensities of ink, but apparently all the same hand.

Sudbury was one of those towns which submitted vital records to the county clerk, at a time when Middlesex County had a legal existence, but was still merged with Suffolk County for the purposes of record keeping. These were published many years ago in the series which was erroneously labelled "Early Records of Boston." The Sudbury section of this set of records was headed "Births and burials from 1639 to the 1 month 1646" [NEHGR 6:378-79].

These county submissions were presumably based on the town records, but there are many discrepancies. In the first place, none of the marriages were sent to the county clerk. There was nothing unusual in this, for that was the requirement, and other towns also omitted their marriages.

As noted above, the page of early deaths in the town volume contained eleven entries, but only seven of these appear in the county copy; the remaining four entries were for 1647 and 1648, after the date of the submission to the county. But the county copy includes one entry not found in the town volume, the burial of Thomas Axdell on "8 (1) 1646," apparently very close to the date that the records were submitted to the county clerk; in fact, this is the very last entry in the county copy. Perhaps the Sudbury town clerk, as he was preparing the list to go to the county, added this new entry directly to the county copy and failed to enter it in the town volume which he retained.

For this first period, the town copy contains many entries which were not sent in to the county clerk, and there is no apparent pattern to the omissions. For instance, on the first of the four town pages, there are twelve entries from 1639 through 1641, seemingly all made at one sitting, and then another fourteen entries, from 1641 and 1642, in a more cramped version of the same hand. Of the first twelve of these entries, the last three did not make it to the county: Joseph, the son of Joseph Bent, born 16 May 1641; Samuel, the son of William Ward, born 14 September 1641; and Johanna, the daughter of Solomon Johnson, born 16 February 1641[/2]. Of the second group of fourteen entries, one was left out: John, the son of Richard Newton and Anne his wife, born 20 October 1641. Even more births from the remaining three pages of the town book were omitted from the county submission.

RECENT LITERATURE

Paul C. Reed and Leslie Mahler, "The Correct Origin of Thomas[1] Millett of Dorchester, Massachusetts," *The American Genealogist* 75 (2000):81-93. The authors present evidence showing that Thomas Millett, who came to New England in 1635 and settled in Dorchester, was baptized at Newbury, Berkshire. They then identify three generations of agnate ancestry for the immigrant.

Susan E. Roser, "Two Daniel Coles of Eastham, Massachusetts, and Two Wives Named Mercy: A *Mayflower* Line," *The American Genealogist* 75 (2000):124-29. Roser untangles the identities of the wives of two men named Daniel Cole, proposing that Mercy Fuller, daughter of Samuel Fuller and granddaughter of Samuel Fuller of the Mayflower, married Daniel Cole, son of the immigrant Job Cole, while Mercy Freeman, daughter of Samuel Freeman and granddaughter of the immigrant Samuel Freeman, married Daniel Cole, son of the immigrant Daniel Cole.

Nathan J. Rogers, "Mary (Farr) (Mycall) Niles of Braintree, Massachusetts, and Mary (Farr) Farnsworth of Lynn and Groton, Massachusetts," *The American Genealogist* 75 (2000):149-50. In our sketch of George Farr of Lynn, we erroneously identified his daughter Mary as wife of James Mycall and Joseph Niles [GMB 3:2077-79]. Rogers demonstrates that this Mary Farr married Matthias Farnsworth, and that no parentage can currently be assigned to the Mary Farr who married Mycall and Niles.

Jane Fletcher Fiske, "The English Background of Nicholas Easton of Newport, Rhode Island," *New England Historical and Genealogical Register* 154 (2000):159-71. Following up on a number of clues which have long been available, Fiske has found extensive English records for Nicholas Easton, resident in Ipswich and Newport in New England. Easton's father and grandfather resided at Lymington, Hampshire, and this parish was probably the birthplace of the immigrant. Nicholas Easton resided for several years at Romsey, Hampshire, and all of his children were baptized there in the 1620s.

Clifford L. Stott and Myrtle Stevens Hyde, "The English Bullard Family Revisited and Their Bignett Connection," *New England Historical and Genealogical Register* 154 (2000):172-88. Stott and Hyde have uncovered additional information on the family of William Bullard of Barnham, Suffolk, father of the four Bullard brothers (William, John, George and Robert) who came to New England in the 1630s, in the process including data on the paternal grandfather and greatgrandfather of the immigrant brothers. They then go on to present extensive information on Grace Bignett, the mother of the immigrant brothers, and on her father and grandfather.

Helen Schatvet Ullmann, "Richard Mills, Seventeenth-Century Schoolmaster in Connecticut and New York," *New England Historical and Genealogical Register* 154 (2000):189-210. Ullmann demonstrates convincingly that, contrary to claims made by some earlier authors, Richard Mills of Stratford and Stamford, Connecticut, was the same man as Richard Mills of Southampton, Newtown and Westchester, New York. Richard Mills had arrived in New England no later than about 1640, by which time he was married to a daughter of Sergeant Francis Nichols of Stratford.

Barbara MacAllan, "The Great Yarmouth Company of Migrant Families," *New England Historical and Genealogical Register* 154 (2000):215-17. MacAllan has found an ecclesiastical court record of 1635 naming nine former residents of Great Yarmouth, Norfolk, as being "in New England." Prominent among these were William Goose and his wife and Joseph Grafton and his wife, all of whom settled in Salem.

Douglas Richardson, "Plantagenet Ancestry of Thomas[1] Rainsford (1609-1680) of Boston, Massachusetts," *New England Historical and Genealogical Register* 154 (2000):219-26. The author presents evidence for a descent from Henry III, King of England, for Thomas Rainsford of Boston, through his mother, Mary Kirton.

Laura J. Murray, "Joining Signs with Words: Missionaries, Metaphors and the Massachusetts Language," *The New England Quarterly* 74 (2001):62-93. The author investigates "a range of conventional ideas about the gestural and metaphorical nature of Indian languages." She does this mainly by examining various reports made by New England ministers of the seventeenth-century as a result of their attempts to convert the Indians of Massachusetts. Many of these reports, not surprisingly, involve the Rev. John Eliot of Roxbury.

Murray shows that there were many barriers to communication between the representatives of the two cultures, beginning with the problem of translating between the two languages. She notes especially that both cultures relied heavily upon figurative uses of language, and that the English especially were hampered by their preconceptions about the assumed primitive nature of the Massachusett language. These ministers were further hindered by their Puritan doctrines, which ignored and attempted to suppress reference to the bodily, gestural aspects of communication.

Michael P. Winship, "Were There Any Puritans in New England?" *The New England Quarterly* 74 (2001):118-38. For some years now, historians, and especially English historians, have been arguing the exact meaning of the term "Puritan." They have claimed, among many other things, that many of the aspects of New England culture that have been called "Puritan" are in fact nothing more than facets of contemporary English culture, and that "Puritan" has been spread so broadly as to become meaningless.

Winship notes that the term came into existence within the mainstream of the Church of England as a pejorative term for those who held very stringent views on church government, church membership, and other ecclesiological matters. When conditions in England drove some of these so-called Puritans to the New World, the context changed, and the immigrants suddenly found themselves in an environment where almost all opposition to their practices had vanished. Should they still be called Puritans in this new situation?

Winship points out that "Puritanism ... is unavoidably a contextual, imprecise term, not an objective one, a term to use carefully but not take too seriously."

Roger Thompson, "Life on the Margins," *The New England Quarterly* 74 (2001):139-50. In a previous issue of this same journal, Roger Thompson published an article on Watertown town government, which was part of a larger study on the early history of Watertown (see GMN 9:15). In the article under discussion here, Thompson presents two detailed case studies of early Watertown settlers who were on "the social and economic periphery." For the purposes of his study, he is interested in marginal persons and families who were long-term residents; he is not focussed on vagrants and transients.

The first of Thompson's subjects is John Whittaker, who appeared in Watertown in 1660 as a single man, not from a Great Migration family. "Because of fines imposed upon him for jilting Mary Linfield in 1660, John began his married life in Watertown with a stained reputation and heavy debts." Whittaker's fortunes did not improve over the next two decades, as he was in constant disputes over livestock and fencing for the remainder of his years in Watertown. Whittaker started at the bottom and stayed there.

Thompson then shifts his attention to John Page and his family. Page had arrived in Watertown in 1630 with a wife and two children, and with connections through his wife to such other prominent early settlers as William Paine and Simon Eyre. Page participated fully in the early and extensive grants of land in Watertown, but the family did not prosper in the same way as others who started out on an equal footing. Their only daughter, Phoebe, was constantly in trouble with the court for her sexual dalliances. Their two surviving sons, John and Samuel, engaged in lengthy disputes over the paternal estate, both before and after the death of their parents. The promise of the immigrant generation was not passed on to the sons.

As usual Thompson makes extensive and effective use of a wide variety of contemporary documents, especially county court records. Also, we are pleased to say, he frequently cites Great Migration Study Project publications.

Great Migration Study Project
101 Newbury Street
Boston, MA 02116

Great Migration Newsletter

Vol. 9   October-December 2000   No. 4

HOW MANY HENRY GLOVERS?

An early step in the preparation of any Great Migration volume is the decision as to which immigrants should be included in a given volume. At the very beginning of the Great Migration Study Project, and then again at the beginning of the second phase, a preliminary checklist of sketches was compiled, the goal being to include all families or persons who came to New England during the stated time period.

For the second phase, covering the years 1634 and 1635, we first compiled a complete list of all records which were generated in New England during that two-year period. We then read systematically through those records, and compiled a list of all names which first appeared during those two years. (The majority of the names in these records, of course, would be for persons already covered in the three volumes of the first series.)

The list created in this way will not be final and complete. We may, for example, discover a deposition, made perhaps in the 1670s, in which the deponent states clearly and credibly that he arrived in New England in 1634, even though no contemporary record of him appears until some years later. Even so, the preliminary list of immigrants compiled in the manner described in the paragraph above will be more than ninety-five percent complete and correct.

Following the creation of the checklist of immigrants, and as we begin the actual composition of sketches, we face a different problem in deciding who should be included in a given volume. We may have a record which clearly shows that a person of a given name arrived in New England in 1634 or 1635, but, as we begin our research, we discover that there was more than one early immigrant of that name.

For the remainder of this article, we will examine the ways in which we resolve such problems by examining the case of Henry Glover. The passenger list of the *Elizabeth*, sailing from Ipswich, Suffolk, on the last day of April in 1634, included "Henery Glover," aged 24 [Hotten 280]. What became of this man?

We note first that the *Elizabeth*, and its sister vessel, the *Francis*, sailing from Ipswich, carried passengers almost exclusively from a narrow band of parishes in southern Suffolk and northern Essex, along the river Stour. We would expect that this Henry Glover would have come from the same area.

No record for a Henry Glover is found anywhere in New England prior to 12 June 1641, when a man of that name had a daughter Mary baptized at New Haven [FANH 660, citing NHChR]. Then, on 2 January 1642/3, a Henry Glover, clearly distinct from the New Haven man, was admitted a townsman at Dedham [DeTR 1:93].

Which, if either, of these men was the passenger of 1634? Savage thought that Henry of New Haven was the 1634 passenger [Savage 2:261], but Pope thought that this record pertained to the Dedham man [Pope 188]. In order to answer this question, we must trace the later history of each of these men, to see if there is anything which could connect one of them with the 1634 passenger list.

Henry Glover of New Haven had seven children in all, baptized between 1641 and 1655 [FANH 660-61]. His wife was named Helena, and she was related in some way to Thomas Cooper of Springfield [GM 2:2:205-12, and the sources cited there]. Connections of this family with Springfield continued, as Henry's daughter Hannah married in 1663 David Ashley of Springfield.

(continued on page 26)

EDITOR'S EFFUSIONS

The *Great Migration Newsletter* is approaching its tenth anniversary, and with that anniversary will come a number of changes and announcements.

With the completion of Volume Nine, we will soon move on to Volume Ten, and will celebrate the completion of ten full volumes of the *Great Migration Newsletter* early next year. Long-time subscribers to this Newsletter will remember that after the completion of the first five volumes, we combined those first twenty issues into a single volume, with a consolidated index.

We plan to produce a similar publication, comprising volumes six through ten of the Newsletter. Purchasers of the earlier similar volume remarked that it was extremely useful to have all the issues in one place, with an index of names, places and subjects to help them in finding useful articles.

In addition, consideration is being given to other changes in content, production and distribution of the newsletter, as we move into the second decade of its publication. Pending the resolution of these considerations, we will for the present be accepting subscription renewals only through Volume Ten.

Once the plans for the future of the Newsletter are complete, they will be presented here, in a future edition of this editor's column. Watch for the announcement!

****

We have had much to say recently in this column about the transformation from XyWrite to XML as the environment in which Great Migration sketches are to be written. As this issue of the Newsletter is being written, our work on XML has advanced to the point that we have completed the first sketch written from beginning to end in XML.

The subject of this first XML sketch is Henry Glover, whose name appears on a 1634 passenger list. This Henry Glover poses a problem frequently encountered in this project, and so provides the fodder for the lead article in this issue.

Robert Charles Anderson, FASG Editor
Gabrielle Stone Production Assistant

The Great Migration Newsletter is published quarterly by the Great Migration Study Project, a project of the New England Historic Genealogical Society, 101 Newbury Street, Boston MA 02116
www.newenglandancestors.org

The subscription rate for Volume 10 is $15.

(continued from page 25)

Henry died at New Haven on 2 September 1689, and left a will, dated 20 August 1689, in which he made bequests to daughters Mercy Mansfield, Abigail Burr and Sarah Ball, to the children of deceased son John Glover, and to wife "Ellin Glover" [NHPR 2:29]. The widow Helen, in her turn, died on 1 March 1697/8, intestate. The participants in the division of her estate were Moses Mansfield (who had married Mercy Glover), David Ashley (who had married Hannah Glover), John Ball (who had married Sarah Glover), Abigail (Glover) Burr, widow of Daniel Burr, and the surviving children of "Mr. John Glover late of New Haven deceased" [NHPR 2:203-4]. (Why Hannah (Glover) Ashley, who was certainly alive at the time of her father's death, was not included in his will is not evident.)

All the heirs listed in these two estates were among the children born at New Haven between 1641 and 1655 (or were children of these children). Thus, there is no evidence that this couple were married any earlier than 1641, and so on this evidence we would place the birth of this Henry Glover at about 1616. (The Torrey entry for Henry Glover of New Haven states his year of birth as 1610, but this is not supported by any New Haven records. This date of birth was almost certainly derived by assuming that which is to be proved, that the passenger of 1634 was the New Haven settler.)

We have only two small bits of information about the 1634 passenger which allow comparison, his age and his probable general area of English origin. Henry Glover of New Haven would seem to be somewhat younger than the 1634 passenger, but the identification is not impossible on these grounds. Very few early New Haven settlers were from southern Suffolk or norther Essex. We do not have enough information to think that the 1634 passenger might be the New Haven Henry Glover.

On 2 January 1642/3, Henry Glover was admitted a townsman at Dedham [DeTR 1:93]. He was granted small parcels of land, and appeared regularly in the Dedham tax lists through 1652, always at the lower end of the assessments [DeTR 1:152, 158, 161, 186, 198, 205]. He moved to Medfield, and died on 21 July 1655; his inventory was presented at court by his widow, Abigail Glover [SPR 2:31]. There is no evidence that this couple had any children.

Based on the date of admission as a townsman, we conclude that this Henry Glover was born no later than 1622. (The Torrey entry for Henry Glover of Dedham states that his year of birth was 1603. This is derived from the erroneous claim that he was baptized at Prescot, Lancashire, on 15 February 1602/3, and was a younger brother of John Glover

(continued on page 32)

Focus on WARWICK

SETTLEMENT OF WARWICK

The three earlier settlements within the present bounds of Rhode Island - Providence, Portsmouth and Newport - were all made by outcasts from Massachusetts Bay Colony. Roger Williams, Anne Hutchinson, William Coddington, John Coggeshall and their ilk all departed in some important way from the orthodoxy set down by John Winthrop and the ministers allied with him.

Warwick too was settled by outcasts, but in this case the principals went beyond anything seen before. Samuel Gorton, the leader of the settlers of Warwick, was dismissed from Massachusetts Bay Colony, Plymouth Colony, Aquidneck (Rhode Island), and Providence.

Realizing that they were running out of options. Gorton and his colleagues purchased a tract of land from the Indians for their own accommodation. On 12 January 1642[/3], "Myantinomy, Chief Sachem of the Nanheygansett," conveyed to Randall Holden, John Greene, John Wickes, Francis Weston, Samuel Gorton, Richard Waterman, John Warner, Richard Carder, Sampson Shotten and William Wardell a parcel of land "lying upon the west side of that part of the sea called Sowhomes Bay from Copassenetuxett over against a little island in the said bay, being the north bounds, and the outermost point of that neck of land called Shawhomett being the south bound from the sea shore of each boundary upon a straight line westward twenty miles" [RICR 1:130-31].

In late 1643 Gorton and some of his crew were carried to Boston, and were placed in jail in various Massachusetts Bay locations. At length, the Massachusetts Bay authorities became disgusted with them, and could think of nothing better than to send them back to Warwick [MBCR 2:51-52; WJ 2:165-67, 171-79, 188-89].

No town records for Warwick exist prior to 1647, although some late recorded deeds, found in a number of the early town record books, document some of the early land transactions.

When the colony of Rhode Island began functioning under the charter which Roger Williams had brought back from England in 1644, Warwick was represented on 19 May 1647 at the first meeting of the four towns by Randall Holden, who was elected Assistant [RICR 1:148]. At a General Court on 16 May 1648, Warwick was represented by a full slate of deputies: Mr. John Smith, Ezekiel Holliman, John Warner, Robert Potter, Christopher Helmes and Peter Greene [RICR 1:210].

EARLY WARWICK RECORDS

In most early New England towns, the first volume or two of records could contain just about everything, from land grants to vital records to town meetings to earmarks to deeds. In time these various types of records were parcelled out into separate volumes by record type, and, in Massachusetts, the recording of deeds was slowly shifted from the town to the county level.

This situation obtained also in the Rhode Island towns, and generally to an even greater degree, since the probating and recording of wills took place at the town level. Furthermore, the recording of deeds and of wills and other estate documents remained with the towns, and does so down to the present.

The records of the town of Warwick demonstrate this phenomenon in the same manner as other Rhode Island towns. The first volume of Warwick records consists mostly of town meeting records and transfers of land from person to person, but a variety of other record types are included. This first volume was published in 1926 [*The Early Records of the Town of Warwick*, edited in accordance with a Resolution of the General Assembly by the Librarian of the Rhode Island Historical Society (Providence, R.I.: E.A. Johnson Company, 1926)].

The introduction to this volume tells us that "The record book originally consisted of two parts. The entries in one part ran from page one for one hundred and thirty three leaves, and the entries in the other part began at the back and continued for one hundred and five leaves, meeting the other section" [p. iv]. (Further citations to this volume will be to the original page numbers, two to a leaf, as noted in the printed volume.)

The first seventy-two pages seem to be intrusive. On most of these pages, the top half was written in shorthand, apparently recording sermons and other religious material. The bottom halves of these pages contain a variety of records, including court actions and earmarks. Some of these are from the 1650s, but more than half are from the early eighteenth century. The paper and binding of the original of this volume should be examined to see whether this grouping of pages could in the late 1640s have been bound with the following pages.

Page seventy-three, the upper left corner of which is torn, begins with some fragmentary text, which appears to be the founding document of the town, like the covenants found in Massachusetts Bay towns. At the end of this text is the phrase "Confirmed this 23d January 1648," with the remainder of this page and all of page seventy-four containing the signatures or marks of all those who had consented to this agreement.

Pages seventy-five through seventy-eight record a series of seventeen town orders, undated, but apparently from the earliest years of the plantation. Page seventy-nine is a list of "Inhabitants received in order as they came first," also undated. Page eighty must have been left blank in these early years, for it contains only eighteenth century earmarks.

Finally, on page eighty-one commences the regular run of records of town meetings, the first being dated 5 June 1648. The first act of the town on this date was to elect the town officers: two magistrates, a clerk, a constable, a sergeant and a treasurer. This act was followed by a number of orders similar to those listed on the previous pages.

From this point through page 266, comprising the remainder of the first section of this first volume, we find a continuous and apparently complete run of records of town meetings down to early 1668. These meetings were concerned mostly with the election of town officers, and of town delegates for colony business, and with the promulgation of various orders relating to town matters.

As published, the volume is now turned over, and the second section of pages is printed. Pages 266 through 306 repeat the pattern found at the beginning of the first section. The top of most pages is covered with shorthand, and then the bottom half contains a wide variety of records, from seventeenth century liquor excise taxes to eighteenth century earmarks.

Pages 307 through 314 contain the actions of the town court of trials from 1649 to 1659 (probably not complete). (Another session of this court, for 30 August 1659, had been included earlier, on the bottom half of page 302.) These proceedings included both civil and criminal matters, as well as a coroner's inquest on the "carcass of a dead Indian being found dead in the limits of this town of Warwick" [p. 314].

The bulk of this second section of the first volume, pages 315 through 476, is taken up with various types of land records (although, as elsewhere, unused portions were a century and more later utilized to record earmarks). Most of this section consists of deeds from person to person, beginning in 1654 and ending in 1668 (although some deeds of earlier date are interspersed with this run of documents).

There are also in this section some records of grants of land from the town to various residents (to be discussed in the next section). And then there are a few records of testamentary proceedings (Robert Potter, in 1661 [page 389]; and John Smith, in 1663 [pages 415-17]), along with a handful of apprenticeships and other miscellaneous documents

The volume concludes as it began, with a single leaf, half of each side of which has shorthand and the other half a variety of seventeenth and eighteenth century records.

The second volume of Warwick town records has recently been published (along with another later volume) [*More Early Records of the Town of Warwick, Rhode Island: "The Books with Clasps" and "General Records,"* transcribed by Marshall Morgan and edited by Cherry Fletcher Bamberg and Jane Fletcher Fiske (Boston: New England Historic Genealogical Society, 2001)].

This second volume, "The Book with Clasps," is much more orderly than its predecessor. This book also is divided into two sections. At one end of the volume are three hundred and fifty pages of deeds, along with some other records, such as town land grants and probate documents. These begin in 1668, where the previous volume left off, and run into 1681.

The reverse section of the book contains a continuous run of town meeting records, picking up in April 1668 (where the first volume left off) and ending with the last meeting of 1680. As with the previous sequence of town meeting records, this volume contains mostly records of elections and town orders.

The volume which was co-published with "The Book with Clasps," called the "General Record Book," was a sort of holding action. Edmund Calverly used it first to enter twenty-five pages of liquor excise tax records, in continuation of similar entries kept in the first volume.

John Potter then employed the volume, noting that "The Town Book with Clasps being written out this 7th day of May 1681 therefore I do record in this town book until the town doth procure a bigger book." Most of these deeds are dated in 1681 and 1682, although a few at the end are dated in the 1690s and early 1700s.

Finally, Potter also used the volume to record "Town Orders the other book being full." The first of these meetings was on 13 March 168[0/]1, with others from 1681 and 1682, and then a few miscellaneous town meetings from the late 1690s and early 1700s.

John Potter eventually got what he wanted, for a volume now referred to as "Land Evidence No. 1" is devoted almost entirely to deeds. Although it is stated in some places to cover the years from 1683 to 1721, the actual range of years of recording is much shorter. The earliest deeds were recorded in 1682, and so this becomes continuous with the brief recording of deeds in 1681 and 1682 in the "General Record Book." Deeds were recorded through late 1705 or early 1706. As with so many similar record books, there are a number of late-recorded deeds, some dating all the way back to the foundation of the town in 1643.

The deeds, now firmly established as a separate series of volumes, continue with another volume in which these documents were recorded from 1705 through 1721. The first six pages of this volume contain late-recorded deeds dated from 1705 through 1721. This volume also includes an assortment of records of town meetings, from a few years of about the same period, including 1689, 1700, 1704, 1709 and some others.

The next volume explicitly stated to contain town meeting minutes bears the dates 1713-1776, but this is misleading. The first twenty-four pages contain only brief extracts from some town meetings from early 1714 until 1737. Only with 1738 does the full and regular recording of town meeting records recommence.

Having used the "General Record Book" as a stopgap in 1681 and 1682, pending the purchase of a "bigger book," we would expect that John Potter would have done for town meetings as he had done for deeds, and started a new book for them in 1681. If he did, that book appears not to survive.

To summarize, then, the first volume of town records has town meetings from 1648 to 1668, and deeds from 1654 through 1668. The "Book with Clasps" contains both varieties of records from 1668 to 1681, and the "General Record Book" has deeds and town meetings for 1681 and 1682.

The separate series of deed volumes commences in 1682, but there is a gap in the continuous recording of town meeting minutes, with only a scattering of records for the period from 1682 to 1738.

For most of this period, probate matters are mixed in with the deed records, until in 1703 a separate series of probate records was begun, and beginning in 1759 the Town Council records were also established as a distinct record series.

EARLY LANDHOLDING

In many New England towns, we have extensive lists of grants of land to all the proprietors of a town. In other instances we have complete land inventories, made some years after the original grants, but covering all the proprietors at the time of the inventory. And in some cases we have both of these types of records.

For Warwick, unfortunately, we are left with a much smaller collection of records from which we might attempt to reconstruct the early granting of land in the town.

At the very commencement of the regular run of town meeting minutes, on 2 April 1649, are recorded some isolated grants of land to individuals. Christopher Unthank is given a piece of meadow; John Moore is granted "10 acres

of land in the Neck where it is not yet laid out" [pp. 82-83 (again using the original pagination)].

In the midst of the sequence of recorded deeds, undated but probably about 1655, are recorded a number of previous grants from the town to individuals.

Thomas Greene being received a free inhabitant to the town of Warwick the 3d of December 1647 having a piece of land granted & confirmed to him for a house lot containing six acres more or less ... [p. 320].

Richard Carder being an Inhabitant of the town of Warwick & having his lot granted to him being about three acres more or less ... having also an acre of land upon Quinnimmocuk more or less granted by the town being lot 28 according to order [p. 321].

The first of these records is for the son of an original settler, and so 1647 may be the date that he came of age and was considered eligible for a grant from the town. But the second record is for an early settler, and, as the language indicates, takes notice of grants made at an earlier date.

In April 1660 the recording of deeds was interrupted to write down a series of grants to individuals, mostly of six acres, and mostly pertaining to their houselots.

Laid out to Richard Carder six acres of land more or less appertaining to his house lot ... [p. 369].

Laid out to Richard Harcutt a six acre lot fronting over against his own house lot ... [p. 370].

Laid out to Peter Buzicott six acres of land upon the account of his last grant ...[p. 371].

Again on 27 January 1664[/5] we find a few more miscellaneous grants to individuals.

Laid out to John Lippett Senior one acre of land more or less on the northeasterly side of a maple tree at the end of John Garyardy's late lot now in possession of said Lippett ... [p. 435].

Then on 12 September 1667 there is entered what appears to be a unique record, a listing of landholdings of Richard Carder, comprising six parcels: thirty acres in Warwick Neck; nine acres in Warwick Neck; a share of meadow in Warwick Neck; a share of meadow at Touskeyonke; a great lot in the second division at Warwick Neck; and a little lot in the same division [pp. 463-64]. Richard Carder apparently was granted one more piece of land, six acres of meadow, sometime prior to 3 April 1668 [p. 474].

Given all these records of grants of land to Richard Carder, we still cannot be sure that we have a complete picture of the grants of land made to him. And we have more information about him than about any of the other early Warwick settlers. A better picture of early Warwick land grants will emerge from a broader study of wills and deeds.

EARLY VITAL RECORDS

The earliest Warwick vital records are found in a separate volume, labelled simply "Marriages." This book of records is, however, much more than just a marriage register. There are two separate sections in this volume, separately paginated, one supposedly dedicated to births and the other to marriages, but neither section retains this distinction.

The first page of the first section has the following introductory passage:

A Record of the birth of the children of the Inhabitants of the Town of Warwick in the Colony of Rhoade Iland & Providence Plantationes in New England begun the first of May Anno Domini 1664 in the sixteenth year of the reign of our sovereign lord King Charles the Second of England, Scotland, France & Ireland &c. per me James Greene Clerk

This opening description was followed by a list of "The birth of the children of John Greene as follows," the first of whom was daughter Deborah, born on 10 August 1649. Eight more children of John Greene are entered on this page, followed by two more on the top of page two, in a different hand. To this list are appended the death records for Captain John Greene and his wife, ending about half-way down the page. Much later, the page was filled out with entries for events in the 1740s.

The third page, again written in the hand seen on the first page, is headed "The birth of the children of me James Greene are as followeth," after which James Greene listed his first four children in his own careful hand. But he was not as careful with the dates. The third of these children was son Elisha, said to be born on 17 March 1662/3, and the fourth was daughter Sarah, said to be born on 7 August 1663. If the town clerk could not get the dates straight for his own children, born just a year or two before the date of the entries, how much reliance can we place on the rest of his records?

At later dates, six more children were entered on this same page, and, on the top of page four, the birth of one final child, in 1685, was recorded. This was then followed by the record of the death of James Greene, in 1698, and, as with page two, the page was filled out with records from 1712, 1713, and other dates from 1735 to 1740.

The chirography of the seven birth entries from 1666 to 1685 is not the same as for the first four entries, but there are enough similarities in the letter forms that we might think that these were also made by James Greene, but not so carefully as the first four entries.

On the other hand, James Greene was replaced as town clerk in 1665 by Edmund Calverly, and so the more likely solution is that Calverly continued the work of Greene, but not, as we shall see, with as much organization and care.

Given the arrangement of these first four pages, it is clear that James Greene was planning to employ a format seen in many other New England towns, in which the records would be grouped by family, in this case with a new family beginning on each recto page, with space left on the unused part of that page, and on the verso of the same leaf, for later entries in this same family.

James Greene was not, however, able to maintain this plan for very long. On page five he began the family of Thomas Greene (including the marriage of Thomas before entering the list of children), and then on page seven he commenced the family of James Sweet.

As we have noted, James Greene ended his term as town clerk in 1664, and with him went this careful plan for entereing town records that he had begun. For many years thereafter, beginning at the top of page eight, the births and deaths are entered in something approaching chronological order, although even this is not maintained at all times.

The hand of John Potter is easily recognized when he entered office as town clerk in 1677, and he continued the format of entering vital events which had been used by Calverly. Occasional attempts were made, however, to enter families as groups, such as Randall Holden [p. 13] and Thomas Smith [p. 15, clearly retrospective, giving only the ages on the date of entry].

In 1687 Peter Green, son of James Greene, was elected as town clerk. He had been trained well by his father, since his was also a clean and forceful hand. He also attempted to restore some of the order which had been initiated by his father nearly three decades earlier.

The second section of the book, at first devoted only to marriages, was begun by Edmund Calverly, with the first entry being for the marriage on 15 August 1664 of David Shippe and Margaret Scranton. This section of the book continued as a marriage register into the term of office of John Potter, but Potter also began to include death records.

When Peter Greene took over the book, he began to use this marriage section in much the way his father had started the first section. On page nine of this second section is recorded the marriage of James Green Junior (brother of Peter) and Mary Fones in early 1689, followed by the births of their many children. (The death of this James Green in 1712, and some other later records of this family, have been crammed into the spaces between entries, apparently in the hand of John Wickes, successor to Peter Greene as town clerk.)

On the next page we find the marriage and the births of the children of "Richard Greene, son of Major John Greene." Because the most meticulous of the early Warwick town clerks were James and Peter Greene, the members of this family are exceptionally well represented in this volume.

RECENT LITERATURE

Robert R. Freeman, "Henry[2] Freeman, Immigrant to Massachusetts Bay in 1630, and His Descendants Through the End of the Eighteenth Century," *The American Genealogist* 75 (2000):169-77, 293-99. Henry Freeman was the son of Samuel Freeman, an immigrant to Watertown in 1630. The author traces the life and descendants of this Henry, demonstrating that, contrary to statements in the published literature, he had posterity at least until the fifth generation.

Paul C. Reed, "The English Origin of Samuel[1] Scullard of Newbury, Massachusetts," *The American Genealogist* 75 (2000):181-86. Reed presents the will of Robert Scullard of Abbots Ann, Hampshire, which names a son Samuel Scullard. Further analysis of the records for Samuel Scullard of Newbury, Massachusetts, establishes that this Robert was the father of the immigrant to New England, who arrived in Newbury by 1638.

Leslie Mahler, "Garbrand *Alias* Harkes Notes: The Ancestry of Susanna[1] Garbrand, Wife of the Rev. Thomas[1] Hooker of Hartford, Connecticut, and of William[1] Goodwin of Hartford and Farmington," *The American Genealogist* 75 (2000):225-28. Mahler has unearthed the lengthy and interesting will of Garbrand Harkes, the father of Richard Garbrand *alias* Harkes, and the grandfather of Susanna Garbrand, the latter of whom came to New England with her first husband. He also presents some additional biographical data on Richard and his brother John.

George F. Sanborn Jr. and Melinde Lutz Sanborn, "The Dalton Cluster: Timothy Dalton, Philemon Dalton, Richard Everard, and Deborah (Everard) Blake," *The New England Historical and Genealogical Register* 154 (2000):259-89. Through an extensive search of English records, the Sanborns have provided a satisfying solution to the long-outstanding problem of the English origin of the Dalton brothers, Philemon and Timothy. They place the brothers as sons of George Dalton of Denington, Suffolk. A third sibling, Sarah Dalton, married Richard Everard, who settled in Dedham, Massachusetts. A first-cousin once-removed, Anne Dalton, married successively Simon Rewse, Henry Boade and Samuel Winsley, and came to New England with her second husband.

Joyce S. Pendery, "Descendants of George and Margery Wathen of Salem, Massachusetts," *The New England Historical and Genealogical Register* 154 (2000):325-52. George Wathen, his wife, and two of their children arrived in New England by 1638, settling first at Lynn and then moving soon to Salem. Pendery has produced a detailed, compiled genealogical account of the family, with extensive treatment of Deborah Wathen, daughter of George and Margery, and Ezekiel Wathen, their son.

Michael R. Paulick, "Richard Masterson, John Ellis, Christopher Verrall and the Sandwich Separatists 1603-1620," *The New England Historical and Genealogical Register* 154 (2000):353-69. By carrying out a detailed search of a variety of records from Canterbury, Kent, Paulick has discovered some additional evidence on Richard Masterson, the immigrant to Plymouth in 1629, and on several families associated with him.

Mary Lee Settle, *I, Roger Williams* (New York, 2001). We have not in the past reviewed works of fiction in this Newsletter, but the present volume seems worthy of our notice. Most chapters begin and end with a brief passage, set in the years immediately after King Philip's War, in which Williams muses on his and the country's current condition. The core of each chapter then reaches deeper into the past, as Williams remembers his childhood in England, and the years of his education.

Disappointingly for those interested in his activities in the New World, three-quarters of the volume is taken up with his life in England, with an extremely heavy emphasis on his relationship with Sir Edward Coke, the eminent jurist. The historical documentation for this relationship is limited to brief passages in a few letters of later date, but Settle builds from this a rich world of young men learning the ways of scholarship and state. Settle places Williams at many historical events which he may or may not have actually witnessed.

The main line of the story skips briefly through the years of Williams's migration to New England, his brief ministries in Plymouth and Salem, and his banishment to Providence. The narrative ends with Williams in London, at the time of the Westminster Assembly, writing and publishing *The Bloody Tenent of Persecution for Cause of Conscience*. The book might better have been titled "The Education of Roger Williams," or perhaps "The Brief History of an Idea," for the focus is entirely on Settle's perception of Williams's conception of liberty of conscience.

There are unfortunately several factual errors (Isaac Johnson was not the son of Lord Say and Sele, but the son-in-law of the Earl of Lincolnshire; Boston and Charlestown are not on the same neck of land). But there are some brief and perceptive character sketches (John Winthrop "who saved my life and helped convict me all at once, a balance as pretty as a jongler upon a tightrope at Bartholomew Fair, which the dear old man sustained all through his life" [p. 108]).

Read this book not for a rounded view of the life of Williams, but for a fictional reconstruction of the world of the political and religious opposition in England in the 1620s.

(continued from page 26)

of Dorchester [Anna Glover, *An Account of John Glover of Dorchester and His Descendants ...* (Boston 1867), pp. 31-32, 505-6]. However, no record connects Henry Glover of Dedham with John Glover of Dorchester. Furthermore, John Glover of Dorchester was quite wealthy, and held several high offices, whereas Henry Glover of Dedham and Medfield was at the opposite end of the economic scale.

Again making our comparison, we have less to go on with regard to age, but again the Medfield man would seem to be younger than the 1634 passenger. Many Dedham settlers were from Suffolk, but mostly from the northern part of the county, and not southern Suffolk, as were most of the passengers on the *Elizabeth*. We cannot say that Henry Glover of Medfield was not the 1634 passenger, but we do not have much to say that he was, either.

Thus, we do not have strong enough evidence to connect either New England settler with the 1634 passenger, although there is no proof that either could not be that passenger.

Finally, we should note that this example of Henry Glover has an important message which we must take into account in some situations which are slightly different. There are many occasions, especially in 1634 and 1635 when we have so many passenger lists, when there is an entry in these lists for a young man, followed by a gap of several years, and then the appearance somewhere in New England of one person of that name.

There is a strong urge in such cases to make the identification between the passenger and the man who appears several years later. But, as we have seen in the discussion above about the various Henry Glovers, we often cannot be certain of a connection even when we have several later settlers of the name.

Thus, there will be many instances where we will not make such connections after a gap of many years between the passenger list entry (which was, after all, created in England), and the first appearance of the name in New England. When we do make such connections, it will be for explicit, stated, reasons.

The process described in this article is just one variety of a wider principle at work in the Great Migration Study Project, the determination not to make any claims for identity which we cannot support. No doubt, we will fail from time to time to connect two groups of records which should be connected, but we would rather do this than make an unfounded claim which could well be wrong, and which might be disproved by evidence not yet discovered.

Great Migration Study Project
101 Newbury Street
Boston, MA 02116-3007

Great Migration Newsletter

Vol. 10   January-March 2001   No. 1

WHEN DID THE GREAT MIGRATION END?

In the second issue of the *Great Migration Newsletter*, we published a one-page article with this same title [GMN 1:9], but now, after eleven years have passed, we must address the question again.

We begin by quoting the opening paragraph of that article:

The Great Migration Study Project plans to survey all those persons and families who had arrived in New England between 1620 and 1643. The beginning date is obvious enough, being the year of arrival of the *Mayflower* at Plymouth. But the choice of 1643 as the terminus of the Project is less evident. Why not 1640, or 1645, or some other date?

The article then went on to note that Winthrop reported in both 1640 and 1641 that migration to New England had diminished greatly, because of some of the early events in the English Civil War, events which encouraged many potential migrants that they might at last be able to achieve their desired religious goals within the Church of England at home [WJ 2:8, 37].

Because Winthrop addressed this subject twice, and because we do not have passenger lists for either of these years, it is uncertain whether the rate of migration fell immediately to a small number in 1640, or whether the decrease in the rate of migration took place in two steps, only reaching the very low level in 1641. Whether we shall ultimately choose 1639 or 1640 as the last year of heavy immigration, and therefore the last year of the Great Migration, is a question we will not address in the present article, but will leave for another day.

Whatever year we eventually choose as the last of the Great Migration, we will then be faced with the question of a cutoff date in the records for immigrants arriving in that last year. From the beginning of the Project, we have adhered to the principle that the date of the Massachusetts Bay election court, generally held in May, would be the cutoff date for accepting immigrants for the previous year. The reasoning here is that some lapse of time was required after arrival in Massachusetts, before the immigrant could go through the process of church admission, and then ad-

mission to freemanship, and the bulk of the freemen were admitted just before the election court. Given the practice of not sending out the passenger ships from London and the outports until late spring, anyone made free in May of a given year must have arrived during the preceding year, at the latest.

We cannot, however, assume that everyone who arrived in 1639, let us say, would have been admitted to freemanship by May of 1640. Some would wait longer, and some would never aspire to freemanship. So, if we choose 1639 as the last year of the Great Migration, we will almost certainly not make the election court of 1640 the cutoff date in the records for accepting immigrants of a given year.

The question we have to answer, then, is how many years do we wait before we are comfortable that all, or, more realistically, most of the passengers of 1639 (or 1640, if that is what we settle on) have appeared in the records?

The lack of passenger lists for these years makes our task much more difficult, but we can use the knowledge we are gaining from our current work on the abundant 1634 and 1635 passenger lists to assist us in making this determination.

As a first step toward answering that question, we will examine in detail the passengers on one vessel which sailed

(continued on page 2)

EDITOR'S EFFUSIONS

Over the course of nine volumes, all of the articles in the *Great Migration Newsletter* have been written by the editor, except for three contributions to the Focus section, one by Pat Hatcher and two by Melinde Sanborn. Some years ago we discussed with Donna Siemiatkoski the possibility that she would write the Focus article for the town of Windsor, given her well-known knowledge and expertise on that town.

Not long after those discussions, as many readers of this Newsletter will know, Donna was diagnosed with ovarian cancer, against which she fought valiantly for three years. Donna's battle ended recently, when she died at home in Windsor on 6 August 2001.

Donna had elaborated many genealogical projects over the years, most of them related in some way to Windsor and its early settlers. Perhaps the most ambitious of these plans was a multi-volume set of books which would put into print all seventeenth-century documents created in or relating to Windsor. Such publications are much to be desired for all early New England towns, but few have been produced, and none have been as extensive or exhaustive as that planned by Donna.

At the memorial service for Donna on 9 August, 2001, one of the celebrants spoke of discussions with Donna just a short time before she died, in which she laid out her vision of how her various projects might be completed, and who would take over each of them. The Windsor records project has found a volunteer who will finish the work which Donna began, and we will see this set of volumes in print.

The Focus section of this issue of the Newsletter will treat the early days of the town of Windsor, and is dedicated to Donna. The author of this section is the editor of the *Great Migration Newsletter*, and so the article will not benefit from the insights and knowledge which Donna would have brought to the writing, but we hope that the result would be acceptable to her. (We wish to thank Richard Roberts, Unit Head for History and Genealogy at the Connecticut State Library, for his assistance in researching this article.)

Robert Charles Anderson, FASG   Editor
Gabrielle Stone   Production Assistant

The Great Migration Newsletter is published quarterly by the Great Migration Study Project, a project of the New England Historic Genealogical Society, 101 Newbury Street, Boston MA 02116
www.newenglandancestors.org

The subscription rate for Volume 10 is $15.

(continued from page 2)

from Weymouth in 1635, the *Marygould* [Hotten 283-86; GMN 7:9]. This ship carried many West Country families, mostly from the parishes of Batcombe and Broadway in Somersetshire, and mostly destined to settle at Weymouth.

The published version of this list was undoubtedly taken from a second-generation (or later) copy of the original, as there are several clear errors in the text as received. First, the passengers are numbered, but there are half a dozen mistakes in the numbering. Without regard for the marginal numbering, we count 104 passengers on this vessel.

Second, the ages given must be in error in some cases. For example, the last entry is for Rich[ard] Porter, husband[man], aged 3. This cannot be correct, and Richard was more likely 23, or else thirty-something. For the purposes of the present analysis, we have silently corrected these mistakes.

As was typical for passenger ships to New England, most of the immigrants came in family groups, which might include nieces, nephews, cousins and servants, along with father, mother and children. In the present instance, there are seventeen family groups, comprising eighty passengers (counting only the parents and children). The remaining twenty passengers were mostly servants, in their late teens and early twenties, although a few unattached adult males are also included in this twenty, perhaps unmarried, or perhaps travelling alone, in advance of the rest of the family.

In our attempts to determine when these passengers first appear in the records, the family groups are the easiest to deal with, and we will begin with them. Of the seventeen family groups, two are never seen in New England, and may not even have sailed. One other family group, Thomas Dibble and his sister Frances, were coming to join their father Robert Dibble, who had come the year before [GM 2:2:345-47].

Of the heads of the remaining fourteen families, seven were founding members of the Weymouth church, and were admitted to freemanship on 2 September 1635 or 3 March 1635/6 (Joseph Hull, Richard Adams, Angel Hollard, William Read, Henry Kingman, Robert Lovell and John Upham) [MBCR 1:371]. Three others appeared in records of 7 June 1635, 4 January 1635/6 and 25 May 1636, and so on that basis alone, in the absence of the passenger list, would have been accounted as 1635 arrivals (Thomas Holbrook, Richard Wade and William King).

Two more of these heads of families first appear in the records on 6 September 1636 and 9 March 1636/7, and so

(continued on page 8)

Focus   on   WINDSOR

SETTLEMENT OF WINDSOR

As the pace of migration to New England began to increase in late 1633 and then reached its peak levels in 1634 and 1635, the Massachusetts Bay towns founded at the time of the coming of the Winthrop Fleet in 1630 became more and more crowded. Exploration parties went out to explore the land along the Connecticut River, and the reports were favorable.

Nearly all of the population of Cambridge chose to make the migration, settling the town of Hartford [GMN 3:27]. A smaller proportion of the residents of Watertown came at the same time to Wethersfield, just to the south of Hartford [GMN 4:27].

The pattern followed by the inhabitants of Dorchester was very similar to that displayed by Cambridge and Watertown. After the return of the exploratory parties, and the decision to make the move, a number of families made the move to Connecticut in 1635.

For some of these internal migrants, the evidence for making the move in 1635 is very strong. Two excellent examples are Thomas Holcombe and Thomas Dewey, both of whom, on 12 August 1635, sold all their lands in Dorchester to Richard Jones [DTR 12]. This complete divestiture of real estate certainly reveals a plan to leave town, and they are not seen again in Dorchester records. Others also disappear from Dorchester records toward the end of 1635, and a larger number made the move in 1636.

The proportion of the population that left Dorchester in these two years was not as great as with Cambridge, but more than with Watertown. As with Cambridge, the Dorchester church, which had been established in 1630, also made the move to Connecticut, and a new church had to be established in Dorchester to serve those who remained behind, and the new immigrants who came to Dorchester and purchased the land from those who had moved on [GMN 1:29]. This interpretation of the history of the Warham church receives strong support from the list of surviving Windsor church members compiled by Matthew Grant on 22 December 1677, which he began by enumerating the men "yet living that came from Dorchester in full communion," and the "women from Dorchester" [Grant Record 94].

The settlers from Dorchester had to confront two challenges beyond the usual difficulties of clearing the wilderness, providing shelter, and dealing with the indigenous population. The first of these was the presence on the site they had chosen for settlement of a trading post established two years earlier by Plymouth Colony. The Plymouth party resisted, briefly and civilly, the competing claims of the Dorchester immigrants, but by 1637 Plymouth sold fifteen-sixteenths of their land to the settlers from Dorchester.

Then, in mid-1635, at the same time that the vanguard of the Dorchester group was arriving at the site of Windsor, there appeared also the passengers of the *Christian*, mostly single, young men who were skilled at carpentry, or were to be trained in that trade, sent out by Sir Richard Saltonstall and others of the Puritan Lords. This group of wealthy Englishmen with strong Puritan inclinations had been trying for years, and would continue to try for some years more, to create a plantation which would meet their own peculiar requirements, along manorial lines. Despite the wealth and standing of these gentlemen, they were destined to be disappointed every time, and that was again the case with their attempts at Windsor. Many of the passengers on the *Christian* remained at Windsor, but not according to the plan set out by Saltonstall and his partners. (An excellent and fully-documented account of these challenges to the Dorchester settlers was prepared in 1859 by Jabez H. Hayden [Windsor Hist 24-59].)

When courts began to sit on the Connecticut, the first being on 26 April 1636, ostensibly still under Massachusetts Bay authority, the towns retained the names of the towns in Massachusetts from which the majority of the settlers had come. This continued for nearly a year, and then, on 21 February 1636/7, these names were all changed. "It is ordered that the plantation called Dorchester shall be called Windsor" [CCCR 1:7]. This is somewhat reminiscent of the practice in Massachusetts Bay of changing from an Algonkian to an English name when a town reached a certain level of political maturity. Perhaps this name change is the signal that the Connecticut settlers felt that their new plantations were secure, and prepared to set out on their own.

EARLY LANDHOLDING

In February 1639/40, the town clerk of Hartford compiled an inventory of the lands granted to and held by the settlers of the town at that time [GMN 3:29-30]. Beginning in February 1640/1, the town clerk of Wethersfield prepared a similar volume for that town [GMN 4:29-30]. As we shall see shortly, Windsor did much the same.

We should not be surprised that all three of the Connecticut river towns acted in parallel, producing in the space of a little more than a year volumes that included the same sort of information, organized in much the same way, since they were ordered to do so by the Connecticut General Court.

On 10 October 1639, the General Court, at a long session during which a number of fundamental issues were addressed, first ordered that the

towns of Hartford, Windsore and Wethersfield, or any other of the towns within this jurisdiction, shall each of them have power to dispose of their own lands undisposed of [CCCR 1:36].

After enumerating other powers of the towns, the Court went on to order that

the towns aforesaid shall each of them provide a ledger book, with an index or alphabet unto the same; also shall choose one who shall be a Town Clerk or Register, who shall before the General Court in April next, record every man's house and land already granted and measured out to him, with the bounds & quantity of the same [CCCR 1:37].

Hartford complied with this order, and produced its ledger in time for the April 1640 General Court. Wethersfield and Windsor both failed to carry out this order, and were given "liberty, until the General Court in September next, to bring in their record of lands" [CCCR 1:47-48]. The record of the General Court in September does not survive, but neither of the towns had finished their work by that date. Wethersfield, as noted above, did its work in February 1640/1, in time for the April 1641 General Court, and, as we shall see, Windsor also compiled its ledger during that same winter. No further mention of this issue is found in the records of the General Court.

Beginning in October of 1640, Bray Rossiter devoted a day or two a month for five months to the creation of the list of Windsor lands. The earliest entries are dated on 10 October 1640, with other entries on 16 November 1640, 8 and 25 December 1640, 11 and 26 January 1640/1 and 2 February 1640/1.

As one example, we will look at Bigod Eggleston, whose inventory was taken on 8 December 1640. He held five parcels [WiLR 1:23r; GMB 1:621]:

An homelot with the addition eleven acres

Eleven acres of meadow

Over the Great River 25 rod in breadth, length 3 mile

Near Paquannick 20 acres

In the palisado three-quarters of an acre

As another example, on 11 January 1640/1, Stephen Terry held five parcels (the last of these probably granted at a later date, judging by the difference in ink) [WiLR 1:38; GMB 3:1804]:

A homelot with the additions seven acres and half

Meadow adjoining twenty acres

Over the Great River in breadth thirty-six rods, in length three miles

In the Northwest Field sixty-four acres

Twelve acres of woodland … in the head of the swamp

We see here again the basic pattern which we have observed in most of the towns which we have studied in these pages: a homelot, some easily accessible meadow, and some larger lots which are more remote, and usually less valuable. These larger lots are generally not useful in the way that meadow land would be, and might eventually be used for planting or for gathering wood.

A difference between Windsor and the Massachusetts Bay towns we have investigated is the much greater size of the meadow lots, which reflects the size and richness of the Connecticut River bottomlands.

A feature unique to Windsor is the palisado lot seen in the inventory of Bigod Eggleston. Only a handful of Windsor's leading residents had land within the constricted area of the palisado, and these small lots were not intended to supply all the usual functions of a homelot [Windsor Hist 1:133-41]. Note that Eggleston had a larger homelot in addition to the small parcel in the palisado.

EARLY VITAL RECORDS

Researchers familiar with Connecticut records, when looking for vital records in the colonial period, will go first to the Barbour index. This index exists in two forms: a slip index, covering all towns, with individual slips for each vital event; and alphabetized typescripts for each Connecticut town, based on the slip index. (The "set of cards" referred to below was created for each town and used as the basis for the typescript for that town. All of these sets of cards were then interfiled to create the present slip index at the State Library.)

For many of the towns, the index is derived simply from the volumes of vital records created by the town clerks. For some towns, however, the situation is more complicated, and the index has been built from a variety of sources. Windsor is such a town.

An introductory page in the Windsor typescript volume of the Barbour index, dated May 1929, states explicitly the source of the records:

This list was taken from a set of cards based on a copy of the Old Church Record of Matthew Grant, the Windsor entries found in a book published in 1898 by E. Stanley Welles entitled "Births, Marriages and Deaths -- Entered in Volumes 1 and 2 of Land Records and No. D. of Colonial Deeds", a few entries from Vol. 1 of Town Records, and a copy of a book in the Town Clerk's Office in Windsor known as "The Loomis Copy".

We will examine each of these four sources, and compare them with one another, beginning with the last of the four to be created. Timothy Loomis (1691-1740), a greatgrandson of the immigrant Joseph Loomis, was town clerk of Windsor from 1723 until his death in 1740. During his years in office, he maintained records of events occurring at the time, but he also went back and compiled volumes containing earlier events. The first of these volumes covered events from the earliest days of Windsor down to about 1705.

In order to compare the sources in detail, we will look at the events recorded for one family, the descendants of Bigod Eggleston. In the first volume of "The Loomis Copy" there are forty-nine Eggleston entries - thirty-seven births, seven marriages and five deaths. The earliest dated entry was for the birth of Thomas, son of Bigod, in 1638. A number of these entries were from the first few years of the eighteenth century, the last being dated 29 November 1703. The births were from five families, those of Bigod the immigrant, of his sons James and Benjamin, and of John, Thomas and Isaac, three sons of James.

Where did Loomis get these early vital records? Most of them, as we shall see, came from the other three sources listed at the head of the Barbour typescript. The earliest of these was the so-called Old Church Record of Matthew Grant (although, as we shall see, this was really Grant's personal record, retained in the family and only incidentally including some church records). Grant had arrived in Dorchester in 1630, came to Windsor with the earliest settlers in 1635, and took over as Windsor town clerk when Bray Rossiter moved to Guilford in 1651.

The record of vital events maintained by Grant was published in 1930 by the Connecticut Historical Society as part of *Some Early Records and Documents of and Relating to the Town of Windsor[,] Connecticut[,] 1639-1703*, pp. 1-102 [cited hereafter as Grant Record]. The introduction to these published records states that the original was apparently put together from two separate volumes compiled by Grant [Grant Record 4].

The first of these consisted of fourteen leaves, the first six of which have been excised. The editor of these records has numbered the remaining pages 13 through 28 [Grant Record 7-21]. This is the portion which may rightfully be referred to as the Church Record, for here Grant has listed church members and baptisms, along with some items of church business (although this was still Grant's own copy, and not properly a church document). The baptisms are arranged by family, an indication that the record was compiled retrospectively. There are other clues indicating that this book

was put together, and certainly completed, in 1677. There are no records after 1677 (with one exception, apparently added at a later date [Grant Record 13]), and at an early point in the book Grant refers to a burial of 6 February 1677[/8?] as happening "now" [Grant Record 9].

The second of the books compiled by Matthew Grant consisted of forty leaves, which the editor has numbered 29 through 108 [Grant Record 21-102]. The first leaf contains no useful information, but then, perhaps as early as 1668, and certainly no later than 18 May 1674, Grant began a register of births, arranged more or less alphabetically by head of family, which filled the next forty-seven pages [Grant Record 21-72, being original pages 31-77]. Beginning in the middle of the seventy-seventh page, Grant began to make new entries for families begun after 1674, with the marriages of William Phelps and Sarah Pinney on 20 December 1676 and John Saxton and Mary Hill on 30 July 1677. These entries for new families continued through page 85, and over onto page 103, with events as late as late 1681 (Grant himself dying on 16 December 1681) [Grant Record 72-77, 100-1].

The remainder of this second book of the Matthew Grant Record contains a miscellany of items. Page 86 copies out some events from 1639 and 1640 from an old book (now lost) [Grant Record 77-79], and pages 87 through 90 list the deaths in Windsor from 1640 to 1681 [Grant Record 79-86]. Except for the last few years we learn only the year in which each person died, but comparison with other records indicates that within each year's list the names are entered in the order of death, so that some guess can be made as to the time of year of the death. Pages 93 through 95 summarize pages 31 through 77, telling how many children in each family were born in Windsor [Grant Record 90-94].

The second book then reverts to church records, the most interesting of which is a compilation of church members still living on 12 December 1677, including fifteen men and women who had been admitted to the church when it was still in Dorchester [Grant Record 94-96, being page 97 of the original].

Of the forty-nine Eggleston entries in "The Loomis Copy," twenty-one are found in the Matthew Grant record. Seven of these are for the births of children of Bigod Eggleston, and eight for the children of his son James [Grant Record 35-36]. The other six items are the death of Bigod Eggleston, the death of his daughter Mercy (year only) and four marriages.

Loomis missed several Eggleston items in the Grant Record, however. Among these were the birth of Hannah, daughter of James, on 19 December 1676, and the marriage of John Denslow and Mary Eggleston on 7 June 1655 [Grant Record 33, 36]. Furthermore, Loomis was not always accurate in making his copy, as for example when he reported the birthdate of Rebecca, daughter of Bigod, as 8 September 1644, when Grant gave the month as December.

As an aside, it should be noted that in 1851 Samuel H. Parsons published the "Records of Marriages and Births" in Windsor, stated to be "from the first book of Records in Windsor" [NEHGR 5:63-66, 225-30, 359-65]. These are, in fact, the entries from the Matthew Grant record, but have been supplemented by other material, not always labelled as editorial additions. The Grant Record as published in 1930 should be used in preference to this earlier version of the same record.

Next we will examine the vital records submitted to and recorded by the colony, transcribed and edited by Edwin Stanley Welles and published in 1898 as *Births, Marriages and Deaths Returned from Hartford, Windsor and Fairfield and Entered in the Early Land Records of the Colony of Connecticut, Volumes I and II of Land Records and No. D of Colonial Deeds* (cited hereafter as Colonial VRs). The earliest of these records, containing events from the earliest days of Windsor down to 1657, were entered into Volume II [Colonial VRs 30-45]. Included here were the records from "Mr. [Bray] Roseter's old book," prior to 1652, along with records maintained by Matthew Grant from 1652 to 1657 [Colonial VRs 7]. Rossiter was Windsor town clerk from 1636 to 1651, and Matthew Grant from 1652 until his death in 1681.

The next batch of Windsor vital records recorded in the colonial volumes is to be found in Volume I, covering the years from 1659 to 1681, all during the tenure of Matthew Grant as town clerk [Colonial VRs 9-29]. Finally, Grant's successor as town clerk sent in records for the years 1681 through 1691, and these were recorded in Volume D [Colonial VRs 46-57].

Of the forty-nine Eggleston entries in "The Loomis Copy," seventeen are found in the Colonial VRs. Nine of these seventeen were also in the Grant Record.

Finally, the introduction to the Barbour typescript lists the first volume of Town Records as a source for some of the vital records, but the original of this volume could not be consulted in the preparation of this article, and the microfilm copy was almost totally illegible. For the Eggleston family, at least, this source was not very important, as there were only two items entered in this volume, both on the first page: the marriage of Benjamin Eggleston on 6 March 1678 and the marriage of Hester Eggleston, widow of James, on 29 April 1680. In both instances these events appear four times in the Barbour compilation, having been entered in the Grant Record, the Colonial VRs, the Loomis Copy and the first volume of Town Records. Matthew Grant had presumably entered these two marriages in his own records, and had submitted them to the colony, and so they had then been picked up by Loomis to be incorporated in his own copy.

What reason there was for recording them also in the Town Records is unclear.

In summary, then, of the forty-nine entries in "The Loomis Copy," twenty-nine had earlier been entered in one or more of the Grant Record, the Colonial VRs or the first volume of Town Records.

Twenty of the Loomis entries are found only in "The Loomis Copy," and eighteen of these are for events after 1691, and therefore after the period covered by the Grant Record and the Colonial VRs. These eighteen entries are therefore presumably copied from some other source, now lost. The other two entries unique to "The Loomis Copy" are births in 1687, which should have been included in the material submitted for Volume D of the colony records (Benjamin, son of Benjamin; and Grace, daughter of Thomas). Examination of the items in Volume D shows dozens of entries for every year between 1681 and 1691, except for 1687 and 1688, for which there were none. The Windsor clerk must have failed to submit the records for these two years to the colony, and Loomis must have had access to some other source which covered these years.

What are we to make of all this, then? Which record is the original? Which is more trustworthy? The answer to the last two questions, in this instance, would seem to be "None of them" or "All of them." When Matthew Grant was town clerk, he was diligent in recording vital events. But most of the items in his record were copied from some earlier source, created either by him or by his predecessor. The entries in the colony records were copies made by Grant or by the colony clerk from an earlier record made by Grant or his predecessor. The copy made by Loomis was taken from the Grant Record, or from the Colony VRs, or from some other source created by Grant or his successor, which may or may not have been more reliable than the Grant Record or the Colonial VRs.

There is, then, no simple rule we can elaborate by which we can evaluate a given entry in any of these records. We must determine as best we can when the entry was made for each event relative to the time the event itself took place (and the time interval here can vary, within the same document, from days to decades). We must attempt to determination what generation of record we are seeing. Is this a record Matthew Grant made himself, or is it a copy of a record he made earlier somewhere else, or is it copy he made of an entry made earlier by Bray Rossiter, or is Loomis copying from the Grant Record, or from a lost volume of town records? If more than one version of a record exists, and those versions are in conflict, we must go to the original in each case, and not rely on the published version.

In other words, the interpretation of the record of any vital event in seventeenth-century Windsor is a case unto itself. There is no simple recipe for analysis of these entries.

RECENT LITERATURE

Neil D. Thompson, "The English Origin of Sergeant Francis[1] Nichols of Stratford, Connecticut," *The American Genealogist* 75 (2000):267-71. Thompson demonstrates that Francis Nicholas, settler in Stratford, Connecticut, by 1639, and the first nine of his children were baptized at Sedgeberrow, Worcestershire. The author also identifies the father and paternal grandfather of the immigrant.

Paul C. Reed and Leslie Mahler, "The Correct English Origin of Thomas[1] Millett of Dorchester, Massachusetts," *The American Genealogist* 75 (2000):310-19. The authors provide some additional data on the English ancestry of Thomas Millett, following up on their earlier article on the same subject [TAG 75:81-93]. Most importantly, they have examined the registers of St. Saviour, Southwark, and have verified the marriage date for Thomas Millett and Mary Greenaway, and the baptismal dates for their first two children.

Leslie Mahler, "The Maternal Ancestry of Allen[1] Converse of Woburn, Massachusetts," *The American Genealogist* 75 (2000):329-30. Mahler has identified the mother of Allen Converse as Sarah Knight, daughter of John Knight of Doddinghurst, Essex.

Jeremy Dupertuis Bangs, "Pilgrim Homes in Leiden," *The New England Historical and Genealogical Register* 154 (2000):413-45. Bangs identifies the locations of a number of houses in which resided members of the congregation of John Robinson of Leiden. A number of these persons, including William Bradford and William Brewster, later came to Plymouth in New England. Bangs also describes in details the typical architectural features of these Leiden dwellings.

Scott C. Steward, "The Thorndikes of Aby in Greenfield, Lincolnshire, and Essex County, Massachusetts," *The New England Historical and Genealogical Register* 154 (2000):459-76. Steward demonstrates that John Thorndike of Salem was son of Francis Thorndike of Scamblesby, Lincolnshire, who was in turn son of Nicholas Thorndike of Aby in the same county. Cousins by the same name resided nearby in Great Carlton, Lincolnshire, and the immigrant had in the past been improperly linked directly to that parish. The present article corrects a serious error made in the third volume of *The Great Migration Begins* [GMB 3:1812].

Robert Battle, "An Addition to 'The Godbold Ancestry of Fishers and Fiskes of Early New England,'" *The New England Historical and Genealogical Register* 154 (2000):495-96. The author adds some detail to our knowledge of the Godbold family of East Anglia.

Sargent Bush, Jr., editor, *The Correspondence of John Cotton* (Chapel Hill, North Carolina: University of North Carolina Press, 2001). Sargent Bush has completed his long-awaited project of identifying, editing and publishing all surviving letters written or received by the Rev. John Cotton of Boston, Lincolnshire, and Boston, Massachusetts.

The introductory essay evaluates "Cotton as Letter-Writer" and his "Epistolary Career," placing Cotton's life and correspondence in historical context. The introduction also presents in great detail the editorial methods used in dealing with abbreviations, omissions, and the like. Anyone interested in the minutiae of historical editing should read this section.

The editor describes at length the history of the various manuscript collections which hold the surviving Cotton letters. "The wonder is, not that so few have survived, but that we have as many letters from that distant day as we do. Although these 125 letters or partial letters are but a small fraction of the number Cotton wrote and received in his lifetime, we know of only three other contemporaries in New England (John Winthrop, Roger Williams, and John Davenport) for whom so many still exist" [p. 79].

Most of the letters are from the Winthrop, Prince, Mather and Hutchinson collections. The editor has, however, made great efforts to include material from a wide variety of others locations, including the British Library, the Gemeente Archief in Leiden, and the Beinecke Library at Yale. In many cases, the actual letters have not survived, but have been included in various publications by other authors. Sometimes the entire letter is published, but more frequently we must be satisfied only with a fragment, even as little as a sentence or two. Facsimiles of a number of the original documents have been included, in part to demonstrate the difficulties encountered in editing some of the letters.

The first letter in the collection dates from 1621, when Cotton was in his mid-thirties and already established at Boston, Lincolnshire. The last item is dated 12 October 1652, just two months before his death.

As one might expect, the content of the letters leans heavily toward the theological, but there are many items of individual interest. For instance, in a letter of 26 August 1640 to "Mr. Elmeston of Crenbrooke in Kent," Cotton refers to "Your old neighbour John Compton," providing an excellent clue to the origin of that Roxbury inhabitant.

Whatever the interest of the reader, this volume provides powerful insights into the character of a man who attracted hundreds of immigrants to New England.

(continued from page 2)

would be accounted as 1636 arrivals on the basis of these records alone. Musachiell Bernard first appears in New England records on 27 September 1637, and George Allen on 5 March 1638/9, and so would be considered immigrants of 1637 and 1638, respectively.

By the election court of 1636, ten of the fourteen heads of families are accounted for in New England records, nearly three-quarters of the total. By the election court of 1639, all fourteen are accounted for. Translating this for the year that marks the end of the Great Migration, and assuming that we settle on 1639 as that year, then using the 1640 election court as the cutoff would give us nearly three-quarters coverage, and using the 1643 election court would result in complete coverage.

The analysis of one passenger list does not give us sufficient data to answer the question at hand. This group of passengers may have been unusual, because of their association with the Rev. Joseph Hull, or because most of them settled in a town with reasonably good record survival. Many more lists, perhaps all of the lists of 1634 and 1635, will have to be studied before we can be satisfied on this matter, but we have at least made a small beginning.

In summary, we need to answer two questions before we can decide which immigrants to New England should be considered to be part of the Great Migration. What was the last year of the Great Migration, 1639 or 1640? How many years after that date do we wait until we are confident that we have captured most of the immigrants of that year in New England records?

Whatever the answer to these two questions may be, we will certainly exclude some persons who should have been included as part of the Great Migration, and include others who should not. This is one of the inevitable consequences of the overall approach of the Great Migration Study Project, which is to establish consistent, objective criteria for inclusion or exclusion, and to attempt to adhere as closely as possible to those criteria.

In our 1990 article of this same title, we established the election court of 10 May 1643 as the cutoff date for inclusion in the Great Migration. When we have fully examined the two questions stated above, we may decide to change to another election court as the cutoff date. But the final choice will clearly not be far from 1643, and it may eventually turn out to be 1643. We will certainly be revisiting this question.

Great Migration Study Project
101 Newbury Street
Boston, MA 02116-3007

NON-PROFIT ORG.
U.S. POSTAGE PAID
Burlington, VERMONT
Permit No. 579

Great Migration Newsletter

Vol. 10   April-June 2001   No. 2

RHODE ISLAND FREEMEN OF 1655

The earliest records of freemen in Rhode Island are found embedded in the records of the individual towns, a circumstance common to almost all categories of records in that colony. Once the four original Rhode Island towns (Providence, Portsmouth, Newport and Warwick) had formed a unified government, admissions to freemanship were occasionally entered in the colony court records, but these records are certainly not complete.

The single most extensive compilation of Rhode Island freemen made in the seventeenth century is "The Roll of the Freemen of the Colony of every Town," dated 1655 [RICR 1:299-302]. This list contains the names of 247 men, of whom 42 were from Providence, 71 from Portsmouth, 96 from Newport and 38 from Warwick.

The fundamental question we must ask is whether this list contains precisely those men who had been admitted to freemanship in or prior to 1655, and were alive and not disenfranchised in that same year. At first glance, the answer would seem to be a simple "Yes." For each town, the names are listed roughly in alphabetical order (in the published version). For two of the towns, Portsmouth and Newport, there are apparent brief additions, in which the number "1656" is entered, next to one name for Portsmouth, and next to one name at the head of a list of six for Newport. The simplest explanation would be that the list was carefully compiled in and as of 1655, that a few additional, newly-minted, freemen were added in 1656, and that no further changes were made thereafter.

The first apparent discrepancy which caused us to doubt this simple explanation came when we were drafting the sketch of John Coggeshall of Roxbury, Boston, Portsmouth and Newport [GMB 1:405-9]. The 1655 list includes in the Newport section two relevant entries, one for "John Coggeshall" and one for "John Coggeshall, Jun[io]r" [RICR 1:300-1].

The difficulty is that the immigrant died in 1647, and the grandson John Coggeshall was not born until 1649 [NEHGR 149:372], so that in 1655 there should have been only one adult John Coggeshall available to be freeman.

This condition should have obtained at least from 1647 until 1670, when the third-generation John Coggeshall reached adulthood.

How do we escape from this dilemma? Does the so-called "1655" list include persons already deceased or removed from the town in question? And, if so, does it include all such men? Or was the list created in 1655, and then amended and modified over a number of years thereafter? The appearance of the few 1656 entries at the end of two of the town sections would seem to be evidence in favor of the first of these options, but we can only be certain if we study the list in more detail.

The first step in the process of examining this list more closely was to look at the original of the list, rather than the printed version. The first surprise is that the names were not entered in alphabetic order, and that Bartlett had rearranged them, crudely, in preparing them for publication. The few names listed under "1656" were at the ends of the Portsmouth and Newport section, but again Bartlett had alphabetized the six Newport names of 1656.

Setting aside the 1656 entries, the remainder of the list is written in the same hand, with the same ink, so we may state as a first conclusion that the list was entered at one sitting, by one clerk. Then, within a year, another clerk, or the same clerk using different ink, added a few names of those made free in 1656.

(continued on page 10)

EDITOR'S EFFUSIONS

As we have observed often in the pages of the *Great Migration Newsletter*, the careful analysis of lists of names provides us with some of our most useful evidence in our studies. In the past, we have looked at a number of lists of freemen, as these are among our most valuable sources.

In 1990, in the third issue of the *Newsletter*, we published a short article entitled "The Value of Freemen's Lists" [GMN 1:17, 24], in which we briefly examined the Massachusetts Bay Colony lists, and at the end of that article noted that "These examples do not exhaust the possibilities for analyzing the lists of freemen...."

In the *Focus* section of this issue, we take a much deeper look at this same set of lists, looking first at the institution of freemanship itself, and the changing requirements for that designation, and then studying in more detail the types of information that can be squeezed out of the lists, beyond the simple appearance of the name in the lists.

In 1994 we investigated the lists of freemen maintained in Plymouth Colony [GMN 5:17-18, 24]. These records were organized in a different manner than were those of Massachusetts Bay, and as a result the extra information which can be extracted from them is of a different kind than what we are able to get from the Massachusetts Bay lists.

In the lead article in this issue we look at a single list from another colony, Rhode Island. In this case, there is a single list, explicitly arranged by town, and ostensibly representing a snapshot of freemen at a single point in time, the year 1655. But our analysis comes up with some surprises, and again provides us with some unexpected additional data.

List analysis propagates synergistically. In 1997 Pat Hatcher analyzed the earliest membership records of Roxbury Church, and made excellent use of our knowledge of the lists of freemen in carrying out her analysis. A list is not just one name after another; it is names in context. If we can understand that context, we will understand much more about the people in that list, and about the society in which they lived.

Robert Charles Anderson, FASG   Editor
Gabrielle Stone   Production Assistant

The Great Migration Newsletter is published quarterly by the Great Migration Study Project, a project of the New England Historic Genealogical Society, 101 Newbury Street, Boston MA 02116
www.newenglandancestors.org

The subscription rate for Volume 10 is $15.

(continued from page 9)

Another result of examining the original is that we have been able to correct some misreadings in the published version, and also to read some entries that were not deciphered by Bartlett. In two cases in the Portsmouth section of the list, the given name of the freeman was published incorrectly: "Arthur Paine" should be "Antho: Paine" (a correction which will be important in our later analysis), and "Fred. Sheffield" should be "Icob. Sheffield" [i.e., Ichabod] (an error which was corrected years ago by Austin). And in one instance, also in Portsmouth, the surname is wrong: "Thomas Warde" should be "Tho[mas] Waite."

In six places, Bartlett indicated entries which he could not read, two in Portsmouth and four in Newport. Examination of the original shows that the Portsmouth names are "Robert Ballewe" and "Henrie Eaves," while the Newport names are "John Cawdall," "John Hornden," "Robert Hinds" and "Daniell Gould." Finally, Bartlett omitted one name from the Portsmouth list, because a line had been drawn through it; the name so erased is "Henrie Knowles," which name also appears at the end of the Warwick section of the list.

Having studied the original version of the list, we now move on to the analysis of the names themselves. For the purposes of the present article, and given the limitations of space, we will examine only the town of Portsmouth. This will lead us to a firm conclusion, which may or may not apply to the other three towns. Further study is certainly indicated.

Most of the men in this list resided in Portsmouth for many decades, and so are not very helpful in pinning down the date of the list to a narrow range of dates. For example, John Albro lived in Portsmouth from 1639 to 1712 [GM 2:1:15-20]; William Baulston from 1638 to 1678 [GMB 1:133-37]; John Porter from 1638 to at least 1665 [GMB 3:1501-4]; and William Freeborn from 1638 to 1670 [GM 2:2:573-75].

For some of the men, we have very few records, and all of these from years before 1655; without this 1655 list of freemen, we would have no reason to believe that they were anywhere in New England in 1655. Gregory Cole appears in a single Portsmouth record, being granted two acres "next the land he liveth upon" on 29 April 1650 [PoTR 45]. This indicates that he resided in Portsmouth for some time before 1650, but we do not hear of him thereafter. Similarly, John Ford appears only once, receiving eight acres of land on 28 November 1643 [PoTR 23]. We cannot demonstrate that these two men did not still reside in Portsmouth in 1655, but, setting aside the 1655 list, there is no evidence that they did.

(continued on page 16)

Focus on MASSACHUSETTS BAY FREEMEN

BECOMING A FREEMAN

Throughout the seventeenth century, the criteria for freemanship in Massachusetts Bay Colony changed frequently. These changes in criteria brought with them alterations in the processes by which freemanship was obtained.

Massachusetts Bay Colony began life as the "Governor and Company of the Mattachusetts Bay in Newe England," receiving its royal charter on 4 March 1628/9 [MBCR 1:3-20]. This charter named twenty-six individuals as members of the company, and at the outset these men would have been the only ones eligible to vote in company affairs.

The company had actually begun to hold meetings in London in February, some weeks before the charter was engrossed [MBCR 1:23-27], and these London meetings continued right up until the departure of the Winthrop Fleet for New England in late March 1630, with the last few meetings being held in Southampton and on board the *Arbella* as the fleet moved down the English Channel [MBCR 1:27-70, 361-65, 383-409].

During this year of meetings of the company in England, a number of men were joined to the charter members, and these new members had generally done so by making an investment in the company [e.g., MBCR 1:46]. But when the Winthrop Fleet sailed, relatively few of the company members actually made the voyage. Winthrop carried with him the charter, and upon arrival in New England the company meetings were held on this side of the ocean, the first such meeting being held at Charlestown on 23 August 1630 [MBCR 1:73-74].

The transfer of the charter and the active leadership to New England was the critical step in the transformation of the enterprise from company to colony. This political change was certainly not what the King and his Council had intended, and conflicts would arise because of this step, but the carrying of the charter to the New World was crucial to the future of Massachusetts Bay.

Because of these events, the only men who could participate in, and vote in, the company meetings were those few who had sailed with Winthrop, or had come earlier in 1628 and 1629, such as John Endicott and the Browne brothers. The number of such men was so small that virtually all of them were immediately pressed into service as officers or assistants of the company.

The first evidence we have that changes to this arrangement were being contemplated came on 19 October 1630 at a General Court held at Boston, where

for the establishing of the government, it was propounded if it were not the best course that the freemen should have the power of choosing Assistants when there are to be chosen, & the Assistants from amongst themselves to choose a Governor & Deputy Governor, who with the Assistants should have the power or making of laws & choosing officers to execute the same. This was fully assented unto by the general vote of the people, & erection of hands [MBCR 1:79].

Appended to the record of this court was a list of "The Names of such as desire to be made Freemen," enumerating one hundred and eight men [MBCR 1:79-80]. These men were presumably "the people" who erected their hands in consenting to this proposal.

We hear nothing further about this issue for some months, in large part because the General Court did not meet during the winter months. Then, on 17 May 1631, Governor John Winthrop reported "A general court in Boston. The former governor was chosen again, and all the freemen of the commons were sworn to this government" [WJ 1:66-67].

The General Court actually met a day later, on 18 May 1631, and at that time one hundred and eighteen men were made free [MBCR 1:366]. Seventy of these had been on the earlier list, from 19 October 1630; of the remaining thirty-eight, several had died or returned to New England in the interim, and some attained freemanship at a later date [GMN 1:17].

This group of freemen had only had to ask in order to attain the privilege (although we may assume that much unrecorded politicking lay behind these events). But at this same court, the agreement noted above regarding elections was confirmed, and was then extended, as follows:

To the end the body of the commons may be preserved of honest & good men, it was likewise ordered and agreed that for time to come, no man shall be admitted to the freedom of this body politic, but such as are members of some church within the limits of the same [MBCR 1:87].

At this time, the process of being admitted to a Massachusetts Bay church was relatively simple, consisting of a confession of faith followed by acceptance by the minister, the ruling elders, and the congregation. Acceptance was not necessarily immediate and automatic, but it was not terribly difficult.

This state of affairs changed around the middle of the decade. In 1634, 1635 and 1636, during a time of heavy immigration, and of the departure of hundreds of inhabitants of Cambridge, Dorchester, Watertown and Roxbury for the Connecticut River valley, new church admission procedures were initiated. With heavy participation by Rev. John Cotton, the requirement was added that applicants for church membership "declare what work of grace the Lord had wrought in them" [WJ 1:215]. (In 1963 Edmund S. Morgan gave us our best description of this part of the history of the early New England church [*Visible Saints: The History of a Puritan Idea*].)

The upshot of this change was the so-called conversion narrative, a small number of which have survived [GMN 5:9-10, 16]. The most immediate consequence for our present purposes is that the time that might elapse between application for church membership and admission would frequently be much longer after this change than before. (For an example of the hurdles that a potential church member had to clear, read the record of the founding of the Dedham church, especially the case of "Thomas Morse," who was actually Samuel Morse [DeChR 1-23].)

The system of creating freemen set in place in 1631 remained unchanged, except in minor detail, for thirty years. The "Body of Liberties" of 1641 delineates the duties and obligations of freemen, but does not restate the criteria for freemanship [*The Colonial Laws of Massachusetts* ... (Boston, 1889), hereafter *Colonial Laws*, pp. 47, 49]. In *The Book of the General Laws and Libertyes* of 1660, we find exactly the same language as was set forth at the General Court in 1631 [*Colonial Laws* 153].

Note that, to this point, there has been no reference to a property requirement for freemanship. Most of those men who attained freemanship were proprietors in one of the towns, but we are unaware of any study which attempts to demonstrate whether or not all of the freemen were also landholders. Such a study should be undertaken, but will not be attempted here. It may be that there was an understanding among those involved in the process of creating freemen that they would be landholders, but there is during the early years no such statutory requirement.

On 28 June 1662, Charles II wrote a letter to the General Court of Massachusetts Bay, partly "concerning admission of freemen." In response, on 3 August 1664, the General Court repealed the act of 1631, and stated that

Henceforth all English men presenting a certificate under the hand of the Ministers, or Minister of the place where they dwell, that they are orthodox in religion, and not vicious in their lives, and also a certificate under the hands of the selectmen of the place, or of the major part of them, that they are freeholders; and are for their own proper estate ... rateable to the Country in a single Country Rate ... to the full value of ten shillings, or that they are in full communion with some church amongst us, ... being twenty-four years of age,

may present themselves for election to freemanship, by a majority vote in the General Court [Colonial Laws 229; MBCR 4:2:117-18].

This law of 1664 obviously represents a radical change in the criteria for admission to freemanship. Very few of the men of interest to us in the Great Migration Study Project attained freemanship in 1664 or later, so for the remainder of this article, we will be looking at those lists created from 1631 to the middle of 1664, during which period we may assume that each new freeman was a church member, and, presumably, also twenty-one years old, although this also is not stated explicitly.

So the path to freemanship in the first decades in Massachusetts Bay began with the church admission procedure. This could take some time, especially after the institution of the conversion narrative as an essential part of the procedure.

When this time delay for church admission is combined with the usual practice of not sending out passenger ships from London until April or later, we conclude that none of those admitted as freemen at the Election Court in May of a given year could have arrived in that year, but must have landed in New England in the previous year, or perhaps even earlier. For this reason, we use the date of the Election Court of each year as the cutoff date for those who had arrived in the year before.

Once admitted to church, a man could be admitted as a freeman very quickly. For example, Thomas Hazard was admitted to Boston church on 22 May 1636, and was admitted to freemanship just three days later, on 25 May 1636 [BChR 21; MBCR 1:372]. The controlling factor in the time required to become a freeman was obviously the church admission and not the freeman admission.

No early examples of the actual documents used in applying for freemanship exist, but some do from later in the century. On 22 May 1677, George Barber, town clerk at Medfield, prepared the following document:

These may certify the much honored General Court sitting in Boston the 23 of the 3 [May] 77 that the persons whose names are underwritten being in full communion with the Church of Christ in Medfield and otherwise qualified according to law desire that they may be admitted to the freedom of this commonwealth.

Obediah Morse	Edward Adams
Jonathan Morse	Eliezur Adams
Joseph Bullin	[NEHGR 3:43].

This paper very likely represents the procedure employed in earlier years. At various times during the year ministers and town clerks across Massachusetts Bay Colony were reviewing the church records for the preceding months, and perhaps for the entire preceding year. The colony clerk would then collect these brief lists created by each church, and consolidate them into a single list which would be presented to the General Court at each of its meetings during the year. The five Medfield names listed above appear in the list for the 23 May 1677 court [MBCR 5:537].

ANALYZING THE LISTS

After 18 May 1631, a regular pattern of admissions to freemanship set in. Each year, the largest numbers of new freemen were admitted at the time of the Court of Elections in May. On 14 May 1634, for example, 104 names appear on the list, and, on 6 May 1635, 69 men were admitted.

The next largest lists of new freemen were entered at the time of the March General Court. On 4 March 1634/5, 61 freemen were admitted, and, on 3 March 1635/6, an additional 49. This March court was the first after the long winter hiatus in court activity, and so one would expect that there were many men who had been admitted to one or another of the churches in the preceding months, and were waiting to advance to freemanship. Smaller numbers of freemen would be admitted at the time of other General Courts during the year.

As described above, each town (and for the most part this meant each church) submitted to the colony lists of those who had met the requirements for freemanship. Had the colony clerk systematically and unerringly created his list for the General Court simply by stringing together the town lists end to end, our task would be very simple, and there wouldn't be much to talk about.

This was not, however, the case. On 4 March 1632/3, for instance, at the time of the first General Court after the winter hiatus, eighteen men were admitted as freemen [MBCR 1:367]. In examining this piece of the list, we will display the techniques we use in determining which town (or church) submitted these names.

The first five of these men (William Curtis through William Heath) had been admitted to Roxbury church, the early records of which survive, so this part of the analysis is not difficult [RChR 74-75]. Four of these men, along with their wives, were admitted to church at the same time.

The next five names were associated with Dorchester in these early years (George Hull through John Newton). In this case the records of the Dorchester church for this period do not exist, and so we fall back on other records for these men, mostly from the town minutes and the colony records. To a certain extent, we are arguing here from the lack of evidence that any of these men resided elsewhere by the date of this list.

The remaining eight names in the list are more difficult to assign. John White and William Spencer were clearly from Cambridge at this time, but we have no early Cambridge church records to help us here. This causes difficulties with the next two names, John Kirman and Timothy Tomlins, men who were associated with a number of towns [GMB 2:1133-35, 3:1828-30]. For each of these men the earliest connection is with Cambridge, after which they removed to

Lynn. Inasmuch as there was no church established at Lynn at this date, we assume that Kirman and Tomlins had been admitted to Cambridge church prior to 4 March 1632/3, and had had their names submitted to the colony clerk by Cambridge authorities. So we have a sequence of four men from Cambridge.

This leaves us with four more names, which do not form any sort of pattern. Henry Harwood had been admitted to Boston church among the earliest members, and then in October 1632 was dismissed to Charlestown church, so he should probably be counted here as a solitary submission from Charlestown [BChR 13, 15, 16]. Richard Collicott was associated only with Dorchester for the first few decades of his presence in New England [GMB 1:439-46]. Then we come to William Brackenbury, who was admitted to Charlestown church on 27 December 1632 [ChChR 8; GMB 1:199-202].

This brings us to the last name in the list, "John Smyth." Had this name appeared in the midst of a long string of names which could be firmly identified as coming from one town, we could say something useful about this man with the most common of names. But coming as it does at the very end of the list, at the tail end of a section of the list which was not well-organized, we are at a loss to tie this record up with others for the same name [GMB 3:1693-94].

This same procedure has been followed for each of the sections of the list, for each of the General Courts at which freemen were admitted. Some of these lists are more structured than others, and so each presents its own problems. The list for 6 May 1635, for example, is much larger than the one we have just studied, and it too has long strings of names which come from one church or another.

About halfway through this list, however, is a troublesome sequence of four names: John Hall, Samuel Allen, Humphrey Bradstreet and Thomas Pyne. Humphrey Bradstreet is firmly associated with Ipswich, and so his name was almost certainly submitted by that town, whose church had been established the year before. But the early Ipswich church records do not survive, and we get no additional assistance from that direction.

Samuel Allen is a fascinating case. No other record for this name appears in New England for the next three years, and then three Samuel Allens spring up in 1639, in Braintree, Windsor and Newport [GM 2:1:39-40]. Is the 1635 record of freemanship for one of these men, or none of these men? We cannot tell, and are left wishing that this name had occurred in a more structured part of the list.

With John Hall we have a similar problem. There was an earlier record for a John Hall being made free on 14 May 1634, and we have assigned this record to the John Hall who was early of Boston and then Charlestown [GMB 2:840-44]. We still have the task of deciding whether or not this freemanship record of 1635 belongs to one of the several other John Halls who arrived early in New England. This record falls within the period of study of the Great Migration volume currently in preparation, and our analysis of the many John Halls is a task we must face very soon.

Finally, the name Thomas Pyne appears nowhere else in early New England, unless we accept Pope's claim that he was the same as the Thomas Pinny who made a letter of attorney in Weymouth in 1640 [Lechford 281]. The gap of five years, and the difference in spelling, make this identification difficult. In this instance, we have little to go on in placing Thomas Pyne.

LOOKING FOR CHURCHES

As we have seen, several men from one town, and therefore from one church, are entered in the lists at one time. We may reverse the process, and use this feature of the lists to learn something about the founding of some of the churches, something we have done in the past in various *Focus* sections of the *Newsletter*.

A relatively straightforward case is that of Ipswich. No record has survived of the founding date for that church, but with the help of the lists of freemen we can establish a relatively narrow range of dates within which this event must have occurred. Rev. Thomas Parker, one of the two founding ministers at Ipswich, had left England in late March of 1634, and so probably arrived in New England in the latter part of May. Some weeks or months of preparation were necessary in the establishment of a New England church, so we may be reasonably sure that Ipswich church was not organized in June, and probably not in July.

In the list of freemen for 3 September 1634, however, we find clear evidence that the Ipswich church was in place by that date. Very near the end of the list for that date we find "Mr. Tho[mas] Parker" and "Mr. James Noise," the two founding ministers, and earlier under the same date we find the names of four other Ipswich men, presumably some of the founding members: Mr. John Spencer, Robert Mussey, Henry Short and Philip Fowler. Nine more Ipswich names are found in the next list of freemen, dated 4 March 1634/5 (Thomas Scott through Richard Kent). Ipswich church was almost certainly organized in August 1634, or perhaps in July [MBCR 1:369-70; GMN 3:19-20].

A more complex, and perhaps a more interesting, story is that of the church at Saugus, or Lynn. This village was not so large as others settled at and immediately after the coming of the Winthrop Fleet, and did not have so many prominent men as inhabitants. When Rev. Stephen Bachiler appeared to partake in the founding of the church, there were many difficulties, some of them recounted by Governor John Winthrop [GMN 1:20].

At the end of the list for 6 May 1635 we find a sequence of nine names, six of which are readily identified as Lynn residents, and the last of which is "Mr. Steven Batchel[e]r" [MBCR 1:371]. This surely indicates that a church had been founded at Lynn in the preceding months.

Having picked out this grouping of nine names, we now may say something useful about those men who are not so readily associated with Lynn. An especially interesting case is that of John Ravensdale, who appears in only one other record associated with New England. Our ability to associate him in 1635 with the town of Lynn allows us to suggest something about this man beyond his sparing appearance in the records [GMB 3:1551].

As a part of the migrations to Connecticut in 1635 and 1636, the churches first founded at Cambridge and Dorchester also made that move, and new churches were organized at those two towns. The evidence for the founding of the second church at Cambridge is seen very clearly in these records, for on 3 March 1635/6 "Mr. Tho[mas] Shepeard" and thirteen other Cambridge residents were admitted as freemen [MBCR 1:371]. (Interestingly, "Mr. Hugh Peters" is imbedded in that sequence of Cambridge men. Is it possible that he resided briefly at Cambridge, before moving on to Salem?)

The situation for the second Dorchester church is not so clear, in part because we have no record that Rev. Richard Mather, the first minister of the second church of Dorchester, was ever made a freeman. We do know, however, that this second church was founded on 23 August 1636 [DChR 1-2]. In the list of freemen of 7 December 1636 we find a grouping of seven Dorchester men, all of whom were among the earliest members of this church [MBCR 1:372; GMN 1:29].

As with every set of records we study, the flow of information proceeds in both directions. For those churches whose early records exist, we use those records as a major tool in recovering some of the structure in the lists of freemen. We then look to other records to identify other sections of the lists that are also arranged by town.

Finally, we can take this a step further, and collect from the lists of freemen the names of those persons who came from a given town, and rebuild the church membership rolls for those towns whose early church records do not survive.

In the case of Cambridge, we have the extra possibility of merging the Cambridge names from the lists of freemen with the surviving conversion narratives for that church [*Thomas Shepard's Confessions*]. Those narratives, which were given by both men and women, were recorded by Shepard in chronological order, and so we may blend these two sets of records to recreate a very complete picture of the Cambridge church in the late 1630s.

RECENT LITERATURE

Robert Charles Anderson, John C. Brandon and Paul C. Reed, "The Ancestry of the Royally Descended Mansfields of the Massachusetts Bay," *The New England Historical and Genealogical Register* 155 (2001):3-35. Three Mansfield siblings arrived in Boston in the 1630s: John Mansfield; Elizabeth (Mansfield) Wilson, wife of Rev. John Wilson; and Anne (Mansfield) Keayne, wife of Robert Keayne. The three authors explore several of the genealogical ramifications of this family, including treatment of the father and paternal grandfather of these immigrants, and a convincing demonstration that John[2] Mansfield, son of John[1], removed to Windsor, Connecticut, and has left many descendants.

Johann Winsser, "Ann Burden, From Dissenting Puritan to Quaker 'Troubler'," *The New England Historical and Genealogical Register* 155 (2001):91-104. Winsser traces the full career of Ann (Soulby) Burden, wife of George[1] Burden of Boston. He focusses on her religious activities, which led from support of Anne Hutchinson in 1637 to her conversion to Quakerism. During the last two decades of her life she travelled widely in New England among Quaker communities.

Leslie Mahler, "The English Ancestry of Anne Tutty, Wife of Alexander[1] Knight and Robert[1] Whitman of Ipswich, Massachusetts: With the Ancestry of Benjamin[1] Ling and Ellis[1] Mew of New Haven, Connecticut, and Sarah[1] (Mew) Cooper of Southampton, Long Island," *The American Genealogist* 76 (2001):1-16. Building on earlier research by Henry FitzGilbert Waters and Thomas W. Cooper II, Mahler has extended the network of immigrants related to Anne Tutty and her half-brother Nathaniel Micklethwaite. Benjamin Lyng of Charlestown and New Haven was uncle of the half-blood, through his father, to the above two immigrants. Furthermore, through his mother, Benjamin Lyng was uncle of the half-blood to Ellis Mew of New Haven and Sarah (Mew) Cooper of Southampton.

Neil D. Thompson, "Hannah Fisher, First Wife of the Rev. George[2] Burroughs, Executed for Witchcraft in Salem, Massachusetts, 1692," *The American Genealogist* 76 (2001):17-19. Thompson has identified the first wife of George[2] Burroughs (Nathaniel[1]) as Hannah[3] Fisher, daughter of Joshua[2] Fisher (Joshua[1]).

Paul C. Reed and John C.B. Sharp, "The English Ancestry of Richard[1] Belden of Wethersfield, Connecticut, With an Account of the Death in England of Richard Baildon, Son of Sir Francis Baildon of Kippax, Yorkshire," and "With the Probable Ancestry of William[1] Belden of Wethersfield," *The American Genealogist* 76 (2001):20-28, 122-28. Reed and Sharp first demonstrate that Richard Belden, resident at

Wethersfield by 1641, had married at Heptonstall, Yorkshire, in 1622 and had six children baptized there. The authors then investigate the claim that this immigrant was the same as Richard Baildon, son of Sir Francis Baildon of Kippax, Yorkshire, concluding that this Richard was buried in 1630 at Sherburn, Yorkshire, and so was not available to be the immigrant to New England. Finally, they present evidence and arguments which suggest that Richard Belden of Wethersfield was brother of William Belden of the same place, and that these two men were sons of Lawrence Baildon of Heptonstall and grandsons of Richard Baildon of Gisburn, Yorkshire.

Neil D. Thompson, "The Baptism of Isaac[2] Nichols of Stratford, Connecticut," *The American Genealogist* 76 (2001):38. Supplementing his earlier article on Francis[1] Nichols [TAG 75:267-71], Thompson adds here the baptism of another child of this immigrant.

Todd A. Farmerie, "Disproof of a Novel Descent of Oliver[1] Mainwaring of New London, Connecticut, From King Edward III of England: Henry Holland, Duke of Exeter, and Robert Holland, 'Bastard of Exeter'," *The American Genealogist* 76 (2001):46-49. As part of an investigation of potential royal ancestry of Oliver Mainwaring, immigrant to New London, Connecticut, Farmerie examines one possible line of ancestry, through his maternal grandmother, Loveday Moyle, to Henry Holland, Duke of Exeter. The author shows that there are fatal chronological problems with this line of descent as published. He adds additional information on some of the illegitimate sons of Henry Holland.

Harry Macy, Jr., "The Family of Daniel[1] Whitehead: A Century and a Half of Fact and Fiction," *The New York Genealogical and Biographical Record* 131 (2000):263-75. Daniel Whitehead was an original proprietor of Hempstead in 1644. Using the recently discovered original of Whitehead's will as a springboard [NYGBR 118:154-55], Macy undertakes a detailed investigation of this immigrant. Whitehead's first wife was a daughter of Thomas Armitage of Hempstead and elsewhere [GM 2:1:76-81]; Macy demonstrates that his second wife was Jane Ireland, and not Jane Skidmore.

Examining a wide variety of records, including primary and secondary sources, and the private correspondence of some prominent genealogists, Macy addresses a number of problems. He compiles an accurate list of the children of Daniel Whitehead, and assigns them to one or the other of Daniel's wives. In the process, he explodes the theory that there were two unrelated Daniel Whiteheads, one in Hempstead and one in Huntington; they were the same man, the immigrant, Daniel Sr.

(continued from page 10)

In at least two cases, prominent men who were early settlers are known to have been residing elsewhere in 1655 and for some years before and after. William Brenton arrived in Boston by 1633, moved with the earliest settlers to Portsmouth in 1638, and then on to Newport in 1639. He then returned to Portsmouth by 1643, but after a few years there removed to Boston, where he is well documented from 1648 to 1657. He returned to Rhode Island by 1659, but to Newport and not to Portsmouth, and then made one last move to Taunton by 1670 [GMB 1:218-24].

Samuel Wilbore Senior made fewer moves than did William Brenton, but he too seems to have been elsewhere in 1655. Wilbore also arrived in Boston by 1633, and moved with the earliest settlers to Portsmouth in 1638. By 1648 Wilbore was residing in Taunton, and he died there in 1656 [GMB 3:1986-88].

The most important case for our current argument is Anthony Paine (published as "Arther Paine"). Like so many others, he arrived in Portsmouth in 1638, where he was recorded infrequently. He made his will in 1649, and was dead within a year [PoTR 384-86]. He had two daughters and no sons [Austin 144], so there was no Anthony Paine available to be in the 1655 list.

So far we have seen examples of men who were probably or certainly not in Portsmouth in 1655. Are there any who could not have been in Portsmouth until after 1655, or were not yet adults by that date? None have yet been found. Possible candidates would be sons of the immigrant generation. Samuel Wilbore Jr. is in the list, but he was clearly adult well before 1655 [PoTR 33], and he remained in Portsmouth long after his father left. Thomas and Francis Borden, two sons of Richard Borden, appear in the list, but they both served on a jury in 1648 [PoTR 37-38].

For Portsmouth, at least, we conclude that the list contains many names of men who had been freemen there at an earlier date, but not in 1655, and so appearance in the list does not guarantee residence in Portsmouth on that date. Whether the Portsmouth town clerk misunderstood his instructions, or the colony clerk unwittingly used an outdated list, we cannot tell. Detailed investigation of the other three towns might determine whether the problem lay with the colony or the towns.

Returning to our original problem with John Coggeshall, we have not carried out a detailed analysis of Newport, but if the same situation obtains with that town as with Portsmouth, we would conclude that John Coggeshall of the 1655 list was the immigrant, who died in 1647, and John Coggeshall Junior was his son.

Great Migration Study Project
101 Newbury Street
Boston, MA 02116-3007

Great Migration Newsletter

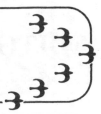

Vol. 10   July-September 2001   No. 3

THE HISTORIAN'S PERSPECTIVE

Although the primary motivation and the largest expected audience for the Great Migration Study Project has always been genealogical, there has from the beginning been a desire to make these sketches useful to academic historians interested in the social history of seventeenth-century New England. Progress on this front has been slow, but during the last year a number of monographs have appeared which refer in one way or another to Great Migration sketches. Three of these publications will be examined here, to determine the varieties of historical usage of our publications.

In the fall of 2000, James and Patricia Scott Deetz published *The Times of Their Lives: Life, Love, and Death in Plymouth Colony* (W.H. Freeman and Co., New York). (James Deetz, a prominent historical archaeologist who worked extensively both in New England and the Chesapeake, died on 25 November 2000, shortly after the book appeared.) The authors cover a variety of aspects of social life in Plymouth Colony, including both normative and deviant behavior. As one might expect, discussions of material objects and excavations of dwellings predominate.

The authors make explicit use of Great Migration sketches in a few places in the text. The most satisfying instance appears in a chapter which analyzes probate inventories, the first of which is from the estate of William Wright, who died in Plymouth in 1633. The Great Migration sketch for this immigrant took note of the many tools in his inventory, and suggested that he was a joiner, or a woodworker of some sort [GMB 3:2075-76]. Deetz and Deetz cite this sketch, noting that it "makes a convincing argument for Wright having been a joiner" [pp. 196-97].

Deetz and Deetz make use of two other sketches in their text, taking note of our characterization of Isaac Allerton and his activities [pp. 220-21], and of the estimate in the sketch of John Alden of the date of his move from Plymouth to Duxbury [p. 239].

Deetz and Deetz make more frequent, but less evident, use of the sketches in the notes at the end of the volume. On numerous occasions when the text refers to a particular Plymouth Colony inhabitant, the explanatory notes will refer directly to a particular sketch. For instance, the third chapter of the book opens with an imagined reconstruction of the last days of William Wright [pp. 82-84]. The supporting note states that "[t]he reconstruction is based on details contained in these documents as well as some biographical information concerning Priscilla Carpenter and Will Wright in … *The Great Migration Begins*" [p. 322].

In summary, Deetz and Deetz rely frequently on our volumes, and always do so by reference to specific sketches in support of textual comments on individual immigrant.

The second study we will examine is Roger Thompson's *Divided We Stand: Watertown, Massachusetts, 1630-1680* (University of Massachusetts Press: Amherst, Massachusetts, 2001). Building on his earlier studies on sexual behavior in Middlesex County and on immigration to New England from East Anglia, Thompson looks at the first fifty years of existence of Watertown, a Middlesex town settled mostly by East Anglians.

Thompson studies many aspects of the social life in this plantation, with sections on town government, land granting, the church, agriculture, welfare, and so on. He challenges claims of earlier historians that the local power structure was a self-perpetuating oligarchy of the elite.

(continued on page 18)

EDITOR'S EFFUSIONS

WHEN ALL ELSE FAILS, TRY SERENDIPITY

The most frustrating part of writing Great Migration sketches is the search for evidence in support of undocumented statements of fact. Much time is consumed in the latter stages of composing many sketches in attempting to track down the evidence for one marriage or death. Recently, we stumbled on a source which resolved a problem in a sketch which had already been completed. The most recently published volume includes the sketch of Henry Flint of Boston and Braintree [GM 2:2:534-37]. Henry Flint was a moderately prominent man, but there were a number of pieces of information which were not easily found.

Two of the younger children of Henry Flint were Seth and Ruth, born in Braintree but not found in later records. Savage tells us that "Seth d. at Dedham, 12 May 1673, being in his 2d yr. at H[arvard] C[ollege]; and Ruth d. next mo." [Savage 2:174]. The obvious places to search for the support for this statement were the Dedham vital records and the Harvard College records, but nothing relevant appeared in either of those places. Casting about in other likely sources, we did find in one of the annotated almanacs of Samuel Sewall these two entries: "1673 May 12. 3 (Tuesday) morning, Seth Flynt died" and "21.7. night, Ruth Flynt died" [NEHGR 7:205]. This was the best we could do at the time, but was clearly not Savage's source.

Current work on the sketch of John Hart of Ipswich led to the death notice of his remarried widow in the journal of Rev. William Adams of Dedham. And there, on the very next page, were the following items: "[May] 12. Mr. Seth Flint, student at Harvard Coll. In his second years standing, died at Dedham," and "[June] 19. Mrs. Ruth Flint died at Braintree a little before sunset" [MHSC 4:1:19, 20]. This points up again the great advantage of the Great Migration Study Project approach. By continually surveying and re-surveying all available records, we frequently come to solutions which we would not reach simply by focussing on one immigrant.

Robert Charles Anderson, FASG   Editor
Gabrielle Stone   Production Assistant

The Great Migration Newsletter is published quarterly by the Great Migration Study Project, a project of the New England Historic Genealogical Society, 101 Newbury Street, Boston MA 02116
www.newenglandancestors.org

The subscription rate for Volume 10 is $15.

(continued from page 17)

Thompson agrees that most of those who held the office of selectmen were from the upper reaches of Watertown's social strata. But he argues that these men were not returned to office repeatedly and automatically simply as a result of their social position. They had to earn the trust and respect of their neighbors, or they would be replaced by other members of the elite.

Thompson builds his study of Watertown on an intimate knowledge of each individual resident of Watertown. For the most part, Thompson has developed this depth of knowledge from his years of work in the Middlesex Court files and other contemporary sources. But many of his subjects are immigrants treated in the Great Migration volumes, and he also relies on these for support of his arguments.

One example of this use is in his description of kinship networks among the immigrant, such as the "Child-Bond-Warren-Goddard links," for which he cites both *The Great Migration Begins* and his own earlier work, *Mobility and Migration* [p. 209, fn. 15]. Another example may be found in his section on land, where virtually all of the "insider" grantees of the early farms have been treated in Great Migration sketches [p. 218, fn. 9].

In a few instances, Thompson uses the Great Migration data in a statistical rather than an individual manner. In his chapter on "The Family," he undertakes "[a]n analysis of recoverable ages of 134 marriages recorded … for Watertown people" in *The Great Migration Begins*, and presents the results in tabular form [p. 239, fn. 3].

Thompson's use of the Great Migration material differs somewhat from that of Deetz and Deetz. Whereas the Plymouth study focusses on one settler at a time, and so points to one sketch at a time, the Watertown book frequently treats people in small groups, whether as migrating "companies," or as classes of selectmen or other town officers. Even when examining groups of people, Thompson most frequently names the individuals involved in each of these groups, and so at least implicitly cites individual sketches. But in a few instances he also carries out statistical analyses, which bring together data from whole clumps of sketches.

Finally, we look at Gloria L. Main's *Peoples of a Spacious Land: Families and Cultures in Colonial New England* (Harvard University Press: Cambridge, Massachusetts, 2001). The scope of Main's work is broader than that of the other two works studied here. She examines the Native American culture into which the English moved, she covers much of New England, and she takes her analysis into the eighteenth century.

(continued on page 24)

Focus   *on*   *BRAINTREE*

BORN FROM BOSTON

All the towns we have studied so far in these Focus sections have been carved out of the wilderness, out of land which had not previously been part of an earlier town. As the number of settlers and the number of settlements increased, more and more towns were created by splitting up existing towns. Among the earliest of these was the separation of Braintree from Boston. Other early instances which we see in our period are the creation of Malden from Charlestown, and of Beverly from Salem. From the viewpoint of the writing of Great Migration sketches, one of the consequences of the creation of such towns is that we are not able to state even an approximate date of removal. The immigrant and his family did not move; rather, the town boundary was removed around them.

The area that would become Braintree, lying between Weymouth and Dorchester, was the scene of two interesting events before it was annexed to Boston. For nearly a decade before the arrival of the Winthrop Fleet, this was the site of Merrymount, Thomas Morton's headquarters for his decidedly non-Puritan activities, and one of the first tasks undertaken by Winthrop was to send Morton on his way [GMB 2:1299]. Then, in the summer of 1632, the "Braintree company, which had begun to sit down at Mount Wollaston, by order of court, removed to Newtown. These were Mr. Hooker's company" [WJ 1:104-5].

On 14 May 1634, the General Court "ordered that Boston shall have convenient enlargement at Mount Wooliston," and this order was repeated on 25 September 1634 [MBCR 1:119, 130]. Boston soon began making grants of land at Mount Wollaston, some very large grants to prominent residents, and many smaller grants to others [BTR 1:passim].

On 13 May 1640, the "petition of the inhabitants of Mount Woollaston was voted, & granted them to be a town according to the agreement with Boston ..., & the town is to be called Braintree" [MBCR 1:291].

Much of the land at Braintree was granted away by the town of Boston before or soon after the establishment of Braintree as a town, and so landholding records and the patterns of landholding there were somewhat different than for other early Massachusetts Bay towns. Because of the various interesting features of the town's vital records, discussed at length below, there is not space here to give the subject of land its usual due. A future Newsletter will take up the subjects of land granting and landholding in Braintree, and also the usual discussion of the establishment of various town institutions.

BRAINTREE CHURCH

The desire for a separate church at Braintree was first raised in September of 1636, but the authorities feared the damage that would be done to Boston by "the removal of so many chief men as would go thither," and nothing was done [WJ 1:233-34]. Very soon after this the problems in the Boston church revolving around Anne Hutchinson and Rev. John Wheelwright arose, and in late October of 1636, after discussion within Boston church, "the church gave way, that [Wheelwright] might be called to a new church, to be gathered at Mount Wollaston [WJ 1:241]. As the Antinomian Controversy deepened, in May of 1637, some prominent Bostonians "upon the day of the general fast, they went from Boston to keep the day at the Mount with Mr. Wheelwright" [WJ 1:267]. Less than a year later Wheelwright and his followers had been banished from Massachusetts Bay Colony, and there is no evidence that a church was properly organized at Mount Wollaston at this time [WJ 1:311].

After a hiatus of more than a year, a church was properly gathered on 7 September 1639. "Mount Wollaston had been formerly laid to Boston; but many poor men having lots assigned them there, and not able to use those lands and dwell still in Boston, they petitioned the town first to have a minister there, and after to have leave to gather a church there, which the town at length (upon some small composition) gave way unto. So, this day, they gathered a church after the usual manner, and chose one Mr. Tomson, a very gracious, sincere man, and Mr. Flint, a godly man also, their ministers" [WJ 1:376-77].

On 24 November 1639, "[o]ur brother James Mattocke was by the Church's silence licensed to be recommended to the Church at Mount Woolliston for the winter season" [BChR 26]. Then, on 16 February 1639/40, "these our brethren and sisters were recommended to the Church of Christ at Mount Wollystone, viz: Willyam Cheesbrough and Anne his wife, James Pennyman and Lydia his wife, Thomas Matson and Amye his wife, George Ruggle and Elizabeth his wife, Alexander Winchester, Richard Wright, Rachell the wife of Martin Saunders, Rachaell the wife of Francis Newcombe, and Thomas Mekins the younger" [BChR 27-28].

Rev. William Thompson and Rev. Henry Flint served this congregation for nearly three decades, Thompson dying in 1666 and Flint in 1668. They were succeeded in 1672 by Rev. Moses Fiske, and no records for the church prior to 1672 survive. This is frequently seen in early New England, and one wonders whether the earliest records for Braintree church are residing quietly in the attic of some descendant of Thompson or Flint.

EARLY VITAL RECORDS

The published vital records of Braintree commence with an informative title page:

Braintrey's Book of Records
Of
Births, Marriages & Deaths
Beginning in the year 1643

As first kept by Henry Addams
Then by Capt. Richard Brackett
Then by Jno. Mills
Then by Christopher Webb

and the list goes on, covering all clerks down to 1776 [BrVR 627].

The first original volume of Braintree vital records covers the period from 1643 to 1762 (with, as we shall see, some earlier records included) [BrVR 628-820], but some records for the years before 1643 were also collected separately, submitted to the county, and not included in the town book.

In 1644 most of the towns of the newly-erected Suffolk and Middlesex counties submitted to the county clerk a record of "who hath been born, & who hath died, since the first founding of their towns" [MBCR 2:15], resulting in the incorrectly named "Early Boston Records." As we have noted in an earlier issue of this Newsletter, most of the towns submitted records for events prior to 1 March 1643/4, and limited themselves to events which had actually occurred in that town, and to events pertaining to families which actually resided in the town on 1 March 1643/4 [GMN 2:17-18, 24]. Braintree was one of the towns which submitted records in this first round of county submissions [NEHGR 3:126-27, 247-48].

In our earlier discussion of these records, we used the apt example of George Ruggles, who first appears in the records of the Boston church, where he was admitted in November of 1633. He then had children baptized at this church on 8 December 1633, 3 January 1635/6 and 31 December 1637. Not long after this last baptism he moved to Braintree. In the Braintree section of the colony submission are listed children of George Ruggles born on 5 May 1640 and 15 February 1642/3. The children born to Ruggles in Boston do not appear in the Braintree records [GMB 3:1604-7].

For most of the towns preparing their vital records early in 1644, "the first founding of their towns" reaches back to the earliest European settlement at that location. But what does this mean for Braintree? Is it the date on which Boston was granted "enlargement at Mount Wooliston" (14 May 1634)? Or is it the date the church was gathered (17 September 1639)? Or is it the date on which the name of the town was changed to Braintree (13 May 1640)? Or did it vary from family to family, depending on when they actually moved from Boston proper to their grants at the Mount?

There are one hundred and five dated records in this first submission to the county, distributed year-by-year as follows: 1637 (1); 1638 (5), 1639 (5), 1640 (24), 1641 (24), 1642 (30) and 1643 (16). Of the five events in 1639 three occurred prior to the gathering of the church, and two after. Thus, only eight of the one hundred and five entries antecede the founding of the church.

For several of these eight exceptional cases, the first and only appearance in Boston town records is when they were granted a lot "at the Mount" on a date after the gathering of the Braintree church. Gregory Belcher received his grant 30 December 1639, and John Merchant, Henry Maudsley and Thomas Symons on 24 February 1639/40 [BTR 1:44, 49, 50]. Apparently, these families settled in Braintree before the establishment of the church and never resided in Boston proper, receiving their grant of Braintree land after the formation of the church.

The conclusion, then, is that for most families, and especially for those who had earlier resided in Boston, only births and deaths occurring after the founding of the Braintree church on 17 September 1639 were included in the Braintree submission. A few exceptions were made for families which had not come to Braintree from Boston. The consequence of this is that any births or deaths occurring prior to 17 September 1639 among these families which had earlier resided in Boston would not be recorded in either the Boston or Braintree records, or anywhere else, for that matter. (We can reject the possibility that all the Boston families moved to their lots precisely at the time the church was gathered; had there not been many families who had already removed, their would have been no need for the petition for a separate church.)

Fortunately, many of these families had had one or more of the parents admitted to Boston church, so many of these "unrecorded" births appear as baptisms in the Boston church. This was the case with George Ruggles, and we may here refine our analysis of his family to suggest that he probably made the move to the Mount well before 17 September 1639, but continued to have his children baptized at Boston until he was dismissed to the newly organized church at Braintree.

The only clear exception to this suggested resolution of the problem is James Penniman, who settled at Boston in 1631, had three children baptized at Boston before 1639, then had son Joseph whose birth was recorded at Braintree on 1 August 1639, and baptized at Boston on 29 September 1639, after which he was recommended from Boston to Braintree church on 16 February 1639/40 [GMB 3:1426-30]. Since the birth occurred so close to the critical date, this may denote nothing more than a clerical error.

We return now to the published first volume of Braintree vital records, as described briefly at the beginning of this section. We reproduced from the cover page of this volume the beginning of the list of town clerks, and we will attempt here to assign the appropriate pages of records to each of the first three clerks, whose total span of service encompasses much of the lifetime of the first generation of settlers. (We are limited to a certain extent in this effort, because the original pages of this volume have not been microfilmed, and so we are dependent totally on what is in print. As we shall see, the pages of this book as presented in print almost certainly do not reflect the original order of those pages.)

As a starting point, we note that Henry Adams was listed as clerk when this volume was initiated in 1643, an inaccurate statement. On 7 March 1643/4, "Peter Bracket is allowed clerk of the writs at Braintree" [MBCR 2:57], so it was presumably he who compiled the county submission at about this same time. But he apparently made no further records of vital events after this first burst of effort.

On 4 November 1646, "Henry Adams is appointed clerk of the writs, & one of the three men to end small causes in Braintree, in the room of Peter Bracket" [MBCR 2:165, 3:81]. No evidence of Peter Brackett holding this office appears in the first volume of vital records, and the earliest pages were entered by Henry Adams. On page 144 of the original we find "A Record of Burials in Brantry. Henry Adams Clerk," with only two entries, the death of his father-in-law Moses Paine on 2 June 1643, and of his own father, Henry Adams, on 8 October 1646 [p. 731 as published]. The first two deaths recorded on page 145, both in 1647, were entered by Henry Adams, but the remaining entries on that page, from 1651 on, were almost certainly entered by Richard Brackett. This change of office reflects the removal of Henry Adams to Medfield in 1650.

Original pages 3 through 6 [p. 628 as published] apparently incorporate all the births entered by Adams, a total of twenty-one for eight years, far fewer per year than for 1640, 1641 and 1642 in the county submission. Only a handful of marriages were entered by Adams, on pages 9 and 10, perhaps only his own marriage in 1643 [p. 629].

The clearest indication of the transition to Richard Brackett as town clerk is found on page 7, which is headed "Records of Births, Richard Brackett Clerk," which contains entries from 1649 to 1654 [p. 629]. This was the only page of births entered by Richard Brackett, and for this five-year period there are only fourteen births, again apparently an incomplete record. Brackett also inscribed a few marriages on page 9 and a few deaths on page 145 [pp. 629, 731].

For some of these items there is uncertainty as to whether Henry Adams or Richard Brackett actually entered the event; examination of the original might permit a correct assignment based on handwriting. This close examination of

who wrote what may seem overly nice, but both of these men failed to record many events that occurred in Braintree during their time in office, and it may eventually be useful to learn in detail the biases of each. As noted above, Henry Adams was careful to enter marriages and deaths within his own immediate family, and not much else.

With the coming of John Mills as clerk of the writs, the situation improved greatly. The heading on page 125 of the original says "John Mills Clerk, Records of Marriages, 6th mo. 10th. 1654 [10 August 1654]." The first marriage entered was that of his own son, John Mills Jr., on 26 April 1653. He then entered a few other earlier marriages from the early 1650s, after which he launches into regular entries over the next quarter-century [pp. 715-19]. In the middle of original page 126 is a new heading, representing a smooth transition of duties: "Christopher Webb, Clerk May 18th. 1678" [p. 719]. (John Mills died on 5 July 1678 [GMB 2:1259-62]).

The section on deaths commenced by Mills has a similar heading, with the same date of initiation. We find here some of the evidence that the original order of the pages has probably not been maintained. Mills begins the death section on original page 24, and continues on to page 25, packing the page very densely with entries [pp. 636-40]. The last entry on page 25 is for 1677, after which there is a jump to page 34, with two additional entries for 1677, and then the usual heading indicating that Christopher Webb had taken over the office [p. 656]. Eight pages (four leaves) of births intervene between these two sections of deaths maintained by Mills.

The situation with births under John Mills is more complicated. On original page 23 we find the following heading: "John Mills Clerk of the Writs for Braintree 6 mo. 10. Record of Births" [p. 635]. The year is omitted, but is clearly meant for 1654, as with the other sections. The rest of this page contains births dating back to 1648, and as late as 1657, sometimes with more than one entry for a given family. From the printed version, the continuation from this page is not absolutely certain, but a pattern emerges. Original pages 11, 13, 15, 16 and 19 contain birth records, many of which reach back as far as 1636, but none of which is later than 1657 [pp. 630-35]; we will have more to say about these pages momentarily.

Original page 26 seems to be a transitional page, as it begins with a birth in 1649, along with some others prior to 1654, but by the end of the page includes several records from 1658 [p. 641]. Original page 27 has births from 1659 and 1660 [pp. 641-43], after which there is an apparent gap, which is filled by a stray page which is apparently not part of this first volume, but is published here [pp. 818-19].

The birth records maintained by John Mills continue on original pages 28, 29, 30 and 31, with entries for the years

1662 through early 1678 [pp. 643-53]. Again, in the middle of original page 31 we find the expected header indicating the assumption of duties by Christopher Webb, with the year date given incorrectly as 1673, an error either by Webb himself or by the transcriber.

We now return to the earliest pages of births kept by John Mills. Remember that both of his predecessors were derelict in their duties, and many vital events went unrecorded between 1643 and 1654. Mills made a deliberate attempt to fill in the gaps left by Adams and Brackett.

As noted above, original page 23 was the first begun by Mills, and, as with his section of marriages, his first entry is the birth of one of his own grandchildren on 1 July 1654. Some records on this page are as late as 1657, with one as early as 1648. We get a taste on this page of what Mills was up to, for there are three consecutive births for children of Thomas and Jewell Grizell, in 1648, 1651 and 1653. Interestingly, Jewell had died not long before Mills took office, as his will was probated on 21 July 1654.

Original pages 11, 13, 15, 16 and 19 were apparently compiled all at one time, since they all reach back some years before Mills came to office, and they all end in 1657. Note that in each case Mills apparently wrote on only one side of a leaf, and neither he nor any later clerk used the blank reverse.

Mills took his duties so seriously that he assiduously gathered birth records family by family, going back as much as twenty years in some cases. On original page 11, after a partially defaced entry and a single birth to John and Mary Saunders, we find a series of family groupings. There are six births each for Moses and Elizabeth Paine (1646-1657), Francis Newcomb (1640-1654) and Daniel Shed (1647-1656). The page then concludes with a single entry for a child of David and Hannah Walsbee, born in 1655.

This pattern is repeated on original pages 13, 15, 16 and 19. It appears that Mills adopted for a while one of the standard New England formats, of grouping all family entries together, with two or three families per page. Did he begin these pages in 1654, and then make additions for births down to 1657? If so, examination of the original manuscript should show differences in the ink, and to a limited extent in the handwriting, from one entry to another within a given family.

Some support for this being the correct interpretation is found in the number of entries on each page. Original page 11 has twenty-one entries. Later pages maintained by Mills, which are arranged in chronological order rather than by family, have many more entries (103 on original page 28, for example). When recording births by family group, one has to leave an uncertain amount of blank space, which may or may not be used, whereas in the chronological format, there is no need to manage the space in this manner. Again, examination of the manuscript would be enlightening on this point.

Examination of the birth records for two of these families is revealing. On original page 15 we find four children born to "John Hoidon and Susanna his wife": Jonathan in 1640, Hannah in 1642, Ebenezer in 1645 and Nehemiah in 1647 [pp. 631-32]. This is John Hayden, who settled in Dorchester in 1632 and then moved to Braintree [GMB 2:890-93].

The first two of these children were also recorded many years earlier, in the county submission [NEHGR 3:127]. The third and fourth births occurred during the term of Henry Adams, but were not recorded by him or by Richard Brackett. Mills made the effort, then, to collect data from a family which had had its last child seven years before he took office. Note, however, that he adhered to the rules of the game, and did not include records for the three early Hayden children who must have been born in Dorchester.

On original page 19 Mills included records for seven children of "John Niles and Jane his wife," from 1636 (the earliest event recorded by Mills) to 1650. The first four of these births occurred within the period covered by the county submission, but were not included in that document. Like Hayden, John Niles first resided in Dorchester, apparently from 1634 to 1638 [DTR 7, 8, 30]. In this case, Mills slipped away from the accepted practice here, and included one or two events which did not occur in Braintree.

These first pages of births prepared by Mills are immensely valuable, and further analysis of them will be highly rewarding. After 1657, Mills settled down to straightforward chronological entry of Braintree births.

SOURCES FOR BRAINTREE

In 1878 William S. Pattee published a typical nineteenth-century town history, with the material arranged topically for the most part: *A History of Old Braintree and Quincy, with a Sketch of Randolph and Holbrook* (Quincy 1878).

In 1886 Samuel A. Bates edited *Records of the Town of Braintree: 1640 to 1793* (Randolph 1886). This has two sections, comprising the early town meeting records (which are very sparse for the earliest years) and the vital records discussed above.

Waldo Chamberlain Sprague compiled his *Genealogies of the Families of Braintree, Massachusetts: 1640-1850* on index cards, which for years have been available only at the New England Historic Genealogical Society. These genealogies are now conveniently available on CD-ROM, available for $39.99 (plus $1.50 shipping) from NEHGS Sales Dept., One Watson Place, Framingham MA 01701.

RECENT LITERATURE

Gordon L. Remington and Roberta Stokes Smith, "Thomas Clemence of Providence, Rhode Island, and Four Generations of His Descendants," *The New England Historical and Genealogical Register* 155 (2001):131-66. The authors have compiled a standard, five-generation agnate genealogy for Thomas Clemence, who arrived in Providence by 1647. Although this immigrant falls outside our usual range, he was closely related to Gregory Dexter, who had arrived in the same town by 1643.

Richard LeBaron Bowen, Jr., "Notes on George Allen of Weymouth and Sandwich," *The New England Historical and Genealogical Register* 155 (2001):212-14. The author offers some corrections to the sketch of George[1] Allen of Weymouth and Sandwich [GM 2:1:27-35].

John C. Brandon, "Genealogical Notes: Shepard of Taunton, Massachusetts," *The New England Historical and Genealogical Register* 155 (2001):215-16. Brandon demonstrates that William Shepard, son of John Shepard of Towcester, Northamptonshire, had died by 1653, and therefore could not be identical with William Shepard of Taunton.

Doris Schreiber Willcox, with David Willcox and Helga Andrews,"'One Wilson' - Servant of Thomas Beard: John Wilson and Mary (Wilson) Wheeler, Younger Children of William[1] and Patience (Grindall) (Trustram) Wilson of Boston," *The New England Historical and Genealogical Register* 155 (2001):217-24. The author explores a number of ramifications of the family of William[1] Wilson of Boston, and particularly of his son John, who is proposed to be the man of that name who married Hester (Chandler) Gage, and resided in Bristol, Rhode Island, and Elizabeth, New Jersey. In the course of her argument, Willcox provides the evidence that Philip[1] Fowler of Ipswich did have a daughter who married William Chandler of Newbury [EQC 5:20; GM 2:2:564].

Donald S. Kenney, "Martha Edwards, First Wife of William Cleaves of Beverly, Massachusetts: A Correction to Torrey's New England Marriages," *The New England Historical and Genealogical Register* 155 (2001):225-26. Kenney demonstrates conclusively that the first wife of William Cleaves of Beverly was not a daughter of Giles Corey, but was instead a daughter of Rice[1] Edwards, a resident of Wenham by 1642.

Leslie Mahler, "The English Origin of Jane (Galland) Paine, Wife of Thomas[1] Mayhew of Martha's Vineyard," *The American Genealogist* 76 (2001):94-98. Working from the clues long available from Lechford and Aspinwall, Mahler located the first marriage of the second wife of Thomas Mayhew. Building on this, he went on to identify her father

and grandfather, and found her baptism in Wantage, Berkshire.

Myrtle Stevens Hyde, "Another Downing Addendum," *The American Genealogist* 76 (2001):137. The author, in collaboration with Leslie Mahler, sets forth some adjustments to that portion of her Downing article which relates to John and Abigail[A] (Downing) Hill.

Thomas A. Foster, "Deficient Husbands: Manhood, Sexual Incapacity, and Male Marital Sexuality in Seventeenth-Century New England," *William and Mary Quarterly*, 3d Series, 56 (1999):723-44. The author argues that in Puritan New England marital intercourse was not promoted only for its procreative consequences, but also as a pleasurable activity. Pertinent data is drawn from several divorce cases, some of them involving children of Great Migration immigrants.

Michael G. Ditmore, "A Prophetess in Her Own Country: An Exegesis of Anne Hutchinson's 'Immediate Revelation'," *William and Mary Quarterly*, 3d Series, 57 (2000):349-92. Ditmore undertakes yet another interpretation of the climactic moment in the Antinomian Controversy, when Anne Hutchinson was being interrogated during her civil trial on 8 November 1637. To do this, he carries out a detailed examination of that portion of the trial record referred to as her confession of "immediate revelation." First, he analyzes the text of the confession carefully, taking note of how much of her discourse consists of direct quotations or paraphrases of Biblical passages. In addition to identifying these passages, he argues that Hutchinson depended on at least three different editions of the Bible: two versions of the Geneva Bible and one of the King James.

Second, Ditmore investigates the actual claims made by Hutchinson, and how they were received by the members of the court. He divides the confession into two parts, the first of which he believes was carefully prepared by Hutchinson in advance, and the second of which was more extemporaneous, in response to the questions of her inquisitors. Ditmore interprets the first part as cleaving closely to the teachings of her mentor, Rev. John Cotton, in that it maintained a close tie between Biblical text and personal revelation, and as such this portion of the confession was not threatening to the colony leaders. But in the second part of the confession, she revealed a mode of Biblical interpretation which was more immediate, and which was more inclined to erase the psychological boundary between the self and the Biblical prophets, than Winthrop and Dudley were willing to permit. This, Ditmore claims, is what Hutchinson revealed to those who were judging her, and this was her downfall.

(continued from page 18)

The core of Main's study is a series of four chapters on the family: "Sexuality, Courtship, and Marriage"; "Bearing and Losing Children"; "Childrearing and the Experience of Childhood"; and "Youth and Old Age." She makes her greatest use of Great Migration materials in these chapters.

As with Deetz and Deetz and with Thompson, Gloria Main uses Great Migration sketches to support her discussions of individual immigrants: Jeremy Adams (p. 258 [fn. 15]), Thomas Dudley (p. 261 [fn. 45]), and John Winthrop (p. 274 [fn. 44]).

Also as with Thompson, Main uses the full range of Great Migration sketches for making statistical statements, and indeed takes this usage even further. In her second chapter, "Newcomers," she compiles three tables, one on immigrant origins in England and two on occupations of the immigrants, in the latter two comparing Great Migration material with data from other sources [pp. 33-34].

Then, using information from many published genealogies and vital records, along with data in *The Great Migration Begins*, she creates a graph on "Seasonality of marriage in rural New England" [p. 81].

In summary, then, scholars of colonial social and family history have begun to find the work of the Great Migration Study Project useful, and are employing our sketches both singly and in bulk, to support detailed studies of individual immigrants, and broader statements about New England society in the seventeenth century.

All of this is very gratifying, of course, but also points out the burden of being as complete and as accurate as possible. As the Project has progressed, there have been modifications and improvements in what is included in the sketches. On a small scale, for example, greater attention has been paid to data on education, occupation and officeholding.

Also, with particular reference to the use of Great Migration sketches for drawing statistical conclusions, attempts are being made to make it easier for interested shcolars to find and extract the data, without detracting from the readability of the prose. In part this has been done by tightening up on the format in the biographical and genealogical sections of the sketches. The change to an underlying XML format has also helped in this regard.

We will continue to make improvements in the sketches we produce, in the scope of the sources consulted, in the way the material is presented, and in the analysis of the material.

Great Migration Study Project
101 Newbury Street
Boston, MA 02116-3007

NON-PROFIT ORG.
U.S. POSTAGE PAID
Burlington, VERMONT
Permit No. 579

Great Migration Newsletter

Vol. 10   October-December 2001   No. 4

THE MARSHAL AND THE MESSENGER

Both Plymouth and Massachusetts Bay began life as colonies with two levels of jurisdiction: colony and town. At each level there were officers of several varieties. In the towns the constable was the legal arm of the town and colony, delivering summonses and sequestering goods and lands because of debt. The colonies also needed officers to carry out similar duties. In Plymouth Colony this persons was initially called the messenger, and in Massachusetts Bay the marshal.

As the colonies grew, the need eventtually arose for an intermediary level of jurisdiction, the county, which came in 1643 in Massachusetts Bay and in 1685 in Plymouth Colony. The duties of the messenger and the marshall became largely based at the county level, and in the long run gave rise to the office of sheriff. We will take a brief look at the evolution of this office in Plymouth Colony in the seventeenth century.

On 1 January 1633/4, the Plymouth General Court appointed constables for the three plantations of Plymouth, Duxbury and Scituate. This record is sof great importance in many respects. First, it tells us just which towns were in existence at this date. Second, this is the first instance of a listing of the towns in the order of their founding, a practice which would continue throughout the life of the colony.

For our present purposes, the importance is that Christopher Wadsworth is chosen constable for Duxbury and Anthony Annable for Scituate, but "Josuah Pratt [is] chosen to the office of messenger & constable for Plymoth" [PCR 1:21]. This record does not describe the duties of the office, and does not make it explicit that this officer's jurisdiction was the entire colony and not just the town of Plymouth, but that would become clear in later records.

For the next two years the choice of constable for the town of Plymouth is not recorded, although those for the other two towns are, and no mention is made of the messenger. But on 3 January 1636/7 the choices for all three towns are given, and on 7 March 1636/7, these three men were sworn: "Josua Pratt was sworn the Messenger for the

whole government, and Constable for the town of New Plymouth; Edmond Chaundler, Constable, of Ducksburroug, sworn; James Cudworth, Constable of Scituate, sworn" [PCR 1:48, 54]. This arrangement was continued for another election cycle [PCR 1:80, 86].

On 4 December 1638, "Mr. John Holmes is sworn messenger for the whole government," and "Josua Pratt is sworn constable of Plymouth until June next, and the Court gives him the measuring of lands, and the sealing of weights and measures, and the fees due for the same" [PCR 1:105]. The Court does not state its reasons, but this record itself suggests two related reasons. First, Pratt as constable is given additional duties, which point forward to the creation of the administrative functions of the county system. These extra responsibilities would make it more difficult for him to carry out the core duties of the messenger. And so the Court had the opportunity to split the offices, and place them in the hands of two different men, so that the messenger answered only to the colony, and not to the town. (In 1986 Eugene A. Stratton prepared a detailed account of the life of John Holmes and of his agnate progeny to the fifth generation [NGSQ 74:83-110, 203-23].)

Problems immediately arose with the conduct of the office of messenger. The colony and the officer had obviously not agreed upon how the officer would be compensated, for on 5 March 1638/9, just four months after his appoint-

(continued on page 26)

EDITOR'S EFFUSIONS

This issue of the *Great Migration Newsletter* completes the tenth volume, forty issues, and thus presents an appropriate occasion for summing up what we believe we have accomplished in these pages.

The format and the content of the issues has been constant for these forty issues, with a few exceptions. We have filled the eight pages with four pages which Focus on a given town (although this has once or twice been more than four pages, and has occasionally been on some subject other than a given town), with a lead article of about two pages (which usually described a class of records or investigated some aspect of the methodology of the Great Migration Study Project), with a page of Recent Literature (which was occasionally more than a page, and sometimes summarized books as well as articles), and with half a page of the editor's maunderings (which might be on anything at all).

We like to believe that the Newsletter has fulfilled its primary mission of informing our readers about the Project and about the early years of New England, and we also wish to believe that our readers are occasionally entertained as well. And we are encouraged in these beliefs by the constancy of our many subscribers, far more subscribers than we had dreamed of at the inception of the Project.

We are certain that the work devoted to preparing the *Newsletter* has been of inestimable value to the research and writing of the Great Migration sketches, the very core of the Project. In this issue, for example, in the Focus section on Rowley, we study in great detail an early inventory of landholding in that town. Having finished this analysis, we are now able to utilize this document in more extensive and more creative ways than if we had simply opened the books and looked at the entries for Humphrey Reyner or Jane Brocklebank. This sort of added knowledge has enriched many of the Great Migration sketches.

There are about three dozen New England towns settled by 1645 which have not yet been treated in this *Newsletter*, and so there is much work yet to be done.

Robert Charles Anderson, FASG   Editor
Gabrielle Stone   Production Assistant

The Great Migration Newsletter is published quarterly by the Great Migration Study Project, a project of the New England Historic Genealogical Society, 101 Newbury Street, Boston MA 02116
www.newenglandancestors.org

The subscription rate for Volume 10 is $15.

(continued from page 25)

ment, "John Holmes, the messenger," was presented by the Plymouth grand jury "for taking five shillings for serving of a warrant" [PCR 1:118].

Finally, in early 1643, we get a clear view of what the messenger was supposed to be doing. On 3 January 1642/3, a Court of Assistants was held at Plymouth, and attached to the minutes of the court is a document headed "Mr. John Holmes, the Messenger's Account this Court" [PCR 2:51].

In this account, Holmes requests compensation of £10 8d., listing eleven items, which may be gathered into four categories. The first three entries are for his annual wages: "Remaining for the first year's wages," £1 6s. 8d.; "For the second year," 10s.; and "For the third year," £1 5s. 2d. We conclude that he received partial payments in each of these first three years of his service, but at the date of this accounting was owed some sums dating back to the time we was appointed messenger.

Three other items ask to have his travel expenses covered: "For his going to Taunton," £1; "For going to Sandwich," 10s.; and "For going to Scittuate," 10s. He must have made more than three official trips in the course of three years, and so again we assume that he had already been paid for some of his travel.

The third category of expenses involves the operation of the colony's prison: "For two bushels of corn to the prison," 6s.; "For a latch for the prison door," 6d.; and "For x weeks diet for Granger," £1. And, finally, two of the entries are for the marshal's payment for carrying out the punishment decreed by the Court: "For whipping 3 malefactors, &c.," £1 2s. 6d.; and "For executing Granger and viij beasts," £2 10s.

At this early stage of the development of the office, then, the messenger was not only serving summonses, but was acting as the jailer and executioner for the colony.

On 28 October 1645, the court issued a number of orders regarding the conduct of several offices, and among the orders was one that "the marshal shall have ijd. per shilling for gathering of fines, if they be not brought in by the parties themselves," and that "for correction by whipping, the marshal shall have 5s., in this manner to be paid by the offender, viz: ijs. vjd. for his imprisonment, & ijs. vjd. his releases" [PCR 2:93].

So, without any fanfare, the title for the office was changed from messenger to marshal, presumably in imitation of the more powerful colony to the north.

(continued on page 32)

Focus   *on*   *ROWLEY*

SETTLEMENT OF ROWLEY

The settlement of Rowley differed from that of earlier towns of Massachusetts Bay in a number of ways. One of the most interesting is that its preliminary name was not the name of the place in the native language, but the name of the leader of the settlement process.

On 2 December 1638, Gov. John Winthrop noted that "Ezekiel Rogers, son of Richard Rogers of Weathersfield in Essex, a worthy son of so worthy a father, [was] lying at Boston with some who came out of Yorkshire with him, where he had been a painful preacher many years" [WJ 1:334-35].

At a General Court on 13 March 1638/9, "Mr. Ezechi[el] Rogers, Mr. John Philips, & their company had granted them 8 miles every way into the country, where it may not trench upon other plantations already settled" [MBCR 1:253]. In April of 1639 Winthrop reported that "a plantation was begun between Ipswich and Newbury … there came over one Mr. Ezekiel Rogers …, and with him some twenty families, godly men, and most of them of good estate" [WJ 1:354-55]. This relatively narrow strip of land, wedged between Ipswich and Newbury, was not "8 miles every way into the country," and in fact included some tracts of land already granted to the adjoining towns.

On 4 September 1639, "Mr. Ezechi[el] Rogers plantation shall be called Rowley" [MBCR 1:271]. This simple statment is a tribute to the reputation and the skill of this minister.

On 13 May 1640, it is "declared, that Rowley bounds is to be 8 miles from their meeting house, in a straight line, & then a cross line diameter from Ipswich River to Merrimack River, where it doth not prejudice any former grant" [MBCR 1:292]. So the town did gets its eight miles, but only in one dimension. And even here there was an error, for on 7 October 1640 a further addition to the west had to be made [MBCR 1:305].

On 7 October 1640, William Bellingham, brother of Richard Bellingham, was appointed to take acknowledgement of deeds, there being no magistrate resident [MBCR 1:307].

The town wasted no time in being represented at the General Court. On 13 May 1640, Mr. Thomas Nelson, the leading layman at Rowley, represented the town. At the midyear General court, on 7 October 1640, Mr. Thomas Nelson and Francis Parret were the representatives, and on 2 June 1641, Maximilian Jewett and Matthew Boyes [MBCR 1:288, 301, 318].

ROWLEY CHURCH

In his entry of 2 December 1638, noted in the previous column, Winthrop described the desire of Ezekiel Rogers and his company to partake of communion with the Boston congregation. After much discussion, Rogers and his company then and there, in Boston, "entered a covenant together, to walk together in all the ordinances, etc." [WJ 1:335]. Winthrop then entered a follow-up note, a year out of chronological sequence, dated 3 December 1639: "Being settled at Rowley, they renewed their church covenant, and their call [blank] of Mr. Rogers to the office of pastor, according to the course of other churches, etc." [WJ 1:335]. One presumes that in the intervening year they carried on as a church body at Rowley, even though they had not yet taken all the canonical steps in the founding of a church in the New England Way.

Richard Rogers, father of Ezekiel, was one of the most renowned of the Puritan ministers in the late Elizabethan and early Jacobean period. He lectured at Wethersfield, Essex, and therefore was well known to all of the lay leaders of the Massachusetts Bay Company.

His son attended Christ's College, Cambridge, and in 1621 became rector at Rowley St. Peter, Yorkshire. In nearly two decades of his ministry there, he attracted many to his Puritan sermons, thus creating one of the strongest of the "ministerial companies" of immigrants, as described by Roger Thompson.

Perhaps the closer analogy to the manner in which Rowley was formed is the somewhat earlier town of Hingham, where virtually all the settlers of the New England town were from Hingham in Norfolk. Most of the Rowley settlers were from Rowley and vicinity. One of the most fruitful parishes for sending settlers to Rowley in New England was Holme-Upon-Spalding-Moor, no more than five or six miles away. In 1980 Walter Lee Sheppard Jr. published a very interesting article, "Ancestral Clues: Some Early Settlers of Rowley, Mass.," in which he mined the parish registers of this parish to find clues on the origins of seven Rowley families [NGSQ 68:9-14].

Rogers was such a strong personality that he did not always have during his lifetime a full partner in the ministry, as was the case in many other New England churches. Rogers died early in 1661, and his replacement did not enter office for four years. Following a pattern seen in other early churches, no records survive for the ministry of Ezekiel Rogers at Rowley. One wonders if there is a cache of Rogers papers somewhere, where this register is quietly lying.

EARLY LANDHOLDING

The earliest town records of Rowley are poorly preserved, and the manner in which they have been published has not been helpful. In 1894 Benjamin P. Mighill and George B. Blodgette published a volume entitled *The Early Records of the Town of Rowley, Massachusetts. 1639-1672. Being Volume One of the Printed Records of the Town*. (This has been reissued, combined with two other books of early Rowley records, one on church records and one on cemetery inscriptions, by Heritage Press under the title *Rowley Massachusetts Records: Town, Church & Cemetery*.)

Mighill and Blodgette tell us that

> The book used for recording the general affairs of the town of Rowley from 1638 to 1672 is much worn, mutilated, and nearly illegible, many leaves are missing, so that nothing remains of record before August, 1647. The printed copy begins on page 51.
>
> Another book, containing the record of the laying out of lands and division of fences, was begun in 1643. It appears herein on the first fifty pages and thence chronologically in connection with the first named record.
>
> There is a third book, styled "Book No. 1" of the town records, into which some matters from the first book have been imperfectly copied. Records therein, not found in the other two books, appear herein in proper order.

In other words, these two compilers have taken material from three volumes, already imperfect before they laid their editorial hands upon them, and have selected from and rearranged this material. Partly because of this dubious process, and partly because there is nothing else earlier than 1643, we will concentrate in this section on the material in the second of these source books, on the laying out of land and related matters.

Despite the reservations noted above, we will for the purposes of our present analysis take the material published in the first fifty pages, which appears to be a coherent whole, at face value. This section is headed as follows:

> The survey of the Town of Rowley taken the tenth of the eleventh Anno Domini 1643 by Mr. Thomas Nelson, Mr. Edward Carlton, Humphrey Reyner, Francis Parrat, appointed for that purpose by the freemen of the said Town who also are to register the several lots of all the inhabitants granted and laid out, and to leave thereof a copy with the Recorder of the Shire according to the order of the General Court.

This is, then, another instance of the category of records which we have encountered in many other Massachusetts Bay towns, and elsewhere in New England, called in other places the Book of Possessions or something similar. The date of the present record we take to be 10 January 1643/4, which is consistent with the statement that the document was to be submitted to the county recorder, the counties having been erected on 10 May 1643, with Rowley placed in Essex County.

Ostensibly, then, this compilation is a snapshot of Rowley landholding as of the stated date. As we look more closely, though, we will find that this is not the case.

The register is organized by the different types of land grants, rather than by the grantees, as we find in so many other similar records. The first section describes the houselots, followed by several sections on uplands, meadows and marshes. We will focus here on the first nine sections, which make up the first two-thirds of the register. In its latter sections, the grants are less well organized, and not so easy to interpret.

The first section, then, describes the houselots:

> A register of all the house lots in such several streets, as are formerly mentioned in the book.

The meaning of "formerly mentioned in the book" remains unexplained. There are in this section fifty-nine entries, laid out along only two streets, Bradford Street and Wethersfield Street.

The vast majority of these houselots are of two standard sizes, twenty-eight being of one acre and a half, and twenty-two being two acres. Of the remaining nine houselots, there is one of one acre, three of three acres, three of four acres and two of six acres. The usual New England arrangment applied here as well, in which the houselot carried with it the proprietorial right to further land grants in the town. As we follow through the various categories of land grants, we shall see how these differences in houselot size are reflected in the later grants.

The two largest grants were to Rev. Ezekiel Rogers, the founder of the town and first minister, and to Thomas Nelson, who was clearly the leading layman in town. The four-acre houselots were held by William Bellingham, Thomas Barker and Sebastian Brigham, and the three-acre houselots by Edward Carleton, Humphrey Reyner and Thomas Mighill. And the solitary one-ace lot was held by the widow Margaret Stanton.

These differences in lot sizes were, of course, intended to reflect and reward social and economic status. William Bellingham, for instance, was brother of one of the leading citizens of the colony, Richard Bellingham, a man who held colony office every year he resided in New England, and who was several times governor.

We should note, however, one peculiarity. A regular sign of social status was the designation of "Mr.," for those too grand to be called "Goodman" or nothing at all. But the use of "Mr." in these records is not consistently correlated with the size of the grant. For example, "Mr. Henry Sands" had a two-acre houselot, and never moved out of that level of grant, whereas Humphrey Reyner, with a three-acre houselot, and Sebastian Brigham, with a four-acre houselot, are never referred to in this document as "Mr." Perhaps the use of the term of respect indicates an earlier ranking, based on English background, whereas the size of the Rowley grants demonstrates the actual social, or, more likely, economic, power of these individuals in the New World.

After the houselots comes a grant of upland:

...A register of the first division of planting lots, in the several fields known by their several names above mentioned in the book.

Again we have an unexplained reference to an earlier book, or an earlier part of this book. There are two fields mentioned, Bradford Street Field and Northeast Field. In the first of these fields, most of the lots were contiguous with the grantee's houselot.

Of the fifty-nine houselot grantees, four received nothing in these planting lots: Hugh Chaplin, Margaret Stanton, Margery Shove and Thomas Miller. Hugh Chaplin continued to receive lots in later grants, while Thomas Miller was omitted for several grants.

The case of the two widows mentioned here is worth some special exploration. Margaret Stanton received no other grants, although she lived until 15 April 1646. Margery Shove, on the other hand, although omitted here, received lots in the next seven grants. There were three other widows in these lists, Jane Brocklebank, Constance Crosby and Jane Grant. The first two of these also received regular grants, both here among the planting lots and elsewhere, while Jane Grant received nothing after the first two. So the failure of Margaret Stanton to receive any further land, and her receipt of the only one-acre houselot in the first place, were not solely a consequence of her widowhood. The difference presumably was that the other four widows had children, whereas there is no evidence that Margaret Stanton was accompanied by any other family members.

Although there are some minor variations, in most cases the size of these planting lot grants was closely correlated with the size of the houselot. Of the twenty-eight recipients of one acre and a half houselots, twenty-two were granted planting lots of four acres and a half. Of the twenty-two two-acre houselots, four were given four acres and a half of planting ground, while fifteen had eight acres. (Perhaps this represents a further level of distinction within the group of two-acre grantees.) As we move up the socioeconomic ladder, we find that the three-acre houselots had twelve or thirteen acres of upland, and the four-acre houselots had thirteen, fourteen or fifteen acres. Finally, Ezekiel Rogers was granted twenty-one acres and Thomas Nelson twenty-four.

We come next to the first division of meadow land:

A register of the first division of fresh meadows ...

An interesting situation appears here. The list begins with fourteen grants, thirteen of which are for half an acre and one for one acre, all of these grants being made to proprietors who held houselots of an acre and a half. At other places in this division are an additional twelve one-acre grants to holders of the same size houselot. Then, at the end of this group of grants, nine of the thirteen who had earlier received half an acre were given an additional half an acre. The implication is that the lotlayers initially felt that half an acre was appropriate, or perhaps all that was available; but, as the laying out of these lots proceeded, the officials saw that the proportion was not right, or that there was more land available than had been initially thought, and so an adjustment was made.

With one exception, all those with two-acre houselots were given one acre and a quarter in this first grant of fresh meadow. The three-acre houselots received three acres, the four-acre houselots various parcels of three acres or more, and the six-acre houselots were given ten acres.

The fourth division of land moved on to salt marsh:

A register of the first division of salt marsh

In this instance, although a few of the houselots did not receive anything, the grants made were totally regular, with no variations. One acre and a half houselots received one acre; two acres received two acres; three acres received six, four acres received ten; and six acres received twenty.

A new wrinkle appears with this grant of salt marsh. Whereas the three previous grants had omitted a few names which held houselots, we find here the first instance of a new name appearing: John Smith was given two acres of salt marsh, which would indicate that he had somehow acquired a two-acre houselot. But this is not the case. At a much later point in this register, we find a series of four grants of land to this John Smith, including a houselot of an acre-and-a-half. This is our first hint that the register was not a snapshot of Rowley landholding at one date, but was an evolving document.

We will remark only briefly on the next five divisions which we are looking at here. There were two more grants of fresh meadow, two more grants of salt marsh, and an additional grant of upland. As with the earlier grants, the lot sizes were in general proportional to the size of the original houselot granted. For the most part, however, the grantees of one-acre-and-a-half houselots did not participate in the third division of fresh meadow or in the third division of salt marsh.

Having outlined the overall pattern of early landgranting in Rowley, we will now look at a few specific cases which will tell us more about this register as an evolving document. Our first case is that of William Bellingham, brother of Richard Bellingham of Boston. As we noted above, William was near the top of the social strata in Rowley, having received a four-acre houselot. His next grant was thirteen acres of upland (along with an extra three added on), after which his grants were very regular, and precisely attuned to what the other recipients of four-acre houselots were given: five acres in each of the three divisions of fresh meadow, ten acres in the second division of upland, and ten acres in the first and second divisions of salt marsh.

When we reach the last of the grants we are studying here, the third division of salt marsh, there is no entry for William Bellingham, but, at the appropriate place in the list, there is a grant of ten acres to Samuel Bellingham. When we look into the latter part of the register, we find no further references to William Bellingham, but there are additional grants to Samuel Bellingham.

William Bellingham died about 1643 (although the evidence for the date of his death is somewhat imprecise [EQC 2:400]), and left all his land to his nephew Samuel, son of Richard Bellingham. It would appear, then, that as soon as the estate passed from William to Samuel, the town began to record grants to the propriety to the new owner. If William did in fact die before 10 January 1643/4, the date of this register, then the entries do not present the landholder on that date, but the original grantee.

A second example is that of Thomas Crosby, who does not appear in the first six divisions we are studying here, but did receive one acre in the third division of fresh marsh, followed by grants of two acres in the second division of upland and two acres in the third division of salt marsh. Grants of this size would be consonant with a two-acre houselot.

This man was the father of Simon Crosby of Cambridge, who came to New England after his son, and resided for a while in Cambridge before moving to Rowley. Examination of the full list of grants shows that there was one and only one two-acre proprietor who ceased receiving grants at the same time that Thomas Crosby began receiving grants. This man was Henry Sands, who moved from Rowley to Boston early in the 1640s.

These two examples serve to reinforce our earlier impression that this register was a living document. The entries apparently show the original grantees of each lot. Further investigation of the entire document will be necessary to answer the more detailed questions we would like to ask. Does the register only include grants made prior to 10 January 1643/4, or does it include later grants? Since each type of land was granted separately, do we have enough information to date each of the grants, and reach a few years back into the history of Rowley?

Next, let us describe a few of the typical estates that would be built up for different levels of grantees in this system. For the holders of one acre and a half houselots, we will choose as an example Peter Cooper, whose collection of lots looked like this: houselot, one acre and a half; first upland division, four acres and a half; first and second fresh meadow divisions, one acre each; first and second salt marsh divisions, one acre each; and second upland division, 107 rods (which was slightly less that three-quarters of an acre).

A few other examples with precisely this distribution were John Burbank, Thomas Palmer and Hugh Smith. Then there were some with slight variations. John Dresser received only half an acre in the first fresh meadow grant, and Thomas Tenney received only four acres in the first planting ground division. Further investigation might reveal whether these variances are the result of real differences in the granting process, or defects in the record itself.

The most usual grouping of lands at the next rung up the ladder was a two-acre houselot, eight acres in the first division of upland and two acres in the second, an acre and a quarter in the first fresh division, and one acre each in the second and third divisions; and two acres in each of the three salt marsh divisions.

With the Bellingham sample we have seen what the four-acre houselot ended up with. Our last example will be Thomas Nelson, the leading layman in town: six-acre houselot; twenty-four acres in the first upland division and twenty in the second; ten acres in the first grant of fresh meadow, eight and a quarter acres in the second and eleven in the third; and twenty acres in the first salt marsh division, thirteen in the second and twenty in the third.

When we compare our findings here with what we have seen in other towns, we see many similarities, such as the usual spread of types of land based on agricultural usage, and the different treatment based on status. But there are also differences, first in the basic arrangment of the records, and then, by comparison with Watertown, for example, no apparent use of household size as a direct measure of lot sizes. The theme is constant, but the variations are endless.

SOURCES FOR ROWLEY

George Brainard Blodgette, comp., *Early Settlers of Rowley, Massachusetts: A Genealogical Record of the Families Who Settled in Rowley Before 1700 With Several Generations of Their Descendants* (1933; rpt. 1981).

Amos Everett Jewett and Emily Mabel Adams Jewett, *Rowley, Massachusetts: "Mr. Ezechi: Rogers Plantation"* (1946; rpt. 1986).

David Grayson Allen, *In English Ways: The Movement of Societies and the Transferal of English Local law and Custom to Massachusetts Bay in the Seventeenth Century* (1981). Based on detailed study of five towns: Rowley, Hingham, Newbury, Ipswich and Watertown.

RECENT LITERATURE

Leslie Mahler, "A Note on Sir Richard[1] Saltonstall of Watertown, Massachusetts," *The American Genealogist* 76 (2001):173. Mahler has found the baptism of one of Saltonstall's children in All Saints Barking, London, in 1628.

Neil D. Thompson, "The English Origin of John[1] Parker of Boston, Massachusetts," *The American Genealogist* 76 (2001):185-89. That John Parker, who came to New England in 1635 and settled in Boston, was from Marlborough, Wiltshire, has long been known from the passenger lists. Thompson now provides a number of entries from the registers of both Marlborough parishes which give us much more detail. We learn the baptismal date for the immigrant, and this also gives us the name of his father. These parish register entries also include the marriage of the immigrant and the baptisms of the first five children of this couple.

Leslie Mahler, "The Family Origin of Frances Brett, Mother of William[1] Pynchon of Roxbury and Springfield, Massachusetts," *The American Genealogist* 76 (2001):211-216. Building on previous knowledge about the mother of William Pynchon, Frances Brett, Mahler has unearthed more information on her family. He demonstrates that she was the daughter of John Brett of Broomfield, Essex, and his third wife, Isabel Brooke, and provides information on the siblings of Frances Brett.

Leslie Mahler, "The Baptism of Sarah, Daughter of the Rev. Thomas[1] Hooker of Hartford, Connecticut," *The American Genealogist* 76 (2001):216. The author has found that Sarah, the daughter of Rev. Thomas Hooker, was baptized in Broomfield, Essex.

David Jay Webber, "Major William[2] Bradford's Second Wife: Was She the Widow of Francis[2] Griswold?" *The New England Historical and Genealogical Register* 155 (2001):245-50. The identity of the second wife of Major William Bradford has long been a vexed question, with little evidence available bearing on the question. Webber has reopened the inquiry, and presents circumstantial evidence that she was the widow of Francis[2] Griswold (Edward[1]). This conclusion is intriguing and highly probable, but not fully proved.

Norbert R. Bankert, "More on the Identity of Abigail (Graves) Dibble, and Her Tragic Death and Suspicions of Witchcraft," *The New England Historical and Genealogical Register* 155 (2001):273-78. The author explores the death of the first wife of Samuel[3] Dibble (Thomas[2], Robert[1]), and provides the evidence that she was Abigail Graves, daughter of William Graves, who had arrived in Stamford by 1642, and later resided at Newtown on Long Island.

Gale Ion Harris, "Peter Brackett of Braintree and Boston, With Notes on his Daughter Sarah (Brackett) (Shaw) (Benjamin) Jimmerson," *The New England Historical and Genealogical Register* 155 (2001):279-94. Building on the work of three earlier genealogists, Harris first studies carefully the family of Peter[1] Brackett, who settled in Braintree by 1639. Harris demonstrates the Brackett had eleven children by two (and perhaps three) wives. The author then looks closely at daughter Sarah and her three husbands, and presents evidence on the seven children she had with the first two of these husbands.

Matthew Wood, "The Descendants of Timothy Wood of Long Island," *The New York Genealogical and Biographical Record* 132 (2001):37-45, 119-28, 186-94. In earlier work, this author has researched a number of connected families from Halifax, Yorkshire, and vicinity, among whom was Edmund[1] Wood, who appeared in New England in 1636 [NYGBR 120:1-9]. In the present multi-part article, Wood undertakes a detailed examination of Timothy Wood of Hempstead and Huntington, one of the sons of Edmund Wood, and traces his agnate progeny to the fifth generation.

Ann M. Little, "'Shoot That Rogue, for He Hath an Englishman's Coat On!': Cultural Cross-Dressing on the New England Frontier, 1620-1760," *The New England Quarterly* 74 (2001):238-73. The author ranges over the whole colonial period, addressing the question of the importance of cloth and clothing in the relationships between Europeans and Native Americans. Of direct interest to us are her discussions of some events in the Pequot War, and her reference to her own doctoral dissertation, which is based on a thorough examination of seventeenth century New Haven probate records.

James E. McWilliams, "Work, Family, and Economic Improvement in Late-Seventeenth-Century Massachusetts Bay: The Case of Joshua Buffum," *The New England Quarterly* 74 (2001):355-84. McWilliams has carried out a detailed analysis of the account book, covering the years from 1677 to 1705, of Joshua[2] Buffum, son of Robert[1] Buffum of Salem. After noting the early tribulations of Joshua Buffum as a Quaker, the author is able to describe in great detail the evolution of the occupational pursuits and the economic fortunes of Joshua and his family. In 1677, Joshua is employed largely as a common laborer, and the family is just barely surviving at a subsistence level. Thirty years later, Joshua has become a respected artisan, and his family is living very comfortably, even enjoying some luxuries. (A footnote unfortunately repeats the discredited Yorkshire ancestry of this family; the Buffums are known to be from Great Yarmouth, Norfolk [TAG 33:199-201].)

(continued from page 26)

On 3 June 1652, the court again addressed the problem of how this office was to be conducted. The office was finally divided, by the creation of the new office of undermarshal. Oaths of office for each of these positions were drafted, and from these documents we learn the details of the new division of labor.

The marshal is first to attend the courts, and in particular to be available to the governor. Second, this officer is to collect fines, serve attachments and "shall safely keep, as head marshall, all such persons as shall be committed to his custody by the government, Governor, or any of his Assistants" [PCR 3:11].

The duties of the undermarshal, as might be expected, were more limited: to attend the courts; to "readily execute and inflict all such censures and punishments as by authority of this present government shall be adjudged to be inflicted upon any delinquents and offenders"; and, as "underkeeper, or undermarshal, keep all such delinquents, and malefactors, and felons as shall be committed unto him" [PCR 3:12].

On the following day, 4 June 1652, "Lieutenant Samuell Nash was chosen and approved by the Court to serve in the office of chief marshal … and is to have for his wages 20 marks per annum, besides his ordinary fees allowed by the Court" [PCR 3:12]. (The timing of this appointment of a new marshal, and the splitting of the office, was probably determined by the death of John Holmes, as no certain record of him has been found later than 7 October 1651 [NGSQ 74:86].)

At the same court, "Thomas Savory is indented with by the court to serve in the office of undermarshal, or executioner … and is to have 20 nobles per annum, besides his ordinary fees allowed by the Court" [PCR 3:12]. (A mark was two-thirds of a pound, and a noble was one-third of a pound, so the undermarshal's wages were exactly half those of the marshal.)

Finally, the Court set out a schedule of fees, for serving an attachment, for serving an execution, and for several other actions, including a travel allowance of two pence per mile [PCR 2:12].

For the remainder of the existence of Plymouth Colony, these offices remained in effect, although additional deputy officers were created, as the population grew, and the creation of counties loomed in the near future. Eventually, the marshal would be transformed into the sheriff, much as we understand the office today.

Great Migration Study Project
101 Newbury Street
Boston, MA 02116-3007

INDEX OF SUBJECTS

INDEX OF PLACES

BINGHAM
   Anne (Fenton) 270
   Richard C. 270
   Thomas 270
BIRCHARDE
   Mary (---) 185
   Thomas 185
BIRD
   Prudence 187
BISCO
   Nathaniel 219, 220
BISHOP
   -- (Master) 243
   John 241
BLACKBORNE
   Walter 215
BLACKBURN
   [Walter] 185
BLACKETT
   Martha 204
BLACKLEECH
   -- (Mr.) 271
BLACKMAN
   Deliverance 255
   Hannah (Osborne) (Ashcraft)
      255
BLACKSTONE
   William 172
BLAISDALE/BLAISDELL
   Ralph 224, 260, 261
BLAKE 247
   Deborah (Everard) 295
   Dorothy (---) 187
   Francis E. 247
   Mary 187
   Nicholas 187
BLAKEMAN
   Adam 255
BLIGH
   Elizabeth (Stevens) 204
BLISS
   Jonathan 207
   Thomas 207
BLODGETTE
   George Brainard 324, 326
BLOIS
   Richard 220
BLOTT
   Mary 184
   Robert 200
BLOWER

Alice (Frost) 187, 215
   Thomas 187, 215
BOADE
   Anne (Dalton) (Rewse) 295
   Henry 295
BOBBITT
   Edward 245
BOCKSTRUCK
   Lloyd DeWitt 199
BONNEY
   Thomas 200
BORDEN
   Francis 312
   Richard 312
   Thomas 312
BOSTON
   Sarah see BARSTOW, Sarah
BOSVILE
   Elizabeth 279
BOSWORTH
   Jonathan 212
   Zaccheus 235
BOULTER
   Nathaniel 238
BOURNE
   Hannah (---) 205
   Nehemiah 205
BOWEN
   Richard LeBaron, Jr. 319
BOWES
   -- (Mr.) 192
BOWIS
   Elizabeth (---) 185
BOWMAN
   Robert E. 239
BOWNE
   John 242
BOYCE
   Eleanor (Plover) 231
   Joseph 231
BOYES/BOYSE
   Johanna (---) 185
   Mathew 185, 323
BOYKETT see BOYKIN
BOYKIN/BOYKETT
   Jarvis 164
   Nathaniel 164
BOYSE see BOYES
BOYSON
   Thomas 4
BOZWORTH

Mercy 204
BRABRICK
   John 220
BRACKENBURY
   William 309
BRACKET/BRACKETT
   Peter 317, 327
   Richard 316, 317, 318
   Sarah 327
BRADBURY
   Judith 262
   Mary (---) 262
   Thomas 260, 261, 262, 263
   Wymond 262
BRADFORD
   -- (---) (Griswold) 327
   Moses 206
   William 327
BRADISH
   James 279
   Robert 212, 279
BRADSTREET
   Humphrey 309
   Simon 186
BRANDON
   John C. 199, 223, 231, 239,
      255, 311, 319
BREMER
   Francis J. 215
BRENTON
   William/Willyam 204, 312
BRETT
   Frances 327
   Isabel (Brooke) 327
   John 327
BREWER
   Daniel 184
   Joanna (---) 184
BRIDGE
   Dorcas 277
   Dorcas (---) 277
   Elizabeth (---) 277
   John 212, 213, 216, 219, 277,
      278, 283
   Thomas 277
BRIDGES
   Edward 185
BRIDGHAM
   Elizabeth (Pounding) 204
   Jonathan 206
BRIGDEN

Thomas 200
BRIGGS
Hannah 207
Jonathan 245
Mary (---) 207
Richard 244
William 207, 244
BRIGHAM
Mercy (---) 280
Sebastian 324, 325
Thomas 280
BRISCO
-- (Mr.) 258
BROCKETT
John 164
BROCKLEBANK
Jane (---) 325
BROCKWAY
Hannah (Briggs) (Harris) 207
Wolston 207
BRONSON/BRUNSON
Isaac 199
John 199
Mary (Root) 199
Brook, Lord 171
BROOKE
Isabel 327
BROOKING
Elizabeth 204
BROOKS
Elis 271
BROTHERTON
Alice 207
BROUGIITON
William 220
BROWN/BROWNE
Abraham 186
Christian 260
Edmond 283
Francis 239
Hannah 186
Henry 260, 262
James 235
Mary 186
Mary (---) 232
Mary (Healy) 239
Nicholas 239
Robert 278
Thomas 239, 283, 285
William 232
BRYANT

Abigail 270
Abigail (Bryant) 270
Abigail (Shaw) 270
John 270
Stephen 270
BUCK
Roger 221
BUCKLEY/BULKELY
Eleanor 205
Ester/Hester
(Lockstone/Loxton/Luxton)
204, 205
Thomas 205
BUCKNALL
Roger 197
BUFFUM
Joshua 327
Robert 327
BUGBY
Judith (---) 184
Richard 184
BULGAR
Richard 236-238
BULKELEY
Grace (Chetwode) 255
BULKELY see BUCKLEY
BULL
Henry 185
Susanna (---) 234
Thomas 234, 271
BULLARD
George 220, 287
Grace (Bignett) 287
John 287
Robert 287
William 207, 287
BULLIEERE
Elis: (Brooks) 271
Julian 271
BULLIN
Joseph 308
BUMSTEAD
Hannah 204
Mary 204
Thomas 204
BUNDY
John 244
BUNKER
George 200
BUR
-- (Mrs.) 184

BURBANK
John 326
BURDEN
Ann (Soulby) 311
George 235, 311
BURDETT
George 173–174
BURGES/BURGESS
James 203, 206
BURKE
Anthony Hale 167
BURNA[M]
Anne 272
Tho: 272
BURNAP
Sarah 221
BURNELL
Cassandra 199
William 199
BURNHAM
Anna (Wright?) 247
Thomas 247
BURR
Abigail (Glover) 290
Daniel 290
Esther 230
Hannah 230
Jehu 184
Simon 230
BURRELL
[John] 185
Sarah (---) 185
BURROUGIIS
George 311
Hannah (Fisher) 311
Nathaniel 311
BURSLEY
John 238
BUSH
Sargent 47
Sargent, Jr. 303
BUSIEL
Alice E. 221
BUSWELL
Isaac 260
BUTLER
Sarah (Stone) 168
Thomas 168
William 212
BUTTERICK
William 221

COLDHAM
  Peter Wilson 33, 40, 183, 202, 208
COLE 239
  -- (Mr.) 133
  -- (Widow) 219, 220, 222
  Amias 59
  Daniel 287
  Elizabeth 233
  Gregory 306
  Isaac 200
  James 77, 103
  Job 199, 287
  John 260, 261, 271
  Mary (---) 184
  Mercy (Freeman) 287
  Mercy (Fuller) 287
  Rachel (Hart) 271
  Robert 83, 184
  Ryce 69
  Samuel 121, 199, 235
  William 235, 236, 238
COLEBOURNE see COLBORN
COLEMAN
  Frances (Albright) (Wells) 79, 87
  Thomas 79, 117
COLES see COLE
COLLICOTT
  Richard 30, 309
COLLIER
  Thomas 230
  William 77
COLLINS
  Edward 144
  Henry 47
COLT
  John 255
COLWELL
  Margaret (White) 231
COMBE
  Francis 199
COMINS
  John 247
COMPTON
  John 185, 235, 236, 303
COMSTOCK
  William 126
CONANT
  Christopher 119
  Jane 255

Roger 27, 52, 53, 59, 119, 143, 255
  Sarah (Horton) 119
CONKLIN
  Ananias 199
CONVERSE
  Allen 303
  Edward 87, 129, 247
  Esther (Champney) 14
  James 221
  Sarah (Parker) 247
COO see COE
COOKE
  Elizabeth (Haynes) 151
  George 212, 226
  John 77
  Joseph 151, 212, 226
  Margaret (---) 204
  Mary 151
  Richard 235
  Susanna 95
COOLE see also COLE
  William 236
COOLIDGE
  John 99
COOMBS
  John 199
COOPER
  John 7, 40, 81
  Peter 326
  Sarah (Mew) 47, 311
  Thomas 47, 119, 131, 134, 229, 231, 289
  Thomas W. 7, 23, 47, 81
  Thomas W., II 311
  William 61, 209
COPELAND
  Lawrence 235, 236
COQUILLETTE
  Daniel R. 143
CORBER
  Richard 192, 197
CORBIN
  John 65
COREY see CORY
CORLET
  Ammi Ruhamah 276, 277
  Barbara (---) 276
  Elijah 276
  Hephzibah 276, 277
  Rebeccah 276, 277

CORLISS
  George 31
CORNISH
  Thom[as] 238
CORNWALL
  Joane (---) 184
  William 182, 184
CORTEIS
  John 182
CORWIN
  Elizabeth (Herbert) (White) 187, 270
  George 187, 270
  Margaret (Shatswell) 187
  Matthias 187
CORY/COREY
  Anne (---) 55
  Giles 319
  John 55, 111
  Mary (Earle) 111
  William 55, 111
COSENS
  John 191
COSTELLO
  Margaret F. 2, 10, 18, 26
COTTA/COTTY
  Robert 52, 53
COTTON
  John 11, 44, 63, 66, 68, 70, 105, 135, 137, 163, 176, 186, 204, 213, 303, 308, 319
  Mary (Mainwaring) 7
  Richard 7
COTTY see COTTA
COURIER
  Richard 260
COYTMORE
  Martha (Rainsborough) 98, 104
  Thomas 104
COZENS
  Martha (Stanbury) 204
CRACKBONE
  -- (Mrs.) 144
  Benjamin 2
  Elizabeth (---) 2, 14
  Gilbert 2, 14, 144
  Grace 167
CRADDOCK/CRADOCK
  -- (Mr.) 89

340

Matthew 37
CRAFTS
Griffin 45, 46, 186
Samuel 186
Stephen 186
CRAIG
F. N. 103, 143, 254
CRAM/CRAME
John 236, 238
CRANE
Jasper 242
John 182
CRANMER
Leon E. 34
CRASE
Jos[eph] 192
CRAWFORD/CRAFORD
-- (Mr.) 153
CRAWLEY
[Thom]as 236
CRESSY
David 18, 71, 112
CRISPE
William 215
CROCKIT
Thomas 61
CROFTS
Alice (---) 184
Griffin 184
CROOKE
Samuel 175
Sarah (Risley) 175
CROSBY
Constance (---) 325
Simon 326
Thomas 326
CROSS
Robert 31
CROSSMAN
Robert 244
CROW/CROWE
-- (Mr.) 271
-- (Mrs.) 37, 190
John 37, 145, 190
CROWELL
-- (Mrs.) 37
Margaret (Knight) 31
CRUGOTT
James 89
CRUMP
Lydia 150

CUDWORTH
James 37, 38, 45, 128, 139,
140, 321
Ralph 82
CULVERWELL 143
Ezekiel 97
CUMMINGS
Abbott Lowell 247
Isaac 63
Richard 197, 198
CUMPTON see COMPTON
CURTIS
Ephraim 15
Mary (Tainter) 15
Samuel 199
Sarah (---) 184
Sarah (Salmon) (Edwards)
199
William 44, 129, 184, 309
CUSHING
Daniel 7, 227, 230, 234
Deborah 230
Lydia (Gilman) 230
CUSHMAN
Robert 23
Thomas 77
CUTLER
James 4, 5
CUTTANCE
Edward 209
CUTTER
Elizabeth (---) 270
Richard 221, 270
William 13
CUTTRISS
Henry 6
DADY
William 38, 190
DALTON
Anne 295
George 295
Philemon 99, 100, 119, 159,
295
Samuel 238
Sarah 295
Timothy 99, 100, 117, 118,
135, 295
DAMFORD
Richard 58
DANE
-- 55

DANFORTH
Nicholas 212
Samuel 45
Thomas 219, 220
DANIELS
William 61
DARNIL
William 61
DAVENPORT
Elizabeth 199
John 131, 163, 166, 199, 303
Richard 58, 121
DAVIE/DAVEY
Elizabeth 204, 205
DAVIES
-- (Bills) 154
Ephraim 154
DAVIS
Cicely (Tayer) 231
Dolor/Dollerd 212, 216, 223
James 231
John 235, 238
DAVIS, cont.
Nicholas 242
Walter Goodwin 39, 103, 171,
174, 191, 192, 197, 198,
218, 222
DAWES
Ambrose 204
Mary (Bumstead) 204
DAY
Mathew 219
Robert 24
DAYE
Dorothy 263
Joane (Morris) 263
Thomas 263
DEACON
Goodwife 206
DEAN
H. Clark 119
DEANE
Eleanor (Cogan) 119
John 243, 244
Samuel 141
Walter 119, 243
DEARBORN/DEARBARNE
Godfrey 118, 236
DEARING/DEARINGE
George 192
DEETZ

John 99
Steven 221
GAYLORD
  William 29, 257
GEARY
  Arthur 185
  [Francis] (---) 185
GEDNEY
  John 54
  Sarah (---) 54
GEE
  Ralph 61
GELDERSLEEVE/
    GILDERSLEEVE
  Richard 267, 268
GENERE see CHENERY
GENESON
  -- (Mr.) 160
GENISON
  Robert 220
GEORGE
  Dorothy 255
  John 31
GERNON 255
GERRISH/GERISH
  -- (Aunt) 206
  Ann 206
  Ann (Manning) 204
GIBBONS/GIBBONS
  Ambrose 30, 60, 61, 62, 173,
    176
  Edward 37
  Richard
GIBBS
  Giles 27, 257
  John 233
GIBSON
  Christopher 30
  Rebecca (Phippen) (Baldwin)
    (Prince) 205
GIDDINGS
  George 83
GILBERT
  Amy 125
  Benjamin 125
  Elizabeth (---) 125
  Gilbert 272
  John, Sr. 243
  Josiah 125
  Lydia (---) 95
  Nathaniel 221

Thomas 85, 95, 246
GILES
  Bridget (---) (Verry) 223
GILL
  Arthur 239
GILLETT
  Jonathan 1, 10
  Mary (Dolbiar) 1
GILMAN
  Charles 241
  Edward 229, 238
  John 238
  Lydia 230
GILREATH
  James 47
GILSON
  William 139, 140
GIRLING/GURLING
  Richard 212, 216
GLOVER
  Abigail 290
  Abigail (---) 290
  Anna 296
  Ellin (---) 290
  Hannah 289, 290
  Helen (---) 290
  Helena (---) 289
  Henry 289, 290, 296
  John 35, 206, 290, 296
  Mary 289
  Mercy 290
  Ralph 17, 35, 90, 160
  Sarah 290
GLYMAN see GILMAN
GOADE
  Abigail 263
  Abigail (Downing) 263
GOBLE
  Thomas 219
GODBOLD 215, 303
GODFREY
  Edward 60
  Richard 245
GODSOME
  Francis 21
GOFFE
  Edward 276
GOLLOP see GALLOP
GOODALE
  Richard 260
GOODENOW/GOODNER

Edmund 222, 283
  John 285
GOODMAN
  -- 12
GOODNER see GOODENOW
GOODRICH
  William 126
GOODWIN
  -- 12
  Elizabeth (Clesby) 204
  Susanna (Garbrand) (Hooker)
    295
  William 11, 93, 212, 295
GOODYEAR/GOODYEARE
  Moses/Moyses 191
GOOKIN
  Daniel 275
GOOSE
  William 287
GORE
  John 135, 185
  Rhoda (---) 135, 185
GORGES
  -- 57
  Ferdinando (Sir) 59, 60, 61,
    62, 171, 173, 176
  Robert 59, 155
GORTON
  Samuel 143, 291
GOSMER
  John 132
GOSSE
  John 151
  Phebe 151
  Phebe (---) 151
GOTT
  Charles 52
  Deborah 52
GOTTFRIED
  Marion H. 9
GOUGE
  William 21
GOULD
  Christopher 73
  Daniell 306
  Rachell (Beake) 73
GOULDING
  William 242
GOULDTHWAIGHT
  Thomas 184
GRAFTON

Joseph 230, 287
GRAGG
Larry D. 127
GRANGER
-- 322
GRANT
-- (Mr.) 66
Abigail 6
Christopher 6
Jane (---) 325
Joshua 6
Mary (---) 6
Matthew 299, 300, 301, 302
GRANTHAM
Alice 39
Walter 39
GRAVES
-- (Mr.) 160, 210
Abigail 327
John 44, 185
Thomas 89
William 148, 327
GRAY
Joseph 245
GREELEY
Andrew 260
GREEN/GREENE
Bartholomew 213, 277
David L. 55, 119, 207, 223, 255
Deborah 294
Elisha 294
Elizabeth (---) 277
James 294
James, Jr. 294
John 35, 36, 189, 200, 291, 294
Mary (Fones) 294
[Mary?] (Widow) 185
Peter 291, 294
Peter 294
Richard 294
Samuel 213
Sarah 277, 294
Thomas 293, 294
GREENAWAY/GREENWAY 263
John 263
Mary 303
GREENFIELD
Samuel 238

GREENHILL
Samuel 212
GREENLEAF
Enoch 260
GREENWAY see
    GREENAWAY
GREET
John 207
Mary (Hart) 207
GREVILLE
Dorothy 279
Elizabeth (Willoughby) 279
Fulke 279
GRIDLEY
Richard 69, 235
GRIGGS
-- 7, 23
George 40
[Thomas] 182, 185
GRINDALL
Patience 319
GRINNELL
Matthew 103
Rose (French) 103
GRISWOLD
Edward 327
Francis 327
GRIZELL
Jewell (---) 318
Thomas 318
GROSS
Isaac 235, 236, 237, 279
Simon 279
GROVER
Edmund 186
James 242
John 186
Prudence (---) 186
GROVES
Elizabeth (Brooking) 204
GROW
Matthew J. 175
GRUBB
Farley 7
GULL
Ann (---) 231
William 231
GUNDISON
Hugh 235
GUNN
Jasper 185

GURA
Philip F. 143
GURLING see GIRLING
GURNELL
John 167
GUY
Jane 219
Jane (---) (Tainter) 15
Nicholas 15
HACKET
Jabez 244
HACKLETON
Hannah (Wakeman) 215
HADDON
Jarret 260
HAFFIELD
Richard 83
HAGBOURNE
Katteren 185
Samuel 185
HAINES
Richard 188
Samuel 218, 224
William 188
HALE
Thomas 159, 184
HALL
Elizabeth 245
John 260, 261, 309, 310
Nicholas 245
Ralph 219, 220, 236, 238
Rebecca (Swaine) 260
Samuel 244, 245, 260, 262
Sarah (---) 260
HALSTEAD 268
HAM
William 197, 198
HAMBY
Katherine 55
HAMLIN
-- 7
HAMMANT
Willyam 264
HAMMOND
Elizabeth (Bartram) 175
Lawrence 220
Marjery (---) 184
Sarah 39
Thomas 229
William 39, 199
William, Sr. 175

347

HANNUM
    Honor (Capen) 73, 74
    William 73
HANSEN
    Charles M. 103
    James L. 151
HANSON
    Robert Brand 100, 101
HAPGOOD
    Joan (Scullard) 187
    Shadrack 187
    Thomas 187
HARBETTLE
    Dorothy 185
HARCUTT
    Richard 293
HARDY
    John 54
    Thomas 31, 83
HARKER
    Margaret 159
    Miles 159
    Ralph 159
    William 131
HARKES
    Garbrand 295
HARLAKENDEN 31
    Elizabeth (Bosvile) 279
    Roger 212, 226
HARLOW
    Robert 158
HARMAN
    Francis 232
    John 232
    Sarah 232
HARRIMAN
    John 187
    Leonard 187
    Matthew 187
HARRIS
    Gale Ion 7, 79, 95, 135, 151,
        167, 175, 187, 199, 207,
        215, 247, 255, 270, 271,
        279, 327
    Hannah (Briggs) 207
    James 279
    John 207
    Sarah (?Eliot) 279
HARRISON
    Hannah 204
    Joan 167

John 260
William 232
HART/HARTE
    -- 12
    Charity 207
    Edmund 167, 186, 207
    Experience 167
    Frederick C., Jr. 166, 187,
        215
    John 314
    Mary 207
    Rachel 271
    Stephen 212, 271
HARVEY
    Joane (Hucker) 243
    William 243
HARWOOD
    Henry 35, 153, 309
    Mary (Woodward) 203, 204
    Rachel (Woodward) 203, 204
HASLAM
    Patricia L. 270
HASTINGS
    Samuel 221
    Thomas 4, 5
HATCH
    Mary 55
    Thomas 29, 55
HATCHER
    Patricia Law 159, 178, 179,
        210, 239, 255, 263, 275,
        306
HATHERLEY
    Timothy 65, 77, 139, 140,
        141, 143
HATHORNE
    William 257
HAUGH/HAUGHE/HOUGH
    Atherton 36, 66, 95, 219, 222
HAUKIN see HAWKINS
HAUPTMAN
    Laurence M. 39
HAUTE
    Joan (Wydevill) 103
    Margaret (Berwick) 103
    William 103
HAUXWORTH/
    HAUXWORTHS
    -- (Widow) 262
    Thomas 260
HAVEN

Samuel F. 62
HAVENZ
    W. T. 109
HAWARD
    Henry 181
HAWKINS
    -- (Goody) 220
    Narias 192, 197, 198, 201
    Robert 200
    Thomas (Capt.) 207
HAY
    Edith Carman 41
HAYDEN
    Ebenezer 318
    Hannah 318
    Jabez H. 299
    James 200
    John 318
    Jonathan 318
    Nehemiah 318
    Susanna (---) 318
HAYNES/HAYNE
    Elizabeth 151
    John 11, 12, 66, 130, 133,
        151, 211
    Mary (Thornton) 151
    Walter 283
HAYWARD see also HOWARD
    Margery 135
HAZARD
    Thomas 308
HEALY
    Grace (---) 276
    Mary 239
    Nathaniel 276
    William 276
HEARD
    Luke 260
HEARST
    William Randolph 235
HEATH
    Agnes (Cheney) 167
    Bartholomew 31
    Isaac 44, 45, 46, 87, 167, 185
    Mary 87
    Mary (---) 184
    Peleg 46
    Prudence 87
    William 44, 45, 46, 87, 129,
        167, 184, 309
HEATON

Edmund S. 14, 20, 137, 308
Marshall 292
MORIARTY
George Andrews 88
MORIS
Richard 236
MORISON
Samuel Eliot 75, 78, 134, 141, 157, 213
MORRILL/MORRELL
Abraham 13, 213, 260, 262
Isaac 44, 184
Sarah (---) 184
MORRIS
Ann (Holyoke) 103
Edward 87
Elizabeth 87
Joane 263
Lenora (---) 237
Mary 103
Prudence (Heath) 87
Richard 41, 237
MORSE
Jeremiah 221
John 204
Jonathan 308
Joseph 86, 102
Margaret 101
Obediah 308
Samuel 99, 101, 102, 308
Thomas 101, 308
MORTON
Thomas 59, 61, 103, 155, 171, 173, 315
MOSLEY
Mary 105
MOSSE
Anthony 117
MOTLEY see MATTLE
MOTT
Adam 185
Sarah (---) 185
MOULTHROP
Jane (Nicholl) 255
Mathew 255
MOULTON
-- 111
Abigail (Goade) 263
Dorothy 167
Elizabeth 111
James 31, 54

MOULTON, cont.
Joy Wade 31
Robert 26, 79, 167, 189, 190, 263
Thomas 116
MOUSALL
Ralph 26
MOW
John 109
MOXON
Henry 147
MOYCE
Joseph 260
MOYLE
Loveday 311
MUNDAY see MONDAY
MUNDIE see MONDAY
MUNN
Benjamin 94
MURRAY
Laura J. 287
MUSSEY
Abraham 84
John 84
Robert 83, 84, 85, 310
MUST/MUSTE
Edward 11, 12
Hester (---) 12, 212
MYCALL
James 287
Mary (Farr) 287
MYERS
Marya 207
MYGATE
Joseph 24
NAMIER
Lewis 284
NANEY
[Katherine] 204
NASH
Alice (---) 207
James 207
Rebecca (Stone) 168
Samuell 328
NAYLOR
[Katherine] (Naney) 204
NEAL/NEALE
Walter 60, 61, 62
NEEDHAM/NEEDOME
-- (Brother) 206
Ann (Potter) 231

Anthony 231
Nicholas 235, 236
NELSON
Dorothy (Stapleton) 143
Thomas 143, 259, 323, 324, 325, 326
NEWALL see NEWHALL
NEWBERRY/NEWBURY
Thomas 27, 28, 257
NEWCOMB/NEWCOMBE
Francis 315, 318
Rachaell (---) 315
NEWELL
Abraham 181, 185
Fayth 181
Francis (---) 181, 185
Grace 181
Margaret E. 167
Ruth 181
NEWGATE
Anne (---) 69
John 69
NEWHALL
-- 23
Anthony 47, 81, 231
Elizabeth 47
Thomas 47, 81, 231, 247
NEWMAN
Ann 181
Samuel 157, 158
Simon P. 63
NEWTON
Anne (---) 286
Anthony 15
Hannah 15
Joan 15
John 286, 309
Richard 7, 286
Roger 15
NICHOLL
Dorothy (George) 255
Ellen 255
Jane 255
Thomas 255
NICHOLS
Barbara J. 119
Francis 119, 287, 303, 311
Isaac 311
Phebe (---) (Gosse) 151
Robert 151
NICHOLSON

Cassandra (Burnell) 199
Lawrence 199
SOWARD *see* SEWARD
SOWL
LeRoy W. 159
SPARROWHAWK
Nathaniel 276
SPENCER/SPENSER
Elizabeth 161
John 41, 42, 83, 115, 310
Michael 220, 222
Thomas 12
William 12, 13, 42, 48, 94,
161, 212, 213, 214, 309
SPICER
Samuel 242
SPISOR
Christian 185
SPRAGUE
-- 27, 35, 60
Ralph 42, 69, 189, 190
Waldo Chamberlain 318
William 186
SPRING
John 220
SQUIRE
John 205
Margaret 127
Thomas 38
STACKPOLE
Everett S. 60
STANBOROUGH
-- (Mr.) 133
STANBURY
Martha 204
STANDISH
Myles 57
STANDLAKE
Mary 168
Richard 168
STANFORD
Thomas 239
STANLEY
John 154
Ruth 154
Thomas 154
Timothy 154
STANTON
Margaret (---) 324, 325
Robert 108
STANYAN

Anthony 238
STAPLE
Geofrey 156
Martha 156
STAPLES
Joseph 245
STAPLETON
Dorothy 143
Philip 143
STARES
Thomas 208
STARR
Frank Farnsworth 92, 93
STEARNS
Isaac 3, 168, 220
John/Jno. 168
Sarah (Mixer) 168
STEBBING/STEBINGE
Edward 212, 213
STEBBINS
-- 12
Edmund 11
John 46
STEBINGE see STEBBING
STEDMAN
Isaac 140, 151
John 144, 221
STEELE
George 12
John 11, 12, 212
STEINER
Bernard C. 114
STENTON
Anne 270
Sterling, Earl of 131, 132
STERNS *see* STEARNS
STETSON
Benjamin 215
Joseph 215
Robert 215
Thomas 215
William 221
STEVENS
Elizabeth 204
John 260
STEWARD
Scott C. 303
STICKLAN *see*
STRICKLAND
STILEMAN
Elias 52, 53

STILES
Francis 208, 209
Henry R. 123, 124
STOCKBRIDGE
John 106, 146
STOCKER
Thomas 47
STOCKING
George 212
STOCKTON
Prudence 111
STONE
Elizabeth 63, 168
Gregoroy 5, 6, 63
Gregory 214, 219
John 87, 285
Mary 168
Rebecca 168
Samuel 11, 66, 91, 92, 168,
176, 211, 212, 276
Sarah 168
STOR/STORRE
Augustine 235, 236
Susannah (Hutchinson) 236
STOTT
Clifford L. 127, 135, 159,
167, 175, 187, 215, 231,
247, 270, 287
STOUGHTON
-- (Rev.) 10
[Elizabeth] 223
Elizabeth (---) 82
Israel 16, 29, 38, 42, 64, 82,
223, 257
John 38, 82, 128
Margaret (Baret) (Huntington)
128
Thomas 16, 38, 82, 128, 223
STOUT
Richard 242
STOW
Elizabeth (---) 185
John 185
STOWERS
John 5
STRANGE
Lott 110
Mary (---) 110
STRATTON
Eugene A. 75, 78, 321
John 220

Samuel 119, 219, 221
STREAME
-- (Widow) 158
STREATE
-- (Master) 243
STRICKLAND/STICKLAN/
    STICKLAND
John 124, 134
STRONG
John 27, 119, 243
STRUTT
-- 39
STUBBS
Joshua 220
SUTTON
Richard 46
SWADDOCK
Ann 31
John 31
SWADDON
Philip 173
SWAIN
William 123
SWAINE/SWAYNE
Francis 238
Mary 185
Nicholas 238
Rebecca 260
Richard 116, 270
SWAN
John 221
SWAYNE see SWAINE
SWEET
James 294
SWIFT
Elizabeth (Capen) 73
Thomas 27, 73
SYLVESTER
Nathaniel 242
Richard 14, 17, 29
SYMMES
Zachariah 188
SYMMONS
John 197
SYMONDES
Samuel 238
SYMONDS
Mark 255
Rebecca (Swaine) (Hall)
    (Biley) (Worcester) 260
Samuel 167, 260

SYMONS
Thomas 316
TABER/TABOR
Elizabeth (Tillinghast) 223
Hannah (---) 223
Joseph 223
Lydia 223
Philip 223
TAINTER
Jane (---) 15
Joseph 15, 220
Mary 15
Mary (Eire) 15
TALBOT
Jared 244
Moses 173
TALBY
Difficulty 52
John 52
TALCOTT/TAYLCOTT
John 11, 94, 130, 212, 213
Mary (Cooke) 151
TALMAGE
[Elizabeth] (---) 184
William 184
TANNENBAUM
Rebecca J. 199
TAPP
Edmund 166, 207
TAPPAN
Andrew 241
TARBOX
William 218, 224, 240
TATMAN
John 184
TAYER see THAYER
TAYLOR
-- (Capt.) 217
Elizabeth (Davie/Davey) 204,
    205
Gregory 8
John 234
Richard 205
TEDD
John 238
TEDDER
Stephen 173
TEFFT
John 95
William 95
TEMPLE

Richard 219
TENNEY
Elizabeth 239
Thomas 215, 326
William 215
TERRY
Stephen 1, 10, 300
THATCHER
Anthony 146, 240
Hannah (---) 278
Samuel 278
Thomas 157, 218, 240
THAYER
Cicely 231
Richard 231
Thomas 231
THEALE
Nicholas 8
THISTLETHWAITE
Frank 18
THOMAS
Elizabeth 175
M. Halsey 122
THOMPSON
Amias (Cole) 59
David 30, 59, 60
John/Jo: 119, 126
Neil D. 7, 103, 223, 255, 263,
    303, 311, 327
Roger 81, 87, 183, 222, 279,
    288, 313, 314, 320, 323
William 315
THOMSON
David 119, 171
James 255
John 119
THORNDALE
William 50, 135
THORNDIKE
Francis 303
John 303
Nicholas 303
THORNEDICKE
-- (Mr.) 83
THORNTON
Anne (Smith) 151
John Wingate 198
Mary 151
Robert 151
THORP
John 90

Henry 68, 225
VAN LAER
   Arnold J. F. 131
VASSALL/VASSAILE
   Anna (---) 185
   Judith 186
   William 39, 140, 141, 146,
      186
VAUGHN
   Alden T. 37
   George 62
VELKE
   Bob 278
VENNARD
   Christopher 216
VEREN
   Philip 52, 53
VERRAL
   Christopher 295
VERRY
   Bridget (---) 223
VINALL
   Mary 142
   Steven 142
VINES
   Richard 191
VIVION/VYVION
   John 197, 198
WADE
   Richard 298
WADSWORTH
   -- 12, 130
   -- (Mr.) 271
   Christopher 77, 186, 246, 321
   William 11, 129
WAIT
   Gamaliel 70, 103
   Grace 70
   Margaret (Carter) 103
   Moses 70
   Samuel 70
   Thomas 103
WAITE
   Deborah 204
   Richard 235
   Tho[mas] 306
WAKEFIELD
   Robert S. 76, 79, 103, 111,
      116, 143, 151, 175, 199,
      223
   William 116

WAKELEY/WAKELY/
   WAKELIE
   Thomas 228, 229
WAKEMAN
   Elizabeth (---) 184
   Hannah 215
   Samuel/Samuell 26, 184, 215
WALDEGRAVE/WALGRAVE
   -- (Mr.) 283, 284
   Jemima 284
   Thomas 284
WALDERNE
   Richard 238
WALDRON
   -- 235
WALES
   Nathaniel 217
WALGRAVE see
      WALDEGRAVE
WALKER
   George Leon 92
   John 184
   [Katherine] (---) 184
   Samuel/Samuell 236, 238
WALL
   James 176, 235, 236, 238
   Robert Emmet, Jr. 229
WALLEN
   Joyce (---) 79
   Mary 79
   Ralph 79, 231
WALLER
   -- 127
WALLES
   James 236
WALLING
   Margaret (White) (Colwell)
      231
   Thomas 231
WALLIS
   Ann 185
WALSBEE
   David 318
   Hannah (---) 318
WALTON
   -- 236
   George 236
   William 228, 229
WANNERTON
   Thomas 60, 61
WARD/WARDE

Andrew 123, 124, 126, 267,
   268, 269
Esther 36
Henry 39
Mary (Dyre) 39
Nathaniel 63, 84
Robert Leigh 199, 231
Samuel 229, 286
Thomas 89, 306
William 285, 286

WARDWELL/WARDELL
   Thomas 235, 236, 237, 238
   William 235, 236, 237, 291
WARFIELD
   John 231
   Samuel 231
WARHAM
   John 29, 81, 214, 257
WARNER
   Andrew 12, 212
   Frederick C. 223
   John 291
   William 86
WARREN
   John 221
WARRENER
   William 148
WASHBURN
   John 199
   Rebecca (Lapham) 199
WATERBURY
   John 8
WATERMAN
   Mercy 254
   Richard 63, 291
   Thomas 182
WATERS
   Frances (---) 69
   Henry FitzGilbert 114, 118,
      311
   John 69
WATHEN
   Deborah 295
   Ezekiel 295
   George 135, 295
   Margery (---) 295
   Margery (Hayward) 135
WATSON
   George 77
   Ian 175